THE MACMILLAN READER

SECOND EDITION

Judith Nadell
Glassboro State College

John Langan
Atlantic Community College

Macmillan Publishing Company

New York

Editor: *Eben W. Ludlow*
Production Supervisor: *Linda Greenberg*
Production Manager: *Pam Kennedy Oborski*
Text and Cover Designer: *Eileen Burke*
Cover photograph: *Mount McKinley, Denali National Park, Alaska. From Comstock, Inc./Bob Grant.*

This book was set in Galliard by Digitype, Inc., and printed and bound by Fairfield Graphics. The cover was printed by Lehigh Press.

Acknowledgments appear on pages 656–660, which constitute an extension of the copyright page.

Macmillan Publishing Company
866 Third Avenue, New York, New York 10022

Library of Congress Cataloging-in-Publication Data

Nadell, Judith.
    The Macmillan reader / Judith Nadell, John Langan. — 2nd ed.
        p.   cm.
    Includes index.
    ISBN 0-02-385871-0
    1. English language — Rhetoric.   I. Langan, John
    II. Title
    PE1417.N33   1990   89-2639
    808′ .0427 — dc20   CIP

Printing: 3 4 5 6 7   Year: 0 1 2 3 4 5 6

For Our Parents

PREFACE

Our bookshelves, and perhaps yours, sag under the weight of all the readers published over the years. Semester after semester we switched texts until we finally realized we wanted more than was being offered. For one thing, many of the readers contained an all-too-predictable blend of selections, with the same pieces cropping up from one book to the next. Also, the books provided students with little guidance on ways to read, think, and write about the selections. And so, when we first began working on *The Macmillan Reader*, we aimed for a different kind of text—one that would offer fresh examples of professional prose, one that would take a more active role in helping students become stronger readers, thinkers, and writers.

In the second edition, as in the first, our primary goal has been to enliven the mix of selections commonly appearing in readers. Although *The Macmillan Reader* includes many popular and classic essays, a number of selections have not yet appeared in other anthologies. Among these are "Eloise" by Garrison Keillor, "Allene Talmey" by Betty Rollin, "Handled with Care" by Bob

Greene, "The Beekeeper" by Sue Hubbell, and "A Well-Regulated Militia" by Paul Fussell. We've been careful to choose selections that range widely in subject matter and approach, from the humorous to the informative, from personal meditation to polemic. We've also made sure that each selection captures students' interest and clearly illustrates a specific rhetorical pattern or combination of patterns.

Our second concern has remained the quality of instruction accompanying the selections. As before, our objective has been to prepare a reader that projects the voice of a real teacher working with students in a knowledgeable and helpful way. Buoyed by compliments about the first edition's teachability, we haven't tinkered with the book's underlying format. Such a structure, we've been told, does indeed help students read more critically, think more logically, and write more skillfully. The book's basic format thus remains as follows:

- **The first chapter, "The Reading Process,"** describes a three-part process for reading with close attention, careful thought, and a high level of interpretive skill. This step-by-step process sharpens students' understanding of the book's selections and promotes the rigorous thinking needed to write effective essays. An activity at the end of the chapter gives students a chance to use the three-step process. First, they read an essay by Pulitzer Prize-winning journalist Ellen Goodman. Then we show them how to apply the suggested sequence to the selection. Last, they respond to sample questions and writing assignments, all similar to the kind following each selection in the book. The chapter thus does more than pay lip service to sharpening students' reading abilities; it presents a class-tested plan for developing higher-level reading skills.

- **The second chapter, "The Writing Process,"** introduces students to essay writing. The chapter emphasizes that writing is a process, a gradual transformation of random ideas into polished prose. We divide the process into six stages: prewriting, stating the thesis, developing the thesis with evidence, organizing the evidence, writing the first draft, and revising. From the start, though, we stress that the composing process is ultimately a personal matter, with each writer adopting his or her own version of the process. A series of activities allows students to practice the skills involved in each stage.

To demonstrate the connection between the reading and writing processes, the writing chapter ends with an annotated student paper written in response to Ellen Goodman's "At a Nuclear Age," the essay presented in the reading chapter. Commentary following the student paper highlights the essay's strengths and points out spots that could use additional work.

- **The next nine chapters** of *The Macmillan Reader* contain selections grouped according to **nine rhetorical patterns**: description, narration, exemplification, process analysis, comparison – contrast, cause – effect, definition, division – classification, and argumentation – persuasion. The sequence progresses from the more experiential to the more analytic modes, but because each chapter is self-contained, the patterns may be covered in any order. Instructors preferring a thematic approach will find the alternative thematic table of contents helpful.

The Macmillan Reader treats the rhetorical patterns separately because such an approach helps students grasp the distinctive characteristics of each pattern. At the same time, the book continually shows the way writers usually combine patterns in their work. We also encourage students to view the patterns as strategies for exploring ideas. Writers, we explain, rarely set out to compose an essay in a specific rhetorical pattern. Rather, they choose a pattern or combination of patterns because it suits their purpose, audience, and subject.

Each of the nine rhetorical chapters follows this format:

1. **A detailed explanation of the pattern** begins the chapter. We describe the pattern's general characteristics, explain when to use the pattern, and then offer practical suggestions for writing an essay or part of an essay using that pattern.

2. Next, we present **a student essay** using the pattern. Written in response to one of the professional selections in the chapter, each essay illustrates the characteristic features of the method of development discussed in the chapter.

3. **Commentary** following each student essay helps students identify the paper's strengths and locate areas needing improvement. "Before" and "after" versions of part of the student essay illustrate the crucial role revision plays in the writing process.

4. The **professional selections** in the rhetorical chapters are accompanied by these items:

    - *A biographical note and preview* give students a perspective on the author and create interest in the piece.
    - *Questions for Close Reading* encourage students to dig into and interpret the selection. The first question asks them to identify the selection's thesis; the last provides work on vocabulary development.
    - *Questions About the Writer's Craft* deal with such matters as purpose, audience, tone, organization, sentence structure, diction, and figures of speech. The first question in the series focuses on the distinctive features of the rhetorical pattern(s) used in the selection.
    - *Questions for Further Thought* inspire lively classroom discussion and help students refine their thoughts before beginning to write.
    - *Writing Assignments*, four in all, follow each selection. Packed with suggestions on how to proceed, the assignments use the selection as a springboard. The first two assignments ask students to write an essay using the same pattern(s) as the selection; the last two prompt students to develop their essays using various combinations of rhetorical patterns.

5. At the end of each rhetorical chapter are **two sets** of **additional writing assignments**: "General Assignments" and "Assignments with a Specific Audience and Purpose." The first set provides open-ended topics that encourage students to discover the best way to use a specific pattern; the second develops their sensitivity to

rhetorical context by asking them to apply the pattern in a real-world situation.

   The Macmillan Reader also includes a glossary listing all the key terms presented in the text. In addition, a comprehensive *Instructor's Manual* contains the following: detailed answers to the "Questions for Close Reading" and "Questions About the Writer's Craft"; suggested activities; pointers about using the book; a detailed syllabus; and a list of the book's paired writing assignments, which encourage students to draw on several selections when writing their essays.

WHAT'S NEW IN THE SECOND EDITION

In preparing the second edition of *The Macmillan Reader*, we looked closely at scores of questionnaires completed by instructors using the book. Their comments (as well as those of students responding to the questionnaire at the back of the book) helped identify essays people liked most. Selections receiving the most enthusiastic endorsements were retained, leaving us with room for 16 new selections. Many of these new readings were suggested by instructors across the country; others were chosen after a lengthy search through magazines, nonfiction collections, newspapers, autobiographies, and the like. Whether written by such recognized pros as Garrison Keillor and Annie Dillard or by such relative newcomers as William McKibben and Beth Johnson Ruth, all 16 new selections are bound to engage students and stimulate thoughtful writing. Each new selection clearly exemplifies the pattern under discussion, and we've taken special care that the comparison–contrast essays reflect practical approaches for organizing essays in that pattern.
   Here are other new features of *The Macmillan Reader*:

- A *revised reading chapter* that makes a stronger connection between the reading and writing processes.
- More *emphasis* on the *rhetorical patterns* as *strategies*, as ways for thinking about a subject and organizing material.

- *Greater attention* to the way writers *blend rhetorical patterns* in their work.
- An *expanded discussion of purpose, audience*, and *tone*.
- *More focus* on *invention* strategies, especially *journal writing*.
- *Increased attention* to *process*, particularly evident in the sections on *thesis statements, first drafts*, and *revision*.
- A *fuller treatment* of *argumentation – persuasion*, including more on *logical fallacies* and *refutation strategies*, as well as *two sets of pro – con essays* on controversial issues.
- A *For Further Reading* section consisting of *four essays*: two by *Martin Luther King, Jr.*, and two by *Joan Didion*. This new section gives students a more *in-depth* look at two outstanding prose stylists.
- Numerous *paired writing assignments*. Worded so that students have the option of reading a related selection in another part of the book, such assignments encourage students to make connections between essays, giving them a richer background of material to draw on in their writing. *Signaled by an asterisk (*)*, these paired assignments should be especially welcome to instructors stressing themes and recurring ideas. A list of all paired assignments can be found near the beginning of the *Instructor's Manual*.

ACKNOWLEDGMENTS

We would like to thank Eben W. Ludlow for his continued enthusiasm and insightful advice. Our appreciation also goes to Linda Greenberg for her skillful attention to the countless details involved in the production process. The following writing instructors reviewed the text and responded to a detailed questionnaire about the book's selections and pedagogy. Their comments guided our work every step of the way: James C. Addison, Jr., West Carolina University; Ken Anania, Massasoit Community College; Chris Anson, University of Minnesota; Bruce Coad, Mountain View College; David Cole, Quinnipiac College; F. Marino D'Amato, Manchester Community College; Benjamin Fiester, Wilkes College; Sister Pauline Fox, Mt. Mercy College; Margaret Franson, Valparaiso University; Lois Friesen, Butler County Community College; Loris Galford, McNeese State University; Gary Griswold, California State University, Long Beach; Betty Boyd Heard, Averett College; Patricia Hummel, Albright

College; Eleanor D. James, Montgomery County Community College; Shakuntala Jayswal, University of New Haven; Kellie Jones, University of Tennessee at Martin; Robert Lesman, Northern Virginia Community College; Barry Maid, University of Arkansas at Little Rock; Catherine Mau, Leeward Community College; Brian McRea, University of Florida; Elizabeth Metzger, University of South Florida; Kathy Mincey, Morehead State University; R. H. Moody, Madison Area Tech College; Steve Odden, University of Wisconsin at Stevens Point; Michael G. O'Hara, Muscatine Community College; Marie Secor, The Pennsylvania State University; Carl Singleton, Fort Hays State University; Carolyn Smith, University of Florida; Eric R. Smith, SUNY College at Cortland; James Gregory Smith, Lamar University; Cynthia Somin, Long Beach City College; Charles Staats, Broward Community College–North; Judith Stanford, Merrimack College; Jacqueline Stark, Los Angeles Valley College; Virginia Stein, Community College of Allegheny County; George Stoll, Broward Community College–North; Ralph Sturm, Edinboro University of Pennsylvania; Vivian Tortorici, Hudson Valley Community College; Larry K. Uffelman, Mansfield University; Anna Villegas, San Joaquin Delta College; David Wickham, Mountain View College; Dorena Allen Wright, Loyola Marymount University.

We are also grateful for the assistance of Joan Dunayer and Santi Buscemi, two creative composition teachers. Their level-headed approach to what does and does not work in the classroom was most helpful. As always, we owe thanks to the unflappable Dorothy Carroll. Her efficiency and good humor kept us on an even (well . . . an almost even) keel. Extra-special thanks go to Linda McMeniman, our co-author on an upcoming Macmillan project. Her work on that book helped highlight areas needing clarification in the second edition of *The Macmillan Reader*. Finally, we are thankful to our students. Their reaction to various drafts of material helped focus our work. And we are especially indebted to the ten students whose essays are included in the book. Their thoughtful, carefully revised papers dramatize the potential of student writing and the power of the composing process.

Judith Nadell
John Langan

CONTENTS

Beware the bony clutches of the thin person, says the author. Anyone who doesn't appreciate double-fudge brownies can't possibly understand the mysteries of life.

Ecologist Rachel Carson warns us that what sounds like a nightmare will become all too real if we fail to protect the earth.

The author goes to a Saturday matinee and finds it doesn't compare with the matinees of his youth.

A stroll into the busy village of Concord after the silence of Walden Pond provides the author with fodder for reflection.

A summer job teaches a college student some important things about himself and the world of work.

Introduction:
   What Is Cause–Effect?
   When to Use Cause–Effect
   Suggestions for Using Cause–Effect in an Essay

ARGUMENTATION – PERSUASION 521

If neither acquiescence nor violence is the proper response to an
unjust system, what is?

Tired of being considered a hypochondriac, a migraine sufferer
argues convincingly that her pain is real and not imagined.

Didion's spare prose evokes a shudder, a recoiling from the
frightening power of the Santa Ana wind.

THEMATIC
CONTENTS

COMMUNICATION AND LANGUAGE

EDUCATION AND WORK

ETHICS AND MORALITY

FAMILY AND CHILDREN

GOVERNMENT AND LAW

HEALTH AND MEDICINE

HUMAN GROUPS AND SOCIETIES

HUMOR AND SATIRE

MEANING IN LIFE

MEMORIES AND AUTOBIOGRAPHY

NATURE AND SCIENCE

THE
READING
PROCESS

More than 200 years ago, the celebrated essayist Joseph Addison wrote, "Of all the diversions of life, there is none so proper to fill up its empty spaces as the reading of useful and entertaining authors." Addison might have also added that reading is challenging and eye-opening.

Reading *is* magical. We can best see this magic in the faces of young children who suddenly realize that all those mysterious, odd-shaped symbols on the page are the passport to vivid scenes and exciting adventures. The pride and pleasure children feel when they first learn to read stem from the power reading gives them. Without consciously realizing it, they know at some level that reading gives them access to worlds that would otherwise remain closed.

But children often lose this sense of wonder as they grow older. They begin to associate reading with tests and homework —both to be avoided at all costs. And there is another reason why some people dislike reading. Quite simply, as pleasurable as reading can be, it requires work. It is almost impossible to remain passive while reading. Even a slick, easy-to-digest bestseller demands that the reader decode, visualize, react to, and interpret what is on the page. The more challenging the reading material, the more actively involved the reader must be.

The selections in this book demand active reading on your part. Representing a broad mix of styles and subjects, the essays range from the classic to the contemporary. Despite this variety, there is a common thread binding the selections together. Each has something important to say; each is intended to stimulate thinking.

The selections serve other purposes as well. They will help you develop a strong repertoire of reading skills—abilities that will benefit you throughout life. Three sets of questions follow each selection: *Questions for Close Reading, Questions About the Writer's Craft,* and *Questions for Further Thought.* These questions illustrate that reading occurs at different levels, moving from the literal to an increasingly analytic and interpretive level. Giving serious thought to the questions will help you achieve a high level of reading proficiency.

As you become more adept at reading the selections, you will undoubtedly find that your own writing becomes more insightful and polished. For one thing, the selections will provide a rich source of background material, encouraging you to explore interesting ideas in your own essays. Second, as you develop an understanding of the techniques experienced writers use, you will learn to apply these strategies in your own essays, for, as novelist Saul Bellow has observed, "A writer is a reader moved to emulation."

In the pages ahead, we describe a suggested approach for reading the selections in this book. Not only will the suggestions enlarge your understanding of the essays, but they will also help you read a variety of written material with ease and assurance.

STEP 1: READ THE SELECTION

Ideally, you should get settled in a quiet place that encourages concentration. If you can focus your attention while sprawled on a bed or curled up in a chair, that's fine. But if you find that being very comfortable is more conducive to daydreaming and dozing off than it is to studying, be sure to avoid getting too relaxed.

Once you are settled, it's time to read the selection. To ensure a good first reading, try the following hints:

- Get an overview of the piece and its author. Start by reading the preview and biographical note that precede the selection. The preview introduces you to the general subject of the essay and often raises questions to consider as you read the selection. The biographical note, by providing information about the author's background, helps you evaluate the writer's credibility as well as his or her slant on the subject. For example, if you know that Lewis Thomas graduated from Harvard Medical School and has held top positions at several prestigious medical facilities, you can better assess whether he is a credible source for the analysis he presents in the essay "The Lie Detector."

    You should then consider the title of the selection. A good title often expresses the main idea of the piece, giving you insight into the selection even before reading it. The title "Making Medical Mistakes," for instance, signals that the essay will focus on the issue of doctors' fallibility. A title may also hint at the tone of a selection. "How to Live to Be 200" points to an essay that is light in spirit, whereas "College Pressures" suggests a piece with a more serious mood.

- Read the selection straight through purely for pleasure. Allow yourself to be drawn into the world the author has created. Just as you first see a painting from the doorway of a room and form an overall impression without perceiving the details, so you can have a preliminary, subjective feeling about the selection. Because you bring your own experiences and viewpoints to the piece, your reading will be unique. As Emerson said, "Take the book, my friend, and read your eyes out; you will never find there what I find."

- After finishing the selection, focus your first impressions by asking yourself — very simply — if you like the selection or not. Try to think of a few words that describe the piece and your reaction to it.

STEP 2: DEEPEN YOUR SENSE OF THE SELECTION

At this point, you are ready to move further into the selection. This second reading will help you identify the specific features of the selection that triggered your initial reaction. Here are some suggestions on how to proceed:

- Mark off the selection's main idea, or thesis, often found near the beginning or end. If the thesis is not stated explicitly, write down your own version of the selection's main idea.
- Locate the main supporting evidence used to develop the thesis. You may even want to number in the margin each supporting point.
- Go back to any unclear passages you encountered during the first reading. The feeling you now have for the whole piece will probably help you make sense of these spots that were initially confusing. On the other hand, this second reading may reveal that the writer's thinking in places is not as clear as it could be.
- Use the dictionary to check the meaning of unfamiliar words.
- Take a minute to write "Yes" or "No" beside points with which you strongly agree or disagree. Your reaction to these points often explains your feelings about the aptness of the selection's ideas.
- Ask yourself if your initial impression of the selection has changed in any way. If your feelings *have* changed, try to determine why you reacted differently on this reading.

STEP 3: EVALUATE THE SELECTION

Now that you have a good grasp of the essay, you may want to read it again, especially if the essay is complex or lengthy. This time, your goal is to make some judgments about the effectiveness of the piece. Keep in mind, though, that you shouldn't evaluate the selection until after you have a strong hold on the piece. A negative or even a positive reaction is valid only if it is based on an accurate reading of the selection.

At first, you may feel uncomfortable evaluating the work of a professional writer. But remember: Written material set in type only *seems* perfect; all writing can be fine-tuned. If you can identify what does and does not work in others' writing, you are taking an important first step toward developing your own power as a writer. You might find it helpful at this point to get together with other students to discuss the selection. Comparing viewpoints often opens up a piece, enabling you to gain a clearer perspective on the selection and the author's approach.

To evaluate the essay, ask yourself the following questions:

1. *Is there adequate and logical support for the selection's thesis?* Does the author provide valid and logical support for the thesis? Are the supporting facts, arguments, and examples pertinent and convincing?
2. *Is the selection unified?* Does everything in the selection belong? Are there any digressions or off-target detours?
3. *Does the selection move smoothly from beginning to middle to end?* What techniques does the writer use to create an easy flow between ideas? Are any parts of the selection abrupt and jarring?
4. *Are various stylistic techniques used effectively in the selection?* What pattern or combination of patterns does the writer use to develop the piece? Why were those patterns selected? How do paragraph development, sentence structure, and word choice contribute to the overall effect of the piece? What tone does the writer adopt? Does the writer use figures of speech to good effect? (The glossary at the back of the book explains these and other terms.)
5. *Does the selection make the reader think?* Does the piece offer a new way of thinking about an issue? Are the ideas in the selection worthy of consideration?

It takes some work to follow the three steps described in this chapter. But the selections in *The Macmillan Reader* are worth the effort. Bear in mind that the sections reprinted here did not spring full-blown from the pens of their authors. The selections are the result of hours of work—hours of writing, rethinking, and revising. As a reader, you should show the same willingness to work with the selections, to read them carefully and thoughtfully. Henry David Thoreau, an avid reader and prolific writer, emphasized the importance of this kind of attentive reading when he advised that "books must be read as deliberately and reservedly as they were written."

To understand the implications of such thoughtful reading,

try applying the three-step process just described to the professional essay that follows: "At a Nuclear Age," written by Ellen Goodman. Start by reading the preview and biographical note that precede the selection. Then, after thinking for a moment about the title of the piece, read the selection straight through once, pausing to collect your first impressions. Next, reread the selection, paying special attention to the essay's thesis and supporting evidence. Finally, evaluate the selection, using the five questions above to gauge the piece's effectiveness. (We provide brief answers to the questions so that you can assess your grasp of the selection.)

Ellen Goodman

The recipient in 1980 of a Pulitzer Prize for distinguished commentary, Ellen Goodman was educated at Radcliffe College. Goodman worked for *Newsweek* and the *Detroit Free Press* before joining the staff of the *Boston Globe* in the mid-1970s. A resident of the Boston area, Goodman writes a popular column that is syndicated in newspapers throughout the country. Goodman's pieces appear in a number of national publications, including *The Village Voice* and *McCalls*. Collections of her columns have been published in *Close to Home* (1979), *Turning Points* (1979), and *At Large* (1981).

At a Nuclear Age

Our age is different from other times. We have medical technology, space exploration, and global communication. But these developments are not what set our age apart from all others. The one factor that most distinguishes this era is our capability to destroy the entire world. How does this knowledge affect us? In the following selection, Ellen Goodman writes about the shadow that haunts us, especially those with the most to lose — the young.

The girl is worrying about The Bomb.   1

It is, a friend assures me, a passing thing. It is, he says, just a   2
symbol of childhood feelings of impotence in a wider and scary
world.

But I think it is a symbol of her fear of the bomb.   3

I saw her staring into space when the idea goose-bumped   4
across her body. She shivered and said simply, "I was worrying
about the bomb."

I wanted to say the right thing to her. It is a parental flaw,   5
wanting to say the right thing. We always want to say the right
thing and end up telling them to brush their hair. So, about the
bomb, I said: "It is worth worrying about." That was
dumb . . . unsatisfactory.

7

She asked for a second opinion. It's what resourceful children do when the first answer is dumb or the source is as historically unreliable as a parent. She looked across the table and questioned a friend of ours: "Do you think I will die from old age, disease, or the bomb?" 6

My friend was taken aback, but he is congenitally reassuring. At least, he has been reassuring me since I was eighteen and worried about making a fool of myself in *Damn Yankees*. He said then that I would be great. My friend is often more reassuring than accurate. 7

So, of course, he told the girl that there wouldn't be a nuclear war because it would be disastrous for everyone. People were too sane to drop the bomb. 8

The girl, however, has had a good deal of experience with the use of ultimate weapons on school playgrounds. She is not convinced that the reasonable human mind is a deterrent to violence. 9

So it was my turn again. This time the best I could do was wryly point out one of the values of living in Boston, one which goes unadvertised by realtors. In the event of a nuclear war, anyone this close to MIT will never know what hit her. 10

Double dumb. 11

What I wanted to be, of course, was both honest and reassuring, both accurate and comforting. But it is sometimes impossible to be both. Ground Zero is not a great comfort, especially if you are eleven years old. 12

This isn't the first time I have flunked my own self-administered, self-corrected, take-home parenting test. Maybe I'm a tough grader, maybe we all are, or maybe the world has raised the standards over our heads. 13

It's not just about the bomb. It's hard to be simultaneously realistic and comforting about almost anything that makes life stable, or the future certain. 14

When we were young, most of us were fed three square meals of certainties. I don't know if our parents believed them all or if they just thought that security, like milk, was good for children. But it was a pretty constant and even nourishing diet. 15

We didn't hear much about bad times, bad marriages, bad wars. The survivors of the Depression didn't talk much about it; the survivors of World War II were proud; divorce was a secret scandal. 16

Most of us grew up expecting a stable world. I don't think we   17
were betrayed; at worst, most of our parents believed they could
build us that world. They thought we needed to be assured instead of prepared. Instead, we were surprised.

The way we live is unexpectedly, surprisingly, insecure. We   18
live in a state of flux.

And lurking in the background is the epitome of human   19
foolishness and insecurity: The Bomb.

All these things cannot help but affect the way we live with   20
our own children. I suspect that they, too, want a stable, secure
world. They want consistency; they want answers to questions
and solutions for problems.

But we can't give them what we don't have. Instead we offer   21
ambiguity, contingency plans, history, alternatives. And we call
this "preparation for the real world."

I don't know whether they are learning insecurity and fear, or   22
learning how to cope. Or perhaps learning how to cope with
insecurity and fear. But I suppose we do what parents always do:
our best. We try to share what we know of the world and what we
assume they will need to know.

With any luck we will have been too pessimistic.   23

The following questions will help crystallize your reactions
to Goodman's essay.

1. Is there adequate and logical support for the selection's thesis?

The most explicit statement of Goodman's thesis may be, "The way
we live is unexpectedly, surprisingly insecure. We live in a state of
flux. And lurking in the background is the epitome of human foolishness and insecurity: The Bomb." But these two sentences are not the
most complete statement of Goodman's main idea because they do
not mention the major concern of her piece — trying to give children
a sense of security in a world governed by the possibility of annihila-
tion. Stating the thesis in your own words may be best: "It is difficult
for parents to provide a sense of security in today's world when
children must live with the specter of nuclear war."

Goodman dramatizes her thesis with a single strong example —
her daughter's fears and questions. She also gives examples of parents'
answers to their children's questions, showing how inadequate such

responses are. Finally, Goodman compares a pre-Bomb childhood with a modern one and points out how much easier it was to provide certainties when such an overwhelming threat did not exist.

2. Is the selection unified?

At first, paragraphs 15–17 seem like a digression. Yet these paragraphs are important because they contrast the simplicity of the world Goodman experienced when growing up with the world her daughter must face. Admittedly, the chatty aside in paragraph 7 is slightly jarring. Goodman includes the paragraph to show that her "congenitally reassuring" friend tends not to be convincing—not to Goodman at eighteen, not to her daughter at eleven. But the paragraph, with its focus on Goodman and its reference to *Damn Yankees*, distracts somewhat from the unity of the piece.

3. Does the selection move smoothly from beginning to middle to end?

Goodman's essay progresses from the dinner-table conversation with her daughter (paragraphs 1–12) to her thoughts about why our children face such an uncertain world. In keeping with conventional newspaper format and her informal style, Goodman writes short, crisp paragraphs—paragraphs that are much briefer than those appropriate for most student writing. And she is careful about providing transitional words to ease the reader from one idea to another: "*But* I think . . . ," "The girl, *however*, . . . ," "*So* it was my turn *again*. . . ." She also uses transitional sentences that echo previous ideas while also introducing new points: "It's not just about the bomb . . . ," "All these things cannot help but affect. . . ."

4. Are various stylistic techniques used effectively in the selection?

Goodman develops her essay by using several patterns of organization. For example, *narration* and *examples* are used in the first twelve paragraphs, while *comparison–contrast* provides the focus for paragraphs 15–17. She uses *short, dramatic sentences* to begin the essay ("The girl is worrying about The Bomb") and to punctuate her ideas ("Double dumb"; "We live in a state of flux"). The essay concludes with a similarly spare but striking sentence: "With any luck we will have been too pessimistic." Goodman achieves an *informal tone* through the use of the first person ("I think . . . ," "I saw . . .") and colloquial language ("never know what hit her"; "that was dumb"; "I have flunked"). In paragraph 15, Goodman uses *figurative language* ("three square meals of certainty" and "security, like milk, was considered good for children") to dramatize how much simpler life was a generation ago. Finally, Goodman leavens her weighty subject with dashes of humor, as when she states, "It is a parental flaw, wanting to say the right thing."

5. Does the selection make the reader think?

Goodman's essay treats a broad issue that is crucial to all of us — the nuclear peril. Her specific concern is the dilemma parents face dealing with their children's fears. Although Goodman offers no solutions, her personal account sharpens our awareness of the problem.

If, for each essay you read, you consider the evaluative questions above, you will be able to respond thoughtfully to the *Questions for Close Reading, Questions About the Writer's Craft,* and *Questions for Further Thought* presented after each selection. In turn, your responses to these items will prepare you for the writing assignments following the questions. Interesting and varied, the assignments invite you to examine issues raised by the selections and encourage you to experiment with various writing styles and organizational patterns.

The following are some sample questions and assignments based on the Goodman essay; all are similar to the sort you will find in this book. Note that the final writing assignment serves as the springboard for several activities and a full student essay in the next chapter, "The Writing Process."

Questions for Close Reading

1. What is the reason Goodman's daughter rejects the family friend's contention that people are too sane ever to drop the bomb?
2. Why does living in Boston create special anxiety for a child concerned about nuclear war?

Questions About the Writer's Craft

1. How would you characterize the tone of Goodman's essay? Is it formal and objective? Informal and subjective? What techniques does Goodman use to achieve this tone?
2. Why does Goodman begin and end her essay with a brief, one-sentence paragraph? What is the effect of such short paragraphs?

Questions for Further Thought

1. What specifically can parents do to minimize the anxiety their children feel living in a nuclear age?
2. Do you think that movies that dramatize the impact of nuclear war have any value? Or are they sensationalized, popular entertainment, having no real significance?

Writing Assignments

1. Ellen Goodman feels powerless when confronted by her daughter's fear of nuclear war. Write an essay explaining the steps parents and/or schools can take to help minimize children's anxieties about another contemporary danger—AIDS, drugs, sexual abuse, whatever.
2. In the essay "At a Nuclear Age," Ellen Goodman contends that the world today is a difficult, even dangerous place for children. Write an essay that provides evidence to support Goodman's view.

The benefits of active reading are many. Books in general and the selections in *The Macmillan Reader* in particular will bring you face to face with issues that concern all of us as thinking and feeling beings. If you study closely the selections and the questions that follow them, you will be on your way to discovering ideas for your own papers. The next chapter, "The Writing Process," offers practical suggestions for turning those ideas into well-organized, thoughtful essays.

THE WRITING PROCESS

Not many people retire at 38. But Michel Montaigne, a sixteenth-century French attorney, did exactly that. Montaigne retired at such a young age because he wanted time to read, think, and write about all the subjects that interested him. After spending years getting his ideas down on paper, Montaigne finally published his short prose pieces. He called them *essais*—French for "trials" or "attempts."

In fact, all writing is an attempt to transform ideas into words, thus giving order and meaning to life. By using the term *essai*, Montaigne acknowledged that a written piece is never really complete or finished. Of course, writers have to stop at some point, especially if they have deadlines to meet. But, as all experienced writers know, even after they dot the final *i*, cross the final *t*, and say "That's it," there is always something that could have been explored further or expressed a little better.

Because writing is a process, changes of direction, even false starts, are not uncommon. Although there is no way to eliminate the work needed to write effectively, certain strategies can make

13

the process more manageable and rewarding. This chapter describes a six-step sequence for you to follow when writing essays. The sequence will help you discover the pleasure and sense of accomplishment that come from expressing your ideas with clarity and force.

We present the sequence as a series of steps, but we urge you not to view it as a rigid formula that must be followed step by unchanging step. Most people develop personalized approaches to writing. Some mull over a topic, then move quickly into a promising first draft; others outline their essays in detail before beginning to write. Between these extremes are any number of variations. The sequence described here can be streamlined, juggled, or otherwise modified to fit such individual needs and styles. The six stages in the sequence are as follows:

1. Prewrite
2. Identify the thesis
3. Support the thesis with evidence
4. Organize the evidence
5. Write the first draft
6. Revise the essay

STAGE 1: PREWRITE

Prewriting refers to a number of strategies you can use *before* starting the first draft of a paper. Tentative and exploratory, prewriting loosens you and helps reduce the anxiety you may feel when you stare at a blank page, wondering how to start and what to say. Moreover, since the preliminary, rooting-around quality of prewriting encourages unhurried, imaginative exploration, you are bound to discover what interests you most about your subject.

Although prewriting is a critical step in the writing process, many people disregard this stage and plunge into the first draft without first thinking through what they want to say. This "let's get the #&%!* thing over with" approach is a little like building a house without a blueprint and *then* discovering all kinds of structural defects in the building. Prewriting provides a blueprint for your writing. It focuses your thinking early in the writing process, steering you away from potential pitfalls.

Keep a Journal

Of all the prewriting techniques, daily (or almost daily) writing in a journal is the one most likely to make writing a part of your life. In journals, you emphasize not the events of a day but your reflections on those events. Some journal entries may focus on a single theme; others may wander from topic to topic. Your starting point may be a dream, a snippet of overheard conversation, a video on MTV, a political cartoon, an issue raised in class or in your reading—anything that surprises, interests, angers, depresses, confuses, or amuses you.

Since journal writing is a private, relaxed activity, you needn't be overly concerned with spelling, grammar, sentence structure, or organization. The important thing is to let your journal serve as a springboard to new insights, providing you with material to draw on in your writing. If you reread your journal entries every week, you can identify recurrent themes and concerns. Keep a list of these issues at the back of your journal, under the heading "Possible Essay Subjects."

Journal writing stimulates thinking in a loose, unstructured way. But when you have a specific piece to write, you need to approach prewriting in a purposeful, focused manner. Here is what you want to do:

- Understand the boundaries of the assignment
- Determine your purpose, audience, and tone
- Discover the limited subject of your essay
- Generate raw material about your limited subject
- Organize the raw material

We will discuss each of these steps in turn. But first, here is a practical tip: Use pencil and scrap paper during the prewriting stage. Less intimidating than typewriter or pen and perfectly blank paper, they reinforce the notion that prewriting is intended to be open and inventive.

Understand the Boundaries of the Assignment

You should not start writing a paper until you know what is expected. First of all, clarify the *kind of paper* the instructor has in mind. Assume the instructor asks you to discuss the key ideas in an assigned reading. What does the instructor want you to do? Should you include a brief summary of the selection? Should you compare the author's ideas with your view of the subject? Should you determine if the author's view is supported by valid evidence?

If you are not sure about an assignment, ask your instructor —not the student behind you, who is probably as confused as you — to make the requirements clear. Most instructors are more than willing to provide an explanation. They would rather take a few minutes of class time to explain an assignment than spend hours reading dozens of student essays that miss the mark.

Also try to find out *how long* the paper should be. Many instructors will indicate the approximate length of the papers they assign. If no length requirements are provided, discuss with the instructor what you plan to cover and indicate how long you think your paper will be. The instructor will either give you the go-ahead or will help you refine the direction and scope of your work.

Determine Your Purpose, Audience, and Tone

Once you understand the requirements of an assignment, you are ready to consider your purpose, audience, and tone. First, what is your essay's broad *purpose*? What do you want the essay to accomplish? The papers you write in college are usually meant to *inform* or *explain*, to *convince* or *persuade*, and sometimes to *entertain*.

In practice, writing often combines purposes. You might, for example, write an essay trying to *convince* people to support a new trash-recycling program in your community. But before you win readers over, you most likely would have to *explain* something about current waste disposal technology. When writing blends purposes in this way, the predominant purpose determines the essay's content, organization, emphasis, and choice of words. Assume you are writing about a political campaign. If your primary goal is to *entertain,* to take a gentle poke at two candidates, you might start with several accounts of one candidate's "foot in mouth" disease and then describe the attempts of the other candidate, a multi-millionaire, to portray himself as an average Joe.

Your language, full of exaggeration, would reflect your objective. But if your primary purpose is to *persuade* readers that the candidates are incompetent and should not be elected, you might adopt a serious, straightforward style. Rather than poke fun at one candidate's gaffes, you would use them to illustrate her insensitivity to important issues. Similarly, the other candidate's posturing would be presented not as a foolish pretension but as evidence of his lack of judgment.

To write effectively, you also need to focus on your *audience,* taking readers' expectations and needs into account. An essay about the artificial preservatives in the food served by the campus cafeteria would take one form if submitted to your chemistry professor and a very different one if written for the college newspaper. The chemistry paper would probably be formal and technical, complete with chemical formulations and scientific data. But such technical information would be inappropriate in a column intended for general readers. Instead, you might provide specific examples of cafeteria foods loaded with additives and suggest ways to eat more healthfully.

To analyze your audience, ask yourself the following questions: What are my readers' age, sex, and educational level? What are their political, religious, and other beliefs? What interests and needs motivate them? How much do my readers already know about my subject? Do they have any misconceptions? What biases do they have about me, my subject, my opinion?

Just as your voice may project a range of feelings, your writing can convey any number of *tones,* or emotional states — enthusiasm, anger, resignation, and so on. Integral to meaning, tone reflects your attitude toward yourself, your purpose, your subject, and your readers. To project the tone you intend, you should pay close attention to *sentence structure* and *word choice*.

Sentence structure refers to the way sentences are shaped. Although the subject matter is exactly the same in the brief paragraphs below, note how differences in sentence structure create sharply dissimilar tones.

> As recently as the 1960s, many minorities considered the police an occupying force, an oppressive agent of control. Accordingly, in poorer neighborhoods, violence against police grew, as did the number of residents killed by police.

> An occupying force. An agent of control. An oppressor. That's how many minorities in the '60s viewed the police patrolling their neighborhoods. Violence against police soared. Police killings of minorities mounted.

Informative in its approach, the first paragraph projects a neutral, dispassionate tone. The sentences are fairly long and impersonal, with clearcut transitions ("As recently as," "Accordingly") marking the progression of thought. But the second paragraph, with its dramatic, almost alarmist tone, seems intended to elicit a strong emotional response, its short sentences, fragments, and abrupt transitions reflecting the turbulence of earlier times.

The words you select also contribute to the feeling that pervades your writing. Words have *denotations,* neutral dictionary meanings, as well as *connotations,* strong emotional associations. The word *beach,* for instance, is defined in the dictionary as "a nearly level stretch of pebbles and sand beside a body of water." This definition, however, does not capture individual responses to the word. For some, *beach* suggests warmth and relaxation; for others, it calls up images of hospital waste and sewage.

Since tone and meaning are tightly bound, you must be sensitive to the emotional nuances of words. If you were writing a respectful piece about police officers, you would not talk about *cops, narcs,* or *flatfoots,* because such terms convey insolence and contempt. Similarly, your words must convey tone clearly. Suppose you were writing a satirical piece criticizing a local beauty pageant. Dubbing the participants "livestock on view" would leave no question about your tone, whereas referring to the participants as "attractive young women" would reveal little about your attitude. Remember, readers can't read your mind, only your paper.

Discover the Limited Subject of Your Essay

Once you have a firm grasp of the assignment's boundaries and have determined your purpose, audience, and tone, you are ready to focus on a limited aspect of the general assignment. Because too broad a subject can result in a diffuse, rambling essay, be sure to restrict your general subject before starting to write.

The following examples show the difference between general subjects that are too broad for an essay and limited subjects that are appropriate and workable. The examples, of course, represent only a few among many possibilities.

General Subject	Less General	Limited
Education	Computers in education	How computers improve on human teachers
Transportation	Bus travel	The unspoken rules of riding in a bus
Work	Planning for a career	Preparing for the jobs of the future

How do you move from a general to a narrow or focused subject? Imagine that you are asked to prepare a straightforward, informative essay for your class. The assignment, based on the selection in the "Reading Process" chapter, is as follows:

> In the essay "At a Nuclear Age," Ellen Goodman contends that the world today is a difficult, even dangerous place for children. Write an essay that provides evidence to support Goodman's point.

You might feel unsure about how to proceed. But two techniques can help you limit such a general assignment. Keeping your purpose, audience, and tone in mind, you may *question* or *brainstorm* the general subject. These two techniques — both explained in detail below — have a paradoxical effect. They encourage you to roam freely over a subject, but they also help focus and restrict the discussion by revealing which aspects of the subject interest you most.

1. Question the general subject.   One way to narrow your subject is to ask a series of questions beginning with words like *who, how, why,* and *what*. Following is an example of the way the questioning technique could help limit the Goodman assignment. Keep in mind, though, that the same questions could lead to different limited subjects — just as other questions would.

> *General Subject:* We live in a world that is difficult, even dangerous for children.

Question	Limited Subject
Who is to blame for the difficult conditions under which children grow up?	An essay describing the effect on children of a weakening family structure
How can parents provide their children with some sense of security in a world filled with uncertainties?	An essay giving examples of the ways parents give children a surer sense of control over their lives
Why do some people claim that our world offers children more security than other periods in history?	An essay comparing the harsh world of children in the past with the relatively easy world of childhood today
What things, other than nuclear war, contribute to the dangers children face?	An essay describing the range of problems that make it difficult to raise children today

2. Brainstorm the general subject.   Another way to focus is to list quickly everything that pops into your mind about the general subject. Working vertically down the page, jot down brief words, phrases, and abbreviations to capture your free-floating thoughts. Don't try to organize or censor your ideas. Even the most fleeting, random, or seemingly outrageous thought can lead to an appropriate limited subject. Here is an example of brainstorming based on the Goodman assignment.

> *General Subject:* We live in a world that is difficult, even dangerous for children.

- too many divorces, bad for kids
- child abuse

- families move a lot, so kids feel insecure
- drug abuse, even in elementary school
- kids not innocent — politicians corrupt, sex everywhere
- AIDS
- adults have less respect for teachers, not good for kids
- TV distorts values — money all important, so much violence
- two-career families mean absent parents

After questioning and brainstorming, reread the raw material generated. Look for recurring themes, for ideas that interest you. Then write a couple of sentences or phrases summarizing possible limited subjects. For example, we will focus in the pages ahead on one limited subject discovered through brainstorming and questioning the Goodman assignment: "The special problems that parents face raising children today."

Generate Raw Material About Your Limited Subject

When a limited subject strikes you as having possibilities, your next step is to see if you have enough interesting and insightful things to say about the subject to write an effective essay. To find out if you do, you may use any or all of the following techniques:

1. Freewrite on your limited subject.   Freewriting means jotting down in rough sentences or phrases everything that comes to mind. To capture this continuous stream of thought, write non-stop for ten minutes or more; don't reread, edit, or pay attention to organization, spelling, or grammar. Simply get your ideas down on paper. If your mind goes blank, repeat words until another thought emerges. The raw material generated will probably yield interesting ideas about your limited subject.

Imagine you are freewriting about the following limited subject: "The special problems that parents face raising children today." You might produce something like this:

Parents today have tough problems to face. Lots of dangers. Drugs and alcohol for one thing. Also crimes of violence against kids. Parents also have to keep up with cost of living, everything costs more, kids want and expect more. Television? Another thing is <u>Playboy</u>, <u>Penthouse</u>. Sexy ads on TV, movies deal with sex. Kids grow up too fast, too fast, too fast. Drugs. Little kids can't handle knowing too much at an early age. Both parents at work much of the day. Another problem is getting kids to do homework, lots of other things to do. Malls, arcades, stereos in kids' rooms. When I was young, we did homework after dinner, no excuses accepted by my parents. . . .

2. Brainstorm your limited subject.   Let your mind wander freely, jotting down every idea, fact, and example that occurs to you about your limited subject. Use brief words and phrases so that you don't get bogged down writing full sentences. Don't worry whether ideas fit together or whether the points listed make sense. When you are finished, you will probably find that you have generated considerable material about the limited subject.

Here is a brainstormed list on the limited subject for the Goodman assignment:

> *Limited Subject:* The special problems that parents face raising children today
>
> - trying to raise kids when both parents work
> - prices of everything
> - sex on TV, in movies, in magazines
> - violence against children
> - violence in movies and on television
> - more distractions, like shopping malls
> - TV, phones, stereos in kids' rooms
> - drugs everywhere
> - schools not as good as they used to be
> - pressures on kids to drink

3. Use group discussion.   Brainstorming can sometimes be conducted as a group activity. Thrashing out ideas with other people stretches the imagination, propelling you in directions you might not have considered otherwise. Because group brain-storming occurs in an atmosphere of creative competition, the process often yields a wealth of prewriting material.

4. Map out the limited subject.   Instead of freewriting or brainstorming, you may want to generate raw material through mapping, sometimes called diagramming. Like other prewriting techniques, mapping proceeds rapidly. With mapping, however, you use tree diagrams (with ideas growing out from each other), balloons, or arrows to depict your free-floating thoughts. If you are the kind of person who doodles while thinking, you may find that mapping prompts imaginative exploration. Visualizing how ideas fit together can encourage, quite literally, new ways of seeing things.

5. Go to the library.   Depending on your topic, you may find it helpful to look in the subject file of the main catalogue for the titles of books dealing with your limited subject. At this stage in the writing process, it is not necessary to read the books you find. Just skim them and perhaps take a few brief notes on ideas and points that could be useful to you. You may also look in the *Readers' Guide to Periodical Literature* or another more special-ized index to find the titles of magazine articles related to your limited topic. A third approach might be to check the library's vertical file for pamphlets on your limited subject.

When researching the Goodman assignment, for instance, you might look under the following headings in the *Readers' Guide:*

    Drug abuse
    Mass media
    Family
    Parent – child relationship:
        Child abuse
        Children — Management and training
        Children of divorced parents
        Children of working mothers
    School and the home

Organize the Raw Material

Once you have generated raw material about your limited subject, you are ready to shape those rough, preliminary ideas. Preparing a scratch outline is an effective strategy. Start by crossing out items not appropriate for your purpose, audience, and tone. Next, eliminate points not closely related to your limited subject, and add items that didn't originally occur to you. Finally, group related ideas under a common heading, and determine what seems to be the best order for those headings.

A scratch outline makes the writing process more manageable because it gives you a preliminary idea of what should be discarded or added, what should come first, what should come last, and what sections need more development. You are not creating a formal outline but a flexible one that can be reshaped along the way. Here is an example of a scratch outline that begins to organize the material for the Goodman assignment.

Limited Subject: The special problems that parents face raising children today

1. Distractions from schoolwork
   - Stereos, televisions in room at home
   - Places to go — malls, video arcades, fast food restaurants
2. Sexually explicit materials
   - Magazines and books
   - Television
   - Movies
3. Life-threatening dangers
   - Violent crimes against children
   - Drugs
   - Drinking

The work done during prewriting is crucial since it provides a solid foundation for the next stages in the writing process. But don't think that once prewriting is completed, invention and imaginative exploration are no longer needed. Remaining open to new ideas is crucial in all phases of the writing process.

Activities: Prewrite

1. Five general subjects are listed below. Use the techniques indicated in parentheses to limit each general topic to a more focused subject.

 Medicine (questioning)
 Sports (freewriting)
 Women (brainstorming)
 Leisure (mapping)
 Law (group discussion)
 Television (journal writing)

2. Each set below contains five scrambled items for a scratch outline. Number the items in each set from 1 (broadest subject) to 5 (most limited subject).

Set A	Set B
Abortion	Business majors
Controversial social issues	Students divided by major
Cutting off state abortion funds	College students
Federal funding for abortions	Kinds of students on campus
Social issues	Why many students major in business

STAGE 2: IDENTIFY THE THESIS

The process of prewriting—discovering a limited subject and generating ideas about it—prepares you for the next stage in writing an essay: identifying the paper's *thesis*, or controlling idea. Representing your slant on a subject, the thesis should focus on an interesting and significant issue, one that engages your energies and merits your consideration. You may think of the thesis as the essay's hub—the central point around which all the other material revolves. Your thesis determines what does and does not belong in the essay. When the thesis occurs early in the essay, it helps focus readers on your central point.

Developing a sound thesis usually does not happen all at once. Willingness to work at shaping a thesis is a crucial part of your job as a writer. Typically, the thesis evolves over time. You may have a clear idea of your thesis early in the prewriting stage. Or you may have to sift through your prewriting material to identify the thesis. In either case, the first thesis formulated may change as the writing process continues. You may find, after writing a while, that feelings, thoughts, and examples emerge that force you to reexamine, or reword, your thesis. Such ongoing clarification is to be expected. As Peter Elbow, author of many books on writing, says, "Writing is a way of thinking something you couldn't have started out saying."

Generally expressed in one or two sentences, a thesis state-ment often has two parts. One part presents the *limited subject* of your paper; the other presents your *attitude* about the limited subject. Here are some examples of the way you might move from general subject to limited subject to thesis statement. In each thesis, the limited subject has been underlined once and the attitude toward the limited subject has been underlined twice.

General Subject	Limited Subject	Thesis
Education	How computers improve on human teachers	Computer programs in mathematics can individualize instruction more effectively than the average teacher can.
Transportation	The unspoken rules of riding a bus	Violating the unspoken rules of bus travel is risky.
Work	Preparing for the jobs of the future	Accounting positions in the decade ahead will demand good comunication skills.
Our anti-child world	Special problems that parents face raising children today	Being a parent today is much more difficult than it was a generation ago.

As you can see, the thesis statement is an important step toward writing a sharply focused essay. For this reason, you want to avoid the following three common problems.

Making an announcement. Some people merely announce the limited subject of their paper and forget to indicate their attitude toward the subject. Such statements are announcements of intent, not thesis statements.

Compare the following three announcements with the thesis statements beside them.

Announcements	Thesis Statements
My essay will discuss whether a student pub should exist on campus.	This college should not allow a student pub on campus.
Handgun legislation is the subject of this paper.	Banning handguns is the first step toward controlling crime in America.
I want to discuss cable television.	Cable television has not delivered on its promise to provide an alternative to network programming.

Making a factual statement. An essay should focus on an issue capable of being developed. If a fact is used as a thesis, you have no place to go. A fact is a fact. It does not invite much discussion. Studying the following two groups will help you see the difference between factual and thesis statements.

Factual Statements	Thesis Statements
Many businesses pollute the environment.	Tax penalities should be levied against businesses that pollute the environment.
Many movies today are violent.	Movie violence provides a healthy outlet for aggression.
America's population is growing older.	The aging of the American population will eventually create an economic crisis.

Making a broad statement.   You also want to avoid stating your thesis in vague, general, or sweeping terms. Broad statements make it easy for readers to misinterpret the point of your essay and the scope of your discussion. Moreover, if you start with a broad thesis, you are saddled with the impossible task of trying to develop a book-length idea with an essay that runs only several pages.

The following examples contrast statements that are too broad with thesis statements that are focused effectively.

Broad Statements	**Thesis Statements**
A high school education is often meaningless nowadays.	High school diplomas have been devalued by grade inflation.
The newspaper industry is catering to the taste of the American public.	The success of *USA Today* indicates that people want their newspapers easy to read and entertaining.
The computer revolution is not all that we have been led to believe it is.	Home computers are still an impractical purchase for many people.

Although every effective essay has a thesis, writers have considerable freedom regarding the presentation of this central idea. The thesis is often stated near the beginning of an essay, but it may be delayed until the middle or end. The thesis may even be reiterated—in different words—at several spots in an essay. Some writers imply the thesis rather than state it explicitly, using their supporting evidence to broadcast—loud and clear—the essay's central thought. The important point is that every essay has a thesis, whether stated or implied. That central concept is the essay's reason for being.

Activities: Identify the Thesis

1. Four possible thesis statements are listed for each of the limited subjects on the next page. Indicate whether each thesis is an announcement (A), a factual statement (FS), too broad a statement (TB), or an acceptable thesis (OK).

Limited Subject: The ethics of treating severely handicapped infants

Some babies born with severe handicaps have been allowed to die.
There are many serious issues involved in the treatment of handicapped newborns.
The government should pass legislation requiring medical treatment for handicapped newborns.
This essay will analyze the controversy surrounding the treatment of severely handicapped babies who would die without medical care.

Limited Subject: Privacy and computerized records

Computers raise some significant and crucial questions for all of us.
Computerized records keep track of consumer spending habits, credit records, travel patterns, and other personal information.
Computerized records have turned our private lives into public property.
In this paper, the relationship between computerized records and the right to privacy will be discussed.

2. Each of the following sets lists the key points in an essay. Based on the information provided, prepare a possible thesis for each essay.

Set A

- One example of evidence of this growing conservatism is the resurgent popularity of fraternities and sororities.
- Beauty contests, ROTC training, and corporate recruiting — once rejected by students on many campuses — are again popular.
- Most important, many students no longer choose risky careers that enable them to contribute to society but select, instead, safe fields with money-making potential.

Set B

- We do not know, first of all, how engineering new forms of life might affect the earth's delicate ecological balance.
- Another danger of genetic research is its potential for unleashing new forms of disease on the population.
- Even beneficial attempts to eliminate genetic defects could contribute to the dangerous idea that only perfect individuals are entitled to live.

3. Supplied here are four sets of general and limited subjects. Generate an appropriate thesis statement for each set of subjects.

General Subject	Limited Subject
Music	Fads in music
Psychology	The power struggles in a classroom
Politics	The separation of church and state
Health	Doctors' attitude toward patients

STAGE 3: SUPPORT THE THESIS WITH EVIDENCE

After creating a thesis statement, you are ready to develop the evidence needed to support that central idea. This supporting material — reasons, facts, examples, opinions, personal observations, quotations, and so forth — lends substance to your viewpoint and gives your writing the specificity that makes an essay convincing and enjoyable. In typical college essays of 500 to 1,500 words (the approximate length of many essays assigned in English and other classes), you usually need at least three major points of evidence to develop the thesis. These major points — each focusing on related but separate aspects of the thesis — eventually will become the supporting paragraphs in the body of the essay.

Where do you find the evidence to support the thesis? Where do you find the essay's major supporting points and secondary details, examples, and facts? A good deal of evidence is generated during the prewriting stage when you keep a journal, brainstorm, freewrite, use the mapping technique, and discuss your ideas with others. The library, with its abundant material, is another rich source for supporting evidence. Moreover, the patterns of development described in later chapters of *The Macmillan Reader* often point the way to specific kinds of support and evidence.

Regardless of its source, strong supporting evidence has the following characteristics.

It is unified. All the evidence in an essay must clearly support the thesis. No matter how riveting evidence might be, supporting material that does not relate directly to the central point of the essay should be eliminated. Such off-target material distracts the reader from the paper's controlling idea.

The paragraphs below, both about the benefits of cable television, illustrate the importance of unified evidence. As you will see, the first paragraph lacks unity because it contains points unrelated to the paragraph's main idea. Specifically, the comments about the foul language on cable television versus the "clean" language on network shows should be deleted. Although these observations bring up interesting points, their inclusion in this paragraph shifts the focus of the writer's thought. If the writer wants to present a balanced view of the pros and cons of cable versus network television, these points *should* be discussed, but they should be covered in another paragraph. By way of contrast, the second paragraph is unified, because all its supporting evidence is appropriate and relevant.

Nonunified Support

Cable television is a real improvement over network television. For one thing, the movies shown on cable are better than those on network TV. Cable movies are usually only months old, they have not been edited by censors, and they are not interrupted by commercials. In addition, the specials on cable television are superior to the ones the networks grind out, usually tired Bob Hope variety shows and boring awards ceremonies. Cable viewers, however, can enjoy such pop stars as Bruce Springsteen, Tina Turner, or Eddie Murphy in concert. But there is one problem with these comedians. The foul language many of them use makes it hard to watch these cable specials with children. The networks, on the other hand, generally present "clean" shows that parents and children can watch together. Finally, programs on cable TV are scheduled at various times over the month. People who work night shifts or attend evening classes can see movies in the afternoon, and viewers who miss the first twenty minutes of a program can always catch them later. It's not surprising that cable viewership is growing while network ratings have taken a plunge.

Unified Support

Cable television is a real improvement over network television. For one thing, the movies shown on cable are better than those on network TV. Cable movies are usually only months old, they have not been edited by censors, and they are not interrupted by commercials. In addition, the specials on cable television are superior to the ones the networks grind out, usually tired Bob Hope variety shows and boring awards ceremonies. Cable viewers, however, may enjoy such pop stars as Bruce Springsteen, Tina Turner, or Eddie Murphy in concert. Finally, programs on cable TV are scheduled at various times over the month. People who work night shifts or attend evening classes can see movies in the afternoon, and viewers who miss the first twenty minutes of a show can always catch them later. It's not surprising that cable viewership is growing while network ratings have taken a plunge.

It is adequate.   Readers will not automatically accept the idea expressed in your thesis; they have to be convinced that your point is valid. The credibility of your position depends, in part, on whether you provide enough evidence to support your viewpoint. On occasion, one extended example or lengthy, complex piece of evidence will be sufficient. But usually you will need a range of evidence to support your thesis. Look at the following paragraphs, both on the subject of limited-service gas stations. You will see how additional examples and details make the second paragraph stronger and more convincing than the first.

Inadequate Support

Gas stations still provide gas, but they no longer provide service. At many stations, attendants have even stopped pumping gas. Motorists pull up to a combination convenience store and gas island where the attendant is enclosed in a glass booth, with a tray for taking money. The driver must get out of the car, pump the gas, and walk over to the booth to pay. That's a real inconvenience, especially when compared with the way service stations used to be run. Friendly service seems to have faded into the past.

Adequate Support

Gas stations still provide gas, but they no longer provide service. At many stations, attendants have even stopped pumping gas. Motorists pull up to a combination convenience store and gas island where the attendant is enclosed in a glass booth, with a tray for taking money. The driver must get out of the car, pump the gas, and walk over to the booth to pay. Even at stations that still employ "pump jockeys," the workers seldom ask, "Check your oil?" They rarely wash windshields, although they may grudgingly point out the location of the bucket and squeegee. Finally, many gas stations have eliminated on-duty mechanics. The skillful mechanic who could replace a belt or fix a tire in a few minutes has been replaced by a teenager in a jumpsuit who doesn't know a carburetor from a charge card. Is the demise of service the result of a decrease in owner-operated businesses and the rise in chain operations? Is it part of a general lack of courtesy in our society? Whatever the reason, it's clear that most gas stations today are mere fuel stops that provide minimal service.

It is specific.   When evidence is vague and general, readers tend to tune out, unconvinced that you have supported your thesis with authority. Specific material, though, engages readers and, equally important, convinces them that your opinion rests on solid ground. In the following paragraphs about flexible working hours, note how interesting and convincing the second paragraph is — particularly when compared to the vague generalities of the first paragraph.

Nonspecific Support
Employees should be allowed more freedom to set their own work schedules. One benefit of such a change would concern traffic problems. Hours would be different, so traffic patterns, especially around urban areas, would be altered. This would eliminate the difficulties that motorists now confront. Companies would also benefit from the change. As soon as they realized that flexible hours would improve employees' work, their objections would lessen. A final benefit would involve working parents. Two-career families might solve many of the tough problems they now face, for the new hours would mean that child care would be easier to arrange. Emotionally, parents would feel better. Making work hours more flexible is a step we should take now.

Specific Support
Employees should be allowed more freedom to set their own work schedules. One benefit of such a change would be a reduction in traffic problems. If employees could report to work any time between 6 A.M. and 11 A.M., for example, rush hour would vanish, traffic jams would be eliminated, accidents would be reduced, and

employees would arrive at work in a more relaxed frame of mind. Companies would also benefit from the new system. Studies sponsored by the journal <u>Corporate Quarterly</u> show that satisfied employees increase productivity by working harder and taking fewer days off. The same studies also point out that contented employees are less susceptible to costly stress-related accidents at work. Most important, flexible hours would solve some of the dilemmas that many working parents face. Child care, for instance, would be easier to arrange if parents were freed from a strict 9-to-5 schedule. In fact, a flexible work schedule might mean that many two-career families could avoid day care altogether, since one parent could be at home with children during non-school hours. Flexible hours seem to be a sensible alternative to the current rigid system.

It is accurate. When you have a strong belief and want readers to see things your way, you may be tempted to skew evidence by exaggerating or downplaying facts, disregarding information, misquoting, or inventing details. Suppose you plan to write an essay making the point that dormitory security is lax on your campus. You begin by supporting your thesis with your personal observations about the situation. Realizing the essay would be more persuasive if you mentioned other people's experiences, you invent a number of incidents and quote several non-existent students. Yes, you have supported your point — but at the expense of truth.

It is representative. Using representative evidence means that you rely on the typical, the usual, to show that your point is valid. Contrary to the maxim, exceptions don't prove the rule. Perhaps you plan to write an essay contending that the value of seat belts has been exaggerated. To support your position, you mention a friend who survived a head-on collision without wearing a seat belt. Such an example is not representative because the facts and figures on accident survival suggest your friend's survival was a matter of luck.

An essay without solid evidence is unlikely to convince readers of the validity of the writer's views. Such writing also tends to be flat and dull, more likely to put readers to sleep than to engage their interest. Taking the time to accumulate supporting material that is specific, adequate, appropriate, accurate, and representative is an important step toward writing effective essays.

Activities: Support the Thesis with Evidence

1. For each of the two thesis statements below, develop three points of relevant support.

   Thesis: The trend toward disposable, throw-away products has gone too far.

   Thesis: All first-year college students should be required to participate in an orientation program conducted the week before the start of the academic year.

2. Each of the following sets includes a thesis statement and four points of support. In each set, identify the one point that is off target.

   ### Set A

   Thesis: Colleges should put less emphasis on sports.

   Encourages grade fixing
   Creates a strong following among former graduates
   Distracts from real goals of education
   Causes extensive and expensive injuries

   ### Set B

   Thesis: America is becoming a homogenized country.

   Regional accents vanishing
   Chain stores blanket country
   Americans proud of their ethnic identities
   Metropolitan areas almost indistinguishable from one another

STAGE 4: ORGANIZE THE EVIDENCE

Having generated your supporting evidence, you are now ready to organize that material. Organizing means arranging material in a sequence that helps you achieve your purpose. The most compelling support in the world will not illustrate the validity of your thesis or achieve your purpose if the reader must plow through a mass of unorganized evidence. Some writers can move quickly from generating support to writing a clear first draft (they usually say they have done their organizing in their heads). But such individuals are rare. Most people need to spend some time organizing their thoughts on paper before starting the first draft; otherwise, they tend to lose their way in a tangle of ideas. Planning and organizing demand hard thought, but they provide the surest route to a well-reasoned essay.

Use Rhetorical Patterns

The rhetorical patterns described in *The Macmillan Reader* help writers organize material. The patterns, each with its own internal logic, are strategies for imposing order on ideas. Some writers in this book use a single pattern throughout their essays. More often, though, the selections (and the essays you will write) blend patterns, with the predominant pattern providing the organizational framework for the piece. For example, an essay arguing a debatable issue might start with a *narrative* to dramatize the controversy, then move to a *definition* of terms, then *compare* and *contrast* competing viewpoints. Still, the essay as a whole would be categorized as argumentation – persuasion because its purpose is to advance a particular position on a controversial issue.

In composition class, you may be asked to write an essay organized around a single pattern. Such assignments are meant to give you practice in that pattern, so you will come to understand its unique demands. Helpful as such assignments are, you should keep in mind that most writing begins not with a specific pattern but with a specific purpose. The pattern or combination of patterns used to organize and develop a piece evolves as you work to meet that larger purpose.

The list below summarizes the purposes of the nine patterns discussed in this book. These patterns are not artificial formats concocted by composition instructors. Not at all. Because they help writers explore their subjects and organize their thoughts, you will see the patterns over and over, in various combinations, as you read the professional and student essays in this book.

Pattern	Purpose
Description	To detail what a person, place, or object is like
Narration	To relate an event
Exemplification	To provide specific instances or illustrations
Process analysis	To explain how something is done
Comparison – contrast	To point out similarities and/or differences
Cause – effect	To analyze reasons and consequences
Division – classification	To divide something into parts or to group related things in categories
Definition	To explain the meaning of a term or concept
Argumentation – persuasion	To convince readers about a controversial point of view

Use Three Basic Organizational Approaches

No matter which pattern(s) of development you select, you need to know three general approaches for organizing supporting evidence. These are explained below.

Chronological approach. Some essays are best organized chronologically; that is, the supporting material is arranged in a clear time sequence, usually starting with what happened first and ending with what happened last. Occasionally, chronological sequences can be rearranged to create flashback or flashforward effects, two techniques discussed later in the chapter on narration. Essays using narration or process analysis, either as the dominant or supporting patterns, are most likely to organize material chronologically.

Spatial approach. When you arrange supporting evidence spatially, you discuss details as they occur in space. This strategy is particularly appropriate for description. Imagine you are planning to write an essay describing the joyous times you spent as a child playing near a fondly remembered tree in the neighborhood park. Using spatial organization, you might start by describing the games you and your friends played at the foot of the tree. Next, you might recall the cozy feeling you experienced sitting on a large branch in the middle of the tree. Finally, you might end by describing the beautiful view of the world from the top of the tree.

Although spatial arrangement is flexible (the essay could, for example, start at the top of the tree), it should always proceed systematically. And once you choose a spatial sequence, you should — to avoid confusing readers — usually stay with that pattern to the end.

Emphatic method. In emphatic order, the most compelling, most striking evidence is saved for last. This arrangement works well because it is based on the psychological principle that people remember best what they experience last. To use emphatic order effectively, you should create a momentum, starting with the least important point and building to the most significant. Emphatic order is especially effective in argumentation – persuasion essays, in papers presenting series of examples, and in pieces involving causal analysis, comparison – contrast, or division – classification.

Depending on your purpose, any one of these three approaches for arranging evidence might be appropriate. Assume, for example, that you want to develop the following thesis for the Goodman assignment discussed earlier in this chapter: "Being a parent today is much more difficult than it was a generation ago." If you want to emphasize the difficulties parents face at various stages in their children's lives, you will probably select a chronological sequence. If you want to focus on the challenges parents face when children are at home, at school, and in the world at large, you most likely will choose a spatial sequence. If you want to show the range of problems parents face (from less to more serious), you will probably use an emphatic sequence. The ordering principle selected will depend on your essay's purpose.

Prepare an Outline

Having an outline—a skeletal version of your paper—can help ease you into the first draft. The outline encourages you to organize your thoughts *before* writing the first draft and serves as a road map once writing begins. Even though ideas continue to evolve during the draft, an outline clarifies the relationship among points, exposes gaps in logic, and identifies places where evidence is weak—underscoring the need, perhaps, for more brainstorming, freewriting, or research.

Like earlier writing stages, the outlining process is flexible. Outlining will often go quickly, with points falling easily into place. But there will also be times when you have to work hard to figure out how points relate to each other. Also keep in mind that the amount of detail in an outline will vary according to the length of the paper and the instructor's requirements. Often a scratch outline—an example of which appears on page 24— will serve you well; at other times you will need a longer, more formal outline. The following suggestions will help if you prepare a structured outline. As always, feel free to modify these guidelines to fit your needs.

- Keeping your purpose, audience, and tone in mind, write your thesis at the top of the outlining page.
- Reevaluate your supporting material. Cross out anything that doesn't develop the thesis, or that isn't consistent with your purpose, audience, and tone.
- Add any new points or material.
- Sort the evidence and group related items. Give each group a heading that represents a main point in support of your thesis.
- Label these main points with Roman numerals (I, II, III, and so on). Let the numerals identify what you think is the best order for these points.
- Identify supporting points and group them under the appropriate major points. Indent and label these subordinate points with capital letters (A, B, C, and so on). Let the order of the letters identify what you think is the most effective order for these secondary points.
- Identify specific details (facts, statistics, examples, expert authority, and so on) and group them under the appropri-

ate supporting points. Indent and label these specific details with Arabic numbers (1, 2, 3, and so on). Let the numbers identify the best order for the details.

- Examine your outline, looking for places where evidence is weak. Where appropriate, add new evidence: major points, supporting points, specific details.
- Evaluate the relationship between the thesis and the various levels of support. Make whatever changes are needed until you are satisfied that you have organized your material in a logical fashion.

Here is an example of a student's somewhat formal outline. It was prepared in response to the assignment on Ellen Goodman's essay "At a Nuclear Age."

Purpose: To write an informative essay
Audience: Instructor and class members, mostly 18–20 years old
Tone: Serious and straightforward
Thesis: Being a parent today is much more difficult than it was a generation ago.

I. Distractions from schoolwork
  A. At home
    1. Stereos, radios, tapes
    2. Television
  B. Outside home
    1. Malls
    2. Video arcades
    3. Fast-food restaurants

II. Sexually explicit materials
  A. In print
    1. Sex magazines
    2. Pornographic books
  B. In movies
    1. Seduction scenes
    2. Casual sex
  C. On television
    1. Soap operas
    2. R-rated movies on cable

III. Increase in life-threatening dangers
  A. Violent crimes against children
  B. Drugs
  C. Alcohol

A brief suggestion: Show your outline to several people (your instructor, friends, classmates) before beginning to write a draft. Their reactions will let you know whether your proposed organization is appropriate for your purpose, audience, tone, and thesis; their comments can highlight areas needing additional work.

If you are asked to submit an outline, you may feel tempted to prepare the outline *after* the paper has been finished. But such a reversing of the process defeats the whole purpose of outlining. If you adapt our suggestions to suit your needs, you will find that outlining, far from being mechanical busywork, can guide your writing and provide a sound structure for the work that follows.

Activities: Organize the Evidence

Following each thesis statement below is a scrambled list of supporting points for an essay. Prepare an outline for each potential essay, being sure to distinguish between major and secondary points.

1. Thesis: Our schools, now in crisis, could be improved in several ways.

Certification requirements for teachers
Schedules
Teachers
Longer school year
Merit pay for outstanding teachers
Curriculum
Better textbooks for classroom use
Longer school days
More challenging content in courses

2. Thesis: Supermarket fruits and vegetables are far from being natural products.

Dyes used to brighten colors
Techniques for growing produce
Pesticide sprays in the fields
Preservative treatments in the warehouse or market
Wax coatings to create shininess
Use of chemical fertilizers
Cosmetic treatments in the warehouse or market
Injections to retard spoilage
Chemical dips to extend shelf life

STAGE 5: WRITE THE FIRST DRAFT

After prewriting, writing a thesis, developing supporting evidence, and organizing the evidence, you are in good shape to write a first draft—a rough, provisional version of your essay. Because of your work in the preceding stages, the first draft may flow rather smoothly. But don't be discouraged if it sometimes goes slowly. You may find, for example, that your thesis needs reshaping, that a point no longer fits, that you have to return to a prewriting activity to generate additional supporting material. Such stopping and starting is to be expected. Writing involves continual clarification and refining of ideas, with your thoughts evolving as you work on the first draft. As E. M. Forster, the British novelist and essayist, remarked, "How do I know what I think until I see what I say?"

There is no right way to prepare a first draft. Some people glance at their outlines or scratch lists only occasionally, while others rely on them heavily. Although outlines and lists are valuable for guiding your work, you don't want to be so dependent on them that you shy away from new ideas that surface during the first draft. If promising new thoughts pop up, jot them down in the margin. Then, at the appropriate point, go back and evaluate the new ideas. Do they support your thesis? Are they consistent with the essay's purpose, audience, and tone? If so, include the material in your draft.

It is easy to get bogged down while preparing the first draft if you edit as you go along. Remember, a draft is not intended to be perfect. For the time being, adopt a relaxed non-critical attitude. Don't stop to look up spelling, check grammar, or polish sentence structure. Save these for later. You may even find it helpful to write messily on scrap paper or a yellow pad, using pencil rather than pen. Writing on alternate lines also underscores that you intend to return later to polish your writing.

If you get stuck while writing your draft, keep calm and try to push ahead. If words just won't come, write down anything—even if it is awkward and imprecise. Or leave a blank space to hold a spot for the right words when they finally break loose, jotting a reminder to yourself in the margin ("Fix this" or "Redo") to fine-tune later on. Another tactic is to reread—out loud is best—what you have already written. Getting a sense of the larger context is often enough to get you moving again. And if a section strikes you as particularly difficult, don't try to wrestle it to the ground. Instead, move on to an easier section, write that, and then return to the challenging part. If, after trying these techniques, you are still getting nowhere, take a break. Watch television, listen to music, talk with friends. While you are distracted, your unconscious mind may take over and untangle the section that has been giving you trouble.

Students sometimes have difficulty with their drafts because they think they have to write the essay's introduction before anything else. There is no rule that says you must. Instead, you may find it helpful to follow the sequence below:

- Write the essay's supporting paragraphs
- Connect the ideas in the supporting paragraphs
- Write the introduction
- Write the conclusion
- Write a title

Working in this sequence encourages you to focus on the supporting paragraphs of the essay. These key paragraphs, in turn, influence how you tie your points together and what you say in your introduction and conclusion.

Write the Essay's Supporting Paragraphs

Drawn from the main sections in your outline or scratch list, each *supporting paragraph* in an essay develops an aspect of your thesis. The rhetorical patterns described in this book (narration, process analysis, whatever) provide the organizational framework for the paragraphs, and *topic sentences* often focus the paragraphs further. One or two sentences in length, the topic sentence is often — but not always — the first sentence in a paragraph. A kind of mini-thesis, the topic sentence signals the paragraph's subject and frequently indicates the writer's attitude toward that subject. The rest of the paragraph provides support for the topic sentence in the form of examples, facts, observations, expert opinion, and so on. In the topic sentences below, the subject of the paragraph is underlined once, and the attitude toward the subject is underlined twice.

Students often select their majors for the wrong reasons.
The ocean dumping of radioactive waste is a ticking time bomb.
Several contemporary rock groups show unexpected sensitivity to social issues.
Political candidates are being sold like products.

Sometimes you may write a supporting paragraph without paying too much attention to a topic sentence. Just be sure to evaluate the paragraph later on, providing a topic sentence if the paragraph needs a sharper focus. Or you may find after writing a paragraph that you have to recast a topic sentence to reflect the unexpected direction the paragraph took. Occasionally, if a paragraph has a clear focus, you may eliminate the topic sentence altogether, letting the content of the paragraph imply your point.

Connect Ideas in the Supporting Paragraphs

While writing the supporting paragraphs, you may want to smooth out the progression of ideas within and between paragraphs. In a *coherent* essay, the relationship between points is clear; readers can easily follow the development of your thoughts. (Sometimes, working on coherence causes a first draft to get bogged down; if you find this happening, move on, and wait until the revision stage to focus on such matters.)

Using a clear chronological, spatial, or emphatic sequence is a first step in making writing coherent (see pages 37–38). Another way is to include *signaling* or *connecting devices* that tell readers where you have been and where you are going. A light touch should be your goal when you provide such devices; overused, they call attention to themselves and make the progression of thoughts plodding and mechanical. In any case, these are some signaling devices to consider:

1. Transitions. Transitions are words and phrases that give simple, clear signals to readers, telling them how the ideas in a paper are connected. Among such signals are the following:

Time	Space	Addition	Examples
First	Above	Moreover	For instance
Next	Below	Also	For example
Now	Next to	Furthermore	To illustrate
Finally	Behind	In addition	As an example

Contrast		Comparison	Summary
But		Similarly	Therefore
However		Also	Thus
Otherwise		Likewise	In short
On the other hand		Too	In conclusion

Here is an earlier paragraph from this chapter. Note how the italicized transitions link ideas together.

Having generated your supporting evidence, you are *now* ready to organize that material. The most compelling support in the world will not illustrate the validity of your thesis or achieve your purpose if the reader must plow through a mass of unorganized evidence. Some writers can move quickly from generating support to writing a clear first draft (they usually say they have done their organizing in their heads). *But* such individuals are rare. Most people need to spend some time organizing their thoughts on paper before starting the first draft; *otherwise*, they tend to lose their way in a tangle of ideas. Planning and organizing demand hard thought, *but* they provide the surest route to a well-reasoned essay.

2. Linking sentences. Linking sentences tie paragraphs together by mentioning what has gone before and what is yet to come. Such sentences remind readers of the material they have just read and introduce them to new ideas. Look again at the first sentence in the paragraph reprinted above, noting the way the sentence performs two functions: It links back to the previous discussion about generating evidence, *and* it signals that this new section will focus on the organization of such evidence.

3. Repeated words, synonyms, and pronouns. Repeating key words, using synonyms, and using pronouns all maintain continuity by creating a tightly woven network of ideas. The repetition of important words produces an echo effect that firmly plants key ideas in the reader's mind. Synonyms, words that are similar in meaning to key words or phrases, also link parts of the essay and make it possible to avoid unimaginative and tedious repetitions. Finally, pronouns act as automatic connecting devices, causing readers to think back to the original word, or antecedent, the pronoun replaces. Be sure, however, that there is no ambiguity about the pronoun's antecedent.

Reprinted here is another paragraph from this chapter. Repeated words have been underlined once, synonyms underlined twice, and pronouns printed in italic type to illustrate how these techniques were used to link the paragraph's ideas.

The process of prewriting—discovering a limited subject and generating ideas about *it*—prepares you for the next stage in writing an essay: stating the paper's thesis, or controlling ideas. Representing your slant on a subject, the thesis should focus on an interesting and significant issue, *one* that engages your energies and merits your consideration. You may think of the thesis as the essay's hub—the central point around which all the other material revolves. Because the thesis often appears early in the essay, *it* helps focus readers on your central point. The thesis is equally valuable to you as a writer, for *it* helps determine what does and does not belong in the essay.

Write the Introduction to the Essay

Some writers wait until the revision stage to write the introduction, but many feel more comfortable if the first draft includes in basic form *all* parts of the final essay. If that is how you feel, you will probably write the introduction as you complete your first draft. No matter when you generate the introduction, you should keep in mind how crucial it is to the success of your essay. Specifically, the introduction serves three important purposes. First, it introduces the subject of your paper. Second, it arouses interest, spurring readers on to look at the whole essay. Third, it presents the thesis, your special angle on the topic.

The length of the introduction will vary according to your paper's scope and purpose. Most of the essays you write will be served best by a one- or two-paragraph beginning. Accomplishing the three tasks of an introduction in just one or two paragraphs can be a challenge; fortunately, you can use any of the following methods, singly or in combination. Note that the thesis statement in each introduction has been underlined.

A Broad Statement Narrowing to a Limited Subject

For generations, morality has been molded primarily by parents, religion, and schools. Children traditionally acquired their ideas about what is right and wrong, which goals are important in life, and how other people should be treated from these three sources. But now there is another powerful force influencing youngsters. Television is implanting in children negative values about sex, work, and family life.

A Brief Anecdote

At a local high school recently, students in a psychology course were given a hint of what it is like to be the parents of a newborn. Each "parent" had to carry a raw egg around at all times to symbolize the responsibilities of parenthood. The egg could not be left alone; it limited the "parents'" activities; it placed a full-time emotional burden on "Mom" and "Dad." This class exercise illustrates a common problem facing the majority of new mothers and fathers. Most people receive little preparation for the job of being parents.

An Idea or Situation That Is the Opposite of the One to Be Developed

We hear a great deal about the disastrous effect of divorce on children. We are deluged with advice on ways to make divorce as painless as possible for youngsters; we listen to heartbreaking stories about the confused, grieving children of divorced parents. Little attention has been paid, however, to a radically different kind of divorce. If children are deeply unhappy with their homelife, they should be allowed to "divorce" their parents.

A Series of Short, Stimulating Questions

What happens if your child is caught vandalizing school property? What happens if your child goes for a joyride in a stolen car and accidentally hits a pedestrian? Are you, as a parent, liable for your children's mistakes? Will you end up being sued for hundreds of thousands of dollars in damages? Parents have begun to think seriously about such questions because the laws concerning the limits of parental responsibility are changing rapidly. <u>With unfortunate frequency, courts are beginning to hold parents liable for their children's mistakes.</u>

A Thought-Provoking Quotation

Educator Neil Postman believes that television has blurred the lines between childhood and adulthood. According to Postman, "All the secrets that a print culture kept from children . . . are revealed all at once by media that do not, and cannot, exclude any audience." <u>This media barrage of information once intended only for adults has changed childhood for the worse.</u>

A Dramatic Fact or Statistic

Seventy percent of the respondents in a poll conducted by columnist Ann Landers stated that, if they could live their lives over, they would choose not to have children. This startling statistic makes one wonder what these people believed parenthood would be like. <u>Most parents, it seems, have unrealistic expectations about their children.</u> Parents want their children automatically to accept their values, follow their paths, and succeed where they failed.

Introductory paragraphs sometimes end with *a plan of development:* a quick preview of the essay's major points in the order in which those points will be discussed. The plan of development may be part of the thesis (as in the first introduction above), or it may immediately follow the thesis (as in the last introduction above).

Because the plan of development highlights the organizational structure of the essay, it helps focus attention on the logical progression of ideas in the essay. A plan of development may not be needed in a brief essay, for your audience will often be able to keep track of your ideas without this extra help. In a longer essay, though, a plan of development can be a unifying device because it points to the main ideas the reader will soon encounter.

Write the Conclusion to the Essay

You have probably read essays that sputtered to a tired close. Perhaps there were no conclusions at all, making the pieces end abruptly, in a jarring, disorienting way. Or the essays might have had conclusions, but they were weak and lifeless, a sure sign that the writers had run out of steam and wanted to finish as quickly as possible. But a strong conclusion is an important part of an effective essay. Generally one or two paragraphs in length, the conclusion should give the reader a feeling of completeness and finality. Because people remember most clearly the points they read last, the conclusion is a good spot to remind readers of your thesis. You may also use the conclusion to echo an idea presented in the introduction or to express a final thought about your subject.

Illustrated briefly here are several strategies for writing sound conclusions. These techniques may be used singly or in combination.

A Summary

Parent-child divorce should not be seen as frivolous and impractical. Studies show that such divorces can save marriages, create a calmer atmosphere at home, and help troubled children develop a new outlook on life. Perhaps such an extreme measure is exactly what is needed to keep families together during these confusing times.

A Prediction

The growing tendency on the part of the judicial system to hold parents responsible for the reactions of their wayward children can have a disturbing impact on all of us. Parents will feel bitter toward their own children and cynical about a system that allows such an injustice. Children, continuing to escape the consequences of their actions, will become even more lawless and destructive. Society cannot afford two such possibilities.

A Quotation

The comic W. C. Fields is reputed to have said, "Anyone who hates children and dogs can't be all bad." Most people do not share Fields' cynicism. Viewing childhood as a time of purity, they are alarmed at the way television exposes children to the seamy side of life, stripping youngsters of their innocence and giving them a glib sophistication that is a poor substitute for wisdom.

A Recommendation or Call for Action

It is a mistake to leave parenting to instinct. Instead, we should make parenting skills a required course in schools. In addition, a nationwide hotline should be established to help parents deal with crises. Such training and continuing support would help adults deal more effectively with many of the problems they face as parents.

Create a Title for the Essay

Some professional writers say that they began a certain piece with only a title in mind. But for most people, a title is a finishing touch. Although creating a title for your paper is usually one of the last steps in writing an essay, it should not be done haphazardly. It may take time to write an effective title — one that hints at the essay's thesis and snares the reader's interest.

Good titles may make use of the following techniques: repetition of sounds ("Why I Want a Wife"); twists on familiar sayings ("To Win or Not to Win: That Is the Question"); and humor ("How to Say Nothing in 500 Words"). More often, though, titles are straightforward phrases derived from the essay's subject or thesis: "Shooting an Elephant" and "TV Addiction," for example.

Pull It All Together

Now that you understand how to write the various parts of an essay, you might find it helpful to see a diagram illustrating how the different paragraphs can fit together. Keep in mind that not every essay you write will take this shape. As your purpose, audience, and tone change, so will the structure of your essay. An introduction or conclusion, for instance, may be developed in more than one paragraph; the thesis statement may be implied or delayed until the middle or end of the essay; not all paragraphs will have topic sentences; and several supporting paragraphs may be needed to develop an important point. Even so, the basic format presented below offers a strategy for organizing a variety of writing assignments, from term papers to lab reports. Once you feel comfortable with the structure, you have a foundation on which to plan your variations. (The variations possible are illustrated in this book's student essays and professional selections.) Moreover, even when using a specific format, you always have room to give your spirit and imagination free play. The language you use, the details you select, and the perspective you offer are highly personal and uniquely yours. They are what make your essay different from everyone else's.

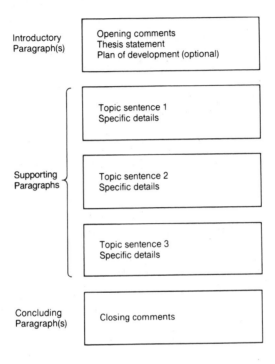

Introductory Paragraph(s)
- Opening comments
- Thesis statement
- Plan of development (optional)

Supporting Paragraphs
- Topic sentence 1
- Specific details
- Topic sentence 2
- Specific details
- Topic sentence 3
- Specific details

Concluding Paragraph(s)
- Closing comments

Activity: Write the First Draft

Following is an outline for a potential essay. The thesis statement, major points, secondary points, and supporting details are given. Write an essay, using this outline as a guide, but feel free to make changes as needed.

Assume that your essay will appear as an informative article in a local high school newspaper. Your audience consists of high school students about to start their first jobs; you want to tell these students what the world of work is like. The tone of the essay should be personable and friendly; you want to sound helpful, not intimidating. The essay should include the following: a title; an introduction that includes the thesis and, if needed, a plan of development; supporting paragraphs, some of which are focused by topic sentences; expanded specific details; transitions and linking sentences; and a conclusion.

If you would rather prepare an essay on a different subject, that's fine. Be sure, however, that your essay includes a title, an introduction, and so on. Also, before writing the essay, clarify to yourself the essay's purpose, audience, and tone.

Thesis: Most employers are neither angels nor ogres; they are simply human beings with varying degrees of management skill.

   I. Bosses who exercise strict control
     A. Bosses who enjoy exercising authority
       1. Give orders at every opportunity
       2. Want to make all decisions themselves
     B. Worriers
       1. Watch employees closely to prevent mistakes
       2. Redo employees' work until it is perfect

  II. Bosses who have relinquished control
     A. Absentee bosses
       1. Never available at critical moments
       2. Employees forced to make all decisions
     B. Burned-out bosses
       1. Uninterested in how job is done
       2. Unreliable — never on time, many supposed sick days

 III. Bosses with good management skills
     A. Skilled supervisors
       1. Good at giving feedback
       2. Willing to delegate authority
     B. Mentors
       1. Help employees get promotions
       2. Provide emotional support

STAGE 6: REVISE THE ESSAY

By now, you have probably abandoned any preconceptions you might have had about good writers sitting down and creating a finished product in one easy step. Alexander Pope's comment that "true ease in writing comes from art, not chance" is as true today as it was more than 200 years ago. Writing that seems effortlessly clear is often the result of sustained work, not of good luck or even inborn talent. And much of this work takes place during the final stage of the writing process when ideas, paragraphs, sentences, and words are refined and reshaped.

    People who make their living as writers — reporters, novelists, columnists, textbook authors — seldom submit a piece of writing that has not undergone revision. They recognize that raw, unrevised work does not do them justice. What's more, they often look forward to revising. Columnist Ellen Goodman puts it this way: "What makes me happy is rewriting. . . . It's like cleaning house, getting rid of all the junk, getting things in the right order, tightening up."

In a sense, revision occurs throughout the writing process: at some point or another, you might have dropped an idea, overhauled your thesis, rejuggled paragraph order. What, then, is different about the refashioning that occurs in this final stage? To answer that question, consider the literal meaning of the word *revision*. Revision means to resee or see again, to cast a clear eye on your work, viewing it as though you were someone else. You go looking for trouble, ready to pick a fight with your own writing. And then you must sit down and rewrite, making the changes needed for your writing to be as effective as possible.

Revision is more than changing a word here, correcting a spelling error there, typing a neat final copy. Revision means eliminating deadwood, rearranging paragraphs, substituting new words for old ones, recasting sentences, improving coherence, even generating new material when appropriate. Because such work is challenging, you may resist revision or feel shaky about how to proceed. The following pointers should help to get you going if you balk at or feel overwhelmed by revising.

First, if time allows, set your writing aside for a while before revising. When you pick up your paper again, you will have a fresh, more objective perspective. Also, try to work from typed material. Having your essay in neutral typed letters instead of your own familiar writing helps you see the paper impartially, as if you did not write it. And whenever possible, read your essay aloud. Hearing how your writing sounds helps you pick up things that passed you by before: places where sentences are awkward, meaning is ambiguous, words are imprecise. Even better, have another person read to you what you have written. If the reader stumbles over an awkward transition or trips over a convoluted paragraph, you know where you have to do some rewriting.

Getting feedback from a group of classmates is another way to make revision easier. You want to leave such peer feedback sessions with specific, pointed comments about what does and does not work in your writing, so be sure to ask your readers focused questions requiring more than a simple "yes" or "no." The checklist questions below should help you solicit feedback. Or you may develop your own targeted questions: "My introduction seems bland. Any ideas on how I could perk it up?" or "The essay seems choppy when it moves to the third point. How could I make the transition smoother?"

Here's a final hint. When revising, don't try to tackle all at once everything needing work. Instead, view revision as a process and proceed step by step. Whenever possible, read your essay several times, each time focusing on different issues and asking yourself different questions. Move from a broad overview of the essay to an up-close look at its mechanics.

The checklist below describes a number of questions you can ask as you move through the various steps in the revising process. As always, adapt our suggestions to suit your needs.

Revision Checklist

- First Step: Focus on Overall Meaning and Content
  - Considering the essay's purpose, audience, and tone, in what ways does or doesn't the paper accomplish what was intended?
  - What is the essay's thesis? Is it stated explicitly, or is it implied?
  - What main points support the thesis? Does any material not support the thesis?
- Second Step: Focus on Organization and Development
  - What pattern or combination of patterns develops the essays? Are the patterns effective?
  - Is the evidence in any supporting paragraph irrelevant, vague, or insufficient? Where?
  - What organizational strategy (chronological, spatial, emphatic) sequences the supporting paragraphs? Is the strategy effective?
  - What connecting devices are used to link ideas? Are there enough devices? Too many?
  - What strategies are used to open and close the essay? Are the strategies effective?
- Third Step: Focus on Sentences and Words
  - What sentences are not particularly crisp and varied? How can they be improved?

- What words are not particularly specific and concrete? How can they be improved?
- Fourth Step: Proofread
  - What spelling, grammar, punctuation, and typographical errors need to be corrected?

A note about proofreading: although proofing seems to involve relatively minor matters, an accumulation of small errors — misspellings, typos, misplaced commas — can distract readers and sabotage an otherwise strong essay. So before handing in the final draft of your essay, proofread it closely, keeping a dictionary and English handbook nearby. When proofing, people tend to see what they think is on the page rather than what really is there. Reading the essay out loud and backwards, starting with the last word first, can highlight errors that might ordinarily slip by.

The six-stage writing process is not meant to be a fixed, unchanging formula for preparing essays. As you gain more experience writing papers, you will learn how to adapt the stages to fit your needs and the demands of specific assignments. You will also learn how to move through the stages more quickly, taking shortcuts when appropriate. But until you feel real confidence as a writer, the six-stage process can provide a welcome series of steps to follow.

STUDENT ESSAY AND COMMENTARY

The student essay that follows was written by Harriet Davids, a 38-year-old college student who is the mother of two teenagers. Harriet set out to write an informative paper with a straightforward, serious tone. While preparing her essay, she kept in mind that her audience included the course instructor as well as other students in the class — most of whom are considerably younger than she. This is the assignment that provided the springboard for Harriet's essay:

> In the essay "At a Nuclear Age," Ellen Goodman contends that the world today is a difficult, even dangerous place for children. Write an essay that provides evidence to support Goodman's point.

The essay has been annotated so you can see how it illustrates the essay format described in this chapter. As you read the essay, try to determine how well it reflects the principles of effective writing. The commentary following the paper will help you look at Harriet's essay more closely.

Challenges for Today's Parents

INTRODUCTION

Reruns of situation comedies from the fifties and early sixties dramatize the kinds of problems that parents used to have with their children. The Cleavers scold Beaver for not washing his hands before dinner; the Andersons ground Bud for not doing his homework; the Nelsons dock little Ricky's allowance because he keeps forgetting to clean his room. But times have

Thesis

changed dramatically. Being a parent today is much more difficult than it was a generation

Plan of development

ago. Parents nowadays must protect their children from a growing number of distractions, from sexually explicit material, and from life-threatening situations.

FIRST SUPPORTING PARAGRAPH

Topic sentence

Today's parents must try, first of all, to control all the new distractions that tempt children away from schoolwork. At home, a child may have a room furnished with a stereo and television. Not many young people can resist the urge to listen to an album or watch MTV—especially if it is time to do schoolwork. Outside the home, the distractions are even more alluring. Children no longer "hang out" on a neighborhood corner within earshot of Mom or Dad's reminder to come in and do homework. Instead, they concentrate in vast shopping malls, buzzing video arcades, and gleaming fast-food restaurants. Parents and school assignments have obvious difficulty competing with such enticing alternatives.

SECOND SUPPORTING PARAGRAPH

Topic sentence

Besides dealing with these distractions, parents also have to shield their children from a flood of sexually explicit materials. Today, children can find sex magazines and pornographic paperbacks in the same corner store that once offered only comics and candy. Children will not see the fuzzily photographed nudes that a previous generation did but will encounter the hard-core raunchiness of <u>Hustler</u> or <u>Penthouse</u>. Moreover, the movies young people attend often focus on highly sexual situations. It is difficult to teach children traditional values when films show teachers seducing students and young people treating sex as a casual sport. An even more difficult matter for parents is the heavily sexual content of programs on television. With just a flick of the dial, children can see soap opera stars cavorting in bed or watch cable programs where nudity is common.

THIRD SUPPORTING PARAGRAPH

Topic sentence

Most disturbing to parents today, however, is the increase in life-threatening dangers that face young people. When children are small, parents fear that their youngsters may be victims of violence. Every news program seems to carry a report about a mass murderer who preys on young girls, a deviant who has buried six boys in his cellar, or an organized child pornography ring that molests preschoolers. When children are older, parents begin to worry about their kids' use of drugs. Peer pressure to experiment with drugs is often stronger than parents' warnings. This pressure to experiment can be fatal if the drugs have been mixed with dangerous chemicals. Finally, even if young people escape the hazards associated with drugs, they must still resist the pressure to drink. Although alcohol has always held an attraction for teenagers, reports indicate that they are drinking more than ever before. As many parents know, the consequences of this attraction can be deadly — especially when drinking is combined with driving.

CONCLUSION

Within one generation, the world as a place to raise children has changed dramatically. One wonders how yesterday's parents would have dealt with today's problems. Could the Andersons have kept Bud away from MTV? Could the Nelsons have shielded Ricky from sexually explicit material? Could the Cleavers have protected Beaver from drugs and alcohol? Parents must be aware of all these distractions and dangers, yet be willing to give their children the freedom they need to become responsible adults. It is not an easy task.

"Challenges for Today's Parents" is an essay with many positive points. Although the paper — like most writing — could be shaped and polished further, it is clear that Harriet knows how to write a strong essay.

The essay's *introduction* attracts the reader's interest by recalling several vintage television shows that have almost become part of our cultural heritage. Harriet begins with these examples from the past because they present such a sharp contrast to the idea expressed in the *thesis:* "Being a parent today is much more difficult than it was a generation ago." This reversing of direction is a common and effective technique for starting an essay. Note, too, the way Harriet's thesis states the paper's subject (being a parent) as well as her attitude toward the subject (the job is more demanding than it was years ago).

Harriet follows her thesis statement with a *plan of development* that anticipates the three major points to be covered in the essay's supporting paragraphs. But the plan of development is somewhat mechanical, with the major points being trotted past the reader in one long, awkward sentence. To deal with this problem, Harriet could have rewritten the sentence or eliminated the plan of development altogether, ending the introduction after the thesis.

Although Harriet develops her thesis primarily through *examples*, she also draws on *two other rhetorical patterns*. The whole paper is characterized by an implied *contrast* between the way life is now and the way it used to be, a contrast spelled out in the introduction. The essay also contains an element of *causal analysis*, since all the factors Harriet cites affect children and the way they are raised.

Organizing the essay around a series of *relevant* and *specific* examples, Harriet uses *emphatic order* to sequence the paper's three main points — that a growing number of distractions, sexually explicit materials, and life-threatening situations make parenting difficult nowadays. The words that open the third supporting paragraph ("Most disturbing to parents today . . .") signal Harriet's particular concern about the physical dangers children face. Moreover, Harriet uses basic organizational strategies to sequence the supporting examples within each paragraph. The details in the first supporting paragraph are organized *spatially*, starting with distractions at home and moving to those outside the home. In the second supporting paragraph, Harriet orders her examples *emphatically*. She starts with sexually explicit publications and ends with the "even more difficult matter" of sexuality on television. The final supporting paragraph is organized *chronologically*; it begins by discussing dangers to small children and concludes by talking about teenagers.

The essay displays Harriet's familiarity with other kinds of organizational strategies. Each supporting paragraph opens with a *topic sentence*. Further, *connecting devices* are used throughout the paper to show the relationship among ideas: *Transitions* ("Instead, they congregate in vast shopping malls"; "Moreover, the movies young people attend often focus on highly sexual situations"); *repetition* ("sexual situations" and "sexual content"); *synonyms* ("distractions . . . enticing alternatives" and "life-threatening . . . fatal"); *pronouns* ("young people . . . they"); and *linking sentences* ("Besides dealing with these distractions, parents also have to shield their children from a flood of sexually explicit material"). In the last case, note how the linking sentence echoes the previous paragraph and states the focus of the new paragraph.

You might have found the structure of Harriet's essay a bit predictable. It might have been better, for instance, had she rewritten one of the paragraphs, perhaps embedding the topic sentence in the middle of the paragraph or saving it for the end. Harriet's use of connecting devices is also somewhat routine ("Today's parents must try, *first of all* . . ."). Even so, an essay with a clear focus and obvious links is preferable to one with a confusing or inaccessible structure. Harriet can continue to work on making the design of her essays more subtle as she gains writing experience.

Given the essay's *purpose* and *audience*, Harriet adopts a serious *tone*, providing no-nonsense evidence to support her thesis. But assume she had been asked by her daughters' school newspaper to write a humorous column about the trials and tribulations parents face raising children. Because of the shift in tone, purpose, and audience, Harriet would have proceeded differently. Drawing on her experience as a mother of two teens, she might have described how she manages to survive the flash and dazzle of MTV and the din of stereos blasting rock music at all hours: she stuffs her ears with cotton, hides her daughters' most raucous tapes, and even cuts off the electricity. This material—with its personalized perspective and exaggerated, light tone—would be appropriate, given Harriet's purpose and readers.

Harriet's *conclusion* brings the essay to a satisfying close by reminding readers of the paper's central idea and three main points. The final paragraph also extends the scope of the essay by introducing a new but related issue—that parents have to strike a balance between their need to provide limitations and their children's need for freedom.

Like the rest of her essay, Harriet's conclusion went through a number of changes before reaching its final form. Comparing the final version of her concluding paragraph with the first draft version below will give you a sense of Harriet's approach to revision.

First Draft Version
Most people love their children and work hard at being good parents. But the job gets harder in a world that is, in many ways, hostile to young people. Even Holden Caulfield, with his rage against a phony society, didn't face the confusing pressures of our world. Today's parents must somehow find ways to give children a reasonable amount of freedom, yet still exercise greater caution than before.

As soon as Harriet read her paper aloud during a group feedback session, she realized her conclusion needed work. Rather than bringing the essay to a satisfying finish, the final paragraph seemed tacked on, like a tired afterthought. Here's how Harriet proceeded when revising the conclusion.

First, she replaced the shopworn opening sentence ("Most people love their chilcren . . .") with three interesting questions ("Could the Andersons . . . Could the Nelsons . . . Could the Cleavers . . . ?"). Because these three rhythmical questions recall the essay's main points and echo the introduction's reference to old TV shows, they help round out and unify Harriet's paper.

When revising the final paragraph, Harriet also took into

account a comment made by another student during the feedback session. As the student pointed out, Harriet's paper discusses children of all ages, not just teens. The allusion to *The Catcher in the Rye* thus misrepresented the focus of the essay. Harriet's decision to omit the Holden Caulfield reference helped the paper come together as a unified whole.

These are just a few of the changes Harriet made when reworking her essay. Realizing that writing is a process, she left herself enough time to make such changes. She was also gratified by her classmates' response to what she had written and pleased by the lively discussion her essay provoked. Early in her composition course, she learned that attention to the various stages in the writing process yields satisfying results — for writer and reader alike.

DESCRIPTION

WHAT IS DESCRIPTION?

Animals live — or die — by their senses. Scenting danger, detecting the slightest rustle, spotting the lion camouflaged in the grass: All are crucial to survival. Although human senses are weak compared to those of most other animals, and although we compensate for this weakness by favoring our brains over our sensory organs, we are still animal enough to respond in a strong way to sensory stimulation. The sweet perfume of a candy shop takes us back to childhood; the stale medicine smell of the campus infirmary reminds us of long vigils at a hospital while a grandmother lay dying; the clang and thud of a city sets our nerves on edge; a splendid meal, pleasing to both eye and palate, usually revives even the most beleaguered among us.

Without any sensory stimulation, we sink into a less-than-human state. Neglected babies, left alone with no human touch, no colors, no lullabies, become withdrawn and unresponsive. And prisoners dread solitary confinement, knowing that the sensory deprivation can be unbearable, even to the point of madness.

Because sensory impressions are so important, descriptive writing has a power and a basic appeal unlike any other kind of writing. Description can be defined as the expression — in vivid word pictures — of what the five human senses experience. A richly rendered description freezes a subject in time, evoking sights, smells, sounds, textures, and tastes in such a way that the reader becomes one with the writer's world and vision.

WHEN TO USE DESCRIPTION

Description can be a supportive technique that develops part of an essay, or description can be the dominant technique used within an entire essay. Your essay's overall purpose will help you determine the amount of description needed. Here are some examples of the way description can help you meet the broad objective of an essay developed chiefly through another pattern of development:

- In an *argumentation-persuasion* essay urging more rigorous handgun control, you might start with a description of a violent family confrontation that ended in murder.
- In a *causal analysis* showing the *consequences* of pet overpopulation, you might describe the desperate appearance of a pack of starving stray dogs.
- In a *process analysis* explaining the pleasure of making ice cream at home, you might describe the beauty of an old-fashioned, hand-cranked ice cream maker.
- In a *narrative essay* recounting the spirited day in the life of a street musician, you might describe the energy of the musician and the joyous, appreciative response of passersby.

Your readers are as important as your purpose in determining how much or how little description to use. As you plan your paper, keep asking yourself, "What do these particular readers need to know to understand and experience keenly what I am describing?" "What descriptive details will they enjoy most?" Your answers to these and similar questions will help you tailor your description to specific readers. Consider an article in a newsletter for professional horticulturists, the purpose of the article being to explain a new technique for controlling spider mites.

Because of the readers' expertise, there would be little need for a lengthy description of the insects. But assume the article appeared in a college newsletter. Rewritten to advise students in dorms how to keep their plants healthy, the article would probably provide a detailed description of the mites so student gardeners could tell the difference between these pesky parasites and random flecks of dust.

While your purpose and audience define *how much* to describe, you have great freedom deciding *what* to describe. Description is especially suited to objects (your car or desk, for example), but you can also describe a person, a place, a time, or a phenomenon or concept. Effective descriptions might be written about a friend who runs marathons (person), the kitchen of a fast-food restaurant (place), a period when you were unemployed (time), the "flight or fight" syndrome (phenomenon or concept).

Depending on your approach to the subject, description can be divided into two types: *objective* and *subjective*. In an *objective description*, you describe the subject but do not reveal your attitude or feelings about it. Instead, you are concerned with transmitting a straightforward and literal portrait of the subject, without fusing your own point of view onto the description. For example, a reporter may write an unemotional account of a township meeting that ended in a fistfight between town council members and residents. Or a marine biologist may write a factual report describing the way sea mammals are killed by the plastic refuse (sandwich wrappings, straws, fishing lines) that humans throw into the ocean. Reporters as well as technical and scientific writers specialize in objective description; their jobs depend on their ability to detail experiences without emotional bias.

On the other hand, in a *subjective description*, you convey a highly personal view of your subject and seek to elicit a strong emotional response from your readers. Such subjective descriptions are often reflective pieces or character studies. For example, you might describe the rich plant life in an inner-city garden, using the piece to reflect on people's longing to connect with the soil and arousing readers' appreciation for the gardeners' hard work. Or in a character study of your grandfather, you might describe the contradiction between his stern appearance and gentle behavior, hoping your description will convey his complexity and move readers to share your esteem for him.

The tone of a subjective description is derived from your

purpose, your attitude toward the subject, and the reader response you hope to evoke. If you were writing about a dynamic woman who runs a center for disturbed children, for example, your tone would depend upon several factors. If your goal were to make readers admire the woman, you would use a serious, appreciative tone. But if you wanted to criticize the woman's high-pressure tactics and create distaste for such a management style, your tone would be disapproving and critical.

Descriptive language changes, depending on whether your purpose is primarily objective or subjective. If the description is objective, the language is straightforward, precise, and factual. Such *denotative* language is concerned with neutral dictionary meanings. For example, if you wanted to describe as dispassionately as possible the violent behavior of fans at a football game, you might write about the "large crowd" and its "mass movement onto the field." But assume you were shocked by the fans' behavior and decided to write a subjective piece, inspiring similar outrage in your readers. Then you might write about the "swelling mob" and its "rowdy stampede onto the field." In the latter case, the language used would be connotative, emotionally charged so that readers would share your feelings.

Subjective and objective descriptions often overlap. Sometimes a single sentence will continue objective *and* subjective elements ("Although his hands were large and misshapen by arthritis, they were gentle to the touch, inspiring confidence and trust"). Other times, part of an essay may provide a factual description (the physical appearance of a summer cabin your family rented), while another part of the essay may be highly subjective (how you felt in the cabin, sitting in front of a fire on a rainy day).

SUGGESTIONS FOR USING DESCRIPTION IN AN ESSAY

The following suggestions will be helpful whether you use description as a dominant or supportive pattern of development.

1. Focus a descriptive essay around a dominant impression.   Like other kinds of writing, a descriptive essay must have a main idea or point. The point usually centers on the *dominant impression* you have about your subject. Suppose you decide to write a paper about your unforgettable ninth-grade history teacher, Mrs. Hazzard. You want to write an essay that conveys Mrs. Hazzard's unconventional, flamboyant nature. The essay could, of course, focus on a different dominant impression — how insensitive she could be to students, for example. What is important is that you establish for yourself the dominant impression of the essay. Because many descriptive essays do not have thesis statements, the essay's dominant impression may be implied. Even so, there never should be any question about what the dominant impression is.

2. Be selective in your choice of details. The power of description — especially description with a subjective slant — hinges on the details chosen to support the dominant impression. You should include only those details that contribute to this impression and leave out all others, no matter how vivid or interesting they might be. If you are describing how flamboyant Mrs. Hazzard could be, the details in the following paragraph would be appropriate.

A large-boned woman, Mrs. Hazzard wore her bright red hair piled on top of her head, where it perched precariously. By the end of class, wayward strands of hair tumbled down and fell into eyes fringed by spiky false eyelashes. Mrs. Hazzard's nails, filed into crisp points, were painted either bloody burgundy or neon pink. Plastic bangle bracelets, also either burgundy or pink, clattered up and down her ample arms as she scrawled on the board the historical dates that had, she claimed, "changed the world."

The details you chose — the heavy eye makeup, the stiletto-like nails, the gaudy bracelets — contribute to the impression of a flamboyant, unusual person. Even if you remembered times that Mrs. Hazzard seemed perfectly conventional and understated, you would most likely omit those details, because they would detract from the unity your essay achieves by being rooted in a single, dominant impression.

You must also be selective in the number of details you include in the essay. Having a dominant impression helps you eliminate many inappropriate details, but there will still be choices to make. For example, you would not want to describe in exhaustive detail everything in a messy room:

The brown desk, made of a grained plastic laminate, is directly under a small window covered by a torn yellow-and-gold plaid curtain. In the left corner of the desk are four crumbled balls of blue-lined yellow paper, three red markers, two fine-point blue pens, an ink eraser, and four letters, two bearing special wildlife stamps. A green down-filled vest and a red cable knit sweater are thrown over the back of the bright blue metal bridge chair pushed under the desk. Under the chair is an oval braided rug, its once brilliant blues and greens spotted by old coffee stains.

Your readers will be reluctant to wade through these undifferentiated specifics. Even more important, such obsessive detailing dilutes the focus of the essay. You end up with a seemingly endless list of specifics, rather than with a carefully crafted picture in words. In this regard, sculptors and writers are similar — what they take away is as important as what they leave in.

Perhaps you are wondering how to generate the details that support your dominant impression. As you can imagine, you have to develop heightened powers of observation and recall. To sharpen these key faculties, it can be helpful to make up a chart with separate columns for each of the five senses. If you can observe your subject directly, enter in the appropriate columns what you see, hear, taste, and so on. If you are attempting to remember something from the past, try to recollect details under each of these sense headings. Ask yourself questions ("How did it smell? What did I hear?") and list each memory recaptured. You will be surprised how this simple technique can tune you in to your experiences, helping uncover the specific details needed to develop your dominant impression.

3. Organize the descriptive details.   It is important to select the organizational pattern (or combination of patterns) that best supports your dominant impression. The paragraphs that make up a descriptive essay are most frequently organized *spatially* (from top to bottom, from interior to exterior, from near to far) or *chronologically* (as the subject is experienced in time). But the paragraphs can also be organized *emphatically* (ending with the most striking elements of your subject). Or you may decide to sequence the paragraphs according to *sensory impressions* (first smell, then taste, then touch, and so on). Although descriptive paragraphs do not always have topic sentences, each paragraph should have its own clear focus.

You might, for instance, use a spatial pattern to organize a description of a large city, detailing your view of the city from the air, from a taxi, and from your vantage points as you walked around the city. A description of your first day at a new job might move chronologically from how you felt when you woke up that morning to the events that occurred during the course of the day. In a paper describing a bout with the flu, you might arrange details emphatically, starting with a description of your low-level aches and pains, concluding with an account of the raging fever that made you feel as though you were burning up. An essay about a neighborhood garbage dump, euphemistically called an "ecology landfill" by its owners, could be organized by sense impression: the sights of the dump, its smells, its sounds.

4. Use vivid and varied language. The connotative language used in subjective descriptions must be rich and evocative. Vague, dull generalizations cannot convey the highly personal impression you wish to share with your readers. The words selected must have the power to etch in their minds the same picture that you have in yours. For this reason, you must use language involving the readers' senses. Consider the differences in the following pairs of descriptions:

The food was unappetizing.	The stew congealed into an oval pool of milky-brown fat.
The toothpaste was refreshing.	The toothpaste, tasting minty sweet, felt good against slippery teeth, free finally from braces.
Filled with passengers and baggage, the car moved slowly down the road.	Burdened with its load of clamoring children and well-worn suitcases, the car labored down the interstate on bald tires and worn shocks, emitting puffs of blue exhaust and an occasional backfire.

The general, abstract sentences on the left are not effective. Unlike the concrete, sensory-packed images on the right, these vague sentences fail to create a strong impression or engage the reader. While all good writing is a blend of abstract and concrete language, descriptive writing demands an abundance of specific sensory language.

Description often uses an especially vivid and creative form of language called *figures of speech*. Figures of speech involve nonliteral, imaginative comparisons between two usually dissimilar things. *Similes* use the words *like* or *as* when making the comparisons; *metaphors* imply that two things are alike; and *personification* involves attributing human characteristics to inanimate things.

The examples that follow show how effective figurative language can be in descriptive writing.

Moving as jerkily as a marionette on strings, the old man picked himself up off the sidewalk and staggered down the street. (simile)

Stalking their prey, the hall monitors remained hidden in the corridors, motionless and ready to spring on any unsuspecting student who dared to sneak into class late. (metaphor)

The scoop of vanilla ice cream, plain and unadorned, cried out for hot fudge sauce and a sprinkling of sliced pecans. (personification)

When writing descriptive passages, you also want to be sure to *vary* your *sentence structure*; you do not want to use the same subject–verb pattern in all your sentences. In the second example above, for instance, the sentence could have been written as follows: "The hall monitors stalked their prey. They remained hidden in the corridors. They remained motionless and ready to spring on any unsuspecting student who dared to sneak into class late." But note how much richer and more interesting the sentence is when the descriptive elements are embedded in the sentence, eliminating what would otherwise be a clipped and predictable subject–verb pattern.

Henry James, American novelist and master of description, gave this advice to beginning writers: "Try to be one of the people on whom nothing is lost." If you work to become the kind of writer "on whom nothing is lost," you will find you have a rich mine of sensory impressions to explore and transmute into written form. To develop your descriptive powers, you must be alert to your inner and outer worlds. And you must develop sensitivity to the nuances of language, finding just the right words to convey the essence of your experiences. It is no wonder that descriptive writing can be a source of such pleasure for writer and reader alike.

STUDENT ESSAY AND COMMENTARY

The following student essay was written by Marie Martinez in response to this assignment:

> The essay "Once More to the Lake" is an evocative piece about a spot that had special meaning in E. B. White's life. Write an essay about a place that holds rich significance for you, centering the description on a dominant impression.

While reading Marie's paper, try to determine how well it applies the principles concerning the use of description. The commentary following the paper will help you look at Marie's essay more closely.

Salt Marsh

In one of his journals, Thoreau told of the difficulty he had escaping the obligations and cares of society: "It sometimes happens that I cannot easily shake off the village. The thought of some work will run in my head and I am not where my body is--I am out of my senses. In my walks I . . . return to my senses." All of us feel out of our senses at times. Overwhelmed by problems or everyday annoyances, we lose touch with sensory pleasures as we spend our days in noisy cities and stuffy classrooms. Just as Thoreau walked in the woods to return to his senses, I have a special place where I return to mine: the salt marsh behind my grandparents' place. 1

My grandparents live on the East Coast, a mile or so inland from the sea. Between the ocean and the mainland is a wide fringe 2 of salt marsh. A salt marsh is not a swamp, but an expanse of dark spongy soil threaded with salt-water creeks and clothed in a kind of grass called salt meadow hay. All the water in the marsh rises and falls daily with the ocean tides, an endless cycle that changes the look of the marsh--partly flooded or mostly dry--as the day progresses.

Heading out to the marsh from my grandparents' house, I follow a short path through the woods. As I walk along, a sharp smell of salt mixed with the rich aroma of peaty soil fills my nostrils. I am always amazed by the way the path changes with the seasons. Sometimes I walk in the brilliant green of spring, sometimes in the tawny gold of autumn, sometimes in the grayish-tan of winter. No matter the season, the grass flanking the trail is often flattened into swirls, like the paintings by Van Gogh where thick brushstrokes of paint curve and recurve in circular patterns. No people come here. The peacefulness heals me like a soothing drug.   3

After a few minutes, the trail suddenly opens up to a view that calms me no matter how upset or discouraged I might be: a line of tall waving reeds bordering and nearly hiding the salt marsh creek. To get to the creek, I part the reeds.   4

The creek is a narrow body of water, no more than fifteen feet wide, and it ebbs and flows as the ocean currents sweep toward the land or rush back toward the sea. The creek winds in a sinuous pattern so that I cannot see its beginning or end, the places where it trickles into the marsh or spills into the open ocean. Little brown birds dip in and out of the reeds on the far shore of the creek, making a special "tweep-tweep" sound peculiar to the marsh. When I stand at low tide on the shore of the creek, I am on a miniature cliff, for the bank of the creek falls abruptly and steeply into the water. Below me, green grasses wave and shimmer under the water while tiny minnows flash their silvery sides as they dart through the underwater tangles.   5

The creek water is often much warmer than the ocean, so I can swim there in three seasons. Sitting on the edge of the creek, I scoop some water in my hand, rubbing my face and neck, then ease into the water. Where the creek is shallow, my feet sink into a foot of muck that feels like mashed potatoes mixed with motor oil. But once I become accustomed to it, I enjoy squishing the slimy mud through my toes. Sometimes I feel brushing past my legs the blue crabs that live in the creek. Other times, I hear the splash of a turtle or otter as it slips from the shore into the water. Otherwise, it is silent. The salty water is buoyant and lifts my spirits as I stroke through it to reach the middle of the creek. There in the center, I float weightlessly, surrounded by tall reeds that reduce the world to water and sky. I am at peace.   6

The salt marsh is not the kind of dramatic landscape found on   7
picture postcards. There are no soaring mountains, sandy beaches,
or lush valleys. The marsh is a flat world that some consider dull
and uninviting. I am glad most people do not respond to the marsh's
subtle beauty because that means I can be alone there. Just as the
rising tide sweeps over the marsh, floating debris out to the ocean,
the marsh washes away my concerns and restores me to my senses.

Marie responded to the assignment by writing a moving
tribute to a place having special meaning for her: the salt marsh
near her grandparents' home. Like most *descriptive pieces*, Marie's
essay is organized around a *dominant impression*: the peaceful
solitude and gentle natural beauty of the marsh. The essay's
introduction provides a context for the dominant impression by
comparing the pleasure Marie experiences in the marsh to the
happiness Thoreau felt in his walks around Walden Pond.

Before developing the essay's dominant impression, Marie
uses the second paragraph to present a *definition* of a salt marsh.
Rooted in an *objective description*, the definition clarifies that a salt
marsh, with its spongy soil, haylike grass and ebbing tides, is not
to be confused with a swamp. Because she offers such a factual
definition, readers are now in a position to understand what
Marie is talking about; they have the background needed to enjoy
the personalized view that follows.

At times, Marie develops the essay's dominant impression
explicitly, as when she writes "No people come here" (paragraph
3) and "I am at peace" (6). But Marie generally uses the more
subtle techniques characteristic of *subjective description* to convey
the dominant impression. First of all, she fills the essay with
strong *connotative language*, rich with *sensory images*. In the third
paragraph, she describes what she smells (the "sharp smell of salt
mixed with the rich aroma of peaty soil") and what she sees
("brilliant green," "tawny gold," and "grayish-tan"). The fifth
paragraph tells us that she hears the chirping sounds of small
birds. And the sixth paragraph includes vigorous descriptions of
how the marsh feels to Marie's touch. She splashes water on her
face and neck; she digs her toes into the mud at the bottom of the
creek; she delights in the delicate brushing of crabs against her
legs.

You might have noted that *figurative language* and *varied
sentence patterns* also play an important role in conveying the

descriptive power of the essay. Marie develops a *simile* in the third paragraph when she compares the flattened swirls of swamp grass to the brush strokes in a painting by Van Gogh. Later in the paper, she uses another simile when she writes that the thick mud in the creek feels "like mashed potatoes mixed with oil." Marie adds further impact to her description by varying the length of her sentences. Long, fairly elaborate sentences are interspersed with short, dramatic statements. In the third paragraph, for example, the long sentence describing the circular swirls of swamp grass is followed by the brief statement "No people come here." And the sixth paragraph uses two short sentences ("Otherwise, it is silent" and "I am at peace") to punctuate the longer sentences in the paragraph.

We can follow Marie's journey through the marsh with ease because she *organizes her descriptive details* effectively. She uses a combination of *spatial, chronological,* and *emphatic* patterns to sequence her experience. Perhaps you realized that the four paragraphs making up the body of the essay focus on the different spots that Marie reaches: first, the path behind her grandparents' house (3); then the area bordering the creek (4); next, her view of the creek (5); and last, the creek itself, with its extraordinary restorative powers (6). Clear *signals* (marked by italics here) indicate the passage of time as well as Marie's location, thus clarifying the sequence of her journey: "*As* I walk along, a sharp smell . . . fills my nostrils" (3); "*After* a few minutes, the trail suddenly opens up . . ." (4); "*Below* me, green grasses wave . . ." (5); and "*There* in the center, I float weightlessly . . ." (6).

Although the four paragraphs in the body of the essay focus on the distinctive qualities of each location, Marie runs into a minor problem generating appropriate material for the third paragraph. Take a moment to reread the last sentence in that paragraph. Comparing the peace of the marsh to the effect of a "soothing drug" is jarring. The effectiveness of Marie's essay hinges on her ability to create a picture of a pure, natural world. This reference to drugs is inappropriate. Now, reread the paragraph aloud, stopping after "No people come here." Note how much more effective the paragraph is, how much more in keeping it is with the essay's dominant impression.

The concluding paragraph brings the essay to a graceful

close. The powerful *simile* found in the last sentence contains an implied reference to Thoreau and her statement about the joy to be found in special places having restorative powers. Such an illusion echoes, with good effect, the paper's opening comments.

When Marie met with some classmates during a group feedback session, the students agreed that Marie's first draft was strong and moving. But they also said that they had difficulty following her route through the marsh; they found her third paragraph especially confusing. The original draft of the third paragraph is reprinted below.

First Draft Version

As I head out to the marsh from the house, I follow a short trail through the woods. A smell of salt mixed with the aroma of soil fills my nostrils. The end of the trail suddenly opens up to a view that calms me no matter how upset or discouraged I might be: a line of tall waving reeds bordering the salt marsh creek. Civilization seems far away as I walk the path of flattened grass and finally reach my goal, the salt marsh creek hidden behind the tall waving reeds. The path changes with the seasons; sometimes I walk in the brilliant green of spring, sometimes in the tawny gold of autumn, sometimes in the quiet grayish-tan of winter. In some areas, the grass is flattened into swirls that make the marsh resemble one of those paintings by Van Gogh. No people come here. The peacefulness heals me like a soothing drug. The path stops at the line of tall waving reeds, standing upright at the border of the creek. I part the reeds to get to the creek.

When Marie looked more carefully at the paragraph, she realized it was indeed baffling. For one thing, in the paragraph's third and fourth sentences, she wrote that she came to the end of the path and reached the reeds bordering the creek. But in the following sentences she said she was on the path again. Then, at the end of the paragraph, she indicated she was once more back at the creek and the reeds, as if she had just arrived there. When revising, Marie resolved this confusion by breaking the single paragraph into two separate paragraphs — one describing the walk along the path, the other describing her arrival at the creek. The restructuring, especially when combined with the addition of clearer transitions, eliminated the confusion.

While revising her essay, Marie also decided to intensify the sensory images in her original version of the paragraph. The "smell of salt mixed with the aroma of soil" was changed to the "sharp smell of salt mixed with the rich aroma of peaty soil." And when she added the phrase "thick brushstrokes of paint curving and recurving in circular patterns," she made the comparison between the grass swirls and a Van Gogh painting more vivid.

These represent some of the changes Marie made while reworking her paper. Her skillful revising provided the polish needed to make an already strong essay even more powerful and evocative.

All the selections ahead use description to make their subjects come alive and to provide supporting evidence for a controlling idea or impression. Larry Woiwode's "Wanting an Orange" is an exuberant and sensuous account of one of life's small pleasures, while Russell Baker's "In My Day" is a wistful memoir of the author's aging mother. Annie Dillard's "In the Jungle" depicts timeless quality of primeval places. In "Once More to the Lake," E. B. White recalls his youth when visiting a childhood vacation spot with his son. Finally, Peggy Anderson's "Children's Hospital" describes an environment especially designed to heal and nurture.

Larry Woiwode

Larry Woiwode (1941–   ) was born and raised in Carrington, North Dakota. He is a freelance writer whose short stories, poems, and essays have appeared in *The New Yorker, Atlantic Monthly, The New York Times,* and the *Paris Review.* His first two novels, *What I'm Going to Do, I Think* (1969) and *Beyond the Bedroom Wall: A Family Album* (1975), won prestigious literary awards; his most recent novels are *Poppa John* (1981) and *Born Brothers* (1988). The following essay originally appeared in the *Paris Review.*

Wanting an Orange

When we look back on our childhoods, it is often the small things we remember most vividly—swinging on a backyard gate, the taste of dreaded lima beans, a grandfather's way of being funny. In this essay, Larry Woiwode celebrates such a seemingly minor experience—the eating of an orange. Using a multitude of sensory details, he shows how youthful enthusiasm can transform the commonplace into sacred ritual.

Oh, those oranges arriving in the midst of the North Dakota winters of the forties—the mere color of them, carried through the door in a net bag or a crate from out of the white winter landscape. Their appearance was enough to set my brother and me to thinking that it might be about time to develop an illness, which was the surest way of receiving a steady supply of them. 1

"Mom, we think we're getting a cold." 2

"*We?* You mean, you two want an orange?" 3

This was difficult for us to answer or dispute; the matter seemed moved beyond our mere wanting. 4

"If you want an orange," she would say, "why don't you ask for one?" 5

"We want an orange." 6

"'We' again. '*We want an orange.*'" 7

"May we have an orange, please."

"That's the way you know I like you to ask for one. Now, why don't each of you ask for one in that same way, but separately?"

"Mom . . ." And so on. There was no depth of degradation that we wouldn't descend to in order to get one. If the oranges hadn't wended their way northward by Thanksgiving, they were sure to arrive before the Christmas season, stacked first in crates at the depot, filling that musty place, where pews sat back to back, with a springtime acidity, as if the building had been rinsed with a renewing elixir that set it right for yet another year. Then the crates would appear at the local grocery store, often with the top slats pried back on a few of them, so that we were aware of a resinous smell of fresh wood in addition to the already orangy atmosphere that foretold the season more explicitly than any calendar.

And in the broken-open crates (as if burst by the power of the oranges themselves), one or two of the lovely spheres would lie free of the tissue they came wrapped in — always purple tissue, as if that were the only color that could contain the populations of them in their nestled positions. The crates bore paper labels at one end — of an orange against a blue background, or of a blue goose against an orange background — signifying the colorful otherworld (unlike our wintry one) that these phenomena had arisen from. Each orange, stripped of its protective wrapping, as vivid in your vision as a pebbled sun, encouraged you to picture a whole pyramid of them in a bowl on your dining room table, glowing in the light, as if giving off the warmth that came through the windows from the real winter sun. And all of them came stamped with a blue-purple name as foreign as the other-world that you might imagine as their place of origin, so that on Christmas day you would find yourself digging past everything else in your Christmas stocking, as if tunneling down to the country of China, in order to reach the rounded bulge at the tip of the toe which meant that you had received a personal reminder of another state of existence, wholly separate from your own.

The packed heft and texture, finally, of an orange in your hand — that is it! — and the eruption of smell and the watery fireworks as a knife, in the hand of someone skilled, like our mother, goes slicing through the skin so perfect for slicing. This gaseous spray can form a mist like smoke, which can then be lit with a match to create actual fireworks if there is a chance to hide alone with a match (matches being forbidden) and the peel from one. Sputtery ignitions can also be produced by squeezing a peel near a candle (at least one candle is generally always going at Christmastime), and the leftover peels are set on the stove top to scent the house.

And the ingenious way in which oranges come packed into their globes! The green nib at the top, like a detonator, can be bitten off, as if disarming the orange, in order to clear a place for you to sink a tooth under the peel. This is the best way to start. If you bite at the peel too much, your front teeth will feel scraped, like dry bone, and your lips will begin to burn from the bitter oil. Better to sink a tooth into this greenish or creamy depression, and then pick at that point with the nail of your thumb, removing a little piece of the peel at a time. Later, you might want to practice to see how large a piece you can remove intact. The peel can also be undone in one continuous ribbon, a feat which maybe your father is able to perform, so that after the orange is freed, looking yellowish, the peel, rewound, will stand in its original shape, although empty.

The yellowish whole of the orange can now be divided into sections, usually about a dozen, by beginning with a division down the middle; after this, each section, enclosed in its papery skin, will be able to be lifted and torn loose more easily. There is a stem up the center of the section like a mushroom stalk, but tougher; this can be eaten. A special variety of orange, without any pits, has an extra growth, or nubbin, like half of a tiny orange, tucked into its bottom. This nubbin is nearly as bitter as the peel, but it can be eaten, too; don't worry. Some of the sections will have miniature sections embedded in them and clinging as if for life, giving the impression that babies are being hatched, and should you happen to find some of these you've found the sweetest morsels of any.

If you prefer to have your orange sliced in half, as some people do, the edges of the peel will abrade the corners of your mouth, making them feel raw, as you eat down into the white of the rind (which is the only way to do it) until you can see daylight through the orangy bubbles composing its outside. Your eyes might burn; there is no proper way to eat an orange. If there are

13

14

15

pits, they can get in the way, and the slower you eat an orange, the more you'll find your fingers sticking together. And no matter how carefully you eat one, or bite into a quarter, juice can always fly or slip from a corner of your mouth; this happens to everyone. Close your eyes to be on the safe side, and for the eruption in your mouth of the slivers of watery meat, which should be broken and rolled fine over your tongue for the essence of orange. And if indeed you have sensed yourself coming down with a cold, there is a chance that you will feel it driven from your head — your nose and sinuses suddenly opening — in the midst of the scent of a peel and eating an orange.

And oranges can also be eaten whole — rolled into a spongy mass and punctured with a pencil (if you don't find this offensive) or a knife, and then sucked upon. Then, once the juice is gone, you can disembowel the orange as you wish and eat away its pulpy remains, and eat once more into the whitish interior of the peel, which scours the coating from your teeth and makes your numbing lips and the tip of your tongue start to tingle and swell up from behind, until, in the light from the windows (shining through an empty glass bowl), you see orange again from the inside. Oh, oranges, solid *o*'s, light from afar in the midst of the freeze, and not unlike that unspherical fruit which first went from Eve to Adam and from there (to abbreviate matters) to my brother and me.

"Mom, we think we're getting a cold."

"You mean, you want an orange?"

This is difficult to answer or dispute or even to acknowledge, finally, with the fullness that the subject deserves, and that each orange bears, within its own makeup, into this hard-edged yet insubstantial, incomplete, cold, wintry world.

Questions for Close Reading

1. What is the thesis (or dominant impression) of the selection? Locate the sentence(s) in which Woiwode states his main idea. If he does not state the thesis explicitly, express it in your own words.
2. Why were Woiwode and his brother, growing up as children in North Dakota, so fond of oranges? What was it about the oranges that made them so appealing?

3. How could the oranges be enjoyed even before they were eaten? What uses, for example, did the author and his brother find for the peel?
4. According to Woiwode, there is no one way to eat an orange. Why is this? How many ways does he describe?
5. Refer to your dictionary as needed to define the following words used in the selection: *degradation* (paragraph 10), *wended* (10), *elixir* (10), *ingenious* (13), *detonator* (13), *morsels* (14), and *disembowel* (16).

Questions About the Writer's Craft

1. Descriptive writing often appeals to our senses, especially to the sense of sight. Which of the senses does "Wanting an Orange" focus on? Why?
2. What method or combination of methods (chronological, sensory, spatial, or emphatic) does Woiwode use to organize his description?
3. Figurative language is another tool the author uses to make his description memorable. One example is the comparison of the green nib at the top of an orange to a detonator in paragraph 13. Find other examples of metaphors and similes in the essay. What qualities of an orange does Woiwode evoke with these images?
4. Why does Woiwode begin this description of an orange by recounting a typical conversation of his youth, one among himself, his brother, and his mother? How does this opening serve as an enticing introduction? In what way does the conversation help support the thesis?

Questions for Further Thought

1. After reading Woiwode's description of oranges, do you feel differently about them? Are there other foods or ordinary things you now realize you take for granted?
2. Do you still remember and treasure any childhood experiences, even those as mundane as eating a favorite food? What memories of special events or objects from childhood do you have that would correspond to Woiwode's of eating oranges?
3. Anything can be special if we pay attention, if we suddenly see it in a close-up or new way. Are there any objects or events in your life that, like the orange, would benefit from such careful examination and appreciation? Could any of these objects and events take on symbolic significance, like the orange?
4. Eating an orange is a simple pleasure. Have we lost sight of such basic appreciations? Do we rely too much on manufactured products, such as electronic gadgets and gourmet delicacies, for our enjoyments?

Writing Assignments Using Description as a Method of Development

1. Write an essay celebrating another food, household item, or ordinary object that people take for granted but that is actually very special and precious, even magical. For example, a pencil, candy bar, paper clip, or favorite pair of shoes or jeans could be the subject of your ode. Use vivid sensory description to convey the significance and vitality of your topic.

2. Describe a recurring event of your childhood that was much anticipated by you and other members of your family. The essay could focus on a cherished family ritual like the celebration of Christmas, a birthday, or Thanksgiving. Or you might write about a family vacation, an annual trip to see a particular sports team play, or even the yearly spring cleaning. Evoke the specialness of this ritual by describing how you anticipated it and the details of the day when it came. If food played an important part in the event, be sure to include the appropriate sensory details.

Writing Assignments Using Other Methods of Development

3. Woiwode describes in great detail how to eat an orange. Pick some other food you enjoy and write an essay describing the process of enjoying it to the fullest. For example, you might write about how to eat an ice cream cone, spaghetti, pizza, tacos, lobster or crab, bacon and eggs, or a Chinese dish.

4. Most people don't pay enough attention to the ordinary things of life. Write an essay arguing this point of view, giving reasons why we should be more observant, even reverent, about the details of what is around us. Support your essay by giving examples of the benefits and advantages of being an aware and appreciative person.

Russell Baker

In his regular column "The Observer" for *The New York Times*, Russell Baker applies his unique brand of humor to social commentary. Born in Virginia in 1925, Baker received his B.A. from Johns Hopkins University and spent several years working as a reporter for the *Baltimore Sun* before joining the *Times* in the mid-fifties. In 1979, Baker won a Pulitzer Prize, journalism's highest honor. Baker's columns have been collected in several books, including *So This Is Depravity* (1980). The following selection is from his 1982 autobiography, *Growing Up*, which became a bestseller and received critical acclaim.

In My Day

We often expect the most from—and are most intolerant of—the people we counted on when we were young. In the following selection, Russell Baker describes his aging mother and the tangled feelings she arouses in him as she takes refuge in her memories. Her mental deterioration leads Baker to ponder the weaving of past and present that flows through all families.

At the age of eighty my mother had her last bad fall, and after 1 that her mind wandered free through time. Some days she went to weddings and funerals that had taken place half a century earlier. On others she presided over family dinners cooked on Sunday afternoons for children who were now gray with age. Through all this she lay in bed but moved across time, traveling among the dead decades with a speed and ease beyond the gift of physical science.

"Where's Russell?" she asked one day when I came to visit at 2 the nursing home.

"I'm Russell," I said. 3

She gazed at this improbably overgrown figure out of an 4 inconceivable future and promptly dismissed it.

"Russell's only this big," she said, holding her hand, palm down, two feet from the floor. That day she was a young country wife with chickens in the backyard and a view of hazy blue Virginia mountains behind the apple orchard, and I was a stranger old enough to be her father.

Early one morning she phoned me in New York. "Are you coming to my funeral today?" she asked.

It was an awkward question with which to be awakened. "What are you talking about, for God's sake?" was the best reply I could manage.

"I'm being buried today," she declared briskly, as though announcing an important social event.

"I'll phone you back," I said and hung up, and when I did phone back she was all right, although she wasn't all right, of course, and we all knew she wasn't.

She had always been a small woman — short, light-boned, delicately structured — but now, under the white hospital sheet, she was becoming tiny. I thought of a doll with huge, fierce eyes. There had always been a fierceness in her. It showed in that angry, challenging thrust of the chin when she issued an opinion, and a great one she had always been for issuing opinions.

"I tell people exactly what's on my mind," she had been fond of boasting. "I tell them what I think, whether they like it or not." Often they had not liked it. She could be sarcastic to people in whom she detected evidence of the ignoramus or the fool.

"It's not always good policy to tell people exactly what's on your mind," I used to caution her.

"If they don't like it, that's too bad," was her customary reply, "because that's the way I am."

And so she was. A formidable woman. Determined to speak her mind, determined to have her way, determined to bend those who opposed her. In that time when I had known her best, my mother had hurled herself at life with chin thrust forward, eyes blazing, and an energy that made her seem always on the run.

She ran after squawking chickens, an axe in her hand, determined on a beheading that would put dinner in the pot. She ran when she made the beds, ran when she set the table. One Thanksgiving she burned herself badly when, running up from the cellar oven with the ceremonial turkey, she tripped on the stairs and tumbled back down, ending at the bottom in the debris of giblets, hot gravy, and battered turkey. Life was combat, and victory was not to the lazy, the timid, the slugabed, the drugstore cowboy, the libertine, the mushmouth afraid to tell people exactly what was on his mind whether people liked it or not. She ran.

But now the running was over. For a time I could not accept   16
the inevitable. As I sat by her bed, my impulse was to argue her back to reality. On my first visit to the hospital in Baltimore, she asked who I was.

"Russell," I said.   17

"Russell's way out west," she advised me.   18

"No, I'm right here."   19

"Guess where I came from today?" was her response.   20

"Where?"   21

"All the way from New Jersey."   22

"When?"   23

"Tonight."   24

"No. You've been in the hospital for three days," I insisted.   25

"I suggest the thing to do is calm down a little bit," she   26
replied. "Go over to the house and shut the door."

Now she was years deep into the past, living in the neighbor-   27
hood where she had settled forty years earlier, and she had just been talking with Mrs. Hoffman, a neighbor across the street.

"It's like Mrs. Hoffman said today: The children always   28
wander back to where they come from," she remarked.

"Mrs. Hoffman has been dead for fifteen years."   29

"Russ got married today," she replied.   30

"I got married in 1950," I said, which was the fact.   31

"The house is unlocked," she said.   32

So it went until a doctor came by to give one of those oral   33
quizzes that medical men apply in such cases. She failed cata-strophically, giving wrong answers or none at all to "What day is this?" "Do you know where you are?" "How old are you?" and so on. Then, a surprise.

"When is your birthday?" he asked.   34

"November 5, 1897," she said. Correct. Absolutely correct.   35

"How do you remember that?" the doctor asked.   36

"Because I was born on Guy Fawkes Day," she said.   37

"Guy Fawkes?" asked the doctor, "Who is Guy Fawkes?"   38

She replied with a rhythm I had heard her recite time and   39
again over the years when the subject of her birth date arose:

"Please to remember the Fifth of November,
Gunpowder treason and plot.
I see no reason why gunpowder treason
Should ever be forgot."

Then she glared at this young doctor so ill informed about Guy
Fawkes' failed scheme to blow King James off his throne with
barrels of gunpowder in 1605. She had been a schoolteacher, after
all, and knew how to glare at a dolt. "You may know a lot about
medicine, but you obviously don't know any history," she said.
Having told him exactly what was on her mind, she left us again.

The doctors diagnosed a hopeless senility. Not unusual, they   40
said. "Hardening of the arteries" was the explanation for laymen.
I thought it was more complicated than that. For ten years or
more the ferocity with which she had once attacked life had been
turning to a rage against the weakness, the boredom, and the
absence of love that too much age had brought her. Now, after
the last bad fall, she seemed to have broken chains that imprisoned her in a life she had come to hate and to return to a time
inhabited by people who loved her, a time in which she was
needed. Gradually I understood. It was the first time in years I
had seen her happy.

She had written a letter three years earlier which explained   41
more than "hardening of the arteries." I had gone down from
New York to Baltimore, where she lived, for one of my infrequent
visits and, afterwards, had written her with some banal advice to
look for the silver lining, to count her blessings instead of bur-
dening others with her miseries. I suppose what it really
amounted to was a threat that if she was not more cheerful during
my visits I would not come to see her very often. Sons are capable
of such letters. This one was written out of a childish faith in the
eternal strength of parents, a naive belief that age and wear could
be overcome by an effort of will, that all she needed was a good
pep talk to recharge a flagging spirit. It was such a foolish,
innocent idea, but one thinks of parents differently from other
people. Other people can become frail and break, but not parents.

She wrote back in an unusually cheery vein intended to   42
demonstrate, I suppose, that she was mending her ways. She was
never a woman to apologize, but for one moment with the pen in

her hand she came very close. Referring to my visit, she wrote: "If I seemed unhappy to you at times — " Here she drew back, reconsidered, and said something quite different:

"If I seemed unhappy to you at times, I am, but there's really   43
nothing anyone can do about it, because I'm just so very tired and lonely that I'll just go to sleep and forget it." She was then seventy-eight.

Now, three years later, after the last bad fall, she had man-   44
aged to forget the fatigue and loneliness and, in these free-wheel-ing excursions back through time, to recapture happiness. I soon stopped trying to wrest her back to what I considered the real world and tried to travel along with her on those fantastic swoops into the past. One day when I arrived at her bedside she was radiant.

"Feeling good today," I said.   45

"Why shouldn't I feel good?" she asked. "Papa's going to   46
take me up to Baltimore on the boat today."

At that moment she was a young girl standing on a wharf at   47
Merry Point, Virginia, waiting for the Chesapeake Bay steamer with her father, who had been dead sixty-one years. William Howard Taft was in the White House, Europe still drowsed in the dusk of the great century of peace, America was a young country, and the future stretched before it in beams of crystal sunlight. "The greatest country on God's green earth," her father might have said, if I had been able to step into my mother's time machine and join him on the wharf with the satchels packed for Baltimore.

I could imagine her there quite clearly. She was wearing a   48
blue dress with big puffy sleeves and long black stockings. There was a ribbon in her hair and a big bow tied on the side of her head. There had been a childhood photograph in her bedroom which showed all this, although the colors of course had been added years later by a restorer who tinted the picture.

About her father, my grandfather, I could only guess, and   49
indeed, about the girl on the wharf with the bow in her hair, I was merely sentimentalizing. Of my mother's childhood and her peo-ple, of their time and place, I knew very little. A world had lived and died, and though it was part of my blood and bone I knew little more about it than I knew of the world of the pharaohs. It

was useless now to ask for help from my mother. The orbits of her mind rarely touched present interrogators for more than a moment.

Sitting at her bedside, forever out of touch with her, I wondered about my own children, and their children, and children in general, and about the disconnections between children and parents that prevent them from knowing each other. Children rarely want to know who their parents were before they were parents, and when age finally stirs their curiosity there is no parent left to tell them. If a parent does lift the curtain a bit, it is often only to stun the young with some exemplary tale of how much harder life was in the old days. 50

I had been guilty of this when my children were small in the early 1960s and living the affluent life. It galled me that their childhoods should be, as I thought, so easy when my own had been, as I thought, so hard. I had developed the habit, when they complained about the steak being overcooked or the television being cut off, of lecturing them on the harshness of life in my day. 51

"In my day all we got for dinner was macaroni and cheese, and we were glad to get it." 52

"In my day we didn't have any television." 53

"In my day . . ." 54

"In my day . . ." 55

At dinner one evening a son had offended me with a inadequate report card, and as I leaned back and cleared my throat to lecture, he gazed at me with an expression of unutterable resignation and said, "Tell me how it was in your days, Dad." 56

I was angry with him for that, but angrier with myself for having become one of those ancient bores whose highly selective memories of the past become transparently dishonest even to small children. I tried to break the habit, but must have failed. A few years later my son was referring to me when I was out of earshot as "the old-timer." Between us there was a dispute about time. He looked upon the time that had been my future in a disturbing way. My future was his past, and being young, he was indifferent to the past. 57

As I hovered over my mother's bed listening for muffled signals from her childhood, I realized that this same dispute had existed between her and me. When she was young, with life ahead of her, I had been her future and resented it. Instinctively, I 58 wanted to break free, cease being a creature defined by her time, consign her future to the past, and create my own. Well, I had finally done that, and then with my own children I had seen my exciting future become their boring past.

These hopeless end-of-the-line visits with my mother made   59 me wish I had not thrown off my own past so carelessly. We all come from the past, and children ought to know what it was that went into their making, to know that life is a braided cord of humanity stretching up from time long gone, and that it cannot be defined by the span of a single journey from diaper to shroud.

Questions for Close Reading

1. What is the thesis (or dominant impression) of the selection? Locate the sentence(s) in which Baker states his main idea. If he does not state the thesis explicitly, express it in your own words.
2. What was Mrs. Baker's philosophy of life? How did it change in her old age?
3. Why does Baker feel "forever out of touch" with his mother? Does he feel equally out of touch with his children?
4. Why does Baker stop trying to get his eighty-year-old mother to return to the real world? Is he being kind or unkind?
5. Refer to your dictionary as needed to define the following words used in the selection: *inconceivable* (paragraph 4), *libertine* (15), *banal* (41), *wrest* (44), *exemplary* (50), *galled* (51), and *consign* (58).

Questions About the Writer's Craft

1. How does the series of scenes in "In My Day" develop the dominant impression of the essay?
2. Baker describes his mother by using details about her actions and her appearance, as well as by quoting things she said. Both are typical techniques for revealing character in a descriptive piece. Which technique is more effective in conveying Mrs. Baker's personality?
3. Baker repeats the word *ran* as he describes his mother's energy in paragraph 15. He also speaks several times of her *falls*. What is the purpose of repeating these words? What do they suggest about the pattern of his mother's life?
4. In paragraph 28, Mrs. Baker says, "The children always wander back to where they come from." How is this comment by Baker's mother ironic? Find some other examples of irony in the essay.

Questions for Further Thought

1. Baker writes, "Other people can become frail and break, but not parents" (41). What does he mean? What illusions do we have about our parents?
2. On the whole, would you say Russell Baker has been a good son? A good father? What do you think he would do differently if he had another chance? Will reading this essay affect your behavior toward your parents or children?
3. Baker feels that there is no way for parents and children truly to know each other. Do you agree or not—and why?
4. Is it inevitable that children will reject their parents' values and their parents' lives? What forms might this rejection take?

Writing Assignments Using Description as a Method of Development

1. Write a description of a parent or relative at a certain age, for example, "My Brother at Fourteen" or "My Mother at Fifty-five." Your description should create a dominant impression by conveying the person's characteristic approach to life. Be sure to select lively details that support this dominant impression.
2. Describe one or more active, vital older people who have not retreated into the past to find happiness. Your examples could be people you know, people you have heard about, or people in the public eye. Choose vivid details that show how such people's actions and attitudes keep them "young." Draw some conclusions about what older people can do to stay involved with life.

Writing Assignments Using Other Methods of Development

3. Russell Baker's essay concerns a crisis in his family. Write an essay about a crisis situation in a family—your own or someone else's. The crisis might be a divorce, serious or chronic illness, loss of a job, financial difficulties, or some other serious problem. Your essay might explore the causes and/or effects of the crisis; it might outline the steps the family has taken to deal with the crisis; it might be a narrative that points to some conclusion about how people deal with crises.
4. In the past, most elderly parents lived in an extended family—children, grandchildren, and other relatives were all part of the house-

hold. Now, many old people are isolated from families. In addition, our culture does not revere older people as many cultures do; we seem to care little about their experience, wisdom, and traditions. In what way might these factors affect the mental and physical health of older people? Write an essay showing how society's attitudes toward older people have affected their lives.

Annie Dillard

Pilgrim at Tinker Creek (1974) is probably Annie Dillard's best-known work. A collection of lyrical observations and reflections about the natural world, *Pilgrim* was awarded a Pulitzer Prize for general nonfiction. Born in 1945, Dillard is currently Adjunct Professor at Wesleyan University in Connecticut and a contributing editor at *Harper's*. Over the years, she has published a variety of books: *Tickets for a Prayer Wheel* (1974), a book of poetry; *Holy the Firm* (1978) and *Teaching a Stone to Talk* (1982), both collections of essays; *Living by Fiction* (1982), literary criticism; *Encounters with Chinese Writers* (1984), narrative nonfiction; and her most recent work, the autobiographical *An American Childhood* (1987). "In the Jungle" is taken from *Teaching a Stone to Talk*.

In the Jungle

In the world inhabited by most North Americans, the quality of life is often defined in terms of possessions: cars, stereos, apartments. But in the Ecuadorian jungle, Annie Dillard discovers that such items have no meaning. Indeed, the richness of the rain forest underscores how impoverished contemporary life may be.

Like any out-of-the-way place, the Napo River in the Ecuadorian jungle seems real enough when you are there, even central. Out of the way of *what*? I was sitting on a stump at the edge of a bankside palm-thatch village, in the middle of the night, on the headwaters of the Amazon. Out of the way of human life, tenderness, or the glance of heaven? 1

A nightjar in a deep-leaved shadow called three long notes, and hushed. The men with me talked softly in clumps: three North Americans, four Ecuadorians who were showing us the jungle. We were holding cool drinks and idly watching a hand- 2 sized tarantula seize moths that came to the lone bulb on the generator shed beside us.

It was February, the middle of summer. Green fireflies spattered lights across the air and illumined for seconds, now here, now there, the pale trunks of enormous, solitary trees. Beneath us the brown Napo River was rising, in all silence; it coiled up the sandy bank and tangled its foam in vines that trailed from the forest and roots that looped the shore.

Each breath of night smelled sweet, more moistened and sweet than any kitchen, or garden, or cradle. Each star in Orion seemed to tremble and stir with my breath. All at once, in the thatch house across the clearing behind us, one of the village's Jesuit priests began playing an alto recorder, playing a wordless song, lyric, in a minor key, that twined over the village clearing, that caught in the big trees' canopies, muted our talk on the bankside, and wandered over the river, dissolving downstream.

This will do, I thought. This will do, for a weekend, or a season, or a home.

Later that night I loosed my hair from its braids and combed it smooth — not for myself, but so the village girls could play with it in the morning.

We had disembarked at the village that afternoon, and I had slumped on some shaded steps, wishing I knew some Spanish or some Quechua so I could speak with the ring of little girls who were alternately staring at me and smiling at their toes. I spoke anyway, and fooled with my hair, which they were obviously dying to get their hands on, and laughed, and soon they were all braiding my hair, all five of them, all fifty fingers, all my hair, even my bangs. And then they took it apart and did it again, laughing, and teaching me Spanish nouns, and meeting my eyes and each other's with open delight, while their small brothers in blue jeans climbed down from the trees and began kicking a volleyball around with one of the North American men.

Now, as I combed my hair in the little tent, another of the men, a free-lance writer from Manhattan, was talking quietly. He was telling us the tale of his life, describing his work in Hollywood, his apartment in Manhattan, his house in Paris. . . . "It makes me wonder," he said, "what I'm doing in a tent under a tree in the village of Pompeya, on the Napo River, in the jungle of Ecuador." After a pause he added, "It makes me wonder why I'm going *back*."

The point of going somewhere like the Napo River in Ecuador is not to see the most spectacular anything. It is simply to see what is there. We are here on the planet only once, and might as well get a feel for the place. We might as well get a feel for the fringes and hollows in which life is lived, for the Amazon basin, which covers half a continent, and for the life that—there, like anywhere else—is always and necessarily lived in detail: on the tributaries, in the riverside villages, sucking this particular white-fleshed guava in this particular pattern of shade.   9

What is there is interesting. The Napo River itself is wide (I mean wider than the Mississippi at Davenport) and brown, opaque, and smeared with floating foam and logs and branches from the jungle. White egrets hunch on shoreline deadfalls and parrots in flocks dart in and out of the light. Under the water in the river, unseen, are anacondas—which are reputed to take a few village toddlers every year—and water boas, stingrays, croco-diles, manatees, and sweet-meated fish.   10

Low water bares gray strips of sandbar on which the natives build tiny palm-thatch shelters, arched, the size of pup tents, for overnight fishing trips. You see these extraordinarily clean people (who bathe twice a day in the river, and whose straight black hair is always freshly washed) paddling down the river in dugout canoes, hugging the banks.   11

Some of the Indians of this region, earlier in the century, used to sleep naked in hammocks. The nights are cold. Gordon MacCreach, an American explorer in these Amazon tributaries, reported that he was startled to hear the Indians get up at three in the morning. He was even more startled, night after night, to hear them walk down to the river slowly, half asleep, and bathe in the water. Only later did he learn what they were doing: they were getting warm. The cold woke them; they warmed their skins in the river, which was always ninety degrees; then they returned to their hammocks and slept through the rest of the night.   12

The riverbanks are low, and from the river you see an unbroken wall of dark forest in every direction, from the Andes to the Atlantic. You get a taste for looking at trees: trees hung with the   13 swinging nests of yellow troupials, trees from which ant nests the size of grain sacks hang like black goiters, trees from which seven-colored tanagers flutter, coral trees, teak, balsa and breadfruit, enormous emergent silk-cotton trees, and the pale-barked *samona* palms.

When you are inside the jungle, away from the river, the trees   14
vault out of sight. It is hard to remember to look up the long trunks and see the fans, strips, fronds, and sprays of glossy leaves. Inside the jungle you are more likely to notice the snarl of climbers and creepers round the trees' boles, the flowering bromeliads and epiphytes in every bough's crook, and the fantastic silk-cotton tree trunks thirty or forty feet across, trunks buttressed in flanges of wood whose curves can make three high walls of a room — a shady, loamy-aired room where you would gladly live, or die. Butterflies, iridescent blue, striped, or clear-winged, thread the jungle paths at eye level. And at your feet is a swath of ants bearing triangular bits of green leaf. The ants with their leaves look like a wide fleet of sailing dinghies — but they don't quit. In either direction they wobble over the jungle floor as far as the eye can see. I followed them off the path as far as I dared, and never saw an end to ants or to those luffing chips of green they bore.

Unseen in the jungle, but present, are tapirs, jaguars, many   15
species of snake and lizard, ocelots, armadillos, marmosets, howler monkeys, toucans and macaws and a hundred other birds, deer, bats, peccaries, capybaras, agoutis, and sloths. Also present in this jungle, but variously distant, are Texaco derricks and pipelines, and some of the wildest Indians in the world, blowgun-using Indians, who killed missionaries in 1956 and ate them.

Long lakes shine in the jungle. We traveled one of these in   16
dugout canoes, canoes with two inches of freeboard, canoes paddled with machete-hewn oars chopped from buttresses of silk-cotton trees, or poled in the shallows with peeled cane or bamboo. Our part-Indian guide had cleared the path to the lake the day before; when we walked the path we saw where he had impaled the lopped head of a boa, open-mouthed, on a pointed stick by the canoes, for decoration.

The lake was wonderful. Herons, egrets, and ibises plodded   17
the sawgrass shores, kingfishers and cuckoos clattered from sunlight to shade, great turkeylike birds fussed in dead branches, and hawks lolled overhead. There was all the time in the world. A

turtle slid into the water. The boy in the bow of my canoe slapped stones at birds with a simple sling, a rubber throng and leather pad. He aimed brilliantly at moving targets, always, and always missed; the birds were out of range. He stuffed his sling back in his shirt. I looked around.

The lake and river waters are as opaque as rain-forest leaves; they are veils, blinds, painted screens. You see things only by their effects. I saw the shoreline water roil and the sawgrass heave above a thrashing *paichi*, an enormous black fish of these waters; one had been caught the previous week weighing 430 pounds. Piranha fish live in the lakes, and electric eels. I dangled my fingers in the water, figuring it would be worth it. 18

We would eat chicken that night in the village, and rice, yucca, onions, beets, and heaps of fruit. The sun would ring down, pulling darkness after it like a curtain. Twilight is short, and the unseen birds of twilight wistful, uncanny, catching the heart. The two nuns in their dazzling white habits—the beautiful-boned young nun and the warm-faced old—would glide to the open cane-and-thatch schoolroom in darkness, and start the children singing. The children would sing in piping Spanish, highpitched and pure; they would sing "Nearer My God to Thee" in Quechua, very fast. (To reciprocate, we sang for them "Old MacDonald Had a Farm"; I thought they might recognize the animal sounds. Of course they thought we were out of our minds.) As the children became excited by their own singing, they left their log benches and swarmed around the nuns, hopping, smiling at us, everyone smiling, the nuns' faces bursting in their cowls, and the clear-voiced children still singing, and the palm-leafed roofing stirred. 19

The Napo River: it is not out of the way. It is *in* the way, catching sunlight the way a cup catches poured water; it is a bowl of sweet air, a basin of greenness, and of grace, and, it would seem, of peace. 20

Questions for Close Reading

1. What is the thesis (or dominant impression) of the selection? Locate the sentence(s) in which Dillard states her main idea. If she does not state the thesis explicitly, express it in your own words.

2. To what extent do the non-natives of the Ecuadorian jungle—the North Americans, priests, and nuns—harmonize with the place and its Indian inhabitants? Are there any times the non-natives seem out of place or ludicrous? When?

3. What can we infer about Dillard's attitude toward the natives who display severed snake heads, sling stones at birds, and eat other human beings?

4. Although Dillard writes that the Napo River is a place "of peace" (paragraph 20), an undercurrent of menace runs throughout her essay. Where does she mention threatening possibilities? What do these dangers suggest about the jungle? About life?

5. Refer to your dictionary as needed to define the following words used in the selection: *tributary* (paragraphs 9 and 12), *opaque* (10, 18), *bole* (14), *buttressed* (14), *derrick* (15), and *impaled* (16).

Questions About the Writer's Craft

1. In descriptive essays, writers often use a fairly straightforward organizational structure. Why doesn't Dillard use strict chronological, sensory, spatial, or emphatic order to structure her essay? Why, for example, does she delay the account of her arrival until paragraph 7?

2. Dillard is a master of rich sensory detail. For example, she writes that the Napo River "coiled up the sandy bank and tangled its foam in vines" (paragraph 3). Find additional examples of words and phrases that appeal powerfully to the senses. How do these word choices support Dillard's thesis?

3. Dillard places descriptions of the sweet and peaceful directly beside descriptions of the sinister and violent. In one sentence, for example, she matter-of-factly mentions refreshing drinks and a tarantula attacking its prey. Find other instances of these startling juxtapositions. What do they suggest about the jungle? About life?

4. Although Dillard relies heavily on visual details, she also refers repeatedly to the invisibly present (paragraphs 10, 14, 15, 18). What is her purpose in reminding readers of what is unseen?

Questions for Further Thought

1. Dillard seems to accept all creatures and behaviors as a natural part of life. Do you have the same attitude, or are you more judgmental? What are the dangers of being either too judgmental or too accepting?

2. What effect does Dillard's not understanding Spanish or Quechua have on her experience with the natives? Were you ever in a region

where you didn't understand the language? What effect did this have on your impression of the place?

3. Were you disturbed when you read about the moths being eaten by the tarantula? Were you more disturbed when you read about the boy attempting to pelt the birds with stones? Perhaps only the references to cannibalism and man-eating animals upset you. What might your reactions reveal about your attitude toward living things?

4. Dillard depicts a continuous cycle of life and death in which chronological time is of little importance. Do you feel society is too conscious of schedules and deadlines? If you think it is, what do we lose by such regimentation? What do we gain?

Writing Assignments Using Description as a Method of Development

*1. Dillard suggests that many of us feel frazzled by our everyday lives. Where do you go when you want to get away from it all? Do you shut yourself in your room and turn on the music? Do you go to a gym? Write an essay describing where you feel most at peace. Like Dillard, use vivid sensory details and figurative language to convey your paper's dominant impression. Before writing the essay, you might want to read Anne Morrow Lindbergh's "Channelled Whelk" (page 200) and/or Henry David Thoreau's "The Village" (page 327), two essays filled with rich descriptive details of peaceful places.

*2. Write a description of a place that seems ugly, harmful, or otherwise offensive — cigarette stubs and debris on the beach, tipped-over trash cans and cracked sidewalks in a nearby neighborhood. Organized around a clear dominant impression, your description should capture the look, smell, sound, and feel of this unpleasant place. Use the description to make a point about humans' interaction with their environment. Thomas Wolfe's "O Rotten Gotham" (page 381) might give you some good ideas for your essay.

Writing Assignments Using Other Methods of Development

3. Write an essay arguing that living in what Dillard calls "out of the way places" is superior to city living. Or take the opposing stance and argue that urban living is preferable. Support your contention through vivid examples of the inconvenience, danger, and unhappiness experienced by those dwelling in the area you find unpleasant. The essay's tone may be serious or playful. One part of the paper, perhaps the introduction, should recognize the opposing viewpoint.

4. Dillard seems to suffer little or no culture shock in the Ecuadorian jungle. Narrate a time you felt out of place — in a new school, foreign country, another region of the country, a stranger's home. Tell what happened by focusing on the experience's humorous, embarrassing, or threatening elements. What did the experience teach you about yourself and your ability to adapt?

E. B. White

Elwyn Brooks White (1899–1985) is considered one of America's finest essayists. For many years, White was a member of *The New Yorker* magazine staff and wrote the magazine's popular column, "The Talk of the Town." He also wrote children's books, including the classic *Charlotte's Web* (1952), and was the coauthor with William Strunk, Jr., of the renowned guide for writers, *The Elements of Style* (1959). But most memorable are the essays White produced during his life—gems of clarity, wit, and heartfelt expression. White's contribution to literature earned him many awards, including the Presidential Medal of Freedom and the National Medal for Literature. The classic essay reprinted here is taken from *The Essays of E. B. White* (1977).

Once More to the Lake

In this celebrated essay, E. B. White describes his return to a vacation spot he had known intimately in his childhood, a cabin on a lake in Maine. This time White is accompanied by his son. In many ways the lake, the cabin, and the surrounding fields and woods are the same, but in other respects they are different. With great skill, White describes his past and present experiences at the lake, exploring the nature of life cycles and of change itself.

One summer, along about 1904, my father rented a camp on 1 a lake in Maine and took us all there for the month of August. We all got ringworm from some kittens and had to rub Pond's Extract on our arms and legs night and morning, and my father rolled over in a canoe with all his clothes on; but outside of that the vacation was a success and from then on none of us ever thought there was any place in the world like that lake in Maine. We returned summer after summer—always on August 1 for one month. I have since become a salt-water man, but sometimes in summer there are days when the restlessness of the tides and the fearful cold of the sea water and the incessant wind that blows across the afternoon and into the evening make me wish for the placidity of a lake in the woods. A few weeks ago this feeling got so strong I bought myself a couple of bass hooks and a spinner and returned to the lake where we used to go, for a week's fishing and to revisit old haunts.

I took along my son, who had never had any fresh water up his nose and who had seen lily pads only from train windows. On the journey over to the lake I began to wonder what it would be like. I wondered how time would have marred this unique, this holy spot — the coves and streams, the hills that the sun set behind, the camps and the paths behind the camps. I was sure that the tarred road would have found it out, and I wondered in what other ways it would be desolated. It is strange how much you can remember about places like that once you allow your mind to return into the grooves that lead back. You remember one thing, and that suddenly reminds you of another thing. I guess I remembered clearest of all the early mornings, when the lake was cool and motionless, remembered how the bedroom smelled of the lumber it was made of and of the wet woods whose scent entered through the screen. The partitions in the camp were thin and did not extend clear to the top of the rooms, and as I was always the first up I would dress softly so as not to wake the others, and sneak out into the sweet outdoors and start out in the canoe, keeping close along the shore in the long shadows of the pines. I remembered being very careful never to rub my paddle against the gunwale for fear of disturbing the stillness of the cathedral.

The lake had never been what you would call a wild lake. There were cottages sprinkled around the shores, and it was in farming country although the shores of the lake were quite heavily wooded. Some of the cottages were owned by nearby farmers, and you would live at the shore and eat your meals at the farmhouse. That's what our family did. But although it wasn't wild, it was a fairly large and undisturbed lake and there were places in it that, to a child at least, seemed infinitely remote and primeval.

I was right about the tar: it led to within half a mile of the shore. But when I got back there, with my boy, and we settled into a camp near a farmhouse and into the kind of summertime I had known, I could tell that it was going to be pretty much the same as it had been before—I knew it, lying in bed the first morning, smelling the bedroom and hearing the boy sneak quietly out and go off along the shore in a boat. I began to sustain the illusion that he was I, and therefore, by simple transposition, that I was my father. This sensation persisted, kept cropping up all the time we were there. It was not an entirely new feeling, but in this setting it grew much stronger. I seemed to be living a dual existence. I would be in the middle of some simple act, I would be picking up a bait box or laying down a table fork, or I would be saying something, and suddenly it would be not I but my father who was saying the words or making the gesture. It gave me a creepy sensation.

We went fishing the first morning. I felt the same damp moss covering the worms in the bait can, and saw the dragonfly alight on the tip of my rod as it hovered a few inches from the surface of the water. It was the arrival of this fly that convinced me beyond any doubt that everything was as it always had been, that the years were a mirage and that there had been no years. The small waves were the same, chucking the rowboat under the chin as we fished at anchor, and the boat was the same boat, the same color green and the ribs broken in the same places, and under the floorboards the same fresh-water leavings and débris—the dead helgramite, the wisps of moss, the rusty discarded fishhook, the dried blood from yesterday's catch. We stared silently at the tips of our rods, at the dragonflies that came and went. I lowered the tip of mine into the water, tentatively, pensively dislodging the fly, which darted two feet away, poised, darted two feet back, and came to rest again a little farther up the rod. There had been no years between the ducking of this dragonfly and the other one—the one that was part of memory. I looked at the boy, who was silently watching his fly, and it was my hands that held his rod, my eyes watching. I felt dizzy and didn't know which rod I was at the end of.

We caught two bass, hauling them in briskly as though they were mackerel, pulling them over the side of the boat in a businesslike manner without any landing net, and stunning them with a blow on the back of the head. When we got back for a swim before lunch, the lake was exactly where we had left it, the same number of inches from the dock, and there was only the merest suggestion of a breeze. This seemed an utterly enchanted sea, this lake you could leave to its own devices for a few hours and come back to, and find that it had not stirred, this constant and trustworthy body of water. In the shallows, the dark, water-soaked sticks and twigs, smooth and old, were undulating in clusters on the bottom against the clean ribbed sand, and the track of the mussel was plain. A school of minnows swam by, each minnow with its small individual shadow, doubling the attendance, so clear and sharp in the sunlight. Some of the other campers were in swimming, along the shore, one of them with a cake of soap, and the water felt thin and clear and unsubstantial. Over the years there had been this person with the cake of soap, this cultist, and here he was. There had been no years.

Up to the farmhouse to dinner through the teeming, dusty field, the road under our sneakers was only a two-track road. The middle track was missing, the one with the marks of the hooves and the splotches of dried, flaky manure. There had always been three tracks to choose from in choosing which track to walk in; now the choice was narrowed down to two. For a moment I missed terribly the middle alternative. But the way led past the tennis court, and something about the way it lay there in the sun reassured me; the tape had loosened along the backline, the alleys were green with plantains and other weeds, and the net (installed in June and removed in September) sagged in the dry noon, and the whole place steamed with midday heat and hunger and emptiness. There was a choice of pie for dessert, and one was blueberry and one was apple, and the waitresses were the same country girls, there having been no passage of time, only the illusion of it as in a dropped curtain — the waitresses were still fifteen; their hair had been washed, that was the only difference — they had been to the movies and seen the pretty girls with the clean hair. 7

Summertime, oh, summertime, pattern of life indelible, the fade-proof lake, the woods unshatterable, the pasture with the sweetfern and the juniper forever and ever, summer without end; this was the background, and the life along the shore was the design, the cottagers with their innocent and tranquil design, their tiny docks with the flagpole and the American flag floating against the white clouds in the blue sky, the little paths over the roots of the trees leading from camp to camp and the paths leading back to the outhouses and the can of lime for sprinkling, 8 and at the souvenir counters at the store the miniature birch-bark canoes and the postcards that showed things looking a little better than they looked. This was the American family at play, escaping the city heat, wondering whether the newcomers in the camp at the head of the cove were "common" or "nice," wondering whether it was true that the people who drove up for Sunday dinner at the farmhouse were turned away because there wasn't enough chicken.

It seemed to me, as I kept remembering all this, that those times and those summers had been infinitely precious and worth saving. There had been jollity and peace and goodness. The arriving (at the beginning of August) had been so big a business in itself, at the railway station the farm wagon drawn up, the first smell of the pine-laden air, the first glimpse of the smiling farmer, and the great importance of the trunks and your father's enormous authority in such matters, and the feel of the wagon under you for the long ten-mile haul, and at the top of the last long hill catching the first view of the lake after eleven months of not seeing this cherished body of water. The shouts and cries of the other campers when they saw you, and the trunks to be unpacked, to give up their rich burden. (Arriving was less exciting nowadays, when you sneaked up in your car and parked it under a tree near the camp and took out the bags and in five minutes it was all over, no fuss, no loud wonderful fuss about trunks.)

Peace and goodness and jollity. The only thing that was wrong now, really, was the sound of the place, an unfamiliar nervous sound of the outboard motors. This was the note that jarred, the one thing that would sometimes break the illusion and set the years moving. In those other summertimes all motors were inboard; and when they were at a little distance, the noise they made was a sedative, an ingredient of summer sleep. They were one-cylinder and two-cylinder engines, and some were make-and-break and some were jump-spark, but they all made a sleepy sound across the lake. The one-lungers throbbed and fluttered, and the twin-cylinder ones purred and purred, and that was a quiet sound, too. But now the campers all had outboards. In the daytime, in the hot mornings, these motors made a petulant, irritable sound; at night, in the still evening when the afterglow lit the water, they whined about one's ears like mosquitoes. My boy loved our rented outboard, and his great desire was to achieve single-handed mastery over it, and authority, and he soon learned the trick of choking it a little (but not too much), and the adjustment of the needle valve. Watching him I would remember the things you could do with the old one-cylinder engine with the heavy flywheel, how you could have it eating out of your hand if you got really close to it spiritually. Motorboats in those days didn't have clutches, and you would make a landing by shutting off the motor at the proper time and coasting in with a dead rudder. But there was a way of reversing them, if you learned the trick, by cutting the switch and putting it on again exactly on the final dying revolution of the flywheel, so that it would kick back against compression and begin reversing. Approaching a dock in a strong following breeze, it was difficult to slow up sufficiently by the ordinary coasting method, and if a boy felt he had complete mastery over his motor, he was tempted to keep it running beyond its time and then reverse it a few feet from the dock. It took a cool nerve, because if you threw the switch a twentieth of a second too soon you would catch the flywheel when it still had speed enough to go up past center, and the boat would leap ahead, charging bullfashion at the dock.

We had a good week at the camp. The bass were biting well and the sun shone endlessly, day after day. We would be tired at night and lie down in the accumulated heat of the little bedrooms after the long hot day and the breeze would stir almost imperceptibly outside and the smell of the swamp drift in through the rusty screens. Sleep would come easily and in the morning the red squirrel would be on the roof, tapping out his gay routine. I kept remembering everything, lying in bed in the mornings — the small steamboat that had a long rounded stern like the lip of a Ubangi, and how quietly she ran on the moonlight sails, when the older boys played their mandolins and the girls sang and we ate doughnuts dipped in sugar, and how sweet the music was on the water in the shining night, and what it had felt like to think about girls then. After breakfast we would go up to the store and the things were in the same place — the minnows in a bottle, the plugs and spinners disarranged and pawed over by the youngsters from the boys' camp, the Fig Newtons and the Beeman's gum. Outside, the road was tarred and cars stood in front of the store.

Inside, all was just as it had always been, except there was more Coca-Cola and not so much Moxie and root beer and birch beer and sarsaparilla. We would walk out with the bottle of pop apiece and sometimes the pop would backfire up our noses and hurt. We explored the streams, quietly, where the turtles slid off the sunny logs and dug their way into the soft bottom; and we lay on the town wharf and fed worms to the tame bass. Everywhere we went I had trouble making out which was I, the one walking at my side, the one walking in my pants.

One afternoon while we were there at the lake a thunderstorm came up. It was like the revival of an old melodrama that I had seen long ago with childish awe. The second-act climax of the drama of the electrical disturbance over a lake in America had not changed in any important respect. This was the big scene, still the big scene. The whole thing was so familiar, the first feeling of oppression and heat and a general air around camp of not wanting to go very far away. In midafternoon (it was all the same) a curious darkening of the sky, and a lull in everything that had made life tick; and then the way the boats suddenly swung the other way at their moorings with the coming of a breeze out of the new quarter, and premonitory rumble. Then the kettle drum, then the snare, then the bass drum and cymbals, then cackling light against the dark, and the gods grinning and licking their chops in the hills. Afterward the calm, the rain steadily rustling in the calm lake, the return of light and hope and spirits, and the campers running out in joy and relief to go swimming in the rain, their bright cries perpetuating the deathless joke about how they were getting simply drenched, and the children screaming with delight at the new sensation of bathing in the rain, and the joke about getting drenched linking the generations in a strong indestructible chain. And the comedian who waded in carrying an umbrella.

When the others went swimming, my son said he was going in, too. He pulled his dripping trunks from the line where they had hung all through the shower and wrung them out. Languidly, and with no thought of going in, I watched him, his hard little body, skinny and bare, saw him wince slightly as he pulled up around his vitals the small, soggy, icy garment. As he buckled the swollen belt, suddenly my groin felt the chill of death.

Questions for Close Reading

1. What is the thesis (or dominant impression) of the selection? Locate the sentence(s) in which White states his main idea. If he does not state the thesis explicitly, express it in your own words.
2. Why does White return to the lake in Maine he had visited as a child? Why do you think he has waited to revisit it until he has a young son to bring along?
3. Several times in the essay, White notes that he felt as if he were his own father — and that his son became his childhood self. What event first prompts this sensation? What actions and thoughts cause it to recur?
4. How is the latest visit to the lake similar to White's childhood summers? What differences does White notice? What effects do the differences have on him?
5. Refer to your dictionary as needed to define the following words used in the selection: *incessant* (paragraph 1), *placidity* (1), *primeval* (3), *transposition* (4), *undulating* (6), *indelible* (8), *petulant* (10), and *languidly* (13).

Questions About the Writer's Craft

1. Through vivid language, descriptive writing evokes the experiences of the five senses. In "Once More to the Lake," White overlays two sets of sensory details: those of the present-day lake and those of the lake as it was in his boyhood. Which set of details is more objective? Which seems sharper and more powerful? Why?
2. White chooses many words and phrases with religious connotations as he describes the lake. Give some examples. Why does he use such language?
3. In paragraph 12, White describes a thunderstorm. Explain the metaphors he uses in this passage.
4. White's thought concerning "the chill of death" in the final paragraph may seem surprising. What brings on this feeling? Why does he feel it "in his groin"? Where has this idea been hinted at previously in the essay?

Questions for Further Thought

1. In paragraph 9, White says about his boyhood visits to the lake that "those times and those summers had been infinitely precious and worth saving." From your own perspective, what makes an experience worth savoring and storing in the memory in all its detail?

2. When White refers to his son, he never uses the boy's first name (he calls him "the boy" or "my boy"); only in the last scene does he call him "my son." Why does White use this impersonal form of reference? Could this essay have been written if the author's child had been a girl?

3. In your opinion, was the visit to the lake a good experience for White—or a bad one? In general, is it or is it not a good idea to try to relive the past?

4. This essay touches on a universal human feeling—the sensation that time is slipping by, that our lives are spinning out their allotted spans every moment of the day. When do people first become aware of their own mortality? What events or phases of life heighten this feeling?

Writing Assignments Using Description as a Method of Development

1. Write a descriptive essay about a special place in your life. It need not be a natural setting like White's lake; it could be a place in a city or house, for example, that has meant a great deal to you or has had an effect on your life. Use sensory details and figurative language, as White does, to give energy to your description. Explain the effects the place has on you, but avoid long narrative passages concerning events that may have occurred there.

*2. White was fortunate that his lake had remained virtually unchanged. But many other special spots have been destroyed or are threatened with destruction. Write a descriptive essay about a place (a park, a school, an old fashioned ice cream parlor) that is "infinitely precious and worth saving." Your dominant theme should be the qualities or aspects of your subject that make it worthy of being preserved intact for future generations. Before writing your essay, you may want to read Art Spikol's "High Noon" (318) and Rachel Carson's "A Fable for Tomorrow" (313), two essays that mourn the loss of special places.

Writing Assignments Using Other Methods of Development

3. Sometimes we are suddenly reminded of the nearness of death: a crushed animal lies on the road, a politician is assassinated, a classmate is killed in a car crash. Write an essay about a time you were forced to think about mortality. Explain what happened and describe your thoughts and feelings afterward.

4. Have your older relatives made an attempt to transfer the special
experiences of their younger years to you in some way? Or have you
done the same with your own children or younger relatives? You
may have visited a special place, as White did, or listened to stories,
or looked at photographs or objects. Write an essay recounting such
a moment (or moments) and explain the motivations of the older
generation — and the effects on the younger one.

Peggy Anderson

Peggy Anderson was born and raised in Chicago and educated at Augustana College in Rock Island, Illinois. She served in the Peace Corps in Togo, West Africa, and later worked as a writer for the Peace Corps in Washington. Now a freelance writer, Anderson has published articles in *Family Circle, The New York Times*, and *Ms*. She is also the author of three books: *The Daughters* (1974), a profile of the Daughters of the American Revolution; *Nurse* (1977), which was made into a television movie and series; and *Children's Hospital* (1985), from which this selection is taken.

Children's Hospital

Most hospitals are the dreariest of places, but the children's hospital described by Peggy Anderson is attractive and friendly. With its impressive atrium, brightly trimmed rooms, and ample play and gathering areas, the hospital imparts a sense of community and hope to young patients and their visitors.

Children's Hospital stands beside a busy boulevard in a   1
major American city. Its nearest neighbors are a massive civic center, a high-rise hotel, and the medical school and hospital of a distinguished university. For decades Children's was housed in a turn-of-the-century edifice of red brick which had grown dingier and more cramped with every passing year. The new facility is a classy, modern, energy-efficient structure of gleaming brown, striped horizontally by brown-tinted windows, with three times the square footage of the old building and space for twice the number of intensive care beds. Its defining characteristic is a one-million-cubic-foot atrium which rises from the lobby through all nine floors and lets in the sky through a stepped glass roof. The new Children's was designed to please children and to allay

their fears. To a visitor, the dominant impressions are of openness, color, and natural light

It is light that first strikes a person coming into the hospital in the daytime. One has passed through an entrance, one is definitely inside, yet the light makes the lobby feel out-of-doors. As if drawn by pulleys, the visitor's eye climbs the nine stories to the source. Only when the light has been accounted for does one look around at ground level and begin to appreciate the lobby itself.

It's enormous. It compares favorably in size with the multipurpose lobbies of the newest hotels. Like many hotel lobbies, the lobby at Children's features live trees and a working fountain. Wooden planters, a quarry tile floor, and molded plastic benches in orange and yellow contribute further to the visitor's sense of being in a park.

But in common with few if any hotels, the Children's lobby is occupied on one side by a McDonald's restaurant. Seating is arranged in the manner of a sidewalk café. Across the floor from McDonald's is a carpeted play pit where a child who feels well enough may roughhouse with siblings in reasonable safety, or a patient in a wheelchair may picnic quietly with parents. At some remove from the pit and right next to the main entrance stands a distorting mirror that could have come straight from a fun house.

The rear of the ground floor is occupied by the hospital cafeteria. Beneath the cafeteria and lobby is a two-level parking garage. The floor below that is the province of computers, equipment, and building engineers. Short wings off the lobby house the Emergency Room, a small chapel, the day surgery unit, and a branch bank as well as the Admissions Office. Floors One through Three are for offices and outpatient clinics.

Four is given over to the operating room complex and four intensive care units. Five and Six are likewise for inpatients. On each of these floors the choicest space has been designated for the children. Head nurses' offices do not have windows at Children's, nor do many doctors' offices. But half of one wall in every patient room is a large window overlooking either the city or the center court. Each wall opposite contains a window through which patients may see into the hall. Every playroom at Children's has huge windows. Some playrooms actually jut out into the court like enclosed balconies with windows on three sides.

Halls play an important role on the first six floors at Children's. The major hallways all overlook the court through tempered glass partitions. From a distance that honors privacy, these halls afford a look into patient rooms, playrooms, clinic waiting rooms, and offices around the court from lobby to skylight. This view diminishes the mystery one usually associates with hospitals. To a parent or child immersed in private misery, the view also offers perspective. Other children are sick enough to be in here too, it says. Some may be worse off. Some are getting well. The view provides a glimpse of institutional business-as-usual which can serve as a reminder that while one's personal world may have stopped, the large world goes on as dependably as the tides. At night someone standing in a main hallway at Children's can look up through the skylight and see stars.   7

The tops of the tempered glass partitions do not meet the hall ceilings. For this reason and because planners sought to isolate sick children as little as possible from life around them, sounds of the hospital reach the hallways from many parts of the building. Somewhere a baby cries. Somewhere a toddler laughs. Somewhere a mother reprimands a clinic patient springing for the elevator. *"Anthony! You get back here!"*   8

Somewhere a child demands a milkshake *and* french fries. The fall of water from the lobby fountain reaches the sixth floor. So does the aggregate of voices from the lobby—a hum of many people with many different missions, much like the buzz one hears in a shopping mall on a weekday afternoon. Together the sounds impart an air of informality and normalcy.   9

Varnished benches of light wood run along the low walls supporting the glass partitions. Though most units have small waiting rooms off the halls, the benches get heavier use. Patients come out to sit on them for a change of scene. Parents give themselves moments alone on the benches. Aunts and uncles and grandparents spread out on them while waiting their turn to visit a child. Doctors or social workers or the chaplain join families on the benches to talk. Secretaries relax on the benches with sandwiches or yogurt. Parents wait out surgery there.   10

As hours pass, or days, the groups in the halls become small cultures. Each has its own habits, its own personality, its own pitch. Cigarette stubs and ashes build up in disposable silvery ashtrays. People stretch out and nap. Group weather brightens or   11 darkens with news. When the news is grave, the sorrow touches anyone who passes. But the halls are long. The benches are long. No one culture can dominate. Traffic continues to go by. Nurses and doctors talk to each other in ordinary voices. Usually in the hallways at Children's, and often in the units themselves, there is notable absence of hush.

Color abounds on the first six floors. In some rooms painters   12
made big orange circles on ceilings. They stenciled big yellow *C*'s and *D*'s on clean and dirty linen bins. Floor experts laid red and blue paths of linoleum tiles in the halls and added red and blue baseboards to match. For clinic waiting areas Purchasing ordered child-sized tables and chairs in orange and green. The color is meant to lift heavy spirits, as is the lilt of popular music which permeates the hospital day and night so unobtrusively as to escape conscious notice.

For all the resemblance they bear in mood to the floors   13
below, the top three floors of Children's might as well be in another city. Floors seven through nine are for research. They are not for patients but for scientists, not for parents but for technicians. On these floors decorators bothered little with color. The rooms are white. The halls are white. The linoleum is gray with white flecks. Hospital sounds seem remote. One imagines bacteria shushing each other in saucers. On three floors of odoriferous laboratories, small and large medical questions are being addressed with such aids as microscopes, scalpels, chemical solutions, government grants, dogs, cats, mice, rabbits, petri dishes, and equations that only scientists comprehend. For all this activity, the atmosphere of these floors feels quiet and white, as after heavy snow.

Questions for Close Reading

1. What is the thesis (or dominant impression) of the selection? Locate the sentence(s) in which Anderson states her main idea. If she does not state the thesis explicitly, express it in your own words.
2. How have the builders of Children's Hospital brought light into the structure? What other aspects of outdoors have they included inside?
3. Anderson says that halls play an important role in the hospital. What is that role? How are the halls different from those of most hospitals?
4. How has color been used throughout the nine floors of Children's Hospital? What is the purpose of the various colors or their absence?

5. Refer to your dictionary as needed to define the following words used in the selection: *edifice* (paragraph 1), *atrium* (1), *siblings* (4), *province* (5), *aggregate* (9), *abounds* (12), *unobtrusively* (12), and *odoriferous* (13).

Questions About the Writer's Craft

1. Anderson says that the dominant impression of the hospital is one of "openness, color, and natural light." What details in the description support that overall impression? Are there any that do not?
2. How does the author use transitions to keep the reader oriented in space throughout the description? Where does the author use repeated words to provide coherence between paragraphs?
3. Anderson's description is primarily visual, but she also refers to the other senses. Where does she point out smells and sounds? How do these details contribute to the overall impression of the hospital being a pleasant, comfortable place?
4. Why does Anderson describe the upper floors of the hospital in only one paragraph? Does this paragraph make an effective conclusion?

Questions for Further Thought

1. The new Children's Hospital "was designed to please children and to allay their fears." Which of the features do you think children will find most appealing? Can you think of other improvements that would add to the hospital's friendly feeling?
2. Why do you think the designers did not decorate the research floors the same way as the patient care floors? What is the effect of the whiteness of the walls?
3. According to psychologists, colors affect our moods: green is calming, red is stimulating, and so on. How responsive are you to colors in your environment? When have you been particularly aware of color or the lighting in your surroundings?
4. In such institutional buildings as schools, hospitals, and government facilities, do you feel enough attention is paid to the visual appeal of the rooms and halls and to the comfort of the users? What positive or negative experiences have you had with such institutional architecture?

Writing Assignments Using Description as a Method of Development

1. Write a description of another children's place, such as a playground, day care center, school, or swimming pool. Include vigor-

ous sensory details that show why the place is appealing to children, or why it is not.

2. Prepare a descriptive essay about a building or room you find uncomfortable, unattractive, and inhospitable. The specifics in your essay should convey your belief that the building or room needs significant changes to make it more appealing to the people who must work in it or use it.

Writing Assignments Using Other Methods of Development

*3. Write a narrative about a stressful time you spent at a clinic, court, hospital, or other institutional setting. Explain what happened during the visit, being sure to provide plentiful details to support your narrative point. You might want to read Tom Wolfe's "O Rotten Gotham—Sliding Down into the Behavioral Sink" (page 381). Wolfe's essay should sharpen your understanding of the way environment can influence people's moods and behaviors.

4. You have probably visited someone who has been hospitalized, or perhaps you have been a patient yourself. Prepare an essay showing how to be a cooperative—or difficult—patient. The essay may be serious or light in tone.

Additional Writing Topics
DESCRIPTION

General Assignments

Write an essay using description to develop any of the following topics. Remember that an effective description focuses on a dominant impression and arranges details in a way that best supports that impression. Your details — vivid and appealing to the senses — should be carefully chosen so that the essay is not overburdened with material of secondary importance. When writing, keep in mind that varied sentence structure and imaginative figures of speech are ways to make a descriptive piece compelling.

1. A favorite item of clothing
2. The world as a certain kind of animal sees it
3. An athletic shoe or high-heeled shoes
4. An individualist's appearance
5. A coffee shop, bus shelter, newsstand, or some other small place
6. A parade or victory celebration
7. A banana, squash, or other fruit or vegetable
8. A particular drawer
9. A house plant
10. A "media event"
11. A dorm room
12. An elderly person
13. An attractive man or woman
14. A prosthetic device or wheelchair
15. A TV, film, or music celebrity
16. A student lounge
17. A once-in-a-lifetime event
18. The inside of something, such as a cave, boat, shed, or machine
19. A friend, roommate, or other person you know well
20. An essential gadget or a useless gadget

Assignments with a Specific Audience and Purpose

1. You have been asked to speak to next year's freshman class at your college on the topic of the registration process. The more the students

know what to expect, the less confused or frustrated they will be. Describe what registration day is like, using specific details and lively language to make the experience vivid and realistic. Choose an adjective that represents your dominant impression of the experience and keep that in mind as you write.

2. As a subscriber to a dating service, you have been asked to submit a description of the kind of person you'd like to meet. Describe your ideal date. Focus on specific information about physical appearance, personal habits, character traits, and interests.

3. Your college has decided to tear down a campus structure and replace it with a new version (it could be a dorm, a dining hall, a special landmark, or any other structure). Write a letter of protest to the administration, describing the place so vividly and appealingly that its value and need for preservation are unquestionable.

4. You have recently joined the staff of the campus newspaper, and you have been asked to write an entertaining column of social news and gossip. For your first column, you are supposed to write a description of a recent campus event—a mixer, party, concert, or other social activity. Write the description, focusing on the places in which the event was held, the appearance of the people who attended, and so on. Your column could be straightforward or tongue-in-cheek.

5. Some students at your college have complained that the college catalog is inaccurate. Its course descriptions are too scanty, misleading, or both. You are on the team charged with revising the catalog. Write an *accurate* description of a course (or courses) with which you are familiar. Tell exactly what the course is about, who teaches it, and how it is run.

6. As a resident of a particular town, you are angered by the appearance of (and activities taking place in) a certain spot—a video game arcade, an adult bookstore, a bar, a bus or train station, or any other place. Write a letter to the town council, describing in detail the undesirable nature of this place.

NARRATION

WHAT IS NARRATION?

Human beings are instinctively storytellers. In prehistoric times, our ancestors huddled around campfires to hear tales of hunting and magic. In ancient times, warriors gathered in halls to listen to bards praise in song the exploits of epic heroes. Things are no different today. Boisterous children invariably settle down to listen when their parents read to them; millions of people tune in day after day to the ongoing drama of their favorite soap operas; vacationers sit motionless on the beach, caught up in the latest bestsellers; and all of us enjoy saying, "Just listen to what happened to me today." Our hunger for storytelling is a basic part of us.

Narration means telling a single story or several related stories. As you will see, the story can be a means to an end, a way to support a main idea or thesis. For instance, to demonstrate that television has become the constant companion of many children, you might narrate a typical child's day in front of the television — starting with frantic cartoons in the morning and ending with dizzy situation comedies at night. Or to support the point that the college registration process should be reformed, you could tell the tale of a chaotic morning spent trying to enroll in classes.

Narration is powerful. Every public speaker, from politician to classroom teacher, knows that stories can capture the attention of listeners in a way that nothing else can. Narration speaks to us strongly because it is about us; we want to know what happened to others, not simply because we are curious, but because their experiences shed light on the nature of our own lives. Narration lends force to opinions, triggers the flow of memory, and evokes places and times in ways that are compelling and affecting.

WHEN TO USE NARRATION

Since narratives tell a story, you may think that narratives can be found only in novels or short stories. But the narrative technique is often used as a supplemental pattern of development to help make a point in various kinds of essays. For example, if your purpose is to *persuade* apathetic readers that airport security regulations must be followed strictly, you might lead off with a brief account of an armed terrorist who easily boarded a plane. In an essay *defining* good teaching, you might keep readers engaged by including satirical anecdotes about one hapless instructor, the antithesis of an effective teacher. Or an essay on the *effects* of an overburdened judicial system might provide — in an attempt to involve readers — a dramatic account of the way one clearly guilty murderer plea bargained his way to freedom.

In addition to providing effective support in one section of your paper, narration can also serve as an essay's dominant pattern of development. In fact, most of this chapter shows how to use a single extended narrative to convey the central point of an essay. In such narrative essays, you tell a story (either your own or someone else's), sharing with readers your view of what happened. You might choose to narrate the events of a day spent with your three-year-old nephew as a way of explaining your rediscovery of the importance of family life. Or you might relate the story of your roommate's mugging, evoking the powerlessness and terror of being a victim. Any story can form the basis for a narrative essay as long as you convey the essence of the experience and evoke its meaning.

SUGGESTIONS FOR USING NARRATION IN AN ESSAY

The following suggestions will be helpful whether you use narration as a dominant or supportive pattern of development.

1. Identify the conflict in the event. The power of many narratives is rooted in a special kind of tension that "hooks" readers and makes them want to follow the story to its end. This narrative tension is often a by-product of some form of *conflict* within the story. Many narratives revolve around an internal dilemma experienced by a key person in the story. Or the conflict may be between people in the story or between a pivotal character and some social institution or natural phenomenon.

2. Determine the point of the narrative. In *The Adventures of Huckleberry Finn*, Mark Twain warned: "Persons attempting to find a motive in this narrative will be prosecuted; persons attempting to find a moral in it will be banished; persons attempting to find a plot in it will be shot." Twain was, of course, being ironic, for his novel's richness lies in its "motives" and "morals." Similarly, any narrative you write should—in addition to conveying a conflict—make a point.

Suppose you decided to write about the time you got locked in a mall late at night. Your narrative might focus on the way the mall looked after hours and how you struggled with mounting terror. But you would also use the narrative to make a point. Perhaps you want to emphasize that fear can be instructive. On the other hand, your point might be that malls have a disturbing, surreal underside. You could state this thesis or narrative point explicitly ("After hours, the mall shed its cheerful daytime demeanor for a more sinister quality"). Or you could refrain from stating the thesis directly, relying on your details and language ("The mannequins stared at me with glazed eyes and frozen smiles"; "The steel grates pulled over each store glinted in the cold light, making each shop look like a prison cell") to convey the point of the narrative.

3. Select details that advance the narrative point.   You know from experience that nothing is more boring than a storyteller who gets sidetracked and drags out a story with nonessential details. If a friend started to tell about the time his car broke down in the middle of an expressway — but interrupted his story to complain at length about the slipshod work done by his auto repair shop — you might clench your teeth in annoyance, wishing your friend would hurry up and get back to the interesting part of the story.

Brainstorming ("What happened? When? Where? Who was involved? Why did it happen?") can be valuable for helping you amass narrative details. Then, after generating the specifics, you cull out the nonessential, devoting your energies to the key specifics needed to advance your narrative point. When telling a story, you maintain an effective narrative pace by focusing on that point and eliminating details that do not support it. A good narrative depends not only on what is included, but also on what has been left out.

But how do you determine which specifics to omit, which to treat briefly, and which to emphasize? Knowing your audience and having a clear sense of your narrative point are crucial. Assume you were writing a narrative about a disastrous get-acquainted dance sponsored by your college the first week of the academic year. In addition to telling what happened, you would want the narrative to make a point; perhaps you want to emphasize that, despite the college's good intentions, such "official" events actually make it difficult to meet people. With that purpose in mind, you might write about how stiff and unnatural students seemed, all dressed up in their best clothes; you might narrate snatches of strained conversation you overheard; you might describe the way males gathered on one side of the room, females on the other — reverting to behaviors supposedly abandoned in fifth grade. All these details would support your narrative point.

Because you do not want to get waylaid by detours that lead away from that point, you would leave out details about the topnotch band and the appetizing refreshments at the dance. The music and food may have been surprisingly good, but since these details do not advance the point you want to make, they should be omitted.

You also need to keep your audience in mind when selecting narrative details. If the audience consists of your instructor and other students — all of them familiar with the new student center where the dance was held — specific details about the center would probably not have to be provided. But imagine that the essay is going to appear in the quarterly magazine published by the college's community relations office. Many of the magazine's readers are former graduates who have not been on campus for several years. They may need some additional specifics about the student center: its location, how many people it holds, how it is furnished.

As you write, keep asking yourself a number of questions: "Is this detail or character or snippet of conversation essential to my purpose? Does my audience need this particular detail to know what I'm talking about?" Borderline details that have some importance but do not deserve lengthy treatment should be summarized ("Two hours went by . . ."). Passing over such specifics quickly allows you to move the story along to its finish. Just as movies use the "quick cut" as storytelling shorthand (the camera lingers on the bags of money being loaded into the armored truck that will soon be held up by a gang of thieves but pans rapidly over the interior of the truck), you need to strike a balance between summarized and fully developed narrative detail.

Sometimes, especially if the narrative recreates an event from the past, you will not be able to remember what happened detail for detail. In such a case, you should take advantage of what is called *dramatic license*. Using as a guide your powers of recall as well as the perspective you now have of that particular time, feel free to reshape events to suit your narrative point.

4. Select and organize the narrative sequence. All of us know the traditional beginning of fairy tales: "Once upon a time. . . ." Every narrative begins somewhere, presents a span of time, and ends at a certain point. Frequently, you will want to use a straightforward time order, following the event chronologically from beginning to end: first this happened, next this happened, finally this happened.

But sometimes a strict chronological recounting may not be effective — especially if the high point of the narrative gets lost somewhere in the middle of the time sequence. To avoid that possibility, you may want to disrupt chronology, plunge the reader into the middle of the story, and then return in a *flashback* to the beginning of the tale. You are probably familiar with the way flashback is used on television and in film. You see someone appealing to the main character for financial help, then return to an earlier time when both were students in the same class, before learning how the rest of the story unfolds. Narratives can also use *flashforward* to tell a story. You get a glimpse of the future (the main character being jailed) before the story continues in the present (the events that led to the arrest). These techniques add texture to the narrative, shifting the story onto several time planes rather than following a straight, linear path from beginning to end. Here are examples of how flashback and flashforward can be used in narrative writing:

Standing behind the wooden counter. Greg wielded his knife expertly as he shucked clams--one every ten seconds--with practiced ease. The scene contrasted sharply with his first day on the job, when his hands broke out in blisters and when splitting each shell was like prying open a safe. (Flashback)

Rushing to move my car from the no-parking zone, I waved a quick good-bye to Karen as she climbed the steps to the bus. I didn't know then that by the time I picked her up at the bus station later that day, she had made a decision that would affect both our lives. (Flashforward)

Whether or not you choose to include flashbacks or flashforwards, remember to limit the time span covered by the narrative. Otherwise, you will have trouble generating the details needed to give the story depth and meaning.

Regardless of the time sequence you select, you also want to guard against organizing the narrative so that it trails off into minor, anticlimactic details. Effective narratives drive toward a strong finish.

Finally, readers should be able to follow with ease your organization of the narrative action. Although narrative paragraphs often do not have topic sentences, each paragraph should be organized clearly. Describing each distinct time phase in separate paragraphs — with or without topic sentences — helps the reader grasp the flow of events. You should also be sure to use time signposts when recounting a story. Words such as *now, then, next, after,* and *later* ensure that your reader will not get lost as the story progresses.

5. Make the narrative vigorous and immediate. A compelling narrative provides abundant specific details, making readers feel as if they are experiencing the story being told. Readers must be able to see, hear, touch, smell, and taste the event being narrated. *Vivid sensory description* is, therefore, an essential part of an effective narrative. Not only do these specific sensory details make writing a pleasure to read — we all enjoy learning the particulars about people, places, and things — but they also give the narrative the stamp of reality. The specifics convince the reader that the event being described actually did, or could, occur. Compare the following excerpts from a narrative essay; the first version is lifeless and dull, while the revised version grabs readers with its sense of foreboding:

> That eventful day started out like every other summer day. My sister Tricia and I made several elaborate mudpies which we decorated with care. A little later on, as we were spraying each other with the garden hose, we heard my father walk up the path.

> That sad summer day started out uneventfully enough. My sister Tricia and I spent a few hours mixing and decorating mudpies. Our hands caked with dry mud, we sprinkled each lopsided pie with alternating rows of dandelion and clover petals. Later when the sun got hotter, we tossed our white T-shirts over the red picket fence--forgetting my grandmother's frequent warnings to be more ladylike. Feeling as tough as boys, our sweaty backs bared to the sun, we doused each other with icy sprays from the garden hose. Caught up in the primitive pleasure of it all, we barely heard my father as he walked up the garden path, the gravel crunching under his heavy work boots.

Another way to create an aura of narrative immediacy is to use *dialogue* while telling a story. Our sense of other people comes, in part, from what they say and from the way they sound. Conversational exchanges allow the reader to experience characters directly, gaining better understanding of the people in the narrative. Compare the following fragments of a narrative, one with dialogue and one without:

When I finally found my way back to the campsite, the trail guide commented on my disheveled appearance.

When I finally found my way back to the campsite, the trail guide took one look at me and drawled, "What on earth happened to you, Daniel Boone? You look as though you've been dragged through a haystack backwards."

A final way to make narratives lively and vigorous is to use *varied sentence structure*. Sentences that plod along predictably (subject–verb, subject–verb) put readers to sleep. Experiment with your sentences by juggling length and sentence type; mix long and short sentences, simple and complex. Comparing the following original and revised versions will give you an idea how effective varied sentence rhythm can be in narrative writing.

Original
The store manager went to the walk-in refrigerator every day. The heavy metal door clanged shut behind her. I had visions of her freezing to death among the hanging carcasses. The shiny door finally swung open. She waddled out.

Revised
Each time the store manager went to the walk-in refrigerator, the heavy metal door clanged shut behind her. Visions of her freezing to death among the hanging carcasses crept into my mind until the shiny door finally swung open and she waddled out.

Original
The yellow-and-blue-striped fish struggled on the line. Its scales shimmered in the sunlight. Its tail waved frantically. The fish gave my brother a real fight.

Revised
Scales shimmering in the sunlight, tail waiving frantically, the yellow-and-blue-striped fish struggled on the line, giving my brother a real fight.

6. Narrate the story using a consistent point of view. All stories have a *narrator*: the person who tells the story. If you, as narrator, tell a story as you experienced it, the story is written in the *first person point of view* ("I saw the dog pull loose . . ."). But if you, as narrator, observed the event and want to tell how someone else experienced it, you would use the *third person point of view* ("Anne saw the dog pull loose . . ."). Each point of view has advantages and limitations. First person recreates with power the event as you, the narrator, actually experienced it. This point of view is limited, though, in its ability to describe the inner reactions of other people involved in the event. By way of contrast, third person makes it easier for you as narrator to provide insight into all the participants; however, this increased objectivity may undercut some of the subjective immediacy typical of the "I was there" point of view.

Effective narratives may be exciting or charming or moving; writing them can be great fun and devilishly difficult at the same time. It is no mean feat to recreate an event, drawing on your powers of recall as well as your skill with language to make the narrative action come alive.

Although some narratives relate unusual experiences, most tread familiar ground, telling tales of joy, love, loss, frustration, fear—all common emotions experienced during a life. Do not think, however, that writing about the familiar makes your story predictable. On the contrary. All of us feel an energizing shock of recognition whenever the human condition is written about with grace and power. Narratives can take the ordinary and transmute it into something significant, even extraordinary. As Willa Cather, the American novelist, wrote: "There are only two or three human stories and they go on repeating themselves as fiercely as if they had never happened before." The challenge lies in applying your own vision to a tale, thereby making it unique.

STUDENT ESSAY AND COMMENTARY

The student essay that follows was written by Paul Monahan in response to this assignment.

In "Shooting an Elephant," George Orwell tells about an incident that forced him to act in a manner that ran counter to his better instincts. Write a narrative about a time when you faced a disturbing conflict and ended up doing something you later regretted.

While reading Paul's paper, try to determine how well it applies the principles concerning the uses of narration. The commentary following the paper will help you look at Paul's essay more closely.

If Only

Having worked at a 7-Eleven store for two years, I thought I had become successful at what our manager calls "customer relations." I firmly believed that a friendly smile and an automatic "sir," "ma'am," and "thank you" would see me through any situation that might arise, from soothing impatient or unpleasant people to apologizing for giving out the wrong change. But the other night an old woman shattered my belief that a glib response could smooth over the rough spots of dealing with other human beings. 1

The moment she entered, the woman presented a sharp contrast to our shiny store with its bright lighting and neatly arranged shelves. Walking as if each step were painful, she slowly pushed open the glass door and hobbled down the nearest aisle. She coughed dryly, wheezing with each breath. On a forty-degree night, she was wearing only a faded print dress, a thin, light-beige sweater too small to button, and black vinyl slippers with the backs cut out to expose calloused heels. There were no stockings or socks on her splotchy, blue-veined legs. 2

After strolling around the store for several minutes, the old woman stopped in front of the rows of canned vegetables. She picked up some Del Monte corn niblets and stared with a strange intensity at the label. At that point, I decided to be a good, courteous employee and asked her if she needed help. As I stood close to her, my smile became harder to maintain; her red-rimmed eyes were partially closed by yellowish crusts; her hands were covered with layer upon layer of grime, and the stale smell of sweat rose in a thick vaporous cloud from her clothes. 3

"I need some food," she muttered in reply to my bright, "Can I help you?" 4

"Are you looking for corn, ma'am?" 5

"I need some food," she repeated. "Any kind." 6

"Well, the corn is ninety-five cents," I said in my most helpful voice. "Or, if you like, we have a special on bologna today." 7

"I can't pay," she said. 8

For a second, I was tempted to say, "Take the corn." But the
employee rules flooded into my mind: Remain polite, but do not let
customers get the best of you. Let them know that you are in control.
For a moment, I even entertained the idea that this was some sort of
test, and that this woman was someone from the head office, testing
my loyalty. I responded dutifully, "I'm sorry, ma'am, but I can't give
away anything free."

9

The old woman's face collapsed a bit more, if that were possible, and her hands trembled as she put the can back on the shelf.
She shuffled past me toward the door, her torn and dirty clothing
barely covering her bent back.

10

Moments after she left, I rushed out the door with the can of
corn, but I never spotted her. For the rest of my shift, the image of
the woman haunted me. I had been young, healthy, and smug. She
had been old, sick, and desperate. Wishing with all my heart that I
had acted like a human being rather than a robot, I was saddened to
realize how fragile a hold we have on our better instincts.

11

Paul chose to write "If Only" from the first person (I was
there) *point of view*, a logical choice because he appears as a main
character in his own story. Using the past tense, Paul recounts an
incident fraught with *conflict* — between him and the woman, and
between his fear of breaking the rules and his instinct to help
someone in need.

It is not always necessary to state the *narrative point* of an
essay; it can be implied. But Paul decided to express the controlling idea of his narrative in two spots — in the introduction ("But
the other night an old woman shattered my belief that a glib
response could smooth over the rough spots of dealing with other
human beings") and in the conclusion where he expands his idea
about rote responses overriding impulses of kindness and compassion. All the *narrative details* in the essay contribute to the
point of the piece; Paul does not include any extraneous information that would detract from the central idea he wants to convey.

The narrative is *organized chronologically*, from the moment
the woman enters the store to Paul's reaction after she leaves.
Paul limits the time span of the narrative. The entire incident
probably occurs in under ten minutes, yet the introduction serves
as a kind of flashback by providing some necessary background
about Paul's past experiences. To help the reader follow the
course of the narrative, Paul uses *time signals*: "*The moment* she
entered, the woman presented a sharp contrast . . ." (paragraph

2); "*At that point*, I decided to be a good, courteous employee . . ." (3); "*For the rest of my shift*, the image of the woman haunted me . . ." (11). And he breaks his narrative into separate paragraphs, each paragraph dealing with a distinct block of time: the woman's actions when she first enters the store, the encounter that takes place after several minutes, the woman's reaction, Paul's delayed reaction.

A number of techniques are used to add energy and interest to the narrative. Paul dramatizes his conflict with the woman through *dialogue*, the words he and the woman spoke. (Note that a new line is used to indicate a shift from one speaker to another.) Paul also uses *descriptive detail* to give the narrative sharp immediacy. For instance, the sentence "her red-rimmed eyes were partially closed by yellowish crusts . . ." (3) recreates vividly the woman's appearance while also suggesting Paul's inner response. Moreover, Paul achieves a vigorous narrative pace by *varying the length and structure of his sentences*. In the second paragraph, a short sentence ("There were no stockings or socks on her splotchy, blue-veined legs") alternates with a longer one ("On a forty-degree night, she was wearing only a faded print dress, a thin, light-beige sweater too small to button, and black vinyl slippers with the backs cut out to expose calloused heels"). Some sentences in the essay open with a subject and verb ("She coughed dryly . . ."), while others start with dependent clauses or phrases ("As I stood close to her, my smile became harder to maintain"; "Walking as if each step were painful, she slowly pushed open the glass door . . ."), or with a prepositional phrase ("For a second, I was tempted . . .").

Comparing the final version of the essay's third paragraph, shown above, with the preliminary version reprinted below reveals some of the decisions Paul made while revising the essay.

First Draft Version

After sneezing and hacking her way around the store, the old woman stopped in front of the vegetable shelves. She picked up a can of corn and stared at the label. She stayed like this for several minutes. Then I walked over to her and asked if I could be of help.

After putting the original draft aside for a while, Paul reread his paper and added the following sentence to the third paragraph: "I decided to be a good, courteous employee." These few words introduce an appropriate note of irony and serve to echo the controlling idea of the piece. When revising the paragraph, Paul also decided to enlarge the descriptive detail, thus giving readers a more compelling picture of the woman.

You probably noted that the sentences in Paul's first draft were choppy and clipped, whereas the revised paragraph has an easy, graceful rhythm. The stilted quality in the original was eliminated when Paul expanded some sentences and combined others. Much of the time, revision involves paring down excess material. In this case, though, Paul made the right decision to elaborate his sentences.

As he reworked the third paragraph, Paul decided to omit the words "sneezing and hacking" because he realized they were too comic or light for his subject. Still, the first sentence in the final version of the paragraph is somewhat jarring. The word *strolling* is not quite appropriate since it implies a leisurely grace inconsistent with the impression he wants to convey. Changing "strolling" to "shuffling" would bring the image more into line with the essay's mood.

Despite this slight problem, Paul's revisions are solid and right on the mark. The changes he made strengthened his essay, turning it into a more evocative, more polished piece of narrative writing.

The following selections are examples of skillfully written narratives, each with vivid characters and scenes, dramatic conflicts and vigorous language. In George Orwell's classic "Shooting an Elephant," a man confronts a crowd, a rampaging animal, and his own conscience. Bob Greene's "Handled with Care" tells about people's surprising reactions when a naked woman wanders through the streets of Chicago. In "Little Deaths," T. H. Watkins joins a professional trapper on his rounds and learns something important about the complexity of life. Langston Hughes in the essay "Salvation" recounts his wrenching loss of innocence. Finally, in "Eloise," Garrison Keillor spins several tales, showing us that small-town life can be simultaneously warm-hearted and mean-spirited, bitter and joyful.

George Orwell

Born Eric Blair in the British colony of India, George Orwell (1903–1950) is probably best known as the author of *Nineteen Eighty-Four* (1949), a frightening portrayal of a totalitarian society watched over by the ubiquitous Big Brother. Orwell was also the author of numerous books and essays, many based on his diverse life experiences. He served with the Indian imperial police in Burma, worked at various jobs in London and Paris, and fought in the Spanish Civil War. His experiences in Burma are the basis for the following essay, which is taken from his collection, *Shooting an Elephant and Other Essays* (1950).

Shooting an Elephant

At one time or another, most of us have done something just so people would not laugh at or think badly of us. In this essay, George Orwell describes how he felt pressured into taking an action against his better judgment — killing an elephant that had strayed into the center of a town in Burma. In addition to its powerful insights into human behavior, Orwell's essay also presents a vivid and horrifying picture of the death of an animal.

In Moulmein, in Lower Burma, I was hated by large numbers 1 of people — the only time in my life that I have been important enough for this to happen to me. I was sub-divisional police officer of the town, and in an aimless, petty kind of way anti-European feeling was very bitter. No one had the guts to raise a riot, but if a European woman went through the bazaars alone somebody would probably spit betel juice over her dress. As a police officer I was an obvious target and was baited whenever it seemed safe to do so. When a nimble Burman tripped me up on the football field and the referee (another Burman) looked the other way, the crowd yelled with hideous laughter. This happened more than once. In the end the sneering yellow faces of young men that met me everywhere, the insults hooted after me when I was at a safe distance, got badly on my nerves. The young Buddhist priests were the worst of all. There were several thousand of them in the town and none of them seemed to have anything to do except stand on street corners and jeer at Europeans.

All this was perplexing and upsetting. For at that time I had already made up my mind that imperialism was an evil thing and the sooner I chucked up my job and got out of it the better. Theoretically—and secretly, of course—I was all for the Burmese and all against their oppressors, the British. As for the job I was doing, I hated it more bitterly than I can perhaps make clear. In a job like that you see the dirty work of Empire at close quarters. The wretched prisoners huddling in the stinking cages of the lock-ups, the grey, cowed faces of the long-term convicts, the scarred buttocks of the men who had been flogged with bamboos—all these oppressed me with an intolerable sense of guilt. But I could get nothing into perspective. I was young and ill-educated and I had had to think out my problems in the utter silence that is imposed on every Englishman in the East. I did not even know that the British Empire is dying, still less did I know that it is a great deal better than the younger empires that are going to supplant it. All I knew was that I was stuck between my hatred of the empire I served and my rage against the evil-spirited little beasts who tried to make my job impossible. With one part of my mind I thought of the British Raj as an unbreakable tyranny, as something clamped down, in *saecula saeculorum*,[1] upon the will of prostrate peoples; with another part I thought that the greatest joy in the world would be to drive a bayonet into a Buddhist priest's guts. Feelings like these are the normal by-products of imperialism; ask any Anglo-Indian official, if you can catch him off duty.

One day something happened which in a roundabout way was enlightening. It was a tiny incident in itself, but it gave me a better glimpse than I had had before of the real nature of imperialism—the real motives for which despotic governments act. Early one morning the sub-inspector at a police station the other end of the town rang me up on the 'phone and said that an

[1]For ever and ever.

elephant was ravaging the bazaar. Would I please come and do something about it? I did not know what I could do, but I wanted to see what was happening and I got on to a pony and started out. I took my rifle, an old .44 Winchester and much too small to kill an elephant, but I thought the noise might be useful *in terrorem*.[2] Various Burmans stopped me on the way and told me about the elephant's doings. It was not, of course, a wild elephant, but a tame one which had gone "must." It had been chained up, as tame elephants always are when their attack of "must" is due, but on the previous night it had broken its chain and escaped. Its mahout, the only person who could manage it when it was in that state, had set out in pursuit, but had taken the wrong direction and was now twelve hours' journey away, and in the morning the elephant had suddenly reappeared in the town. The Burmese population had no weapons and were quite helpless against it. It had already destroyed somebody's bamboo hut, killed a cow and raided some fruit-stalls and devoured the stock; also it had met the municipal rubbish van and, when the driver jumped out and took to his heels, had turned the van over and inflicted violence upon it.

The Burmese sub-inspector and some Indian constables were waiting for me in the quarter where the elephant had been seen. It was a very poor quarter, a labyrinth of squalid bamboo huts, thatched with palm-leaf, winding all over a steep hillside. I remember that it was a cloudy, stuffy morning at the beginning of the rains. We began questioning the people as to where the elephant had gone and, as usual, failed to get any definite information. That is invariably the case in the East; a story always sounds clear enough at a distance, but the nearer you get to the scene of events the vaguer it becomes. Some of the people said that the elephant had gone in one direction, some said that he had gone in another, some professed not even to have heard of any elephant. I had almost made up my mind that the whole story was a pack of lies, when we heard yells a little distance away. There was a loud, scandalized cry of "Go away, child! Go away this instant!" and an old woman with a switch in her hand came round the corner of a hut, violently shooing away a crowd of naked children. Some more women followed, clicking their

4

[2]As a warning.

tongues and exclaiming; evidently there was something that the children ought not to have seen. I rounded the hut and saw a man's dead body sprawling in the mud. He was an Indian, a black Dravidian coolie, almost naked, and he could not have been dead many minutes. The people said that the elephant had come suddenly upon him round the corner of the hut, caught him with its trunk, put its foot on his back and ground him into the earth. This was the rainy season and the ground was soft, and his face had scored a trench a foot deep and a couple of yards long. He was lying on his belly with arms crucified and head sharply twisted to one side. His face was coated with mud, the eyes wide open, the teeth bared and grinning with an expression of unendurable agony. (Never tell me, by the way, that the dead look peaceful. Most of the corpses I have seen looked devilish.) The friction of the great beast's foot had stripped the skin from his back as neatly as one skins a rabbit. As soon as I saw the dead man I sent an orderly to a friend's house nearby to borrow an elephant rifle. I had already sent back the pony, not wanting it to go mad with fright and throw me if it smelt the elephant.

The orderly came back in a few minutes with a rifle and five 5
cartridges, and meanwhile some Burmans had arrived and told us that the elephant was in the paddy fields below, only a few hundred yards away. As I started forward practically the whole population of the quarter flocked out of the houses and followed me. They had seen the rifle and were all shouting excitedly that I was going to shoot the elephant. They had not shown much interest in the elephant when he was merely ravaging their homes, but it was different now that he was going to be shot. It was a bit of fun to them, as it would be to an English crowd; besides they wanted the meat. It made me vaguely uneasy. I had no intention of shooting the elephant — I had merely sent for the rifle to defend myself if necessary — and it is always unnerving to have a crowd following you. I marched down the hill, looking and feeling a fool, with the rifle over my shoulder and an ever-growing army of people jostling at my heels. At the bottom, when you got away from the huts, there was a metalled road and beyond that a miry waste of paddy fields a thousand yards across, not yet ploughed but soggy from the first rains and dotted with coarse grass. The elephant was standing eight yards from the road, his left side towards us. He took not the slightest notice of the

crowd's approach. He was tearing up bunches of grass, beating them against his knees to clean them and stuffing them into his mouth.

I had halted on the road. As soon as I saw the elephant I   6
knew with perfect certainty that I ought not to shoot him. It is a serious matter to shoot a working elephant—it is comparable to destroying a huge and costly piece of machinery—and obviously one ought not to do it if it can possibly be avoided. And at that distance, peacefully eating, the elephant looked no more dangerous than a cow. I thought then and I think now that his attack of "must" was already passing off; in which case he would merely wander harmlessly about until the mahout came back and caught him. Moreover, I did not in the least want to shoot him. I decided that I would watch him for a little while to make sure that he did not turn savage again, and then go home.

But at that moment I glanced round at the crowd that had   7
followed me. It was an immense crowd, two thousand at the least and growing every minute. It blocked the road for a long distance on either side. I looked at the sea of yellow faces above the garish clothes—faces all happy and excited over this bit of fun, all certain that the elephant was going to be shot. They were watching me as they would watch a conjurer about to perform a trick. They did not like me, but with the magical rifle in my hands I was momentarily worth watching. And suddenly I realized that I should have to shoot the elephant after all. The people expected it of me and I had got to do it; I could feel their two thousand wills pressing me forward, irresistibly. And it was at this moment, as I stood there with the rifle in my hands, that I first grasped the hollowness, the futility of the white man's dominion in the East. Here was I, the white man with his gun, standing in front of the unarmed native crowd—seemingly the leading actor of the piece; but in reality I was only an absurd puppet pushed to and fro by the will of those yellow faces behind. I perceived in this moment that when the white man turns tyrant it is his own freedom that he destroys. He becomes a sort of hollow, posing dummy, the conventionalized figure of a sahib. For it is the condition of his rule that he shall spend his life in trying to impress the "natives," and so in every crisis he has got to do what the "natives" expect of him. He wears a mask, and his face grows to fit it. I had got to

shoot the elephant. I had committed myself to doing it when I sent for the rifle. A sahib has got to act like a sahib; he has got to appear resolute, to know his own mind and do definite things. To come all that way, rifle in hand, with two thousand people marching at my heels, and then to trail feebly away, having done nothing—no, that was impossible. The crowd would laugh at me. And my whole life, every white man's life in the East, was one long struggle not be laughed at.

But I did not want to shoot the elephant. I watched him   8 beating his bunch of grass against his knees, with that preoccupied grandmotherly air that elephants have. It seemed to me that it would be murder to shoot him. At that age I was not squeamish about killing animals, but I had never shot an elephant and never wanted to. (Somehow it always seems worse to kill a *large* animal.) Besides, there was the beast's owner to be considered. Alive, the elephant was worth at least a hundred pounds; dead, he would only be worth the value of his tusks, five pounds, possibly. But I had got to act quickly. I turned to some experienced-looking Burmans who had been there when we arrived, and asked them how the elephant had been behaving. They all said the same thing: he took no notice of you if you left him alone, but he might charge if you went too close to him.

It was perfectly clear to me what I ought to do. I ought to   9 walk up to within, say, twenty-five yards of the elephant and test his behavior. If he charged, I could shoot; if he took no notice of me, it would be safe to leave him until the mahout came back. But also I knew that I was going to do no such thing. I was a poor shot with a rifle and the ground was soft mud into which one would sink at every step. If the elephant charged and I missed him, I should have about as much chance as a toad under a steam-roller. But even then I was not thinking particularly of my own skin, only of the watchful yellow faces behind. For at that moment, with the crowd watching me, I was not afraid in the ordinary sense, as I would have been if I had been alone. A white man mustn't be frightened in front of "natives"; and so, in general, he isn't frightened. The sole thought in my mind was that if anything went wrong those two thousand Burmans would see me pursued, caught, trampled on and reduced to a grinning corpse like that Indian up the hill. And if that happened it was quite probable that some of them would laugh. That would never do. There was only one alternative. I shoved the cartridges into the magazine and lay down on the road to get a better aim.

The crowd grew very still, and a deep, low, happy sigh, as of people who see the theatre curtain go up at last, breathed from innumerable throats. They were going to have their bit of fun after all. The rifle was a beautiful German thing with cross-hair sights. I did not then know that in shooting an elephant one would shoot to cut an imaginary bar running from ear-hole to ear-hole. I ought, therefore, as the elephant was sideway on, to have aimed straight at his ear-hole; actually I aimed several inches in front of this, thinking the brain would be further forward.   10

When I pulled the trigger I did not hear the bang or feel the kick — one never does when a shot goes home — but I heard the devilish roar of glee that went up from the crowd. In that instant, in too short a time, one would have thought, even for the bullet to get there, a mysterious, terrible change had come over the elephant. He neither stirred nor fell, but every line of his body had altered. He looked suddenly stricken, shrunken, immensely old, as though the frightful impact of the bullet had paralyzed him without knocking him down. At last, after what seemed a long time — it might have been five seconds, I dare say — he sagged flabbily to his knees. His mouth slobbered. An enormous senility seemed to have settled upon him. One could have imagined him thousands of years old. I fired again into the same spot. At the second shot he did not collapse but climbed with desperate slowness to his feet and stood weakly upright, with legs sagging and head drooping. I fired a third time. That was the shot that did for him. You could see the agony of it jolt his whole body and knock the last remnant of strength from his legs. But in falling he seemed for a moment to rise, for as his hind legs collapsed beneath him he seemed to tower upward like a huge rock toppling, his trunk reaching skywards like a tree. He trumpeted, for the first and only time. And then down he came, his belly towards me, with a crash that seemed to shake the ground even where I lay.   11

I got up. The Burmans were already racing past me across the mud. It was obvious that the elephant would never rise again, but he was not dead. He was breathing very rhythmically with long rattling gasps, his great mound of a side painfully rising and   12 falling. His mouth was wide open — I could see far down into caverns of pale pink throat. I waited a long time for him to die, but his breathing did not weaken. Finally I fired my two remaining shots into the spot where I thought his heart must be. The thick blood welled out of him like red velvet, but still he did not die. His body did not even jerk when the shots hit him, the tortured breathing continued without a pause. He was dying, very slowly and in great agony, but in some world remote from me where not even a bullet could damage him further. I felt that I had got to put an end to that dreadful noise. It seemed dreadful to see the great beast lying there, powerless to move and yet powerless to die, and not even to be able to finish him. I sent back for my small rifle and poured shot after shot into his heart and down his throat. They seemed to make no impression. The tortured gasps continued as steadily as the ticking of a clock.

In the end I could not stand it any longer and went away. I heard later that it took him half an hour to die. Burmans were bringing dahs and baskets even before I left, and I was told they had stripped the body almost to the bones by the afternoon.   13

Afterwards, of course, there were endless discussions about the shooting of the elephant. The owner was furious, but he was only an Indian and could do nothing. Besides, legally I had done the right thing, for a mad elephant has to be killed, like a mad dog, if its owner fails to control it. Among the Europeans opinion was divided. The older men said I was right, the younger men said it was a damn shame to shoot an elephant for killing a coolie, because an elephant was worth more than any damn Coringhee coolie. And afterwards I was very glad that the coolie had been killed; it put me legally in the right and it gave me a sufficient pretext for shooting the elephant. I often wondered whether any of the others grasped that I had done it solely to avoid looking a fool.   14

Questions for Close Reading

1. What is the thesis (or narrative point) of the selection? Locate the sentence(s) in which Orwell states his main idea. If he does not state the thesis explicitly, express it in your own words.
2. How did Orwell feel about the Burmans? What words does Orwell use to describe them?
3. What reasons does Orwell give for shooting the elephant?

4. In paragraph 3, Orwell says that the elephant incident gave him a better understanding of "the real motives for which despotic governments act." What do you think he means? Before you answer, reread paragraph 7 carefully.
5. Refer to your dictionary as needed to define the following words used in the selection: *imperialism* (paragraph 2), *prostrate* (2), *despotic* (3), *mahout* (3), *miry* (5), *conjurer* (7), *futility* (7), and *sahib* (7).

Questions About the Writer's Craft

1. Most effective narratives encompass a restricted time span. How much time elapses from the moment Orwell gets his gun to the time the elephant dies? What time signals does Orwell provide to help the reader follow the sequence of events in this limited time span?
2. Orwell does not actually begin his narrative until the third paragraph. What purposes do the first two paragraphs serve?
3. In paragraph 6, Orwell says that shooting a working elephant "is comparable to destroying a huge and costly piece of machinery." This kind of comparison is called an *analogy* — describing something unfamiliar, often abstract, in terms of something more familiar and concrete. Where else in "Shooting an Elephant" does Orwell use analogies to make a point? Find at least three additional examples in the essay.
4. Much of the power of Orwell's narrative comes from his ability to convey sensory impressions — what he saw, heard, smelled. Orwell's description becomes most vivid when he writes about the death of the elephant in paragraphs 11 and 12. Find some evocative words and phrases that give the description its power.

Questions for Further Thought

1. In the first paragraph of "Shooting an Elephant," Orwell tells us he was "hated by large numbers of people — the only time in my life that I have been important enough for this to happen to me." What is Orwell implying about people's attitudes toward authority? Do you think Orwell has a valid point? To decide, think about the people who have power over you and how you feel about their authority.
2. The Burmese population was eager to see Orwell shoot the elephant. Why do you believe this incident held such significance for them?
3. In paragraph 7, Orwell comments that "when the white man turns tyrant it it his own freedom that he destroys." This is a *paradox* — a statement that seems to contradict itself. Explain the meaning of this paradox.

4. At the end of his essay, Orwell says he is glad the elephant had killed someone because it put him "legally in the right" for shooting the animal. Think of actions today considered legally right that you, or others, feel are morally wrong.

Writing Assignments Using Narration as a Method of Development

*1. Orwell recounts a time he acted under great pressure. Write a narrative about an incident in your life when you did something you didn't want to do (or wouldn't normally do) simply because you felt pressured: perhaps you didn't want to be laughed at, or maybe you wanted to live up to someone else's expectations. Like Orwell, use vivid details to make the incident come alive. Langston Hughes' "Salvation" (page 157) may lead to some insights into the way stress influences behavior.

2. Write a narrative essay about an experience that gave you, like Orwell, a deeper insight into your own nature. You may have discovered, for instance, that you can be naive, compassionate, petty, cowardly, brave, rebellious, hypocritical, or surprisingly good at something.

Writing Assignments Using Other Methods of Development

3. Was Orwell justified in shooting the elephant? Write an essay arguing that Orwell was justified *or* that he was not. To develop your thesis, cite several specific reasons, each supported by details drawn from the essay. Here are some points you might consider: the legality of Orwell's act; the temperament of the elephant; the influence of the crowd; Orwell's state of mind; the aftermath of the elephant's death; the actual death of the elephant.

4. Orwell's essay concerns, in part, the all-too-human tendency to cover up indecision and confusion just to maintain a façade of authority. Write an essay about the way people in authority often *pretend* to know what they are doing rather than seem insecure to those subordinate to them. You might consider discussing examples of such behavior that you have seen in parents, teachers, police officers, politicians, or other authority figures. You may use actual incidents you have witnessed or hypothetical examples of common responses.

Bob Greene

Bob Greene is a journalist whose column for the *Chicago Tribune* is syndicated in more than 200 newspapers across the
country. Greene also serves as a contributing editor of *Esquire*
magazine, which carries his "American Beat" column each
month. His bestselling 1984 book, *Good Morning, Merry Sunshine*, recounts his experiences as a father. His observations of
American life have been published in two books, *American
Beat* (1983), from which the following essay is taken, and
Cheeseburgers (1985).

Handled with Care

Life in cities is tough, cruel, harsh, dangerous — or so we are
told all the time by the media. We come to expect wrenching
stories of vulnerable people ignored or even injured by hardened passersby on city streets. But in the following essay, Bob
Greene describes what actually happened one day in Chicago
when a woman took off her clothes on a busy downtown
street.

1   The day the lady took her clothes off on Michigan Avenue,
people were leaving downtown as usual. The workday had come
to an end; men and women were heading for bus and train
stations, in a hurry to get home.

2   She walked south on Michigan; she was wearing a white robe,
as if she had been to the beach. She was blond and in her thirties.

3   As she passssed the Radisson Hotel, Roosevelt Williams, a
doorman, was opening the door of a cab for one of the hotel's
guests. The woman did not really pause while she walked; she
merely shrugged the robe off, and it fell to the sidewalk.

4   She was wearing what appeared to be the bottom of a blue
bikini bathing suit, although one woman who was directly next to
her said it was just underwear. She wore nothing else.

5   Williams at first did not believe what he was seeing. If you

hang around long enough, you will see everything: robberies, muggings, street fights, murders. But a naked woman on North Michigan Avenue? Williams had not seen that before and neither, apparently, had the other people on the street.

It was strange; her white robe lay on the sidewalk, and by all   6
accounts she was smiling. But no one spoke to her. A report in the newspaper the next day quoted someone: "The cars were stopping, the people on the buses were staring, people were shouting, and people were taking pictures." But that is not what other people who were there that afternoon said.

The atmosphere was not carnival-like, they said. Rather, they   7
said, it was as if something very sad was taking place. It took only a moment for people to realize that this was not some stunt designed to promote a product or a movie. Without anyone telling them, they understood that the woman was troubled, and that what she was doing had nothing to do with sexual titillation; it was more of a cry for help.

The cry for help came in a way that such cries often come.   8
The woman was violating one of the basic premises of the social fabric. She was doing something that is not done. She was not shooting anyone, or breaking a window, or shouting in anger. Rather, in a way that everyone understood, she was signaling that things were not right.

The line is so thin between matters being manageable and   9
being out of hand. One day a person may be barely all right; the next the same person may have crossed over. Here is something from the author John Barth:

> She paused amid the kitchen to drink a glass of water; at that instant, losing a grip of 50 years, the next-room-ceiling plaster crashed. Or he merely sat in an empty study, in March-day glare, listening to the universe rustle in his head, when suddenly a five-foot shelf let go. For ages the fault creeps secret through the rock; in a second, ledge and railings, tourists and turbines all thunder over Niagara. Which snowflake triggers the avalanche? A house explodes; a star. In your spouse, so apparently resigned, murder twitches like a fetus. At some trifling new assessment, all the colonies rebel.

The woman continued to walk past Tribune Tower. People 10 who saw her said that the look on her face was almost peaceful. She did not seem to think she was doing anything unusual; she was described as appearing "blissful." Whatever the reaction on the street was, she seemed calm, as if she believed herself to be in control.

She walked over the Michigan Avenue bridge. Again, people 11 who were there report that no one harassed her; no one jeered at her or attempted to touch her. At some point on the bridge, she removed her bikini bottom. Now she was completely undressed, and still she walked.

"It was as if people knew not to bother her," said one woman 12 who was there. "To tell it, it sounds like something very lewd and sensational was going on. But it wasn't like that at all. It was as if people knew that something very . . . fragile . . . was taking place. I was impressed with the maturity with which people were handling it. No one spoke to her, but you could tell that they wished someone would help her."

Back in front of the Radisson, a police officer had picked up 13 the woman's robe. He was on his portable radio, advising his colleagues that the woman was walking over the bridge.

When the police caught up with the woman, she was just 14 standing there, naked in downtown Chicago, still smiling. The first thing the police did was hand her some covering and ask her to put it on; the show was over.

People who were there said that there was no reaction from 15 the people who were watching. They said that the juvenile behavior you might expect in such a situation just didn't happen. After all, when a man walks out on a ledge in a suicide attempt, there are always people down below who call for him to jump. But this day, by all accounts, nothing like that took place. No one called for her to stay undressed; no one cursed the police officers for stopping her.

"It was as if everyone was relieved," said a woman who saw 16 it. "They were embarrassed by it; it made them feel bad. They were glad that someone had stopped her. And she was still smiling. She seemed to be off somewhere."

The police charged her with no crime; they took her to Read 17 Mental Health Center, where she was reported to have signed herself in voluntarily. Within minutes things were back to as they always are on Michigan Avenue; there was no reminder of the naked lady who had reminded people how fragile is the everyday world in which we live.

Questions for Close Reading

1. What is the thesis (or narrative point) of the selection? Locate the sentence(s) in which Greene states his main idea. If he does not state the thesis explicitly, express it in your own words.
2. What does the newspaper say about this event? Why does its report differ from Greene's?
3. How do the other passersby react to the woman's disrobing on the street? How do the police treat the woman?
4. Why does Greene interpret the woman's disrobing as a call for help?
5. Refer to your dictionary as needed to define the following words used in the selection: *titillation* (paragraph 7), *trifling* (9), and *blissful* (10).

Questions About the Writer's Craft

1. What is the source of the narrative tension that keeps you reading this essay? What conflict underlies this narrative?
2. Why does Greene use the title, "Handled with Care"? What is being "handled with care" in this case?
3. What does the quotation from John Barth add to the essay? Why does Greene interrupt his narrative with this quotation, rather than include it in a concluding interpretive paragraph?
4. How does Greene know what happened that day? Would you believe his account over that of the newspaper? Why? What in this essay makes it different from a straightforward newspaper report?

Questions for Further Thought

1. Why do you think none of the bystanders interfered with the woman's actions? Do you agree with the person who said the onlookers handled it "with maturity"? What could or should people have done before the police came?
2. Should people "get involved" when strangers are in trouble? Are we our brothers' or sisters' keepers?
3. What is so "very sad" about this woman's action? If this woman is so sad, why do you think she had a "blissful" appearance?
4. The author writes, "The line is so thin between matters being manageable and being out of hand." Do you agree? Do you know of anyone who has abruptly given in to the feeling that life is unmanageable?

Writing Assignments Using Narration as a Method of Development

1. "Handled with Care" is an example of a "slice of life" narrative. It consists of a single incident, vividly told, that illustrates the author's main point. Think of a similar incident that suggests a larger meaning. The incident may be one you have experienced or heard about. Brainstorm to gather the details, and then write a narrative essay in the third person. In addition to relating the incident, be sure to clarify—through implicit or explicit means—the significance of the experience.

2. Greene's essay uses a quotation to focus the events of the narrative effectively. Find a quotation or a familiar saying that appeals to you or seems wise and true. Write a narrative essay in which an incident or event illustrates the quotation. Some examples of quotations on which essays might be based include the following:

   • What a tangled web we weave/When first we practice to deceive. (Walter Scott)
   • When the going gets tough, the tough get going.
   • Trees that bend with the wind live longer. (fortune cookie)
   • Experience is a tough teacher. She tests first and teaches afterwards. (Salada tea bag "tag line")

Writing Assignments Using Other Methods of Development

3. Write an essay explaining the reasons for the bystanders' reaction to the naked woman. You may choose to analyze one cause in depth, or you may examine several causes; for example, city dwellers' habitual treatment of others, people's attitudes toward aberrant behavior, and so on.

*4. Write an essay arguing that we should or should not get involved when we see people in trouble. Explain in what cases we should offer assistance and what we should do if we decide not to offer help. You might consider any of the following: a person in tears, a street person asleep on a sidewalk, a person talking to himself or herself or screaming or cursing at the air. To give you more of a sense of some people's response to the less fortunate, you might want to read William McKibben's "Ugly" (page 427).

T. H. Watkins

T. H. Watkins is a historian and environmentalist who has written nine books and numerous articles for such magazines as *American Heritage, Cry California, The American West,* and *The Sierra Club Bulletin.* One of his books, *California: An Illustrated History* (1973), was nominated for a Pulitzer Prize. He currently lives on a houseboat moored in San Francisco Bay. This selection first appeared in *The Sierra Club Bulletin.*

Little Deaths

We Americans coddle our pets; yet every year, thousands of cats and dogs are abandoned by their owners. We take our children to zoos to see the beauty of wild animals, but we wear furs from the pelts of nearly extinct species. In this selection, T. H. Watkins describes an expedition he took with his cousin, a professional trapper whose job is to "clear the varmints" from the land. As Watkins accompanies his cousin, he experiences some conflicting emotions.

It has been more than ten years since the day my cousin let me walk his traplines with him. We never see each other now. Our worlds, never very close, have grown even farther apart. He left California several years ago to become a trapping supervisor somewhere in Nevada, while I have joined the ranks of those who would cheerfully eliminate his way of life. He would, rightly enough, consider me one of his natural enemies, and it is not likely that we would have much to say if we did meet. Still, I am grateful to him for giving me a glimpse into the reality of a world normally hidden from us, a dark little world where death is the only commonplace. 1

At the time, my cousin was a lowly field trapper at the beck and call of any rancher or farmer who made an official complaint to the trapping service about varmint troubles — coyotes or wildcats getting after newborn lambs, foxes sneaking into chicken 2 coops, that sort of thing. His current assignment was to trap out the varmint population of some ranchland high in the Diablo Hills southeast of Oakland, a country of rolling grassland, scrub oak, and chaparral dominated by the 3,000-foot upthrust of Mount Diablo. His base was a house trailer planted on the edge of one of the ranches he was servicing near Livermore, although he got into Oakland quite a lot for weekend visits to a lady of his acquaintance. I lived in Oakland at the time, and he usually made a point of stopping by to see my children, of whom he was particularly fond.

I was then a practicing student of western history and thor-   3
oughly intrigued by the glittering adventure that pervaded my reading—especially in the stories of the mountain men, those grizzled, anarchic beings with a lust for far places and far things, stubborn individualists who had lived freer than any Indian and had followed their quest for beaver pelts into nearly all the mysterious blanks of the American West, from Taos, New Mexico, to Puget Sound, from the Marys River of the northern Rockies to the Colorado River of the Southwest; hopelessly romantic creatures with a predilection for Indian women, a talent for profanity, and a thirst for liquor profound enough to melt rivets. And here was my cousin, the literary—if not lineal—descendant of the mountain man. True, he was neither grizzled nor given much to profanity, nor had he, so far as I knew, ever offered his blanket to an Indian woman. Still, he was a *trapper*, by God, and when on one of his visits he invited me to accompany him on his rounds, I was entranced with the notion.

Late one spring afternoon I bundled wife and children into   4
the car and drove down to Livermore and out to the ranch where he was staying. After a dinner cooked in the trailer's tiny kitchen, my wife and the children bedded down in the trailer's two little bunks. "When we get back tomorrow afternoon," my cousin told the children, "I'll take you out and show you some spring lambs. You'd like that, right?" he added, giving them a pinch and tickle that set them to giggling in delight. He and I bundled up in sleeping bags on the ground outside.

It was pitch black when he woke me that next morning at five   5
o'clock. After shocking ourselves out of sleep by bathing our faces in water from the outside faucet, we got into his pickup and drove off for breakfast at an all-night diner on the road. Dawn was

insinuating itself over the dark hills by the time we finished breakfast, and had laid a neon streak across the sky when we finally turned off the highway and began climbing a rutted dirt road that led to the first trapline (we would be walking two traplines, my cousin explained, one on the western side of the hills, one on the eastern; these were two of the six he had scattered over the whole range, each of them containing between 15 and 20 traps and each checked out and reset or moved to a new location every ten days or so). As we bumped and rattled up the road, daylight slowly illuminated the hills. For two or three months in the spring, before the summer sun turns them warm and brown, these hills look as if they had been transplanted whole from Ireland or Wales. They are a celebration of green, all shades of green, from the black-green of manzanita leaves to the bright, pool-table green of the grasses. Isolated bunches of cows and sheep stood almost motionless, like ornaments added for the effect of contrast, and morning mist crept around the base of trees and shrouded dark hollows with the ghost of its presence. Through all this, the exposed earth of the road cut like a red scar, and the sounds of the pickup's engine and the country-western music yammering out of its radio intruded themselves on the earth's silence gracelessly.

We talked of my cousin's father, whom he worshipped and emulated. My cousin was, in fact, almost literally following in his father's footsteps, for "the old man" had been a state trapper himself and was now a trapping supervisor. Before that, back in the deep of the Depression, he had been a lion hunter for the state, when a mountain lion's ears were good as money, and before that he had "cowboyed some," as he put it; at one time, according to family tradition, his grandfather's ranch had encompassed much of what became the town of San Bernardino in Southern California. At one point in his life, he had led jaguar-hunting trips to the jungles of northwestern Mexico, and he was still a noteworthy hunter, though now he confined himself principally to an occasional deer, antelope, or bear. My cousin had grown up in a house where skins of various types served as rugs and couchthrows, where stuffed heads glared unblinkingly from the walls, where sleek hounds were always in-and-out, where hunting magazines dominated the tables, hunting talk dominated the conversations, and everywhere was the peculiarly masculine

6

smell of newly oiled guns, all kinds of guns — pistols (including an old Colt once used by my cousin's great-grandfather, legend had it, to kill a man), rifles, shotguns. It was a family that had been killing things for a long time, sometimes for meat, sometimes for a living, sometimes for what was called the sport of it, and one of my cousin's consuming ambitions was to bag a bighorn sheep, something his father had never managed to do.

I had never killed anything in my life except fish, and since fish neither scream, grunt, squeal, nor moan when done in, it had never seemed like killing at all. In any case, I was by no means prepared for the first sight of what my cousin did to earn his bread. I don't know what I had expected with my romantic notions of the trapper's life, but surely it was something other than what I learned when we crawled up the road through increasingly heavy underbrush and stopped to check out the first of my cousin's traps.   7

We got out of the truck and beat our way through the brush to a spot perhaps 30 feet from the road. I did not see the animal until we were nearly on top of it. It was a raccoon, the first raccoon I had ever seen in person, and at that moment I wished that I never had seen one. It was dead, had been dead for several days, my cousin informed me. "Hunger, thirst, and shock is what kills them, mostly," he said in response to my question. "That, and exhaustion, I reckon." The animal seemed ridiculously tiny in death. It lay on its side, its small mouth, crawling with ants, open in a bared-tooth grin, and its right rear leg in the clutch of the steel trap. It was easy to see how the animal had exhausted itself; it had been at its leg. A strip of flesh perhaps three inches in width had been gnawed away, leaving the white bone and a length of tendon exposed. Tiny flies sang about the ragged wound and over the pool of dried blood beneath the leg. There was a stink in the air, and it suddenly seemed very, very warm to me there in the morning shadows of the brush.   8

"Once in a while," my cousin said, prying open the curved jaws of the trap, "one of them will chew his way loose, and if he doesn't lose too much blood he can live. I caught a three-legged coyote once. Too stupid to learn, I guess."   9

"Do you ever find one of them still alive?" I asked.   10

"Sometimes."   11

"What do you do with them?"   12

He looked up at me. "Do with them? I shoot them," he said, patting the holstered pistol at his waist. He lifted the freed raccoon by the hind legs and swung it off into the brush. "Buzzard meat," he said. He then grabbed the steel stake to which the trap was attached by a chain and worked it out of the ground. "I've had this line going for over a month, now. The area's just about trapped out." He carried the trap back to the road, threw it in the back of the pickup, and we drove up the increasingly rough road to the next trap. It was empty, as was the one after it. I was beginning to hope they would all be empty, but the fourth one contained a small skunk, a black-and-white pussycat of a creature that had managed to get three of its feet in the trap at once and lay huddled in death like a child's stuffed toy. It, too, was disengaged and tossed into the brush. A little further up the ridge, and we found a fox, to my cousin's visible relief. "Great," he said. "That has to be the mate to the one I got a couple of weeks ago. Pregnant, too. There won't be any little foxes running around this year." Into the brush the animal went.

By the time we reached the top of the long ridge on which my cousin had set his traps, the morning had slipped toward noon and our count had risen to seven animals: three raccoons, three skunks, and the pregnant fox. There was only one trap left now, but it was occupied by the prize of the morning, a bobcat. "I'll be damned," my cousin said, "I've been after that bugger all month. Just about give up hope." The bobcat had not died well, but in anger. The marks of its rage and anguish were laid out in a torn circle of earth described by the length of the chain that had linked the animal to its death. Even the brush had been ripped and clawed at, leaves and twigs stripped from branches, leaving sweeping scars. Yellow tufts of the animal's fur lay scattered on the ground, as if the bobcat had torn at its own body for betraying it, and its death-mask was a silent howl of outrage. My cousin took it out of the trap and heaved it down the side of the hill. Buzzard meat.

We had to go back down the hills and around the range in order to come up the eastern slopes and check out the second trapline, and on the way we stopped at a small roadhouse in Clayton for a hamburger and a beer. I found I could eat, which surprised me a little, and I certainly had a thirst for the beer. We sat side-by-side at the bar, not saying much. Something Wallace

Stegner had once written kept flashing through my mind. "Like most of my contemporaries," he had said, "I grew up careless. I grew up killing things." I wondered if my cousin would know what Stegner had been talking about, and decided it would be best not to bring it up. I could have cancelled out right there, I suppose, asking him to take me back to his camp, explaining that I had seen enough, too much, of the trapper's life. I could always plead exhaustion. After all, the day's hiking had been more real exercise than I had had in months, and I was, in fact, tired. A stubborn kernel of pride would not let me do it. I would see the day through to the end.

So the ritual continued. We climbed back up into the hills on the east side of the range in the oven-heat of a strong spring sun. The day's count rose even more as the pickup bounced its way up the ragged weedgrown road: two more skunks, another fox, two more raccoons. The work went more slowly than the morning's run, for this was a new line, and each trap had to be reset. My cousin performed this task with an efficient swiftness and the kind of quiet pride any craftsman takes in his skill, snapping and locking the jaws of the traps, covering them with a thin scattering of earth and twigs, sprinkling the ground about with dog urine from a plastic squeeze bottle to cover up the man-smell. By the time we were ready to approach the last three traps of the line, it was well after three o'clock. We were very high by then, well up on the slopes of Mount Diablo itself, and we had to abandon the pickup to hike the rest of the way on foot. We broke out of the brush and walked along a spur of the hills. About 1,500 feet below us and some miles to the east, we could see the towns of Pittsburgh and Martinez sending an urban haze into the air. Ahead of me, my cousin suddenly stopped.   16

"Wait a minute. Listen," he said.   17

A distant thrashing and rattling sound came from the slope below us. "That's where the trap is," he said. "Might be a bobcat, but I didn't expect to get him so soon. Come on."   18

The slope was very steep, and we slid much of the way down to the trap on our bottoms, slapped at and tangled by brush. The animal was not a bobcat. It was a dog, a large, dirty-white mongrel whose foreleg was gripped in the trap. The dog snarled at us as we approached it. Saliva had gathered at its lips and there was a wildness in its eyes.   19

"Dammit," my cousin said. He had owned dogs all his life.   20

"A wild dog. Probably abandoned by somebody. They do it all the time. Dogs turn wild and start running in packs. Some people ought to be shot."

I didn't know what he wanted to do. He hadn't pulled out his gun. "Can we turn him loose? Maybe he isn't wild. Maybe he just wandered up here on his own." 21

My cousin looked at me. "Maybe. There's a noose-pole in the back of the truck—a kind of a long stick with a loop of rope at the end. Why don't you get it?" 22

I scrambled back up the slope and made my way back to the pickup, where I found the noose-pole. As thick as a broomhandle and about five feet in length, it looked like a primitive fishing-pole. When I got back down to the trap, the dog was still snarling viciously. My cousin took the pole from me, opened the loop at the end, and extended it toward the dog. "If I can hook him," he said, "I'll hold his head down while you open the trap. You've seen how I do it." 23

It was useless. The dog fought at the loop frantically in a madness of pain and fear. After perhaps 15 minutes, my cousin laid the pole down. "He just isn't going to take it." 24

"What'll we do?" I asked, though I'm sure I knew. 25

He shrugged. "Can't just leave him here to die." He unsnapped his holster and pulled out the gun. He duck-walked to within a couple of feet of the animal, which watched him suspiciously. "I'll try to do it with one shot," he said. The gun's discharge slammed into the silence of the mountain. The dog howled once, a long, penetrating song of despair that ran in echoes down the hill. My cousin nudged the animal with his boot. It was dead. He opened the trap, freed the leg, and heaved the body down the slope. The crashing of its fall seemed to go on for a long time. My cousin reset the trap. "Come on," he said. "It's getting late." 26

The last trap of the day held a dead raccoon. 27

My cousin was pleased with the day's work. "If it keeps up like this," he said as we rattled down the highway toward his trailer, "I could be out of here in a month." 28

"What's the hurry?" 29

He indicated a small housing development by the side of the road. "Too much civilization around here for me. Too many people. I need to get back up into the mountains." 30

There was plenty of light left when we got back, and true to 31 his promise, my cousin took the children out into the fields to see a newborn lamb. While its mother bleated in protest, he ran one down and brought it to my children so they could pet it. I watched his face as he held the little creature. There was no hint in it of all the death we had harvested that day, no hint of the half-eaten legs we had seen, no hint of the fearful thrashing agony the animals had endured before dying. No hint, even, of the death-howl of the dirty white dog that may or may not have been wild. There was neither irony nor cynicism in him. He held the lamb with open, honest delight at the wonder my children found in touching this small, warm, live thing.

My cousin is not an evil man. We are none of us evil men.   3*

Questions for Close Reading

1. What is the thesis (or narrative point) of the selection? Locate the sentence(s) in which Watkins states his main idea. If he does not state the thesis explicitly, express it in your own words.
2. Watkins explains that even ten years ago, he and his cousin were not close or much alike. Why, then, was Watkins so eager to accompany his cousin on a trapping expendition? What fascination did trapping hold for Watkins?
3. Although Watkins does not approve of what his cousin does for a living, he is fair to him. Find places in the essay where Watkins points out (a) his cousin's good qualities, (b) his cousin's reasons for trapping.
4. What is the difference between the incident of the trapped dog and the other trapping incidents described in the essay? Why do you think Watkins described the episode with the dog at such length?
5. Refer to your dictionary as needed to define the following words used in the selection: *chaparral* (paragraph 2), *anarchic* (3), *predilection* (3), *lineal* (3), *emulated* (6), and *encompassed* (6).

Questions About the Writer's Craft

1. Narratives rely on vivid description for much of their impact. As a narrator, Watkins is a master of sensory detail, particularly when he wants us to see the death agonies of the trapped animals. Locate two paragraphs in which his descriptions of death are especially vivid. Which words and phrases in these paragraphs make you understand the pain and horror of the animals' deaths?
2. What are some of the time signals that Watkins uses to indicate the sequence of events in his essay?

3. Watkins skillfully employs *simile*, a technique that uses the words *like* or *as* to highlight the similarities between two seemingly unlike objects. One example of simile can be found in paragraph 13, where Watkins describes the dead skunk as looking "like a child's stuffed toy." Find two more examples of similes in "Little Deaths."

4. How does Watkins use dialogue to reveal his cousin's attitudes toward animals? How do these comments help us understand Watkins' thesis?

Questions for Further Thought

1. In what ways are the animals' deaths "little" deaths? In what ways are they significant deaths? What else might have "died" during Watkins' experience?

2. The last paragraph of the selection reads, "My cousin is not an evil man. We are none of us evil men." Do you think Watkins is correct about his cousin? About humanity in general?

3. How might Watkins' cousin, so gentle with young children and a newborn lamb, justify to himself what he does for a living? Is there necessarily a conflict between the two sides of his character?

4. The essay raises the question of justifiable killing. Was the trapper justified in killing the animals because they were "varmints"? Should human needs and desires take precedence over an animal's right to live?

Writing Assignments Using Narrative as a Method of Development

1. As Watkins has done, write a narrative about a moment of harsh discovery in your life. Describe how someone or something you had idealized turned out to be sharply different from what you had expected. Be sure you describe briefly, perhaps in the introduction, your original expectations.

2. Undoubtedly, Watkins feels that his cousin treats life too casually. Write a narrative about a time when you treated life too lightly. The life could be an animal's, another person's, even your own. Use specific details to tell what happened.

Writing Assignments Using Other Methods of Development

3. Write an essay on either the pros or cons of hunting. To prepare for this assignment, look up "Hunting" or "Wildlife Management" in the *Readers' Guide to Periodical Literature*. In addition, you might talk

to people you know about their attitudes toward hunting. Then take a position. Direct your essay to a confirmed nonhunter and prove that hunting is beneficial. Or direct the essay to an enthusiastic hunter and support the nonhunting position.

4. The philosopher Hannah Arendt refers in her writings to "the banality of evil." Evil may sometimes be part of the most ordinary, most normal people or activities. Write an essay about one commonly accepted activity that you believe is evil — or at least immoral. Offer detailed support about how or why this activity is wrong. You may consider any of the following: killing animals for fur or food; our treatment of old people or children; our neglect or abuse of our environment.

Langston Hughes

One of the foremost members of the 1920s literary movement known as the Harlem Renaissance, Langston Hughes (1902–1967) committed himself to portraying the richness of black life in America. A poet and a writer of short stories, Hughes was greatly influenced by the rhythms of blues and jazz. In his later years, he published two autobiographical works, *The Big Sea* (1940) and *I Wonder as I Wander* (1956), and he wrote a history of the National Association for the Advancement of Colored People (NAACP). The following selection is from *The Big Sea*.

Salvation

Disillusionment is part of growing up. As children, we start out expecting the best from people and life. But as we grow older, experiences tend to chip away at our cherished beliefs and trusting expectations. In "Salvation," Langston Hughes uses humor and poignancy to recount a time in his own child-hood when he faced such a moment of disillusionment.

I was saved from sin when I was going on thirteen. But not really saved. It happened like this. There was a big revival at my Auntie Reed's church. Every night for weeks there had been much preaching, singing, praying, and shouting, and some very hardened sinners had been brought to Christ, and the member-ship of the church had grown by leaps and bounds. Then just before the revival ended, they held a special meeting for children, "to bring the young lambs to the fold." My aunt spoke of it for days ahead. That night I was escorted to the front row and placed on the mourners' bench with all the other young sinners, who had not yet been brought to Jesus. 1

My aunt told me that when you were saved you saw a light, and something happened to you inside! And Jesus came into your life! And God was with you from then on! She said you could see 2

157

and hear and feel Jesus in your soul. I believed her. I had heard a great many old people say the same thing and it seemed to me they ought to know. So I sat there calmly in the hot, crowded church, waiting for Jesus to come to me.

The preacher preached a wonderful rhythmical sermon, all   3
moans and shouts and lonely cries and dire pictures of hell, and then he sang a song about the ninety and nine safe in the fold, but one little lamb was left out in the cold. Then he said: "Won't you come? Won't you come to Jesus? Young lambs, won't you come?" And he held out his arms to all us young sinners there on the mourners' bench. And the little girls cried. And some of them jumped up and went to Jesus right away. But most of us just sat there.

A great many older people came and knelt around us and   4
prayed, old women with jet-black faces and braided hair, old men with work-gnarled hands. And the church sang a song about the lower lights are burning, some poor sinners to be saved. And the whole building rocked with prayer and song.

Still I kept waiting to *see* Jesus.   5

Finally all the young people had gone to the altar and were   6
saved, but one boy and me. He was a rounder's son named Westley. Westley and I were surrounded by sisters and deacons praying. It was very hot in the church, and getting late now. Finally Westley said to me in a whisper: "God damn! I'm tired o' sitting here. Let's get up and be saved." So he got up and was saved.

Then I was left all alone on the mourners' bench. My aunt   7
came and knelt at my knees and cried, while prayers and songs swirled all around me in the little church. The whole congregation prayed for me alone, in a mighty wail of moans and voices. And I kept waiting serenely for Jesus, waiting, waiting—but he didn't come. I wanted to see him, but nothing happened to me. Nothing! I wanted something to happen to me, but nothing happened.

I heard the songs and the minister saying: "Why don't you   8
come? My dear child, why don't you come to Jesus? Jesus is waiting for you. He wants you. Why don't you come? Sister Reed, what is this child's name?"

"Langston," my aunt sobbed.   9

"Langston, why don't you come? Why don't you come and
be saved? Oh, Lamb of God! Why don't you come?"   10

Now it was really getting late. I began to be ashamed of   11
myself, holding everything up so long. I began to wonder what
God thought about Westley, who certainly hadn't seen Jesus
either, but who was now sitting proudly on the platform, swinging his knickerbockered legs and grinning down at me, surrounded by deacons and old women on their knees praying. God
had not struck Westley dead for taking his name in vain or for
lying in the temple. So I decided that maybe to save further
trouble, I'd better lie, too, and say that Jesus had come, and get
up and be saved.

So I got up.   12

Suddenly the whole room broke into a sea of shouting, as   13
they saw me rise. Waves of rejoicing swept the place. Women
leaped in the air. My aunt threw her arms around me. The minister took me by the hand and led me to the platform.

When things quieted down, in a hushed silence, punctuated   14
by a few ecstatic "Amens," all the new young lambs were blessed
in the name of God. Then joyous singing filled the room.

That night, for the last time in my life but one — for I was a   15
big boy twelve years old — I cried. I cried, in bed alone, and
couldn't stop. I buried my head under the quilts, but my aunt
heard me. She woke up and told my uncle I was crying because
the Holy Ghost had come into my life, and because I had seen
Jesus. But I was really crying because I couldn't bear to tell her
that I had lied, that I had deceived everybody in the church, and I
hadn't seen Jesus, and that now I didn't believe there was a Jesus
any more, since he didn't come to help me.

Questions for Close Reading

1. What is the thesis (or narrative point) of "Salvation"? If the thesis is
   not explicitly stated, express it in your own words.
2. During the revival meeting, what pressures are put on the young
   Langston to get up and be saved?
3. How does Westley's attitude differ from Langston's?

4. Does the narrator's Auntie Reed really understand him? Why can't he tell her the truth about his experience in the church?

5. Refer to your dictionary as needed to define the following words in the selection: *revival* (paragraph 1), *knickerbockered* (11), *punctuated* (14), and *ecstatic* (14).

Questions About the Writer's Craft

1. The power of a narrative can often be traced to a conflict within the event being recounted. What conflict does the narrator of "Salvation" experience? How does this conflict create tension in the reader?

2. What key role does Westley serve in the resolution of the narrator's dilemma? How does the inclusion of Westley in the story help us to understand Langston better?

3. The thirteenth paragraph develops a metaphor of the church as an ocean. What images create this metaphor? What does the metaphor tell us about Hughes' feelings and those of the church people at this point?

4. The singing of hymns is a major part of this religious service. Why does the narrator reveal the subjects and even the lyrics of some of the hymns?

Questions for Further Thought

1. What did Hughes expect to happen when he was "saved"? Was he led to have unrealistic expectations about this religious moment? Do you think children often understand religious ideas differently than adults?

2. Given the circumstances, do you think young Langston Hughes did the right thing?

3. Young people often feel excessively pressured by family and community to adopt certain values, beliefs, or traditions. What are some examples of this pressure from your own experience? Should young people accept that the older generation knows more about what to believe and do?

4. Is disillusionment with adults and with society's institutions a necessary part of growing up? Why or why not?

Writing Assignments Using Narration as a Method of Development

1. Like Hughes, we sometimes believe that deception is our best alternative. Write a narrative about a time you felt deception was the best

way either to protect those you care about or to maintain the respect of those important to you.

2. Write a narrative essay about a chain of events that caused you to become disillusioned about a person or institution you had held in high esteem. Begin as Hughes does by presenting your initial beliefs. Relate the sequence of events that brought about a change in your evaluation of the person or organization. In the conclusion, explain the short- and long-term effects of the incident.

Writing Assignments Using Other Methods of Development

3. Hughes writes, "My aunt told me that when you were saved, you saw a light, and something happened to you inside! And Jesus came into your life!" What causes people to change their beliefs? Can such changes come from waiting calmly, as Hughes tried to do in church, or must they come from a more active process? Write an essay explaining why or how a change or conversion in beliefs might take place. You may use process analysis, causal analysis, or some other organizational pattern to develop your thesis. Be sure to include specific examples of what you are describing.

*4. Write a persuasive essay arguing either that lying is sometimes right or that lying is always wrong. Support your thesis by showing the consequences of your position for society and the individual. Apply your thesis to particular situations and show how lying is or is not the right course of action. Reading Lewis Thomas' "The Lie Detector" (page 400) may help you define your position. You might even mention Thomas' point of view in your essay.

Garrison Keillor

Garrison Keillor, best known as the host of the popular public radio program *A Prairie Home Companion*, was born in 1942 in Anoka, Minnesota. For years, Keillor wrote wry pieces for *The New Yorker* and other publications. But it was not until *Prairie Home Companion* that he earned a large national following, with fans eagerly turning their radio dials to listen to Keillor's tales of fictional Lake Wobegon, "the little town that time forgot and the decades cannot improve." Nostalgic but not saccharine, *Companion* aired from 1974 until 1987, when Keillor moved to Denmark to concentrate on writing. Keillor's essays are collected in three books: *Happy to Be Here* (1982), *Lake Wobegon Days* (1985), and *Leaving Home: A Collection of Lake Wobegon Stories* (1987). "Eloise," the piece below, is taken from *Leaving Home*.

Eloise

As fans of *A Prairie Home Companion* know, the weeks in Lake Wobegon are quiet. But the stillness is not always a contented one. Garrison Keillor knows that small-town life, along with its satisfactions and joys, has its share of bitterness and spite. The nearby forest may be ablaze with color, but, Keillor warns us, the only trail through this "magical wood . . . is a cowpath, so you have to watch where you step."

It has been a quiet week in Lake Wobegon. It was warm and 1 bright and the trees were in full color, magnificent, explosive, like permanent fireworks — reds and yellows, oranges, some so brilliant that Crayola never put them in crayons for fear the children would color outside the lines. Maple trees the color of illicit romance, blazing red sumac and oaks and aspen, such color that you weren't sure you were in this world but perhaps had stepped through a seam in the tapestry and walked into a magical wood.

162

But the only trail through there is a cowpath, so you have to watch where you step.

Florian and Myrtle Krebsbach went driving Tuesday to look 2 at the beautiful trees, which neither of them enjoys, but they go because they've done it for years. Myrtle gets carsick more easily now since she bumped her head on the cupboard. The bright colors only made her dizziness more vivid. Florian was grumpy because he hates to see the odometer roll on his '66 Chev (like new, only forty-seven thousand miles on her). Low mileage is a form of youth to Florian, it means plenty of mileage to come. He drove slowly toward Millet and back and Myrtle hung on to the strap. She said, of the fall colors, "Well, if this don't prove to them there's an Almighty, I don't know what in hell will." They drove 6.2 miles at twenty-five mph and returned to home base, where he wiped the engine clean with a rag soaked in gasoline. The smell of gas makes Florian perk up.

The leaves reached their peak about Thursday and then, in 3 late afternoon, seemed to dim. Friday morning we woke up and could see that we had passed our apex and were heading for the nadir.

It was still warm, though, so when Ranger Steve came to the 4 third grade with a boxful of snakes, they were pretty lively. Snakes are our friends, not slimy, not evil, but really very beautiful and nothing to be afraid of, he said. "I'm sure Mrs. Hughes isn't afraid of snakes — look," he said, and draped a black one on her shoulder as her body shrank and then stiffened. "See? Snakes aren't slimy at all. Actually their skin is rather dry — right, Mrs. Hughes? This is called a bridle snake; it bites, but only if you bother it."

Ranger Steve smiled. "It's all right, there's nothing to worry 5 about," he said to Mrs. Hughes, whose eyes were shut, and took the snake in his big manly hand, and set it on his broad shoulder. Instantly the harmless reptile dove into the V of his collar and disappeared. Ranger Steve said, *"Oh God,"* and grabbed at it. He was wearing a green jump suit, with no belt for a roadblock, and he turned his back to the children and bent over and tried to grab the bridle snake in the jump suit. It was warm under there and the snake was excited, and the children heard a cry, and Steve staggered and the snake came out his left pants leg. They all helped catch it. Steve talked more about snakes but his smile had slipped to the side and gone out of focus. The passage of the bridle snake through the jump suit had worn him out, the exertion of being cool and hysterical at the same time.

Afterward, some of the boys did an imitation of Ranger Steve   6
with the snake in his pants, and Mrs. Hughes said, "I don't consider that one bit funny," even though it was hilarious.

That's what wears out a grown-up person: the con-   7
tradictions.

After school, a girl from the third grade jumped on her old   8
blue coaster bike and tore off toward the woods to find snakes and put them on her brothers. Then, coasting down Branch Street, she saw her little brother standing looking at their dog Fatso lying by the tree, covering him up with leaves. She swerved and headed straight for the innocent little child and yelled, "I can't stop! No brakes! I can't stop," but he stood there like a stone so she stopped. She said, "You coulda been killed. Why'ntcha move? That was a close call, y'know." Fatso stood up and tottered around back of the tree but the little boy was too scared to move. "You're dumb, you know that? You're as dumb as a dog." Fatso blinked. The little boy's eyes filled with tears to hear his sweet sister talk to him like that, two pools of pale-blue tears in his blue eyes, and then he made a decision that certainly changed his life: he took one step toward her with his left foot and with his right he kicked the big jerk in her ankle as hard as he could. He held back nothing. A swift hard kick.

More happened then: she chased him, caught him, threw him   9
down, pounded him. But it wasn't important. He had done something. (The wrong thing — it's wrong to kick your sister — but sometimes the wrong thing is exactly the right thing to do.) His mother ran out and hauled her off him. "What is going on out here?"

"He kicked me — here," said Amy, and to show how much it   10
hurt, her big brown eyes filled up with tears.

"What did you do to him?"   11

"Nothing. I was riding my bike."   12

"Paul! How could you do a thing like that?"   13

He looked up at his mother. He wasn't sure.   14

"Just for that, you come inside."   15

That was fine with him. He preferred inside.   16

These are Florian and Myrtle Krebsbach's grandchildren and   17 their daughter Eloise, who lives around the corner from Carl. She's got three kids, these two plus a tall lonesome boy named Charlie, one in a long tradition of tall skinny lonesome boys who grew up there. Eloise's name is Best. She married Chuck Best out of high school, a handsome friendly boy, and three years ago he decided he'd been married long enough to her. He came home to pack his bags.

Eloise cried and then, when he went to the garage for his golf   18
clubs, she locked him out of the house without so much as a warm jacket. She told him she was going to give all his clothes to the church clothing drive. When he asked for his car keys she laughed at him through the letter slot. "You want to start over, then *start* over," she said. "Don't be such a drip. This isn't a halfway house, mister, this is my home. You want to go away, go ahead, but don't ask me to give you a ride."

This took place on Greener Avenue South in Minneapolis   19
one bright summer day in 1983. The neighbors were out working on their yards, and when they noticed the Bests' conversation — the shouts from the slot, the man in the blue blazer and tan slacks saying, "Please, Ellie. Try to control yourself" — the neighbors shut off their mowers and got busy doing quiet things. They studied trees for signs of drought, snipped at a hedge with silent little snips, quietly pulled crabgrass.

"Ellie, please. Let's discuss this. Let me in and let's talk."   20

"I am talking!" she said and called him a bunch of words   21
that moms don't use. "All right," he said. "That's it. That's all I'm going to take from you." And he walked gravely and respectably down the walk. He stood at the end of his walk, glancing left and right, then turned left as she opened the door and yelled, "You . . . are a . . . lousy lover!" Her voice echoed off the frame and brick houses — "lousylousylousylousyloverlousyloverloverlover" — far up the pleasant street where they'd had a sweet comfortable ten years, and he heard the lawn sprinklers whisper, "It's true, it's true, it's true, it's true."

More happened then. He came after her with excellent legal   22
talent and pounded her pretty hard in court, and she wound up in a two-bedroom tumble-down stucco house in Lake Wobegon, where, well — to be a single woman with three children, you might as well paint the house chartreuse and convert to Islam and make it complete.

Her mother, Myrtle, says, "Eloise, you're the first one in this 23
family ever to collect a welfare check, it's a disgrace. People talk
about us. Do you know that? They never useta, and now you can
hear em all over town."

She said, "Mother, don't get too ashamed now, because I've 24
got a long way to go."

"I don't see why you can't get yourself a job." 25

"I'm trying." 26

"Try harder." 27

So last Thursday her little ad appeared in the *Herald-Star*. 28
Harold himself called her Sunday and asked, "Is this legit?" So
there it was: "Dancing Taught in My Home or Yours. Individual
lessons. Polka, Waltz, Foxtrot, or Lindy. Eloise Krebsbach Best."

Ella Anderson called her Thursday night. "Ellie," she said, "I 29
didn't know you could dance."

"Well, Ella, you never asked me." 30

"I wonder if this wouldn't help my bad hip." 31

Ella is old and has a hard life taking care of herself and 32
Henry. People don't visit them, because they're embarrassed to
see him, a man once important in our town, now old and sleepy.
Suddenly he'll sit up and talk about your horse and somebody
named David and where did the girls go? The girls went away and
became middle-aged a long time ago. Ella is lonely. Her daughter
Charlotte called one night and suddenly said, "Well? Mother? Do
you want to or not?" And Ella couldn't remember the question.
Charlotte said, "Just say yes or no," and Ella said, "Yes." And
now she wonders what she said yes to.

"What's it like to be old?" Ellie asked her. 33

"Old age is like birds in the winter. It's hard to keep going. 34
But you still have your good days, and one good day makes you
want to keep on. I used to get so upset if any little thing went
wrong. Now everything goes wrong and it doesn't bother me,
and some little thing is so wonderful — if my son writes me a
letter, that's wonderful. And if he puts in a picture of my grandchildren, then that's just about everything."

Ellie rolled up the rag rug and pushed back the coffee table 35
and chairs. "What'll it be, a waltz?" she said. A waltz it was, the
"Blue Skirt Waltz," and if you walked by on Thursday night and
saw in the window two women dancing, one with white hair and
the other with red, smiling, turning, would you have thought it

was strange? Would you have stopped? Or would you have walked on, taking the sweetness of it to heart on a fall night turning cold, the bright colors, magnificence and glory all around us everywhere in the air.

Questions for Close Reading

1. What is the thesis of the selection? Locate the sentence(s) in which Keillor states his main idea. If he does not state the thesis explicitly, express it in your own words.
2. Myrtle Krebsbach's reaction to a car ride is motion-sickness; her husband Florian's reaction is annoyance over the accumulated mileage. What do these reactions reveal about the couple's outlook on life?
3. Keillor writes that Paul's kicking his sister is both the wrong thing and the right thing to do. Resolve this apparent paradox. In whose eyes is the action wrong? In what sense is it right?
4. Keillor briefly tells the circumstances in which Eloise and Chuck Best married, then vividly relates the confrontation that ends in their separation. What can you infer about their years of married life and about their reasons for having married each other in the first place?
5. Refer to your dictionary as needed to define the following words used in the selection: *illicit* (paragraph 1), *odometer* (2), *apex* (3), and *chartreuse* (22).

Questions About the Writer's Craft

1. Keillor structures "Eloise" around a series of interwoven narratives. Identify these various subplots. What common threads run through all of them?
2. In several spots, Keillor's sudden shift in point of view creates a sharp ironic contrast. One such shift occurs at the beginning of the essay: The narrator sees the autumn foliage as "magnificent and explosive," but the Krebsbachs view it out of duty, simply because "they've done it for years." Find other examples of such shifts. How do these ironic contrasts support Keillor's main point?
3. Like all skilled narrative writers, Keillor makes effective use of dialogue. What do the snippets of conversation reveal about each speaker's character?
4. Keillor narrates episodes in the lives of several people. Why does he single out Eloise as the title character?

Questions for Further Thought

1. Many of us have a romantic, idealized picture of small-town life—exactly the sort of picture Keillor shatters in "Eloise." Do you think that life in a small town is better or worse than life in a city? Explain.
2. In Lake Wobegon, children in a family often fight each other—and none too gently. What can be learned from such conflicts? How should parents deal with children's squabbles?
3. Growing old has been difficult for Ella and the Krebsbachs. What can families do to make the aging process easier for elderly parents?
4. In Keillor's world, the relationship between child and parent is filled with tensions. How would you characterize these tensions? How do they change over the years?

Writing Assignments Using Narrative as a Method of Development

1. Keillor celebrates Ella and Eloise's inner strength and resilience. Have you or has someone you know ever triumphed over a difficult experience? In a narrative or series of narratives, recount a time you (or someone else) survived and were strengthened by a trying time. At the end, reach some conclusions about why some people survive while others do not.
2. Keillor tells us that Krebsbachs drive every year to view the autumn foliage—although neither of them enjoys these excursions. Using a series of narratives, recount some ritual your family observed year after year. Order the narratives so that the sequence highlights a sudden or gradual change that took place in your feelings about the ritual. Reach some conclusions about why the ritual became more or less significant to you as time went by.

Writing Assignments Using Other Methods of Development

3. Eloise asks Ella, "What's it like to be old?" Write an essay defining what it means to be your age—eighteen, twenty-seven, whatever. No matter which strategies you use to develop the definition (description, comparison–contrast, narration, and so on), the essay should convey the physical and emotional reality of being your age.
4. Myrtle Krebsbach disapproves of her daughter's being on welfare. Focusing on one aspect of your life (social, academic, or professional), compare and contrast what your parents expect or expected of you with what you yourself want. What are or were the points of conflict and agreement? Your paper should lead you to some conclusions about the ways in which your values are like and unlike your parents'.

Additional Writing Topics

NARRATION

General Assignments

Prepare an essay on any of the following topics, using narration as the paper's dominant method of development. Be sure to select details that advance the narrative purpose of the essay; you may even want to experiment with flashback or flashforward. In any case, keep the sequence of events clear by using transitional cues. Within the limited time span covered, use vigorous details and varied sentence structure to enliven the narrative. Tell the story from a consistent point of view.

1. An emergency that brought out the best or worst in you
2. The hazards of taking children out to eat
3. An incident that made you believe in fate
4. Your best or worst day at school or work
5. A major decision
6. An encounter with a machine
7. An important learning experience
8. A narrow escape
9. Your first date, day on the job, or first anything
10. A memorable childhood experience
11. A fairy tale the way you would like to hear it told
12. A painful moment
13. An incredible but true story
14. A significant family event
15. An experience in which a certain emotion (pride, anger, regret, or some other) was predominant

Assignments with a Specific Audience and Purpose

1. A friend comes to you with a question of ethics. Your friend has seen someone cheat, or shoplift, or perform some dishonest action. Should your friend speak up to the teacher, the store owner, the employer? Convince your friend that he or she should act by narrating an incident in which someone did (or did not) speak up in such a situation. Tell what happened as a result.
2. As fundraiser for a particular organization (SPCA, Red Cross, Big Brothers/Sisters, and so on), you are sending a newsletter to contributors. Support your cause by telling the story of one time when your

organization made all the difference—the blood donation that saved a life, the animal that was saved from the gas chamber, and so on.

3. You have had a disturbing encounter with one of the people who seem to have "fallen through the cracks" of society—a street person, an unwanted child, or anyone else who is alone and abandoned. Write a letter to the local newspaper describing this encounter. Your purpose is to arouse people's indignation and compassion and to get help for such unfortunates.

4. Write an article for your old high school newspaper. The article will be read primarily by seniors who are planning to go away to college next year. In the article, narrate a story that points to some truth about the "breaking away" stage of life—that first experience of moving away from home.

5. Your best friend has had a terrible experience with a teacher, employer, doctor, repairperson (or any other kind of professional) and is completely disillusioned. Balance the cynical picture your friend has by narrating a story that shows the "flip side" of this profession—a good experience you had when such a person went all out to help you.

6. Your younger brother or sister can't wait to be your age. Tell your sibling that your age isn't as wonderful as he or she thinks by narrating a story that shows the disadvantage of being your age. Make the story one that a young person could understand.

EXEMPLIFICATION

WHAT IS EXEMPLIFICATION?

If someone asked you, "Have you been to any good restaurants lately?" you probably wouldn't answer "Yes" and then immediately change the subject. You would go on, most likely, to explain your answer with examples. You might give the names of restaurants you had enjoyed and talk briefly about the specific things you liked: the attractive prices, the tasty main courses, the pleasant service, the tempting desserts. Such examples and details are needed if you want to convince others that your opinion — in this or any matter — is valid. Similarly, when you talk about larger and more important issues, people will not pay much attention to your opinion if all you do is string together vague generalizations: "We have to do something about acid rain. We have a real problem. The impact of acid rain on the environment has been considerable. Acid rain has serious effects on all of us." Without specific supporting examples, such an argument is a toothless tiger, blustery but ineffective. People must have examples (the forests in the Adirondacks are dying; yesterday's rainfall was fifty times more acidic than normal; Pine Lake, in the northern part of the state, was once a great fishing spot but now has no fish population) to be convinced that your point is well founded.

Examples are equally important when you write an essay. Facts, anecdotes, statistics, details, opinions, and observations are at the heart of effective writing, giving your work substance and solidity. Don't worry that you are padding your essay when you use examples. Don't assume that general statements and abstract phrasing somehow elevate your work, making it sound more impressive. Strong writing is concrete and down-to-earth, the most skillful writers achieving their effects through specific examples.

WHEN TO USE EXEMPLIFICATION

The wording of assignments and essay exam questions may indicate clearly the need for specific illustrations:

> Soap operas, whether shown during the day or in the evening, are among the most watched programs on television. Why is this so? Be sure to provide specific examples to support your position.

> Many observers claim that college students are interested less in learning than in getting ahead in their careers. Cite evidence to demonstrate the validity—or lack of validity—of this claim.

> A growing number of people feel that parents should not allow their children to participate in highly competitive, highly organized team sports. Basing your conclusion on your own experiences and observations, indicate whether you think these people have a reasonable point of view.

Phrases like "provide specific examples," "cite evidence," and "basing your conclusion on your own experiences and observations" signal that each essay would be developed with examples.

Usually, though, you will not be told to provide examples.

Instead, as you think about the best way to achieve your essay's purpose, you will see the need for illustrations and details. You will also discover that all essays — no matter the rhetorical patterns used — require examples. For instance, to *persuade* skeptical readers that the country needs a national health system, you might mention specific cases to dramatize the inadequacy of our current health care system: a family bankrupted by medical bills; an uninsured accident victim turned away by a hospital; a chronically ill person rapidly deteriorating because he didn't have enough money to visit a doctor. Or imagine a lightly satiric piece that pokes fun at cat-lovers. Insisting that cat-people are pretty strange creatures, you might make your point — and make readers chuckle — with a series of examples *contrasting* cat-lovers and dog-lovers: the qualities admired by each group (loyalty in dogs versus aloofness in cats) and the different expectations each group has for its pets (dog-lovers want Fido to be obedient and lovable, while cat-lovers are satisfied with Felix's occasional spurts of docility and affection). Similarly, you would supply examples in a *causal analysis* examining the impact of a proposed tuition increase on students at your college. To inform the college administration of the negative effects of such a hike, you might cite the following: articles reporting an upswing in student transfers to less expensive schools; statistics indicating a significant drop in grades among already employed students forced to work more hours to make ends meet; interviews with students too strapped financially to continue their college education.

Whether you use examples as a primary or supplemental method of development, they serve a number of important purposes. For one thing, examples make writing interesting. Assume you are writing an essay about sexism in TV commercials but forget to include examples of commercials presenting stereotyped views of men and women. Your essay would be lifeless and boring if all it did was repeat over and over, in a general way, that commercials are sexist:

> Sexism is rampant in television commercials. It is very much alive, and most viewers seem to take it all in stride. Few people protest the obviously sexist characters and statements on such commercials. Surely, these commercials misrepresent the way most of us live.

Without interesting particulars, readers may respond, "Who cares?" But if you provide specific examples, readers will be pulled into the essay, and their attention will be drawn to the point being made:

> Sexism is rampant in television commercials. Although millions of women hold responsible jobs outside the home, commercials continue to portray women as simple creatures who spend most of their time thinking about wax buildup, cottony-soft bathroom tissue, and static-free clothes. Men, apparently, have better things to do than to fret over such mundane household matters. How many commercials can you recall that depict men proclaiming the virtues of squeaky-clean dishes or sparkling bathrooms? Not many.

Examples also make writing *persuasive.* Most writing conveys a point, but many readers are reluctant to accept someone else's point of view without evidence to demonstrate the validity of that position. Imagine that you are writing an essay showing that latchkey children are more self-sufficient and emotionally secure than children who return from school to a home where a parent awaits them. Your thesis is obviously controversial. Without specific examples — from your own experience, from personal observations, or from research studies — your readers would undoubtedly question the validity of your position.

Moreover, examples *help explain* difficult, abstract, or unusual ideas. Suppose you have been assigned an essay on a complex subject, such as inflation, zero population growth, or radiation exposure. As a writer, you have a responsibility to make these difficult concepts concrete and easily understandable. If you were writing an essay on radiation exposure in everyday life, you might start by providing specific examples of home appliances that emit radiation — color televisions, computers, and microwave ovens — and tell exactly how much radiation we absorb in a typical day from this equipment. To illustrate further the extent of our radiation exposure, you could also provide specifics about unavoidable sources of natural radiation (the sun, for instance) and details about the widespread use of radiation in medicine (x-rays, radiation therapy). These specific examples ground your discussion, making it immediate and concrete, preventing it from flying off into a vague and theoretical realm.

Finally, examples *help ensure clear communication.* All of us have experienced the frustration of not being understood, of having someone misinterpret what we said. In face-to-face communication, we often can detect when someone doesn't understand what we're saying and can provide on-the-spot clarification. Because instantaneous feedback is not available to you when writing, it's crucial that you make your meaning as clear as possible. Examples will help.

Let's assume that you are writing an essay asserting that ineffective teaching is on the rise in today's high schools. Through examples, you clarify what you mean by "ineffective." You might mention the following: the teacher who spent so much time disciplining unruly students that he never got around to teaching assigned lessons; the moonlighting teacher who was so tired in class that she regularly took naps during tests; the teacher who accepted obviously plagiarized reports simply because he was grateful that students handed in something.

Without these concrete examples, your readers will supply or fill in their own ideas — and these may not be what you had in mind. Readers might imagine "ineffective" to mean uncreative or unimaginative, whereas your examples show you intend it to mean irresponsible and out of control. Such specific examples help prevent misunderstanding and imprecise communication.

SUGGESTIONS FOR USING EXEMPLIFICATION IN AN ESSAY

The following suggestions will be helpful whether you use examples as a dominant or supportive pattern of development.

1. Generate examples.   Where do you get the examples to develop your essay? The first batch of examples is generated during the prewriting stage. With your audience and thesis in mind, you should brainstorm and freewrite, making a broad sweep for examples. Search your own experience; recall or ask about other people's experience; visit the library.

Examples can take several forms, including specific names (people, places, products, for instance), anecdotes, events, and factual details gathered through research. Be sure, however, to exercise caution with any statistics you come across. An old saying warns that there are lies, damn lies, and statistics — meaning that statistics can be misleading; they can be manipulated easily to suit varying ends. A commercial may claim that "in a taste test, eighty percent of those questioned indicated that they preferred Fizzy Cola." Impressed? Don't be — at least, not until you find out how the test was conducted. Perhaps the subjects had to choose between Fizzy Cola and battery acid, or perhaps there were only five subjects, including Fizzy Cola's four vice presidents and a hapless stranger.

During the prewriting stage, try to generate more examples than you think you can use. Starting with abundance — and then picking out the strongest examples — will give you a firm base on which to construct the essay. If you have a great deal of trouble finding examples to support your thesis, you may need to revise the thesis; you may be trying to support an idea that has little validity. On the other hand, while prewriting, you may unearth numerous examples but may find that many of them contradict the point you started out to support. If that happens, don't hesitate to recast your central point, always remembering that your thesis and examples must fit.

2. Select the examples to include.   If you have generated as many specifics as possible, you are now ready to narrow down your examples to the strongest items. At this point, keeping your thesis and audience in mind, you should ask yourself several key questions: "How many examples do I need? Should the examples be brief? Should they be extended?"

You may decide to include several brief examples within a single sentence:

The French people's fascination with some American literary figures, such as Poe and Hawthorne, is understandable. But their great respect for "artists" like comedian Jerry Lewis is a mystery.

Or you may elect to develop a paragraph with a number of "for instances":

A uniquely American style of movie-acting reached its peak in the 1950s. Certain charismatic actors completely abandoned the stage techniques and tradition that had been the foundation of acting up to that time. Instead of articulating their lines clearly, the actors mumbled; instead of making firm eye contact with their colleagues, they hung their heads, shifted their eyes, even talked with their eyes closed. Marlon Brando, and then James Dean, were two actors who exemplified this new trend.

Generally, you will need to provide *more than one example.* An essay with the thesis "Rock videos are dangerously violent" would not be convincing if only one example of a video were given. Several strong examples would be needed before anyone felt that enough support had been provided to illustrate the point. Occasionally, one *extended example,* fully developed with many details, can support an essay. It might be possible, for example, to support the thesis that "Federal legislation should be passed to raise the legal drinking age to twenty-one" with one compelling, highly detailed example describing the effects of one teenager's drunken driving spree.

You want to be sure your examples are *relevant* and develop the points they are intended to support. This may sound obvious, but writers sometimes use weak or inappropriate examples to support their positions. You would have a hard time convincing readers that Americans have callous attitudes toward the elderly if you described the wide range of new programs, all staffed by volunteers, at a well-financed center for senior citizens. Similarly, you would not convince your reader that pollution from landfills poses a serious health risk if you discussed legislation needed to control automobile emissions. Because these examples do not support their respective thesis statements, the logic of the essay would collapse, and your credibility would be compromised.

Finally, you need to select *representative* examples. Picking the oddball or one-in-a-million example to support a point — and passing it off as typical or usual — is dishonest. For instance, since the 1960s, some people have tagged feminists with the label "bra-burner." But how many liberationists actually burned bras? If such an incident happened only once, it is unfair to use it as proof that the women's movement is frivolous or destructive.

3. Develop examples with sufficient detail.   To ensure that readers grasp the significance of your examples, you should develop key specifics in enough detail. If you were asked to write an essay on the types of heroes that reappear in American movies, you could not string together a series of paragraphs, each of them like the one below.

Heroes in American movies usually fall into types. One kind of hero is the tight-lipped loner, men like Clint Eastwood or Humphrey Bogart. Another movie hero is the quiet, shy, or fumbling type who has appeared in movies since the beginning. The main characteristic of this hero is lovableness, as seen in actors like Jimmy Stewart. Perhaps the most one-dimensional and predictable hero is the superman who battles tough odds. This kind of hero is best illustrated by Sylvester Stallone as Rocky and Rambo.

If the essay were developed this way — if you moved quickly from one undeveloped example to another, without providing supporting specifics — you would not be writing an essay; you would be doing little more than making a list. To be effective, key examples must be expanded in sufficient detail. You could, for instance, develop the first example this way:

Heroes can be tight-lipped loners who appear out of nowhere, form no permanent attachments, and walk, drive, or ride off into the sunset. In many of his Westerns, from the low-budget "spaghetti Westerns" of the 1960s to <u>Pale</u> <u>Rider</u> in 1985, Clint Eastwood personifies this kind of hero. He is remote, mysterious, and has few lines of dialogue. Yet he cleans the villains out of town, helps a little crippled girl, and shoots down an evil sheriff--acts that cement his heroic status. The loner might also be Humphrey Bogart as Sam Spade, a man with few true friends and no meaningful romantic attachments. Spade solves the crime and sends the guilty off to jail in a clearly heroic way, yet he holds his emotions in check and has no permanent ties beyond his faithful secretary and shabby office. One gets the feeling that he could walk away from these, too, if necessary. Even in <u>The</u> <u>Right</u> <u>Stuff</u>, a fairly factual account of America's early astronauts, the scriptwriters mold Chuck Yeager, the man who broke the sound barrier, into a classic loner. Yeager has a wife. But, as played by lanky, aloof Sam Shepard, the astronaut is insular. Depending only on himself, he rarely confides in anyone, taking mute pride in the knowledge that he is the best at what he does.

4. Organize the examples. If, as is usually the case, several examples are provided to support a point, you should be sure there is a reason for presenting the examples in the order you do. The examples cannot be presented randomly, without design. Instead, you should select a sequence that most effectively illustrates your thesis. Imagine you are writing an essay about the period of adjustment many students experience during the first months of college. The supporting examples could be arranged *chronologically*. You might start by providing examples of the ambivalence students feel the first day of college when their parents leave to go home; you might then offer an anecdote or two about students' frequent calls to Mom and Dad during the opening weeks of the semester; the essay might end with an account that details students' reluctance to leave campus at the midyear break. An essay demonstrating that the furnishings in a room often reflect the character of its occupant might be organized *spatially:* from the empty soda cans on the floor to the spitballs on the ceiling. The *emphatic sequence*—in which you lead steadily from your first example to your final, most significant or dramatic example—is also an effective way to organize an essay containing many examples. A paper about Americans' characteristic impatience might progress from minor examples (dependence on fast food, obsession with ever-faster mail delivery services) to more disturbing manifestations of impatience (using drugs as quick solutions to problems, advocating simple answers to complex international problems: "Bomb them!").

Without appropriate and dynamic examples, an essay is a dry, bloodless thing. Even provocative and intriguing ideas lose their power—or may be misunderstood—if writers do not provide the specific details needed to explain and develop their central points. Remember that most readers will not take seriously a writer who has been too lazy to do anything but spout a series of vague generalities. If you examine a stirring speech, a riveting newspaper article, an informative book, you are sure to find clear, well-developed examples. These specifics engage the reader and provide the writing with its distinctive energy.

STUDENT ESSAY AND COMMENTARY

The student essay that follows was written by Michael Pagano in response to this assignment:

> Anne Morrow Lindbergh states in "Channelled Whelk"
> that Americans impose unnecessary complications on

their lives. Observe closely the way you and others conduct your daily lives. Use your observations to generate evidence for an essay that supports or refutes Lindbergh's point of view.

While reading the paper, try to determine how effectively it applies the principles concerning the use of exemplification. The commentary following the paper will help you look at Michael's essay more closely.

Pursuit of Possessions

In the essay, "Channelled Whelk," Anne Morrow Lindbergh   1
states that Americans "who could choose simplicity, choose complication." Lindbergh herself is a prime example of the phenomenon she discusses. A wife and a mother as well as a writer, Lindbergh has many obligations which make for a complicated life. Even so, Lindbergh attempts to simplify her life by escaping to a beach cottage that is bare except for driftwood and shells for decoration; there she is happy. But very few of us would be willing to simplify our lives as Lindbergh does. Instead, we choose to clutter our lives with a stream of material possessions. And what is the result of this mania for possessions? Much of our time goes to buying new things, dealing with the complications they create, and working madly to buy more things or pay for the things we already have.

We devote a great deal of our lives to acquiring the material   2
goods we imagine are essential to our well-being. Hours are spent planning and thinking about our future purchases. We windowshop for designer jogging shoes; we leaf through magazines looking at ads for elaborate stereo equipment; we research back issues of <u>Consumer Reports</u> to find out about recent developments in exercise equipment. Moreover, once we find what we are looking for, more time is taken up when we decide to actually buy the purchases. How do we find this time? That's easy. We turn evenings, weekends, and holidays--time that used to be set aside for family and friends--into shopping expeditions. No wonder that family life is deteriorating and that children spend so much time in front of television sets. Their parents are seldom around.

As soon as we take our new purchases home, they begin to   3
complicate our lives. A sleek new sports car has to be washed, waxed, and vacuumed. A fashionable pair of skintight jeans can't be thrown in the washing machine but has to be taken to the dry cleaners. New stereo equipment has to be connected with a tangled

network of cables to the TV, radio, and cassette deck. Eventually, of course, the inevitable happens. Our indispensable possessions break down and need to be repaired. The home computer starts to lose data, the microwave has to have its temperature controls adjusted, and the videotape recorder has to be serviced when a cassette becomes jammed in the machine.

After more time has gone by, we sometimes discover that our   4
purchases don't suit us anymore, and so we decide to replace them. Before making our replacement purchases, though, we have to find ways to get rid of the old items. If we want to replace our black-and-white 19-inch television set with a 25-inch color set, we have to find time to put an ad in the classified section of the paper. Then we have to handle phone calls and set up times people can come to look at the TV. We could store the set in the basement--if we are lucky enough to find a spot that isn't already filled with other discarded purchases.

Worst of all, this mania for possessions often influences our   5
approach to work. It is not unusual for people to take a second or even a third job to pay off the debt they fall into because they have overbought. After paying for food, clothing, and shelter, many people see the rest of their paycheck go to Visa, MasterCard, department store charge accounts, and time payments. Panic sets in when they realize there simply is not enough money to cover all their expenses. Just to stay afloat, people may have to work overtime or take on additional jobs.

It is clear that many of us have allowed the pursuit of posses-   6
sions to dominate our lives. We are so busy buying, maintaining, and paying for our worldly goods that we do not have much time to think about what is really important. We should try to step back from our compulsive need for more of everything and get in touch with the basic values that are the real point of our lives.

In his essay, "Pursuit of Possessions," Michael analyzes the mania in American society for acquiring material goods. He begins with a quotation from Anne Morrow Lindbergh's "Channelled Whelk" and briefly explains Lindbergh's strategy for uncomplicating her life. The reference to Lindbergh gives Michael a chance to *contrast* the way she tries to lead her life with the acquisitive and frenzied way many of us lead ours. This contrast leads logically to the essay's *thesis*: "We choose to clutter our lives with a stream of material possessions."

In the last sentence of the introductory paragraph, Michael provides a *plan of development* that reveals the paper's major supporting points and the order in which they will be discussed: (1) we spend a good deal of time buying things, (2) our possessions create complications, and (3) we have to work hard to pay for all our possessions. Essays of this length often do not need a plan of development. But Michael's paper is supported mainly through *exemplification* and thus is filled with many specific illustrations; the plan of development presents readers with the paper's overall structure, making it easier for them to see how all the details relate to the essay's central points. The plan of development also helps readers see that Michael's paper contains an element of *causal analysis*: the examples illustrate that our pursuit of possessions adversely affects our lives.

The *support* for the thesis consists of examples organized around the three major points. Michael uses one paragraph to develop his first and third points and two paragraphs to develop his second point. Each of the four supporting paragraphs is focused by a *topic sentence* which appears at the start of the paragraph: "We devote a great deal of our lives to acquiring the material goods we imagine are essential to our well-being" (paragraph 2); "As soon as we take our new purchases home, they begin to complicate our lives" (3); "After more time has gone by, we sometimes discover that our purchases don't suit us anymore, and so we decide to replace them" (4); and "Worst of all, this mania for possessions often influences our approach to work" (6). The transitional phrase "Worst of all" signals that Michael has sequenced his major points *emphatically,* saving for last the issue he considers most significant.

Now let's look more closely at some of the other techniques Michael uses to organize the essay. When reading the paper, you probably felt that there was an easy flow from one supporting paragraph to the next. How does Michael achieve such a graceful progression? Look closely at the topic sentences that introduce the third and fourth paragraphs. Note the way the beginning of each sentence (in italics) *links back* to the preceding paragraph: "*As soon as we take our new purchases home,* they . . . complicate our lives," and "*After more time has gone by,* we . . . discover . . . our purchases don't suit us. . . ."

Similar organizing strategies are used within the paragraphs to link material. For instance, the details in the supporting paragraphs are sequenced *chronologically.* Thus, the third paragraph starts by describing purchases that have just been brought home and then moves to what happens to the purchases after they have been home for a while. To help readers follow the chronological progression of points within the supporting paragraphs, Michael uses strong *transitional signals:* "*Moreover, once* we find what we are looking for, more time is taken up . . ." (2); "*Eventually,* of course, the inevitable happens" (3); "*Then* we have to handle phone calls . . ." (4).

As you read Michael's essay, you might have noticed that his paragraph development is not always consistent. You probably recall that an essay developed primarily through examples must include illustrative material that is *interesting, relevant, convincing,* and *sufficiently detailed.* On the whole, Michael's specifics are fairly successful in meeting these requirements. The third and fourth paragraphs especially include vigorous details that show how our mania for buying things can govern our lives. We may even laugh with self-recognition when reading about "skintight jeans that can't be thrown in the washing machine" or a "basement . . . filled with . . . discarded purchases."

But in other spots, Michael runs into trouble preparing well-developed paragraphs. Consider the second paragraph. The sentences "No wonder children spend so much time in front of the television set. Their parents are seldom around" disrupt the unity of the paragraph by introducing an issue unrelated to the paragraph's controlling idea. And once these two sentences are deleted, it becomes apparent that the paragraph is not very substantial. Indeed, the fact that the paragraph is now shorter than the introduction signals that more material is needed. To give the paragraph more solidity, Michael could go into more detail about a typical weekend shopping spree or an elaborate ritual preceding the purchase of some nonessential item.

The fifth paragraph is similarly underdeveloped. We know that this paragraph presents what Michael considers his most significant point, but the details in the paragraph are flat and unconvincing. When compared to the energetic specifics found in the third and fourth paragraphs, this section of the paper seems anticlimactic. More support and vigorous details are needed to round out this final supporting section. Michael could, for instance, mention specific people he knows who overspend, revealing how much they are in debt and how much they have to work to become solvent again. Or he could cite a television documentary or magazine article dealing with the issue of consumer debt. Such specifics would give the paragraph the solidity it now lacks.

The fifth paragraph has a second, more subtle problem; it presents an abrupt *shift in tone*. Although critical of our possession-mad culture, up to now Michael has poked fun at our obsession, keeping his tone conversational and gently satiric. But in this paragraph, Michael suddenly adopts a serious tone. And he assumes a preachy, somewhat moralistic stance in the next paragraph. It is, of course, legitimate to have a serious message in a lightly satiric piece. In fact, most satiric pieces have such an additional layer of meaning. But because Michael has trouble blending these two moods, there is a jarring shift in the feeling of the essay.

Although the essay needs work in spots, it is much stronger than Michael's first draft. To see the kind of rethinking Michael did when revising the paper, take a moment to compare the second and third supporting paragraphs above with what he originally wrote.

First Draft Version

Our lives are spent not only buying things but in dealing with the inevitable complications that are created by our newly acquired possessions. First, we have to find places to put all the objects we bring home. More clothes demand more closets; a second car demands more garage space; a home entertainment center requires elaborate shelving. We shouldn't be surprised that the average American family moves once every three years. A good many families move simply because they need more space to store all the things they buy. In addition, our possessions demand maintenance time. A person who gets a new car will spend hours washing it, waxing it, and vacuuming it. A new pair of jeans has to go to the dry cleaners. New stereo systems have to be connected to already existing equipment. Eventually, of course, the inevitable happens. Our new items need to be repaired. Or we get sick of them and decide to replace them. Before making our replacement purchases, though, we have to get rid of the old items. That can be a real inconvenience.

When Michael looked more closely at this paragraph, he realized it rambled and lacked energy. He started to revise the paragraph by tightening the first sentence, making it more focused and less awkward. Certainly, the revised sentence ("As soon as we take our new purchases home, they begin to complicate our lives") is crisper than the original. Next, he decided to omit the discussion about finding places to put new possessions; these sentences about inadequate closet, garage, and shelf space were so exaggerated that they undercut the valid point he wanted to make. He also chose to eliminate the sentences about the mobility of American families. This was, he felt, an interesting point, but it introduced an issue too complex to be included in the paragraph.

Next, Michael strengthened the rest of the paragraph by making the details more specific. A "new car" became a "sleek new sports car," and a "pair of jeans" became a "fashionable pair of skintight jeans." Michael also realized he had to do more than merely write, "Eventually, . . . our new items need to be repaired." This point had to be dramatized by sharp, convincing details. And so, for the revision, he generated lively specifics describing how things — microwaves, home computers, VCRs — break down. Similarly, Michael realized it wasn't enough simply to say, as he had in the original, that we run into problems when we try to replace out-of-favor purchases. Vigorous details were again needed to make such a point. Michael thus used a typical "replaceable," an old black-and-white TV, as his key example, showing the nuisance involved in handling phone calls and setting up appointments so people can see the TV.

After adding these specifics, Michael realized he had enough material to devote a separate paragraph to the problems associated with replacing old purchases. By dividing his original paragraph in two, Michael ended up with two well-focused paragraphs, neither of which has the rambling quality found in the draft version.

In short, Michael's revisions show that he understands how to make writing stronger through rigorous editing. One more round of attentive revising would have made his essay considerably stronger. But even without this additional work, Michael has prepared an interesting essay that provides a helpful perspective on one of our cultural preoccupations.

The selections that follow use abundant examples to make their points. At the heart of Paul Fussell's "A Well-Regulated

Militia" is a series of hypothetical examples, all illustrating Fussell's view on the gun-control issue. Betty Rollin uses lively anecdotes to sketch a memorable character study of a hard-to-please supervisor in "Allene Talmey." In "Channelled Whelk," Anne Morrow Lindbergh provides examples of two lives, one busy and chaotic, the other stripped to essentials. "Sexism and Language," by Alleen Pace Nilsen, presents numerous instances of the way our language discriminates against women. Last, hilarious examples of college misadventures make James Thurber's "University Days" a longstanding favorite.

Paul Fussell

Paul Fussell, a professor at Rutgers University for many years, now holds the Donald T. Regan Chair of English Literature at the University of Pennsylvania. Born in California in 1924, Fussell took his Ph.D. at Harvard after serving in World War II as an infantryman, an experience that influenced him profoundly. Fussell's reputation as a literary critic was firmly established by *Poetic Meter and Poetic Form,* published in 1965. Another book, *The Great War and Modern Memory* (1976), won Fussell much popular acclaim, earning the National Book Award. Currently a contributing editor at *Harper's* and *The New Republic,* Fussell's generally wry approach to his subjects is evident in *The Boy Scout Handbook and Other Observations* (1982) and in *Class: A Guide Through the American Status System* (1983), both well-received collections of essays. The selection below is taken from Fussell's most recent book, *Thank God for the Atom Bomb* (1988).

A Well-Regulated Militia

Poll after poll reveals that most Americans favor additional gun-control legislation. But the National Rifle Association resists further restrictions, contending that the Second Amendment guarantees the right to own firearms. Paul Fussell invites NRA advocates to look more closely at the Second Amendment and shows — with a winning combination of irony and logic — what would happen if the first part of the Amendment were taken as literally as the last.

In the spring Washington swarms with high school graduating classes. They come to the great pulsating heart of the Republic — which no one has yet told them is Wall Street — to be impressed by the White House and the Capitol and the monuments and the Smithsonian and the space capsules. Given the

187

state of public secondary education, I doubt if many of these young people are at all interested in language and rhetoric, and I imagine few are fascinated by such attendants of power and pressure as verbal misrepresentation and disingenuous quotation. But any who are can profit from a stroll past the headquarters of the National Rifle Association of America, its slick marble façade conspicuous at 1600 Rhode Island Avenue, NW.

There they would see an entrance flanked by two marble   2
panels offering language, and language more dignified and traditional than that customarily associated with the Association's gun-freak constituency, with its T-shirts reading GUNS, GUTS, AND GLORY ARE WHAT MADE AMERICA GREAT and its belt buckles proclaiming I'LL GIVE UP MY GUN WHEN THEY PRY MY COLD DEAD FINGERS FROM AROUND IT. The marble panel on the right reads, "The right of the people to keep and bear arms shall not be infringed," which sounds familiar. So familiar that the student naturally expects the left-hand panel to honor the principle of symmetry by presenting the first half of the quotation, namely: "A well-regulated Militia, being necessary to the security of a free state, . . ." But looking to the left, the inquirer discovers not that clause at all but rather this lame list of NRA functions and specializations: "Firearms Safety Education. Marksmanship Training. Shooting for Recreation." It's as if in presenting its well-washed, shiny public face the NRA doesn't want to remind anyone of the crucial dependent clause of the Second Amendment, whose latter half alone it is so fond of invoking to urge its prerogatives. (Some legible belt buckles of members retreat further into a seductive vagueness, reading only, "Our American Heritage: the Second Amendment.") We infer that for the Association, the less emphasis on the clause about the militia, the better. Hence its pretense on the front of its premises that the quoted main clause is not crucially dependent on the now unadvertised subordinate clause—indeed, it's meaningless without it.

Because flying .38- and .45-caliber bullets rank close to   3
cancer, heart disease, and AIDS as menaces to public health in this country, the firearm lobby, led by the NRA, comes under liberal attack regularly, and with special vigor immediately after an assault on some conspicuous person like Ronald Reagan or John Lennon. Thus *The New Republic,* in April 1981, deplored the state of things but offered as a solution only the suggestion

that the whole Second Amendment be perceived as obsolete and amended out of the Constitution. This would leave the NRA with not a leg to stand on.

But here as elsewhere a better solution would be not to fiddle   4
with the Constitution but to take it seriously, the way we've done with the First Amendment, say, or with the Thirteenth, the one forbidding open and avowed slavery. And by taking the Second Amendment seriously I mean taking it literally. We should "close read" it and thus focus lots of attention on the grammatical reasoning of its two clauses. This might shame the NRA into pulling the dependent clause out of the closet, displaying it on its façade, and accepting its not entirely pleasant implications. These could be particularized in an Act of Congress providing:

(1) that the Militia shall now, after these many years, be   5
"well regulated," as the Constitution requires.

(2) that any person who has chosen to possess at home a gun   6
of any kind, and who is not a member of the police or the military or an appropriate government agency, shall be deemed to have enrolled automatically in the Militia of the United States. Members of the Militia, who will be issued identifying badges, will be organized in units of battalion, company, or platoon size representing counties, towns, or boroughs. If they bear arms while not proceeding to or from scheduled exercises of the Militia, they will be punished "as a court martial may direct."

(3) that any gun owner who declines to join the regulated   7
Militia may opt out by selling his firearms to the federal government for $1,000 each. He will sign an undertaking that if he ever again owns firearms he will be considered to have enlisted in the Militia.

(4) that because the Constitution specifically requires that   8
the Militia shall be "well regulated," a regular training program, of the sort familiar to all who have belonged to military units charged with the orderly management of small arms, shall be instituted. This will require at least eight hours of drill each Saturday at some convenient field or park, rain or shine or snow or ice. There will be weekly supervised target practice (separation from the service, publicly announced, for those who can't hit a barn door). And there will be ample practice in digging simple defense works, like foxholes and trenches, as well as necessary sanitary installations like field latrines and straddle trenches. Each

summer there will be a six-week bivouac (without spouses), and this, like all the other exercises, will be under the close supervision of long-service noncommissioned officers of the United States Army and the Marine Corps. On bivouac, liquor will be forbidden under extreme penalty, but there will be an issue every Friday night of two cans of 3.2 beer, and feeding will follow traditional military lines, the cuisine consisting largely of shit-on-a-shingle, sandwiches made of bull dick (baloney) and choke-ass (cheese), beans, and fatty pork. On Sundays and holidays, powdered eggs for breakfast. Chlorinated water will often be available, in Lister Bags. Further obligatory exercises designed to toughen up the Militia will include twenty-five-mile hikes and the negotiation of obstacle courses. In addition, there will be instruction of the sort appropriate to other lightly armed, well-regulated military units: in map-reading, the erection of double-apron barbed-wire fences, and the rudiments of military courtesy and the traditions of the Militia, beginning with the Minute Men. Per diem payments will be made to those participating in these exercises.

(5) that since the purpose of the Militia is, as the Constitu-   9
tion says, to safeguard "the security of a free state," at times when invasion threatens (perhaps now the threat will come from Nicaragua, national security no longer being menaced by North Vietnam) all units of the Militia will be trucked to the borders for the duration of the emergency, there to remain in field conditions (here's where the practice in latrine-digging pays off) until Congress declares that the emergency has passed. Congress may also order the Militia to perform other duties consistent with its constitutional identity as a regulated volunteer force: for example, flood and emergency and disaster service (digging, sandbag filling, rescuing old people); patrolling angry or incinerated cities; or controlling crowds at large public events like patriotic parades, motor races, and professional football games.

(6) that failure to appear for these scheduled drills, practices,   10
bivouacs, and mobilizations shall result in the Militiaperson's dismissal from the service and forfeiture of badge, pay, and firearm.

.   .   .   .

Why did the Framers of the Constitution add the word *bear* to the phrase "keep and bear arms"? Because they conceived that keeping arms at home implied the public obligation to bear them in a regulated way for "the security of" not a private household but "a free state." If interstate bus fares can be regulated, it is hard to see why the Militia can't be, especially since the Constitution says it must be. *The New Republic* has recognized that "the Second Amendment to the Constitution clearly connects the right to bear arms to the 18th-century national need to raise a militia." But it goes on: "That need is now obsolete, and so is the amendment." And it concludes: "If the only way this country can get control of firearms is to amend the Constitution, then it's time for Congress to get the process under way."

I think not. Rather, it's time not to amend Article II of the   11
Bill of Rights (and Obligations) but to read it, publicize it, embrace it, and enforce it. That the Second Amendment stems from concerns that can be stigmatized as "18th-century" cuts little ice. The First Amendment stems precisely from such concerns, and no one but Yahoos wants to amend it. Also "18th-century" is that lovely bit in Section 9 of Article I forbidding any "Title of Nobility" to be granted by the United States. That's why we've been spared Lord Annenberg and Sir Leonard Bernstein, Knight. Thank God for the eighteenth century, I say. It understood not just what a firearm is and what a Militia is. It also understood what "well-regulated" means. It knew how to compose a constitutional article and it knew how to read it. And it assumed that everyone, gun lobbyists and touring students alike, would understand and correctly quote it. Both halves of it.

Questions for Close Reading

1. What is the thesis of the selection? Locate the sentence(s) in which Fussell states his main idea. If he does not state the thesis explicitly, express it in your own words.
2. Why is the subordinate clause that mentions "a well-regulated Militia" so crucial to the meaning of the Second Amendment? How does the author explain the NRA's reluctance to refer to this clause when the organization argues for the right to "keep and bear arms"?
3. Why does *The New Republic* propose that we repeal the Second Amendment? What is the author's response to this idea? Would his proposal have the same or different effect as *The New Republic*'s? Explain.

4. Explain what Fussell means when, in paragraph 1, he tells us that "verbal misrepresentation and disingenuous quotation" are "attendants of power and pressure." In what way does his discussion of the NRA help illustrate this point?
5. Refer to your dictionary as needed to define the following words in the selection: *disingenuous* (paragraph 1), *façade* (1), *constituency* (2), *avowed* (4), *bivouac* (8), *rudiments* (8), *per diem* (8), *stigmatized* (11), and *Yahoos* (11).

Questions About the Writer's Craft

1. Fussell provides, in the form of a facetious proposal to be passed by Congress, six examples of what would happen if the Second Amendment were to be taken seriously. What principle has Fussell used to organize this list of examples? Why does he wait until item six to explain the penalties for failing to attend scheduled drills, bivouacs, and mobilizations?
2. Why might Fussell have chosen to begin his essay with a description of the high school students who visit Washington each spring? How does what he says about them help him introduce his discussion of the firearms controversy?
3. Fussell's tone is aggressive and often sarcastic. Identify several examples of sarcasm in the essay. Does Fussell's caustic humor and sometimes raw language enhance or diminish the persuasiveness of his argument? Explain.
4. Why does Fussell end his essay with a sentence fragment? What purpose does the fragment serve?

Questions for Further Thought

1. Is the author being fair in his characterization of NRA members? If you know anyone who belongs to this organization, discuss the way he or she does or does not fit Fussell's stereotype.
2. What do you think is the best way to resolve the controversy surrounding the Second Amendment? Do you side with Fussell? Do you believe that we ought to adopt the plan advanced by *The New Republic,* or do you think we should rewrite the Second Amendment altogether? Explain.
3. In paragraph 1, the author suggests that Wall Street, not Washington, is "the great pulsating heart of the Republic." Is there any truth to this notion, or is this just an example of gratuitous sarcasm? Explain.
4. Fussell emphasizes that the Second Amendment calls for a Militia that is "well-regulated." What do you think he means? How would you define this term? What measures do you believe we should take to keep our armed forces "well-regulated"?

Writing Assignments Using Exemplification as a Method of Development

*1. What examples of linguistic manipulation or doublespeak have you observed in the remarks of public figures, in the language used by the media, in the world of advertising? Select one area and, with a series of detailed, specific examples, develop the point that, as Fussell says, "verbal misrepresentation and disingenuous quotation" are all around us. Before you begin writing, you might want to read Ann McClintock's "Propaganda Techniques in Today's Advertising" (page 502) and/or H. L. Mencken's "The Politician" (page 437) to gather details and insights.

2. Try your hand at Fussell's kind of tongue-in-cheek satire. Draw on a series of facetious examples to illustrate the desirability or undesirability of a proposed or already existing regulation or policy. You could, for instance, show how absurd it would be for colleges to enforce dorm curfews or how beneficial it would be if public school teachers had to pass periodic competency tests. Whatever topic you select, be sure the facetious examples reinforce your opinion of the policy.

Writing Assignments Using Other Methods of Development

3. Do you believe that individual citizens should have the right to bear arms? Citing examples from your own or other people's experience and from what you have read or heard, write an essay in which you defend your position. Part of the essay should acknowledge, perhaps even refute, the opposing viewpoint. As needed, use the *Readers' Guide to Periodical Literature* to locate relevant articles that will help you develop your thesis.

4. Near the end of his essay, Fussell tells us that no one but a "Yahoo" would want to amend the First Amendment. Use a dictionary to look up the meaning and origin of this term. Then write an essay offering *your* definition of a Yahoo. The definition should be developed with numerous examples of the characteristics and personality traits you think make a person a Yahoo.

Betty Rollin

Betty Rollin has been a writer and editor at *Vogue* and *Look* magazines. More recently, she has been a correspondent for ABC News. Her 1976 book describing her battle with breast cancer, *First You Cry,* attracted much praise and notoriety, as has her most recent book, *Last Wish* (1985), about her terminally ill mother's suicide. The following excerpt is taken from Rollin's second book, *Am I Getting Paid for This?,* written in 1982.

Allene Talmey

Everyone has a horror story about a demanding boss or teacher. We complain to friends about unpaid overtime, 20-page papers due in two weeks, impossible standards. Betty Rollin had this kind of tough boss when she was a writer for *Vogue.* But Rollin does not write to criticize Miss Talmey. Instead, with a shiver and a touch of humor, she praises her boss and thanks her for the important lesson she taught: "good enough" is just not good enough.

Vogue was tough. The fashion department was tough because it was supposed to be the best—and, under Diana Vreeland, it was. And the features department was tough because fashion, not features, sold the magazine, so the features department could afford to be the best—which, among the women's magazines, under Allene Talmey, *it* probably was. Operative words: Allene Talmey. When she wanted to, Miss Talmey had a special ability to make those who thought they were tough cower. And she wanted to a lot. Those of us who did not think we were tough did not cower; we crumbled. We shriveled. We dissolved. I know Joan Didion only slightly, but we share a unique Pavlovian symptom: to this day should we see or speak to or run into Allene Talmey —and Joan says the same holds true on coast-to-coast telephone calls—our knees give. And the funny thing is, we both love her.

Throughout my tenure at *Vogue*, mercifully brief though it

1

2

was, on an average of once or twice a week, something Miss Talmey said — sometimes it was just a look — would lead me to close my office door, lean against it, and cry. It wasn't that Miss Talmey raised her voice, nor even that she got angry. It was simply her way of making everyone who entered her office and stood on the other side of her desk feel like a worm. Say, God forbid, you wrote a convoluted sentence. She would call you into her office (you never knew at those times what you had done, only that it was bad), you would then lower yourself onto the straight-backed polished mahogany chair that faced her desk, hoping, all the while, that your beating heart would not rupture your chest wall. Whereupon she would look at you and, with her eyes fixed on your face, she'd hold up with two fingers — as if it were a soiled bedsheet — this execrable thing you had written. Slowly, she would read the offending sentence, lingering and slightly increasing the volume of her voice, when she got to the (particularly) offensive passage. Then she would place the paper down on her desk and look at you again.

"What is it you are trying to say, dear?" she would ask, pronouncing the word *dear* in the same tone of voice that is normally used for the word *moron*. Then, falteringly, you would say what you were "trying to say." You always knew what would come next, but it had the same sting as a surprise: 3

"Why didn't you *write* it that way, dear?" Unless you were so stupid as to try to explain, you would then rise, bite your lip (or your hand, whichever was nearer), take your paper back, and, as rapidly as possible, leave the room. 4

Convolution, however, was not the greatest sin. Writing a cliché was. In that event, the meeting would be shorter and less cordial. Sometimes she would stand behind her desk and, as you entered, spit the cliché at you: "*High as a kite?*" Then, again, louder and slower, letting each syllable drip like slime: "*High — as — a — KITE?*" Then she would thrust the article or caption or whatever it was at you, as if it had been used to wrap a flounder, with a final, deadly: "Change it." 5

There were two other women writers in the department and two secretaries, clustered in a small suite of offices, which, except for the bright green carpeting (leftovers from the fashion floor), looked like an accounting firm. Each of us dealt with the Talmey 6 situation differently. The secretaries dealt with it by being perfect. The most senior other writer dealt with it by being cool (I never figured out if it was an act or if she had something surgical done to sever her nerve endings). The third woman, who was married to a French diplomat, handled it by being lah-dee-dah. "Really, how *boring* of her," she would say, swishing past me in the small office we shared, having just retrieved one of her pieces from the meat grinder.

Miss Talmey's reactions to pieces were not always delivered   7
in person. Sometimes she wrote down what she thought in the margin and sent it back.

Once I submitted an idea for a piece for the Beautiful People   8
series, which was in full swing then. Almost every issue of the magazine had a spread on the Beautiful People of Rome, the Beautiful People of Tangiers, the Beautiful People of Palm Beach, and so forth. The previous evening I had gone to a dinner party in Brooklyn Heights—a rather fancy section of Brooklyn—at which there were a number of social types who, it seemed to me, made the grade as Beautiful People. So, the next morning, I wrote a memo to Miss Talmey, suggesting *Vogue* do the Beautiful People in Brooklyn. I went to lunch before getting a reply. When I returned, I walked into my office and noticed that the memo had been placed back on my desk. I read the comment in the margin upside down: "*Good, Good!*" I was thrilled—and not too surprised. I *knew* I had a winner—an idea which was in keeping with the concept, yet it had a fresh twist. To think I had actually hesitated before submitting it! I shook my head and smiled to myself. Go with your instincts, I thought, go with your instincts. (I was at the stage where I liked to make lessons out of things.)

Then I walked around to the front of my desk and read the   9
comment right side up. "Good God!" it said.

One reason for Miss Talmey's power over people—aside   10
from the fact that she was the boss, aside from the fact that she knew how, and loved, to terrorize—was that Miss Talmey was always right. Also, she knew everything. She thought we writers should know everything, too. Now and then, probably to make sure that we *knew* that she thought we should know everything, she gave quizzes. The quizzes were not formal. They just felt formal. It wasn't so bad when they were given to the three of us, together. That way, at least, you could usually count on someone

else besides yourself making a mistake. To be quizzed alone, however, was excruciating. Usually, a quiz followed a transgression. Once, for example, I spelled the choreographer George Balanchine's name wrong. Miss Talmey *hated* spelling errors. *Vogue* has a "checker" whose job it was to check spelling and punctuation, so there was little danger of an error going uncorrected (only the Lord could save her if she overlooked one) into the magazine; but Miss Talmey held that the writer should *never* depend on the checker and a writer who made a spelling error was simply and inexcusably *sloppy*. In addition to which, an error connoted *ignorance* and even more contemptible than *slop* was *ignorance*.

"How do you spell Balanchine, dear?" I was standing. She 11
was seated at her desk. Her eyes were on the paper.

"D-did I spell it wrong?" I said, trying to keep my voice in a 12
normal range.

"You spelled it B-a-l-*e*. There is only one *e*" — she was look- 13
ing at me now — "in Mr. Balanchine's name and that is at the end."

"Of course — I — I knew that — I don't know why I — " 14

"Do you ever go to the ballet, dear?" Oh, God, it was going 15
to be a ballet quiz. But maybe not: "Do you read newspapers, dear?"

"I read the *Times*," I said, confused now. 16

"Is that all?" she said. 17

I had no idea where this was leading — only that it was 18
making me feel faint. "S-sometimes I read the *Post* — and, occasionally, *The Wall Street Journal*." (That was a lie. I never read *The Wall Street Journal*.)

"Do you read all sections of the newspaper?" she asked. 19

"Well, I try to," I said. (Another lie.) 20

"Who is Willie Mays?" My mouth went dry and my toes 21
curled under in my shoes.

"He's a baseball player, I think." 22

"You *think*?" said Miss Talmey. "What team does he play 23
for?"

"I'm not sure," I whispered, knowing all was lost. 24

"He plays for the Giants, dear," she said, pronouncing each 25
word as if I were a lip-reader. "His batting average last year was three fourteen. You should know that. From now on, when you

read the newspapers, dear, read every section. *Every* section of *every* newspaper." And then, as she was wont to do sometimes when the beating was over, she moved the corners of her mouth sideways (her version of a smile). "Okay?"

"Yes, Miss Talmey," I said, backing out.   26

Questions for Close Reading

1. What is the thesis of the selection? Locate the sentence(s) in which Rollin states her main idea. If she does not state the thesis explicitly, express it in your own words.
2. What was Miss Talmey's function at *Vogue?* What department did she rule? Who worked in the department?
3. What were Talmey's standards for her staff? What things did she hate?
4. How did Talmey reveal her displeasure? What were the reactions of her staff?
5. Refer to your dictionary as needed to define the following words in the selection: *cower* (paragraph 1), *convoluted* (2), *cordial* (5), *excruciating* (10), and *transgression* (10).

Questions About the Writer's Craft

1. Rollin provides several examples of Talmey's treatment of her staff. Why does she put Talmey's reaction to the "sin" of convolution first in the essay? Why does she save the example of the "quiz" for last?
2. The author reveals Allene Talmey to us by showing her effect on her subordinates. Why does Rollin keep strictly to this external view of her subject, rather than, for example, report Talmey's point of view on editing or running a magazine?
3. What is striking about the sentence patterns in the first paragraph? Why do you think Rollin chose this style for her introduction to Allene Talmey? How do these sentences affect you?
4. Rollin uses strong images and comparisons to convey the effect that Talmey had on her subordinates. Find some of these images. Are any of them exaggerated or humorous? How do they affect the tone of the essay?

Questions for Further Thought

1. Why would a writer, or any employee, stay in a job with a boss like Talmey? What positive effects might there be?
2. Does Rollin's account of her editor challenge or confirm common stereotypes about "lady editors" and female bosses?

3. What is the best way to handle a boss who loves "to terrorize"? Would you use one of the techniques described in paragraph 6 or handle Talmey another way if you worked under her?

4. It has been said there are two types of authority figures, those we love and those we fear. Which type do you prefer? Which is more effective? When you become a parent, boss, or a leader, which type will you try to be?

Writing Assignments Using Exemplification as a Method of Development

*1. Drawing on your past employment and educational experiences, write an essay explaining whether you prefer a demanding or supportive work/school environment. Use numerous examples from your experience to support the essay's thesis. Before planning the paper, you may find it helpful to read two other essays on work: Sue Hubbell's "The Beekeeper" (page 253) and Richard Rodriguez's "Workers" (page 333).

2. For *Vogue* staffers under Allene Talmey, there were some mistakes that were "unforgivable"—using a cliché, for example. Write an essay that gives examples of some unforgivable mistakes of another occupation or role. For example, you might describe what errors would be unforgivable for a parent, a driver, a roommate, a student, a salesperson, and so on. Your essay may be serious or playful. In either case, provide specific examples and anecdotes drawn from your experiences.

Writing Assignments Using Other Methods of Development

3. Write a descriptive character sketch of the toughest boss, teacher, or leader you ever had to work under. Follow Rollin's example in providing examples, dialogue, anecdotes, and sharp images to make your subject come alive.

4. What is the best style for a boss or manager to use with his or her staff? Read in the library about leadership or management styles. There are a number of magazines that regularly discuss techniques helpful to supervisors. Decide what approach you would take if and when you found it necessary to manage people. Write an essay explaining how you would manage effectively. To back up your analysis, use the information, quotations, facts, and so on found in your reading.

Anne Morrow Lindbergh

Anne Morrow Lindbergh (1906–) has had a successful career as a novelist, diarist, essayist, poet. In 1962, she published her first novel, *Dearly Beloved,* a book about the Apollo moon mission, to be followed in 1969 by *Earth Shine,* and several well-received volumes of collected letters and diaries. The following selection first appeared in *Gift from the Sea* (1955).

Channelled Whelk

"The world is too much with us, late and soon/Getting and spending, we lay waste our powers." Poet William Wordsworth wrote these lines in the early nineteenth century, but they still characterize our lives today. Like human pinballs, many of us bounce from one set of responsibilities to another —from career to family life to school and community service. In this essay, Anne Morrow Lindbergh reflects on the longed-for goal of simplicity and explains why it often eludes us in everyday living.

1   The shell in my hand is deserted. It once housed a whelk, a snail-like creature, and then temporarily, after the death of the first occupant, a little hermit crab, who has run away, leaving his tracks behind him like a delicate vine on the sand. He ran away, and left me his shell. It was once a protection to him. I turn the shell in my hand, gazing into the wide open door from which he made his exit. Had it become an encumbrance? Why did he run away? Did he hope to find a better home, a better mode of living? I too have run away, I realize, I have shed the shell of my life, for these few weeks of vacation.

2   But his shell—it is simple; it is bare, it is beautiful. Small, only the size of my thumb, its architecture is perfect, down to the finest detail. Its shape, swelling like a pear in the center, winds in a gentle spiral to the pointed apex. Its color, dull gold, is whit-

ened by a wash of salt from the sea. Each whorl, each faint knob, each criss-cross vein in its egg-shell texture, is as clearly defined as on the day of creation. My eye follows with delight the outer circumference of that diminutive winding staircase up which this tenant used to travel.

My shell is not like this, I think. How untidy it has become!   3
Blurred with moss, knobby with barnacles, its shape is hardly recognizable any more. Surely, it had a shape once. It has a shape still in my mind. What is the shape of my life?

The shape of my life today starts with a family. I have a   4
husband, five children and a home just beyond the suburbs of New York. I have also a craft, writing, and therefore work I want to pursue. The shape of my life is, of course, determined by many other things; my background and childhood, my mind and its education, my conscience and its pressures, my heart and its desires. I want to give to and take from my children and husband, to share with friends and community, to carry out my obligations to man and to the world as a woman, as an artist, as a citizen.

But I want first of all — in fact, as an end to these other   5
desires — to be at peace with myself. I want a singleness of eye, a purity of intention, a central core to my life that will enable me to carry out these obligations and activities as well as I can. I want, in fact — to borrow from the language of the saints — to live "in grace" as much of the time as possible. I am not using this term in a strictly theological sense. By grace I mean an inner harmony, essentially spiritual, which can be translated into outward harmony. I am seeking perhaps what Socrates asked for in the prayer from the *Phaedrus* when he said, "May the outward and inward man be at one." I would like to achieve a state of inner spiritual grace from which I could function and give as I was meant to in the eye of God.

Vague as this definition may be, I believe most people are   6
aware of periods in their lives when they seem to be "in grace" and other periods in their lives when they feel "out of grace," even though they may use different words to describe these states. In the first happy condition, one seems to carry all one's tasks before one lightly, as if borne along on a great tide; and in the opposite state one can hardly tie a shoe-string. It is true that a large part of life consists in learning a technique of tying the shoe-string, whether one is in grace or not. But there are tech-

niques of living too; there are even techniques in the search for grace. And techniques can be cultivated. I have learned by some experience, by many examples, and by the writings of countless others before me, also occupied in the search, that certain environments, certain modes of life, certain rules of conduct are more conducive to inner and outer harmony than others. There are, in fact, certain roads that one may follow. Simplification of life is one of them.

I mean to lead a simple life, to choose a simple shell I can 7 carry easily — like a hermit crab. But I do not. I find that my frame of life does not foster simplicity. My husband and five children must make their way in the world. The life I have chosen as wife and mother entrains a whole caravan of complications. It involves a house in the suburbs and either household drudgery or household help which wavers between scarcity and non-existence for most of us. It involves food and shelter; meals, planning, marketing, bills, and making the ends meet in a thousand ways. It involves not only the butcher, the baker, the candlestickmaker but countless other experts to keep my modern house with its modern "simplifications" (electricity, plumbing, refrigerator, gas-stove, oil-burner, dish-washer, radios, car, and numerous other labor-saving devices) functioning properly. It involves health; doctors, dentists, appointments, medicine, cod-liver oil, vitamins, trips to the drugstore. It involves education, spiritual, intellectual, physical; schools, school conferences, carpools, extra trips for basket-ball or orchestra practice; tutoring; camps, camp equipment and transportation. It involves clothes, shopping, laundry, cleaning, mending, letting skirts down and sewing buttons on, or finding someone else to do it. It involves friends, my husband's, my children's, my own, and endless arrangements to get together; letters, invitations, telephone calls and transportation hither and yon.

For life today in America is based on the premise of ever-wid- 8 ening circles of contact and communication. It involves not only family demands, but community demands, national demands, international demands on the good citizen, through social and cultural pressures, through newspapers, magazines, radio programs, political drives, charitable appeals, and so on. My mind reels with it. What a circus act we women perform every day of our lives. It puts the trapeze artist to shame. Look at us. We run a tight rope daily, balancing a pile of books on the head. Baby-carriage, parasol, kitchen chair, still under control. Steady now!

This is not the life of simplicity but the life of multiplicity that the wise men warn us of. It leads not to unification but to fragmentation. It does not bring grace; it destroys the soul. And this is not only true of my life, I am forced to conclude; it is the life of millions of women in America. I stress America, because today, the American woman more than any other has the privilege of choosing such a life. Woman in large parts of the civilized world has been forced back by war, by poverty, by collapse, by the sheer struggle to survive, into a smaller circle of immediate time and space, immediate family life, immediate problems of existence. The American woman is still relatively free to choose the wider life. How long she will hold this enviable and precarious position no one knows. But her particular situation has a significance far above its apparent economic, national or even sex limitations.   9

For the problem of the multiplicity of life not only confronts the American woman, but also the American man. And it is not merely the concern of the American as such, but of our whole modern civilization, since life in America today is held up as the ideal of a large part of the rest of the world. And finally, it is not limited to our present civilization, though we are faced with it now in an exaggerated form. It has always been one of the pitfalls of mankind. Plotinus was preaching the dangers of multiplicity of the world back in the third century. Yet, the problem is particularly and essentially woman's. Distraction is, always has been, and probably always will be, inherent in woman's life.   10

For to be a woman is to have interests and duties, raying out in all directions from the central mother-core, like spokes from the hub of a wheel. The pattern of our lives is essentially circular. We must be open to all points of the compass; husband, children, friends, home, community; stretched out, exposed, sensitive like a spider's web to each breeze that blows, to each call that comes. How difficult for us, then, to achieve a balance in the midst of these contradictory tensions, and yet how necessary for the proper functioning of our lives. How much we need, and how arduous of attainment is that steadiness preached in all rules for holy living. How desirable and distant is the ideal of the contemplative, artist, or saint — the inner inviolable core, the single eye.   11

With a new awareness, both painful and humorous, I begin 12
to understand why the saints were rarely married women. I am
convinced it has nothing inherently to do, as I once supposed,
with chastity or children. It has to do primarily with distractions.
The bearing, rearing, feeding and educating of children; the running of a house with its thousand details; human relationships
with their myriad pulls — woman's normal occupations in general run counter to creative life, or contemplative life, or saintly
life. The problem is not merely one of *Woman and Career,*
Woman and the Home, Woman and Independence. It is more
basically: how to remain whole in the midst of the distractions of
life; how to remain balanced, no matter what centrifugal forces
tend to pull one off center; how to remain strong, no matter what
shocks come in at the periphery and tend to crack the hub of the
wheel.

What is the answer? There is no easy answer, no complete 13
answer. I have only clues, shells from the sea. The bare beauty of
the channelled whelk tells me that one answer, and perhaps a first
step, is in simplification of life, in cutting out some of the distractions. But how? Total retirement is not possible. I cannot
shed my responsibilities. I cannot permanently inhabit a desert
island. I cannot be a nun in the midst of family life. I would not
want to be. The solution for me, surely, is neither in total renun-
ciation of the world, nor in total acceptance of it. I must find a
balance somewhere, or an alternating rhythm between these two
extremes; a swinging of the pendulum between solitude and
communion, between retreat and return. In my periods of retreat,
perhaps I can learn something to carry back into my worldly life. I
can at least practice for these two weeks the simplification of
outward life, as a beginning. I can follow this superficial clue, and
see where it leads. Here, in beach living, I can try.

One learns first of all in beach living the art of shedding; how 14
little one can get along with, not how much. Physical shedding to
begin with, which then mysteriously spreads into other fields.
Clothes, first. Of course, one needs less in the sun. But one needs
less anyway, one finds suddenly. One does not need a closet-full,
only a small suitcase-full. And what a relief it is! Less taking up
and down of hems, less mending, and — best of all — less worry
about what to wear. One finds one is shedding not only clothes
—but vanity.

Next, shelter. One does not need the airtight shelter one has   15
in winter in the North. Here I live in a bare sea-shell of a cottage.
No heat, no telephone, no plumbing to speak of, no hot water, a
two-burner oil stove, no gadgets to go wrong. No rugs. There
were some, but I rolled them up the first day; it is easier to sweep
the sand off a bare floor. But I find I don't bustle about with
unnecessary sweeping and cleaning here. I am no longer aware of
the dust. I have shed my Puritan conscience about absolute tidi-
ness and cleanliness. Is it possible that, too, is a material burden?
No curtains. I do not need them for privacy; the pines around my
house are enough protection. I want the windows open all the
time, and I don't want to worry about rain. I begin to shed my
Martha-like anxiety about many things. Washable slipcovers,
faded and old—I hardly see them; I don't worry about the
impression they make on other people. I am shedding pride. As
little furniture as possible; I shall not need much. I shall ask into
my shell only those friends with whom I can be completely
honest. I find I am shedding hypocrisy in human relationships.
What a result that will be! The most exhausting thing in life, I
have discovered, is being insincere. That is why so much of social
life is exhausting; one is wearing a mask. I have shed my mask.

I find I live quite happily without those things I think neces-   16
sary in winter in the North. And as I write these words, I remember, with some shock at the disparity in our lives, a similar
statement made by a friend of mine in France who spent three
years in a German prison camp. Of course, he said, qualifying his
remark, they did not get enough to eat, they were sometimes
atrociously treated, they had little physical freedom. And yet,
prison life taught him how little one can get along with, and what
extraordinary spiritual freedom and peace such simplification can
bring. I remember again, ironically, that today more of us in
America than anywhere else in the world have the luxury of
choice between simplicity and complication of life. And for the
most part, we, who could choose simplicity, choose complication. War, prison, survival periods, enforce a form of simplicity
on man. The monk and the nun choose it of their own free will.
But if one accidentally finds it, as I have for a few days, one finds
also the serenity it brings.

Is it not rather ugly, one may ask? One collects material   17
possessions not only for security, comfort or vanity, but for

beauty as well. Is your sea-shell house not ugly and bare? No, it is beautiful, my house. It is bare, of course, but the wind, the sun, the smell of the pines blow through its bareness. The unfinished beams in the roof are veiled by cobwebs. They are lovely, I think, gazing up at them with new eyes; they soften the hard lines of the rafters as grey hairs soften the lines on a middle-aged face. I no longer pull out grey hairs or sweep down cobwebs. As for the walls, it is true they looked forbidding at first. I felt cramped and enclosed by their blank faces. I wanted to knock holes in them, to give them another dimension with pictures or windows. So I dragged home from the beach grey arms of driftwood, worn satin-smooth by wind and sand. I gathered trailing green vines with floppy red-tipped leaves. I picked up the whitened skeletons of conchshells, their curious hollowed-out shapes faintly reminiscent of abstract sculpture. With these tacked to walls and propped up in corners, I am satisfied. I have a periscope out to the world. I have a window, a view, a point of flight from my sedentary base.

I am content. I sit down at my desk, a bare kitchen table with 18 a blotter, a bottle of ink, a sand dollar to weight down one corner, a clam shell for a pen tray, the broken tip of a conch, pink-tinged, to finger, and a row of shells to set my thoughts spinning.

I love my sea-shell of a house. I wish I could live in it always. 19 I wish I could transport it home. But I cannot. It will not hold a husband, five children and the necessities and trappings of daily life. I can only carry back my little channelled whelk. It will sit on my desk in Connecticut, to remind me of the ideal of a simplified life, to encourage me in the game I played on the beach. To ask how little, not how much, can I get along with. To say — is it necessary? — when I am tempted to add one more accumulation to my life, when I am pulled toward one more centrifugal activity.

Simplification of outward life is not enough. It is merely the 20 outside. But I am starting with the outside. I am looking at the outside of a shell, the outside of my life — the shell. The complete answer is not to be found on the outside, in an outward mode of living. This is only a technique, a road to grace. The final answer, I know, is always inside. But the outside can give a clue, can help one to find the inside answer. One is free, like the hermit crab, to change one's shell.

Channelled whelk, I put you down again, but you have set 21

my mind on a journey, up an inwardly winding spiral staircase of thought.

Questions for Close Reading

1. What is the thesis of the selection? Locate the sentence(s) in which Lindbergh states her main idea. If she does not state the thesis explicitly, express it in your own words.
2. What appeals to Lindbergh about the shell of the channelled whelk?
3. Why are distraction and "multiplicity" so much a problem for women, in particular? Why are they less of a problem for men, according to the author?
4. Since Lindbergh prefers the life at the beach house, why doesn't she remain there? Why does she take the shell away with her?
5. Refer to your dictionary as needed to define the following words used in the selection: *apex* (paragraph 2), *conducive* (6), *myriad* (12), *periphery* (12), and *sedentary* (17).

Questions About the Writer's Craft

1. Essays developed through exemplification often provide extended illustrations to develop key points. In what paragraphs does Lindbergh include extended illustrations to clarify what she means by "simplification"?
2. Why does Lindbergh begin her essay about the distractions of women's lives with a few paragraphs about a whelk shell? Where does she return to discussing the shell? What does the shell come to represent?
3. In paragraph 6, the author uses the image of "tying a shoe-string." What aspects of life is she referring to through this image? At what point do you recognize that she is using "tying a shoe-string" as a metaphor for a larger part of life?
4. Why does Lindbergh end the essay with a short "speech" or address to the whelk shell? How does this last paragraph extend an idea suggested in the paragraph before it?

Questions for Further Thought

1. Lindbergh writes, "I want first of all . . . to be at peace with myself." Besides her method of simplification, how else could she achieve this inner peace?
2. Could we ever eliminate all the distractions from our lives? Do you think this would be desirable?
3. Lindbergh says the problems she has with distractions is particularly a

woman's problem. Do you agree? Have women's lives—and men's—changed much since she wrote this essay?

4. How would *you* simplify your life, if you were given the opportunity? What would you shed? What would you be unable to shed? What might you be able to shed . . . but only after agonizing over it or getting help?

Writing Assignments Using Exemplification as a Method of Development

1. Write an essay about the excess of possessions in people's lives today. Give examples of people you know or have heard about. Alternatively, you may use fictional characters (from books or TV shows) whose lives are obsessed with possessions. Part of your essay should discuss the effect of these possessions on the quality of people's lives.

2. Lindbergh writes that she often feels fragmented into a series of selves because of the numerous demands—family, community, and political—made on her. Analyze your own life to identify the different roles you play. Write an essay detailing the "balancing act" you perform in your life. When describing each of your roles, be sure to provide specific examples of the demands claiming your attention. In the conclusion, point briefly to some things you could do to make your life less fragmented and more harmonious.

Writing Assignments Using Other Methods of Developments

*3. Imagine simplifying your own life to achieve greater inner harmony. How would you go about it? Before planning your paper, you might want to read Henry David Thoreau's "The Village" (page 327) or Janet Mendell Goldstein's "The Quick Fix Society" (page 512). In different ways, both essays focus on the value of leading less cluttered, more easy-paced lives. Then write an essay describing the process by which you would make your life simpler. For each step, include specific examples of activities, objects, relationships, and the like that you would eliminate.

4. Take a position opposed to Lindbergh's—that the multiplicity of our lives is beneficial to us. Argue that material possessions and our numerous "circles of contact" are necessary and advantageous. Use either a serious or a humorous tone.

Alleen Pace Nilsen

A specialist in children's literature, Alleen Pace Nilsen teaches
at Arizona State University and edits a newsletter on adolescent literature. Nilsen's doctoral dissertation concerned sexism
in the language of books written for children. The following
selection is from *Sexism and Language* (1977), a collection of
essays by various authors published by the National Council of
Teachers of English.

Sexism and Language

Is there anything wrong in calling a woman a "fox" or a
"chick"? Why is it embarrassing for a man to perform a job
labeled "women's work," while it is a compliment for a
woman to do "a man's job"? Would you rather be a female
named "Sam" or a male called "Carroll"? Your response to
these questions most likely results from the attitudes you have
acquired as a speaker of American English. In the following
selection, Alleen Pace Nilsen will make you look more closely
at the language you use, showing how seemingly innocent
words and phrases reflect society's attitudes toward the roles
— and worth — of men and women.

Over the last hundred years, American anthropologists have   1
travelled to the corners of the earth to study primitive cultures.
They either became linguists themselves or they took linguists
with them to help in learning and analyzing languages. Even if
the culture was one that no longer existed, they were interested in
learning its language because besides being tools of communication, the vocabulary and structure of a language tell much about
the values held by its speakers.

However, the culture need not be primitive, nor do the   2
people making observations need to be anthropologists and linguists. Anyone living in the United States who listens with a keen
ear or reads with a perceptive eye can come up with startling new
insights about the way American English reflects our values.

Animal Terms for People — Mirrors of the Double Standard

If we look at just one semantic area of English, that of animal   3
terms in relation to people, we can uncover some interesting
insights into how our culture views males and females. References
to identical animals can have negative connotations when related
to a female, but positive or neutral connotations when related to
a male. For example, a *shrew* has come to mean "a scolding,
nagging, evil-tempered woman," while *shrewd* means "keen-wit-
ted, clever, or sharp in practical affairs; astute . . . businessman,
etc." (*Webster's New World Dictionary of the American Language*,
1964).

A *lucky dog* or a *gay dog* may be a very interesting fellow, but   4
when a woman is a *dog*, she is unattractive, and when she's a *bitch*
she's the personification of whatever is undesirable in the mind of
the speaker. When a man is self-confident, he may be described as
cocksure or even *cocky*, but in a woman this same self-confidence is
likely to result in her being called a *cocky bitch*, which is not only a
mixed metaphor, but also probably the most insulting animal
metaphor we have. *Bitch* has taken on such negative
connotations — children are taught it is a swear word — that in
everyday American English, speakers are hesitant to call a female
dog a *bitch*. Most of us feel that we would be insulting the dog.
When we want to insult a man by comparing him to a dog, we
call him a *son of a bitch*, which quite literally is an insult to his
mother rather than to him.

If the female is called a *vixen* (a female fox), the dictionary   5
says this means she is "an ill-tempered, shrewish, or malicious
woman." The female seems both to attract and to hold on longer
to animal metaphors with negative connotations. A *vampire* was
originally a corpse that came alive to suck the blood of living
persons. The word acquired the general meaning of an unscrupulous person such as a blackmailer and then, the specialized meaning of "a beautiful but unscrupulous woman who seduces men
and leads them to their ruin." From this latter meaning we get the
word *vamp*. The popularity of this term and of the name *vampire
bat* may contribute to the idea that a female being is referred to in
a phrase such as *the old bat*.

Other animal metaphors do not have definitely derogatory   6 connotations for the female, but they do seem to indicate frivolity or unimportance, as in *social butterfly* and *flapper*. Look at the differences between the connotations of participating in a *hen party* and in a *bull session*. Male metaphors, even when they are negative in connotation, still relate to strength and conquest. Metaphors related to aggressive sex roles, for example, *buck, stag, wolf,* and *stud,* will undoubtedly remain attached to males. Perhaps one of the reasons that in the late sixties it was so shocking to hear policemen called *pigs* was that the connotations of *pig* are very different from the other animal metaphors we usually apply to males.

When I was living in Afghanistan, I was surprised at the cruelty and unfairness of a proverb that said, "When you see an old man, sit down and take a lesson; when you see an old woman, throw a stone." In looking at Afghan folk literature. I found that young girls were pictured as delightful and enticing, middle-aged women were sometimes interesting but more often just tolerable, while old women were always grotesque and villainous. Probably the reason for the negative connotation of old age in women is that women are valued for their bodies while men are valued for their accomplishments and their wisdom. Bodies deteriorate with age but wisdom and accomplishments grow greater.

When we returned home from Afghanistan, I was shocked to discover that we have remnants of this same attitude in America. We see it in our animal metaphors. If both the animal and the woman are young, the connotation is positive, but if the animal and the woman are old, the connotation is negative. Hugh Hefner might never have made it to the big time if he had called his girls *rabbits* instead of *bunnies*. He probably chose *bunny* because he wanted something close to, but not quite so obvious as *kitten* or *cat* — the all-time winners for connoting female sexuality. Also *bunny,* as in the skiers' *snow bunny,* already had some of the connotations Hefner wanted. Compare the connotations of *filly* to *old nag; bird* to *old crow* or *old bat;* and *lamb* to *crone* (apparently related to the early modern Dutch *kronje, old ewe* but now *withered old woman*).

Probably the most striking examples of the contrast between young and old women are animal metaphors relating to cats and chickens. A young girl is encouraged to be *kittenish,* but not *catty*. And though most of us wouldn't mind living next door to a *sex kitten,* we wouldn't want to live next door to a *cat house.* Parents might name their daughter *Kitty* but not *Puss* or *Pussy,* which used to be a fairly common nickname for girls. It has now developed such sexual connotations that it is used mostly for humor, as in the James Bond movie featuring Pussy Galore and her flying felines.

In the chicken metaphors, a young girl is a *chick.* When she   10
gets old enough she marries and soon begins feeling *cooped up.* To relieve the boredom she goes to *hen parties* and *cackles* with her friends. Eventually she has her *brood,* begins to *henpeck* her husband, and finally turns into an *old biddy.*

How English Glorifies Maleness

Throughout the ages physical strength has been very impor-   11
tant, and because men are physically stronger than women, they have been valued more. Only now in the machine age, when the difference in strength between males and females pales into insignificance in comparison to the strength of earth-moving machinery, airplanes, and guns, males no longer have such an inherent advantage. Today a man of intellect is more valued than a physical laborer, and since women can compete intellectually with men, their value is on the rise. But language lags far behind cultural changes, so the language still reflects this emphasis on the importance of being male. For example, when we want to compliment a male, all we need to do is stress the fact that he is male by saying he is a *he-man,* or he is *manly,* or he is *virile.* Both *virile* and *virtuous* come from the Latin *vir,* meaning *man.*

The command or encouragement that males receive in sen-   12
tences like "Be a man!" implies that *to be a man* is to be honorable, strong, righteous, and whatever else the speaker thinks desirable. But in contrast to this, a girl is never told to be a *woman.* And when she is told to be a *lady,* she is simply being encouraged to "act feminine," which means sitting with her knees together, walking gracefully, and talking softly.

The armed forces, particularly the Marines, use the positive   13
masculine connotation as part of their recruitment psychology. They promote the idea that to join the Marines (or the Army, Navy, or Air Force) guarantees that you will become a man. But

this brings up a problem, because much of the work that is necessary to keep a large organization running is what is traditionally thought of as *women's work*. Now, how can the Marines ask someone who has signed up for a *man-sized job* to do *women's work*? Since they can't, they euphemize and give the jobs titles that either are more prestigious or, at least, don't make people think of females. Waitresses are called *orderlies,* secretaries are called *clerk-typists,* nurses are called *medics,* assistants are called *adjutants,* and cleaning up an area is called *policing* the area. The same kind of word glorification is used in civilian life to bolster a man's ego when he is doing such tasks as cooking and sewing. For example, a *chef* has higher prestige than a *cook* and a *tailor* has higher prestige than a *seamstress.*

Little girls learn early in life that the boy's role is one to be envied and emulated. Child psychologists have pointed out that experimenting with the role of the opposite sex is much more acceptable for little girls than it is for little boys. For example, girls are free to dress in boys' clothes, but certainly not the other way around. Most parents are amused if they have a daughter who is a *tomboy,* but they are genuinely distressed if they have a son who is a *sissy.* The names we give to young children reflect this same attitude. It is all right for girls to have boys' names, but pity the boy who has a girl's name! Because parents keep giving boys' names to girls, the number of acceptable boys' names keeps shrinking. Currently popular names for girls include *Jo, Kelly, Teri, Chris, Pat, Shawn, Toni,* and *Sam* (short for *Samantha*). *Evelyn, Carroll, Gayle, Hazel, Lynn, Beverley, Marion, Francis,* and *Shirley* once were acceptable names for males. But as they were given to females, they became less and less acceptable. Today, men who are stuck with them self-consciously go by their initials or by abbreviated forms such as *Haze, Shirl, Frank,* or *Ev.* And they seldom pass these names on to their sons.

Many common words have come into the language from people's names. These lexical items again show the importance of maleness compared to the triviality of the feminine activities being described. Words derived from the names of women include *Melba toast,* named for the Australian singer Dame Nellie Melba; *Sally Lunn cakes,* named after an eighteenth-century woman who first made them; *pompadour,* a hair style named after

Madame Pompadour; and the word *maudlin,* as in *maudlin sentiment,* from Mary Magdalene, who was often portrayed by artists as displaying exaggerated sorrow.

There are trivial items named after men — *teddy bear* after Theodore Roosevelt and *sideburns* after General Burnside — but most words that come from men's names relate to significant inventions or developments. These include *pasteurization* after Louis Pasteur, *sousaphone* after John Philip Sousa, *mason jar* after John L. Mason, *boysenberry* after Rudolph Boysen, *pullman car* after George M. Pullman, *braille* after Louis Braille, *franklin stove* after Benjamin Franklin, *diesel engine* after Rudolf Diesel, *ferris wheel* after George W. G. Ferris, and the verb *to lynch* after William Lynch, who was a vigilante captain in Virginia in 1780.

The latter is an example of a whole set of English words dealing with violence. These words have strongly negative connotations. From research using free association and semantic differentials, with university students as subjects, James Ney concluded that English reflects both an anti-male and an anti-female bias because these biases exist in the culture (*Etc.: A Review of General Semantics,* March 1976, pp. 67–76). The students consistently marked as masculine such words as *killer, murderer, robber, attacker, fighter, stabber, rapist, assassin, gang, hood, arsonist, criminal, hijacker, villain,* and *bully,* even though most of these words contain nothing to specify that they are masculine. An example of bias against males, Ney observed, is the absence in English of a pejorative term for women equivalent to *rapist.* Outcomes of his free association test indicated that if "English speakers want to call a man something bad, there seems to be a large vocabulary available to them but if they want to use a term which is good to describe a male, there is a small vocabulary available. The reverse is true for women."

Certainly we do not always think positively about males; witness such words as *jerk, creep, crumb, slob, fink,* and *jackass.* But much of what determines our positive and negative feelings relates to the roles people play. We have very negative feelings toward someone who is hurting us or threatening us or in some way making our lives miserable. To be able to do this, the person has to have power over us and this power usually belongs to males.

On the other hand, when someone helps us or makes our life

more pleasant, we have positive feelings toward that person or that role. *Mother* is one of the positive female terms in English, and we see such extensions of it as *Mother Nature, Mother Earth, mother lode, mother superior,* etc. But even though a word like *mother* is positive it is still not a word of power. In the minds of English speakers being female and being powerless or passive are so closely related that we use the terms *feminine* and *lady* either to mean female or to describe a certain kind of quiet and unobtrusive behavior.

Words Labelling Women as Things

Because of our expectations of passivity, we like to compare   20
females to items that people acquire for their pleasure. For example, in a recent commercial for the television show "Happy Days," one of the characters announced that in the coming season they were going to have not only "cars, motorcycles, and girls," but also a band. Another example of this kind of thinking is the comparison of females to food since food is something we all enjoy, even though it is extremely passive. We describe females as such delectable morsels as a *dish,* a *cookie,* a *tart, cheesecake, sugar and spice,* a *cute tomato, honey,* a *sharp cookie,* and *sweetie pie.* We say a particular girl has a *peaches and cream complexion* or "she looks good enough to eat." And parents give their daughters such names as *Candy* and *Cherry.*

Other pleasurable items that we compare females to are toys.   21
Young girls are called *little dolls* or *China dolls,* while older girls —if they are attractive—are simply called *dolls.* We might say about a woman, "She's pretty as a picture," or "She's a fashion plate." And we might compare a girl to a plant by saying she is a *clinging vine,* a *shrinking violet,* or a *wallflower.* And we might name our daughters after plants such as *Rose, Lily, Ivy, Daisy, Iris,* and *Petunia.* Compare these names to boys' names such as *Martin* which means warlike, *Ernest* which means resolute fighter, *Nicholas* which means victory, *Val* which means strong or valiant, and *Leo* which means lion. We would be very hesitant to give a boy the name of something as passive as a flower although we might say about a man that he is a *late-bloomer.* This is making a comparison between a man and the most active thing a plant can do, which is to bloom. The only other familiar plant metaphor

used for a man is the insulting *pansy*, implying that he is like a woman.

Questions for Close Reading

1. What is the thesis of the selection? Locate the sentence(s) in which Nilsen states her main idea. If she does not state the thesis explicitly, express it in your own words.
2. According to Nilsen, when animal metaphors are used for human females, what do they usually imply? What do male animal metaphors imply?
3. Why, according to Nilsen, do some professions or jobs have different names depending on whether a male or female is performing them? What is implied by the existence of two different terms for the same job?
4. When positive terms are used for women, what personality characteristics do they suggest? Why are there so many words connoting violence that are most often applied to men?
5. Refer to your dictionary as needed to define the following words used in the selection: *unscrupulous* (paragraph 5), *enticing* (7), *connotation* (8), *virile* (11), *lexical* (15), *maudlin* (15), and *vigilante* (16).

Questions About the Writer's Craft

1. Why does Nilsen use so many examples to illustrate each type of sexism in the English language? What point of view is she trying to anticipate and counteract?
2. What are the three main sexist motifs in English that Nilsen examines? How does she signal to us that she is moving from one to another?
3. Why do you think Nilsen begins by discussing animal terms for humans? What effect does placing this section first have on you as a reader?
4. What is Nilsen's tone in this essay? What terms and expressions reveal her personal viewpoint on sexism in our language?

Questions for Further Thought

1. Do you think most users of English are aware of the sexism of many of our everyday expressions? Were you surprised by any of Nilsen's examples? Why or why not?
2. Nilsen writes that "American English reflects our values." Do you

agree that phrases like "man-sized jobs" and "women's work" or "cocky" and "old biddy" mean we are a sexist nation? Should we watch what we say to guard against biased terms and images for males and females?

3. The names for many professions and positions have been gender-identified: consider *policeman, chairman, actor/actress, master* and *journeyman,* and so on. Is it better to change these terms to uniform, nonsexual ones like *police officer, chairperson, actor,* and so on? Do these terms really affect our thinking about people's worth or the decisions young people make about their futures?

4. Can our language ever be made completely nonsexist? What changes would have to occur?

Writing Assignments Using Exemplification as a Method of Development

*1. The author claims that our language glorifies maleness and denigrates femaleness. Are there other areas of our lives where typical male behavior and attitudes are valued more than typical female roles or characteristics? Consider such areas as marriage, sports, clothing, occupations. Focusing on one area, write an essay showing that our culture glorifies one sex over the other. You might develop your essay by mentioning points made by Judy Syfers in "Why I Want a Wife" (page 432).

2. Our language embodies many prejudices besides sexism. There are many words and expressions that are based on or imply prejudice against skin colors, old age, youth, left-handedness, shortness, fatness, and so on. Explore one of these areas in an essay, using specific examples of prejudicial language to show how the words we use reflect our stereotypes and biases.

Writing Assignments Using Other Methods of Development

3. Gender-based stereotyping exists in many areas of our culture besides language. Imagine you are a visitor to the United States who knows nothing about the culture—perhaps you are a visitor from Mars. You observe people, watch TV for a week, and study several issues of a popular general interest magazine, such as *People, Time,* or *Newsweek.* Then you write a report back to your home about the differences in the United States between males and females. Using numerous examples to explain the dissimilarities, cover one or more of the following in your analysis: occupations, recreational activities, friendships, positions of leadership, and so forth.

4. Imagine that you are the opposite sex. How would your life so far have been different? Would you have been treated differently by your parents, teachers, and friends? Are there any specific experiences or events that would have turned out differently had you been a different sex? Write an essay persuading readers that your life would have been essentially the same *or* very different had you been born exactly as you are except for your sex.

James Thurber

American humorist James Thurber (1894–1961) is perhaps best known as the author of "The Secret Life of Walter Mitty." Thurber often wrote about people's longings, using his skill as a satirist to portray the humor and poignancy of the human condition. He was able to give his wit—which often bordered on the acerbic—full play during his long career at *The New Yorker,* where he wrote satiric essays and drew cartoons. He also wrote several humorous books, including *Is Sex Necessary?* (1929), which he coauthored with E. B. White; *Fables for Our Time* (1940); *My World and Welcome to It* (1942); and *Thurber Country* (1953). This selection first appeared in *My Life and Hard Times* (1933).

University Days

University catalogs depict higher education as one of life's loftier experiences, with confident undergrads strolling eagerly toward ivy-covered lecture halls. But in this hilarious essay, James Thurber takes the pomp and circumstance out of higher education. He reveals the bumbling, the incompetence, and the embarrassment that frequently beset him and his fellow students at Ohio State University. He shows professors with gritted teeth trying to educate the ineducable and coach the uncooperative. Even back in the early days of this century, college life was far from the idealized image depicted in the catalogs.

I passed all the other courses that I took at my university, but I could never pass botany. This was because all botany students had to spend several hours a week in a laboratory looking through a microscope at plant cells, and I could never see through a microscope. I never once saw a cell through a microscope. This used to enrage my instructor. He would wander around the laboratory pleased with the progress all the students were making in drawing the involved and, so I am told, interesting structure of

flower cells, until he came to me. I would just be standing there.
"I can't see anything," I would say. He would begin patiently
enough, explaining how anybody can see through a microscope,
but he would always end up in a fury, claiming that I could *too* see
through a microscope but just pretended that I couldn't. "It takes
away from the beauty of flowers anyway," I used to tell him. "We
are not concerned with beauty in this course," he would say. "We
are concerned solely with what I may call the *mechanics* of flars."
"Well," I'd say, "I can't see anything." "Try it just once again,"
he'd say, and I would put my eye to the microscope and see
nothing at all, except now and again a nebulous milky substance
—a phenomenon of maladjustment. You were supposed to see a
vivid, restless clockwork of sharply defined plant cells. "I see what
looks like a lot of milk," I would tell him. This, he claimed, was
the result of my not having adjusted the microscope properly, so
he would readjust it for me, or rather, for himself. And I would
look again and see milk.

I finally took a deferred pass, as they called it, and waited a   2
year and tried again. (You had to pass one of the biological
sciences or you couldn't graduate.) The professor had come back
from vacation brown as a berry, bright-eyed, and eager to explain
cell-structure again to his classes. "Well," he said to me, cheerily,
when we met in the first laboratory hour of the semester, "we're
going to see cells this time, aren't we?" "Yes, sir," I said. Students
to right of me and to left of me and in front of me were seeing
cells; what's more, they were quietly drawing pictures of them in
their notebooks. Of course, I didn't see anything.

"We'll try it," the professor said to me, grimly, "with every   3
adjustment of the microscope known to man. As God is my
witness, I'll arrange this glass so that you see cells through it or
I'll give up teaching. In twenty-two years of botany, I —" He cut
off abruptly for he was beginning to quiver all over, like Lionel
Barrymore, and he genuinely wished to hold onto his temper; his
scenes with me had taken a great deal out of him.

So we tried it with every adjustment of the microscope   4
known to man. With only one of them did I see anything but
blackness or the familiar lacteal opacity, and that time I saw, to
my pleasure and amazement, a variegated constellation of flecks,
specks, and dots. These I hastily drew. The instructor, noting my
activity, came back from an adjoining desk, a smile on his lips and

his eyebrows high in hope. He looked at my cell drawing. "What's that?" he demanded, with a hint of a squeal in his voice. "That's what I saw," I said. "You didn't, you didn't, you *didn't*!" he screamed, losing control of his temper instantly, and he bent over and squinted into the microscope. His head snapped up. "That's your eye!" he shouted. "You've fixed the lens so that it reflects! You've drawn your eye!"

Another course that I didn't like, but somehow managed to   5 pass, was economics. I went to that class straight from the botany class, which didn't help me any in understanding either subject. I used to get them mixed up. But not as mixed up as another student in my economics class who came there direct from a physics laboratory. He was a tackle on the football team, named Bolenciecwcz. At that time Ohio State University had one of the best football teams in the country, and Bolenciecwcz was one of its outstanding stars. In order to be eligible to play it was necessary for him to keep up in his studies, a very difficult matter, for while he was not dumber than an ox he was not any smarter. Most of his professors were lenient and helped him along. None gave him more hints in answering questions or asked him simpler ones than the economics professor, a thin, timid man named Bassum. One day when we were on the subject of transportation and distribution, it came Bolenciecwcz's turn to answer a question. "Name one means of transportation," the professor said to him. No light came into the big tackle's eyes. "Just any means of transportation," said the professor. Bolenciecwcz sat staring at him. "That is," pursued the professor, "any medium, agency, or method of going from one place to another." Bolenciecwcz had the look of a man who is being led into a trap. "You may choose among steam, horse-drawn, or electrically propelled vehicles," said the instructor. "I might suggest the one which we commonly take in making long journeys across land." There was a profound silence in which everybody stirred uneasily, including Bolenciecwcz and Mr. Bassum. Mr. Bassum abruptly broke this silence in an amazing manner. "Choo-choo-choo," he said, in a low voice, and turned instantly scarlet. He glanced appealingly around the room. All of us, of course, shared Mr. Bassum's desire that Bolenciecwcz should stay abreast of the class in economics, for the Illinois game, one of the hardest and most important of the season, was only a week off. "Toot, toot, too-toooooooot!"

some student with a deep voice moaned, and we all looked encouragingly at Bolenciecwcz. Somebody else gave a fine imitation of a locomotive letting off steam. Mr. Bassum himself rounded off the little show. "Ding, dong, ding, dong," he said, hopefully. Bolenciecwcz was staring at the floor now, trying to think, his great brow furrowed, his huge hands rubbing together, his face red.

"How did you come to college this year, Mr. Bolenciecwcz?"   6
asked the professor. "*Chuffa* chuffa, *chuffa* chuffa."

"M'father sent me," said the football player.   7

"What on?" asked Bassum.   8

"I git an 'lowance," said the tackle, in a low, husky voice,   9
obviously embarrassed.

"No, no," said Bassum. "Name a means of transportation.   10
What did you *ride* here on?"

"Train," said Bolenciecwcz.   11

"Quite right," said the professor. "Now, Mr. Nugent, will   12
you tell us — "

If I went through anguish in botany and economics — for   13
different reasons — gymnasium work was even worse. I don't even like to think about it. They wouldn't let you play games or join in the exercises with your glasses on and I couldn't see with mine off. I bumped into professors, horizontal bars, agricultural students, and swinging iron rings. Not being able to see, I could take it but I couldn't dish it out. Also, in order to pass gymnasium (and you had to pass it to graduate) you had to learn to swim if you didn't know how. I didn't like the swimming pool, I didn't like swimming, and I didn't like the swimming instructor, and after all these years I still don't. I never swam but I passed my gym work anyway, by having another student give my gymnasium number (978) and swim across the pool in my place. He was a quiet, amiable blond youth, number 473, and he would have seen through a microscope for me if we could have got away with it, but we couldn't get away with it. Another thing I didn't like about gymnasium work was that they made you strip the day you registered. It is impossible for me to be happy when I am stripped and being asked a lot of questions. Still, I did better than a lanky agricultural student who was cross-examined just before I was. They asked each student what college he was in — that is, whether Arts, Engineering, Commerce, or Agriculture. "What college are

you in?" the instructor snapped at the youth in front of me. "Ohio State University," he said promptly.

It wasn't that agricultural student but it was another a whole   14 lot like him who decided to take up journalism, possibly on the ground that when farming went to hell he could fall back on newspaper work. He didn't realize, of course, that that would be very much like falling back full-length on a kit of carpenter's tools. Haskins didn't seem cut out for journalism, being too embarrassed to talk to anybody and unable to use a typewriter, but the editor of the college paper assigned him to the cow barns, the sheep house, the horse pavilion, and the animal husbandry department generally. This was a genuinely big "beat," for it took up five times as much ground and got ten times as great a legislative appropriation as the College of Liberal Arts. The agricultural student knew animals, but nevertheless his stories were dull and colorlessly written. He took all afternoon on each of them, on account of having to hunt for each letter on the typewriter. Once in a while he had to ask somebody to help him hunt. "C" and "L," in particular, were hard letters for him to find. His editor finally got pretty much annoyed at the farmer-journalist because his pieces were so uninteresting. "See here, Haskins," he snapped at him one day, "why is it we never have anything hot from you on the horse pavilion? Here we have two hundred head of horses on this campus — more than any other university in the Western Conference except Purdue — and yet you never get any real lowdown on them. Now shoot over to the horse barns and dig up something lively." Haskins shambled out and came back in about an hour; he said he had something. "Well, start it off snappily," said the editor. "Something people will read." Haskins set to work and in a couple of hours brought a sheet of typewritten paper to the desk; it was a two-hundred-word story about some disease that had broken out among the horses. Its opening sentence was simple but arresting. It read: "Who has noticed the sores on the tops of the horses in the animal husbandry building?"

Ohio State was a land grant university and therefore two   15 years of military drill was compulsory. We drilled with old Springfield rifles and studied the tactics of the Civil War even though the World War was going on at the time. At 11 o'clock each morning thousands of freshmen and sophomores used to deploy over the campus, moodily creeping up on the old chemistry building. It was good training for the kind of warfare that was waged at Shiloh but it had no connection with what was going on in Europe. Some people used to think there was German money behind it, but they didn't dare say so or they would have been thrown in jail as German spies. It was a period of muddy thought and marked, I believe, the decline of higher education in the Middle West.

As a soldier I was never any good at all. Most of the cadets were glumly indifferent soldiers, but I was no good at all. Once General Littlefield, who was commandant of the cadet corps, popped up in front of me during regimental drill and snapped, "You are the main trouble with this university!" I think he meant that my type was the main trouble with the university but he may have meant me individually. I was mediocre at drill, certainly — that is, until my senior year. By that time I had drilled longer than anybody else in the Western Conference, having failed at military at the end of each preceding year so that I had to do it all over again. I was the only senior still in uniform. The uniform which, when new, had made me look like an interurban railway conductor, now that it had become faded and too tight made me look like Bert Williams in his bellboy act. This had a definitely bad effect on my morale. Even so, I had become by sheer practice little short of wonderful at squad maneuvers. 16

One day General Littlefield picked our company out of the whole regiment and tried to get it mixed up by putting it through one movement after another as fast as we could execute them: squads right, squads left, squads on right into line, squads right about, squads left front into line, etc. In about three minutes one hundred and nine men were marching in one direction and I was marching away from them at an angle of forty degrees, all alone. "Company, halt!" shouted General Littlefield. "That man is the only man who has it right!" I was made a corporal for my achievement. 17

The next day General Littlefield summoned me to his office. He was swatting flies when I went in. I was silent and he was silent too, for a long time. I don't think he remembered me or why he had sent for me, but he didn't want to admit it. He swatted some more flies, keeping his eyes on them narrowly before he let go with the swatter. "Button up your coat!" he 18 snapped. Looking back on it now I can see that he meant me although he was looking at a fly, but I just stood there. Another fly came to rest on a paper in front of the general and began rubbing its hind legs together. The general lifted the swatter cautiously. I moved restlessly and the fly flew away. "You startled him!" barked General Littlefield, looking at me severely. I said I was sorry. "That won't help the situation!" snapped the General, with cold military logic. I didn't see what I could do except offer to chase some more flies toward his desk, but I didn't say anything. He stared out the window at the faraway figures of co-eds crossing the campus toward the library. Finally, he told me I could go. So I went. He either didn't know which cadet I was or else he forgot what he wanted to see me about. It may have been that he wished to apologize for having called me the main trouble with the university; or maybe he had decided to compliment me on my brilliant drilling of the day before and then at the last minute decided not to. I don't know. I don't think about it much any more.

Questions for Close Reading

1. What is the thesis of the selection? Locate the sentence(s) in which Thurber states his main idea. If he does not state the thesis explicitly, express it in your own words.
2. In his writings and cartoons, Thurber reveals a distaste for authority. Find evidence of such an attitude in this selection.
3. Thurber passes gym class by having another student assume his identification number. What does this fact indicate about his gym class in particular and about his university in general?
4. Thurber sets up a comparison between himself and the fly in General Littlefield's office. How is this comparison related to Thurber's thesis?
5. Refer to your dictionary as needed to define the following words used in the selection: *nebulous* (paragraph 1), *lacteal* (4), *opacity* (4), *variegated* (4), *husbandry* (14), and *appropriation* (14).

Questions About the Writer's Craft

1. Thurber develops his piece through a series of examples, each in the form of a brief anecdote. Which two anecdotes does Thurber develop in most detail? What might have been his reason for doing so?

2. *Satire* uses humor to criticize a situation and create awareness of the need for change. One satiric technique is *caricature:* an oversimplified description in which one quality of an individual is exaggerated, resulting in a stereotype. Where in "University Days" does Thurber employ caricature? What is he satirizing?
3. Thurber often uses dialogue rather than commentary to convey humor. Find several places in the essay where dialogue is especially effective in enhancing the essay's humor.
4. The inability to see is a recurrent theme in Thurber's essay. Locate instances of such difficulty. What might this inability symbolize?

Questions for Further Thought

1. Thurber shows an entire class struggling to help a slow-witted athlete. Do you think colleges and universities should make special concessions to athletes who may not be doing well academically? Why or why not?
2. Did Thurber act dishonorably in having another student pass his swimming test for him? Do you view this as cheating or as a way of getting around an unreasonable school requirement?
3. Thurber shows teachers having difficulty explaining concepts to students. Who is at fault when learning grinds to a halt? Teachers? Students? Both? What should teachers and students realistically expect from each other?
4. With great wit, Thurber looks under the surface to disclose some of the inadequacies of the education he received at Ohio State University. What shortcomings do you perceive with the education you received in the past? What were its merits?

Writing Assignments Using Exemplification as a Method of Development

*1. Read William Zinsser's "College Pressures" (page 477). Zinsser sees college students as overly ambitious, driven to achieve credentials that will lead to financial success. But Thurber shows students too dull or apathetic to make much effort to move in any direction. Which view of students is more accurate? Using concrete examples of students you know or have observed, write an essay developing the point that college students are either too competitive or too lackadaisical. Save for last your most convincing example.
2. With great relish, Thurber illustrates ineptitude, showing people unable to master even the simplest of tasks. Write an essay illustrating excellence. Give several vivid examples of skill, even virtuosity, by depicting individuals engaged in tasks they have fully mastered.

You might recall a rock musician you heard in concert, an Olympic gymnast you saw on TV, a mechanic you watched repair a car. The people cited, though at first glance possibly quite dissimilar, should share one common trait: their basic excellence.

Writing Assignments Using Other Methods of Development

3. Thurber and his instructors have different views about what is important. Write a narrative essay relating one or more occasions when your sense of what was important clashed with someone else's. How was the disagreement resolved? You might want to conclude with some generalization about the type of individual with whom you seem to come into conflict.
4. Thurber's instructors show varying degrees of patience, empathy, and success in dealing with their recalcitrant students. In a serious or playful essay, contrast a teacher you consider excellent with one you consider inferior. Address the same aspects of each teacher's style — for example, patience, command of subject matter, ability to create and maintain interest. No matter which tone you select, the essay should make clear those traits you consider most essential to excellent teaching.

Additional Writing Topics
EXEMPLIFICATION

General Assignments

Use examples to develop any of the following topics into a well-organized essay. When writing the paper, choose enough relevant examples to support your thesis. Organize the material into a sequence that most effectively illustrates the thesis, keeping in mind that emphatic order is often the most compelling way to present specifics.

1. Many of today's drivers have dangerous habits.
2. Drug and alcohol abuse is (or is not) a serious problem among many young people.
3. One rule of restaurant dining is, "Management often seems oblivious to problems that are perfectly obvious to customers."
4. Children today are not encouraged to use their imaginations.
5. The worst kind of hypocrite is a religious hypocrite.
6. The best things in life are definitely not free.
7. A part-time job is an important learning experience every student should have.
8. Many TV and magazine ads use sexual allusions to see their products.
9. _____ (name someone you know well) is a _____ (use a quality: open-minded, dishonest, compulsive, reliable, gentle, and so on) person.
10. Television commercials stereotype the elderly (or another minority group).
11. Today, salespeople act as if they are doing you a favor by taking your money.
12. Most people behave very decently in their daily interactions with each other.
13. Pettiness, jealousy, and selfishness abound in our daily interactions with each other.
14. You can tell a lot about people by observing what they wear and eat.
15. Too many Americans are overly concerned with material things.
16. There are several study techniques that will help a student learn more efficiently.

17. Some teachers seem to enjoy turning tests into ordeals.
18. "Learning bad eating habits" is one course all college students take.
19. More needs to be done to eliminate obstacles faced by the physically handicapped.
20. Some of the best presents are those that cost the least.

Assignments with a Specific Audience and Purpose

1. A friend of yours has taken a job in a big city or moved to a small town. You want to warn your friend about what he or she can expect in this new environment. Give examples of what life in a big city or small town is like. You might focus on the benefits, or dangers, of both.
2. You are shopping for a new car. You become annoyed at how expensive the available options are. Or you become angry because the options available *should* be standard equipment. Write a letter of complaint to the auto manufacturer citing at least three examples of options that are too expensive, or options that should be standard, or options that should be required on all models.
3. Many people at your college or workplace have been experiencing stress lately. You have been asked to help them. Write a brochure that will be distributed by the counseling department on the subject of ways to reduce anxiety. Focus on how people can reduce stress, giving examples of each strategy you describe.
4. Assume that you teach in an elementary school. The school principal has asked you to make a speech to parents about the adverse effects of television on children. You decide to focus on just one aspect of this topic: how TV distorts reality. Write out the speech, giving examples to prove your point.
5. A pet food company is having an annual contest to choose a new animal to feature in its advertising and on packages of its product. In addition to appealing pictures of the animal, the company requires contestants to submit an essay proving that the animal of their choice is personable, playful, unique. Write an essay giving examples of your pet's special qualities. Your aim is to win the contest.
6. You have been asked to write a light article on the "three best consumer products of the past twenty-five years." You know that in a magazine article published several years ago, a prominent business-person mentioned disposable diapers, pens, and lighters as examples of such products. What products do you feel are most worthy of this designation? Write an essay for your college humor magazine giving examples of at least three such products.

PROCESS
ANALYSIS

WHAT IS PROCESS ANALYSIS?

You have probably observed and maybe even admired at one time
or another the dogged determination of small children. When
learning to do something like tie their shoelaces or tell time, little
children struggle along, creating knotted tangles, confusing the
hour with the minute hand. But they don't give up. Mastering
such basic skills empowers them and makes them feel less dependent on the adults of the world — all of whom, in the children's
eyes, seem to know how to do everything. Actually, none of us is
born knowing how to do very much. We depend not on inborn
instinct for survival, but on our great capacity for learning. We
spend a good deal of our lives learning — everything from speaking our first word to balancing our first bank statement. Indeed,
many of the milestones in our lives are linked to the processes we
master: how to cross the street alone; how to drive a car; how to
make a speech without being paralyzed by fear.

    Process analysis, a writing technique that explains the steps or

231

sequence involved in doing something, fascinates us because it satisfies our need to learn as well as our curiosity about how the world works. All the self-help books flooding the market today (*Managing Stress, How to Make a Million in Real Estate, Ten Days to A Perfect Body*) are examples of process analysis. The instructions on the federal tax form and the recipes in a cookbook are also process analyses. Several television classics, now seen in reruns, also capitalize on our desire to learn how things happen: "The Wild Kingdom" shows how animals survive in faraway lands, and "Mission Impossible" has great fun detailing elaborate plans for preventing the triumph of evil. But process analysis can deal with more than the merely interesting or entertaining. Process analysis can also focus on critical matters. Consider a waiter hurriedly skimming the "Choking Aid" instructions posted on the restaurant wall or an air traffic controller following emergency procedures in an effort to prevent a mid-air collision. In these last examples, the consequences could be fatal if the process analyses were slipshod, inaccurate, or confusing.

Undoubtedly, all of us have experienced less dramatic effects of poorly written process analyses. Perhaps you have tried to assemble a bicycle and spent hours sorting through a stack of parts, only to end up with one or two extra pieces never mentioned in the instructions. Or maybe you were baffled when putting up a set of wall shelves because the instructions insisted on using such unfamiliar terms as "mitered cleat," "wing nut," and "dowel pin." No wonder many people stay clear of anything that actually admits "assembly required."

WHEN TO USE PROCESS ANALYSIS

You will write a process analysis in one of two situations: Either your purpose is to give readers step-by-step instructions showing them how they can do something, or you would like readers to understand how something happens even though they will not actually follow the steps outlined. The first kind of process analysis is called *directional process analysis;* the second is called *informational process analysis.* When you look at the instructions on a package of frozen vegetables or when you follow the instructions for completing a job application, you are reading directional process analysis. A straightforward letter advising a friend how to interview for a job you once held and a humorous note to your

houseguests telling them how to avoid getting scalded by a tem-
peramental shower are also examples of directional process analysis. Using a variety of tones, informational process analyses can
range over equally diverse topics: how the core of a nuclear power
plant melts down, how television became so important in political campaigns, how to survive a blind date.

College assignments frequently lead to process essays. Take a
moment to consider the following examples.

> The officials of this community have been accused of
> mismanaging the recent unrest over the public housing
> ordinance. Describe the steps the officials took, indicat-
> ing whether you think they acted wisely. If not, how do
> you think the situation should have been handled?

> Many colleges and universities have changed the eligibil-
> ity guidelines for financial aid, with the result that fewer
> students can depend on student loans or scholarships to
> help finance their education. How can students and
> their families cope with the increasing educational costs
> they now have to incur? How can they ease the financial
> burden involved in obtaining a higher education?

> There have been many reports recently citing the abuse
> of small children in day care centers. What can parents
> using day care do to guard against the mistreatment of
> their children?

> Genius has been defined as ten percent inspiration and
> ninety percent perspiration. Do you consider this an apt
> description? Support your point by explaining the pro-
> cess you or someone you know used to achieve a goal
> that required both hard work and imagination.

You will note that, with the exception of the last example, none
of the assignments explicitly requires the essay response to use
process analysis. Instead, the wording of the assignments ("Describe the steps . . . ," "How can they ease . . . ," and "What
can parents . . . do . . .,") suggests that process analysis would
be an appropriate strategy for developing the papers.

It's important to realize that assignments do not always

contain such clear signals to use process analysis. But during the prewriting stage, as you generate material to support your thesis, you will often realize that you can best achieve your purpose by developing the essay—or part of it—using process analysis. Sometimes process analysis will end up being the primary strategy for organizing an essay; other times it will be used to help make a point in an essay organized around another pattern of development. Let's take a moment to illustrate this second use.

Assume that you are writing a *causal analysis* examining the impact of television commercials on people's buying behavior. To make the point that commercials create a need where none exists, you might describe the various stages in an advertising campaign to pitch a new, completely frivolous product. In an essay *defining* a good boss, you could get across the point that effective managers must be skilled at settling disputes by explaining the steps your boss took to resolve a heated disagreement between two employees. If you wrote an *argumentation– persuasion* paper urging the funding of programs to ease the plight of the homeless, you would have to dramatize for readers the tragedy of these people's lives. To achieve your purpose, you could devote part of the paper to an explanation of how the typical street person goes about the desperate jobs of finding a place to sleep and getting food to eat.

SUGGESTIONS FOR USING PROCESS ANALYSIS IN AN ESSAY

The suggestions that follow will be helpful whether you use process analysis as a predominant or supportive pattern of development.

1. Identify the desired outcome of the process analysis.   Many papers developed primarily through process analysis have a clear-cut purpose: simply to *inform* readers as objectively as possible about a process: "Here is a way of making french fries at home that will surpass the best served in your favorite fast-food restaurant." But process essays may also have a *persuasive* edge, with the writer advocating a point of view about the process, perhaps even urging a course of action: "If you do not want your arguments to deteriorate into ugly battles, you should follow a series of foolproof steps for having disagreements that leave friendships intact." Before starting to write, you need to decide if the essay is to be purely factual or if it will include this kind of persuasive dimension.

2. Decide whether the process analysis will be primarily directional or informational. Directional and informational processes are not always distinct. In fact, they may be complementary. Background information about a process often has to be provided before the steps for performing the process can be outlined. A paper might explain how the body burns calories before describing a step-by-step approach for losing weight. Or you could provide some theory about the way organic fertilizers work before detailing a plan for growing your own vegetables. Although both approaches may be appropriate in a paper using process analysis as its predominant pattern, only one approach will provide the focus of the essay.

The kind of process analysis chosen has important implications for the way you relate to your reader. When the process analysis is *directional,* the reader is addressed in the *second person*: "You should first rinse the residue from the radiator by . . . ," or "Wrap the injured person in a blanket and then. . . ." (In the second example, the pronoun *you* is implied or understood.)

If the process analysis has an *informational* purpose, you do not address the reader directly but can take advantage of a number of other options. For example, the *first person* might be used. In a humorous essay explaining how to study for finals, you could cite your own study habits as a perfect example of what *not* to do: "Filled with good intentions, I sit on my bed, pick up a pencil, open my notebook, and fall promptly asleep." The *third person singular or plural* could also be used: "The door-to-door salesperson walks up the front walk, heart pounding, more than a bit nervous, but also challenged by the prospect of striking a deal," or "The new recruits next underwent a series of important balance tests in what they referred to as the 'horror chamber.'" You might have noticed that in the third person examples, the present tense was used in one sentence, the past tense in the other. Past tense is appropriate for events already completed, while present tense is used for habitual or ongoing actions ("A dominant male goose usually flies at the head of the V-wedge during migration"). The present tense is also effective when you want to lend a sense of dramatic immediacy to a process, even if the steps were performed in the past ("The surgeon gently separates the facial skin and muscle from the underlying bony skull").

3. Keep your audience in mind.   When writing a process analysis, you must always consider the audience; only when you gauge how much your readers already know about the process can you determine how detailed your explanation should be. Imagine you plan to write an article informing students of the best way to use the university computer center. The article will be published in a newsletter for computer science majors. You would seriously misjudge your audience—and probably put them to sleep—if you explained in detail how to transfer material from disk to disk or how to delete information from a file. But if the article were prepared for a general audience (your composition class, for instance), such detailed instructions would be appropriate.

4. Identify the steps in the process.   To explain a sequence to your readers, you need to think through the process, exploring it thoroughly, identifying its major parts and subparts, locating possible missteps or trouble spots. With your purpose and audience in mind, use the appropriate prewriting techniques to break the process down into its component parts. When prewriting, it's a good idea to start by generating more material than you expect to use. Then the raw material can be shaped and pruned to fit your purpose and the needs of your audience. The amount of work done during the prewriting stage will have a direct bearing on the clarity of your presentation.

5. Explain the process, one step at a time.   Once the key stages in the process have been determined, you are ready to present the process in an easy-to-follow sequence. At times you will write about a process that follows a fairly fixed chronological sequence consisting of a series of steps agreed upon by most people: how to make pizza, how to pot a plant, how to change a tire. In such cases, you should include all necessary steps, putting them in the correct chronological order, being sure not to omit any steps. Other times you will write about a process with no commonly accepted steps or sequence. If you prepare an essay explaining how to discipline a child or how to pull yourself out of a blue mood, you have to come up with your own definition of the key steps and then put those steps into a logical order. Also, keep in mind that process analyses are not limited to describing a given progression of steps; you may use a process essay to reject or reformulate a traditional sequence. An interesting process analysis, for example, could be written based on the following thesis: "Our system for electing Congressional representatives is inefficient and even undemocratic. It must be reformed."

Whether the essay describes a generally agreed-upon or a not commonly accepted process, you must provide all the details needed to explain the process to your audience. Readers should be able to understand, even visualize, the process. There should be no fuzzy patches or confusing cuts from one step to another. On the other hand, don't overreact to this advice by going into obsessive detail about minor stages or steps. If you dwell for several hundred words on how to butter the pan, your readers will never stay with you long enough to learn how to make the omelet.

It is not unusual, especially in less defined sequences, if some steps occur simultaneously and overlap. When that occurs, you should present the steps in the most logical order, being sure to tell your readers that several steps are not perfectly distinct and may even merge. For example, if explaining how a species becomes extinct, you would have to indicate that overpopulation of hardy strains and destruction of endangered breeds are often simultaneous events. You would also need to clarify that the depletion of food sources both precedes and follows the demise of a species. Moreover, if a strict chronological ordering of steps means that a particularly important part of the sequence gets buried in the middle, the sequence probably should be juggled so that the crucial step receives the attention it deserves.

6. Provide readers with the help needed to follow the sequence. Put yourself in your readers' shoes. Will they need some background about the process before you describe it in depth? Are there technical terms that should be defined? If the essay is directional, you will most likely explain in the beginning the material and equipment needed to perform the process. And as you move through the steps, don't forget to warn readers about difficulties they might encounter. For example, when writing a paper on the artistry involved in butterflying a shrimp, you might say something like this:

Next, make a shallow cut with your sharpened knife along the convex curve of the shrimp's intestinal tract. The tract, usually a faint black line along the outside curve of the shrimp, is faintly visible beneath the translucent flesh. But some shrimp have a thick orange, blue, or gray line instead of a thin black one. In all cases, be careful not to slice too deeply, or you will end up with two shrimp halves instead of one butterflied shrimp.

You have told readers what to look for, citing the exceptions, and have warned them against making too deep a cut. Anticipating spots where communication might break down is a key part of writing an effective process analysis.

Transition words are also critical in helping readers understand the order of the steps being described. Time signals such as *first, next, now, while, after, before,* and *finally* provide the reader with a clear sense of the sequence as it unfolds. Entire sentences can also be used to link parts of the process, reminding the audience of what has already been discussed and indicating what will now be explained: "Once the panel of experts finishes its evaluation of the exam questions, randomly selected items are field-tested in schools throughout the country."

7. Decide what tone you want the process essay to convey. When writing a process essay, be sure to select a tone consistent with your purpose, your attitude towards your subject, and the effect you want to have on the reader. Do you want to use an objective, nonjudgmental tone when explaining how fraternities and sororities recruit new members, or do you want to project an angry, even accusatory tone? And once you settle on the tone of an essay, maintain it throughout the piece. If you are writing a light piece on the way computers are taking over our lives, you wouldn't include a grim, cautionary discussion about the abuse of computerized medical records.

8. Open and close the process analysis effectively. A paper developed primarily through process analysis should make a strong beginning. Your introduction should state the process to be described and clarify whether the essay has an informational or directional intent. Once readers have that information, they should be able to follow your analysis with ease because they have a clear idea where you are going.

If you suspect your readers are indifferent to your subject, the introduction can be used to motivate them, telling them how important the subject is:

> Do you enjoy the salad bars found in many restaurants? If you do, you probably have noticed that the vegetables are always crisp and fresh--no matter how many hours they have been exposed to the air. What are the restaurants doing to make the vegetables look so inviting? There's a simple answer. Many restaurants dip and spray the vegetables with potent chemicals to make them appetizing.

Moreover, if you think the audience might feel intimidated by your subject, the introduction is a perfect spot to reassure them that the process being described is not beyond their grasp:

> Studies show that many people willingly accept a defective product just so they won't have to deal with the uncomfortable process of making a complaint. But once a few easy-to-learn basics are mastered, anyone can register a complaint that gets results.

Most process essays do not end as soon as the last step in the sequence has been explained. Instead, they usually include some brief closing comments that round out the piece and bring it to a satisfying close. This final section of the essay may summarize the main steps in the process — not repeating the steps verbatim but rephrasing and condensing them in several concise sentences. The conclusion can also be an effective spot to underscore the significance of the process, recalling what may have been said in the introduction about the importance of the subject. Or the essay could end by echoing the note of reassurance that may have been included at the start of the piece.

Despite the glut of "how-to" books on the market, effective process writing is not as easy to do as it might appear. Explaining how to do something is often as difficult as responding to the proverbial "How do I get there from here?" And explaining how something happened means recreating often complex events, restructuring the world so that logic and clarity take precedence over cloudiness and confusion. If, after reading your piece, the reader thinks or says, "I understand. I see what you mean," you can be confident that your process analysis has been successful. That is no mean accomplishment.

STUDENT ESSAY AND COMMENTARY

The student essay that follows was written by Robert Berry in response to this assignment:

> Stephen Leacock's "How to Live to Be 200" pokes fun at our obsessive concern with physical fitness. By looking around and observing people, identify another example of an obsessive behavior that borders on the addictive. Then write a light-spirited essay explaining the various stages in the addiction. Since the essay is humorous in tone, be sure to describe an addiction that does not have serious consequences.

While reading the paper, try to determine how effectively it applies the principles concerning the use of process analysis. The commentary following the paper will help you look at Robert's essay more closely.

Becoming a Videoholic

In the last several years, videocassette recorders have become popular additions in many American homes. A recent newspaper article notes that one in three households has a VCR, with sales continuing to climb every day. VCRs seem to be the most popular technological breakthrough since television itself. No consumer warning labels are attached to these rapidly multiplying VCRs, but there should be. VCRs can be dangerous. Barely aware of what is happening, a person can turn into a compulsive videotaper. The descent from innocent hobby to full-blown addiction takes place in several stages.

In the first innocent stage, the unsuspecting person buys a VCR for occasional use. I was at this stage when I asked my parents if they would buy me a VCR as a combined birthday and high school graduation gift. With the VCR, I could tape <u>Star</u> <u>Trek</u> and <u>Miami</u> <u>Vice</u>, shows I would otherwise miss on nights I was at work. The VCR was perfect. I hooked it up to the old TV in my bedroom, recorded the intergalactic adventures of Captain Kirk and the high voltage escapades of Sonny Crockett, then watched the tapes the next day. Occasionally, I taped a movie which my friends and I watched over the weekend. I had just one cassette, but that was all I needed since I watched every show I recorded and simply taped over the preceding show when I recorded another. In these early days, my VCR was the equivalent of light social drinking.

In the second phase on the road to videoholism, an individual 3 uses the VCR more frequently and begins to stockpile tapes rather than watch them. My troubles began in July when my family went to the shore for a week's vacation. I programmed the VCR to tape all five episodes of Star Trek while I was at the beach perfecting my tan. Since I used the VCR's long-play mode, I could get all five Star Treks on one cassette. But that ended up creating a problem. Even I, an avid Trekkie, didn't want to watch five shows in one sitting. I viewed two shows, but the three unwatched shows tied up my tape, making it impossible to record other shows. How did I resolve this dilemma? Very easily. I went out and bought several more cassettes. Once I had these additional tapes, I was free to record as many Star Treks as I wanted, plus I could tape reruns of classics like The Honeymooners and Mission Impossible. Very quickly, I accumulated six Star Treks, four Honeymooners, and three Mission Impossibles. Then a friend--who shall go nameless--told me that only eighty-two episodes of Star Trek were ever made. Excited by the thought that I could acquire as impressive a collection of tapes as a Hollywood executive, I continued recording Star Trek, even taping shows while I watched them. Clearly, my once innocent hobby was getting out of control. I was now using the VCR on a regular basis--the equivalent of several stiff drinks a day.

In the third stage of videoholism, the amount of taping in- 4 creases significantly, leading to an even more irrational stockpiling of cassettes. The catalyst that propelled me into this third stage was my parents' decision to get cable TV. Selfless guy that I am, I volunteered to move my VCR and hook it up to the TV in the living room where the cable outlet was located. Now I could tape all the most recent movies and cable specials. With that delightful possibility in mind, I went out and bought two six-packs of blank tapes. Then, in addition to my regulars, I began to record a couple of additional shows every day. I taped Rocky III, Magnum Force, a James Bond movie, an HBO comedy special with Eddie Murphy, and an MTV concert featuring Mick Jagger. Where did I get time to watch all these tapes? I didn't. Taping at this point was more satisfying than watching. Reason and common sense were abandoned. Getting things on tape had become an obsession, and I was taping all the time.

In the fourth stage, videoholism creeps into other parts of the 5 addict's life, influencing behavior in strange ways. Secrecy becomes commonplace. One day, my mother came into my room and saw my bookcase filled with tapes--rather than with the paperbacks that used to be there. "Robert," she exclaimed, "isn't this getting a bit out of hand?" I assured her it was just a hobby, but I started hiding my tapes, putting them in a suitcase stored in my closet. I also taped at night, slipping downstairs to turn on the VCR after my parents had gone to bed and getting down first thing in the morning to turn off the VCR and remove the cassette before my parents noticed. Also, denial is not unusual during this stage of VCR addiction. At the dinner table, when my younger sister commented, "Robert tapes all the time," I laughingly told everyone--including myself--that the taping was no big deal. I was getting bored with it and was going to stop any day, I assured my family. Obsessive behavior also characterizes the fourth stage of videoholism. Each week, I pulled out the TV magazine from the Sunday paper and went through it carefully, circling in red all the shows I wanted to tape. Another sign of addiction was my compulsive organization of all the tapes I had stockpiled. Working more diligently than I ever had for any term paper, I typed up labels and attached them to each cassette. I also created an elaborate list that showed my tapes broken down into categories such as Westerns, horror movies, and comedies.

In the final stage of an addiction, the individual either succumbs completely to the addiction or is able to tear away from the habit. I broke my addiction, and I broke it cold turkey. This total withdrawal occurred when I went off to college. There was no point in taking my VCR to school because TV's were not allowed in the freshman dorms. Even though there were many things to occupy my time during the school week, cold sweats overcame me whenever I thought about everything on TV I was not taping. I even considered calling home and asking members of my family to tape things for me, but I knew they would think I was crazy. At the beginning of the semester, I also had to resist the overwhelming desire to travel the three hours home every weekend so I could get my fix. But after a while, the urgent need to tape subsided. Now, months later, as I write this, I feel detached and sober. 6

I have no illusions, though. I know that once a videoholic, always a videoholic. Soon I will return home for the holidays, which, as everyone knows, can be a time for excess eating--and taping. But I will cope with the pressure. I will take each day one at a time. I will ask my little sister to hide my blank tapes. And if I feel myself succumbing to the temptations of taping, I will pick up the telephone and dial the videoholics' hotline: (800) VCR-TAPE. I will win the battle. 7

Robert's essay is an example of *informational process analysis,* his purpose being to describe — rather than teach — the process of becoming a "videoholic." The title, with its coined term "videoholic," tips us off that the essay is going to be entertaining. And the introductory paragraph clearly establishes the essay's playful, mock-serious tone with the words. "No consumer warning labels are attached to these rapidly multiplying VCRs, but there should be. VCRs can be dangerous." The tone established, Robert briefly defines the term "videoholic" as a "compulsive videotaper," and then moves to the essay's *thesis*: "The descent from innocent hobby to full-blown addiction takes place in several stages." The thesis lets us know that the paper is going to explain how videoholism develops.

Robert sustains the humor of the introduction throughout the essay, poking fun at his quirks and mocking his own motivations: "Even I, an avid Trekkie, didn't want to watch five shows in one sitting" (paragraph 3); "Selfless guy that I am, I volunteered to move my VCR . . ." (4); "Working more diligently than I ever had for any term paper, I typed up labels. . . ." (5) In addition to the consistent tone underlying the essay, Robert's paper is unified by an *analogy*, the sustained comparison between Robert's video addiction and the obviously more serious addiction to alcohol. Handled incorrectly, the analogy could have been offensive, but Robert makes the comparison work to his advantage. The analogy is used in several spots: "In these early days, my VCR was the equivalent of light social drinking" (2); "I was now using the VCR on a regular basis — the equivalent of several stiff drinks a day" (3). Another place where Robert touches wittily on the analogy occurs in the middle of the fourth paragraph: "I went out and bought two six-packs of blank tapes" (4).

To meet the requirements of the assignment, Robert's major responsibility is to provide a *step-by-step* explanation of the process he has chosen to describe. And because he invented the term "videoholism," Robert likewise must invent the stages in the progression of the addiction. During his prewriting, Robert discovered five stages in his videoholism. These stages provide the organizing focus for his paper. Specifically, each supporting paragraph in the essay is devoted to one of the stages, with the *topic sentence* for each paragraph indicating the stage's distinctive characteristics: "In the first innocent stage, the unsuspecting person buys a VCR for occasional use" (2); "In the second phase on the road to videoholism, an individual uses the VCR more frequently and begins to stockpile tapes rather than watch them" (3); "In the third stage of videoholism, the amount of taping increases significantly, leading to an even more irrational stockpiling of cassettes" (4); "In the fourth stage, videoholism creeps into other parts of the addict's life, influencing behavior in strange ways" (5); and "In the final stage of any addiction, an individual either succumbs completely or is able to tear away from the habit" (6).

Although Robert's essay is playful, it is nonetheless a process analysis and so must have an organizational structure that is easy to follow. Keeping this in mind, Robert wisely includes *transitions* to signal what happened at each stage of his videoholism: "*Once* I had these additional tapes, I was free to record . . ." (3); "*Then,* in addition to my regulars, I began to tape . . ." (4); "*One day,* my mother came into my room . . ." (5); "*But after a while,* the urgent need . . . subsided" (6). In addition to such transitions, crisp questions are also used to move from idea to idea within a paragraph: "How did I resolve this dilemma? Very easily. I . . . bought several more cassettes" (3) and "Where did I get time to watch all these tapes? I didn't" (4). The conversational feel of these questions suits the entertaining tone of Robert's essay.

Robert generates lively details to illustrate the stages in his uncontrollable progression toward videoholism. You might have been amused, for instance, by the image of Robert's sneaking downstairs to tape shows during the night. Robert probably uses a bit of *dramatic license* when reporting some of these details, and we, as readers, understand that he is exaggerating for comic effect. Most likely he didn't break out in a cold sweat at the thought of the TV shows he was unable to tape, and he probably didn't hide his tapes in a suitcase. Nevertheless, this tinkering with the truth is legitimate because it allows Robert to create material that fits the essay's lightly satiric tone.

Even though Robert's specifics are — on the whole — vigorous and appropriate, he runs into a minor problem at the end of the fourth paragraph. Starting with the sentence "Reason and common sense were abandoned . . . ," he begins to ramble and repeat himself. These last two sentences fail to add anything substantial to what has already been said. Take a moment to read this paragraph aloud, omitting the last two sentences. Note how much sharper the new conclusion is: "Where did I get time to watch all these tapes? I didn't. Taping at this point was more satisfying than watching." This new ending says all that needs to be said in a punctuated, upbeat way.

When it was time to revise, Robert decided, in spite of his apprehension, to show his paper to his roommate, asking his roommate to read the essay aloud. Robert knew this strategy would provide an objective perspective on his work. His roommate, at first an unwilling recruit, nonetheless laughed as he read the essay. That was just the response Robert wanted. But when his roommate got to the conclusion, Robert heard that the closing paragraph was flat and anticlimactic. Here is the original version of Robert's conclusion.

First Draft Version
I have no illusions, though, that I am over my videoholism. Soon I will be returning home for the holidays, which can be a time for excess taping. All I can do is ask my little sister to hide my blank tapes. After that, I will hope for the best.

Robert and his roommate brainstormed ways to make the conclusion livelier and more consistent in spirit with the rest of the essay. They decided that the best approach would be to continue the playful, mock-serious tone that characterized earlier parts of the essay. Robert thus made three major changes. First, he tightened the first sentence of the paragraph ("I have no illusions, though, that I am over my videoholism"), making it crisper and more dramatic: "I have no illusions, though." Second, he added a few sentences to sustain the light, self-deprecating tone he had used earlier: "I know that once a videoholic, always a videoholic"; "But I will cope with the pressure"; "I will win the battle." Third, and perhaps most important, he returned to the alcoholism analogy: "I will take each day one at a time. . . . And if I feel myself succumbing to the temptations of taping, I will pick up the telephone and dial the videoholics' hotline. . . ."

These were not the only changes Robert made while reworking his paper, but they give you some sense of how sensitive he was to the effect he wanted to achieve. Certainly, the recasting of the conclusion was critical to the overall success of this amusing essay.

Process analysis is the heart of each of the following essays. In "How to Live to Be 200," Stephen Leacock gives some light-hearted instructions for those who believe exercise is the key to immortality. Sue Hubbell's "The Beekeeper," part narration and part description, centers on the surprising technique that bee-keepers use to develop resistance to bee venom. Jessica Mitford's "The American Way of Death" is a look at a process most of us will never perform but will, instead, have done *to* us. "How to Say Nothing in 500 Words," by Paul Roberts, shows students the way to write essays that will make their professors want to leave teaching. Finally, in "Shopping with Children," Phyllis Theroux presents a series of steps designed to make a potentially frustrating experience somewhat more bearable.

Stephen Leacock

Stephen Leacock (1869–1944) was born in Great Britain but spent most of his life in Canada. Educated at the University of Toronto, Leacock became a professor of economics at McGill University. In later life, he began to write humorous essays which brought him great popularity. Leacock's work was collected in such books as *Literary Lapses* (1910) and *Winnowed Wisdom* (1926). The following essay is from *Literary Lapses*.

How to Live to Be 200

Are you tired of being urged to exercise by talk show hosts and sleek TV celebrities? Are you annoyed by friends who brag about how often they work out or how many miles they run? Do you enjoy a good fast-food meal packed with preservatives, salt, and calories? If so, you have an ally in Stephen Leacock, who many years ago chided the Health Maniacs of his day. Health fanaticism, you see, is not new; there were health nuts even in the early 1900s. But as Leacock points out, they didn't live long enough to enjoy the current health craze.

1   Twenty years ago I knew a man called Jiggins, who had the Health Habit.

2   He used to take a cold plunge every morning. He said it opened his pores. After it he took a hot sponge. He said it closed the pores. He got so that he could open and shut his pores at will.

3   Jiggins used to stand and breathe at an open window for half an hour before dressing. He said it expanded his lungs. He might, of course, have had it done in a shoe-store with a boot-stretcher, but after all it cost him nothing this way, and what is half an hour?

4   After he had got his undershirt on, Jiggins used to hitch himself up like a dog in harness and do Sandow exercises. He did them forwards, backwards, and hind-side up.

5   He could have got a job as a dog anywhere. He spent all his

time at this kind of thing. In his spare time at the office, he used to lie on his stomach on the floor and see if he could lift himself up with his knuckles. If he could, then he tried some other way until he found one that he couldn't do. Then he would spend the rest of his lunch hour on his stomach, perfectly happy.

In the evenings in his room he used to lift iron bars, cannon-balls, heave dumb-bells, and haul himself up to the ceiling with his teeth. You could hear the thumps half a mile. 6

He liked it. 7

He spent half the night slinging himself around his room. He said it made his brain clear. When he got his brain perfectly clear, he went to bed and slept. As soon as he woke, he began clearing it again. 8

Jiggins is dead. He was, of course, a pioneer, but the fact that he dumb-belled himself to death at an early age does not prevent a whole generation of young men from following in his path. 9

They are ridden by the Health Mania. 10

They make themselves a nuisance. 11

They get up at impossible hours. They go out in silly little suits and run Marathon heats before breakfast. They chase around barefoot to get the dew on their feet. They hunt for ozone. They bother about pepsin. They won't eat meat because it has too much nitrogen. They won't eat fruit because it hasn't any. They prefer albumen and starch and nitrogen to huckleberry pie and doughnuts. They won't drink water out of a tap. They won't eat sardines out of a can. They won't use oysters out of a pail. They won't drink milk out of a glass. They are afraid of alcohol in any shape. Yes, sir, afraid. "Cowards." 12

And after all their fuss they presently incur some simple old-fashioned illness and die like anybody else. 13

Now people of this sort have no chance to attain any great age. They are on the wrong track. 14

Listen. Do you want to live to be really old, to enjoy a grand, green, exuberant, boastful old age and to make yourself a nuisance to your whole neighbourhood with your reminiscences? 15

Then cut out all this nonsense. Cut it out. Get up in the morning at a sensible hour. The time to get up is when you have to, not before. If your office opens at eleven, get up at ten-thirty. Take your chance on ozone. There isn't any such thing anyway. Or, if there is, you can buy a thermos bottle full for five cents, and put it on a shelf in your cupboard. If your work begins at seven in 16 the morning, get up at ten minutes to, but don't be liar enough to say that you like it. It isn't exhilarating, and you know it.

Also, drop all that cold-bath nonsense. You never did it when you were a boy. Don't be a fool now. If you must take a bath (you don't really need to), take it warm. The pleasure of getting out of a cold bed and creeping into a hot bath beats a cold plunge to death. In any case, stop gassing about your tub and your "shower," as if you were the only man who ever washed.   17

So much for that point.   18

Next, take the question of germs and bacilli. Don't be scared of them. That's all. That's the whole thing, and if you once get on to that you never need to worry again.   19

If you see a bacilli, walk right up to it, and look it in the eye. If one flies into your room, strike at it with your hat or with a towel. Hit it as hard as you can between the neck and the thorax. It will soon get sick of that.   20

But as a matter of fact, a bacilli is perfectly quiet and harmless if you are not afraid of it. Speak to it. Call out to it to "lie down." It will understand. I had a bacilli once, called Fido, that would come and lie at my feet while I was working. I never knew a more affectionate companion, and when it was run over by an automobile, I buried it in the garden with genuine sorrow.   21

(I admit this is an exaggeration. I don't really remember its name; it may have been Robert.)   22

Understand that it is only a fad of modern medicine to say that cholera and typhoid and diphtheria are caused by bacilli and germs; nonsense. Cholera is caused by a frightful pain in the stomach, and diptheria is caused by trying to cure a sore throat.   23

Now take the question of food.   24

Eat what you want. Eat lots of it. Yes, eat too much of it. Eat till you can just stagger across the room with it and prop it up against a sofa cushion. Eat everything that you like until you can't eat any more. The only test is, can you pay for it? If you can't pay for it, don't eat it. And listen — don't worry as to whether your food contains starch, or albumen, or gluten, or nitrogen. If you are damn fool enough to want these things, go and buy them and eat all you want of them. Go to a laundry and get a bag of starch, and eat your fill of it. Eat it, and take a good long drink of glue after it, and a spoonful of Portland cement. That will gluten you, good and solid.   25

If you like nitrogen, go and get a druggist to give you a   26 canful of it at the soda counter, and let you sip it with a straw. Only don't think that you can mix all these things up with your food. There isn't any nitrogen or phosphorus or albumen in ordinary things to eat. In any decent household all that sort of stuff is washed out in the kitchen sink before the food is put on the table.

And just one word about fresh air and exercise. Don't bother   27 with either of them. Get your room full of good air, then shut up the windows and keep it. It will keep for years. Anyway, don't keep using your lungs all the time. Let them rest. As for exercise, if you have to take it, take it and put up with it. But as long as you have the price of a hack and can hire other people to play baseball for you and run races and do gymnastics when you sit in the shade and smoke and watch them — great heavens, what more do you want?

Questions for Close Reading

1. What is the thesis of the selection? Locate the sentence(s) in which Leacock states his main idea. If he does not state the thesis explicitly, express it in your own words.
2. What is the "Health Habit"? What does it include?
3. Why does Leacock call people who try to eat right "cowards"?
4. Instead of good health, what goals does the author imply should guide a person's daily behavior?
5. Refer to your dictionary as needed to define the following words used in the selection: *ozone* (paragraph 12), *pepsin* (12), and *cholera* (23).

Questions About the Writer's Craft

1. Why does Leacock use the imperative in the essay? What effect does this have on the tone of the piece?
2. What two processes does the author explain in this essay? How are these processes related?
3. Leacock uses exaggeration in the title of his essay. Where else does he use exaggeration? Why?
4. What are the characteristics of Leacock's typical sentences? Why does

he use this sentence style? How does it add to the comedy of the essay?

Questions for Further Thought

1. What kind of person does Leacock reveal himself to be? How serious do you take his objections to health consciousness to be? Do you think he goes overboard into intolerance?
2. Leacock describes a health maniac as an obsessed person. How do people become obsessed? Are obsessions always bad?
3. We are presently in the midst of a health and fitness boom. To what extent has this trend affected our culture in general, and your life in particular?
4. Which is more important, to enjoy life's pleasures or to sacrifice some of them to keep physically fit? Are these two goals necessarily incompatible?

Writing Assignments Using Process Analysis as a Method of Development

1. Write a humorous essay showing how to conquer an addiction to some food, activity, or object that is not normally considered addictive. Since the paper is light in tone, you should choose a topic that can be discussed in a playful manner. You might find it helpful to look at the student essay on pages 240–242.
2. Imagine you are Jiggins, and that Leacock has just "passed on" as a result of his Unhealthy Habit. Write an essay similar to Leacock's, deploring the daily habits of people like Leacock. Describe as specifically as possible how such people live, generating lively details to support your point. Then explain the steps these people should follow if they want to be healthy and live to be 200.

Writing Assignments Using Other Methods of Development

3. Write an essay classifying people's attitudes toward food. In each section, use specific facts and examples to convey how people in each category shop, cook, eat, and talk or think about food. You might choose such types as junk-food addicts, vegetarians, food snobs, health-food fanatics, "chocoholics," finicky eaters, compulsive eaters or dieters, and so on. To make the essay more than a random collec-

tion of categories, you should provide a unifying point for your analysis.

4. Leacock presents Jiggins, the health nut, as motivated by a concern for his health. However, in your experience, do people often have other, perhaps less legitimate motives for going to the gym or running? Write an essay about the "real" reasons why people try to keep fit. Provide specific examples of people you know to illustrate each reason you discuss.

Sue Hubbell

Sue Hubbell keeps bees on her ninety-acre farm in Missouri. Born and raised in Kalamazoo, Michigan, she holds a journalism degree from the University of Southern California and a library science degree from Drexel University in Philadelphia. Hubbell's freelance writing has appeared in such publications as *Time, Sports Illustrated, Country Journal,* and *Harper's.* Her latest works are entitled *A Country Year: Living the Question* (1986) and *A Book of Bees* (1988). The following selection first appeared as one of the "Hers" columns in *The New York Times.*

The Beekeeper

One of nature's miracles is the ability of bees to transform the nectar of flowers into honey. In the following essay, Sue Hubbell describes the removal of honey from the hives so it can be processed. Accomplishing this task means confronting thousands of angry bees. So Hubbell and her co-workers follow a series of unusual steps to protect themselves against the inevitable stings that await them. The interesting process described by Hubbell implies something important about humans' tolerance of stressful situations.

For the past week I've been spending my afternoons out in the honey house getting things ready for the harvest. I'm making sure the screens are all tight because once I get started clouds of bees will surround the place and try to get in, lured by the scent of honey. I've been checking the machinery, repairing what isn't running properly, and I've been scrubbing everything down so that the health inspector will be proud. 1

My honey house contains a shiny array of stainless-steel tanks, a power uncapper for slicing honeycomb open, an extractor for spinning the honey out of the comb and a pump to move it — machinery that whirs, whomps, hums and looks very special. 2

My neighbors call it the honey factory, and I'm not above insinuating slyly that what I'm really running back here in the woods is a still.

The bees have been working since early spring, gathering 3 nectar, first from wild plum, peach, and cherry blossoms, later from blackberries, sweet clover, water willow and other wildflowers as they bloomed. As they have gathered it, their enzymes have changed the complex plant sugars in the nectar to the simple ones of honey. In the hive young bees have formed into work crews to fan the droplets of nectar with their wings, evaporating its water until it is thick and heavy. Summertime heat has helped them, and now the honey is ripe and finished. The bees have capped over each cell of honeycomb with snowy white wax from their bodies, so the honey is ready for my harvest.

The honey that I take from the bees is the extra that they will 4 not need for the winter; they store it above their hives in wooden boxes called supers. When I take it from them I stand behind the hives with a gasoline-powered machine called a bee blower and blow the bees out of the supers while the strong young men that I hire to help me carry the supers, weighing 60 pounds each, and stack them on pallets in the truck. There may be 30 to 50 supers in every one of my bee yards, and we have about half an hour to get them off the hives and stacked before the bees realize what we are up to and begin getting cross about it.

The time to harvest honey is summer's end, when it is hot. 5 The temper of the bees requires that we wear protective clothing: a full set of coveralls, a zippered bee veil and leather gloves. Even a very strong young man works up a sweat wrapped in a bee suit in the heat, hustling 60-pound supers while being harassed by angry bees. It is a hard job, harder even than haying, but jobs are scarce here and I've always been able to hire help.

This year David, the son of friends of mine, is working for 6 me. He is big and strong and used to labor, but he was nervous about bees. After we had made the job arrangement I set about desensitizing him to bee stings. I put a piece of ice on his arm to numb it and then, holding a bee carefully by its head, I put it on the numbed spot and let it sting him. A bee stinger is barbed and stays in the flesh, pulling loose from the body of the bee as it struggles to free itself. The bulbous poison sac at the top of the stinger continues to pulsate after the bee has left, pumping the venom and forcing the stinger deeper into the flesh.

That first day I wanted David to have only a partial dose of venom, so after a minute I scraped the stinger out. A few people are seriously sensitive to bee venom; each sting they receive can cause a more severe reaction than the one before—reactions ranging from hives, breathing difficulties, accelerated heart beat and choking to anaphylactic shock and death. I didn't think David would be allergic in that way, but I wanted to make sure.   7

We sat down and had a cup of coffee and I watched him. The spot where the stinger went in grew red and began to swell. That was a normal reaction, and so was the itching that he felt later on.   8

The next day I coaxed a bee into stinging him again, repeating the procedure, but I left the stinger in place for 10 minutes, until the venom sac was empty. Again the spot was red, swollen and itchy but had disappeared in 24 hours. By that time David was ready to catch a bee himself and administer his own sting. He also decided that the ice cube was a bother and gave it up. I told him to keep to one sting a day until he had no redness or swelling and then to increase to two stings. He was ready for them the next day. The greater amount of venom caused redness and swelling for a few days, but soon his body could tolerate it without reaction and he increased the number of stings once again.   9

Today he told me he was up to six stings. His arms look as though they have track marks on them, but the fresh stings are having little effect. I'll keep him at it until he can tolerate 10 a day with no reaction and then I'll not worry about taking him out to the bee yard.   10

I know what will happen to him there. For the first few days his movements will be nervous and quick and he will be stung without mercy. After that he will relax and the bees, in turn, will calm down.   11

The reason I am hiring David this year is that a young man I have used in the past has moved away. We worked well together and he liked bees though even he was stung royally at first. I admired his courage the first day we were out together, for he stood holding a super from which I was blowing bees while his arm was fast turning into a pin cushion from stings.   12

When we carried the stacked supers to the honey house's   13 loading dock, he would scorn the hot bee veil as he wheeled the supers on the handtruck despite the cross bees flying around the dock. One time, as I opened the door for him to bring in the load, I noticed that his face was contorted in what I took to be the effort of getting the handtruck down the ramp. We quickly wheeled the load of supers up to the scale, where we weigh each load. He was going too fast, so that when he stopped at the scale he fell backward and 350 pounds of supers dropped on him. Pinned down, he loyally balanced himself on one fist so that he didn't harm the honey pump against which he had fallen. The reason for his knotted face and his speed was obvious for the first time: He was being stung on the forehead by three bees.

Good boss that I am, I did not choose that moment to go to the cabin and make myself a cup of coffee; I picked the supers off his chest, scraped off the stingers and helped him to his feet. It became one of our shared legends of working together. This year I miss him. 14

Now it is David, still shy about working for a friend of his parents, still a little nervous about bees. He is 19 and eager to please. But he is going to be fine. In a month we will have finished and he will be easy and relaxed, and he and I will have our own set of shared legends. 15

Questions for Close Reading

1. What is the thesis of the selection? Locate the sentence(s) in which Hubbell states her main idea. If she does not state the thesis explicitly, express it in your own words.
2. Why does the author hire David to harvest the honey? What qualities does David have that make him a good choice?
3. What is desensitization? What role does it play in the honey harvesting process?
4. What are the supers, and what role do they play in the harvesting process? How do the bees use them? How do the people use them?
5. Refer to your dictionary as needed to define the following words used in the selection: *enzymes* (paragraph 3), *desensitize* (6), *bulbous* (6), *pulsate* (6), and *anaphylactic* (7).

Questions About the Writer's Craft

1. How many steps are there in the process of making and gathering

honey? Does Hubbell provide sufficient detail for you to understand this process?

2. What technical terms of the honey-making trade does the author take time to define? Where in the essay does she provide her definitions? What technical terms does she leave undefined? Why?

3. Where does Hubbell break out of the chronological process description? Why does she include this material in the essay? What does it add?

4. What is the author's attitude toward the subject of the essay? Is the job of harvesting just another job, just in the day's work, or is it something more? Find places where this attitude is revealed.

Questions for Further Thought

1. Hubbell says that she has little trouble finding helpers because "jobs are scarce around here." Would you have to be desperate for a job to become a beekeeper's assistant? What other satisfactions might this job offer?

2. Is Hubbell a good boss? How would you describe her treatment of her employees?

3. Would you deliberately allow yourself to be stung by bees so you could work on a bee farm? Can you think of other jobs that require desensitization to pain? What are some of them? What kinds of pain are involved?

4. Is becoming "hardened" to physical or mental pain a good thing? A necessary thing?

Writing Assignments Using Process Analysis as a Method of Development

*1. Many jobs, like Hubbell's, require becoming hardened to pain or discomfort. Write an essay about an experience you have had that desensitized you to physical pain or to emotional distress. Describe the process of becoming used to the pain and growing able to perform the task or job without being unduly upset. One part of the essay should discuss the way the difficulties encountered helped you discover new things about yourself. Before writing the paper, you might want to read Betty Rollin's "Allene Talmey" (page 194) and Richard Rodriguez's "Workers" (page 333), two very different essays on hard, often uncomfortable work.

2. Write an essay describing a process that you know well, but that most people do not. You may have learned the process in school, on a job, from a relative or friend, or on your own. As Hubbell does, explain the steps clearly enough that a wide audience of people

could understand the sequence. Make sure you define any special terms. Possible subjects could be making bread from scratch, moving a piano, carving a decoy, refinishing furniture. The essay should make clear the pleasure derived from mastering the process.

Writing Assignments Using Other Methods of Development

3. Hubbell clearly finds pleasure and satisfaction in her work. Write an essay exploring the three most important satisfactions you hope for in your future career. Be specific about what you want and why you want it. As part of the paper, explain how you became interested in this kind of work.

4. Hubbell's essay concludes with a "shared legend" — a story of a crisis in which the author and her employee helped each other, survived, and became closer. Write a narrative about an experience that became the basis for a shared legend between you and someone else. Explore what it was about the event that made it legendary, showing how your bond with the other person changed or deepened as a result of the experience.

Jessica Mitford

English-born Jessica Mitford came to the United States in 1939 at the age of twenty-one and received her American citizenship during the war. Mitford worked as a bartender and salesperson before becoming an investigator for the Office of Price Administration in Washington. She did not begin her writing career until the age of thirty-eight. Her books include an autobiography, *Daughters and Rebels* (1960), and *Kind and Usual Punishment* (1974), which is a critique of the American penal system. The following selection is from the book that gave Mitford a national reputation as an investigative writer, *The American Way of Death* (1963). A scathing attack on the American funeral industry, this book shocked readers and enraged morticians.

The American Way of Death

If you were in charge of the funeral arrangements for a loved one, would you ask to have that person's lips sewed, eyes glued, blood drained, and face painted? If you answered "No," you probably don't know much about the world of mortuary science. In this world, the appearance of death is to be avoided, and the goal is to make people look as if they are asleep. In the following selection, Jessica Mitford parts the "formaldehyde curtain" to reveal our funeral practices. Such practices, she implies, reflect our deep-seated fear of death.

Embalming is indeed a most extraordinary procedure, and one must wonder at the docility of Americans who each year pay hundreds of millions of dollars for its perpetuation, blissfully ignorant of what it is all about, what is done, how it is done. Not one in ten thousand has any idea of what actually takes place. Books on the subject are extremely hard to come by. They are not to be found in most libraries or bookshops.

In an era when huge television audiences watch surgical 2
operations in the comfort of their living rooms, when, thanks to
the animated cartoon, the geography of the digestive system has
become familiar territory even to the nursery school set, in a land
where the satisfaction of curiosity about almost all matters is a
national pastime, the secrecy surrounding embalming can, surely,
hardly be attributed to the inherent gruesomeness of the subject.
Custom in this regard has within this century suffered a complete
reversal. In the early days of American embalming, when it was
performed in the home of the deceased, it was almost mandatory
for some relative to stay by the embalmer's side and witness the
procedure. Today, family members who might wish to be in
attendance would certainly be dissuaded by the funeral director.
All others, except apprentices, are excluded by law from the
preparation room.

A close look at what does actually take place may explain in 3
large measure the undertaker's intractable reticence concerning a
procedure that has become his major *raison d'être*. Is it possible he
fears that public information about embalming might lead pa-
trons to wonder if they really want this service? If the funeral men
are loath to discuss the subject outside the trade, the reader may,
understandably, be equally loath to go on reading at this point.
For those who have the stomach for it, let us part the formaldehyde curtain. . . .

The body is first laid out in the undertaker's morgue — or 4
rather, Mr. Jones is reposing in the preparation room — to be
readied to bid the world farewell.

The preparation room in any of the better funeral establish- 5
ments has the tiled and sterile look of a surgery, and indeed the
embalmer – restorative artist who does his chores there is beginning to adopt the term "dermasurgeon" (appropriately corrupted
by some mortician-writers as "demisurgeon") to describe his calling. His equipment, consisting of scalpels, scissors, augers, for-
ceps, clamps, needles, pumps, tubes, bowls and basins, is crudely
imitative of the surgeon's, as is his technique, acquired in a nine-
or twelve-month post-high-school course in an embalming
school. He is supplied by an advanced chemical industry with a
bewildering array of fluids, sprays, pastes, oils, powders, creams,
to fix or soften tissue, shrink or distend it as needed, dry it here,
restore the moisture there. There are cosmetics, waxes and paints

to fill and cover features, even plaster of Paris to replace entire limbs. There are ingenious aids to prop and stabilize the cadaver: a Vari-Pose Head Rest, the Edwards Arm and Hand Positioner, the Repose Block (to support the shoulders during the embalming), and the Throop Foot Positioner, which resembles an old-fashioned stocks.

Mr. John H. Eckels, president of the Eckels College of Mortuary Science, thus describes the first part of the embalming procedure: "In the hands of a skilled practitioner, this work may be done in a comparatively short time and without mutilating the body other than by slight incision — so slight that it scarcely would cause serious inconvenience if made upon a living person. It is necessary to remove the blood, and doing this not only helps in the disinfecting, but removes the principal cause of disfigurements due to discoloration." 6

Another textbook discusses the all-important time element: "The earlier this is done, the better, for every hour that elapses between death and embalming will add to the problems and complications encountered. . . ." Just how soon should one get going on the embalming? The author tells us, "On the basis of such scanty information made available to this profession through its rudimentary and haphazard system of technical research, we must conclude that the best results are to be obtained if the subject is embalmed before life is completely extinct — that is, before cellular death has occurred. In the average case, this would mean within an hour after somatic death." For those who feel that there is something a little rudimentary, not to say haphazard, about this advice, a comforting thought is offered by another writer. Speaking of fears entertained in early days of premature burial, he points out, "One of the effects of embalming by chemical injection, however, has been to dispel fears of live burial." How true; once the blood is removed, chances of live burial are indeed remote. 7

To return to Mr. Jones, the blood is drained out through the veins and replaced by embalming fluid pumped in through the arteries. As noted in *The Principles and Practices of Embalming,* "every operator has a favorite injection and drainage point — a fact which becomes a handicap only if he fails or refuses to forsake his favorites when conditions demand it." Typical favorites are the carotid artery, femoral artery, jugular vein, subclavian vein. 8

There are various choices of embalming fluid. If Flextone is used, it will produce a "mild, flexible rigidity. The skin retains a velvety softness, the tissues are rubbery and pliable. Ideal for women and children." It may be blended with B. and G. Products Company's Lyf-Lyk tint, which is guaranteed to reproduce "nature's own skin texture . . . the velvety appearance of living tissue." Suntone comes in three separate tints: Suntan; Special Cosmetic Tint, a pink shade "especially indicated for young female subjects"; and Regular Cosmetic Tint, moderately pink.

About three to six gallons of a dyed and perfumed solution of formaldehyde, glycerin, borax, phenol, alcohol, and water is soon circulating through Mr. Jones, whose mouth has been sewn together with a "needle directed upward between the upper lip and gum and brought out through the left nostril," with the corners raised slightly "for a more pleasant expression." If he should be bucktoothed, his teeth are cleaned with Bon Ami and coated with colorless nail polish. His eyes, meanwhile, are closed with flesh-tinted eye caps and eye cement.

The next step is to have at Mr. Jones with a thing called a trocar. This is a long, hollow needle attached to a tube. It is jabbed into the abdomen, poked around the entrails and chest cavity, the contents of which are pumped out and replaced with "cavity fluid." This done, and the hole in the abdomen sewn up, Mr. Jones's face is heavily creamed (to protect the skin from burns which may be caused by leakage of the chemicals), and he is covered with a sheet and left unmolested for a while. But not for long—there is more, much more, in store for him. He has been embalmed, but not yet restored, and the best time to start the restorative work is eight to ten hours after embalming, when the tissues have become firm and dry.

The object of all this attention to the corpse, it must be remembered, is to make it presentable for viewing in an attitude of healthy repose. "Our customs require the presentation of our dead in the semblance of normality . . . unmarred by the ravages of illness, disease or mutilation," says Mr. J. Sheridan Mayer in his *Restorative Art*. This is rather a large order since few people die in the full bloom of health, unravaged by illness and unmarked by some disfigurement. The funeral industry is equal to the challenge: "In some cases the gruesome appearance of a mutilated or disease-ridden subject may be quite discouraging.

The task of restoration may seem impossible and shake the confidence of the embalmer. This is the time for intestinal fortitude and determination. Once the formative work is begun and affected tissues are cleaned or removed, all doubts of success vanish. It is surprising and gratifying to discover the results which may be obtained."

The embalmer, having allowed an appropriate interval to   12
elapse, returns to the attack, but now he brings into play the skill and equipment of sculptor and cosmetician. Is a hand missing? Casting one in plaster of Paris is a simple matter. "For replacement purposes, only a cast of the back of the hand is necessary; this is within the ability of the average operator and is quite adequate." If a lip or two, a nose or an ear should be missing, the embalmer has at hand a variety of restorative waxes with which to model replacements. Pores and skin texture are simulated by stippling with a little brush, and over this cosmetics are laid on. Head off? Decapitation cases are rather routinely handled. Ragged edges are trimmed, and head joined to torso with a series of splints, wires and sutures. It is a good idea to have a little something at the neck—a scarf or high collar—when time for viewing comes. Swollen mouth? Cut out tissue as needed from inside the lips. If too much is removed, the surface contour can easily be restored by padding with cotton. Swollen necks and cheeks are reduced by removing tissue through vertical incisions made down each side of the neck. "When the deceased is casketed, the pillow will hide the suture incisions . . . as an extra precaution against leakage, the suture may be painted with liquid sealer."

The opposite condition is more likely to present itself—that   13
of emaciation. His hypodermic syringe now loaded with massage cream, the embalmer seeks out and fills the hollowed and sunken areas by injection. In this procedure the backs of the hands and fingers and the under-chin area should not be neglected.

Positioning the lips is a problem that recurrently challenges   14
the ingenuity of the embalmer. Closed too tightly they tend to give a stern, even disapproving expression. Ideally, embalmers feel, the lips should give the impression of being ever so slightly parted, the upper lip protruding slightly for a more youthful appearance. This takes some engineering, however, as the lips tend to drift apart. Lip drift can sometimes be remedied by push-

ing one or two straight pins through the inner margin of the lower lip and then inserting them between the two front upper teeth. If Mr. Jones happens to have no teeth, the pins can just as easily be anchored in his Armstrong Face Former and Denture Replacer. Another method to maintain lip closure is to dislocate the lower jaw, which is then held in its new position by a wire run through holes which have been drilled through the upper and lower jaws at the midline. As the French are fond of saying, *il faut souffrir pour être belle.*[1]

If Mr. Jones has died of jaundice, the embalming fluid will very likely turn him green. Does this deter the embalmer? Not if he has intestinal fortitude. Masking pastes and cosmetics are heavily laid on, burial garments and casket interiors are color-correlated with particular care, and Jones is displayed beneath rose-colored lights. Friends will say, "How *well* he looks." Death by carbon monoxide, on the other hand, can be rather a good thing from the embalmer's viewpoint: "One advantage is the fact that this type of discoloration is an exaggerated form of a natural pink coloration." This is nice because the healthy glow is already present and needs but little attention. 15

The patching and filling completed, Mr. Jones is now shaved, washed and dressed. Cream-based cosmetic, available in pink, flesh, suntan, brunette, and blond, is applied to his hands and face, his hair is shampooed and combed (and, in the case of Mrs. Jones, set), his hands manicured. For the horny-handed son of toil special care must be taken; cream should be applied to remove ingrained grime, and the nails cleaned. "If he were not in the habit of having them manicured in life, trimming and shaping is advised for better appearance — never questioned by kin." 16

Jones is now ready for casketing (this is the present participle of the verb "to casket"). In this operation his right shoulder should be depressed slightly "to turn the body a bit to the right and soften the appearance of lying flat on the back." Positioning the hands is a matter of importance, and special rubber positioning blocks may be used. The hands should be cupped slightly for a more lifelike, relaxed appearance. Proper placement of the body requires a delicate sense of balance. It should lie as high as possi- 17

---

[1]One has to suffer to be beautiful.

ble in the casket, yet not so high that the lid, when lowered, will hit the nose. On the other hand, we are cautioned, placing the body too low "creates the impression that the body is in a box."

Jones is next wheeled into the appointed slumber room   18
where a few last touches may be added — his favorite pipe placed in his hand or, if he was a great reader, a book propped into position. (In the case of little Master Jones a Teddy bear may be clutched.) Here he will hold open house for a few days, visiting hours 10 A.M. to 9 P.M.

Questions for Close Reading

1. What is the thesis of the selection? Locate the sentence(s) in which Mitford states her main idea. If she does not state the thesis explicitly, express it in your own words.
2. Why, according to Mitford, do Americans know so little about the embalming process?
3. Mitford quotes from a textbook on embalming practices (paragraph 11). What does the passage reveal about the goals of mortuary science?
4. In what ways is the body made to look even better than it did when alive?
5. Refer to your dictionary as needed to define the following words used in the selection: *docility* (paragraph 1), *intractable* (3), *raison d'être* (3), *augers* (5), *distend* (5), *stippling* (12), and *jaundice* (15).

Questions About the Writer's Craft

1. What are the main stages of the mortician's craft? What happens in each step? What words and phrases does Mitford use to indicate she is moving from one step to the next?
2. Why does Mitford refer to the body being embalmed as Mr. Jones? What effect does this naming have on the reader?
3. Mitford interweaves her description of the embalming and restoring process with many quotations from mortuary science texts. Why does she do this? What do you notice about the writing style of the authors of these texts?
4. What is Mitford's tone in this essay? Do you feel she is being objective in her description of the funeral industry? Why or why not?

Questions for Further Thought

1. Does embalming strike you as a worthwhile process now that you know more about it? Do you feel it is the proper way to treat the dead?

2. One embalmers' manual states that cleaning and trimming the nails of a working man is "never questioned by kin." Are kin prevented from questioning embalmers' techniques? Do you think the funeral industry as a whole takes advantage of grief and disorientation to sell its products?

3. Mitford describes a method of preparation for burial that is undignified and, at times, ludicrous. How does this practice help confirm the statement that funerals are for the living, not for the dead? What kinds of final rites would show more respect for the dead — and for the process of dying?

4. Once, Mitford says, relatives prepared a body for burial, and death was thus blended into ordinary life. Today, the process of burial is given over to specialists. Do you think this change has harmed the survivors? Have any other natural aspects of life been turned over to "specialists" and thus separated from daily life?

Writing Assignments Using Process Analysis as a Method of Development

1. Many important events or changes in our lives are marked by celebrations or rituals. Often, the basic outlines of these rituals are established by tradition, but we can personalize these traditions by making some changes or additions to fit our special occasion. Select an important change or event that you will celebrate in the future. Explain how you would like to experience the event. Your choice could include any of the following: your marriage, the birth of a child, your graduation, your parent's retirement, or some other notable time.

2. Write a paper telling your survivors how you wish to be treated after death. Explain how they should conduct your funeral, whether they should embalm you, where they should put your remains, and, most important, what you would like said in your eulogy. Be as specific as possible as you outline the steps to be taken.

Writing Assignments Using Other Methods of Development

3. Write an essay describing a funeral or viewing that you have attended. Focus on what seems to you the most important scene. Your thesis should express a dominant feeling about the scene: depression, grief,

discomfort, fear, disbelief, anger, or some other emotion. Alternatively, write a similar essay about any other ceremony or ritual you have experienced (for example, a wedding, bar/bat mitzvah, or graduation). Your dominant feeling may be positive or negative.

4. Write an essay showing that Americans often pretend that death does not exist or is not really happening. Give examples drawn from your own life, your family's, or public events. You might consider such typical situations as the following: the expressions we use with children ("Grandpa's gone away"; "Kitty is sleeping"); the euphemistic language we have for death ("passed away"; "no longer with us"); our obsession with looking young and keeping fit; our beliefs about "eternal life"; people's resistance to making a will; our refusal to discuss the implications of aging, even with close relatives.

Paul Roberts

Paul Roberts (1917–1967) was a scholar of linguistics and a respected teacher whose textbooks helped scores of high school and college students become better writers. Roberts' works include *English Syntax* (1954) and *Patterns of English* (1956). The following selection is from his best-known book, *Understanding English* (1958).

How to Say Nothing in 500 Words

Student essays are written on the bus, in the cafeteria, during television shows, and after midnight. Not surprisingly, many are uninspired last-ditch attempts to fulfill an assignment. Paul Roberts, who spent many bleary-eyed hours reading such papers, has great fun presenting a typical freshman essay for analysis. He then provides students with lively and helpful advice on ways to write essays that are worth something.

Nothing About Something

It's Friday afternoon, and you have almost survived another 1 week of classes. You are just looking forward dreamily to the weekend when the English instructor says: "For Monday you will turn in a five-hundred word composition on college football."

Well, that puts a good big hole in the weekend. You don't 2 have any strong views on college football one way or the other. You get rather excited during the season and go to all the home games and find it rather more fun than not. On the other hand, the class has been reading Robert Hutchins in the anthology and perhaps Shaw's "Eighty-Yard Run," and from the class discussion you have got the idea that the instructor thinks college football is for the birds. You are no fool, you. You can figure out what side to take.

After dinner you get out the portable typewriter that you got
for high school graduation. You might as well get it over with and
enjoy Saturday and Sunday. Five hundred words is about two
double-spaced pages with normal margins. You put in a sheet of
paper, think up a title, and you're off: 3

Why College Football Should Be Abolished

College football should be abolished because it's
bad for the school and also bad for the players. The
players are so busy practicing that they don't have any
time for their studies.   4

This, you feel, is a mighty good start. The only trouble is that
it's only thirty-two words. You still have four hundred and sixty-
eight to go, and you've pretty well exhausted the subject. It comes
to you that you do your best thinking in the morning, so you put
away the typewriter and go to the movies. But the next morning
you have to do your washing and some math problems, and in the
afternoon you go to the game. The English instructor turns up
too, and you wonder if you've taken the right side after all.
Saturday night you have a date, and Sunday morning you have to
go to church. (You shouldn't let English assignments interfere
with your religion.) What with one thing and another, it's ten
o'clock Sunday night before you get out the typewriter again. You
make a pot of coffee and start to fill out your views on college
football. Put a little meat on the bones.   5

Why College Football Should Be Abolished

In my opinion, it seems to me that college football
should be abolished. The reason why I think this to be
true is because I feel that football is bad for the colleges
in nearly every respect. As Robert Hutchins says in his
article in our anthology in which he discusses college
football, it would be better if the colleges had race horses
and had races with one another, because then the horses
would not have to attend classes. I firmly agree with Mr.
Hutchins on this point, and I am sure that many other
students would agree too.   6

One reason why it seems to me that college football   7
is bad is that it has become too commercial. In the olden
times when people played football just for the fun of it,
maybe college football was all right, but they do not play
football just for the fun of it now as they used to in the
old days. Nowadays college football is what you might
call a big business. Maybe this is not true at all schools,
and I don't think it is especially true here at State, but
certainly this is the case at most colleges and universities
in America nowadays, as Mr. Hutchins points out in his
very interesting article. Actually the coaches and alumni
go around to the high schools and offer the high school
stars large salaries to come to their colleges and play
football for them. There was one case where a high
school star was offered a convertible if he would play
football for a certain college.

Another reason for abolishing college football is   8
that it is bad for the players. They do not have time to
get a college education, because they are so busy playing
football. A football player has to practice every afternoon from three to six, and then he is so tired that he
can't concentrate on his studies. He just feels like dropping off to sleep after dinner, and then the next day he
goes to his classes without having studied and maybe he
fails the test.

(Good ripe stuff so far, but you're still a hundred and fifty-one
words from home. One more push.)

Also I think college football is bad for the colleges   9
and the universities because not very many students get
to participate in it. Out of a college of ten thousand
students only seventy-five or a hundred play football, if
that many. Football is what you might call a spectator
sport. That means that most people go to watch it but
do not play it themselves.

(Four hundred and fifteen. Well, you still have the conclusion,
and when you retype it, you can make the margins a little wider.)

These are the reasons why I agree with Mr. Hutchins that college football should be abolished in American colleges and universities.   10

On Monday you turn it in, moderately hopeful, and on Friday it comes back marked "weak in content" and sporting a big "D."   11

This essay is exaggerated a little, not much. The English instructor will recognize it as reasonably typical of what an assignment on college football will bring in. He knows that nearly half of the class will contrive in five hundred words to say that college football is too commercial and bad for the players. Most of the other half will inform him that college football builds character and prepares one for life and brings prestige to the school. As he reads paper after paper all saying the same thing in almost the same words, all bloodless, five hundred words dripping out of nothing, he wonders how he allowed himself to get trapped into teaching English when he might have had a happy and interesting life as an electrician or a confidence man.   12

Well, you may ask, what can you do about it? The subject is one on which you have few convictions and little information. Can you be expected to make a dull subject interesting? As a matter of fact, this is precisely what you are expected to do. This is the writer's essential task. All subjects, except sex, are dull until somebody makes them interesting. The writer's job is to find the argument, the approach, the angle, the wording that will take the reader with him. This is seldom easy, and it is particularly hard in subjects that have been much discussed: College Football, Fraternities, Popular Music, Is Chivalry Dead?, and the like. You will feel that there is nothing you can do with such subjects except repeat the old bromides. But there are some things you can do which will make your papers, if not throbbingly alive, at least less insufferably tedious than they might otherwise be.   13

Avoid the Obvious Content

Say the assignment is college football. Say that you've decided to be against it. Begin by putting down the arguments that come to your mind: it is too commercial, it takes the students'   14 minds off their studies, it is hard on the players, it makes the university a kind of circus instead of an intellectual center, for most schools it is financially ruinous. Can you think of any more arguments just off hand? All right. Now when you write your paper, *make sure that you don't use any of the material on this list.* If these are the points that leap to your mind, they will leap to everyone else's too, and whether you get a "C" or a "D" may depend on whether the instructor reads your paper early when he is fresh and tolerant or late, when the sentence "In my opinion, college football has become too commercial," inexorably repeated, has brought him to the brink of lunacy.

Be against college football for some reason or reasons of   15
your own. If they are keen and perceptive ones, that's splendid. But even if they are trivial or foolish or indefensible, you are still ahead so long as they are not everybody else's reasons too. Be against it because the colleges don't spend enough money on it to make it worth while, because it is bad for the characters of the spectators, because the players are forced to attend classes, because the football stars hog all the beautiful women, because it competes with baseball and is therefore un-American and possibly Communist inspired. There are lots of more or less unused reasons for being against college football.

Sometimes it is a good idea to sum up and dispose of the trite   16
and conventional points before going on to your own. This has the advantage of indicating to the reader that you are going to be neither trite nor conventional. Something like this:

> We are often told that college football should be   17
> abolished because it has become too commercial or because it is bad for the players. These arguments are no doubt very cogent, but they don't really go to the heart of the matter.

Then you go to the heart of the matter.

Take the Less Usual Side

One rather simple way of getting interest into your paper is   18
to take the side of the argument that most of the citizens will want to avoid. If the assignment is an essay on dogs, you can, if

you choose, explain that dogs are faithful and lovable compan-
ions, intelligent, useful as guardians of the house and protectors
of children, indispensable in police work—in short, when all is
said and done, man's best friends. Or you can suggest that those
big brown eyes conceal, more often than not, a vacuity of mind
and an inconstancy of purpose; that the dogs you have known
most intimately have been mangy, ill-tempered brutes, incapable
of instruction; and that only your nobility of mind and fear of
arrest prevent you from kicking the flea-ridden animals when you
pass them on the street.

Naturally, personal convictions will sometimes dictate your   19
approach. If the assigned subject is "Is Methodism Rewarding to
the Individual?" and you are a pious Methodist, you have really
no choice. But few assigned subjects, if any, will fall in this
category. Most of them will lie in broad areas of discussion with
much to be said on both sides. They are intellectual exercises and
it is legitimate to argue now one way and now another, as de-
baters do in similar circumstances. Always take the side that looks
to you hardest, least defensible. It will almost always turn out to
be easier to write interestingly on that side.

This general advice applies where you have a choice of sub-   20
jects. If you are to choose among "The Value of Fraternities" and
"My Favorite High School Teacher" and "What I Think About
Beetles," by all means plump for the beetles. By the time the
instructor gets to your paper, he will be up to his ears in tedious
tales about the French teacher at Bloombury High and assertions
about how fraternities build character and prepare one for life.
Your views on beetles, whatever they are, are bound to be a
refreshing change.

Don't worry too much about figuring out what the instruc-   21
tor thinks about the subject so that you can cuddle up with him.
Chances are his views are no stronger than yours. If he does have
convictions and you oppose them, his problem is to keep from
grading you higher than you deserve in order to show he is not
biased. This doesn't mean that you should always cantankerously
dissent from what the instructor says; that gets tiresome too. And
if the subject assigned is "My Pet Peeve," do not begin, "My pet
peeve is the English instructor who assigns papers on 'my pet
peeve.'" This was still funny during the War of 1812, but it has

sort of lost its edge since then. It is in general good manners to avoid personalities.

Slip Out of Abstraction

If you will study the essay on college football . . . you will 22 perceive that one reason for its appalling dullness is that it never gets down to particulars. It is just a series of not very glittering generalities: "football is bad for the colleges," "it has become too commercial," "football is a big business," "it is bad for the players," and so on. Such round phrases thudding against the reader's brain are unlikely to convince him, though they may well render him unconscious.

If you want the reader to believe that college football is bad 23 for the players, you have to do more than say so. You have to display the evil. Take your roommate, Alfred Simkins, the second-string center. Picture poor old Alfy coming home from football practice every evening, bruised and aching, agonizingly tired, scarcely able to shovel the mashed potatoes into his mouth. Let us see him staggering up to the room, getting out his econ textbook, peering desperately at it with his good eye, falling asleep and failing the test in the morning. Let us share his unbearable tension as Saturday draws near. Will he fail, be demoted, lose his monthly allowance, be forced to return to the coal mines? And if he succeeds, what will be his reward? Perhaps a slight ripple of applause when the third-string center replaces him, a moment of elation in the locker room if the team wins, of despair if it loses. What will he look back on when he graduates from college? Toil and torn ligaments. And what will be his future? He is not good enough for pro football, and he is too obscure and weak in econ to succeed in stocks and bonds. College football is tearing the heart from Alfy Simkins and, when it finishes with him, will callously toss aside the shattered hulk.

This is no doubt a weak enough argument for the abolition 24 of college football, but it is a sight better than saying, in three or four variations, that college football (in your opinion) is bad for the players.

Look at the work of any professional writer and notice how 25 constantly he is moving from the generality, the abstract statement, to the concrete example, the facts and figures, the illustration. If he is writing on juvenile delinquency, he does not just tell you that juveniles are (it seems to him) delinquent and that (in his opinion) something should be done about it. He shows you juveniles being delinquent, tearing up movie theatres in Buffalo, stabbing high school principals in Dallas, smoking marijuana in Palo Alto. And more than likely he is moving toward some specific remedy, not just a general wringing of the hands.

It is no doubt possible to be *too* concrete, too illustrative or   26
anecdotal, but few inexperienced writers err this way. For most the soundest advice is to be seeking always for the picture, to be always turning general remarks into seeable examples. Don't say, "Sororities teach girls the social graces." Say "Sorority life teaches a girl how to carry on a conversation while pouring tea, without sloshing the tea into the saucer." Don't say, "I like certain kinds of popular music very much." Say, "Whenever I hear Gerber Spinklittle play 'Mississippi Man' on the trombone, my socks creep up my ankles."

Get Rid of Obvious Padding

The student toiling away at his weekly English theme is too   27
often tormented by a figure: five hundred words. How, he asks himself, is he to achieve this staggering total? Obviously by never using one word when he can somehow work in ten.

He is therefore seldom content with a plain statement like   28
"Fast driving is dangerous." This has only four words in it. He takes thought, and the sentence becomes:

In my opinion, fast driving is dangerous.

Better, but he can do better still:

In my opinion, fast driving would seem to be rather dangerous.

If he is really adept, it may come out:

In my humble opinion, though I do not claim to be an expert on this complicated subject, fast driving, in

most circumstances, would seem to be rather dangerous
in many respects, or at least so it would seem to me.

Thus four words have been turned into forty, and not an iota of
content has been added.

Now this is a way to go about reaching five hundred words,   29
and if you are content with a "D" grade, it is as good a way as
any. But if you aim higher, you must work differently. Instead of
stuffing your sentences with straw, you must try steadily to get rid
of the padding, to make your sentences lean and tough. If you are
really working at it, your first draft will greatly exceed the required total, and then you will work it down, thus:

> It is thought in some quarters that fraternities do
> not contribute as much as might be expected to campus
> life.
> Some people think that fraternities contribute little
> to campus life.
> The average doctor who practices in small towns or
> in the country must toil night and day to heal the sick.
> Most country doctors work long hours.
> When I was a little girl, I suffered from shyness and
> embarrassment in the presence of others.
> I was a shy little girl.
> It is absolutely necessary for the person employed as
> a marine fireman to give the matter of steam pressure his
> undivided attention at all times.
> The fireman has to keep his eye on the steam gauge.

You may ask how you can arrive at five hundred words at this   30
rate. Simply. You dig up more real content. Instead of taking a
couple of obvious points off the surface of the topic and then
circling warily around them for six paragraphs, you work in and
explore, figure out the details. You illustrate. You say that fast
driving is dangerous, and then you prove it. How long does it
take to stop a car at forty and at eighty? How far can you see at
night? What happens when a tire blows? What happens in a
head-on collision at fifty miles an hour? Pretty soon your paper
will be full of broken glass and blood and headless torsos, and
reaching five hundred words will not really be a problem.

Call a Fool a Fool

Some of the padding in freshman themes is to be blamed not 31
on anxiety about the word minimum but on excessive timidity.
The student writes, "In my opinion, the principal of my high
school acted in ways that I believe every unbiased person would
have to call foolish." This isn't exactly what he means. What he
means is, "My high school principal was a fool." If he was a fool,
call him a fool. Hedging the thing about with "in-my-opinion's"
and "it-seems-to-me's" and "as-I-see-it's" and "at-least-from-my-
point-of-view's" gains you nothing. Delete these phrases whenever they creep into your paper.

The student's tendency to hedge stems from a modesty that 32
in other circumstances would be commendable. He is, he realizes,
young and inexperienced, and he half suspects that he is dopey
and fuzzy-minded beyond the average. Probably only too true.
But it doesn't help to announce your incompetence six times in
every paragraph. Decide what you want to say and say it as
vigorously as possible, without apology and in plain words.

Linguistic diffidence can take various forms. One is what we 33
call *euphemism.* This is the tendency to call a spade "a certain
garden implement" or women's underwear "unmentionables." It
is stronger in some eras than others and in some people than
others but it always operates more or less in subjects that are
touchy or taboo: death, sex, madness, and so on. Thus we shrink
from saying "He died last night" but say instead "passed away,"
"left us," "joined his Maker," "went to his reward." Or we try to
take off the tension with a lighter cliché: "kicked the bucket,"
"cashed in his chips," "handed in his dinner pail." We have
found all sorts of ways to avoid saying *mad*: "mentally ill,"
"touched," "not quite right upstairs," "feeble-minded," "innocent," "simple," "off his trolley," "not in his right mind." Even
such a now plain word as *insane* began as a euphemism with the
meaning "not healthy."

Modern science, particularly psychology, contributes many 34
polysyllables in which we can wrap our thoughts and blunt their
force. To many writers there is no such thing as a bad schoolboy.
Schoolboys are maladjusted or unoriented or misunderstood or
in need of guidance or lacking in continued success toward satis-
factory integration of the personality as a social unit, but they are

never bad. Psychology no doubt makes us better men or women, more sympathetic and tolerant, but it doesn't make writing any easier. Had Shakespeare been confronted with psychology, "To be or not to be" might have come out, "To continue as a social unit or not to do so. That is the personality problem. Whether 'tis a better sign of integration at the conscious level to display a psychic tolerance toward the maladjustments and repressions induced by one's lack of orientation in one's environment or—" But Hamlet would never have finished the soliloquy.

Writing in the modern world, you cannot altogether avoid   35
modern jargon. Nor, in an effort to get away from euphemism, should you salt your paper with four-letter words. But you can do much if you will mount guard against those roundabout phrases, those echoing polysyllables that tend to slip into your writing to rob it of its crispness and force.

Beware of the Pat Expression

Other things being equal, avoid phrases like "other things   36
being equal." Those sentences that come to you whole, or in two or three doughy lumps, are sure to be bad sentences. They are no creation of yours but pieces of common thought floating in the community soup.

Pat expressions are hard, often impossible, to avoid, because   37
they come too easily to be noticed and seem too necessary to be dispensed with. No writer avoids them altogether, but good writers avoid them more often than poor writers.

By "pat expressions" we mean such tags as "to all practical   38
intents and purposes," "the pure and simple truth," "from where I sit," "the time of his life," "to the ends of the earth," "in the twinkling of an eye," "as sure as you're born," "over my dead body," "under cover of darkness," "took the easy way out," "when all is said and done," "told him time and time again," "parted the best of friends," "stand up and be counted," "gave him the best years of her life," "worked her fingers to the bone." Like other clichés, these expressions were once forceful. Now we should use them only when we can't possibly think of anything else.

Some pat expressions stand like a wall between the writer and   39
thought. Such a one is "the American way of life." Many student

writers feel that when they have said that something accords with the American way of life or does not they have exhausted the subject. Actually, they have stopped at the highest level of abstraction. The American way of life is the complicated set of bonds between a hundred and eighty million ways. All of us know this when we think about it, but the tag phrase too often keeps us from thinking about it.

So with many another phrase dear to the politician: "this 40 great land of ours," "the man in the street," "our national heritage." These may prove our patriotism or give a clue to our political beliefs, but otherwise they add nothing to the paper except words.

Colorful Words

The writer builds with words, and no builder uses a raw 41 material more slippery and elusive and treacherous. A writer's work is a constant struggle to get the right word in the right place, to find that particular word that will convey his meaning exactly, that will persuade the reader or soothe him or startle or amuse him. He never succeeds altogether—sometimes he feels that he scarcely succeeds at all—but such successes as he has are what make the thing worth doing.

There is no book of rules for this game. One progresses 42 through everlasting experiment on the basis of ever-widening experience. There are few useful generalizations that one can make about words as words, but there are perhaps a few.

Some words are what we call "colorful." By this we mean 43 that they are calculated to produce a picture or induce an emotion. They are dressy instead of plain, specific instead of general, loud instead of soft. Thus, in place of "Her heart beat," we may write "Her heart *pounded, throbbed, fluttered, danced.*" Instead of "He sat in his chair," we may say, "He *lounged, sprawled, coiled.*" Instead of "It was hot," we may say, "It was *blistering, sultry, muggy, suffocating, steamy, wilting.*"

However, it should not be supposed that the fancy word is 44 always better. Often it is as well to write "Her heart beat" or "It was hot" if that is all it did or all it was. Ages differ in how they like their prose. The nineteenth century liked it rich and smoky. The twentieth has usually preferred it lean and cool. The twentieth century writer, like all writers, is forever seeking the exact word, but he is wary of sounding feverish. He tends to pitch it low, to understate it, to throw it away. He knows that if he gets too colorful, the audience is likely to giggle.

See how this strikes you: "As the rich, golden glow of the 45 sunset died away along the eternal western hills, Angela's limpid blue eyes looked softly and trustingly into Montague's flashing brown ones, and her heart pounded like a drum in time with the joyous song surging in her soul." Some people like that sort of thing, but most modern readers would say, "Good grief," and turn on the television.

Colored Words

Some words we would call not so much colorful as colored 46 —that is, loaded with associations, good or bad. All words— except perhaps structure words — have associations of some sort. We have said that the meaning of a word is the sum of the contexts in which it occurs. When we hear a word, we hear with it an echo of all the situations in which we have heard it before.

In some words, these echoes are obvious and discussable. 47 The word *mother,* for example, has, for most people, agreeable associations. When you hear *mother* you probably think of home, safety, love, food, and various other pleasant things. If one writes, "She was like a mother to me," he gets an effect which he would not get in "She was like an aunt to me." The advertiser makes use of the associations of *mother* by working it in when he talks about his product. The politician works it in when he talks about himself.

So also with such words as *home, liberty, fireside, contentment,* 48 *patriot, tenderness, sacrifice, childlike, manly, bluff, limpid.* All of these words are loaded with favorable associations that would be rather hard to indicate in a straightforward definition. There is more than a literal difference between "They sat around the fireside" and "They sat around the stove." They might have been equally warm and happy around the stove, but *fireside* suggests leisure, grace, quiet tradition, congenial company, and *stove* does not.

Conversely, some words have bad associations. *Mother* sug- 49 gests pleasant things, but *mother-in-law* does not. Many mothers-in-law are heroically lovable and some mothers drink gin all day and beat their children insensible, but these facts of life are beside the point. The thing is that *mother* sounds good and *mother-in-law* does not.

Or consider the word *intellectual*. This would seem to be a   50 complimentary term, but in point of fact it is not, for it has picked up associations of impracticality and ineffectuality and general dopiness. So also with such words as *liberal, reactionary, Communist, socialist, capitalist, radical, schoolteacher, truck driver, undertaker, operator, salesman, huckster, speculator*. These convey meanings on the literal level, but beyond that — sometimes, in some places — they convey contempt on the part of the speaker.

The question of whether to use loaded words or not depends   51 on what is being written. The scientist, the scholar, try to avoid them; for the poet, the advertising writer, the public speaker, they are standard equipment. But every writer should take care that they do not substitute for thought. If you write, "Anyone who thinks that is nothing but a Socialist (or Communist or capitalist)," you have said nothing except that you don't like people who think that, and such remarks are effective only with the most naïve readers. It is always a bad mistake to think your readers more naïve than they really are.

Colorless Words

But probably most student writers come to grief not with   52 words that are colorful or those that are colored but with those that have no color at all. A pet example is *nice*, a word we would find it hard to dispense with in casual conversation but which is no longer capable of adding much to a description. Colorless words are those of such general meaning that in a particular sentence they mean nothing. Slang adjectives, like *cool* ("That's real cool") tend to explode all over the language. They are applied to everything, lose their original force, and quickly die.

Beware also of nouns of very general meaning, like *circum-*   53 *stances, cases, instances, aspects, factors, relationships, attitudes, eventualities*, etc. In most circumstances you will find that those cases of writing which contain too many instances of words like these will in this and other aspects have factors leading to unsatisfactory relationships with the reader resulting in unfavorable attitudes on his part and perhaps other eventualities, like a grade of "D." Notice also what "etc." means. It means "I'd like to make this list longer, but I can't think of any more examples."

Questions for Close Reading

1. What is the thesis of the selection? Locate the sentence(s) in which Roberts states his main idea. If he does not state the thesis explicitly, express it in your own words.
2. According to Roberts, what do students assume they have to do to get a good grade on an English composition?
3. What is the difference between "colorful words," "colored words," and "colorless words"? Which are preferred in essay writing?
4. What are Roberts' most important pieces of advice for the student writer?
5. Refer to the dictionary as needed to define the following words used in the selection: *bromides* (paragraph 13), *insufferably* (13), *inexorably* (14), *dissent* (21), *abolition* (24), *adept* (28), *euphemism* (33), and *insensible* (49).

Questions About the Writer's Craft

1. What two processes does Roberts analyze in this essay? Is each process informational, directional, or a combination of the two?
2. Why does Roberts use the second person "you" throughout the essay? How does this choice of point of view affect your response to the essay?
3. What is Roberts' tone in this essay? Find some typical examples of this tone. What does Roberts do to achieve this tone? Considering his intended audience, is this tone a good choice?
4. Does Roberts "practice what he preaches" about writing? Review the section headings of the essay and find examples of each piece of advice in the essay.

Questions for Further Thought

1. Roberts writes that making "a dull subject interesting . . . is precisely what you are expected to do" in college English. Do you agree that most writing subjects are dull? If so, do you think assignments could be made more interesting? And how could instructors get students to write honestly, instead of writing what they think the instructor wants to read?

2. Is Roberts' suggestion to write about the least obvious topic always appropriate? Would you follow this advice yourself?
3. In paragraph 14, Roberts says the difference between a "C" or a "D" may depend on when the teacher grades the paper. Do you think instructors' grades are usually fair, objective, and appropriate? Or do they often seem arbitrary and subjective?
4. Do you think students on your campus are preoccupied with things like word-counting and guessing the instructor's opinion on a topic? Are you? Why do some students handle writing assignments this way? What could professors do to encourage students to focus more on the challenge of writing?

Writing Assignments Using Process Analysis as a Method of Development

1. Write a humorous essay showing how to avoid doing schoolwork, household chores, or anything else most people tend to put off. You may use the second person as Roberts does. Or you may use the first person and describe your typical method of avoidance.
2. Borrowing some of Roberts' lively techniques, make a routine, predictable process interesting to read about. You might choose an activity such as how to register to vote, apply for a driver's license, sign up for college courses, take care of laundry, play a simple game, study for an exam, or some other familiar process.

Writing Assignments Using Other Methods of Development

3. Is freshman writing a beneficial and valuable experience? Or should the course be scrapped? Write an essay arguing the value — or lack of value — of freshman writing courses. Follow Roberts' advice for writing a lively composition on a time-worn subject: avoid obvious padding, choose unusual points, avoid abstractions, go to the heart of the matter, use colorful words.
4. Write a paper detailing your experiences as a student in English classes — from elementary school up to now. Using several examples, describe how successfully or unsuccessfully English has been taught, and recommend any specific reforms or changes you feel are needed.

Phyllis Theroux

A frequent contributor to the *Washington Post*, *McCall's*, and *Reader's Digest*, Phyllis Theroux (1939–   ) won special recognition for a series of pieces she wrote for *The New York Times*' "Hers" column. Theroux's essays, often about the complex relationship between child and parent, combine wry humor with keen insight. Theroux has collected her work in three books: *California and Other States of Grace: A Memoir* (1980), *Peripheral Visions* (1982), and *Night Lights* (1987), from which the following selection is taken.

Shopping with Children

With characteristic sympathy for both adults and youngsters, Phyllis Theroux recognizes that "shopping with children is exactly as awful as shopping with parents." To make the process more tolerable, she sets down several rules for parents to follow. Though tongue-in-cheek, the guidelines reflect Theroux's gentle wisdom and show that she remembers perfectly what it is like to be a child.

Once upon a time there were three little children. By and large, dressing them was a joyful thing. At a moment's notice, their mother could turn the boys into baby Rothschilds, the girl into a shipping heiress, or even a Kennedy. In those early days of motherhood, I used to take a lot of photographs for the scrapbook. Now I flip through the scrapbook sometimes to remind myself that "those were the days." 1

The eldest son was the first to establish his individuality: sleeveless Army jackets, kneecap bandannas and a pierced ear hidden under a lengthening hair style. Then the youngest son discovered dirt. He formed a club, still active, called "The All Dirt Association." To qualify, one had to roll in the mud. 2

Fortunately, the little girl grows increasingly more tasteful and immaculate. She will get up at 5:30 A.M. to make sure she has 3

284

enough time to wash and curl her hair so that it bounces properly on her shoulders when she goes off to school, and she screams as if bitten by an adder if a drop of spaghetti sauce lands on her Izod. The entire house is thrown into an uproar while she races for the Clorox bottle. This is a family of extremists, and nobody dresses for the kind of success I had in mind.

Time will tell what happens to these children. Who can say   4
whether my son the dirt bomb will wind up sewing buttons on a seersucker sports jacket, or my daughter the Southamptonian will discover the joys of thrift-shop browsing. They are still evolving toward personal statements that are, at this writing, incomplete.

In the meantime, however, they must be dressed, which   5
means taking them to stores where clothing for their growing bodies can be purchased. Shopping with children is exactly as awful as shopping with parents. But if the experience is to be survived there are certain rules all adults must follow. (If you are a child, you may not read any further. This is for your parents, who will deal with you very harshly if you read one more word!)

Rule I: Never shop with more than one child at a time. This   6
rule is closely related to another rule — never raise more than one child at a time. If you understand the second rule, there is no need to elaborate upon the first.

Rule II: Dress very nicely yourself. After the age of nine,   7
children do not like to be seen with their mothers in public. You are a blot upon their reputation, a shadow they want to shake. I, myself, always insisted that my mother walk ten paces behind me, take separate elevators and escalators and speak only when spoken to — which brings me to the next rule.

Rule III: Do not make any sudden gestures, loud noises or   8
heartfelt exclamations such as "How adorable you look in that!" or "Twenty-nine ninety-five! Are you kidding? For a shirt?" Children are terribly embarrassed by our eccentricities, and it goes without saying that you must never buy their articles of "intimate apparel" in their presence. Children, until enough sleazy adults teach them that it is old-fashioned, are very modest creatures. One time I ran out of the store and took the bus home by myself after my mother asked a salesclerk where the "underpants" counter was. Everyone in the store heard her. I had no choice.

RULE IV: Know your child's limits. If he can be coerced into   9
a department store, coaxed into telling you that he wouldn't
mind wearing this shirt or that pair of pants, don't insist that he
go the whole distance — i.e., don't force him to try them on.
Keep the sales slips; if something doesn't fit when he tries it on at
home, return it. If he cannot be made to enter the store at all, say,
"Fine. When you run out of clothes, wear your sister's." Children
who won't go shopping at all save their parents a lot of time.

RULE V: Know your own limits. Do not be dragged to every   10
sneaker store in the metropolitan area to find the exact shoes your
child has in mind. Announce: "We're going to Sears — and Sears
only — unless you want to wait for six more weeks, which is the
next time I am free." Some children, with nothing but time and a
passion to improve their image, will cheerfully go to three stores
they know about and six more they don't, without blinking an
eye.

RULE VI: Keep your hand on your checkbook. This is a very   11
hard rule to follow if you are not strong-minded. Children can
accuse you of ruining their lives because you do not genuflect
before the entire line of Ocean Pacific sportswear, and girls have a
way of filling you with guilt by telling you that every other girl in
their confirmation class is going to be wearing Capezio sandals
and if you want to make her look funny in front of the bishop she
will never forgive you as long as she lives.

RULE VII: Keep on top of the laundry. Or, if you can't keep   12
on top of the laundry, remember that the wardrobe your son or
daughter wants is probably lying in the bottom of a hamper
waiting to be retrieved. When packing a trunk for camp or school,
insist that everything the child owns be washed (preferably by him
or her), folded and ready to be inventoried before you go to the
store to fill in the gaps. Your children will hate you for enforcing
this rule, but remember that true love is strong.

RULE VIII: Avoid designer clothes. Shut your eyes to labels.   13
Do not be intimidated by the "fact" that your daughter cannot
go to the movies without swinging a Bermuda Bag, or that your
son will not be able to concentrate in the library without Top-
siders on his feet. Tell your children that the best thing about
Gloria Vanderbilt is her bank account, fattened by socially insecure people which, thank God, they are not!

Having laid down the rules, it is important to refresh the 14
adult's memory with "remembrances of things past." I have
never met a child who did not remind me of how difficult it is to
present a confident face to the world. Clothing is only the top
blanket shielding them from the elements, and children need all
the protective covering they can get.

As a child, I knew in an inarticulate way that I stood a better 15
chance of surviving a windstorm in a circle of trees. My aim was
to be the tree in the middle, identical and interchangeable with
every other sapling in the grove. How I dressed had everything to
do with feeling socially acceptable and when I inadvertently
slipped into an individualism I could not back up with sustained
confidence, I would try to think what I could do to regain my
place in the grove.

It seemed to me that social success depended on having at 16
least one of three commodities: a fabulous personality, fame, or a
yellow Pandora sweater. These were the building blocks upon
which one could stand.

A fabulous personality was beyond my power to sustain on a 17
daily basis. Fame, like lightning, seemed to strike other people,
none of whom I even knew. But a yellow Pandora sweater could
be purchased at Macy's, if only my mother would understand its
cosmic importance. Fortunately, she did.

For several days, or as long as it took for the sweater cuffs to 18
lose their elasticity, I faced the world feeling buttoned up, yellow
and self-confident — almost as confident as Susan Figel, who had
a whole drawerful of Pandora sweaters in different shades to
match her moods.

Unfortunately, I remember that yellow Pandora sweater a 19
little too vividly. When I am shopping with my children, empathy
continually blows me off course in the aisles. On the one hand,
nobody wants her child to look funny in front of the bishop. On
the other, it has yet to occur to my children that the bishop in full
regalia looks pretty funny himself.

Questions for Close Reading

1. What is the thesis of the selection? Locate the sentence(s) in which
   Theroux states her main idea. If she does not state the thesis explicitly, express it in your own words.

2. What does the author mean when she says that "shopping with a child is exactly as awful as shopping with parents" (paragraph 5)? What factors make it so awful?

3. What does Theroux suggest about children's egos when she warns parents never to make "sudden gestures, loud noises or heartfelt exclamations" (paragraph 8) when shopping with a child?

4. What does Theroux tell us about herself as a child in the last five paragraphs of this essay? How does this information relate to her thesis and her rules for shopping with children?

5. Refer to your dictionary as needed to define the following words in the selection: *adder* (paragraph 3), *seersucker* (4), *coerced* (9), *genuflect* (11), *inarticulate* (15), and *regalia* (19).

Questions About the Writer's Craft

1. Theroux does not list the steps in her process chronologically. Should she have? Is there a logic to the way she has organized her list? Explain.

2. Writers of process analysis often provide some background information before presenting their step-by-step sequence. What background information does Theroux provide? What function does this material serve?

3. How would you describe the tone of Theroux's essay? Is one tone maintained throughout the selection? Explain.

4. Process analyses may be informative and/or persuasive. Which is this essay? How do you know?

Questions for Further Thought

1. Are Theroux's children like most American children? In what ways are they similar or different?

2. Theroux shows us that children attach great, even undue importance to clothing. Trying to counteract this emphasis on appearance, some schools have adopted dress codes, requiring students to wear uniforms or dress alike in some other way. Are such dress codes a good idea? Why or why not?

3. Was there, when you were a child (or is there now), an item in your life as important to you as Theroux's Pandora sweater was to her? If so, what might this item represent?

4. Theroux's rule 8 is "Avoid designer clothes." Yet nowadays, even baby clothes carry designer labels. What tendencies in our society does this phenomenon reflect? Are such tendencies harmless? Why or why not?

Writing Assignments Using Process Analysis as a Method of Development

1. A great deal has been written about how parents should raise children. Now it's your turn. Write a process analysis advising parents how to talk with their children about something: keeping curfews; getting good grades; the facts of life; participating in extracurricular activities; avoiding drugs; getting along with other family members; turning down the stereo. Your essay may be serious or playful, but, like Theroux's, it should make a point about what it is like to be a child.

2. Theroux's essay is a survival guide for parents. Write a process analysis aimed at students entering your college next year. Adopting a serious or humorous tone, focus on a process that will help them survive the demands of college life. Possible topics include registering for classes, taking lecture notes, acquiring good study habits, getting along with a roommate.

Writing Assignments Using Other Methods of Development

*3. Theroux remarks that "children are terribly embarrassed by . . . [parents'] eccentricities." But Mark Twain once observed that time has a way of changing children's perceptions. "When I was a boy of fourteen," Twain remarked, "my father was so ignorant I could hardly stand to have the old man around. But when I got to be twenty-one, I was astonished at how much he had learned in seven years." Write a narrative or a series of narratives showing your sudden or gradual reevaluation of your parents. Russell Baker's "In My Day" (page 83) might spark some interesting thoughts.

4. Theroux believes that youngsters' shaky selfhood finds security in conformity, in being "identical and interchangeable" with others. But part of growing up involves what psychologists call "individuation"—becoming a separate person who, although still wanting acceptance, is willing to do some things differently from others. Drawing on your own or others' experiences, write an essay defining "individuality." To develop your definition, you might provide anecdotes, contrast two people, and/or use division-classification to analyze the characteristics of individuality.

Additional Writing Topics
PROCESS ANALYSIS

General Assignments

Develop one of the following topics through process analysis. Explain the process one step at a time, organizing the steps chronologically. If there is no set, agreed-upon sequence, design your own series of steps. Use transitions to ease the audience through the steps in the process. You may, of course, use any tone you wish, from serious to light.

Directional: How to Do Something

1. How to improve a course you have taken
2. How to drive defensively
3. How to get away with _____
4. How to succeed at a job interview
5. How to relax
6. How to show appreciation to others
7. How to get through school despite personal problems
8. How to be a responsible pet owner
9. How to conduct a garage or yard sale
10. How to look fashionable on a limited budget
11. How to protect a home from burglars
12. How to meet more people
13. How to improve the place where you work
14. How to gain or lose weight
15. How to complain effectively

Informational: How Something Happens

1. How a student becomes burned out
2. How a library card catalog organizes books
3. How a dead thing decays (or some other natural process)
4. How the college registration process works
5. How *Homo sapiens* chooses a mate
6. How a VCR (or some other machine) works
7. How a bad habit develops
8. How people fall into debt

Assignments with a Specific Audience and Purpose

1. You've been asked to write part of a driver's education textbook that deals with one of the following: making a three-point turn, parallel parking, handling a skid, or any other driving maneuver. Explain the process one step at a time. Remember, your audience consists of sixteen-year-olds who are just learning how to drive and who lack self-confidence and experience.

2. An author of books for young children, you want to show youngsters how to do something simple — put on boots, water a plant, or any other task. Explain the process in terms a young child would understand.

3. Write an article for *Consumer Reports* on how to shop for a certain product or service. Give specific steps explaining how to save money, get your money's worth, and so on.

4. Write a process analysis showing how to save a life in a specific way. The paper might be on CPR or rescue breathing or the Heimlich maneuver or any other life-saving method. Your audience will be people from your neighborhood who are taking a first-aid class.

5. Your best friend plans to move into his/her own apartment and doesn't know the first thing about how to choose one. Explain the process of selecting an apartment — where to look, what to investigate, what questions to ask before signing a lease.

6. You write an "advice to the lovelorn" column for the campus paper. A correspondent writes saying that he or she wants to break up with a steady boyfriend/girlfriend but doesn't know how to do it without hurting the person. Advise the writer on the process of ending a meaningful relationship with a minimal amount of pain.

COMPARISON – CONTRAST

WHAT IS COMPARISON – CONTRAST?

As reasoning creatures, we frequently try to make sense of the world by finding similarities and differences in the experiences we encounter. Seeing how things are alike (comparing) and seeing how they are different (contrasting) helps us impose meaning on experiences that otherwise might remain fragmented and disconnected. We may think to ourselves — barely aware of the fact that we are comparing and contrasting — "I woke up in a great mood this morning, but now I feel uneasy and anxious. I wonder why I don't feel the same way. I wonder why I feel so different." This inner questioning, which often occurs in a flash, is just one example of the way we use comparison and contrast to understand ourselves and our world.

Comparing and contrasting also helps us make choices in everyday life. We compare and contrast everything from two brands of soap we might buy to two possible colleges we might attend. We listen to a favorite radio station, watch a preferred

293

nightly news show, select a particular dessert from a menu — all because we have done some degree of comparing and contrasting. We often weigh these alternatives in an unstudied, casual manner, as when we flip from one radio station to another. But if we have to make important decisions, we tend to think rigorously about how things are alike or different: Should I live in a dorm or rent an apartment? Should I accept the higher-paying job or the lower-paying job that offers more challenges? Such a deliberate approach to comparison–contrast may also provide us with needed insight into significant contemporary issues: Do recent events in Central America parallel what happened earlier in Vietnam? What are the merits of the various positions on abortion?

WHEN TO USE COMPARISON–CONTRAST

You need to develop a sure sense of when it is appropriate to use the comparison–contrast method of development. Often the wording of an assignment, as in those that follow, signals that comparison–contrast is called for:

> Compare the way male and female relationships are depicted in *Cosmopolitan, Ms., Playboy,* and *Esquire.* Which publication has the most limited view of men and women? Which has the broadest perspective?

> Many social commentators have observed that college students and their parents share the same view about the purpose of a college education: both expect colleges to equip young people with immediately marketable skills. Indicate whether you think this is an accurate assessment by comparing your own and your parents' beliefs about the purpose of a college degree.

> One has only to watch a few football, basketball, or baseball games to realize that each sport has a special appeal to its fans. Contrast the unique drawing power of each sport, being sure to arrive at some conclusions about the nature of each sport's following.

The issue of prayer in public school has received a good deal of attention lately. Take a position on the controversy by contrasting the views of those who believe prayer should be allowed in public schools with those who believe it should be prohibited.

Comparison – contrast assignments like these are common in college writing classes because they demand logical thinking and sound organizational skills.

At other times, assignments will, upon consideration, lend themselves to comparison – contrast. For instance, although the words *compare* and *contrast* do not appear in the following assignments, essay responses to the assignments could be organized around the comparison – contrast format.

The emergence of the two-career family is one of the major phenomena of our culture. Discuss the advantages and disadvantages of having both parents work, showing how you feel about such two-career households.

Some people believe that the 1950s, often called the golden age of television, produced several never-to-be equaled comedy classics. Do you agree that shows like *I Love Lucy* and *The Honeymooners* are superior to the situation comedies aired on television today?

There has been considerable criticism recently of the news coverage in the city's two leading newspapers, the *Herald* and the *Beacon.* Indicate whether you think the criticism is valid by discussing the similarities and differences in the two papers' news coverage.

Note: The last assignment shows that a comparison – contrast essay may cover both similarities *and* differences, not just one or the other.

As you have seen, comparison – contrast can be the key strategy for achieving an essay's purpose. But comparison – contrast can also be a supplemental method used to help make a point in an essay organized chiefly around another pattern of development. A paper *defining* common sense, for example, might include a section contrasting common sense with book learning. Or a paper analyzing the *effects* of reinstating the draft might spend some time comparing different views toward compulsory military service. Or if you were writing an *argumentation–persuasion* essay urging stricter controls over drug abuse in the workplace, you might compare several companies' approaches for dealing with drug-related work problems.

SUGGESTIONS FOR USING COMPARISON–CONTRAST IN AN ESSAY

The following suggestions will be helpful whether you use comparison–contrast as a dominant or supportive pattern of development.

1. Clarify your purpose.   It is important to keep in mind that comparison–contrast is not an end in itself. The objective is not to turn an essay into a mechanical list of "how *A* differs from *B*" or "how *A* is like *B*." As with all the patterns discussed in this book, comparison–contrast should be viewed as a strategy for making a point or meeting a larger purpose.

Sometimes, your purpose will be to *present information* about your subjects as objectively as possible: "This is what the *Herald*'s news coverage is like. This is what the *Beacon*'s news coverage is like." The purpose of comparison–contrast here is purely *informative*.

More frequently, you will use comparison–contrast to evaluate your subjects. In such a case, your goal will be to reach a conclusion or make a judgment. ("The *Herald* and the *Beacon* spend too much time reporting local news," or "In the recent hostage crisis, the *Herald*'s analysis of negotiation strategies was more insightful than the *Beacon*'s.") Comparison–contrast can also be used to *persuade* readers to agree with your opinion ("Neither the *Herald* nor the *Beacon* provided comprehensive coverage of the recent hostage crisis") or to take action ("People interested in thorough coverage of international events should buy the *Herald*"). Or your persuasive objective may be to propose a change: "If the *Beacon* is to regain its reputation, it must assign more reporters to international stories."

Comparing and contrasting also make it possible to draw an *analogy* between two seemingly unrelated subjects. An analogy is an imaginative comparison that delves beneath the surface differences of the subjects in order to expose their unsuspected similarities or significant differences. Your purpose may be to show that singles bars and zoos share a number of striking similarities. Or you may want to illustrate that wolves and humans raise their young in much the same way, but that wolves go about the process in a more civilized manner. The analogical approach can also make a complex subject easier to understand — as when the national deficit is compared to a household budget gone awry. Analogies are often dramatic and instructive, challenging you and your audience to consider subjects in a new light. But analogies do not speak for themselves. It must be clear to the reader how the analogy demonstrates your purpose.

2. Select subjects that are at least somewhat alike.   Unless you plan to develop an analogy, the subjects you choose to compare or contrast should have in common some obvious characteristics or qualities. It makes sense to compare different parts of the country, two situation comedies, or several college teachers. But an interesting and reasonable paper would probably not result from, let's say, a comparison of a situation comedy with a detective show. Your subjects must belong to the same general group so that your comparison – contrast stays within logical bounds and does not veer off into pointlessness.

3. Present a clear thesis.   An essay developed primarily through comparison – contrast should be focused by a strong thesis. This controlling idea will often do the following:

- Name the subjects being compared and contrasted.
- Indicate whether the essay focuses on the subjects' similarities *or* differences, or whether the essay focuses on the subjects' similarities *and* differences.
- State the main point of comparison or contrast covered.

Here are several examples of well-written thesis statements for comparison – contrast essays. The first thesis statement signals similarities, the second indicates differences, and the last shows similarities and differences:

The confusion many people feel as they approach middle age is much like the upheavals they experienced as adolescents.

Most retired people have different priorities than people in their forties and fifties who are still working.

Nontraditional students struggle with the same problems most students do, but they also have to deal with a special set of pressures.

Not all comparison – contrast essays will contain thesis statements as structured as those above. Moreover, the thesis in a comparison – contrast essay does not have to be placed at the start of an essay; it may appear as a judgment or persuasive statement at the conclusion of the paper. In all cases, though, the thesis should state what you will show or what you have shown about your subjects.

4. Select the points to be discussed.   Once the purpose, subject, and thesis of your essay have been determined, you need to decide which points of similarity or difference to discuss. This means you have to identify which aspects of the subjects to compare or contrast. College professors, for instance, could be compared and contrasted on the basis of their testing methods, ability to motivate students, confidence in front of a classroom, personalities, level of enthusiasm, and so forth.

Brainstorming helps generate possible points to cover. When brainstorming, try to produce more raw material than you will need, so that you have the luxury of narrowing the list down to the most significant points. When you select the points to cover, be sure to consider your readers. Ask yourself: "Will they be familiar with this item? Will I need this item to get my message across? Will my audience find this item interesting or convincing?" What the audience knows, what they do not know, and what you can project about their reactions should influence your choices. And, of course, you need to select points that support your thesis. If your essay explains the differences between healthy, sensible diets and dangerous crash diets, it would not be appropriate to talk about aerobic exercise. Finally, the points discussed must introduce important and interesting issues. It does not make much sense to focus on points of comparison or contrast that are obvious and require little or no thought from you or your reader. Imagine you want to write an essay making the point that, despite their differences, hard rock of the 1960s and punk rock of the 1970s both reflected young people's disillusionment with society. You would probably produce little of value if you contrasted the long uncombed hair of the sixties with the short spikey cuts of the seventies. But contrasting song lyrics (protest versus nihilistic messages) would lead to interesting and significant insights.

5. Organize the points to be discussed.   After selecting the points to include in the essay, you should use a systematic, logical plan when presenting the points of comparison and contrast. If they are not organized, your essay will be little more than a confusing maze of ideas. There are two common ways to organize an essay developed wholly or in part by comparison–contrast: the *one-side-at-a-time* method and the *point-by-point* method. Although both strategies may be used in a paper, one method usually predominates.

One-side-at-a-time method.   In the one-side-at-a-time method, you discuss everything relevant about one subject first and then switch, in turn, to the other subjects. For example, in the assignment that asked you to analyze the news coverage in two local papers, you might first talk about the *Herald*'s coverage of international, national, and local news; then you would discuss the *Beacon*'s coverage of international, national, and local news. Note that the areas discussed should be the same for both newspapers. It would not be logical to review the *Herald*'s coverage of international, national, and local news and then to detail the *Beacon*'s magazine supplements, modern living section, and comics page. Moreover, the areas compared and contrasted should be presented in the same order.

This is how you would organize an essay using the one-side-at-a-time method:

Everything about *A*   *Herald*'s news coverage:
                                                • international
                                                • national
                                                • local

Everything about *B*   *Beacon*'s news coverage:
                                                • international
                                                • national
                                                • local

Point-by-point method. In the point-by-point method of development, you alternate from one aspect of the first subject to the same aspect in your other subject(s). For example, if this method were used when comparing or contrasting the *Herald* and the *Beacon,* you would first discuss the *Herald*'s international coverage and then the *Beacon*'s international coverage; next the *Herald*'s national coverage and then the *Beacon*'s national coverage; and finally, the *Herald*'s local coverage and then the *Beacon*'s local coverage.

An essay using the point-by-point method would be organized like this:

First Aspect of *A* and *B*	*Beacon*: international coverage
	Herald: international coverage
Second Aspect of *A* and *B*	*Beacon*: national coverage
	Herald: national coverage
Third Aspect of *A* and *B*	*Beacon*: local coverage
	Herald: local coverage

Deciding which of these two methods of organization to use is a personal choice, but there are a number of factors to consider. The one-side-at-a-time method tends to convey a more unified feeling since it highlights broad similarities and differences. It is, therefore, an effective pattern when your subjects are fairly uncomplicated. This strategy also works well when essays are brief; the reader won't find it difficult to remember what has been said about *A* when reading about *B*.

Because it permits more extensive coverage of similarities and differences, the point-by-point method is a wise choice when subjects are complex. This pattern is also useful when an essay is lengthy since readers would probably find it difficult to remember, let's say, ten pages of information about *A* while reading the next ten pages of *B*. However, the point-by-point approach may cause readers to lose sight of the broader picture, so remember to keep them focused on your central point.

6. Supply the reader with clear organizational cues. Although an organized comparison – contrast format is important, it does not guarantee that readers will be able to follow your line of thought easily. Organizational cues — especially linking devices that signal similarities or differences — are needed to show readers where they have been and where they are going.

Such organizational cues are essential in all writing, but they are especially crucial in a paper using comparison – contrast. By indicating clearly when subjects are being compared or contrasted, the cues help weave the discussion into a coherent, seamless whole.

The cues in boldface type below could be used to *signal similarities* in an essay discussing the news coverage in the *Herald* and the *Beacon:*

- The *Beacon* **also** allots only a small portion of the front page to global news.
- **In the same way,** the *Herald* tries to include at least three local stories on the first page.
- **Likewise,** the *Beacon* emphasizes the importance of up-to-date reporting of town meetings.
- The *Herald* is **similarly** committed to extensive coverage of high school and college sports.

The following linking cues in boldface type could be used to *signal differences* in the same essay:

- **By way of contrast,** the *Herald*'s editorial page deals with national matters on the average of three times a week.
- **On the other hand,** the *Beacon* does not share the *Herald*'s enthusiasm for interviews with national figures.
- The *Beacon,* **however,** does not encourage its reporters to tackle national stories the way the *Herald* does.
- **But** the *Herald*'s coverage of the Washington scene is much more comprehensive than its competitor's.

When using comparison – contrast, try not to pay obsessive attention to the mechanics of organizing your essay. Although the paper should have a logical structure, you do not want the essay to deteriorate into a rote listing of how things are alike or different. Nor do you want to become a slave to format, forcing points into an artificial or uncomfortable fit, rather like Cinderella's stepsisters hacking off their toes in order to squeeze into the glass slipper. Remember, comparison–contrast is a means to an end; that end is to open up a subject for exploration, providing new ways of thinking about a subject.

STUDENT ESSAY AND COMMENTARY

The following student essay was written by Carol Siskin in response to this assignment:

> In "High Noon," Art Spikol contrasts youthful innocence with mature sophistication, suggesting that he misses "the wonder and the awe" of youth. Given your choice, which would you rather be, younger or older? Your essay should explain why you prefer one time of life to another.

While reading Carol's paper, try to determine how well it applies the principles concerning the use of comparison–contrast. The commentary following the paper will help you look at Carol's essay more closely.

The Virtues of Growing Older

1   Our society worships youth. Advertisements convince us to buy Grecian Formula and Oil of Olay so we can hide the gray in our hair and smooth the lines on our face. Television shows feature attractive young stars with firm bodies, perfect complexions, and thick manes of hair. Middle-aged folks work out in gyms and jog down the street, trying to delay the effects of age.

2   Wouldn't any person over thirty gladly sign with the devil just to be young again? Isn't aging an experience to be dreaded? Perhaps it is un-American to say so, but I believe the answer is "No." Being young is often pleasant, but being older has distinct advantages.

3   When young, you are apt to be obsessed with your outward appearance. When my brother Dave and I were teens, we worked feverishly to perfect the bodies we had. Dave lifted weights, took

megadoses of vitamins, and drank a half-dozen milk shakes a day in order to turn his wiry adolescent frame into some muscular ideal. And as a teenager, I dieted constantly. No matter what I weighed, though, I was never satisfied with the way I looked. My legs were too heavy, my shoulders too broad, my waist too big. When Dave and I were young, we begged and pleaded for the "right" clothes. If our parents didn't get them for us, we felt our world would fall apart. How could we go to school wearing loose-fitting blazers when everyone else would be wearing smartly tailored leather jackets? We would be considered freaks. I often wonder how my parents, and parents in general, manage to tolerate their children during the adolescent years. Now, however, Dave and I are beyond such adolescent agonies. My rounded figure seems fine, and I don't deny myself a slice of pecan pie if I feel in the mood. Dave still works out, but he has actually become fond of his tall lanky frame. The two of us enjoy wearing fashionable clothes, but we are no longer slaves to style. And women, I'm embarrassed to admit, even more than men, have always seemed to be at the mercy of fashion. Now my clothes-- and my brother's--are attractive yet easy to wear. We no longer feel anxious about what others will think. As long as we feel good about how we look, we are happy.

Being older is preferable to being younger in another way. 4 Obviously, I still have important choices to make about my life, but I have already made many of the critical decisions that confront those just starting out. I chose the man I wanted to marry. I decided to have children. I elected to return to college to complete my education. But when you are young, major decisions await you at every turn. "What college should I attend?" "What career should I pursue?" "Should I get married?" "Should I have children?" These are just a few of the issues facing young people. It's no wonder that, despite their carefree facade, they are often confused, uncertain, and troubled by all the unknowns in their future.

But the greatest benefit of being forty is knowing who I am. 5 The most unsettling aspect of youth is the uncertainty you feel about your values, goals, and dreams. Being young means wondering what is worth working for. Being young means feeling happy with yourself one day and wishing you were never born the next. It means trying on new selves by taking up with different crowds. It means resenting your parents and their way of life one minute and then feeling you will never be as good or as accomplished as they are. By way of contrast, forty is sanity. I have a surer self-identity now. I don't laugh at jokes I don't think are funny. I can make a speech in front of a town meeting or complain in a store because I am no longer terrified that people will laugh at me; I am no longer anxious that everyone must like me. I no longer blame my parents for my every personality quirk or keep a running score of everything they did wrong raising me. Life has taught me that I, not they, am responsible for who I am. We are all human beings--neither saints nor devils.

Most Americans blindly accept the idea that newer is automatically better. But a human life contradicts this premise. There is a great deal of happiness to be found as we grow older. My own parents, now in their sixties, recently told me that they are happier now than they have ever been. They would not want to be my age. Did this surprise me? At first, yes. Then it gladdened me. Their contentment holds out great promise for me as I move into the next--perhaps even better--phase of my life.   6

In response to the assignment, Carol decided to disprove the widespread belief that being young is preferable to being old. The *comparison – contrast* pattern allows her to analyze the drawbacks of one and the merits of the other, thus providing the essay with an *evaluative purpose.* Using the title to indicate her point of view, Carol places the *thesis* at the end of her two-paragraph introduction: "Being young is often pleasant, but being older has distinct advantages." Note that the thesis accomplishes several things. It names the two subjects to be discussed and clarifies Carol's point of view about her subjects. The thesis also implies that the essay will focus on the contrasts between these two periods of life.

To support her assertion that older is better, Carol supplies examples from her own life, organizing the examples around three main points: attitudes about appearance, decisions about life choices, and questions of self-concept. These key points are explored in separate supporting paragraphs, with each paragraph focused by a topic sentence: "When young, you are apt to be obsessed with your outward appearance" (paragraph 3); "Being older is preferable to being younger in another way" (4); and "But the greatest benefit of being forty is knowing who I am" (5).

Now let's look more closely at the way these three central points are presented. Carol obviously considers appearances the least important of a person's worries, life choices more important, and self-concept the most critical. And so she uses *emphatic order* to sequence the supporting paragraphs, with the phrase "But the greatest benefit" signaling the special significance of the last issue. Carol is also careful throughout the essay to use *transi-*

tions to help readers follow her line of thinking: *"Now, however,* Dave and I are beyond such adolescent agonies" (3); *"But* when you are young, major decisions await you at every turn" (4); and *"By way of contrast,* forty is sanity" (5).

Although Carol has worked hard to write a well-organized paper — and has on the whole been successful — she does not feel compelled to make the paper fit a rigid format. She does not, for example, use the identical structure in each supporting paragraph. All three supporting paragraphs do use the *one-side-at-a-time format* — that is, everything about one age group is discussed before there is a shift to the other age group. But notice that the third and fifth paragraphs start with young people and then move to adults, whereas the fourth paragraph reverses the sequence by starting with older people.

As you read the third paragraph, you might have noted that Carol ran into a problem. Two sentences in the paragraph disrupt the *unity* of Carol's discussion: "I often wonder how my parents, and parents in general, tolerate their children during the adolescent years," and "Women, I'm embarrassed to admit . . . have always seemed to be at the mercy of fashion." These sentences should be deleted because they do not develop the idea that adolescents are overly concerned with appearances.

Carol's final paragraph brings the essay to a pleasing and interesting close. The conclusion recalls the point made in the introduction: Americans overvalue youth. Carol also uses the conclusion to broaden the scope of her discussion. Rather than continuing to focus on herself, she briefly mentions her parents and the pleasure they take in life. By bringing her parents into the essay, Carol is able to make a gently philosophical observation about the promise that awaits her as she grows older. The implication is that a similarly positive future awaits us, too.

Carol made a number of changes when reworking her essay, but it is especially interesting to see the way she revised the introduction. The original draft of the introduction is reprinted here.

First Draft Version

America is a land filled with people who worship youth. We admire dynamic young achievers; our middle-aged citizens work out in gyms; all of us wear tight tops and colorful sneakers--clothes that look fine on the young but ridiculous on aging bodies. Television shows revolve around perfect-looking young stars, while commercials entice us with products that will keep us young.

Wouldn't every older person want to be young again? Isn't aging to be avoided? It may be slightly unpatriotic to say so, but I believe the answer is "No." Being young may be pleasant at times, but I would rather be my forty-year-old self. I no longer have to agonize about my physical appearance, I have already made many of my crucial life decisions, and I am much less confused about who I am.

After looking closely at her original two-paragraph introduction, Carol was dissatisfied with what she had written. Although not quite sure what bothered her, she knew the paragraphs were flat and failed to start the essay on a strong note. She decided to begin her revision by whittling down the wordy opening sentence, making it crisper and more powerful: "Our society worships youth." That done, she next eliminated two bland sentences ("We admire dynamic young achievers," and "all of us wear tight tops and colorful sneakers"), and she made several vague references more concrete and interesting. "Commercials entice us with products that will keep us young" became "Grecian Formula and Oil of Olay . . . hide the gray in our hair and smooth the lines on our face"; "perfect-looking young stars" became "attractive young stars with firm bodies, perfect complexions, and thick manes of hair." With the addition of these specifics, the first paragraph became more vigorous and interesting.

Carol next made some subtle changes in the two questions that opened the second paragraph of the original introduction. Certainly, the revised sentences ("Wouldn't any person over thirty gladly sign with the devil just to be young again?" and "Isn't aging an experience to be dreaded?") are more emphatic than the originals. Moreover, these rephrased, attention-getting questions convey our national obsession with youth, a point that had to be made dramatically if the essay were to achieve its purpose. Carol also revised the end of the original second paragraph. Because the paper is relatively short, and the subject matter easy to understand, Carol decided to omit her somewhat awkward *plan of development* ("I no longer have to agonize about my physical appearance, I have already made many of my crucial life decisions, and I am much less confused about who I am"). This change made it possible to end the introduction with a strong statement of the essay's thesis.

Once these revisions were made, Carol was able to get her essay off to a solid start. And, on the whole, she maintains this strength to the end, producing an interesting piece that offers food for thought.

The essays that follow use comparison and contrast to explore a wide range of subjects. With no pretense of objectivity, Suzanne Britt ("That Lean and Hungry Look") contrasts fat and thin people and finds the latter an altogether inferior species. Famed ecologist Rachel Carson shows us two pictures in her "Fable for Tomorrow": one of a beautiful, environmentally healthy village, the other of the same village devastated by the irresponsible use of pesticides. In "High Noon," Art Spikol compares the magical movie matinees of years past with the current crop of films that attract youngsters. In "The Village," Henry David Thoreau takes a look at the difference between his quiet life on Walden Pond and the bustling affairs of the townspeople. And Richard Rodriguez's "Workers" is a highly personal account of different work situations.

Suzanne Britt

Freelance writer Suzanne Britt, a native of Winston-Salem, North Carolina, studied at Salem College and Washington University. Her work has been published in the *Baltimore Sun, Newsday,* and *The New York Times.* A regular columnist for a newsletter devoted to the works of Charles Dickens, Britt contributes to Duke University's *Books and Religion,* a publication featuring religious and social commentary. Britt's first book, *Skinny People Are Dull and Crunchy Like Carrots* (1982), is an expansion of the essay below, which first appeared in *Newsweek*'s "My Turn" column. Her second book, *Show and Tell,* was published in 1982.

That Lean and Hungry Look[1]

When was the last time you saw a popular magazine that didn't advertise on its cover a new diet or exercise program? How many health clubs have sprung up in your town in recent years? Everywhere we look, we're bombarded by anti-fat propaganda. Essayist Suzanne Britt is fed up with it all. Here's her case for the idea that fat people have nothing to lose but skinnies have a lot to gain.

Caesar was right. Thin people need watching. I've been watching them for most of my adult life, and I don't like what I see. When these narrow fellows spring at me, I quiver to my toes. Thin people come in all personalities, most of them menacing. You've got your "together" thin person, your mechanical thin person, your condescending thin person, your tsk-tsk thin person, your efficiency-expert thin person. All of them are dangerous.

---

[1]Britt's title is a reference to a line from Shakespeare's *Julius Caesar*. In the play, Caesar says he distrusts Cassius because Cassius has "a lean and hungry look; . . . such men are dangerous." Later in the play, Cassius helps assassinate Caesar, proving Caesar's fears were justified.

308

In the first place, thin people aren't fun. They don't know 2 how to goof off, at least in the best, fat sense of the word. They've always got to be adoing. Give them a coffee break, and they'll jog around the block. Supply them with a quiet evening at home, and they'll fix the screen door and lick S&H green stamps. They say things like "there aren't enough hours in the day." Fat people never say that. Fat people think the day is too damn long already.

Thin people make me tired. They've got speedy little metabo- 3 lisms that cause them to bustle briskly. They're forever rubbing their bony hands together and eyeing new problems to "tackle." I like to surround myself with sluggish, inert, easygoing fat people, the kind who believe that if you clean it up today, it'll just get dirty again tomorrow.

Some people say the business about the jolly fat person is a 4 myth, that all of us chubbies are neurotic, sick, sad people. I disagree. Fat people may not be chortling all day long, but they're a hell of a lot *nicer* than the wizened and shriveled. Thin people turn surly, mean, and hard at a young age because they never learn the value of a hot-fudge sundae for easing tension. Thin people don't like gooey soft things because they themselves are neither gooey nor soft. They are crunchy and dull, like carrots. They go straight to the heart of the matter while fat people let things stay all blurry and hazy and vague, the way things actually are. Thin people want to face the truth. Fat people know there is no truth. One of my thin friends is always staring at complex, unsolvable problems and saying, "The key thing is. . . ." Fat people never say that. They know there isn't any such thing as the key thing about anything.

Thin people believe in logic. Fat people see all sides. The 5 sides fat people see are rounded blobs, usually gray, always nebulous and truly not worth worrying about. But the thin person persists. "If you consume more calories than you burn," says one of my thin friends, "you will gain weight. It's that simple." Fat people always grin when they hear statements like that. They know better.

Fat people realize that life is illogical and unfair. They know 6 very well that God is not in his heaven and all is not right with the world. If God is up there, fat people could have two doughnuts and a big orange drink anytime they wanted it.

Thin people have a long list of logical things they are always 7 spouting off to me. They hold up one finger at a time as they reel off these things, so I won't lose track. They speak slowly as if to a young child. The list is long and full of holes. It contains tidbits like "get a grip on yourself," "cigarettes kill," "cholesterol clogs," "fit as a fiddle," "ducks in a row," "organize," and "sound fiscal management." Phrases like that.

They think these 2,000-point plans lead to happiness. Fat people know happiness is elusive at best and even if they could get the kind thin people talk about, they wouldn't want it. Wisely, fat people see that such programs are too dull, too hard, too off the mark. They are never better than a whole cheesecake.   8

Fat people know all about the mystery of life. They are the ones acquainted with the night, with luck, with fate, with playing it by ear. One thin person I know once suggested that we arrange all the parts of a jigsaw puzzle into groups according to size, shape, and color. He figured this would cut the time needed to complete the puzzle by at least 50 percent. I said I wouldn't do it. One, I like to muddle through. Two, what good would it do to finish early? Three, the jigsaw puzzle isn't the important thing. The important thing is the fun of four people (one thin person included) sitting around a card table, working a jigsaw puzzle. My thin friend had no use for my list. Instead of joining us, he went outside and mulched the boxwoods. The three remaining fat people finished the puzzle and made chocolate, double-fudged brownies to celebrate.   9

The main problem with thin people is they oppress. Their good intentions, bony torsos, tight ships, neat corners, cerebral machinations, and pat solutions loom like dark clouds over the loose, comfortable, spread-out, soft world of the fat. Long after fat people have removed their coats and shoes and put their feet up on the coffee table, thin people are still sitting on the edge of the sofa, looking neat as a pin, discussing rutabagas. Fat people are heavily into fits of laughter, slapping their thighs and whooping it up, while thin people are still politely waiting for the punch line.   10

Thin people are downers. They like math and morality and reasoned evaluation of the limitations of human beings. They have their skinny little acts together. They expound, prognose, probe, and prick.   11

Fat people are convivial. They will like you even if you're irregular and have acne. They will come up with a good reason   12 why you never wrote the great American novel. They will cry in your beer with you. They will put your name in the pot. They will let you off the hook. Fat people will gab, giggle, guffaw, gallumph, gyrate, and gossip. They are generous, giving, and gallant. They are gluttonous and goodly and great. What you want when you're down is soft and jiggly, not muscled and stable. Fat people know this. Fat people have plenty of room. Fat people will take you in.

Questions for Close Reading

1. What is the thesis of the selection? Locate the sentence(s) in which Britt states her main idea. If she does not state the thesis explicitly, express it in your own words.
2. Into what personality types does Britt divide thin people? What do these personality types have in common?
3. Britt writes that thin people use their free time for such activities as jogging, fixing a screen door, and pasting in green stamps. How are these activities similar?
4. Why does Britt approve of fat people's tendency to "let things stay all blurry and hazy and vague"?
5. Refer to your dictionary as needed to define the following words used in the selection: *wizened* (paragraph 4), *nebulous* (5), *fiscal* (7), *mulch* (9), *machinations* (10), *expound* (11), and *convivial* (12).

Questions About the Writer's Craft

1. Which comparison–contrast format does Britt use to develop her essay? Why might she have chosen this format?
2. How does Britt's choice of words and sentence structure establish an informal, light-hearted tone?
3. Why is Britt's carrot simile especially apt?
4. Where in the last paragraph does Britt use alliteration, the repetition of initial consonant sounds? What might have been her reason for using this technique?

Questions for Further Thought

1. Britt pokes fun at thin people who "always got to be adoing." Which do you value most — goal-oriented activity or the ability to relax and have a good time? Why?

2. Britt admires fat people's ability to recognize the limits of logic. How might this ability enrich life? How might it create problems?
3. Britt mocks those who are uncompromisingly principled. How might a person's overly scrupulous principles make life difficult for the individual and others?
4. According to Britt, people in need of reassurance prefer a "soft and jiggly" person to a "muscled and stable" one. Which kind of person comforts you more — someone who seems equally vulnerable or someone who seems more immune to distress? Why?

Writing Assignments Using Comparison – Contrast as a Method of Development

1. Write an essay contrasting two people who represent markedly dissimilar types. Perhaps one person is messy, the other neat. Or maybe one is worldly-wise while the other is unsophisticated. Or one might be punctual while the other is always late. Use the one-side-at-a-time or the point-by-point method to highlight the differences between the two people. Adopting a light, waggish tone, argue — as Britt does — that one type is superior to the other.
2. Britt scoffs at thin people who "believe in logic." Take two decisions you made recently — one fairly logical, the other more emotional. Contrast how you went about making the decisions, the outcomes of the decisions, and so on. Reach some conclusion about the value of logic and emotion in your life.

Writing Assignments Using Other Methods of Development

3. Britt enjoys the pleasures of good food and company. In a descriptive essay, recall a gathering where the food and company were especially satisfying. Through sensory details, convey the aroma, taste, and appearance of the food, as well as the social atmosphere.
4. Britt takes issue with the notion that thin is better than plump. What other prejudicial assumptions do you see at work in contemporary society? Select one and write an essay persuading readers that this idea is unfounded. Your tone may be serious or playful like Britt's.

Rachel Carson

Once accused of being a fearmonger, biologist Rachel Carson (1907–1964) is now recognized as one of the country's first environmentalists. She was the author of three popular books about the marine world: *The Sea Around Us* (1951), *Under the Sea Wind* (1952), and *The Edge of the Sea* (1955). But it was the publication of *Silent Spring* (1962), Carson's alarming study of the use of pesticides and herbicides, that brought her special attention and established her reputation as a passionate advocate for a clean environment. The following selection is taken from *Silent Spring.*

A Fable for Tomorrow

Fairy tales and fables often tell of people suffering under a wicked witch's curse, the evil spell robbing life of its beauty and condemning people to a bleak existence. Soon, though, the clever hero or heroine finds a way to remove the curse and bring the story to a happy ending. But ecologist Rachel Carson's fable is different: the curse is one that we have brought upon ourselves and that we alone have the power to remove.

There was once a town in the heart of America where all life   1
seemed to live in harmony with its surroundings. The town lay in the midst of a checkerboard of prosperous farms, with fields of grain and hillsides of orchards where, in spring, white clouds of bloom drifted above the green fields. In autumn, oak and maple and birch set up a blaze of color that flamed and flickered across a backdrop of pines. Then foxes barked in the hills and deer silently crossed the fields, half hidden in the mists of the fall mornings.

Along the roads, laurel, viburnum and alder, great ferns and   2
wildflowers delighted the traveler's eye through much of the year. Even in winter the roadsides were places of beauty, where countless birds came to feed on the berries and on the seed heads of the dried weeds rising above the snow. The countryside was, in fact,

famous for the abundance and variety of its bird life, and when the flood of migrants was pouring through in spring and fall people traveled from great distances to observe them. Others came to fish the streams, which flowed clear and cold out of the hills and contained shady pools where trout lay. So it had been from the days many years ago when the first settlers raised their houses, sank their wells, and built their barns.

Then a strange blight crept over the area and everything   3
began to change. Some evil spell had settled on the community: mysterious maladies swept the flocks of chickens; the cattle and sheep sickened and died. Everywhere was a shadow of death. The farmers spoke of much illness among their families. In the town the doctors had become more and more puzzled by new kinds of sickness appearing among their patients. There had been several sudden and unexplained deaths, not only among adults but even among children, who would be stricken suddenly while at play and die within a few hours.

There was a strange stillness. The birds, for example — where   4
had they gone? Many people spoke of them, puzzled and disturbed. The feeding stations in the backyards were deserted. The few birds seen anywhere were moribund; they trembled violently and could not fly. It was a spring without voices. On the mornings that had once throbbed with the dawn chorus of robins, catbirds, doves, jays, wrens, and scores of other bird voices there was now no sound; only silence lay over the fields and woods and marsh.

On the farms the hens brooded, but no chicks hatched. The   5
farmers complained that they were unable to raise any pigs— the litters were small and the young survived only a few days. The apple trees were coming into bloom but no bees droned among the blossoms, so there was no pollination and there would be no fruit.

The roadsides, once so attractive, were now lined with   6
browned and withered vegetation as though swept by fire. These, too, were silent, deserted by all living things. Even the streams were now lifeless. Anglers no longer visited them, for all the fish had died.

In the gutters under the eaves and between the shingles of   7
the roofs, a white granular powder still showed a few patches; some weeks before it had fallen like snow upon the roofs and the lawns, the fields and streams.

No witchcraft, no enemy action had silenced the rebirth of new life in this stricken world. The people had done it themselves. 8

This town does not actually exist, but it might easily have a thousand counterparts in America or elsewhere in the world. I know of no community that has experienced all the misfortunes I describe. Yet every one of these disasters has actually happened somewhere, and many real communities have already suffered a substantial number of them. A grim specter has crept upon us almost unnoticed, and this imagined tragedy may easily become a stark reality we all shall know. 9

Questions for Close Reading

1. What is the thesis of the selection? Locate the sentence(s) in which Carson states her main idea. If she does not state the thesis explicitly, express it in your own words.
2. What are some of the delights of Carson's beautiful, healthy countryside?
3. When Carson writes of "a strange blight," an "evil spell" (3), whose point of view is she adopting?
4. What are the effects of the blight?
5. Refer to your dictionary as needed to define the following words used in the selection: *viburnum* (paragraph 2), *alder* (2), *moribund* (4), and *specter* (9).

Questions About the Writer's Craft

1. To develop her essay, Carson uses the one-side-at-a-time method of comparison–contrast. What does this method enable her to do that the point-by-point approach would not?
2. Throughout the essay, Carson appeals to the reader's senses of sight and hearing. Which paragraphs are developed primarily through visual or auditory description? How do the sensory images in these paragraphs reinforce Carson's thesis?
3. Carson's diction (word choice) and sentence rhythm often resembles that of the Bible. For example, we read, "So it had been from the days many years ago" (2), "a strange blight crept over the area" (3), and "Everywhere was a shadow of death" (3). Why do you suppose Carson chose to echo the Bible in this way?
4. How does Carson's approach to her subject change in the last paragraph? What is the effect of this change?

Questions for Further Thought

1. What threat to the environment concerns you the most? Seepage from landfills? Disposal of nuclear wastes? Acid rain? What can the average person do to deal with this threat?
2. Environmentalists are sometimes referred to as "tree huggers." What attitude is suggested by this term? How do you feel about the term? About the attitude?
3. Do you think the concerns of environmentalists can be excessive and counterproductive? Explain.
4. Carson is concerned about the destruction of America's rural environment. Someone raised in a major city, however, may give little thought to flowing brooks, colorful orchards, and bird-songs. Why should someone accustomed to an urban environment care what happens to forests, farmlands, or lakes?

Writing Assignments Using Comparison – Contrast as a Method of Development

1. Carson imagines a fictional town before and after a blight. Consider a place once special to you that has been changed for the worse by some external force. Perhaps the culprit was noise pollution, urban development, a tornado, whatever. Write an essay contrasting the place before and after the change. Reach some conclusion about the future of this formerly treasured place.
2. In her essay, Carson provides descriptive details unique to particular seasons. For example, she writes that "in autumn, oak and maple and birch set up a blaze of color that flamed and flickered across a backdrop of pines" (1). Choosing a place you know well, contrast its sights, sounds, and smells during one season with those you have noticed during another time of year. Use rich sensory details to convey the differences between the two seasons.

Writing Assignments Using Other Methods of Development

3. Carson cites "white granular powder" (7) as the cause of the blight. Write a narrative about a time you noticed a visible environmental problem — say, smog blurring a city skyline, soot coating a window, or medical syringes discarded on the beach. Use vivid narrative details to capture the effect of the experience on you.
*4. Carson shows the effects of herbicides and pesticides on the environment. Focus on some other less global environmental problem with which you have had first-hand experience: graffiti on a building,

landscaping allowed to die, beer cans thrown in a neighborhood park. Analyze the way the situation affects people's attitudes and actions. Then offer some suggestions about how to avoid similar problems in the future. Peggy Anderson's "Children's Hospital" (110) and Tom Wolfe's "O Rotten Gotham—Sliding Down into the Behavioral Sink" (381) will help you appreciate the interaction between environment and human behavior.

Art Spikol

Art Spikol has used his writing talents in many ways. He was editor of *Philadelphia Magazine,* one of the country's most successful city publications; author of *Magazine Writing: The Inside Angle;* founder of The Philadelphia Writer's School. He has lectured widely on the subject of writing, but is probably best known for his "Nonfiction" column, a staple of *Writer's Digest* for over a decade. Today, a self-employed writer, editor, and graphic designer, he divides his time between advertising and his real love, writing; his first novel, a mystery entitled *The Physalia Incident,* was published in 1988. This selection originally appeared in *Philadelphia Magazine.*

High Noon

In some ways, life is a series of losses. Loved ones leave, pets die, neighborhoods are left behind. Yet the things we lose can endure — if we work at remembering them. In the following selection, Art Spikol recreates an experience that was a highlight of his childhood: the Saturday movie matinee. Discovering the extent of his loss when he takes his daughter to a modern-day matinee, Spikol reminisces about the vanished world of cliffhanger serials, newsreels, and cartoons. And behind this nostalgia lies a sense of loss for the world that disappeared along with the Saturday matinee.

The Saturday matinee, for those of you who ever chafed   1
while waiting for the weekend to arrive, is dead. I learned this only recently when I took my seven-year-old daughter, Elizabeth, to one; first I consulted the neighborhood movie guide in the paper, expecting to find dozens of kiddie matinees, and found maybe four or five in the city. The movies I attended as a kid — the Lindley, the Logan and the Rockland in the Logan section of the city — are no longer there. The ones I attended as a teenager — the Benner, the Castor and the Tyson, all on Castor Avenue in

the Northeast — were showing R-rated films and had no matinees listed.

I finally ended up at a theater called the Parkwood Manor in a small shopping center at Academy and Byberry Roads in the Northeast, dragging my daughter, who would rather have gone to a friend's house anyway, behind me.

Driving out there, we talked. I told Elizabeth about the old Saturday matinees, the ones that I grew up with. I told her about the time I was ejected from the Lindley on 5th Street because I ran up on the stage to avoid capture by a neighborhood bully, and how I sat and wept on the steps of the theater, not knowing where to go or what to do. I told her about the harmonica contest I entered at the Logan Theater on Broad Street with what would have seemed a pretty good chance of winning — there was only one other contestant — and how I played "Oh Susannah" and "Old Black Joe" and how nobody recognized either song, and how I turned red and stared at my shoes while the other kid played "The Flight of the Bumble Bee." I told her about the drawings they used to have — they'd give away a bicycle to the lucky kid whose ticket stub number matched the one they called — and how it was always a rich kid who won. The more I told her about these things and other things like the candy boxes that used to honk and popcorn that came out of machines, the more excited and curious she became to arrive at the Parkwood Manor — not so much to see *The Wonders of Aladdin* and the two cartoons, but to relive something of her daddy's world.

The Parkwood Manor, it turned out, is a large theater by today's standards and a good-sized one by yesterday's, not yet having been twinned. It shows signs of wear — many of the seats have been cut or torn and are held intact by wide strips of tape, and some of the wall decorations have seen better days, but overall the theater is pleasant and so are the people who work there: a cheerful ticket-seller who smiled and said hello; an older, gray-haired ticket-taker who chatted amiably about how bad business is these days, and a young woman behind the candy counter who told me that she'd be on duty throughout the picture if I wanted anything else.

We bought our popcorn and Raisinets and Jujyfruits and soda and took our seats, and waited.

I will tell you what I learned at the Parkwood Manor. But 6
first, let me tell you about 1944 and a woman, a gorgeous,
smooth-skinned brunette goddess who managed to move unen-
cumbered despite her tight khaki pants, despite the sleek boots
and the pure white, tight, button-down-the-front blouse which
barely restrained a chest yearning for release. I loved her for
things she had and which I did not understand: her breasts, her
buttocks. I loved the way she moved through the jungle, graceful
and sure of herself, like the ladies in today's deodorant commercials, and I loved it when she moved over rough terrain and what
happened to her hips when she did so. The camera spent a lot of
time following her, as did the native bearers who never thought to
take advantage of their position at the rear, as did I, from the
audience. But while those on the screen were worried about
mean-looking men with too-perfect mustaches, used-car-salesmen
types transplanted, somehow, to darkest Africa, I was worried
about her buttons.

I was eight and in love with Nyoka the Jungle Girl. 7

I had her for only a few minutes each week, but after they 8
were over I took her memory home and thought about her in the
privacy of my bed, in that little tent theater under my covers. I
was old enough to get a tickly feeling in my loins, too young to
know what it was all about: I simply wished she could have been
my mother.

This was the stuff of which the serials were made: 9

Scene: a cavern   Nyoka has been lured there, and now she 10
stands alone, vulnerable and trapped. Suddenly there is a sound
like pistol fire — it is the floor of the cavern cracking beneath her
feet. The whole screen trembles, the theater vibrates from the
noise. And then, with a rip and a gasp, the cavern floor opens — it
is like watching an earthquake — and bubbling up from under it
is molten lava. A thousand little kids are bouncing up and down,
screaming; one of them spills his candy on me.

Nyoka leaps for a hanging vine — and the cavern floor col- 11
lapses. I am, at this point, transfixed; my heart is thumping and I
have forgotten the wad of candy in my cheek. I sit there watching
her hang from the vine (she even *hangs* beautifully) kicking her
wonderful legs, and as the lava bubbles up, almost touching her, I
am wondering about what happens if she falls: will those breasts
and hips and buttocks boil away and become vapor? The vine

begins to tear [*closeup of vine*] thread by thread, each thread snapping like the crack of a whip. When there is only enough left to floss Nyoka's beautiful white teeth, the screen disintegrates into a crescendo of organ music and gives way to a title something like:

NEXT WEEK
LAIR OF EVIL

If that were all there'd been to it — the few minutes of Nyoka or Flash Gordon or Secret Agent X-9 — the serials alone would have been worth the three-block walk to the Lindley. The Saturday matinee was the high point of every kid's week back then; it was the long-awaited moment, like a particularly good dessert after a dreadful meal, filling enough to have been the meal itself. Today you can see some of it on television — the Dead End Kids, Our Gang, the Bowery Boys, the Three Stooges — but watching on a small screen, interrupted by commercials for overpriced games and toys, is not anything like seeing it giant-sized and experiencing it as a member of a concerned multitude. 12

To relieve the tension, cartoons usually followed the serials. The Second World War was being fought, and it was probably fought nowhere as bravely and as brilliantly as in neighborhood theaters: Bugs Bunny, for instance, was pitted against Hitler, and won. Or there was more serious stuff, some of it outright propaganda, subtly indoctrinating us, and we would laugh and cheer in all the right parts, patriotic little bastards that we were. There was a sense of total participation in that war that has never since been duplicated, and the louder we cheered, the surer victory. 13

This was all before television — which made the movies not only the sole visual treat of the week, but the only place to see film coverage of the events that shaped the world, and so the newsreel was an important part of any theater fare, Saturday matinees included. Warner-Pathé News opened with a burst of Sousa-like band music and the crowing of the famous rooster, and it was the Warner-Pathé rooster which told us it was time to go to the bathroom: do it now or you'll miss something important. For me, the rooster was part of a conditioned response. Even if I didn't *have* to go, the rooster made me *want* to go. And when I got back, there was still time to boo the enemy, cheer 14

American advances and FDR, and whistle at the beauty contest queens without knowing why.

Then the coming attractions — small, magic glimpses of our movie future — and then the main feature.

The main feature! You'd almost forgotten there *was* one, and a sort of excitement filled you when you realized that the show was just *starting*. It was at the Lindley that I saw *Cat People*, a film which so terrified me that I sat up in bed for three nights straight, afraid to lie down or close my eyes. I saw *The Purple Heart* at the Lindley, and *Bataan*, and *Guadalcanal Diary*. I saw Frank Sinatra sing *The House I Live In*, a very moving short about brotherhood and working together, things that seemed very possible in those days. I saw every adventure that ever unfolded on the Spanish Main or the Barbary Coast or in Sherwood Forest. It was the fighting we wanted to see, the tales of bravery, although we knew that we had to put up with a little mush when Errol Flynn would have to stop swinging on curtain sashes occasionally to make love to somebody — but in those soft, tender moments we would boo and throw candy at girls. When the action came back on again, the theater fell silent once more until the hero came to the rescue and the good guys attacked the bad guys.

When it was over we ran from the theater and continued the action in the streets on the way home, and what part you took would depend upon how much influence you had with your peers, which usually depended upon how big you were. For us smaller guys, it was a *fait accompli:* I was a Japanese soldier, or the Sheriff of Nottingham, and I was doomed to die soon and in agony. But I was glad to do it for the cause.

I would arrive home soaked with sweat, and my mother, who thought of perspiration of any kind as the first sign of yellow fever, would run her hand through my hair with disapproval and tell me I would probably get sick and miss school, not as bad a fate as she imagined, and then she would ask me how the movie had been. I would always say the same thing: "Great!"

And it was. There was nothing like it, and I guess there will be nothing like it ever again. There was something unrestrained about Saturday matinees, and whatever it was, it's dead now. To remember it is to mourn.

I had hoped to find it alive and well at the Parkwood Manor, a theater which can seat about 1,000 people. But when we went to our seats, we had the theater to ourselves. There were no more than 20 to 25 people there, and that was all there was going to be. There is no question that such a matinee loses money, despite the fact that there is no newsreel, no serial, no coming attractions, no shorts, and only two old and not-very-good cartoons.

But — almost as if they knew what I was there for — they   21
showed as their "main feature" *The Wonders of Aladdin,* with Donald O'Connor, a color extravaganza produced at no small cost back when it was made — about 15 years ago, I would guess. The fact that it was out of another era was not hard to substantiate: in one scene, the Prince, one of the heroes, tells a wounded soldier to chew a little hashish to relieve the pain: in another, the heroine is running across the desert trying to escape from the baddies, and — because she is wearing a very short dress — she is running with one hand holding the dress down over her crotch. Take my word for it, it was an old movie, and I even vaguely remembered seeing it once, long ago. The kids who were there seemed to like it, but it was hard to tell. No one would have dared to cheer; it would have been hollow and presumptuous, like the noise made when a book is dropped in a library.

I remember one whispered comment, from a little boy a few   22
rows behind us. Donald O'Connor races in to rescue the lady in distress, in this case a voluptuous brunette hanging by her wrists, apparently stark naked. She has been tortured. She is also hidden from the viewer's eyes by a large gong, and when she sees O'Connor she twists frantically to turn her body around so that he can't see her private parts. It is one of the movie's funniest moments, this maiden suddenly getting modesty, and one of the kids behind me says wistfully, "If only that thing wasn't in the way, we could see *everything.*" He was about seven years old.

Kids haven't changed much, but the world around them has.   23
The Saturday matinee may be alive and well under certain circumstances — like when a film ballyhooed on TV comes to town for a limited engagement — but then it is simply an event, not *the* event. The circus is over.

Movies used to open with "The Star Spangled Banner." The   24
audience, kids and grownups alike, would rise as one to the music and sing the words, watching the screen as the flag whipped slowly in the wind. I don't think the flag is particularly beautiful, but when I remember myself at eight, I know that it was beautiful once. Occasionally there'd be a serviceman in the audience home

on furlough, and he'd salute while other adults would place their hands over their hearts, and we kids, identifying much more strongly with the guys at the front than with our parents at home, would salute, too. We didn't question the flag. We didn't know that it could be used to cover things up as well as to liberate. It may not have been the best of times back then, but it was certainly the easiest of times; we knew all we had to know, and we knew what we had to do.

Sophistication killed the Saturday matinee, and the kid who watches *Kojak* and *All in the Family* and *Police Woman* and the uncountable news and talk shows gets sophisticated early. There is no Aladdin's lamp, no genie. The wonder and the awe and the innocence are gone.   25

And what's left? What is an appropriate way to say goodbye to an era that meant so much to so many, an era in which you could always tell the good guys from the bad, the right causes from the wrong? Maybe to do it like the old cartoons did — not say *The End,* but have a happy little pig stick his head out through a multicolored circle, wave his white glove across our vanished childhoods, and say, to joyful, upbeat music, "Th-th-tha-that's all, folks!"   26

Questions for Close Reading

1. What is the thesis of the selection? Locate the sentence(s) in which Spikol states his main idea. If he does not state the thesis explicitly, express it in your own words.
2. Why did Spikol enjoy the Saturday matinees he attended as a child? What needs does he say these matinees filled for him?
3. According to Spikol, what factors contributed to the death of the Saturday matinee? Do you agree with his conclusions?
4. The matinees of Spikol's childhood occurred during wartime. What evidence is there in the essay that Spikol's nostalgia for matinees is connected with his nostalgia for a particular era?
5. Refer to your dictionary as needed to define the following words used in the selection: *chafed* (paragraph 1), *transfixed* (11), *crescendo* (11), *indoctrinating* (13), *substantiate* (21), and *furlough* (24).

Questions About the Writer's Craft

1. Find where Spikol moves from the present movie theater to the past,

and where he moves back into the present, thus completing his comparison–contrast. How does Spikol signal that these shifts in time are going to occur?

2. The title "High Noon" is taken from a classic Western movie — filmed in black and white — about a duel between a hero and a villain. Why do you think Spikol chose this title for his essay?

3. In a typical comparison–contrast essay, a writer balances the time given to each side. Why do you think Spikol devotes most of "High Noon" to the Saturday matinees he saw as a child and so little to the show to which he took his daughter?

4. Why does Spikol end his essay with the image of the "happy little pig" waving good-bye? What things have come to an end?

Questions for Further Thought

1. How might Spikol's experience prove the maxim, "You can't go home again"? What experiences have you had that exemplify this saying?

2. Movies tend to reflect the values of contemporary society. What messages do today's movies convey to children? Consider closely specific films and movie characters.

3. If the Saturday matinee is dead, what has replaced it? How do today's children amuse themselves on weekends? Are the new forms of recreation any better — or are they worse?

4. There has been a growing trend toward watching movies at home rather than going out to theaters. What has been gained or lost by this change?

Writing Assignments Using Comparison–Contrast as a Method of Development

1. The adult Art Spikol can now understand and articulate the meaning of his childhood experiences at the Saturday matinee. Spikol obviously did not have this kind of insight at the time. Write an essay about a past experience, contrasting your understanding and feelings about it then with your understanding now. Some possibilities to consider might be a divorce in the family, an argument, an embarrassing event, a frightening moment, or some other experience.

*2. Write an essay comparing and/or contrasting a place as it was in the past with that same place today. Some possibilities to consider might be a house, a school, a playground, a rural area. Use vivid details to make the contrasting images of this place as sharp and clear as a pair of photographs. E. B. White's celebrated "Once More to the Lake" (page 100) shows how a master prose stylist approached such an essay.

Writing Assignments Using Other Methods of Development

*3. Spikol believes that today's Saturday matinees are not as good as they once were. He could be right about other things as well. Remembering that not everyone feels as you do, write an essay in which you argue that something you know well has changed for the worse. Some possible topics might be television shows, restaurants, sports, music, or a special neighborhood or vacation spot. Before planning the essay, you may want to read Rachel Carson's "A Fable for Tomorrow" (313) for some insight into the way things can change.

4. Conduct one or more personal interviews (with a teacher, parent, older brother or sister, or some other person), so you can write an essay describing a vanished activity or thing as it was before your time. You might interview people about an era they lived through or an activity they participated in. Your essay should indicate clearly whether you are pleased or regretful that things have changed. Include only those details that support your dominant impression.

Henry David Thoreau

Henry David Thoreau (1817–1862) died at the age of 44 with little of his written work published. Yet he has come to be remembered as one of the most influential of American writers. His essay on "Civil Disobedience" (1849) was critical in shaping the philosophies of social reformers Mahatma Gandhi and Martin Luther King. *Walden* (1854), Thoreau's account of the more than two years he lived alone on the shore of Walden Pond in Concord, Massachusetts, is a classic celebration of the virtues of simple living. Thoreau's other works include *A Week on the Concord and Merrimack Rivers* (1849), *The Maine Woods* (1864), *Cape Cod* (1865), and numerous poems. "The Village" is excerpted from *Walden*.

The Village

Nowadays we tend to "visit" nature; we may picnic in a deserted meadow or hike a seldom-used trail, but we shortly return to our classrooms and offices, far from nature. Henry David Thoreau, however, spent more than two years immersed in nature, living alone on the shores of Walden Pond. He frequently walked into the nearby village of Concord to visit the townsfolk. There, he briefly enjoyed their gossip and goings-on. Soon, though, he tired of village life and eagerly returned to the only place he felt truly alive.

After hoeing, or perhaps reading and writing, in the forenoon, I usually bathed again in the pond, swimming across one of its coves for a stint, and washed the dust of labor from my person, or smoothed out the last wrinkle which study had made, and for the afternoon was absolutely free. Every day or two I strolled to the village to hear some of the gossip which is incessantly going on there, circulating either from mouth to mouth, or from newspaper to newspaper, and which, taken in homœopathic doses, was really as refreshing in its way as the rustle of leaves and   1 the peeping of frogs. As I walked in the woods to see the birds and squirrels, so I walked in the village to see the men and boys; instead of the wind among the pines I heard the carts rattle. In one direction from my house there was a colony of musk-rats in the river meadows; under the grove of elms and buttonwoods in the other horizon was a village of busy men, as curious to me as if they had been prairie dogs, each sitting at the mouth of its burrow, or running out to a neighbor's to gossip. I went there frequently to observe their habits. The village appeared to me a great news room; and on one side, to support it, as once at Redding & Company's on State Street, they kept nuts and raisins, or salt and meal and other groceries. Some have such a vast appetite for the former commodity, that is, the news, and such sound digestive organs, that they can sit forever in public avenues without stirring, and let it simmer and whisper through them like the Etesian winds, or as if inhaling ether, it only producing numbness and insensibility to pain, — otherwise it would often be painful to hear, — without affecting the consciousness. I hardly ever failed, when I rambled through the village, to see a row of such worthies, either sitting on a ladder sunning themselves, with their bodies inclined forward and their eyes glancing along the line this way and that, from time to time, with a voluptuous expression, or else leaning against a barn with their hands in their pockets, like caryatides, as if to prop it up. They, being commonly out of doors, heard whatever was in the wind. These are the coarsest mills, in which all gossip is first rudely digested or cracked up before it is emptied into finer and more delicate hoppers within doors. I observed that the vitals of the village were the grocery, the bar-room, the post-office, and the bank; and, as a necessary part of the machinery, they kept a bell, a big gun, a fire-engine, at convenient places; and the houses were so arranged as to make the most of mankind, in lanes and fronting one another, so that every traveller had to run the gauntlet, and every man, woman, and child might get a lick at him. Of course, those who were stationed nearest to the head of the line, where they could most see and be seen, and have the first blow at him, paid the highest prices for their places; and the few straggling inhabitants in the outskirts, where long gaps in the line began to occur, and the traveller could get over walls or turn aside into cow-paths, and so escape, paid a very slight ground or

window tax. Signs were hung out on all sides to allure him; some
to catch him by the appetite, as the tavern and victualling cellar;
some by the fancy, as the dry goods store and the jeweller's; and
others by the hair or the feet or the skirts, as the barber, the
shoemaker, or the tailor. Besides, there was a still more terrible
standing invitation to call at every one of these houses, and
company expected about these times. For the most part I escaped
wonderfully from these dangers, either by proceeding at once
boldly and without deliberation to the goal, as is recommended
to those who run the gauntlet, or by keeping my thoughts on
high things, like Orpheus, who, "loudly singing the praises of the
gods to his lyre, drowned the voices of the Sirens, and kept out of
danger." Sometimes I bolted suddenly, and nobody could tell my
whereabouts, for I did not stand much about gracefulness, and
never hesitated at a gap in a fence. I was even accustomed to make
an irruption into some houses, where I was well entertained, and
after learning the kernels and very last sieve-ful of news, what had
subsided, the prospects of war and peace, and whether the world
was likely to hold together much longer, I was let out through the
rear avenues, and so escaped to the woods again.

It was very pleasant, when I stayed late in town, to launch   2
myself into the night, especially if it was dark and tempestuous,
and set sail from some bright village parlor or lecture room, with
a bag of rye or Indian meal upon my shoulder, for my snug
harbor in the woods, having made all tight without and withdrawn under hatches with a merry crew of thoughts, leaving only
my outer man at the helm, or even tying up the helm when it was
plain sailing. I had many a genial thought by the cabin fire "as I
sailed." I was never cast away nor distressed in any weather,
though I encountered some severe storms. It is darker in the
woods, even in common nights, than most suppose. I frequently
had to look up at the opening between the trees above the path in
order to learn my route, and, where there was no cart-path, to feel
with my feet the faint track which I had worn, or steer by the
known relation of particular trees which I felt with my hands,
passing between two pines for instance, not more than eighteen
inches apart, in the midst of the woods, invariably in the darkest
night. Sometimes, after coming home thus late in a dark and
muggy night, when my feet felt the path which my eyes could not
see, dreaming and absent-minded all the way, until I was aroused

by having to raise my hand to lift the latch, I have not been able to recall a single step of my walk, and I have thought that perhaps my body would find its way home if its master should forsake it, as the hand finds its way to the mouth without assistance. Several times, when a visitor chanced to stay into evening, and it proved a dark night, I was obliged to conduct him to the cart-path in the rear of the house, and then point out to him the direction he was to pursue, and in keeping which he was to be guided rather by his feet than his eyes. One very dark night I directed thus on their way two young men who had been fishing in the pond. They lived about a mile off through the woods, and were quite used to the route. A day or two after one of them told me that they wandered about the greater part of the night, close by their own premises, and did not get home till toward morning, by which time, as there had been several heavy showers in the mean while, and the leaves were very wet, they were drenched to their skins. I have heard of many going astray even in the village streets, when the darkness was so thick that you could cut it with a knife, as the saying is. Some who live in the outskirts, having come to town a-shopping in their wagons, have been obliged to put up for the night; and gentlemen and ladies making a call have gone half a mile out of their way, feeling the sidewalk only with their feet, and not knowing when they turned. It is a surprising and memorable, as well as valuable experience, to be lost in the woods any time. Often in a snow storm, even by day, one will come out upon a well-known road and yet find it impossible to tell which way leads to the village. Though he knows that he has travelled it a thousand times, he cannot recognize a feature in it, but it is as strange to him as if it were a road in Siberia. By night, of course, the perplexity is infinitely greater. In our most trivial walks, we are constantly, though unconsciously, steering like pilots by certain well-known beacons and headlands, and if we go beyond our usual course we still carry in our minds the bearing of some neighboring cape; and not till we are completely lost, or turned round, — for a man needs only to be turned round once with his eyes shut in this world to be lost, — do we appreciate the vastness and strangeness of Nature. Every man has to learn the points of compass again as often as he awakes, whether from sleep or any abstraction. Not till we are lost, in other words, not till we have lost the world, do we begin to find ourselves, and realize where we are and the infinite extent of our relations.

Questions for Close Reading

1. What is the thesis of the selection? Locate the sentence(s) in which Thoreau states his main idea. If he does not state the thesis explicitly, express it in your own words.
2. What reasons does Thoreau give for his visits to the village and to other people's homes? What do these reasons reveal about his character and about his relationships with other people?
3. From the selection, what can you infer about Thoreau's daily activities? His living conditions? His means of survival?
4. Why does Thoreau write that the experience of being lost in the woods is "valuable"? What does he believe is gained from such an experience?
5. Refer to your dictionary as needed to define the following words used in the selection: *homœopathic* (paragraph 1), *voluptuous* (1), *caryatid* (1), *hopper* (1), *victual* (1), *gauntlet* (1), and *Orpheus* (1).

Questions About the Writer's Craft

1. Thoreau organizes "The Village" around a number of contrasts. What are they?
2. A master of description, Thoreau provides many details about life in the village. What aspects of village life does he depict most clearly? How do these details support his thesis?
3. "The Village" is divided into two paragraphs; one describes the daytime, the other the night. Why does the night half contain the majority of words with spiritual connotations—for example, "beacon," "infinite," "vastness"?
4. Thoreau's reference to State Street and his allusion to Orpheus indicate certain assumptions about his readers. What audience is he addressing?

Questions for Further Thought

1. Do you, like Thoreau, believe we tend to fritter away our lives, concerning ourselves with too many petty, unimportant matters? Explain.
2. Before going to Walden, Thoreau discarded most of his possessions. Which possessions do you feel are necessary to your comfort, convenience, and happiness? Which are not?
3. Thoreau gains news from conversation or the newspaper. Today, most people get their news from television. What is the difference between newspaper and television news? Which do you trust more? Why?
4. Thoreau acknowledges that the villagers' company could be as "re-

freshing . . . as the rustle of leaves." But he also confesses that after a while he "bolted . . . and escaped to the woods." Why might such a person choose to become a writer? What virtues and flaws might be present in such a person's works?

Writing Assignments Using Comparison–Contrast as a Method of Development

*1. Read Annie Dillard's "In the Jungle" (page 92). Using either the point-by-point or the one-side-at-a-time approach, compare and contrast Dillard and Thoreau's attitudes toward nature and society. Your discussion should focus on several key points and should make clear with whose attitudes you are more in agreement. Use part of the essay to explain the reasons for feeling as you do.

2. Thoreau in the woods is quite different from Thoreau in the village. Write a paper comparing and contrasting the "private" and "public" you. Draw some conclusions about your own temperament and the circumstances in which you feel most like your true self.

Writing Assignments Using Other Methods of Development

3. "The Village" relates instances of people getting lost while going somewhere. Through carefully selected details and close attention to narrative pacing, recount a time you got lost, conveying what you saw and how you felt. Share any insights you gained about your own character, other people, and the world around you.

4. In Thoreau's view, gossip plays a significant role in people's lives. For better or worse, gossip is also an important part of our world, as the popularity of the *National Enquirer, People* magazine, and *Entertainment Tonight* attest. Using specific examples drawn from your experiences and observations, write an essay explaining why humans love gossip. What needs does it meet? Your paper should also discuss the effects of gossip. Are they harmful or harmless?

Richard Rodriguez

In *Hunger of Memory* (1981), from which the following selection is taken, Richard Rodriguez describes his experiences growing up in America as a first-generation Mexican-American. Born in 1944 in San Francisco, Rodriguez spoke only Spanish for the first six years of his life. After winning a scholarship to a private high school, Rodriguez attended Stanford, Columbia, and the University of California at Berkeley where he earned a Ph.D. in English literature. Rodriguez now writes, lectures, and serves as an educational consultant from his home base in San Francisco.

Workers

As a college student, you probably look forward to a working world where individuals feel a sense of accomplishment and prestige, where personal growth is as much a consideration as monetary rewards. Richard Rodriguez discovered a very different world of work during a summer spent as a laborer, a world in which work is survival and the boss is god. For such workers, there are no alternatives, no exits, no chances for fulfillment.

It was at Stanford, one day near the end of my senior year, that a friend told me about a summer construction job he knew was available. I was quickly alert. Desire uncoiled within me. My friend said that he knew I had been looking for summer employment. He knew I needed some money. Almost apologetically he explained: It was something I probably wouldn't be interested in, but a friend of his, a contractor, needed someone for the summer to do menial jobs. There would be lots of shoveling and raking and sweeping. Nothing too hard. But nothing more interesting either. Still, the pay would be good. Did I want it? Or did I know someone who did? 1

I did. Yes, I said, surprised to hear myself say it. 2

In the weeks following, friends cautioned that I had no idea
how hard physical labor really is. ('You only *think* you know what
it is like to shovel for eight hours straight.') Their objections
seemed to me challenges. They resolved the issue. I became happy
with my plan. I decided, however, not to tell my parents. I
wouldn't tell my mother because I could guess her worried reaction. I would tell my father only after the summer was over, when
I could announce that, after all, I did know what 'real work' is
like.

                                             3

The day I met the contractor (a Princeton graduate, it turned
out), he asked me whether I had done any physical labor before.
'In high school, during the summer,' I lied. And although he
seemed to regard me with skepticism, he decided to give me a try.
Several days later, expectant, I arrived at my first construction
site. I would take off my shirt to the sun. And at last grasp desired
sensation. No longer afraid. At last become like a *bracero*. 'We
need those tree stumps out of here by tomorrow,' the contractor
said. I started to work.

                                             4

I labored with excitement that first morning — and all the
days after. The work was harder than I could have expected. But it
was never as tedious as my friends had warned me it would be.
There was too much physical pleasure in the labor. Especially
early in the day, I would be most alert to the sensations of
movement and straining. Beginning around seven each morning
(when the air was still damp but the scent of weeds and dry earth
anticipated the heat of the sun), I would feel my body resist the
first thrusts of the shovel. My arms, tightened by sleep, would
gradually loosen; after only several minutes, sweat would gather
in beads on my forehead and then — a short while later — I would
feel my chest silky with sweat in the breeze. I would return to my
work. A nervous spark of pain would fly up my arm and settle to
burn like an ember in the thick of my shoulder. An hour, two
passed. Three. My whole body would assume regular movements;
my shoveling would be described by identical, even movements.
Even later in the day, my enthusiasm for primitive sensation
would survive the heat and the dust and the insects pricking my
back. I would strain wildly for sensation as the day came to a
close. At three-thirty, quitting time, I would stand upright and
slowly let my head fall back, luxuriating in the feeling of tightness
relieved.

                                             5

Some of the men working nearby would watch me and laugh.   6
Two or three of the older men took the trouble to teach me the
right way to use a pick, the correct way to shovel. 'You're doing it
wrong, too fucking hard,' one man scolded. Then proceeded to
show me — what persons who work with their bodies all their
lives quickly learn — the most economical way to use one's body
in labor.

'Don't make your back do so much work,' he instructed. I   7
stood impatiently listening, half listening, vaguely watching, then
noticed his work-thickened fingers clutching the shovel. I was
annoyed. I wanted to tell him that I enjoyed shoveling the wrong
way. And I didn't want to learn the right way. I wasn't afraid of
back pain. I liked the way my body felt sore at the end of the day.

I was about to, but, as it turned out, I didn't say a thing.   8
Rather it was at that moment I realized that I was fooling myself
if I expected a few weeks of labor to gain me admission to the
world of the laborer. I would not learn in three months what my
father had meant by 'real work.' I was not bound to this job; I
could imagine its rapid conclusion. For me the sensations were to
be feared. Fatigue took a different toll on their bodies — and
minds.

It was, I know, a simple insight. But it was with this realiza-   9
tion that I took my first step that summer toward realizing something even more important about the 'worker.' In the company of
carpenters, electricians, plumbers, and painters at lunch, I would
often sit quietly, observant. I was not shy in such company. I felt
easy, pleased by the knowledge that I was casually accepted, my
presence taken for granted by men (exotics) who worked with
their hands. Some days the younger men would talk and talk
about sex, and they would howl at women who drove by in cars.
Other days the talk at lunchtime was subdued; men gathered in
separate groups. It depended on who was around. There were
rough, good-natured workers. Others were quiet. The more I
remember that summer, the more I realize that there was no
single *type* of worker. I am embarrassed to say I had not expected
such diversity. I certainly had not expected to meet, for example,
a plumber who was an abstract painter in his off hours and
admired the work of Mark Rothko. Nor did I expect to meet so
many workers with college diplomas. (They were the ones who
were not surprised that I intended to enter graduate school in the

fall.) I suppose what I really want to say here is painfully obvious, but I must say it nevertheless: The men of that summer were middle-class Americans. They certainly didn't constitute an oppressed society. Carefully completing their work sheets; talking about the fortunes of local football teams; planning Las Vegas vacations; comparing the gas mileage of various makes of campers — they were not *los pobres* my mother had spoken about.

On two occasions, the contractor hired a group of Mexican aliens. They were employed to cut down some trees and haul off debris. In all, there were six men of varying age. The youngest in his late twenties; the oldest (his father?) perhaps sixty years old. They came and they left in a single old truck. Anonymous men. They were never introduced to the other men at the site. Immediately upon their arrival, they would follow the contractor's directions, start working — rarely resting — seemingly driven by a fatalistic sense that work which had to be done was best done as quickly as possible.   10

I watched them sometimes. Perhaps they watched me. The only time I saw them pay me much notice was one day at lunchtime when I was laughing with the other men. The Mexicans sat apart when they ate, just as they worked by themselves. Quiet. I rarely heard them say much to each other. All I could hear were their voices calling out sharply to one another, giving directions. Otherwise, when they stood briefly resting, they talked among themselves in voices too hard to overhear.   11

The contractor knew enough Spanish, and the Mexicans — or at least the oldest of them, their spokesman — seemed to know enough English to communicate. But because I was around, the contractor decided one day to make me his translator. (He assumed I could speak Spanish.) I did what I was told. Shyly I went over to tell the Mexicans that the *patrón* wanted them to do something else before they left for the day. As I started to speak, I was afraid with my old fear that I would be unable to pronounce the Spanish words. But it was a simple instruction I had to convey. I could say it in phrases.   12

The dark sweating faces turned toward me as I spoke. They stopped their work to hear me. Each nodded in response. I stood there. I wanted to say something more. But what could I say in Spanish, even if I could have pronounced the words right? Perhaps I just wanted to engage them in small talk, to be assured of their confidence, our familiarity. I thought for a moment to ask   13 them where in Mexico they were from. Something like that. And maybe I wanted to tell them (a lie, if need be) that my parents were from the same part of Mexico.

I stood there.   14

Their faces watched me. The eyes of the man directly in front   15
of me moved slowly over my shoulder, and I turned to follow his glance toward *el patrón* some distance away. For a moment I felt swept up by that glance into the Mexicans' company. But then I heard one of them returning to work. And then the others went back to work. I left them without saying anything more.

When they had finished, the contractor went over to pay   16
them in cash. (He later told me that he paid them collectively— 'for the job,' though he wouldn't tell me their wages. He said something quickly about the good rate of exchange 'in their own country.') I can still hear the loudly confident voice he used with the Mexicans. It was the sound of the *gringo* I had heard as a very young boy. And I can still hear the quiet, indistinct sounds of the Mexican, the oldest, who replied. At hearing that voice I was sad for the Mexicans. Depressed by their vulnerability. Angry at myself. The adventure of the summer seemed suddenly ludicrous. I would not shorten the distance I felt from *los pobres* with a few weeks of physical labor. I would not become like them. They were different from me.

After that summer, a great deal—and not very much really   17
—changed in my life. The curse of physical shame was broken by the sun; I was no longer ashamed of my body. No longer would I deny myself the pleasing sensations of my maleness. During those years when middle-class black Americans began to assert with pride, 'Black is beautiful,' I was able to regard my complexion without shame. I am today darker than I ever was as a boy. I have taken up the middle-class sport of long-distance running. Nearly every day now I run ten or fifteen miles, barely clothed, my skin exposed to the California winter rain and wind or the summer sun of late afternoon. The torso, the soccer player's calves and thighs, the arms of the twenty-year-old I never was, I possess now in my thirties. I study the youthful parody shape in the mirror: the stomach lipped tight by muscle; the shoulders rounded by chin-ups; the arms veined strong. This man. A man. I meet him. He laughs to see me, what I have become.

The dandy. I wear double-breasted Italian suits and custom-   18 made English shoes. I resemble no one so much as my father — the man pictured in those honeymoon photos. At that point in life when he abandoned the dandy's posture, I assume it. At the point when my parents would not consider going on vacation, I register at the Hotel Carlyle in New York and the Plaza Athenée in Paris. I am as taken by the symbols of leisure and wealth as they were. For my parents, however, those symbols became taunts, reminders of all they could not achieve in one lifetime. For me those same symbols are reassuring reminders of public success. I tempt vulgarity to be reassured. I am filled with the gaudy delight, the monstrous grace of the nouveau riche.

In recent years I have had occasion to lecture in ghetto high   19
schools. There I see students of remarkable style and physical grace. (One can see more dandies in such schools than one ever will find in middle-class high schools.) There is not the look of casual assurance I saw students at Stanford display. Ghetto girls mimic high-fashion models. Their dresses are of bold, forceful color; their figures elegant, long; the stance theatrical. Boys wear shirts that grip at their overdeveloped muscular bodies. (Against a powerless future, they engage images of strength.) Bad nutrition does not yet tell. Great disappointment, fatal to youth, awaits them still. For the moment, movements in school hallways are dancelike, a procession of postures in a sexual masque. Watching them, I feel a kind of envy. I wonder how different my adolescence would have been had I been free. . . . But no, it is my parents I see — their optimism during those years when they were entertained by Italian grand opera.

The registration clerk in London wonders if I have just been   20
to Switzerland. And the man who carries my luggage in New York guesses the Caribbean. My complexion becomes a mark of my leisure. Yet no one would regard my complexion the same way if I entered such hotels through the service entrance. That is only to say that my complexion assumes its significance from the context of my life. My skin, in itself, means nothing. I stress the point because I know there are people who would label me 'disadvantaged' because of my color. They make the same mistake I made as a boy, when I thought a disadvantaged life was circumscribed by particular occupations. That summer I worked in the sun may have made me physically indistinguishable from the Mexicans working nearby. (My skin was actually darker because,

unlike them, I worked without wearing a shirt. By late August my hands were probably as tough as theirs.) But I was not one of *los pobres*. What made me different from them was an attitude of *mind*, my imagination of myself.

I do not blame my mother for warning me away from the sun 21 when I was young. In a world where her brother had become an old man in his twenties because he was dark, my complexion was something to worry about. 'Don't run in the sun,' she warns me today. I run. In the end, my father was right — though perhaps he did not know how right or why — to say that I would never know what real work is. I will never know what he felt at his last factory job. If tomorrow I worked at some kind of factory, it would go differently for me. My long education would favor me. I could act as a public person — able to defend my interests, to unionize, to petition, to speak up — to challenge and demand. (I will never know what real work is.) I will never know what the Mexicans knew, gathering their shovels and ladders and saws.

Their silence stays with me now. The wages those Mexicans 22 received for their labor were only a measure of their disadvantaged condition. Their silence is more telling. They lack a public identity. They remain profoundly alien. Persons apart. People lacking a union obviously, people without grounds. They depend upon the relative good will or fairness of their employers each day. For such people, lacking a better alternative, it is not such an unreasonable risk.

Their silence stays with me. I have taken these many words to 23 describe its impact. Only: the quiet. Something uncanny about it. Its compliance. Vulnerability. Pathos. As I heard their truck rumbling away, I shuddered, my face mirrored with sweat. I had finally come face to face with *los pobres*.

Questions for Close Reading

1. What is the thesis of the selection? Locate the sentence(s) in which Rodriguez states his main idea. If he does not state the thesis explicitly, express it in your own words.
2. What appealed to Rodriguez about the construction job when his friend first offered it to him?
3. Once on the job, how long does it take Rodriguez to realize he will never be a "laborer"? Why does he feel this way?

4. According to the author, what makes him different from *los pobres*? Is poverty the only thing that makes them distinctive?
5. Refer to your dictionary as needed to define the following words in the selection: *menial* (paragraph 1), *skepticism* (4), *luxuriating* (5), *diversity* (9), *ludicrous* (16), *nouveau riche* (18), and *pathos* (23).

Questions About the Writer's Craft

1. One way Rodriguez develops his essay is by comparing and contrasting himself to the two groups of workers. Which group is he more like? What specifics does Rodriguez provide to show his similarity to this group and his dissimilarity to the other?
2. Rodriguez's main support for his comparison of the two other groups of workers is narrative. How many narrative segments appear in the essay? Why does Rodriguez put the story about the Mexican workers last?
3. Why does the author include some Spanish words in his essay? How is the use of these words related to the overall theme?
4. Rodriguez uses especially vivid language to describe the sun, his sweat, and the sensation of digging. Locate some examples of these descriptions. Which ones particularly stand out?

Questions for Further Thought

1. Why does Rodriguez decide not to tell his parents about his summer job? What do you think his mother's fears would have been? How would your parents and friends react if you went to work in construction after graduating from college?
2. Rodriguez discovers that "there is no single *type* of worker" on the construction job. What do you think his preconceptions about construction workers were? What other kinds of workers are often stereotyped?
3. What does Rodriguez desire to gain from this job that he could not, presumably, learn at Stanford or in graduate school? Have you ever felt a similar need to learn outside the classroom?
4. What are the characteristics of "real work" for Rodriguez at the start of his summer? How would you say his definition of "real work" has changed by the end of the job? Would you agree with his perception that a college-educated person can never know the meaning of "real work"?

Writing Assignments Using Comparison–Contrast as a Method of Development

1. Write an essay comparing and/or contrasting a part-time or sum-

mer job you've had with your (or someone else's) full-time or "real" job. Use examples, description, anecdotes, and illustrations to clarify the points of comparison or contrast.

2. Compare and/or contrast the job you hope to have after graduation with a job you now have or have had in the past. Your analysis should reach conclusions about your interests, skills, and values.

Writing Assignments Using Other Methods of Development

*3. In an essay, define what you mean by the term "real work." Support your definition by citing experiences you have had and/or have heard about. Sue Hubbell's "The Beekeeper" (page 253) and Betty Rollin's "Allene Tallmey" (page 194) should prompt some interesting thoughts about work.

4. Phil Donahue once did a show on people who had "terrible jobs." Guests included a garbage man, toll collector, car repossessor, IRS auditor, and diaper-service truck driver. Write an essay explaining what would be terrible work for you. It might be one or more of the jobs held by Donahue guests or some other type of job. Provide abundant reasons why you would never want to do such work and reach some conclusions about your priorities.

Additional Writing Topics
COMPARISON–CONTRAST

General Assignments

Using comparison–contrast, write an essay on any of the following topics. Your thesis should indicate whether the two subjects are being compared, contrasted, or both. Organize the paper by arranging the details in a one-side-at-a-time or point-by-point pattern. Remember to use organizational cues to help the audience follow your analysis of the subjects.

1. Two-career family versus one-career family
2. Two approaches for dealing with problems
3. Children's pastimes today and yesterday
4. Two rooms where you spend a good deal of time
5. Neighborhood stores versus shopping malls
6. Two characters in a novel or other literary work
7. Living at home versus living in an apartment or dorm
8. Two attitudes toward money
9. A sports team then and now
10. Watching a movie on television versus going out to a theater
11. Two attitudes about a controversial subject
12. Two approaches to parenting
13. Walking or biking versus driving a car
14. Marriage versus living together
15. The atmosphere in two classes
16. Two approaches to studying
17. The place where you live and the place where you would like to live
18. Two comedians
19. The coverage of an event on TV versus the coverage in a newspaper
20. Significant trend versus passing fad
21. Two horror or adventure movies
22. Typewriter versus word processor
23. Two candidates for an office
24. Your attitude before and after getting to know someone
25. Two friends with different lifestyles

Assignments with a Specific Audience and Purpose

1. You have decided you want to change your campus living arrangements next year: you want to switch from a dorm room to an off-campus apartment, or you want to move from home onto campus, or any other change. You will first have to convince your parents, who are paying most of your college costs, that the move will be beneficial. Write your parents a letter contrasting your current situation with your proposed one, explaining why the new arrangement will be better.

2. You have managed a retail store for several years and done a good job—sales are up. Your regional manager has asked you to write a memo to your fellow store managers, explaining how you are able to attract so many customers. Feeling that the key to success lies in the ability to lure all kinds of customers to the store, you write a memo using the comparison–contrast format: you compare/contrast the needs and shopping habits of several different consumer groups (by age, or spending ability, or sex, and so on) and show why each feels comfortable in your store.

3. Some of the students in your school are putting together an alternative/underground booklet called "The Real Guide to College Life," intended primarily for entering freshmen. You are going to write the section on "Taking Exams" and have decided to contrast the right and wrong ways to prepare for and take exams. You have decided that your purpose is basically serious, but that you will leaven the section on how *not* to take exams with a little humor.

4. You work part-time in a medical office and have been asked to write an informational brochure to be placed in the patients' waiting room. The brochure is intended to show people how to avoid stress by changing their behavior patterns. You decide to center the brochure on the contrast between "Type A" and "Type B" personalities: the former is nervous, hard-driving, competitive, while the latter is relaxed and noncompetitive. Give specific examples of how each "type" tends to act in a stressful situation, such as waiting in line, dealing with frustration or failure, coping with job or family crises.

5. Congratulations! You have been tapped to be one of the President's key advisers. Your first assignment is to draft a recommendation for the President on a specific issue: for example, whether to tighten quotas on imported cars or whether to allow the vehicles to come into the country unrestricted. To prepare your analysis, you contrast the advantages and disadvantages of the courses of action available, ending the document with a recommendation about the position the President should take.

6. Your old high school has invited you back to make a speech before an audience of seniors; you will discuss "how to choose the college that is right for you." Write your speech in the form of a comparison – contrast analysis. Focus on the choices available (two-year and four-year, large school and small, local school and faraway one, and so on), showing the advantages and/or disadvantages of each.

CAUSE–EFFECT

WHAT IS CAUSE–EFFECT?

Young children barrage adults with endless questions: "Why do trees grow tall?" "What would happen if the sun didn't shine?" But children aren't the only ones who wonder "what if." All of us think in terms of cause and effect, sometimes consciously, sometimes unconsciously. "Why did they give me such an odd look?" we wonder, or "How would I do at another college?" we speculate. This exploration of reasons and results is also at the heart of most professions. "What led to our involvement in Vietnam?" historians question. "What will happen if we administer this experimental drug?" scientists ask.

Cause–effect writing, often called *causal analysis*, is rooted in this elemental need to make connections. Because the drive to understand reasons and results is so fundamental, causal analysis is a common kind of writing. An article analyzing the unexpected outcome of an election, a report linking poor nutrition to low

345

academic achievement, an editorial analyzing the impact of a proposed tax cut — all are examples of cause – effect writing.

Done well, cause – effect pieces can uncover the subtle and often surprising connections between events or phenomena. By rooting out causes and projecting effects, causal analysis enables us to make sense of our experiences, revealing a universe that is somewhat less arbitrary and chaotic.

WHEN TO USE CAUSE – EFFECT

Many assignments and exam questions in college involve writing essays that analyze causes, effects, or both. Sometimes, as in the following examples, you will be told to write an essay developed primarily through the cause – effect pattern.

> Although divorces have leveled off in the past few years, the number of marriages ending in divorce is still greater than it was a generation ago. What do you think are the causes of this phenomenon?

> Political commentators were surprised that so few people voted in the past election. Discuss the probable causes of this unexpectedly weak voter turnout.

> Americans never seem to tire of gossip about the rich and famous. What effect has this fascination with celebrities had on American culture?

> The federal government is expected to pass legislation that will reduce significantly the funding of student loans. Analyze the possible effects of such a cutback on your life.

Other assignments or exam questions may not specify causes or effects but will use words that suggest that causal analysis would be appropriate. Consider these examples, paying special attention to the italicized words.

> In contrast to the socially involved youth of the 1960s, many young people today tend to remove themselves

from political issues. What do you think are the *sources* of the political apathy found among eighteen- to twenty-five-year-olds? (cause)

A number of experts forecast that drug abuse will be the most significant factor affecting American productivity in the coming decade. Evaluate the validity of this observation by discussing the *impact* of drugs in the workplace. (effect)

According to school officials, a predictable percentage of entering students drop out of college at some point during their first year. What *motivates* students to drop out? What *happens* to them once they leave? (cause and effect)

By now, it's apparent that causal analysis can be the primary strategy for achieving an essay's purpose. But causal analysis can also be a supplemental method used to help make a point in an essay organized chiefly around another pattern of development. For instance, assume you want to write an essay *defining* the term "the homeless." To make the point that most of the homeless are not faceless derelicts but people very much like the rest of us, you might discuss some of the unavoidable, everyday factors causing people to live on streets and in subway stations. In an *argumentation – persuasion* paper advocating the elimination of letter-grade evaluations, you would probably spend some time analyzing the positive impact of such a system on students and faculty.

SUGGESTIONS FOR USING CAUSE–EFFECT IN AN ESSAY

The following suggestions will be helpful whether you use causal analysis as a dominant or supportive pattern of development.

1. Determine the purpose of a paper developed mainly through causal analysis. You should always clarify to yourself the purpose for writing a cause – effect essay. Do you wish to inform? Persuade? Speculate about possibilities? Or do you want to achieve some combination of these purposes? Consider, for example, a paper on the causes of widespread child abuse. Concerned primarily with explaining the problem to your readers, you might take a purely *informative* approach.

> Although parental stress is the immediate cause of child abuse, the more compelling reason for such behavior lies in the way parents were themselves mistreated in their own families.

Or you might want to *persuade* the audience about some point or idea concerning child abuse:

> The tragic consequences of child abuse provide strong support for more aggressive handling of such cases by social workers and judges.

Then again, you could choose a *speculative* approach, your main purpose being to suggest possibilities:

> Psychologists disagree about the potential effect on youngsters of all the media attention to child abuse. Will the children grow up assertive, self-confident, and able to protect themselves, or will they become fearful and distrustful?

These examples illustrate that causal analysis may have more than one purpose. For instance, although the last paper has a primarily speculative purpose, it would probably start by informing readers of the experts' conflicting views. Moreover, the paper would also have a persuasive slant if it ended by urging readers to complain to the media about their sensationalized treatment of the child abuse issue.

2. Adapt the causal analysis to your purpose and readers.   Your objective and audience determine what supporting material and what tone will be most effective in your analysis. Assume you want to direct your essay on child abuse to open-minded general readers who know little about the subject. To *inform* your readers, you would use objective, nontechnical language, providing a straightforward analysis of the causes of child abuse. But imagine that your purpose is to *convince* people intending to become social workers that social service agencies often act negligently in child abuse cases. Hoping to encourage more responsible behavior in the prospective social workers, you would probably adopt a more emotional approach, perhaps citing tragic case histories that dramatize what happens when child abuse is not taken seriously.

3. Think logically about causes and effects. Cause–effect relationships are complex. To write a well-conceived paper, you should do some careful thinking about these relationships. Causes and effects are seldom simple or obvious — as suggested by the ongoing nature of scientific debates (How did humans evolve?), historical analyses (What happened in Vietnam?), and literary criticism (What were Hamlet's motivations?). Children tend to oversimplify causes and effects ("Mommy and Daddy are getting divorced because I was bad the other day"), and barroom arguments are also characterized by hasty, often slipshod thinking ("All these immigrants willing to work cheaply have made us lose our jobs"). But imprecise thinking has no place in essay writing. You should be willing to dig for causes, to think creatively about effects. You should examine your subject in depth, looking beyond the obvious and superficial.

Brainstorming is one way to explore causes and effects thoroughly. When brainstorming, generate as many explanations as possible by asking yourself a battery of questions: *What happened? Why did it happen? What other reasons were there for its happening? What will most likely happen now? What else might happen? How could it be prevented from happening again?*

If you remain open and do not let yourself settle for the obvious, you will discover that a cause may have many effects. Imagine you are writing a paper on the effects of smoking. A number of consequences might be discussed, some more apparent than others: increased risk of lung cancer and heart disease, shortening of breath, lower birth weights in babies of mothers who smoke, nicotine stains on teeth leading to various dental problems, conflicts between smoking and nonsmoking members of the same family, and legal battles regarding the rights of smokers and nonsmokers in public places.

In the same way, brainstorming will help you see that an effect may have multiple causes. An essay analyzing the reasons for world hunger could discuss many causes, again, some more evident than others: overpopulation, climatic changes, poor farming techniques, internal political disruptions, lack of long-range planning by governments, cultural predispositions for large families, and international rivalries that turn the feeding of hungry people into a political rather than an ethical issue.

Brainstorming may also uncover a *causal chain* in which one cause brings about another, which brings about another, and so on. Here is an example of a causal chain: prohibition went into effect; bootleggers and organized crime stepped in to supply public demand for alcohol; ordinary citizens began breaking the law by buying illegal alcohol and patronizing speakeasies; disrespect for legal authority became widespread and acceptable. You can see that a causal chain often leads to interesting points. In this case, the subject of prohibition led not just to the obvious (illegal consumption of alcohol) but to a more complex issue: society's decreasing respect for legal authority.

When determining the validity of the causes and effects generated during brainstorming, you should be careful to avoid the logical fallacy called *post hoc* thinking — a shortened form of a Latin phrase meaning "After this, therefore because of this." This kind of faulty thinking occurs when you assume that simply because one event followed another, the first event *caused* the second. For example, if the Republicans win a majority of seats in Congress and, several months later, the economy collapses, can you conclude that the Republicans caused the collapse? A quick assumption of "Yes" fails the test of logic, for the timing of events could be coincidental and not indicative of any cause – effect relationship. The collapse may have been triggered by uncontrolled inflation that began well before the Congressional elections.

After evaluating the brainstormed material, you need to identify which causes and effects are *primary* and which are *secondary*. How extensively you cover secondary causes and effects will depend on your purpose and the audience for whom you are writing. In an essay intended to inform a general audience of the harmful effects of pesticides, you would most likely concentrate on the effects that are immediately damaging to humans — polluted water, hazardous waste, residues in food. Given your purpose and audience, you would probably decide not to include a full discussion of more scientific and long-range effects (evolution of resistant insects, disruption of ecosystems).

Finally, keep in mind that a rigorous causal analysis involves more than loose talk about causes and effects. Creating plausible connections may require research, interviewing, or a combination of both. Often you will need to provide facts, statistics, details, personal observations, or other corroborative material if readers are going to accept the reasoning behind your analysis.

4. Write a thesis that focuses the paper on causes, effects, or both.   The thesis in a paper developed through causal analysis often indicates whether the essay will deal mostly with causes, effects, or both. Here, for example, are three thesis statements for causal analyses dealing with the public school system. You will see that each thesis indicates the particular emphasis for that essay:

Our school system has been weakened by paltry teaching salaries, an overemphasis on trendy electives, and decreasing parental support. (causes)

An ineffectual school system has led to high illiteracy rates, crippling teachers' strikes, and widespread disrespect for public education. (effects)

Societal neglect and bureaucratic inefficiency have created a school system unresponsive to children's emotional and intellectual needs. (causes and effects)

Note that each thesis statement — in addition to signaling whether the paper will discuss causes or effects or both — also points to the plan of development for the essay. Consider the first thesis statement. The thesis makes clear that the paper will discuss poor salaries first, then gimmicky electives, and last, parental indifference.

The thesis statement in a causal analysis does not have to specify whether the essay will discuss causes, effects, or both. Nor does the thesis have to be worded in such a way that the essay's plan of development is apparent. But when first writing cause–effect essays, you may find that a highly focused thesis will keep your analysis on track.

5. Choose an organizational pattern.   When presenting your cause–effect discussion, you have two basic ways to organize your points. You may select a *chronological* order, discussing causes and effects in the order in which they occur or will occur. Suppose you were writing an essay on the causes for the growing popularity of imported cars. Causes might be discussed in chronological sequence: American plant workers became frustrated and dissatisfied on the job; some workers got careless while others deliberately sabotaged the product; a growing number of defective cars hit the market; consumers grew dissatisfied with American cars and switched to imports.

Chronology might also be used to organize a discussion about effects. Imagine that you were writing an essay about the need to guard against disrupting delicate balances in the country's wildlife population. You might start the essay by discussing the disturbance that occurred when the starling, a nonnative bird, was introduced into the American environment. Because the starling had few natural predators, the starling population soared out of control; the starlings took over food sources and habitats of native species; the bluebird, a native species, declined and is now threatened with extinction.

Although a chronological pattern can be an effective way to organize material, a strict time sequence can present a problem if your primary cause or effect ends up buried in the middle of the sequence. In such a case, you might want to use *emphatic order*, reserving the most significant cause/effect for the end of the essay. For example, an exact time sequence for an essay detailing the reasons behind a candidate's unexpected victory might include the following: less than a month after the candidate's earlier defeat, a full-scale fundraising campaign for the next election was started; the candidate spoke to many crucial power groups early in the campaign; the candidate did exceptionally well in the preelection debates; good weather and large voter turnout on election day favored the candidate. But if you believe that the candidate's appearance before influential groups was the key factor in the victory, it would be more effective to emphasize that point by saving it for the end. This is what is meant by emphatic order—saving for last the point you want to stress.

Emphatic order is an especially effective way to sequence cause–effect points when readers hold what in your view are mistaken or narrow views about a subject. To encourage readers to look more closely at the issues, you present what you consider the erroneous or obvious views first, show why they are unsound or limited, then present what you feel to be the actual causes and effects. Such a sequence nudges the audience into giving further thought to the causes and effects you have discovered. Here are brief outlines for two causal analyses using this approach.

Subject: The causes of the riot at a rock concert

1. Some commentators blame the excessively hot weather.
2. Others cite drug use among the concert-goers.
3. Still others blame the liquor sold at the concessions.
4. But the real cause of the disaster was poor planning by the concert promoters.

Subject: The effects of campus crime

1. Immediate problems
   a. Students feel insecure and fearful.
   b. Many night-time campus activities have been curtailed.

2. More significant long-term problems
   a. Unfavorable publicity about campus crime will affect future student enrollments.
   b. Hiring faculty will become more difficult.

If emphatic order is used in the causal analysis, you might want to word the thesis in such a way that it signals which point your essay will stress. Consider the following thesis statements:

Many recent immigrants lack marketable skills and often are forced to contend with prejudice once they arrive in America. But the most pressing problem is the difficulty they have dealing with an unfamiliar language.

The space program has led to dramatic advances in computer technology and medical science. Even more important, though, the program has helped change many people's attitudes toward the planet we live on.

These statements reflect an awareness of the complex nature of cause – effect relationships. While not dismissing secondary issues, the statements establish the points that are considered most noteworthy. The second paper, for instance, would touch upon the technological and medical advances made possible by the space program but would emphasize the way the program has changed people's attitudes toward the earth.

6. Use language that hints at the complexity of cause–effect relationships. Because it is difficult — if not impossible — to determine that the causes and effects you discuss are the only possible ones, you want to use language that reflects this element of uncertainty. Instead of writing, "There is no doubt that . . . ," you might say, "It is probable that. . . ." or "One likely cause/effect of. . . ." Using such language is not indecisive; it is reasonable and reflects your understanding of the often tangled nature of causes and effects. Be careful, though, of going to the other extreme and being reluctant to take a stand on the issues. If you have thought long and hard about causes and effects, you have a right to state your analysis with conviction. Don't undercut the hard work you have done by writing as if your ideas were unworthy of your reader's attention.

Cause–effect writing is gratifying for both writer and audience. As a writer, you experience the pleasure of stretching your mind, confident that your exploration of causes and effects has gone beyond the obvious. Readers feel a comparable satisfaction, knowing that they have a clearer understanding of an event or phenomenon. Causal analysis also has the potential for generating vigorous discussion and honest disagreement about a variety of issues — from reasons for international terrorism to consequences of reducing support for school lunch programs. Cause–effect writing is certainly one of the most critical ways we have for thinking about matters that concern us.

STUDENT ESSAY AND COMMENTARY

The following student essay was written by Carl Novack in response to this assignment:

> In "The Faltering Family," George Gallup, Jr., points to a number of factors that have caused the decline of the American family. Think of another institution, process, or practice that has changed recently and discuss several factors you believe are responsible for the change.

While reading Carl's paper, try to determine how well it applies the principles concerning the use of causal analysis. The commentary following the paper will help you look at Carl's essay more closely.

Americans and Food

An offbeat but timely cartoon recently appeared in the local newspaper. The single panel showed a gravel-pit operation with piles of raw earth and large cranes. Next to one of the cranes stood the owner of the gravel pit--a grizzled, tough-looking character, hammer in hand, pointing proudly to the new sign he had just tacked up. The sign read, "Fred's Fill Dirt and Croissants." The cartoon illustrates an interesting phenomenon: the changing food habits of Americans. Our meals used to consist of something like home-cooked pot roast, mashed potatoes laced with butter and salt, a thick slice of apple pie topped with a healthy scoop of vanilla ice cream--plain, heavy meals, cooked from scratch, and eaten leisurely at home. But America has changed, and as it has, so has what we Americans eat and how we eat it.

We used to have simple, unsophisticated tastes and looked with suspicion at anything more exotic than hamburger. Admittedly, we did adopt some foods from the various immigrant groups who flocked to our shores. We learned to eat Chinese food, pizza, and bagels. But in the last few years, the international character of our diet has grown tremendously. We can walk into any mall in Middle America and buy pita bread, quiche, and tacos. Such foods are often changed on their journey from exotic imports to ordinary "American" meals (no Pakistani, for example, eats frozen-on-a-stick boysenberry-flavored yogurt), but the imports are still a long way from hamburger on a bun.

Why have we become more worldly in our tastes? For one thing, television blankets the country with information about new food products and trends. Viewers in rural Montana know that the latest craving in Washington, D.C., is Cajun cooking or that something called tofu is now available in the local supermarket. Another reason for the growing international flavor of our food is that many young Americans have traveled abroad and gotten hooked on new tastes and flavors. Backpacking students and young professionals vacationing in Europe come home with cravings for authentic French bread or German beer. Finally, continuing waves of immigrants settle in the cities where many of us live, causing significant changes in what we eat. Vietnamese, Haitians, and Thais, for instance, bring their native foods and cooking styles with them and eventually open small markets or restaurants. In time, the new food will become Americanized enough to take its place in our national diet.

Our growing concern with health has also affected the way we 4 eat. For the last few years, the media have warned us about the dangers of our traditional diet, high in salt and fat, low in fiber. The media also began to educate us about the dangers of processed foods pumped full of chemical additives. As a result, consumers began to demand healthier foods, and manufacturers started to change some of their products. Many foods, such as lunch meat, canned vegetables, and soups, were made available in low-fat, low-sodium versions. Whole grain cereals and high-fiber breads also began to appear on the grocery shelves. Moreover, the food industry started to produce all-natural products--everything from potato chips to ice cream--without additives and preservatives. Not surprisingly, the restaurant industry responded to this switch to healthier foods, luring customers with salad bars, broiled fish, and steamed vegetables.

Our food habits are being affected, too, by the rapid increase in 5 the number of women working outside the home. Sociologists and other experts believe that two important factors triggered this phenomenon: the women's movement and a changing economic climate. Women were assured that it was acceptable, even rewarding, to work outside the home; many women also discovered that they had to work just to keep up with the cost of living. As the traditional role of the homemaker changed, so did the way families ate. With Mom working, there wasn't time for her to prepare the traditional three square meals a day. Instead, families began looking for alternatives to provide quick meals. What was the result? For one thing, there was a boom in fast-food restaurants. The suburban or downtown strip that once contained a lone McDonald's now features Wendy's, Roy Rogers, Taco Bell, Burger King, and Pizza Hut. Families also began to depend on frozen foods as another time-saving alternative. Once again, though, demand changed the kind of frozen food available. Frozen foods no longer consist of foil trays divided into greasy fried chicken, watery corn niblets, and lumpy mashed potatoes. Supermarkets now stock a range of supposedly gourmet frozen dinners--from fettucini in cream sauce to braised beef en brochette.

It may not be possible to pick up a ton of fill dirt and a half- 6 dozen croissants at the same place, but America's food habits are definitely changing. If it is true that "you are what you eat," then America's identity is evolving along with its diet.

Asked to prepare a paper analyzing the reasons behind a change in our lives, Carl decided to write about a shift he had noticed in Americans' eating habits. The title of Carl's essay, "Americans and Food," does identify his subject but needs to be reworked so it is livelier and more interesting.

Despite his uninspired title, Carl starts his *causal analysis* with a sharp, attention-getting opener — the vivid description of a cartoon. He then connects the cartoon to his subject with the following sentence: "The cartoon illustrates an interesting phenomenon: the changing food habits of Americans." To back up his belief that there has been a revolution in our eating habits, Carl uses the first paragraph to provide a capsule summary of the kind of meal that people used to eat, suggesting that such a meal is pretty much a thing of the past. At that point, Carl moves into his thesis: "But America has changed, and as it has, so has what we Americans eat and how we eat it." Note that the thesis implies that Carl's paper will focus on both causes and effects.

Carl's purpose was to write an *informative* causal analysis. But before he could present the causes of the change, he needed to show that such a change had, in fact, taken place. The second paragraph, therefore, documents one aspect of this change — the internationalization of our eating habits.

At the start of the third paragraph, Carl uses a question ("Why have we become more worldly in our tastes?") to signal that his discussion of causes is about to begin. This question also serves as the paragraph's *topic sentence,* indicating that the paragraph will focus on reasons for the increasingly international flavor of our food. The next two paragraphs, also focused by topic sentences, identify two other major reasons for the change in eating habits: "Our growing concern with health has also affected the way we eat" (paragraph 4) and "Our food habits are being affected, too, by the rapid increase in the number of women working outside the home" (5).

Since Carl's essay has an informational intent, he must support the point expressed in each topic sentence. Without convincing specifics, he will not be able to demonstrate the validity of his analysis. Consider for a moment the essay's third paragraph. In this section, Carl asserts that one reason for our new eating habits is our growing exposure to international foods. To illustrate the aptness of his analysis, Carl provides evidence showing that we have indeed become more familiar with international cuisine. Television exposes rural Montana to Cajun cooking; students traveling abroad take a liking to hard-crusted French bread; urban folks enjoy the exotic fare served by numerous immigrant groups settled in the cities.

The fourth and fifth paragraphs use similarly convincing specifics to demonstrate the soundness of the points expressed in the topic sentences. Let's look more closely at the evidence Carl uses to develop these points. As you know, causal analyses rely on clear thinking and logic. And Carl, not satisfied with obvious explanations, thought about his essay carefully, even brainstorming with friends to arrive at as comprehensive an analysis as possible. Not surprisingly, much of the evidence Carl uncovered took the form of *causal chains.* In the fourth paragraph, Carl writes, "The media also began to educate us about the dangers of processed foods pumped full of chemical additives. As a result, consumers began to demand healthier food . . . and manufacturers started to change some of their products." And the next paragraph shows how the changing role of American women caused families to look for alternative ways of eating. This shift, in turn, caused the restaurant and food industries to respond with a staggering range of food alternatives.

Although Carl's analysis digs beneath the surface and reveals complex cause – effect relationships, he wisely limits his pursuit of causal chains. He does not let the complexities distract him from his main purpose: to show why and how the American diet is changing. He knows his analysis must focus on key cause – effect relationships. Carl is also careful to provide his essay with abundant *connecting devices,* making it easy for readers to see the links between the points in his analysis. Consider the use of *transitions* (signaled by italics) in the following sentences: *"Another* reason for the growing international flavor of our food is that many young Americans have traveled abroad . . ." (3); *"As a result,* consumers began to demand healthier foods . . ." (4); and *"As* the traditional role of homemaker changed, *so* did the way families ate" (5).

When reading the essay, you probably noticed that Carl's conclusion is a bit weak. Although his reference to the cartoon works well, the rest of the paragraph limps to a tired close. Ending an otherwise vigorous essay with such a slight conclusion undercuts the effectiveness of the whole paper. Carl spent so much energy developing the body of his essay that he ran out of the stamina needed to conclude the piece more forcefully. Careful budgeting of his time would have allowed him to prepare a stronger concluding paragraph.

When Carl revised his paper, he realized that his fourth paragraph needed extensive work. Here is the original version of that paragraph.

First Draft Version

A growing concern with health has also affected the way we eat, especially because the media has sent us warnings the last few years about the dangers of salt, sugar, food additives, high-fat and low-fiber diets. We have started to worry that our traditional meals may have been shortening our lives. As a result, consumers demanded healthier foods and manufacturers started taking some of the salt and sugar out of canned foods. "All-natural" became an effective selling point, leading to many preservative-free products. Restaurants, too, adapted their menus, luring customers with light meals. Because we now know about the link between overweight and a variety of health problems, including heart attacks, we are counting calories. In turn, food companies made fortunes on diet beer and diet cola. Sometimes, though, we seem a bit confused about the health issue; we drink soda that is sugar-free but loaded with chemical sweeteners. Still, we believe we are lengthening our lives through changing our diets.

Carl's revising of this paragraph started with a reworking of the awkward first sentence. Packed with too much material, the sentence did not function as an effective topic sentence for the paragraph. Carl corrected the problem by breaking the overlong sentence into two shorter ones: "Our growing concern with health has also affected the way we eat. For the last few years, the media have warned us about the dangers of our traditional diet, high in salt and fat, low in fiber." The first of these sentences serves as a crisp topic sentence that focuses the rest of the paragraph.

In addition, Carl decided to omit all references to the way our concern with weight has affected our eating habits. It's true, of course, that calorie-counting has changed how we eat. But as soon as Carl started to discuss this point, he got involved in a causal chain that undercut the unity of the paragraph. He ended up describing the paradoxical situation in which we find ourselves. In an attempt to eat healthily, we stay away from sugar, using instead artificial sweeteners that probably aren't very good for us. This is an interesting issue, but it detracts from the point Carl wants to make: that our concern with health has affected our eating habits in a positive way.

Finally, while revising the paragraph, Carl made many of his details more concrete. He changed "manufacturers started taking some of the salt and sugar out of canned foods" to the more specific "Many foods, such as lunch meats, canned vegetables, and soups, were made available in low-fat, low-sodium versions." Similarly, generalizations about light meals and all-natural products gained life through the addition of concrete examples: "the restaurant industry responded to this switch to healthier foods, luring customers with salad bars, broiled fish, and steamed vegetables" and "the food industry started to produce all-natural products — everything from potato chips to ice cream — without additives and preservatives."

Carl did an equally fine job revising other sections of his paper. With the exception of the weak spots already discussed, he made the changes needed to craft a well-reasoned essay that demonstrated his ability to analyze a complex phenomenon.

The essays in this chapter analyze a range of cause–effect relationships. In "The Faltering Family," George Gallup, Jr., studies why the American family is changing and makes some disturbing predictions about future changes. Peter Farb's "In Other Words" describes a rather surprising cause of some children's poor school performance. In "O Rotten Gotham — Sliding Down into the Behavioral Sink," Tom Wolfe uses black humor to show how overpopulation leads to human aggression. With poignancy, Alice Walker traces, in "Beauty: When the Other Dancer Is the Self," the impact on her life of a disfiguring eye injury. Finally, Lewis Thomas examines why "The Lie Detector" works as it does and comes away encouraged by what he learns about human nature.

George Gallup, Jr.

Born in Illinois in 1930, George Gallup, Jr., is president of the Gallup Poll, the well-known research firm that measures public opinion. Gallup still resides in Princeton, New Jersey, where he graduated from the University, and has served as executive director of the Princeton Religion Research Center. He has published articles about religion, politics, and other current issues. His books include *America's Search for Faith* (1980), with David Poling; *My Kid on Drugs?* (1981), with Art Linkletter; *Adventures in Immortality* (1982) and *Forecast 2000* (1985), both with William Proctor. The following essay is from *Forecast 2000*.

The Faltering Family

For better or worse, the American family—one of society's most important structures—is changing in response to a variety of cultural forces. Based on the results of several national opinion polls, the following selection presents George Gallup's conclusions about the future of the family. According to Gallup, if current trends continue, the traditional family will fade into a mere memory.

In a recent Sunday school class in a United Methodist 1 Church in the Northeast, a group of eight- to ten-year-olds were in a deep discussion with their two teachers. When asked to choose which of ten stated possibilities they most feared happening, their response was unanimous. All the children most dreaded a divorce between their parents.

Later, as the teachers, a man and a woman in their late 2 thirties, reflected on the lesson, they both agreed they'd been shocked at the response. When they were the same age as their students, they said, the possibility of their parents' being divorced never entered their heads. Yet in just one generation, children seemed to feel much less security in their family ties.

Nor is the experience of these two Sunday school teachers an   3
isolated one. Psychiatrists revealed in one recent newspaper investigation that the fears of children definitely do change in
different periods; and in recent times, divorce has become one of
the most frequently mentioned anxieties. In one case, for example, a four-year-old insisted that his father rather than his mother
walk him to nursery school each day. The reason? He said many
of his friends had "no daddy living at home, and I'm scared that
will happen to me" (*The New York Times,* May 2, 1983).

In line with such reports, our opinion leaders expressed great   4
concern about the present and future status of the American
family. In the poll 33 percent of the responses listed decline in
family structure, divorce, and other family-oriented concerns as
one of the five major problems facing the nation today. And 26
percent of the responses included such family difficulties as one
of the five major problems for the United States in the year 2000.

Historical and sociological trends add strong support to   5
these expressions of concern. For example, today about one marriage in every two ends in divorce. Moreover, the situation seems
to be getting worse, rather than better. In 1962, the number of
divorces was 2.2 per 1,000 people, according to the National
Center for Health Statistics. By 1982, the figure had jumped to
5.1 divorces per 1,000 people — a rate that had more than doubled in two decades.

One common concern expressed about the rise in divorces   6
and decline in stability of the family is that the family unit has
traditionally been a key factor in transmitting stable cultural and
moral values from generation to generation. Various studies have
shown that educational and religious institutions often can have
only a limited impact on children without strong family support.

Even grandparents are contributing to the divorce statistics.   7
One recent study revealed that about 100,000 people over the age
of fifty-five get divorced in the United States each year. These
divorces are usually initiated by men who face retirement, and the
relationships being ended are those that have endured for thirty
years or more (*The New York Times Magazine,* December 19,
1982).

What are the pressures that have emerged in the past twenty   8
years that cause long-standing family bonds to be broken?

Many now agree that the sexual revolution of the 1960s   9

worked a profound change on our society's family values and personal relationships. Certainly, the seeds of upheaval were present before that critical decade. But a major change that occurred in the mid-sixties was an explicit widespread rejection of the common values about sexual and family relationships that most Americans in the past had held up as an ideal.

We're just beginning to sort through all the changes in social   10 standards that have occurred. Here are some of the major pressures that have contributed to those changes:

Pressure One: Alternative Lifestyles

Twenty years ago, the typical American family was depicted   11 as a man and woman who were married to each other and who produced children (usually two) and lived happily ever after. This was the pattern that young people expected to follow in order to become "full" or "normal" members of society. Of course, some people have always chosen a different route—remaining single, taking many partners, or living with a member of their own sex. But they were always considered somewhat odd, and outside the social order of the traditional family.

In the last two decades, this picture has changed dramati-   12 cally. In addition to the proliferation of single people through divorce, we also have these developments:

- Gay men and women have petitioned the courts for the   13 right to marry each other and to adopt children. These demands are being given serious consideration, and there may even be a trend of sorts in this direction. For example, the National Association of Social Workers is increasingly supporting full adoption rights for gay people (*The New York Times,* January 10, 1983).
- Many heterosexual single adults have been permitted to   14 adopt children and set up single-parent families. So being unattached no longer excludes people from the joys of parenthood.
- Some women have deliberately chosen to bear children out   15 of wedlock and raise them alone. In the past, many of these children would have been given up for adoption, but no longer.

A most unusual case involved an unmarried psycholo-   16
gist, Dr. Afton Blake, who recently gave birth after being
artificially inseminated with sperm from a sperm bank to
which Nobel Prize winners had contributed (*The New York
Times,* September 6, 1983).

- In a recent Gallup Youth Poll, 64 percent of the teenagers   17
  questioned said that they hoped their lives would be different from those of their parents. This included having more
  money, pursuing a different kind of profession, living in a
  different area, having more free time — and staying single
  longer.

Most surveys show increasing numbers of unmarried   18
couples living together. Also, there are periodic reports of
experiments in communal living, "open marriages," and
other such arrangements. Although the more radical approaches to relationships tend to come and go and never
seem to attract large numbers of people, the practice of
living together without getting married seems to be something that's here to stay. The law is beginning to respond to
these arrangements with awards for "palimony" —
compensation for long-term unmarried partners in a relationship. But the legal and social status of unmarried people who live together is still quite uncertain — especially as
far as any children of the union are concerned.

- Increasing numbers of married couples are choosing to   19
  remain childless. Planned Parenthood has even established
  workshops for couples to assist them in making this decision (*Los Angeles Herald-Examiner,* November 27, 1979).

So clearly, a situation has arisen during the last twenty years   20
in which traditional values are no longer as important. Also, a
wide variety of alternatives to the traditional family have arisen.
Individuals may feel that old-fashioned marriage is just one of
many options.

Pressure Two: Sexual Morality

The shifts in attitudes toward sexual morality have changed   21
as dramatically in the last two decades as the alternatives to

traditional marriage. Hear what a widely used college textbook, published in 1953, said about premarital sex:

> The arguments against premarital coitus outweigh 22
> those in its favor. Except for the matter of temporary
> physical pleasure, all arguments about gains tend to be
> highly theoretical, while the risks and unpleasant conse-
> quences tend to be in equal degree highly practical. . . .
>
> The promiscuity of young men is certainly poor 23
> preparation for marital fidelity and successful family life.
> For girls it is certainly no better and sometimes leads
> still further to the physical and psychological shock of
> abortion or the more prolonged suffering of bearing an
> illegitimate child and giving it up to others. From the
> viewpoint of ethical and religious leaders, the spread of
> disease through unrestrained sex activities is far more
> than a health problem. They see it as undermining the
> dependable standards of character and the spiritual
> values that raise life to the level of the "good society."

(This comes from *Marriage and the Family* by Professor Ray E. Baber of Pomona College, California, which was part of the McGraw-Hill Series in Sociology and Anthropology and required reading for some college courses.)

Clearly, attitudes have changed a great deal in just three 24 decades. Teenagers have accepted the idea of premarital sex as the norm. In one recent national poll, 52 percent of girls and 66 percent of boys favored having sexual relations in their teens. Ironically, however, 46 percent of the teenagers thought that virginity in their future marital partner was fairly important. Youngsters, in other words, display some confusion about what they want to do sexually, and what they expect from a future mate.

But of course, only part of the problem of defining sexual 25 standards lies with young people and premarital sex. The strong emphasis on achieving an active and rewarding sex life has proba-bly played some role in encouraging many husbands and wives into rejecting monogamy. Here's some of the evidence that's been accumulating:

- Half of the men in a recent nationwide study admitted   2
cheating on their wives (*Pensacola Journal,* May 30, 1978).
- Psychiatrists today say they see more patients who are   2
thinking about having an extramarital affair and who
wonder if it would harm their marriage (*New York Post,*
November 18, 1976).
- A psychiatrist at the Albert Einstein College of Medicine   2
says, "In my practice I have been particularly struck by how
many women have been able to use an affair to raise their
consciousness and their confidence."

So the desire for unrestrained sex now tends to take a place   2
among other more traditional priorities, and this can be expected
to continue to exert strong pressure on marriage relationships.

Pressure Three: The Economy

The number of married women working outside the home   30
has been increasing steadily, and most of these women are working out of economic necessity. As a result, neither spouse may
have time to concentrate on the nurturing of the children or of
the marriage relationship.

One mother we interviewed in New Jersey told us about her   31
feelings when she was forced to work full time in a library after
her husband lost his job.

"It's the idea that I have no choice that really bothers me,"   32
she said. "I have to work, or we won't eat or have a roof over our
heads. I didn't mind working part-time just to have extra money.
I suppose that it's selfish, but I hate having to work every day and
then to come home, fix dinner, and have to start doing housework. Both my husband and I were raised in traditional families,
where the father went to work and the mother stayed home and
took care of the house and children. [My husband] would never
think of cooking or doing housework. I've raised my boys the
same way, and now I'm paying for it. Sometimes, I almost hate
my husband, even though I know it's not his fault."

Unfortunately, such pressures probably won't ease in the   33
future. Even if the economy improves and the number of unemployed workers decreases, few women are likely to give up their
jobs. Economists agree that working-class women who have be-

come breadwinners during a recession can be expected to remain in the work force. One reason is that many unemployed men aren't going to get their old jobs back, even when the economy improves.

"To the extent that [the men] may have to take lower-paying service jobs, their families will need a second income," says Michelle Brandman, associate economist at Chase Econometrics. "The trend to two-paycheck families as a means of maintaining family income is going to continue" (*The Wall Street Journal*, December 8, 1982). 34

In addition to the pressures of unemployment, the cost of having, rearing, and educating children is steadily going up. Researchers have found that middle-class families with two children *think* they're spending only about 15 percent of their income on their children. Usually, though, they *actually* spend about 40 percent of their money on them. To put the cost in dollars and cents, if you had a baby in 1977, the estimated cost of raising that child to the age of eighteen will be $85,000, and that figure has of course been on the rise for babies born since then (*New York Daily News*, July 24, 1977). 35

Another important factor that promises to keep both spouses working full time in the future is the attitude of today's teenagers toward these issues. They're not so much concerned about global issues like overpopulation as they are about the high cost of living. Both boys and girls place a lot of emphasis on having enough money so that they can go out and do things. Consequently, most teenage girls surveyed say they expect to pursue careers, even after they get married. 36

So it would seem that by the year 2000 we can expect to see more working mothers in the United States. The woman who doesn't hold down any sort of outside job but stays at home to care for her children represents a small percentage of wives today. By the end of the century, with a few exceptions here and there, she may well have become a part of America's quaint past. 37

As women have joined the work force in response to economic needs, one result has been increased emotional strains on the marriage and family relationships. But there's another set of pressures that has encouraged women to pursue careers. That's the power of feminist philosophy to permeate attitudes in grassroots America during the past couple of decades. 38

Pressure Four: Grassroots
Feminist Philosophy

Many women may not agree with the most radical expres-   39
sions of feminist philosophy that have arisen in the past decade or
so. But most younger women — and indeed, a majority of women
in the United States — tend to agree with most of the objectives
that even the radical feminist groups have been trying to achieve.
The basic feminist philosophy has filtered down to the grass
roots, and young boys and girls are growing up with feminist
assumptions that may have been foreign to their parents and
grandparents.

For example, child care and housework are no longer re-   40
garded strictly as "women's work" by the young people we've
polled. Also, according to the Gallup Youth Poll, most teenage
girls want to go to college and pursue a career. Moreover, they
expect to marry later in life and to continue working after they're
married. Another poll, conducted by *The New York Times* and
CBS News, revealed that only 2 percent of the youngest age
group interviewed — that is, those eighteen to twenty-nine years
old — preferred "traditional marriage." By this, they meant a
marriage in which the husband is exclusively a provider and the
wife is exclusively a homemaker and mother.

If these young people continue to hold views similar to these   41
into later life, it's likely that the changes that are occurring today
in the traditional family structure will continue. For one thing,
more day-care centers for children will have to be established.
Consequently, the rearing of children will no longer be regarded
as solely the responsibility of the family, but will become a community or institutional responsibility.

But while such developments may lessen the strain on   42
mothers and fathers, they may also weaken the bonds that hold
families together. Among other things, it may become psychologically easier to get a divorce if a person is not getting along with a
spouse, because the divorcing spouses will believe it's less likely
that the lives of the children will be disrupted.

So the concept of broadening the rights of women vis-à-vis   43
their husbands and families has certainly encouraged women to
enter the working world in greater numbers. They're also more
inclined to seek a personal identity that isn't tied up so much in
their homelife.

These grassroots feminist forces have brought greater bene-   44
fits to many, but at the same time they've often worked against
traditional family ties, and we remain uncertain about what is
going to replace them. Feminists may argue that the traditional
family caused its own demise — or else why would supposedly
content wives and daughters have worked so hard to transform it?
Whatever its theories, though, feminism is still a factor that, in its
present form, appears to exert a destabilizing influence on many
traditional familial relationships among husbands, wives, and
children.

As things stand now, our family lives are in a state of flux and   45
will probably continue to be out of balance until the year 2000.
The pressures we've discussed will continue to have an impact on
our family lives in future years. But at the same time, counter-
forces, which tend to drive families back together again, are also
at work.

One of these factors is a traditionalist strain in the large   46
majority of American women. The vast majority of women in this
country — 74 percent — continue to view marriage with children
as the most interesting and satisfying life for them personally,
according to a Gallup Poll for the White House Conference on
Families released in June, 1980.

Another force supporting family life is the attitude of Ameri-   47
can teenagers toward divorce. According to a recent Gallup
Youth Poll, 55 percent feel that divorces are too easy to get today.
Also, they're concerned about the high rate of divorce, and they
want to have enduring marriages themselves. But at the same
time — in a response that reflects the confusion of many adult
Americans on this subject — 67 percent of the teens in this same
poll say it's right to get a divorce if a couple doesn't get along
together. In other words, they place little importance on trying to
improve or salvage a relationship that has run into serious
trouble.

There's a similar ambivalence in the experts we polled. As   48
we've seen, 33 percent of them consider family problems as a top
concern today, and 26 percent think these problems will be a big
difficulty in the year 2000. But ironically, less than 3 percent
suggest that strengthening family relationships is an important
consideration in planning for the future! It's obvious, then, that
we're confused and ambivalent in our feelings about marriage

and the family. Most people know instinctively, without having to read a poll or a book, that happiness and satisfaction in life are rooted largely in the quality of our personal relationships. Furthermore, the most important of those relationships usually begin at home. So one of the greatest challenges we face before the year 2000, both as a nation and as individuals, is how to make our all-important family ties strong and healthy. It's only upon such a firm personal foundation that we can hope to venture forth and grapple effectively with more public problems.

Questions for Close Reading

1. What is the thesis of the selection? Locate the sentence(s) in which Gallup states his main idea. If he does not state the thesis explicitly, express it in your own words.
2. According to Gallup, what are the major pressures that have caused the change in American attitudes to marriage and the family?
3. What new styles of pairing up and parenting have entered the American mainstream and now compete with traditional marriage?
4. Why are more and more women choosing to work outside the home? Why does the author believe that this is a permanent lifestyle change for American women?
5. Refer to your dictionary as needed to define the following words in the selection: *explicit* (paragraph 9), *proliferation* (12), *inseminated* (16), *salvage* (47), and *ambivalence* (48).

Questions About the Writer's Craft

1. In this selection, Gallup tries to account for the changes in the American ideals of marriage and family. Why does he use the term *pressures* rather than *causes*? Does he intend the list of pressures to be complete?
2. What techniques does the author use to introduce the selection? What feeling does this introduction create in you toward marriage and the family? How is the introduction related to the data covered in the article?
3. Examine the supporting evidence for each "pressure." For which ones does the author provide facts or statistics? What other kinds of evidence does he provide for the remaining pressures?
4. How does the author create a sense of objectivity about the report? Are there any clues in the author's word choices that reveal his actual opinions about the transformation of American family values?

Questions for Further Thought

1. Gallup places much of the blame for the family's decline on women. Find places in the essay where this is so. Do you think his assessment is fair? Can you think of other, perhaps male-related, reasons for the family's decline?
2. Gallup's statement that "one marriage in two ends in divorce" suggests that 50 percent of the country's marriages dissolve. But the statistics mean that, in a given year, the number of divorces is equal to half the number of new marriages — *not* to the total number of marriages in the country. Can you find other places where Gallup's statistics are open to misinterpretation (look closely at paragraph 4, for example)? How do these instances affect your view of his causal analysis?
3. Do American TV and the other media put pressure on our personal lifestyles? Is the image of family and relationships in the media a reflection of our changing personal values or an influence on them?
4. How widespread are the alternative lifestyles in the lives of people you know and go to school with?

Writing Assignments Using Cause – Effect as a Method of Development

1. Identify two or three additional pressures (besides those Gallup cites) that are changing the family. These pressures may result from societal dislocations such as homelessness and unemployment or from parental factors such as substance abuse or neglect. Write an essay analyzing the effect of these pressures.
2. Write an essay explaining how people are affected when those close to them choose an alternative lifestyle. For example, think of someone you know who has chosen divorce, single parenthood, a gay lifestyle, cohabitation, or some other nontraditional way of life. Decide what positive and/or negative effects resulted from this choice and write an essay outlining these effects. You may wish to evaluate the choice on the basis of how it turned out, but be careful of generalizing from one case to universal rules of behavior.

Writing Assignments Using Other Methods of Development

3. When a family breaks apart, many lives are disrupted. Parents, children, grandparents, relatives, friends, even neighbors must cope with disorder and confusion. Write an essay illustrating the kinds of turmoil that may be felt by one of these groups. Develop the paper by

drawing on your own and/or other people's experience. The essay should include some brief recommendations about ways the group under discussion can learn to cope with the dislocations that occur.

4. Watch prime-time TV for a week and keep a numerical record of how often alternative lifestyles (extramarital affairs, divorce, single parenthood, and so on) appear in the plots of TV dramas. Write up your findings in the form of a letter to *TV Guide,* either criticizing or praising the TV networks for their presentation of these life choices. Support your argument with specific references to the shows you watched.

Peter Farb

Peter Farb (1929–1980) was born in New York and attended Vanderbilt University. Farb served as a consultant to the Smithsonian Institution and as a visiting lecturer at Yale University. A deep interest in language and human cultures led Farb to write *Face of North America* (1963), *Man's Rise to Civilization as Shown by the Indians of North America* (1968), and *Word Play: What Happens When People Talk* (1973). This selection is from *Word Play*.

In Other Words

How can Clever Hans, a horse that solved mathematical problems, provide insight into a serious problem in public education? Surprisingly, there is a strong connection. In the following essay, Peter Farb uses the story of Clever Hans to show how subtly a teacher's body language can affect children's performance in the classroom.

Early in this century, a horse named Hans amazed the people 1 of Berlin by his extraordinary ability to perform rapid calculations in mathematics. After a problem was written on a blackboard placed in front of him, he promptly counted out the answer by tapping the low numbers with his right forefoot and multiples of ten with his left. Trickery was ruled out because Hans's owner, unlike owners of other performing animals, did not profit financially—and Hans even performed his feats whether or not the owner was present. The psychologist O. Pfungst witnessed one of these performances and became convinced that there had to be a more logical explanation than the uncanny intelligence of a horse.

Because Hans performed only in the presence of an audience 2 that could see the blackboard and therefore knew the correct answer, Pfungst reasoned that the secret lay in observation of the audience rather than of the horse. He finally discovered that as soon as the problem was written on the blackboard, the audience bent forward very slightly in anticipation to watch Hans's fore-feet. As slight as that movement was, Hans perceived it and took it as his signal to begin tapping. As his taps approached the correct number, the audience became tense with excitement and made almost imperceptible movements of the head — which signaled Hans to stop counting. The audience, simply by expecting Hans to stop when the correct number was reached, had actually told the animal when to stop. Pfungst clearly demonstrated that Hans's intelligence was nothing but a mechanical response to his audience, which unwittingly communicated the answer by its body language.

The "Clever Hans Phenomenon," as it has come to be known, raises an interesting question. If a mere horse can detect unintentional and extraordinarily subtle body signals, might they not also be detected by human beings? Professional gamblers and con men have long been known for their skill in observing the body-language cues of their victims, but only recently has it been shown scientifically that all speakers constantly detect and interpret such cues also, even though they do not realize it. 3

An examination of television word games several years ago revealed that contestants inadvertently gave their partners body-language signals that led to correct answers. In one such game, contestants had to elicit certain words from their partners, but they were permitted to give only brief verbal clues as to what the words might be. It turned out that sometimes the contestants also gave body signals that were much more informative than the verbal clues. In one case, a contestant was supposed to answer *sad* in response to his partner's verbal clue of *happy* — that is, the correct answer was a word opposite to the verbal clue. The partner giving the *happy* clue unconsciously used his body to indicate to his fellow contestant that an opposite word was needed. He did that by shifting his body and head very slightly to one side as he said *happy,* then to the other side in expectation of an opposite word. 4

Contestants on a television program are usually unsophisticated about psychology and linguistics, but trained psychological experimenters also unintentionally flash body signals which are sometimes detected by the test subjects — and which may distort the results of experiments. Hidden cameras have revealed that the 5 sex of the experimenter, for example, can influence the responses of subjects. Even though the films showed that both male and female experimenters carried out the experiments in the same way and asked the same questions, the experimenters were very much aware of their own sex in relation to the sex of the subjects. Male experimenters spent 16 per cent more time carrying out experiments with female subjects than they did with male subjects; similarly, female experimenters took 13 per cent longer to go through experiments with male subjects than they did with female subjects. The cameras also revealed that chivalry is not dead in the psychological experiment; male experimenters smiled about six times as often with female subjects as they did with male subjects.

The important question, of course, is whether or not such 6 nonverbal communication influences the results of experiments. The answer is that it often does. Psychologists who have watched films made without the knowledge of either the experimenters or the subjects could predict almost immediately which experimenters would obtain results from their subjects that were in the direction of the experimenters' own biases. Those experimenters who seemed more dominant, personal, and relaxed during the first moments of conversation with their subjects usually obtained the results that they secretly hoped the experiments would yield. And they somehow communicated their secret hopes in a completely visual way, regardless of what they said or their paralanguage when they spoke. That was made clear when these films were shown to two groups, one of which saw the films without hearing the sound track while the other heard only the sound track without seeing the films. The group that heard only the voices could not accurately predict the experimenters' biases— but those who saw the films without hearing the words immediately sensed whether or not the experimenters were communicating their biases.

A person who signals his expectations about a certain kind of 7 behavior is not aware that he is doing so—and usually he is indignant when told that his experiment was biased—but the subjects themselves confirm his bias by their performances. Such bias in experiments has been shown to represent self-fulfilling prophecies. In other words, the experimenters' expectations about the results of the experiment actually result in those expectations coming true. That was demonstrated when each of twelve experimenters was given five rats bred from an identical strain of laboratory animals. Half of the experimenters were told that their rats could be expected to perform brilliantly because they had been bred especially for high intelligence and quickness in running through a maze. The others were told that their rats could be expected to perform very poorly because they had been bred for low intelligence. All the experimenters were then asked to teach their rats to run a maze.

Almost as soon as the rats were put into the maze it became   8 clear that those for which the experimenters had high expectations would prove to be the better performers. And the rats which were expected to perform badly did in fact perform very badly, even though they were bred from the identical strain as the excellent performers. Some of these poor performers did not even budge from their starting positions in the maze. The misleading prophecy about the behavior of the two groups of rats was fulfilled — simply because the two groups of experimenters unconsciously communicated their expectations to the animals. Those experimenters who anticipated high performance were friendlier to their animals than those who expected low performance; they handled their animals more, and they did so more gently. Clearly, the predictions of the experimenters were communicated to the rats in subtle and unintended ways — and the rats behaved accordingly.

Since animals such as laboratory rats and Clever Hans can   9 detect body-language cues, it is not surprising that human beings are just as perceptive in detecting visual signals about expectations for performance. It is a psychological truth that we are likely to speak to a person whom we expect to be unpleasant in such a way that we force him to act unpleasantly. But it has only recently become apparent that poor children — often black or Spanish-speaking — perform badly in school because that is what their teachers expect of them, and because the teachers manage to convey that expectation by both verbal and nonverbal channels. True to the teachers' prediction, the black and brown children probably will do poorly — not necessarily because children from minority groups are capable only of poor performance, but because poor performance has been expected of them. The first grade may be the place where teachers anticipate poor performances by children of certain racial, economic, and cultural backgrounds—and where the teachers actually teach these children how to fail.

Evidence of the way the "Clever Hans Phenomenon" works 10 in many schools comes from a careful series of experiments by psychologist Robert Rosenthal and his co-workers at Harvard University. They received permission from a school south of San Francisco to give a series of tests to the children in the lower grades. The teachers were blatantly lied to. They were told that the test was a newly developed tool that could predict which children would be "spurters" and achieve high performance in the coming year. Actually, the experimenters administered a new kind of IQ test that the teachers were unlikely to have seen previously. After IQ scores were obtained, the experimenters selected the names of 20 percent of the children completely at random. Some of the selected children scored very high on the IQ test and others scored low, some were from middle-class families and others from lower-class. Then the teachers were lied to again. The experimenters said that the tests singled out this 20 per cent as the children who could be expected to make unusual intellectual gains in the coming year. The teachers were also cautioned not to discuss the test results with the pupils or their parents. Since the names of these children had been selected completely at random, any difference between them and the 80 per cent not designated as "spurters" was completely in the minds of the teachers.

All the children were given IQ tests again during that school 11 year and once more the following year. The 20 per cent who had been called to the attention of their teachers did indeed turn in the high performances expected of them—in some cases dramatic increases of 25 points in IQ. The teachers' comments about these children also were revealing. The teachers considered them more happy, curious, and interesting than the other 80 per cent —and they predicted that they would be successes in life, a prophecy they had already started to fulfill. The experiment plainly showed that children who are expected to gain intellectually do gain and that their behavior improves as well.

The results of the experiment are clear—but the explanation 12 for the results is not. It might be imagined that the teachers simply devoted more time to the children singled out for high expectations, but the study showed that was not so. Instead, the influence of the teachers upon these children apparently was much more subtle. What the teachers said to them, how and when it was said, the facial expressions, gestures, posture, perhaps even touch that accompanied their speech — some or all of these things must have communicated that the teachers expected improved performance from them. And when these children responded correctly, the teachers were quicker to praise them and also more lavish in their praise. Whatever the exact mechanism was, the effect upon the children who had been singled out was dramatic. They changed their ideas about themselves, their behavior, their motivation, and their learning capacities.

The lesson of the California experiment is that pupil per-   13
formance does not depend so much upon a school's audio-visual equipment or new textbooks or enriching trips to museums as it does upon teachers whose body language communicates high expectations for the pupils — even if the teacher thinks she "knows" that a black, a Puerto Rican, a Mexican-American, or any other disadvantaged child is fated to do poorly in school. Apparently, remedial instruction in our schools is misdirected. It is needed more by the middle-class teachers than by the disadvantaged children.

Questions for Close Reading

1. What is the thesis of the selection? Locate the sentence(s) in which Farb states his main idea. If he does not state the thesis explicitly, express it in your own words.
2. Does Farb consider the "Clever Hans Phenomenon" a true phenomenon, or does he give reasons for it? What kinds of people and animals are likely to detect and interpret body language clues?
3. The author refers to an experiment that used rats in a maze. Who was really the subject of that experiment, the rats or someone else?
4. What did the Harvard experiment in the San Francisco schools prove? In this experiment, who were the "rats"?
5. Refer to your dictionary as needed to define the following words in the selection: *unwittingly* (paragraph 2), *linguistics* (5), and *blatantly* (10).

Questions About the Writer's Craft

1. Scientific experiments are set up to limit the possible causes of an effect. In describing the "Clever Hans Phenomenon," Farb reveals

that naive viewers thought that the cause of the phenomenon was one thing (Hans doing math in his head), while the psychologist Pfungst determined that the cause was something else (Hans reacting to body movements of the audience). Locate this pattern of an effect and two possible causes — one simple, one subtle — in Farb's other examples of the "Clever Hans Phenomenon."

2. This essay begins with a detailed description of a clever horse in Berlin in the early 1900s and follows with an example of game show contestants. Why do you think these examples precede the discussion of modern scientific experiments? Why does Farb save the research on schoolchildren for last?

3. A qualifier is a word that moderates or "tones down" the certainty of a statement. *Often, usually, almost,* and *sometimes* are common qualifiers. Their absence and the use of terms like *always* and *never* produce "unqualified" statements. Look for qualifiers in "In Other Words" —especially at places where Farb interprets research for us. Does he qualify his statements more or less as the essay goes on?

4. Is Farb serious in his closing remarks about who really needs remedial work? Why does he make his final point this way?

Questions for Further Thought

1. What are the "other words" Farb refers to in the title? How are they different from the words we use when we speak aloud?

2. Are you aware of the subtle (and sometimes not-so-subtle) distinctions made by teachers and expressed in their treatment of students? What are some examples from your own experience of these subtle signals?

3. In at least two of the research projects Farb discusses, the scientists lied to their subjects. In the grade school experiment, a direct result of this was that teachers favored some students, and, presumably, looked on others with disfavor. Do you think it was ethical for researchers to set up an experiment on the basis of lies?

4. In our dealings with each other, are we sufficiently careful of our body language? What could we do to make our nonverbal communication more positive?

Writing Assignments Using Cause – Effect as a Method of Development

*1. None of us can escape fully other people's expectations. Such expectations may motivate or discourage us. Analyze the extent to which you or someone you know well has been influenced by others' expectations. Two essays, Langston Hughes' "Salvation" (page

157) and Alice Walker's "Beauty: When the Other Dancer Is the Self" (page 390), should get you thinking about the extent to which our inner worlds are shaped by others.

2. As Farb implies, many game shows test the ability of contestants to guess or "mind-read" the responses of others. Sometimes in our own lives we have the feeling that people have read our minds, or that we have read theirs. Brainstorm a short list of such experiences you have had. Then pick one or two and write an essay in which you examine the experience(s). Analyze the factors that contributed to the effect of "mind reading." These could include detecting someone's body language cues, knowing another person's habits or opinions, being familiar with his or her schedule, or sharing a common or similar past experience.

Writing Assignment Using Other Methods of Development

3. Imagine that you are the principal of a high school attended by disadvantaged students. Write a letter to your faculty briefly explaining the gist of the Rosenthal experiment. Then make three recommendations to your staff about techniques they can use to encourage high achievement in students. When making your recommendations, keep in mind that the students have been in school for many years; they are already suffering the effects of teachers' biases. Take this into account in making your recommendations. Choose your tone and words carefully, for you want to avoid offending the faculty or implying that they are not already doing their best.

4. Write an essay on an interesting person you know or have heard about who surpassed the restricted expectations held by other people. Citing the Rosenthal study in your introduction, prepare a strong argument refuting Rosenthal's research. Support your thesis with dramatic evidence showing how the person overcame the obstacles imposed by others.

Tom Wolfe

Born in Richmond, Virginia, in 1931, Tom Wolfe has worked
as a reporter for the *Washington Post* and other newspapers. In
his articles for *Esquire* and *The New Yorker,* Wolfe pioneered a
prose style known as the "new journalism," which blends the
subjective awareness of the writer with objective reportage.
Wolfe's books focus on subcultures of American society and
include such works as *The Kandy-Kolored, Tangerine-Flake
Streamline Baby* (1965), *The Electric Kool-Aid Acid Test*
(1968), *The Pump-House Gang* (1968), *The Right Stuff*
(1979), and *The Bonfire of the Vanities* (1987). This selection is
from *The Pump-House Gang.*

O Rotten Gotham —
Sliding Down into the
Behavioral Sink

Have you ever looked down from the top of a tall building and
thought, "They all look like ants down there?" We may not
like it, but humans do indeed resemble ants, or any other kind
of communal, social animal. In the following selection, Tom
Wolfe leads a lively tour through overcrowded New York City,
pointing at how we humans react to the pressures of city life.
He then links his observations to the findings of scientists who
have examined how other animals handle the stresses created
by competition and overcrowding. Overall, Wolfe concludes,
the prospects for human life look pretty grim.

I just spent two days with Edward T. Hall, an anthropolo- 1
gist, watching thousands of my fellow New Yorkers short-circuiting themselves into hot little twitching death balls with jolts of
their own adrenaline. Dr. Hall says it is overcrowding that does it.
Overcrowding gets the adrenaline going, and the adrenaline gets
them queer, autistic, sadistic, barren, batty, sloppy, hot-in-the-

381

pants, chancred-on-the-flankers, leering, puling, numb—the usual in New York, in other words, and God knows what else. Dr. Hall has the theory that overcrowding has already thrown New York into a state of behavioral sink. Behavioral sink is a term from ethology, which is the study of how animals relate to their environment. Among animals, the sink winds up with a "population collapse" or "massive die-off." O rotten Gotham.

It got to be easy to look at New Yorkers as animals, especially   2
looking down from some place like a balcony at Grand Central at the rush hour Friday afternoon. The floor was filled with the poor white humans, running around, dodging, blinking their eyes, making a sound like a pen full of starlings or rats or something.

"Listen to them skid," says Dr. Hall.   3

He was right. The poor old etiolate animals were out there   4
skidding on their rubber soles. You could hear it once he pointed it out. They stop short to keep from hitting somebody or because they are disoriented and they suddenly stop and look around, and they skid on their rubber-soled shoes, and a screech goes up. They pour out onto the floor down the escalators from the Pan-Am Building, from 42nd Street, from Lexington Avenue, up out of subways, down into subways, railroad trains, up into helicopters—

"You can also hear the helicopters all the way down here,"   5
says Dr. Hall. The sound of the helicopters using the roof of the Pan-Am Building nearly fifty stories up beats right through. "If it weren't for this ceiling"—he is referring to the very high ceiling in Grand Central—"this place would be unbearable with this kind of crowding. And yet they'll probably never 'waste' space like this again."

They screech! And the adrenal glands in all those poor white   6
animals enlarge, micrometer by micrometer, to the size of cantaloupes. Dr. Hall pulls a Minox camera out of a holster he has on his belt and starts shooting away at the human scurry. The Sink!

Dr. Hall has the Minox up to his eye—he is a slender man,   7
calm, 52 years old, young-looking, an anthropologist who has worked with Navajos, Hopis, Spanish-Americans, Negroes, Trukese. He was the most important anthropologist in the government during the crucial years of the foreign aid program, the 1950's. He directed both the Point Four training program and the Human Relations Area Files. He wrote *The Silent Language*

and *The Hidden Dimension,* two books that are picking up the kind of "underground" following his friend Marshall McLuhan started picking up about five years ago. He teaches at the Illinois Institute of Technology, lives with his wife, Mildred, in a high-ceilinged town house on one of the last great residential streets in downtown Chicago, Astor Street; he has a grown son and daughter, loves good food, good wine, the relaxed, civilized life—but comes to New York with a Minox at his eye to record!—perfect —The Sink.

We really got down in there by walking down into the Lexington Avenue line subway stop under Grand Central. We inhaled those nice big fluffy fumes of human sweat, urine, effluvia, and sebaceous secretions. One old female human was already stroked out on the upper level, on a stretcher, with two policemen standing by. The other humans barely looked at her. They rushed into line. They bellied each other, haunch to paunch, down the stairs. Human heads shone through the gratings. The species North European tried to create bubbles of space around themselves, about a foot and a half in diameter— 8

"See, he's reacting against the line," says Dr. Hall. 9

—but the species Mediterranean presses on in. The hell with bubbles of space. The species North European resents that, this male human behind him presses forward toward the booth . . . *breathing* on him, he's disgusted, he pulls out of the line entirely, the species Mediterranean resents him for resenting it, and neither of them realizes what the hell they are getting irritable about exactly. And in all of them the old adrenals grow another micrometer. 10

Dr. Hall whips out the Minox. Too perfect! The bottom of The Sink. 11

It is the sheer overcrowding, such as occurs in the business sections of Manhattan five days a week and in Harlem, Bedford-Stuyvesant, southeast Bronx every day—sheer overcrowding is converting New Yorkers into animals in a sink pen. Dr. Hall's argument runs as follows: all animals, including birds, seem to have a built-in inherited requirement to have a certain amount of territory, space, to lead their lives in. Even if they have all the food they need, and there are no predatory animals threatening them, they cannot tolerate crowding beyond a certain point. No more than two hundred wild Norway rats can survive on a quarter acre 12 of ground, for example, even when they are given all the food they can eat. They just die off.

But why? To find out, ethologists have run experiments on all sorts of animals, from stickleback crabs to Sika deer. In one major experiment, an ethologist named John Calhoun put some domesticated white Norway rats in a pen with four sections to it, connected by ramps. Calhoun knew from previous experiments that the rats tend to split up into groups of ten to twelve and that the pen, therefore, would hold forty to forty-eight rats comfortably, assuming they formed four equal groups. He allowed them to reproduce until there were eighty rats, balanced between male and female, but did not let it get any more crowded. He kept them supplied with plenty of food, water, and nesting materials. In other words, all their more obvious needs were taken care of. A less obvious need—space—was not. To the human eye, the pen did not even look especially crowded. But to the rats, it was crowded beyond endurance.

The entire colony was soon plunged into a profound behavioral sink. "The sink," said Calhoun, "is the outcome of any behavioral process that collects animals together in unusually great numbers. The unhealthy connotations of the term are not accidental: a behavioral sink does act to aggravate all forms of pathology that can be found within a group."

For a start, long before the rat population reached eighty, a status hierarchy had developed in the pen. Two dominant male rats took over the two end sections, acquired harems of eight to ten females each, and forced the rest of the rats into the two middle pens. All the overcrowding took place in the middle pens. That was where the "sink" hit. The aristocrat rats at the end grew bigger, sleeker, healthier, and more secure the whole time.

In The Sink, meanwhile, nest building, courting, sex behavior, reproduction, social organization, health—all of it went to pieces. Normally, Norway rats have a mating ritual in which the male chases the female, the female ducks down into a burrow and sticks her head up to watch the male. He performs a little dance outside the burrow, then she comes out, and he mounts her, usually for a few seconds. When The Sink set in, however, no more than three males—the dominant males in the middle sections—kept up the old customs. The rest tried everything from satyrism to homosexuality or else gave up on sex altogether. Some of the subordinate males spent all their time chasing females. Three or four might chase one female at the same time, and instead of stopping at the burrow entrance for the ritual, they would charge right in. Once mounted, they would hold on for minutes instead of the usual seconds.

Homosexuality rose sharply. So did bisexuality. Some males   17
would mount anything—males, females, babies, senescent rats, anything. Still other males dropped sexual activity altogether, wouldn't fight and, in fact, would hardly move except when the other rats slept. Occasionally, a female from the aristocrat rats' harems would come over the ramps and into the middle sections to sample life in The Sink. When she had had enough, she would run back up the ramp. Sink males would give chase up to the top of the ramp, which is to say, to the very edge of the aristocratic preserve. But one glance from one of the king rats would stop them cold and they would return to The Sink.

The slumming females from the harems had their adventures   18
and then returned to a placid, healthy life. Females in The Sink, however, were ravaged, physically and psychologically. Pregnant rats had trouble continuing pregnancy. The rate of miscarriages increased significantly, and females started dying from tumors and other disorders of the mammary glands, sex organs, uterus, ovaries, and Fallopian tubes. Typically, their kidneys, livers, and adrenals were also enlarged or diseased or showed other signs associated with stress.

Child-rearing became totally disorganized. The females lost   19
the interest or the stamina to build nests and did not keep them up if they did build them. In the general filth and confusion, they would not put themselves out to save offspring they were momentarily separated from. Frantic, even sadistic competition among the males was going on all around them and rendering their lives chaotic. The males began unprovoked and senseless assaults upon one another, often in the form of tail-biting. Ordinarily, rats will suppress this kind of behavior when it crops up. In The Sink, male rats gave up all policing and just looked out for themselves. The "pecking order" among males in The Sink was never stable. Normally, male rats set up a three-class structure. Under the pressure of overcrowding, however, they broke up into all sorts of unstable subclasses, cliques, packs—and constantly pushed, probed, explored, tested one another's power. Anyone was fair game, except for the aristocrats in the end pens.

Calhoun kept the population down to eighty, so that the   20 next stage, "population collapse" or "massive die-off," did not occur. But the autopsies showed that the pattern—as in the diseases among the female rats—was already there.

The classic study of die-off was John J. Christian's study of   21 Sika deer on James Island in the Chesapeake Bay, west of Cambridge, Maryland. Four or five of the deer had been released on the island, which was 280 acres and uninhabited, in 1916. By 1955 they had bred freely into a herd of 280 to 300. The population density was only about one deer per acre at this point, but Christian knew that this was already too high for the Sikas' inborn space requirements, and something would give before long. For two years the number of deer remained 280 to 300. But suddenly, in 1958, over half the deer died; 161 carcasses were recovered. In 1959 more deer died and the population steadied at about 80.

In two years, two-thirds of the herd had died. Why? It was   22 not starvation. In fact, all the deer collected were in excellent condition, with well-developed muscles, shining coats, and fat deposits between the muscles. In practically all the deer, however, the adrenal glands had enlarged by 50 percent. Christian concluded that the die-off was due to "shock following severe metabolic disturbance, probably as a result of prolonged adrenocortical hyperactivity. . . . There was no evidence of infection, starvation, or other obvious cause to explain the mass mortality." In other words, the constant stress of overpopulation, plus the normal stress of the cold of the winter, had kept the adrenaline flowing so constantly in the deer that their systems were depleted of blood sugar and they died of shock.

Well, the white humans are still skidding and darting across   23 the floor of Grand Central. Dr. Hall listens a moment longer to the skidding and the darting noises, and then says, "You know, I've been on commuter trains here after everyone has been through one of these rushes, and I'll tell you, there is enough acid flowing in the stomachs in every car to dissolve the rails underneath."

Just a little invisible acid bath for the linings to round off the   24 day. The ulcers the acids cause, of course, are the one disease people have already been taught to associate with the stress of city life. But overcrowding, as Dr. Hall sees it, raises a lot more hell with the body than just ulcers. In everyday life in New York— just the usual, getting to work, working in massively congested areas like 42nd Street between Fifth Avenue and Lexington, especially now that the Pan-Am Building is set in there, working in cubicles such as those in the editorial offices at Time-Life, Inc., which Dr. Hall cites as typical of New York's poor handling of space, working in cubicles with low ceilings and, often, no access to a window, while construction crews all over Manhattan drive everybody up the Masonite wall with air-pressure generators with noises up to the boil-a-brain decibel level, then rushing to get home, piling into subways and trains, fighting for time and for space, the usual day in New York — the whole now-normal thing keeps shooting jolts of adrenaline into the body, breaking down the body's defenses and winding up with the work-a-daddy human animal stroked out at the breakfast table with his head apoplexed like a cauliflower out of his $6.95 semi-spread Pima-cotton shirt, and nosed over into a plate of No-Kloresto egg substitute, signing off with the black thrombosis, cancer, kidney, liver, or stomach failure, and the adrenals ooze to a halt, the size of eggplants in July.

One of the people whose work Dr. Hall is interested in on this score is Rene Dubos at the Rockefeller Institute. Dubos's work indicates that specific organisms, such as the tuberculosis bacillus or a pneumonia virus, can seldom be considered "the cause" of a disease. The germ or virus, apparently, has to work in combination with other things that have already broken the body down in some way — such as the old adrenal hyperactivity. Dr. Hall would like to see some autopsy studies made to record the size of adrenal glands in New York, especially of people crowded into slums and people who go through the full rush-hour-work-rush-hour cycle every day. He is afraid that until there is some clinical, statistical data on how overcrowding actually ravages the human body, no one will be willing to do anything about it. Even in so obvious a thing as air pollution, the pattern is familiar. Until people can actually see the smoke or smell the sulphur or feel the sting in their eyes, politicians will not get excited about it, even though it is well known that many of the lethal substances polluting the air are invisible and odorless. For one thing, most politicians are like the aristocrat rats. They are insulated from The Sink by practically sultanic buffers — limousines, chauffeurs, secretaries, aides-de-camp, doormen, shuttered houses, high-floor apartments. They almost never ride subways, fight rush hours, much less live in the slums or work in the Pan-Am Building.

Questions for Close Reading

1. What is the thesis of the selection? Locate the sentence(s) in which Wolfe states his main idea. If he does not state the thesis explicitly, express it in your own words.
2. In paragraph 5, Dr. Hall comments on the high ceiling of Grand Central Station: "They'll probably never 'waste' space like this again." Why is the word "waste" emphasized? Why does Wolfe include this remark in the essay?
3. Why does Dr. Hall come to New York? Who is John Calhoun, and what does he have to do with "rotten Gotham"?
4. How do the male and female rats respond to overcrowding? Are Dr. Hall's observations in Grand Central pertinent to both human sexes? To all races and classes of people in New York?
5. Refer to your dictionary as needed to define the following words used in the selection: *autistic* (paragraph 1), *chancred* (1), *etiolate* (4), *effluvia* (8), *sebaceous* (8), *ethologist* (13), *satyrism* (16), and *adrenocortical* (22).

Questions About the Writer's Craft

1. What is the causal chain of behaviors established in the essay? How does the author organize the results of scientific research to suggest this chain?
2. Locate the points where Wolfe shifts from a discussion of one researcher's work and moves to another's. How does Wolfe achieve these transitions? How much space does he devote to them?
3. Wolfe uses gross exaggeration in the essay: adrenal glands "the size of cantaloupes," for example. What are some other examples of hyperbole in the essay? Is this technique appropriate for an essay on a scientific subject?
4. Dr. Hall seems almost lighthearted as he snaps photos of New Yorkers "short-circuiting themselves" at Grand Central Station. "Listen to them skid," Wolfe reports him saying. What is the tone of the essay? Is the tone an appropriate one for Wolfe's subject?

Questions for Further Thought

1. In what ways do big cities resemble the rat colonies in Calhoun's lab? Is your opinion based on experience or hearsay?
2. How do you react to crowding when you commute, study, shop, attend classes, or engage in other activities? What reactions do you notice in others? Are there any situations in which crowding is *fun*?
3. Are humans able to rise above the level of viciousness exhibited by the

rats—or do we behave in the same manner? What remedies, short- and long-term, can you imagine to prevent humans from becoming mired in a "sink"?

4. Survivalists are people who are preparing for a national disaster— war, riots, economic collapse—by stockpiling weapons, food, and other supplies. Are survivalists being sensible? Are they admirable?

Writing Assignments Using Cause – Effect as a Method of Development

1. Examine the effects of overcrowding, or excessive competition, or a frenzied pace on a particular aspect of American life. You might choose to focus on any of the following: student life, life in cities, life in a large corporation, life in the suburbs, or vacations in crowded resorts or national parks. Choose at least three important effects and write an essay warning readers of the dangers involved in allowing such conditions to continue.

2. Assume you have been assigned to write a guest editorial for your college newspaper. You decide to recommend a small change in student behavior or in college administrative policy, showing how such a change could make a significant difference on campus. Establish a causal chain that demonstrates the value of your proposed change. For example, "If students would bus their own trays in the cafeteria," or "If the college library would allow book renewal by phone. . . ."

Writing Assignments Using Other Methods of Development

*3. If you live in or have visited a large city, you probably have some first-hand knowledge of the conditions Wolfe writes about in "O Rotten Gotham. . . ." Write a narrative of your experience, referring to specific urban problems. Show the reader the low points of human behavior in the city. Make the essay vivid by using a style similar to Wolfe's: full of hyperbole, slang, and vivid imagery. Before writing the paper, you may find it helpful to read what William McKibben ("Ugly," page 427) says about one aspect of city life.

*4. Write an essay arguing that architecture can influence people. Discuss the reasons people are attracted to or feel distaste for certain architectural styles or structures—for example, why people flock to spacious courtyards in cities or why they become prone to violence in stark housing developments. Peggy Anderson's "Children's Hospital" (page 110) might prompt some thoughts on the connection between architecture and human behavior.

Alice Walker

The eighth child of Georgia sharecroppers, Alice Walker (1944–) has built a reputation as a sensitive chronicler of the black experience in America. After studying at Spelman College in Atlanta, Walker graduated from Sarah Lawrence College in New York. Soon after that, she worked in the civil rights movement helping to register black voters and teaching in Mississippi's Head Start Program. The recipient of numerous writing fellowships and the founder of her own publishing company, Walker has written extensively: a biography, *Langston Hughes, American Poet* (1973); poetry, *Revolutionary Petunias and Other Poems* (1973); short stories, collected in *In Love & Trouble* (1973) and *You Can't Keep a Good Woman Down* (1981); essays, gathered in *Living by the Word* (1988); and novels, including *Meridian* (1976) and *The Color Purple* (1982). The last won both the Pulitzer Prize and the American Book Award and was made into a feature film. The following selection comes from her 1983 collection of essays, *In Search of Our Mothers' Gardens*.

Beauty: When the Other Dancer Is the Self

A disfiguring injury can seriously affect anyone's self-esteem. Alice Walker sustained such an injury as a child. In this essay, she describes what happened to her and provides glimpses of her Southern childhood and the people who changed her life for better or worse. Walker's experience is a commentary on the role of good looks in a girl's life, and on the importance of good sense in gaining self-acceptance and esteem as an adult.

It is a bright summer day in 1947. My father, a fat, funny   1
man with beautiful eyes and a subversive wit, is trying to decide
which of his eight children he will take with him to the county
fair. My mother, of course, will not go. She is knocked out from

390

getting most of us ready: I hold my neck stiff against the pressure of her knuckles as she hastily completes the braiding and then beribboning of my hair.

My father is the driver for the rich old white lady up the road.   2
Her name is Miss Mey. She owns all the land for miles around, as well as the house in which we live. All I remember about her is that she once offered to pay my mother thirty-five cents for cleaning her house, raking up piles of her magnolia leaves, and washing her family's clothes, and that my mother—she of no money, eight children, and a chronic earache—refused it. But I do not think of this in 1947. I am two and a half years old. I want to go everywhere my daddy goes. I am excited at the prospect of riding in a car. Someone has told me fairs are fun. That there is room in the car for only three of us doesn't faze me at all. Whirling happily in my starchy frock, showing off my biscuit-polished patent-leather shoes and lavender socks, tossing my head in a way that makes my ribbons bounce, I stand, hands on hips, before my father. "Take me, Daddy," I say with assurance; "I'm the prettiest!"

Later, it does not surprise me to find myself in Miss Mey's   3
shiny black car, sharing the back seat with the other lucky ones. Does not surprise me that I thoroughly enjoy the fair. At home that night I tell the unlucky ones all I can remember about the merry-go-round, the man who eats live chickens, and the teddy bears, until they say: that's enough baby Alice. Shut up now, and go to sleep.

It is Easter Sunday, 1950. I am dressed in a green, flocked,   4
scalloped-hem dress (handmade by my adoring sister, Ruth) that has its own smooth satin petticoat and tiny hot-pink roses tucked into each scallop. My shoes, new T-strap patent leather, again highly biscuit-polished. I am six years old and have learned one of the longest Easter speeches to be heard that day, totally unlike the speech I said when I was two: "Easter lilies/pure and white/blossom in/the morning light." When I rise to give my speech I do so on a great wave of love and pride and expectation. People in the church stop rustling their new crinolines. They seem to hold their breath. I can tell they admire my dress, but it is my spirit, bordering on sassiness (womanishness), they secretly applaud.

"That girl's a little *mess*," they whisper to each other, pleased.   5

Naturally I say my speech without stammer or pause, unlike   6
those who stutter, stammer, or, worst of all, forget. This is before
the word "beautiful" exists in people's vocabulary, but "Oh, isn't
she the *cutest* thing?" frequently floats my way. "And got so
much sense!" they gratefully add . . . for which thoughtful addition I thank them to this day.

It was great fun being cute. But then, one day, it ended.   7

I am eight years old and a tomboy. I have a cowboy hat,   8
cowboy boots, checkered shirt and pants, all red. My playmates
are my brothers, two and four years older than I. Their colors are
black and green, the only difference in the way we are dressed. On
Saturday nights we all go to the picture show, even my mother;
Westerns are her favorite kind of movie. Back home, "on the
ranch," we pretend we are Tom Mix, Hopalong Cassidy, Lash
LaRue (we've even named one of our dogs Lash LaRue); we chase
each other for hours rustling cattle, being outlaws, delivering
damsels from distress. Then my parents decide to buy my
brothers guns. These are not "real" guns. They shoot "BBs,"
copper pellets my brothers say will kill birds. Because I am a girl, I
do not get a gun. Instantly I am relegated to the position of
Indian. Now there appears a great distance between us. They
shoot and shoot at everything with their new guns. I try to keep
up with my bow and arrows.

One day while I am standing on top of our makeshift   9
"garage" — pieces of tin nailed across some poles — holding my
bow and arrow and looking out toward the fields, I feel an
incredible blow in my right eye. I look down just in time to see
my brother lower his gun.

Both brothers rush to my side. My eye stings, and I cover it   10
with my hand. "If you tell," they say, "we will get a whipping.
You don't want that to happen, do you?" I do not. "Here is a
piece of wire," says the older brother, picking it up from the roof;
"say you stepped on one end of it and the other flew up and hit
you." The pain is beginning to start. "Yes," I say. "Yes, I will say
that is what happened." If I do not say this is what happened, I
know my brothers will find ways to make me wish I had. But now
I will say anything that gets me to my mother.

Confronted by our parents we stick to the lie agreed upon.   11
They place me on a bench on the porch and I close my left eye
while they examine the right. There is a tree growing from under-

neath the porch that climbs past the railing to the roof. It is the last thing my right eye sees. I watch as its trunk, its branches, and then its leaves are blotted out by the rising blood.

I am in shock. First there is intense fever, which my father   12
tries to break using lily leaves bound around my head. Then there are chills: my mother tries to get me to eat soup. Eventually, I do not know how, my parents learn what has happened. A week after the "accident" they take me to see a doctor. "Why did you wait so long to come?" he asks, looking into my eye and shaking his head. "Eyes are sympathetic," he says. "If one is blind, the other will likely become blind too."

This comment of the doctor's terrifies me. But it is really   13
how I look that bothers me most. Where the BB pellet struck there is a glob of whitish scar tissue, a hideous cataract, on my eye. Now when I stare at people — a favorite pastime, up to now — they will stare back. Not at the "cute" little girl, but at her scar. For six years I do not stare at anyone, because I do not raise my head.

Years later, in the throes of a mid-life crisis, I ask my mother   14
and sister whether I changed after the "accident." "No," they say, puzzled. "What do you mean?"

What do I mean?   15

I am eight, and, for the first time, doing poorly in school,   16
where I have been something of a whiz since I was four. We have just moved to the place where the "accident" occurred. We do not know any of the people around us because this is a different county. The only time I see the friends I knew is when we go back to our old church. The new school is the former state penitentiary. It is a large stone building, cold and drafty, crammed to overflowing with boisterous, ill-disciplined children. On the third floor there is a huge circular imprint of some partition that has been torn out.

"What used to be here?" I ask a sullen girl next to me on our   17
way past it to lunch.

"The electric chair," says she.   18

At night I have nightmares about the electric chair; and   19
about all the people reputedly "fried" in it. I am afraid of the school, where all the students seem to be budding criminals.

"What's the matter with your eye?" they ask, critically.   20

When I don't answer (I cannot decide whether it was an   21
"accident" or not), they shove me, insist on a fight.

My brother, the one who created the story about the wire,   22
comes to my rescue. But then brags so much about "protecting"
me, I become sick.

After months of torture at the school, my parents decide to   23
send me back to our old community, to my old school. I live with
my grandparents and the teacher they board. But there is no room
for Phoebe, my cat. By the time my grandparents decide there *is*
room, and I ask for my cat, she cannot be found. Miss Yarbor-
ough, the boarding teacher, takes me under her wing, and begins
to teach me to play the piano. But soon she marries an African —
a "prince," she says — and is whisked away to his continent.

At my old school there is at least one teacher who loves me.   24
She is the teacher who "knew me before I was born" and bought
my first baby clothes. It is she who makes life bearable. It is her
presence that finally helps me turn on the one child at the school
who continually calls me "one-eyed bitch." One day I simply
grab him by his coat and beat him until I am satisfied. It is my
teacher who tells me my mother is ill.

My mother is lying in bed in the middle of the day, some-   25
thing I have never seen. She is in too much pain to speak. She has
an abscess in her ear. I stand looking down on her, knowing that
if she dies, I cannot live. She is being treated with warm oils and
hot bricks held against her cheeks. Finally a doctor comes. But I
must go back to my grandparents' house. The weeks pass but I am
hardly aware of it. All I know is that my mother might die, my
father is not so jolly, my brothers still have their guns, and I am
the one sent away from home.

"You did not change," they say.   26
Did I imagine the anguish of never looking up?   27

I am twelve. When relatives come to visit I hide in my room.   28
My cousin Brenda, just my age, whose father works in the post
office and whose mother is a nurse, comes to find me. "Hello,"
she says. And then she asks, looking at my recent school picture,
which I did not want taken, and on which the "glob," as I think
of it, is clearly visible, "You still can't see out of that eye?"

"No," I say, and flop back on the bed over my book.   29

That night, as I do almost every night, I abuse my eye. I rant   30 and rave at it, in front of the mirror. I plead with it to clear up before morning. I tell it I hate and despite it. I do not pray for sight. I pray for beauty.

"You did not change," they say.   31

I am fourteen and baby-sitting for my brother Bill, who lives   32
in Boston. He is my favorite brother and there is a strong bond between us. Understanding my feelings of shame and ugliness he and his wife take me to a local hospital, where the "glob" is removed by a doctor named O. Henry. There is still a small bluish crater where the scar tissue was, but the ugly white stuff is gone. Almost immediately I become a different person from the girl who does not raise her head. Or so I think. Now that I've raised my head I win the boyfriend of my dreams. Now that I've raised my head I have plenty of friends. Now that I've raised my head classwork comes from my lips as faultlessly as Easter speeches did, and I leave high school as valedictorian, most popular student, and *queen,* hardly believing my luck. Ironically, the girl who was voted most beautiful in our class (and was) was later shot twice through the chest by a male companion, using a "real" gun, while she was pregnant. But that's another story in itself. Or is it?

"You did not change," they say.   33

It is now thirty years since the "accident." A beautiful jour-   34
nalist comes to visit and to interview me. She is going to write a cover story for her magazine that focuses on my latest book. "Decide how you want to look on the cover," she says. "Glamorous, or whatever."

Never mind "glamorous," it is the "whatever" that I hear.   35
Suddenly all I can think of is whether I will get enough sleep the night before the photography session: if I don't, my eye will be tired and wander, as blind eyes will.

At night in bed with my lover I think up reasons why I   36
should not appear on the cover of a magazine. "My meanest critics will say I've sold out," I say. "My family will now realize I write scandalous books."

"But what's the real reason you don't want to do this?" he   37
asks.

"Because in all probability," I say in a rush, "my eye won't be   38
straight."

"It will be straight enough," he says. Then, "Besides, I   39
thought you'd made your peace with that."

And I suddenly remember that I have.   40
I remember: 41
I am talking to my brother Jimmy, asking if he remembers   42
anything unusual about the day I was shot. He does not know I
consider that day the last time my father, with his sweet.home
remedy of cool lily leaves, chose me, and that I suffered and raged
inside because of this. "Well," he says, "all I remember is standing by the side of the highway with Daddy, trying to flag down a
car. A white man stopped, but when Daddy said he needed somebody to take his little girl to the doctor, he drove off."
I remember: 43
I am in the desert for the first time. I fall totally in love with   44
it. I am so overwhelmed by its beauty, I confront for the first
time, consciously, the meaning of the doctor's words years ago:
"Eyes are sympathetic. If one is blind, the other will likely become blind too." I realize I have dashed about the world madly,
looking at this, looking at that, storing up images against the
fading of the light. *But I might have missed seeing the desert!* The
shock of that possibility—and gratitude for over twenty-five
years of sight—sends me literally to my knees. Poem after poem
comes—which is perhaps how poets pray.

On Sight   45

I am so thankful I have seen
The Desert
And the creatures in the desert
And the desert Itself.

The desert has its own moon
Which I have seen
With my own eye.
There is no flag on it.

Trees of the desert have arms
All of which are always up
That is because the moon is up
The sun is up
Also the sky
The stars
Clouds
None with flags.

> If there were *flags*, I *doubt*
> the trees would point.
> Would *you?*

But mostly, I remember this: 46

I am twenty-seven, and my baby daughter is almost three.   47
Since her birth I have worried about her discovery that her
mother's eyes are different from other people's. Will she be embarrassed? I think. What will she say? Every day she watches a
television program called "Big Blue Marble." It begins with a
picture of the earth as it appears from the moon. It is bluish, a
little battered-looking, but full of light, with whitish clouds swirl-
ing around it. Every time I see it I weep with love, as if it is a
picture of Grandma's house. One day when I am putting Rebecca
down for her nap, she suddenly focuses on my eye. Something
inside me cringes, gets ready to try to protect myself. All children
are cruel about physical differences, I know from experience, and
that they don't always mean to be is another matter. I assume
Rebecca will be the same.

But no-o-o-o. She studies my face intently as we stand, her   48
inside and me outside the crib. She even holds my face maternally
between her dimpled little hands. Then, looking every bit as
serious and lawyerlike as her father, she says, as if it may just
possibly have slipped my attention: "Mommy, there's a *world* in
your eye." (As in, "Don't be alarmed, or do anything crazy.")
And then, gently, but with great interest: "Mommy, where did
you *get* that world in your eye?"

For the most part, the pain left then. (So what, if my brothers   49
grew up to buy even more powerful pellet guns for their sons and
to carry real guns themselves. So what, if a young "Morehouse
man" once nearly fell off the steps of Trevor Arnett Library
because he thought my eyes were blue.) Crying and laughing I ran
to the bathroom, while Rebecca mumbled and sang herself off to
sleep. Yes indeed, I realized, looking into the mirror. There *was* a
world in my eye. And I saw that it was possible to love it: that in
fact, for all it had taught me of shame and anger and inner vision,
I *did* love it. Even to see it drifting out of orbit in boredom, or
rolling up out of fatigue, not to mention floating back at attention in excitement (bearing witness, a friend has called it), deeply
suitable to my personality, and even characteristic of me.

That night I dream I am dancing to Stevie Wonder's song   50
"Always" (the name of the song is really "As," but I hear it as
"Always"). As I dance, whirling and joyous, happier than I've
ever been in my life, another bright-faced dancer joins me. We
dance and kiss each other and hold each other through the night.
The other dancer has obviously come through all right, as I have
done. She is beautiful, whole and free. And she is also me.

Questions for Close Reading

1. What is the thesis of the selection? Locate the sentence(s) in which Walker states her main idea. If she does not state the thesis explicitly, express it in your own words.
2. How does Walker's injury affect her ability to express herself and relate to others?
3. What is the connection between the loss of young Alice's cat and her teacher's marriage (paragraph 23)?
4. How do you interpret the essay's title — "Beauty: When the Other Dancer Is the Self"? How does the title reinforce Walker's thesis?
5. Refer to your dictionary as needed to define the following words used in the selection: *subversive* (paragraph 1), *chronic* (2), *flocked* (4), *crinoline* (4), *cataract* (13), and *abscess* (25).

Questions About the Writer's Craft

1. Walker's essay is structured around a causal chain that shows the interaction between the external and the internal. Explain how Walker develops this chain throughout the essay.
2. Although Walker records incidents occurring from infancy to mid-life, she writes in the present tense. Why?
3. How does Walker signal the ages at which she experiences a crisis or some other major event? What technique does she use?
4. The refrain "You did not change" occurs in differing contexts throughout Walker's essay. What is the effect of this repetition?

Questions for Further Thought

1. Walker believes that her father's attitude toward her changed after her injury. Has someone's attitude toward you ever changed dramatically? What precipitated the change? What were its consequences?
2. Walker relates that she lied about the cause of her injury partly to protect herself from her brothers' possible retaliation. If a person is

bullied and intimidated, what is the best course of action—to comply with those more powerful, to go against their wishes secretly, or to defy them openly and face the consequences? Why?

3. Walker recalls being "relegated to the position of Indian." Think of a time when you were excluded from participation in some activity because of your age, sex, race, or economic status. How did you feel about being excluded?

4. Walker tells us that although she was the valedictorian and the "most popular student" in her high school class, another student was voted most beautiful. If you could be academically outstanding, extremely well liked, or strikingly good looking, which would you choose? Why?

Writing Assignments Using Cause–Effect as a Method of Development

1. An event initially viewed as handicapping can, as Walker shows, prove to be a blessing. In a causal analysis, explain the effect on your life of an experience that at first seemed negative but turned out for the best.

2. Walker expects her daughter to react with revulsion to her eye injury. To her surprise, her daughter's reaction is tender and gentle. Think of a time you expected someone to treat you with kindness, but instead you were treated harshly, or, conversely, you expected severity but met with generosity. In an essay, trace the causes of your faulty expectation as well as the possible reasons for the other person's unexpected behavior. Draw some conclusion about human nature.

Writing Assignments Using Other Methods of Development

3. Walker writes of an experience in which joyful, exuberant play turned—in an instant—to terror. Write about a time in your own or in someone else's life when there was a sudden reversal of events —a positive experience became negative, or vice versa. Use vivid images, varied sentence structure, and dialogue to capture what happened. Did the event leave a lasting impression? If so, end by writing briefly about this effect.

*4. Walker mentions two elementary school teachers who responded to her in a loving, supportive way. Write a letter to beginning grade school teachers outlining the steps they should (and should not) take to make their students' school experience a positive one. Peter Farb's "In Other Words" (page 373) might give you some ideas to explore.

Lewis Thomas

Lewis Thomas (1913–) has earned a reputation as an out-standing scientist and physician. A graduate of Princeton University and Harvard Medical School, Thomas has held both the deanship of Yale University's medical school and the presidency of Memorial Sloan–Kettering Cancer Center. But more remarkable than Thomas' professional accomplishments is his gift for communicating the wonder of medicine and biology to the average reader. His essays, many of which first appeared in *The New England Journal of Medicine,* are less about medicine than they are about what he calls the "mystery of being." Thomas' work has been collected in three books: *Lives of a Cell* (1974), *The Medusa and the Snail* (1979), and *Late Night Thoughts on Listening to Mahler's Ninth Symphony* (1984), from which the following piece is taken.

The Lie Detector

The evidence against the innate goodness of the human race seems overwhelming at times. But writer/physician Lewis Thomas, expressing himself in typically plain-spoken but elegant prose, takes comfort in what a lie detector reveals about human impulses and instincts.

Every once in a while the reasons for discouragement about 1
the human prospect pile up so high that it becomes difficult to see the way ahead, and it is then a great blessing to have one conspicuous and irrefutable good thing to think about ourselves, something solid enough to step onto and look beyond the pile.

Language is often useful for this, and music. A particular 2
painting, if you have the right receptors, can lift the spirits and hold them high enough to see a whole future for the race. The sound of laughter in the distance in the dark can be a marvelous encouragement. But these are chancy stimuli, ready to work only

if you happen to be ready to receive them, which takes a bit of luck.

I have been reading magazine stories about the technology of 3 lie detection lately, and it occurs to me that this may be the thing I've been looking for, an encouragement propped up by genuine, hard scientific data. It is promising enough that I've decided to take as given what the articles say, uncritically, and to look no further. For a while, anyway.

Lying Is a Strain

As I understand it, a human being cannot tell a lie, even a 4 small one, without setting off a kind of smoke alarm somewhere deep in a dark lobule of the brain, resulting in the sudden discharge of nerve impulses, or the sudden outpouring of neurohormones of some sort, or both. The outcome, recorded by the lie-detector gadgetry, is a highly reproducible cascade of changes in the electrical conductivity of the skin, the heart rate, and the manner of breathing, similar to the responses to various kinds of stress.

Lying, then, is stressful, even when we do it for protection, 5 or relief, or escape, or profit, or just for the pure pleasure of lying and getting away with it. It is a strain, distressing enough to cause the emission of signals to and from the central nervous system warning that something has gone wrong. It is, in a pure physiological sense, an unnatural act.

Now I regard this as a piece of extraordinarily good news, 6 meaning, unless I have it all balled up, that we are a moral species by compulsion, at least in the limited sense that we are biologically designed to be truthful to each other. Lying doesn't hurt, mind you, and perhaps you could tell lies all day and night for years on end without being damaged, but maybe not—maybe the lie detector informs us that repeated, inveterate untruthfulness will gradually undermine the peripheral vascular system, the sweat glands, the adrenals, and who knows what else. Perhaps we should be looking into the possibility of lying as an etiologic agent for some of the common human ailments still beyond explaining, recurrent head colds, for instance, or that most human of all unaccountable disorders, a sudden pain in the lower mid-back.

Truth: Genetically Required?

It makes a sort of shrewd biological sense, and might there-   7
fore represent a biological trait built into our genes, a feature of
humanity as characteristic for us as feathers for birds or scales for
fish, enabling us to live, at our best, the kinds of lives we are
designed to live. This is, I suppose, the "sociobiological" view to
take, with the obvious alternative being that we are brought up
this way as children in response to the rules of our culture. But if
the latter is the case, you would expect to encounter, every once
in a while, societies in which the rule does not hold, and I have
never heard of a culture in which lying was done by everyone as a
matter of course, all life through, nor can I imagine such a group
functioning successfully. Biologically speaking, there is good reason for us to restrain ourselves from lying outright to each other
whenever possible. We are indeed a social species, more interde-
pendent than the celebrated social insects; we can no more live a
solitary life than can a bee; we are obliged, as a species, to rely on
each other. Trust is a fundamental requirement for our kind of
existence, and without it all our linkages would begin to snap
loose.

The restraint is a mild one, so gentle as to be almost imper-   8
ceptible. But it is there; we know about it from what we call guilt,
and now we have a neat machine to record it as well.

It seems a trivial thing to have this information, but perhaps   9
it tells us to look again, and look deeper. If we had better instruments, designed for profounder probes, we might see needles
flipping, lines on charts recording quantitative degrees of mean-
ness of spirit, or a lack of love. I do not wish for such instruments,
I hope they will never be constructed; they would somehow
belittle the issues involved. It is enough, quite enough, to know
that we cannot even tell a plain untruth, betray a trust, without
scaring some part of our own brains. I'd rather guess at the rest.

Questions for Close Reading

1. What is the thesis of the selection? Locate the sentence(s) in which
   Thomas states his main idea. If he does not state the thesis explicitly,
   express it in your own words.

2. For what reasons does Thomas call lying an "unnatural act"? How does he feel about its being "unnatural"?

3. Thomas writes that receptivity to language, music, art, and laughter "takes a bit of luck" (paragraph 2). What do you think he means by this statement?

4. To his "sociobiological" view of truth telling, Thomas contrasts another viewpoint. What is this other interpretation? Does he give this other interpretation equal evidence? Why or why not?

5. Refer to your dictionary as needed to define the following words used in the selection: *irrefutable* (paragraph 1), *receptors* (2), *stimuli* (2), *lobule* (4), *neurohormones* (4), *inveterate* (6), and *etiologic* (6).

Questions About the Writer's Craft

1. At the heart of Thomas' essay is a causal chain consisting of a series of interwoven causes and effects. What is this causal chain?

2. Thomas mixes technical terms from neuroscience with a rather informal style, involving contractions, the personal "I," colloquial expressions ("unless I have it all balled up"), and sentence fragments. Why might he have chosen to blend two such contrasting styles?

3. When presenting his viewpoint, Thomas uses a number of qualifiers: "it occurs to me" (3), "as I understand it" (4), "unless I have it all balled up" (6), and "I suppose" (7). What is the effect of these qualifiers? Do they contribute to or detract from his credibility?

4. Thomas' next-to-last paragraph is shorter than any other in the essay. What function does this brief paragraph serve?

Questions for Further Thought

1. Thomas opens his essay by saying that "reasons for discouragement about the human prospect" sometimes "pile up." But he does not go on to specify these reasons. What might these reasons be? What do you find most discouraging about our future?

2. Thomas does not differentiate between "white" lies and intentionally hurtful ones. For you, what situations might justify lying?

3. Thomas writes that he requires scientific evidence to support an optimistic outlook. Which is more important to you — concrete evidence or faith? Explain.

4. In nature, opossums "play dead," birds feign broken wings, and chimpanzees direct competitors away from a food source by falsely indicating the food is located elsewhere. In what ways might humans' ability to deceive also serve an important function? Explain.

Writing Assignments Using Cause–Effect as a Method of Development

*1. Reasons for lying, Thomas writes, include profit, protection, pleasure, and kindness. Write a causal analysis tracing the reasons for a lie that you or someone else (a parent, friend, or public figure) once told. Also analyze the effect of the lie. Langston Hughes' "Salvation" (p. 157) may provide some insight into the psychology of lying. End the paper with some conclusions about when lying is and is not acceptable.

2. Thomas welcomes the use of the lie detector but has qualms about the development of similar technologies. Focus on one technological breakthrough (word processors, videotape recorders, telephone answering machines, to name a few) and discuss its negative and positive ramifications. Although your causal analysis may be serious or playful, it should have a basically persuasive intent.

Writing Assignments Using Other Methods of Development

3. Thomas claims "Trust is a fundamental requirement for our . . . existence." In an essay, define the word *trust.* Dramatic examples, brief anecdotes, a comparison of two people are possible ways to develop the definition. Your essay should illustrate Thomas' point that without trust "all our linkages would . . . snap loose."

*4. According to Thomas, "we are a moral species by compulsion." Write an essay in which you argue for or against his contention. Remembering to consider the opposing opinion, develop your argument by citing several examples of human behavior. Mark Twain's "The Damned Human Race" (page 564) and Bob Greene's "Handled with Care" (page 142), two essays with sharply different viewpoints, will spark some interesting ideas.

Additional Writing Topics

CAUSE – EFFECT

General Assignments

Write an essay that analyzes the causes and/or effects of any of the following topics. Determine your purpose before beginning to write: Will the essay be informative, persuasive, or speculative? As you prewrite, think rigorously about causes and effects; try to identify causal chains. Provide solid evidence for the thesis and use either chronological or emphatic order to organize your supporting points.

1. Having the parents you have
2. Sleep deprivation
3. Lack of communication in a relationship
4. Overexercising or not exercising
5. A particular TV or rock star's popularity
6. Skill or ineptitude in sports
7. A major life decision
8. Stiffer legal penalties for drunken driving
9. Changing attitudes toward protecting the environment
10. A particular national crisis
11. The mass movement of women into the work force
12. Choosing to attend this college
13. "Back to basics" movement in schools
14. Headaches
15. An act of violence
16. A natural event: leaves turning, birds migrating, animals hibernating, an eclipse occurring
17. Pesticide use
18. Use of computers in the classroom
19. Banning disposable cans and bottles
20. A bad habit
21. A fear of _____
22. Legalizing prostitution or marijuana
23. Abolishing the F grade
24. Joining a particular organization
25. Owning a pet

Assignments with a Specific Audience and Purpose

1. The athletic program on your campus is in a state of crisis. The college has been accused of placing sports above studies (there have been several grade-fixing and recruiting scandals). You do not believe, as some people have suggested, that your school should abandon "big-time athletics." You have been designated to appear on the local TV news show to reply to an anti-sports editorial. Write a script for your brief on-the-air reply, explaining why it would be disastrous for the university to curtail its involvement with sports.

2. Why do students "flunk out" of college? Write an article for the opening-day issue of the campus newspaper outlining the main causes of failure. Your goal is to warn incoming students so they don't fall into the dangerous patterns that lead to poor grades or dropping out.

3. You probably have read many articles in the paper recently about the current "trash crisis" in America, especially in crowded eastern states. Dumps are overflowing, garbage is piling up, people protest waste incinerators in their neighborhoods. Write a letter to the editor, analyzing the causes of this crisis. Be sure to mention the nationwide love affair with disposable items and the general abandonment of the idea of thrift.

4. As a part-time employee of the college employment/work-study office, you have been given the task of drafting a brief pamphlet: "Things to Keep in Mind If You Plan to Work while Attending College." The pamphlet will be given to your fellow students and it will focus on the effects — both negative and positive — of combining a part-time job with college studies.

5. Teenage suicide has been on the rise. Why might this be so? Write a fact sheet to be given to parents of teenagers and to high school guidance counselors, describing the factors that could make a student desperate enough to attempt suicide.

6. Some communities have conducted campaigns encouraging residents to give up television for a fixed period of time. The communities believe that such a move would change life for the better. You feel your community should participate in such an experiment. Write a letter to the PTA or the mayor encouraging a public relations effort in favor of "Turn off the TV Month." Cite specifically the positive effects such a program would have on parents, children, and the community in general.

DEFINITION

WHAT IS DEFINITION?

In Lewis Carroll's wise and whimsical tale, *Through the Looking Glass,* Humpty Dumpty proclaims, "When *I* use a word . . . , it means just what I choose it to mean — neither more nor less." If the world were filled with characters like Humpty Dumpty, all of them bending words to their own purposes and accepting no challenges to their personal definitions, communication would be an exercise in frustration. You would say a word, and it would mean one thing to you but perhaps something completely different to a close friend. Without a common understanding, the two of you would be talking at cross-purposes, missing each other's meanings as you blundered through a conversation.

For language to communicate, words must have accepted definitions. Dictionaries, the source-books for accepted definitions, are compilations of current word-meanings, enabling speakers of a language to understand one another. But as you might suspect, things are not as simple as they first appear. We all know that a word like *discipline* has a standard dictionary definition. We also know, though, that parents argue every day over the meaning of "discipline" and that controversies about the meaning of "discipline" rage within school systems year after year. Moreover, many of the wrenching moral debates of our time also boil down to questions of definition. Much of the controversy over abortion, for instance, centers on what is meant by "life" and when it "begins."

Words can, in short, be slippery. Each of us has unique experiences, attitudes, and values that influence the way we use words and the way we interpret the words of others. Lewis Carroll may have been exaggerating, but Humpty Dumpty's attitude exists—in a very real way—within all of us.

In addition to the idiosyncratic interpretations that may attach to words, some words may shift in meaning over time. The word *pedagogue,* for instance, used to mean "a teacher or leader of children." Over the last several years, though, *pedagogue* has come to mean "a dogmatic, pedantic teacher." And, of course, other words (*modem, byte*) we invent as the need arises.

When writing a definition, you try to answer the basic question: What does _____ mean? What is the special or true nature of _____? The word to be defined may be an object, a complex or abstract concept, a person, a place, or a phenomenon. Potential subjects for definition might be a "user-friendly" computer, animal rights, a respected teacher, your hometown, cabin fever. As you will see, there are various strategies for expanding definitions far beyond the single-word synonyms or brief phrases that dictionaries use to clarify meanings.

WHEN TO USE DEFINITION

Many times, short-answer questions on exams are worded in such a way that a definition is clearly appropriate. Consider the following:

- Define the term *mob psychology.*
- What is the difference between a metaphor and a simile?
- How would you characterize a religious cult? Explain what it is and what it is not.

In such cases, a good response might involve a definition of several sentences or several paragraphs.

Other times definition may be used in part of a longer essay organized mainly around another pattern of development. When this situation occurs, all that is needed is a brief formal definition or a short definition in your own words. For instance, a *process analysis* showing how computers have revolutionized the typical business office might start with a textbook definition of "artificial intelligence." In an *argumentation–persuasion* paper urging the elimination of fraternities and sororities, you could refer to the definitions of "blackballing" and "hazing" found in the university handbook. Or your personal definition of "hero" could be the starting point for a *causal analysis* that examines why there are so few real heroes in today's world.

But the most complex use of definition, and the one we are primarily concerned with in this chapter, involves exploring a subject through an *extended definition*. Extended definition allows you to apply a personal interpretation to a word, to make a case for a revisionist view of a commonly accepted meaning, to analyze words representing complex or controversial issues. "Pornography," "gun control," "secular humanism," and "right-to-life" would be excellent subjects for extended definition — each is multifaceted, often misunderstood, and fraught with emotional meaning. "Junk food," "anger," "leadership," "anxiety" could make interesting subjects, especially if the extended definition helped readers develop a new understanding of the word. You might, for example, write a paper on "anxiety," defining it not as a negative state to be avoided but as a positive force propelling us to significant action.

The extended definitions you write will perhaps run several paragraphs or a few pages. Keep in mind, however, that an extended definition may require a chapter or even an entire book to develop. If this seems unlikely, remember that you can find volumes defining "excellence" and that theologians, philosophers and pop psychologists have devoted entire texts to such concepts as "death" and "love."

SUGGESTIONS FOR USING DEFINITION IN AN ESSAY

The following suggestions will be helpful whether you use definition as a dominant or supportive pattern of development.

1. Decide on the essay's purpose and tone. Since your purpose for writing an extended definition shapes the entire paper, you need to clarify for yourself the essay's goal. A definition essay with a purely *informative* purpose seeks only to explain or make meaning clear. But a definition essay with a *persuasive* slant also tries to win readers over to a particular point of view. Suppose that you decide to write an essay defining "jazz." The paper might lend itself to an *informative* or *persuasive* approach. The essay could be purely explanatory and discuss the origins of jazz, its characteristic tonal patterns, some of the great jazz musicians of the past. Or the essay could move beyond the purely informative and take on a persuasive edge. It might, for example, argue that jazz is the only contemporary form of music worth considering seriously.

Just as your purpose in writing a definition essay will vary, so will the tone you use. A strictly informative definition generally will assume a detached, serious tone ("Apathy is an emotional state characterized by listlessness and indifference"). By way of contrast, a definition essay with a persuasive bent might be urgent in tone ("To combat student apathy, we must design a series of programs to engage students in campus life"), or it might take a light — even satiric — approach ("An apathetic stance is a wise choice for any thinking student").

When deciding on the purpose and tone of the essay, you must remember to consider your audience. Not only does the audience determine what terms have to be defined (and how detailed the definition should be), but the audience also helps you focus on the most appropriate purpose and tone to select. You probably would not, for instance, write a strictly informative, serious piece for the college newspaper about the "mystery meat" served in the campus cafeteria. Instead, you would adopt a light tone as you defined the culinary horror and might even make a persuasive pitch about what could be done to improve the quality of food prepared on campus.

2. Formulate an effective definition. Definition essays sometimes start with a brief *formal definition* — either the dictionary's, a textbook's, or the writer's — and then go on to expand that initial definition with supporting details. Formal definitions are traditionally worded as three-part statements that consist of the following: the *term,* the *class* to which the term belongs, and the *characteristics* that distinguish the term from other members of its class.

Term	Class	Characteristics
The peregrine falcon,	an endangered bird,	is the world's fastest flyer.
A bodice-ripper	is a paperback book,	usually read by women, that deals with highly charged romance in exotic places and faraway times.
Back to basics	is a trend in education	that emphasizes skill mastery through rote learning.

A definition that meets these guidelines will clarify what your subject *is* and what it *is not.* These guidelines also establish the boundaries of your definition, removing unlike items from consideration in your (and your reader's) mind. For example, defining "back to basics" as a trend that emphasizes rote learning signals a certain boundary; other educational trends, such as those that emphasize children's social or emotional development, would not be part of the essay's definition.

If you decide to include a formal definition, avoid the old-hat "the dictionary says" or "according to Webster" approach. Such weak starts are just plain boring and often herald an unimaginative essay. You should also keep in mind that a strict dictionary definition may actually confuse readers. Suppose you were writing a paper on the way all of us absorb ideas and values from the media. Likening this automatic response to the process of osmosis, you decide to open the paper with a dictionary definition. But if you write, "According to the dictionary, osmosis is the tendency of a solvent to disperse through a porous membrane into a more concentrated solution," readers are apt to be baffled, even hostile. Remember, the purpose of a definition is to clarify, not obscure, meaning. A final pitfall to avoid is *circularity*, saying the same thing twice and therefore defining nothing: "A campus tribunal is a tribunal composed of various members of the university community." We do not learn from such a definition what a campus tribunal is, for the writer has said only that *"X is X."*

3. Develop the extended definition. You can choose from a variety of patterns when developing an extended definition. Description, narration, process, comparison, or any of the other patterns discussed in the book can be used — alone or in combination. Imagine that you are planning to write an extended definition of "robotics." You might choose to develop the term by providing *examples* of the ways robots are currently being used in scientific research; by *comparing* and *contrasting* human and robot capabilities; or by *classifying* robots, starting with the most basic and moving to the most advanced or futuristic models.

The patterns of development to use will often become apparent during the prewriting stage. Here is a list of prewriting questions as well as the pattern of development implied by each brainstorming question.

Question	Pattern of Development
What does it look like?	Description
What happened?	Narration
What are some typical instances of it?	Examples
How does it work?	Process
What things is it like or not like?	Comparison – contrast
Why did it happen? What will its impact be?	Cause – effect
What are its subparts? How can it be categorized?	Division – classification

Those questions yielding the most material often suggest effective pattern(s) for developing an extended definition.

4. Organize the material that supports the definition. If you use a single method to develop the extended definition, apply the principles of organization suited to that method, as described in the appropriate chapter of this book. Assume that you are defining "fad" by means of *process analysis.* You might organize your paragraphs according to the steps in the process: a fad's slow start as something avant-garde or eccentric; a fad's wildfire acceptance by the general public; a fad's demise as it becomes familiar or tiresome. If "character" is going to be defined by means of a single *narration,* paragraphs would probably be organized chronologically.

In a definition essay using several methods of development, you should devote separate paragraphs to each pattern. A definition of "relaxation," for instance, might start with a paragraph that *narrates* a particularly relaxing day; then it might move to several *examples* of people who find it difficult to unwind; finally, it might end by explaining a *process* for relaxing the mind and body.

5. Write an effective introduction. It may be helpful to provide—near the start of a definition essay—a brief formal definition of the term you are going to develop in the rest of the paper. Beyond this basic element, the introduction may include a number of other features. You may explain the *origin* of the term being defined: "Acid rock is a term first coined in the 1960s to describe music that was written or listened to under the influence of the drug LSD." Similarly, you may explain the *etymology,* or linguistic origin, of the key word that focuses the paper. "The term *vigilantism* is derived from the Latin word meaning 'to watch and be awake.'"

Second, the introduction may clarify what the subject is *not.* Such *definition by negation* can be an effective strategy at the beginning of a paper, especially if readers do not share your view of the subject. In such a case, you would write something like this: "The gorilla, far from being the vicious killer of jungle movies and popular imagination, is a sedentary, gentle creature living in a closely knit family group." Such a statement provides the special focus of your essay and signals some of the misconceptions or fallacies soon to be discussed.

You may also decide to include in the introduction a *stipulative definition,* one that puts special restrictions on a term:

"Strictly defined, a mall refers to a one- or two-story enclosed building containing a variety of retail shops and at least two large anchor stores. Highway-strip shopping centers or downtown centers cannot be considered true malls." When a term has multiple meanings, or when its meaning has become fuzzy through misuse, a stipulative definition sets the record straight right at the start, so that writer and audience know exactly what is, and is not, being defined.

Finally, the introduction may end with *a plan of development* that implies how the definition essay will unfold. A student who returned to school after having raised a family decided to write a paper defining the midlife crisis that led to her enrollment in college. After providing a brief formal definition of midlife crisis, the student rounded off her introduction with this sentence: "Such a midlife crisis starts with vague misgivings, turns into depression, and ends with a significant change in lifestyle."

Semanticists, those who study the nature of language, have noted that meaning lies in people, not in words. Because words are symbols — and therefore open to multiple interpretations — dictionaries can only be starting points, never ultimate authorities. The complex nature of language makes the formulation of definitions an important part of writing. Extended definitions are one way we can sort out for ourselves the confusing nature of a word or term. We see the importance of definition every day. The courts define "right to privacy"; the campus handbook explains what "plagiarism" is; international negotiators try to forge an agreement on the meaning of "arms parity." Because definition essays can be developed so many ways, they make demands quite different from most other assignments. Definition essays are, in short, a challenge worth mastering.

STUDENT ESSAY AND COMMENTARY

The following student essay was written by Laura Chen in response to this assignment:

> In "Entropy," K. C. Cole takes a scientific term from physics and gives it a broader definition and a wider

application. Choose another specialized term and define it in such a way that you reveal something significant about contemporary life.

While reading Laura's paper, try to determine how well it applies the principles concerning the use of definition. The commentary following the paper will help you look at Laura's essay more closely.

Physics in Everyday Life

A boulder sits on a mountain side for a thousand years. The boulder will remain there forever unless an outside force intervenes. Suppose a force does affect the boulder--an earthquake, for instance. Once the boulder begins to thunder down the mountain, it will remain in motion and head in one direction only--downhill--until another force interrupts its progress. If the boulder tumbles into a gorge, it will finally come to rest as gravity anchors it to the earth once more. In both cases, the boulder is exhibiting the physical principle of inertia: the tendency of matter to remain at rest or, if moving, to keep moving in one direction unless affected by an outside force. Inertia, an important factor in the world of physics, also plays a crucial role in the human world. Inertia affects our individual lives as well as the direction taken by society as a whole. 1

Inertia often influences our value systems and personal growth. Inertia is at work, for example, when people cling to certain behaviors and views. Like the boulder firmly fixed to the mountain, most people are set in their ways. Without thinking, they vote Republican or Democratic because they have always voted that way. They regard with suspicion a couple having no children, simply because everyone else in the neighborhood has a large family. It is only when an outside force--a jolt of some sort--occurs that people change their views. A white American couple may think little about racial discrimination, for instance, until they adopt an Asian child and must comfort her when classmates tease her because she looks different. Parents may consider promiscuous any unmarried teenage girl who has a baby until their 17-year-old honors-student daughter confesses that she is pregnant. Personal jolts like these force people to think, perhaps for the first time, about issues that now affect them directly. 2

To illustrate how inertia governs our lives, it is helpful to compare the world of television with real life. On TV, inertia does not exist. Television shows and commercials show people making all 3 kinds of drastic changes. They switch brands of coffee or try a new haircolor with no hesitation. In one car commercial, an ambitious young accountant abandons her career with a flourish and is seen driving off into the sunset as she heads for a small cabin by the sea to write poetry. In a soap opera, a character may progress from homemaker to hooker to nun in a single year. But in real life, inertia rules. People tend to stay where they are, to keep their jobs, to be loyal to products. A second major difference between television and real life is that, on television, everyone takes prompt and dramatic action to solve problems. The construction worker with a thudding headache is pain-free at the end of the sixty-second commercial; the police catch the murderer within an hour; the family learns to cope with their son's life-threatening drug addiction by the time the made-for-TV movie ends at eleven. But in the real world, inertia persists, so that few problems are solved neatly or quickly. Illnesses drag on, few crimes are solved, and family conflicts last for years.

Inertia is, most importantly, a force at work in the life of our nation. Again, inertia is two-sided. It keeps us from moving and, once we move, it keeps us pointed in one direction. We find ourselves mired in a certain path, accepting the inferior, even the dangerous. We settle for toys that break, winter coats with no warmth, and rivers clogged with pollution. Inertia also compels our nation to keep moving in one direction--despite the uncomfortable suspicion that it is the wrong direction. We are not sure if manipulating genes is a good idea, yet we continue to fund scientific projects in genetic engineering. More than forty years ago, we were shaken when we saw the devastation caused by an atomic bomb. But we went on to develop weapons hundreds of times more destructive. Although warned that excessive television viewing may be harmful, we continue to watch hours of television each day.

We have learned to defy gravity, one of the basic laws of physics; we fly high above the earth, even float in outer space. But most of us have not learned to defy inertia. Those special individuals who are able to act when everyone else seems paralyzed are rare. But the fact that such people do exist means that inertia is not all-powerful. If we use our reasoning ability and our creativity, we can conquer inertia, just as we have conquered gravity.

As the title of her essay suggests, Laura — like the author of "Entropy" — has taken a scientific term from a specialized field and used the term to help explain some everyday phenomena. Laura opens her essay with a vivid *descriptive* example of "inertia," the term at the heart of the paper. This description is then followed by a *formal definition* of inertia: "the tendency of matter to remain at rest or, if moving, to keep moving in one direction unless affected by an outside force." Laura wisely begins the paper with the attention-getting description rather than with the scientific definition. Had the order been reversed, the essay would not have gotten off to nearly as effective a start. Laura then ends her introductory paragraph with a two-sentence *thesis:* "Inertia, an important factor in the world of physics, also plays a crucial role in the human world. Inertia affects our individual lives as well as the direction taken by society as a whole."

Like all effective *definition essays,* Laura's paper helps us look at ourselves and the world in a new light. And since Laura wants us to accept her definition of inertia and her view that it often governs human behavior, her essay also contains a distinct element of *argumentation–persuasion.*

To support her definition of inertia and her belief that it can rule our lives, Laura generates a number of compelling examples. She organizes these examples by grouping them into three major points, each point signaled by a *topic sentence* that appears at the start of the essay's three supporting paragraphs: "Inertia often influences our value systems and personal growth" (paragraph 2); "To illustrate how inertia governs our lives, it is helpful to compare the world of television with real life" (3); and "Inertia is, most importantly, a force at work in the life of our nation" (4).

Note that a definite organizational strategy underpins the sequence of Laura's three central points. The essay moves from the way inertia affects the individual to the way it shapes the life of the nation. And the words "most importantly" at the start of the fourth paragraph indicate that Laura has arranged her points emphatically, believing that inertia's impact on society is most critical.

In addition to using numerous examples to illustrate her points, Laura draws on *several writing patterns* to show that inertia can be a powerful force. In the second and fourth paragraphs, for example, she uses *causal analysis* to explain how inertia can paralyze people and nations. The second paragraph indicates that only "an outside force — a jolt of some sort — " can motivate inert people to change. To support this view, Laura provides two examples of parents who experience such jolts. Similarly, in the fourth paragraph, she contends that inertia causes the persistence of specific national problems: shoddy consumer goods and environmental pollution. Another writing strategy, *comparison–contrast,* is used in the third paragraph to highlight the differences between television and real life: on television, people zoom into action, but in everyday life, people tend to stay put and muddle through. The essay also contains a distinct element of *argumentation–persuasion* since Laura wants readers to accept her definition of inertia and her view that it often governs human behavior.

You might have noticed when reading the rest of the fourth paragraph that Laura's examples are not sequenced as effectively as they could be. To show that we, as a nation, tend to keep moving in the same direction, Laura discusses our ongoing uneasiness about genetic engineering, nuclear arms, and excessive television viewing. The point about nuclear weapons is most significant, yet it gets lost because it is sandwiched in the middle. The paragraph would be stronger if it ended with the point about nuclear arms. Moreover, the idea about excessive television viewing does not belong in this paragraph since — at best — it has limited bearing on the issue being discussed.

Laura's *conclusion* rounds off the essay nicely and brings it to a satisfying close. Laura refers to another law of physics, one with which we are all familiar: gravity. Creating an *analogy* between gravity and inertia, she suggests that our ability to defy gravity should encourage us to try to defy inertia. The analogy enlarges the scope of the essay; it allows Laura to reach out to her readers by challenging them to action. Such a challenge is, of course, appropriate in a definition essay having a persuasive bent.

When it was time to rework her essay, Laura put her paper aside for a while before starting to revise in earnest. Once the revising process began, she made a number of changes but found that the original version of her third paragraph needed special attention. The first draft of the paragraph is reprinted here.

First Draft Version
The ordinary actions of daily life are, in part, determined by inertia. To understand this, it is helpful to compare the world of television with real life, for, in the TV-land of ads and entertainment, inertia does not exist. For example, on television, people are often shown making all kinds of drastic changes. They switch

brands of coffee or try a new hair color with no hesitation. In one car commercial, a young accountant leaves her career and sets off for a cabin by the sea to write poetry. In a soap opera, a character may progress from homemaker to hooker to nun in a single year. In contrast, inertia rules in real life. People tend to stay where they are, to keep their jobs, to be loyal to products (wives get annoyed if a husband brings home the wrong brand or color of bathroom tissue from the market). Middle-aged people wear the hairstyles or makeup that suited them in high school. A second major difference between television and real life is that, on TV, everyone takes prompt and dramatic action to solve problems. A woman finds the solution to dull clothes at the end of a commercial; the police catch the murderer within an hour; the family learns to cope with a son's disturbing lifestyle by the time the movie is over. In contrast, the law of real-life inertia means that few problems are solved neatly or quickly. Things, once started, tend to stay as they are. Few crimes are actually solved. Medical problems are not easily diagnosed. Messy wars in foreign countries seem endless. National problems are identified, but Congress does not pass legislation to solve them.

After rereading what she had written, Laura realized that the paragraph rambled. To tighten and gain control over this section of the paper, Laura did a number of things. First, she eliminated two flat, unconvincing examples: the idea about wives who get annoyed when their husbands bring home the wrong brand of bathroom tissue and the references to hairstyles and makeup. In addition, she condensed the two disjointed sentences that originally opened the paragraph. Note how much more crisp and focused the revised sentences are: "To illustrate how inertia rules our lives, it is helpful to compare the world of television with real life. On TV, inertia does not exist."

Laura also worked to make the details and the language in the paragraph more specific and vigorous. The vague sentence "A woman finds the solution to dull clothes at the end of the commercial" is dropped for the more dramatic "The construction worker with a thudding headache is pain-free at the end of the sixty-second commercial." Similarly, Laura changed a "son's troublesome lifestyle" to a "son's life-threatening drug addiction," and "when the movie is over" to "when the made-for-TV movie ends at eleven." Moreover, the sentence ". . . a young accountant leaves her career and sets off for a cabin by the sea to write poetry" became ". . . an ambitious young accountant abandons her career with a flourish and is seen driving off into the sunset as she heads for a small cabin by the sea to write poetry."

Most important, Laura made some shrewd organizational changes in the paragraph. She removed the last two sentences because they referred to inertia in national affairs: "Messy wars in foreign countries seem endless" and "National problems are identified, but Congress does not pass legislation. . . ." Laura realized that these sentences did not belong in the paragraph because this section of the paper focused on inertia in the life of the individual. Once these sentences were eliminated, she decided to round off the paragraph by adding a powerful summary statement that implied the difference between real life and television: "Illnesses drag on, few crimes are solved, and family conflicts last for years."

These revisions in the third paragraph are similar to the kind Laura made in the other sections of her first draft. Such astute changes enabled her to turn her already effective paper into an especially thoughtful analysis of human behavior.

As the following selections show, definition essays generally use a variety of patterns to develop the concept that is at the heart of the essay. K. C. Cole uses facts, examples, and anecdotes in the essay "Entropy" to show how a specialized concept applies to everyday life. In "Ugly," William McKibben draws on a single dramatic example to redefine a word that has lost its power. In "Why I Want a Wife," Judy Syfers generates examples to clarify her definition of a traditional wife. H. L. Mencken employs examples, description, and brief narratives as he defines the essence of "The Politician." Finally, Marie Winn draws a compelling analogy to clarify her definition of "TV Addiction."

K. C. Cole

K. C. Cole's writings about science, especially physics, have made a great deal of specialized knowledge available to the general public. A graduate of Barnard College, she has contributed numerous articles to such publications as *The New York Times,* the *Washington Post,* and *Newsday.* Most recently, Cole has written a regular column for *Discover* magazine. Her work with the Exploratorium, a San Francisco science museum, led her to write several books on the exhibits there. In 1985, Cole published a collection of essays, *Sympathetic Vibrations: Reflections on Physics as a Way of Life.* The following selection first appeared as a "Hers" column in *The New York Times.*

Entropy

Scientific concepts often sound unintelligible to the layperson. Can any of us state Einstein's theory of relativity, for example? But the natural laws at work in the universe are not just for geniuses. Instead, they are the invisible strings that control all creatures on the planet, including ourselves. In her essay, K. C. Cole takes an odd-sounding, specialized concept from physics and shows how it is a factor in everyone's daily life.

1 It was about two months ago when I realized that entropy was getting the better of me. On the same day my car broke down (again), my refrigerator conked out and I learned that I needed root-canal work in my right rear tooth. The windows in the bedroom were still leaking every time it rained and my son's baby sitter was still failing to show up every time I really needed her. My hair was turning gray and my typewriter was wearing out. The house needed paint and I needed glasses. My son's sneakers were developing holes and I was developing a deep sense of futility.

2 After all, what was the point of spending half of Saturday at the Laundromat if the clothes were dirty all over again the following Friday?

Disorder, alas, is the natural order of things in the universe. 3
There is even a precise measure of the amount of disorder, called
entropy. Unlike almost every other physical property (motion,
gravity, energy), entropy does not work both ways. It can only
increase. Once it's created it can never be destroyed. The road to
disorder is a one-way street.

Because of its unnerving irreversibility, entropy has been 4
called the arrow of time. We all understand this instinctively.
Children's rooms, left on their own, tend to get messy, not neat.
Wood rots, metal rusts, people wrinkle and flowers wither. Even
mountains wear down; even the nuclei of atoms decay. In the city
we see entropy in the rundown subways and worn-out sidewalks
and torn-down buildings, in the increasing disorder of our lives.
We know, without asking, what is old. If we were suddenly to see
the paint jump back on an old building, we would know that
something was wrong. If we saw an egg unscramble itself and
jump back into its shell, we would laugh in the same way we
laugh at a movie run backward.

Entropy is no laughing matter, however, because with every 5
increase in entropy energy is wasted and opportunity is lost.
Water flowing down a mountainside can be made to do some
useful work on its way. But once all the water is at the same level
it can work no more. That is entropy. When my refrigerator was
working, it kept all the cold air ordered in one part of the kitchen
and warmer air in another. Once it broke down the warm and
cold mixed into a lukewarm mess that allowed my butter to melt,
my milk to rot and my frozen vegetables to decay.

Of course the energy is not really lost, but it has defused and 6
dissipated into a chaotic caldron of randomness that can do us no
possible good. Entropy is chaos. It is loss of purpose.

People are often upset by the entropy they seem to see in the 7
haphazardness of their own lives. Buffeted about like so many
molecules in my tepid kitchen, they feel that they have lost their
sense of direction, that they are wasting youth and opportunity at
every turn. It is easy to see entropy in marriages, when the
partners are too preoccupied to patch small things up, almost
guaranteeing that they will fall apart. There is much entropy in
the state of our country, in the relationships between nations —
lost opportunities to stop the avalanche of disorders that seems
ready to swallow us all.

Entropy is not inevitable everywhere, however. Crystals and 8
snowflakes and galaxies are islands of incredibly ordered beauty
in the midst of random events. If it was not for exceptions to
entropy, the sky would be black and we would be able to see
where the stars spend their days; it is only because air molecules in
the atmosphere cluster in ordered groups that the sky is blue.

The most profound exception to entropy is the creation of 9
life. A seed soaks up some soil and some carbon and some sunshine and some water and arranges it into a rose. A seed in the
womb takes some oxygen and pizza and milk and transforms it
into a baby.

The catch is that it takes a lot of energy to produce a baby. It 10
also takes energy to make a tree. The road to disorder is all
downhill but the road to creation takes work. Though combating
entropy is possible, it also has its price. That's why it seems so
hard to get ourselves together, so easy to let ourselves fall apart.

Worse, creating order in one corner of the universe always 11
creates more disorder somewhere else. We create ordered energy
from oil and coal at the price of the entropy of smog.

I recently took up playing the flute again after an absence of 12
several months. As the uneven vibrations screeched through the
house, my son covered his ears and said, "Mom, what's wrong
with your flute?" Nothing was wrong with my flute, of course. It
was my ability to play it that had atrophied, or entropied, as the
case may be. The only way to stop that process was to practice
every day, and sure enough my tone improved, though only at the
price of constant work. Like anything else, abilities deteriorate
when we stop applying our energies to them.

That's why entropy is depressing. It seems as if just breaking 13
even is an uphill fight. There's a good reason that this should be
so. The mechanics of entropy are a matter of chance. Take any
ice-cold air molecule milling around my kitchen. The chances are
that it will wander in the direction of my refrigerator at any point
are exactly 50–50. The chances that it will wander away from my
refrigerator are also 50–50. But take billions of warm and cold
molecules mixed together, and the chances that all the cold ones
will wander toward the refrigerator and all the warm ones will
wander away from it are virtually nil.

Entropy wins not because order is impossible but because 14
there are always so many more paths toward disorder than toward

order. There are so many more different ways to do a sloppy job than a good one, so many more ways to make a mess than to clean it up. The obstacles and accidents in our lives almost guarantee that constant collisions will bounce us on to random paths, get us off the track. Disorder is the path of least resistance, the easy but not the inevitable road.

Like so many others, I am distressed by the entropy I see   15
around me today. I am afraid of the randomness of international events, of the lack of common purpose in the world; I am terrified that it will lead into the ultimate entropy of nuclear war. I am upset that I could not in the city where I live send my child to a public school; that people are unemployed and inflation is out of control; that tensions between sexes and races seem to be increasing again; that relationships everywhere seem to be falling apart.

Social institutions — like atoms and stars — decay if energy is   16
not added to keep them ordered. Friendships and families and economies all fall apart unless we constantly make an effort to keep them working and well oiled. And far too few people, it seems to me, are willing to contribute consistently to those efforts.

Of course, the more complex things are, the harder it is. If   17
there were only a dozen or so air molecules in my kitchen, it would be likely — if I waited a year or so — that at some point the six coldest ones would congregate inside the freezer. But the more factors in the equation — the more players in the game — the less likely it is that their paths will coincide in an orderly way. The more pieces in the puzzle, the harder it is to put back together once order is disturbed. "Irreversibility," said a physicist, "is the price we pay for complexity."

Questions for Close Reading

1. What is the thesis of the selection? Locate the sentence(s) in which Cole states her main idea. If she does not state the thesis explicitly, express it in your own words.
2. How does entropy differ from the other properties of the physical world? Is the image "the arrow of time" helpful in establishing this difference?
3. Why is the creation of life an exception to entropy? What is the relationship between entropy and energy?

4. Why does Cole say that entropy "is no laughing matter"? What is so depressing about the entropy she describes?

5. Refer to your dictionary as needed to define the following words in the selection: *futility* (paragraph 1), *dissipated* (6), *buffeted* (7), *tepid* (7), and *atrophied* (12).

Questions About the Writer's Craft

1. What is Cole's underlying purpose in defining the scientific term *entropy*? Is she being merely informative, or does her essay have a subtle persuasive edge as well?

2. What tone does the author adopt to break down our resistance to reading about a scientific concept? Find some examples where her tone is especially prominent.

3. Cole uses words like *futility, loss,* and *depressing.* How do these words affect you? Why do you think the author chose such terms? Find other similar words in the essay.

4. Many of Cole's sentences follow a two-part pattern: "The road to disorder is all downhill, but the road to creation takes work." "There are so many more different ways to do a sloppy job than a good one. . . ." Find other examples of this sentence pattern. Why do you think Cole finds it useful to explain the effects of entropy by using this pattern?

Questions for Further Thought

1. Besides the examples provided by Cole, what instances of entropy do you see around you?

2. Is entropy in nature the same as entropy in society? In a marriage? In a city? In international relations? Do you accept Cole's application of the term *entropy* to these various realms?

3. Entropy means that paint peels, "people wrinkle, flowers wither." How does our society respond to these phenomena?

4. Cole writes that it's "so hard to get ourselves together, so easy to let ourselves fall apart." If so, why do we bother? Overall, would you say the author is optimistic or pessimistic about humans getting themselves together?

Writing Assignments Using Definition as a Method of Development

1. Define *order* or *disorder* by applying the term to an institution, organization, or system that you know well. You might focus on your

school, dorm, family, workplace, or any other system. Develop your definition through any combination of writing patterns: by supplying examples and instances, by showing contrasts, by analyzing the process of the organization and so on.

2. Choose a technical term that might be unfamiliar to many people. Write a humorous or serious paper defining the term as it is used technically, and then show how the term can be used to explain some aspect of your life. For example, the concept in astronomy of a *supernova* could be used to explain your sudden emergence as a new star on the athletic field, in your schoolwork, on the social scene. Here are a few suggested terms:

Symbiosis	Volatility	Resonance
Velocity	Erosion	Catalyst
Neutralization	Equilibrium	Malleability

Writing Assignments Using Other Methods of Development

3. Can one person make much difference in the amount of entropy— disorder and decay—in the world? Explain your views in an essay. Use examples of people, past or present, who tried—successfully or not—to overcome the tendency of things to "fall apart."

4. How much control do people have over their own lives? Is our sense of self-determination an illusion, given what Cole says about entropy? She claims that "People are often upset by . . . the haphazardness of their own lives. Buffeted about like so many molecules . . . , they feel that they have lost their sense of direction, that they are wasting youth and opportunity at every turn." Write an essay arguing that people either do or do not control their own fates. Use a series of specific examples to support your point.

William McKibben

William McKibben is a 1982 graduate of Harvard University. While in college, he worked on the school newspaper, *The Harvard Crimson,* as well as on the *Lexington Minuteman.* Born in California but raised in Canada, McKibben has worked since graduation as a staff writer for *The New Yorker.* During that time, he has written numerous pieces for the magazine's celebrated "Talk of the Town" section. Appearing in each issue, "Talk of the Town" features brief, unsigned essays, including commentary on national and international events, as well as personal glimpses of people and goings-on in the city. "Ugly," the selection below, was published in "Talk of the Town" in 1984.

Ugly

Have we become so accustomed to horror—cities reduced to rubble by terrorist bombings, political leaders assassinated, children hollow-eyed with hunger—that we have lost the ability to be outraged? Hoping to puncture our complacency, William McKibben focuses on a growing horror of American life—the plight of the homeless—and dramatizes our callous disregard of the situation.

The adjective "ugly" doesn't get around much anymore—it 1
has a restricted range, like the buffalo, which, instead of darkening the plains, is currently crossbred with the occasional cow to create a low-cholesterol steak. Emerson remarked that one man's beauty is another's ugliness, but the years have turned his proverb topsy-turvy, for now all that was ugly is beautiful, or, at least, "interesting." If someone covers the inside of a subway car with his initials, the result is either art or hooliganism to be diligently studied as indicative of social decay; if one comes across a Buick rusting in the woods, it is, you know, stark. What was ugly has become earthy, or industrial, or post-industrial, or "found," and

427

that's fine with us: there *is* some glory in damn near everything —the orange sunsets, say, when the smog is most visible. Anyway, now that the word is not being constantly drained, some force should accumulate behind it, like water building up behind a dam, so that when somebody does put it to use — and shortly we intend to do just that — it will pack some wallop.

There are things we all must do, regardless of race or class or computer literacy: we must eat and sleep and think what we would buy first if we won the lottery. And when our legs get tired we must sit down. In some parts of the world, people have learned to squat, to hunker down, but in America only baseball catchers are really much good at it. Most of us need something to sit on — a chair, perhaps. If you are an average citizen, it is no problem: when you've been shopping a few hours, you can walk into a coffee shop and sit down and order an iced tea and drink it and pay the bill and leave a tip and get up and go home. But imagine for a moment that you have no money at all. Perhaps you are homeless, and what you own you are carrying; it's not so much, but it's more than nothing, because before so very long it will be November and *then* you'll want that parka. You're walking up toward midtown, not because it's midtown but because the daylight lasts fifteen hours this time of year and you have to walk somewhere. You're tired of walking, but you can't go into a restaurant, even a McDonald's, because they'll ask you to leave and then they'll make you leave, and who can blame them? You might go into the Park, but maybe it's on toward evening and you don't want to be hassled. So maybe you head for a ledge in front of a shop or a hotel, or even a church, and when you get there you find they have stuck spikes into the granite or the brick so that you can't sit there. Those spikes — they are *ugly*.

If you try to sit on them, it hurts. We have tried, and if you don't believe us you try. They are meant to hurt; with the exception of a very few places where they are put up to keep people from crashing through windows or falling into cellars, their aim is to deter sitting. Not so much sitting by you or by us. If it was only you and us, the people who put them up wouldn't much mind; if you could design a spike that would afflict the backsides of derelicts and teen-agers but cushion the posteriors of so-called yuppies, you could make some money. The spikes are meant for bums and drunks. It's silly to blame the shopkeepers and the

2

3

hoteliers for setting up such grotesque barriers; a man who counts the receipts in his register at the end of a day develops some feel for what draws customers in and what keeps them out. If his customers won't come past a smelly fellow snoozing in the sun, or a woman drinking Colt 45 and cadging quarters and singing little made-up songs—well, up go the spikes. What makes spiked ledges so ugly is not that they rob the down-and-out of a place to sit. There is always the sidewalk or, for those with the energy to hop the turnstile, the subway. Anyway, the homeless lack plenty of items dearer than a seat—a roof, a job, a dinner, a family. The ugliness is in the gesture. It would be nice to think that the reason poor people wander the streets is that we've yet to figure out just how to help them. But it isn't like that really. What the spikes say is: Don't wander the streets, or, at least, don't sit yourself down, in my neighborhood, where I shop; go somewhere else.

Questions for Close Reading

1. What is the thesis of this selection? Locate the sentence(s) in which McKibben states his main idea. If he does not state the thesis explicitly, express it in your own words.
2. What does McKibben mean when he states that the word *ugly* is not being "constantly drained"? What good does he see in this fact?
3. For whom and for what purpose were spiked ledges designed? What, according to McKibben, makes them so "ugly"?
4. In paragraph 2, McKibben tells us that "there are things we all must do." What are some of these things, and how does mentioning them help the author justify his definition of "ugly"?
5. Refer to your dictionary as needed to define the following words in the selection: *hooliganism* (paragraph 1), *diligently* (1), *deter* (3), *afflict* (3), *derelicts* (3), *hoteliers* (3), and *cadging* (3).

Questions About the Writer's Craft

1. McKibben undoubtedly intends his essay to do more than merely define *ugly*. What evidence do you see in the essay of a broader purpose? What is that purpose?
2. In what parts of his essay does McKibben employ definition by negation? How does this technique help him achieve his purpose?
3. What patterns of development does McKibben rely on to develop his definition? In which paragraphs can these patterns be found?

4. How would you describe McKibben's tone? In what way is this tone appropriate for his purpose and audience?

Questions for Further Thought

1. What signs do you see to support McKibben's opinion that the homeless are spurned by society? What evidence can you find to indicate that the opposite is true?
2. Is there something about large cities that desensitizes people to the plight of the homeless? Would people in small towns be more sensitive? Why or why not?
3. What other examples of spiritual ugliness can you think of? What makes them ugly?
4. McKibben stops short of offering a solution to the spread of homelessness, and he doesn't assign blame for its origins to a particular group of people, government agency, or segment of society. What, in your opinion, has caused this problem, and what should be done, by whom, to alleviate it?

Writing Assignments Using Definition as a Method of Development

1. If you have ever lived in or visited a city with a large homeless population, you probably know something about the plight of the homeless. Define the term *homeless* by focusing on one or more of these individuals. To develop your definition, you might do any of the following: describe what these people look like; show what they have to do to stay alive; contrast them with the hobos of earlier times; explain why they have become homeless.
2. Like McKibben, write an extended definition of an abstract idea. You might define such concepts as the following: "compassion," by citing examples of how your college, church, or synagogue helps the needy; "intelligence," by contrasting two people; "patriotism," by explaining what it is and what it is not. Whichever concept you select, be sure to provide sufficient specific support to make the abstraction clear.

Writing Assignments Using Other Methods of Development

*3. McKibben argues that America has been desensitized to the plight of the homeless. Is such callousness justifiable, even understandable? Write an essay explaining what you think has caused this reaction. Mark Twain's "The Damned Human Race" (page 564) or Thomas

Wolfe's "O Rotten Gotham . . ." (page 381) might give you some ideas to consider.

*4. Write an essay arguing that Americans can be kind and generous-spirited. Bob Greene's "Handled with Care" (page 142) will start you thinking about these more positive aspects of human nature. As you write, assume that some of your readers hold a more jaundiced view, so be sure to marshal compelling evidence to support your contention. You may even want to do some research to find out, for instance, how many Americans are involved in volunteer work, how much the average person contributes every year to charity, and so on.

Judy Syfers

Judy Syfers was born in 1937 in San Francisco and was educated at the University of Iowa. She became a freelance writer during the 1960s and has written articles for a variety of publications. The provocative essay here first appeared in *Ms.* magazine in 1971 and has become a classic of feminist satire.

Why I Want a Wife

According to the dictionary, a wife is a "woman married to a man." But, as many women know, a wife is much more: cook, housekeeper, nutritionist, chauffeur, friend, sex partner, valet, nurse, social secretary, ego-builder, and more. Rather than complain about all the responsibilities she and other women assume, Judy Syfers explains why she herself would like to have a wife.

1 I belong to that classification of people known as wives. I am A Wife. And, not altogether incidentally, I am a mother.

2 Not too long ago a male friend of mine appeared on the scene from the Midwest fresh from a recent divorce. He had one child, who is, of course, with his ex-wife. He is obviously looking for another wife. As I thought about him while I was ironing one evening, it suddenly occurred to me that I, too, would like to have a wife. Why do I want a wife?

3 I would like to go back to school so that I can become economically independent, support myself, and, if need be, support those dependent upon me. I want a wife who will work and send me to school. And while I am going to school I want a wife to take care of my children. I want a wife to keep track of the children's doctor and dentist appointments. And to keep track of mine, too. I want a wife to make sure my children eat properly and are kept clean. I want a wife who will wash the children's clothes and keep them mended. I want a wife who is a good nurturant attendant to my children, arranges for their schooling,

makes sure that they have an adequate social life with their peers, takes them to the park, the zoo, etc. I want a wife who takes care of the children when they are sick, a wife who arranges to be around when the children need special care, because, of course, I cannot miss classes at school. My wife must arrange to lose time at work and not lose the job. It may mean a small cut in my wife's income from time to time, but I guess I can tolerate that. Needless to say, my wife will arrange and pay for the care of the children while my wife is working.

I want a wife who will take care of *my* physical needs. I want a wife who will keep my house clean. A wife who will pick up after my children, a wife who will pick up after me. I want a wife who will keep my clothes clean, ironed, mended, replaced when need be, and who will see to it that my personal things are kept in their proper place so that I can find what I need the minute I need it. I want a wife who cooks the meals, a wife who is a *good* cook. I want a wife who will plan the menus, do the necessary grocery shopping, prepare the meals, serve them pleasantly, and then do the cleaning up while I do my studying. I want a wife who will care for me when I am sick and sympathize with my pain and loss of time from school. I want a wife to go along when our family takes a vacation so that someone can continue to care for me and my children when I need a rest and a change of scene.

I want a wife who will not bother me with rambling complaints about a wife's duties. But I want a wife who will listen to me when I feel the need to explain a rather difficult point I have come across in my course of studies. And I want a wife who will type my papers for me when I have written them.

I want a wife who will take care of the details of my social life. When my wife and I are invited out by my friends, I want a wife who will take care of the babysitting arrangements. When I meet people at school that I like and want to entertain, I want a wife who will have the house clean, will prepare a special meal, serve it to me and my friends, and not interrupt when I talk about the things that interest me and my friends. I want a wife who will have arranged that the children are fed and ready for bed before my guests arrive so that the children do not bother us. I want a wife who takes care of the needs of my guests so that they feel comfortable, who makes sure that they have an ashtray, that they are passed the hors d'oeuvres, that they are offered a second helping of the food, that their wine glasses are replenished when necessary, that their coffee is served to them as they like it. And I want a wife who knows that sometimes I need a night out by myself.

I want a wife who is sensitive to my sexual needs, a wife who makes love passionately and eagerly when I feel like it, a wife who makes sure that I am satisfied. And, of course, I want a wife who will not demand sexual attention when I am not in the mood for it. I want a wife who assumes the complete responsibility for birth control, because I do not want more children. I want a wife who will remain sexually faithful to me so that I do not have to clutter up my intellectual life with jealousies. And I want a wife who understands that *my* sexual needs may entail more than strict adherence to monogamy. I must, after all, be able to relate to people as fully as possible.

7

If, by chance, I find another person more suitable as a wife than the wife I already have, I want the liberty to replace my present wife with another one. Naturally, I will expect a fresh, new life; my wife will take the children and be solely responsible for them so that I am left free.

8

When I am through with school and have acquired a job, I want my wife to quit working and remain at home so that my wife can more fully and completely take care of a wife's duties.

9

My God, who *wouldn't* want a wife?

10

Questions for Close Reading

1. What is the thesis of the selection? Locate the sentence(s) in which Syfers states her main idea. If she does not state the thesis explicitly, express it in your own words.
2. What event sparked Syfers to think about why she would like to have a wife? How is this event related to her thesis?
3. What are the duties of a wife, according to Syfers?
4. How are a wife's duties different from her spouse's? Which roles apply to the wife and not her spouse?
5. Refer to your dictionary as needed to define the following words used in the selection: *nurturant* (paragraph 3), *replenished* (6), *entail* (7), and *adherence* (7).

Questions About the Writer's Craft

1. What is Syfers's tone in this essay? How does this tone help us understand her definition of what it is to be a "wife"?
2. Why does the author repeat "I want a wife" over and over? How does this repetition add to the essay's effectiveness?
3. Are the reasons why Syfers wants a wife listed in any particular order? Why does she save sexual needs and the right to divorce for last?
4. How does Syfers develop her definition of "wife"? Does she ever provide a direct summary statement of what a wife is?

Questions for Further Thought

1. This essay was first published in 1972, when the women's movement was still new. Have times changed? Or is Syfers's message still relevant today?
2. Syfers concludes, "My God, who wouldn't want a wife?" Would you? Why or why not?
3. Syfers casts herself in the role of a spouse of a certain kind of wife. What is your opinion of this spouse? How do you think most husbands would react to reading this essay?
4. Do you know any couples in which the woman is the kind of "wife" that Syfers describes? Are these people happy? Do you see any positive aspects to such a relationship?

Writing Assignments Using Definition as a Method of Development

1. Adopting either a positive or negative viewpoint, write an essay defining a husband. Use either "I want a husband" or "I don't want a husband" as your theme. Build your definition around numerous examples of the way husbands behave.
2. Define what you mean by the phrase "a good marriage"—that is, the kind of marriage you would like to have. Develop your definition in an essay that explains what the two partners should do to make a good marriage a reality.

Writing Assignments Using Other Methods of Development

3. Write an essay from the point of view of a traditional homemaker defending such a lifestyle as fulfilling and important. Remembering to take the opposing viewpoint into account, try to persuade your

audience that it is a worthy lifestyle by giving reasons and examples of its benefits and advantages.

*4. Syfers claims that men and women experience marriage differently. Pick one other area that reflects sharp differences between the sexes. Possibilities include the following:

> Friendships
> Dating protocol
> Academic achievement
> Clothing worn
> Language used

Using the comparison–contrast format to analyze the area selected, discuss what you observe about male and female attitudes and behavior. Your analysis should help explain the role of societal expectations in defining these characteristic patterns. Alleen Pace Nilsen's "Sexism and Language" (page 209) might help you develop your analysis.

H. L. Mencken

With a cool eye and biting wit, H. L. Mencken (1880–1956) examined the mores and foibles of American culture. A prolific writer, Mencken founded the journal *American Mercury,* edited the *Baltimore Sun,* and published dozens of books, including studies of American English and several volumes of autobiography. Known for his ability to puncture pretensions and skewer foolishness, Mencken invented the term "booboisie" to describe the middle class, and insisted that no one ever went broke underestimating the intelligence of the American people. The essay here was published in *A Mencken Chrestomathy* (1949).

The Politician

Politicians are not, for the most part, highly respected. We seem to enjoy electing our public officials so that we can later claim, "They're all crooks." In the following selection, H. L. Mencken denounces the politicians of his day for being dealers in "hokum" and "hooey." Before deciding that Mencken exaggerates, take a long look at the many political scandals that Mencken didn't live long enough to see.

After damning politicians up hill and down dale for many years, as rogues and vagabonds, frauds and scoundrels, I sometimes suspect that, like everyone else, I often expect too much of them. Though faith and confidence are surely more or less foreign to my nature, I not infrequently find myself looking to them to be able, diligent, candid, and even honest. Plainly enough, that is too large an order, as anyone must realize who reflects upon the manner in which they reach public office. They seldom if ever get there by merit alone, at least in democratic states. Sometimes, to be sure, it happens, but only by a kind of miracle. They are chosen normally for quite different reasons, the chief of which is simply their power to impress and enchant the intellectually underprivi-

1

leged. It is a talent like any other, and when it is exercised by a radio crooner, a movie actor or a bishop, it even takes on a certain austere and sorry respectability. But it is obviously not identical with a capacity for the intricate problems of statecraft.

Those problems demand for their solution—when they are soluble at all, which is not often—a high degree of technical proficiency, and with it there should go an adamantine kind of integrity, for the temptations of a public official are almost as cruel as those of a glamor girl or a dipsomaniac. But we train a man for facing them, not by locking him up in a monastery and stuffing him with wisdom and virtue, but by turning him loose on the stump. If he is a smart and enterprising fellow, which he usually is, he quickly discovers there that hooey pleases the boobs a great deal more than sense. Indeed, he finds that sense really disquiets and alarms them—that it makes them, at best, intolerably uncomfortable, just as a tight collar makes them uncomfortable, or a speck of dust in the eye, or the thought of Hell. The truth, to the overwhelming majority of mankind, is indistinguishable from a headache. After trying a few shots of it on his customers, the larval statesman concludes sadly that it must hurt them, and after that he taps a more humane keg, and in a little while the whole audience is singing "Glory, glory, hallelujah," and when the returns come in the candidate is on his way to the White House.

I hope no one will mistake this brief account of the political process under democracy for exaggeration. It is almost literally true. I do not mean to argue, remember, that all politicians are villains in the sense that a burglar, a child-stealer, or a Darwinian are villains. Far from it. Many of them, in their private characters, are very charming persons, and I have known plenty that I'd trust with my diamonds, my daughter or my liberty, if I had any such things. I happen to be acquainted to some extent with nearly all the gentlemen, both Democrats and Republicans, who are currently itching for the Presidency, including the present incumbent, and I testify freely that they are all pleasant fellows, with qualities above rather than below the common. The worst of them is a great deal better company than most generals in the army, or writers of murder mysteries, or astrophysicists, and the best is a really superior and wholly delightful man—full of sound knowledge, competent and prudent, frank and enterprising, and quite as honest as any American can be without being clapped into a madhouse. Don't ask me what his name is, for I am not in politics. I can only tell you that he has been in public life a long while, and has not been caught yet.

But will this prodigy, or any of his rivals, ever unload any 4 appreciable amount of sagacity on the stump? Will any of them venture to tell the plain truth, the whole truth and nothing but the truth about the situation of the country, foreign or domestic? Will any of them refrain from promises that he knows he can't fulfill — that no human being *could* fulfill? Will any of them utter a word, however obvious, that will alarm and alienate any of the huge packs of morons who now cluster at the public trough, wallowing in the pap that grows thinner and thinner, hoping against hope? Answer: maybe for a few weeks at the start. Maybe before the campaign really begins. Maybe behind the door. But not after the issue is fairly joined, and the struggle is on in earnest. From that moment they will all resort to demagogy, and by the middle of June of election year the only choice among them will be a choice between amateurs of that science and professionals.

They will all promise every man, woman and child in the 5 country whatever he, she or it wants. They'll all be roving the land looking for chances to make the rich poor, to remedy the irremediable, to succor the unsuccorable, to unscramble the unscrambleable, to dephlogisticate the undephlogisticable. They will all be curing warts by saying words over them, and paying off the national debt with money that no one will have to earn. When one of them demonstrates that twice two is five, another will prove that it is six, six and a half, ten, twenty, n. In brief, they will divest themselves of their character as sensible, candid and truthful men, and become simply candidates for office, bent only on collaring votes. They will all know by then, even supposing that some of them don't know it now, that votes are collared under democracy, not by talking sense but by talking nonsense, and they will apply themselves to the job with a hearty yo-heave-ho. Most of them, before the uproar is over, will actually convince themselves. The winner will be whoever promises the most with the least probability of delivering anything.

Some years ago I accompanied a candidate for the Presidency 6 on his campaign-tour. He was, like all such rascals, an amusing fellow, and I came to like him very much. His speeches, at the start, were full of fire. He was going to save the country from all the stupendous frauds and false pretenses of his rival. Every time that rival offered to rescue another million of poor fish from the neglects and oversights of God he howled his derision from the back platform of his train. I noticed at once that these blasts of common sense got very little applause, and after a while the candidate began to notice it too. Worse, he began to get word from his spies on the train of his rival that the rival was wowing them, panicking them, laying them in the aisles. They threw flowers, hot dogs and five-cent cigars at him. In places where the times were especially hard they tried to unhook the locomotive from his train, so that he'd have to stay with them awhile longer, and promise them some more. There were no Gallup polls in those innocent days, but the local politicians had ways of their own for finding out how the cat was jumping, and they began to join my candidate's train in the middle of the night, and wake him up to tell him that all was lost, including honor. This had some effect upon him — in truth, an effect almost as powerful as that of sitting in the electric chair. He lost his intelligent manner, and became something you could hardly distinguish from an idealist. Instead of mocking he began to promise, and in a little while he was promising everything that his rival was promising, and a good deal more.

One night out in the Bible country, after the hullabaloo of the day was over, I went into his private car along with another newspaper reporter, and we sat down to gabble with him. This other reporter, a faithful member of the candidate's own party, began to upbraid him, at first very gently, for letting off so much hokum. What did he mean by making promises that no human being on this earth, and not many of the angels in Heaven, could ever hope to carry out? In particular, what was his idea in trying to work off all those preposterous bile-beans and snake-oils on the poor farmers, a class of men who had been fooled and rooked by every fresh wave of politicians since Apostolic times? Did he really believe that the Utopia he had begun so fervently to preach would ever come to pass? Did he honestly think that farmers, as a body, would ever see all their rosy dreams come true, or that the share-croppers in their lower ranks would ever be more than a hop, skip and jump from starvation? The candidate thought awhile, took a long swallow of the coffin-varnish he carried with him, and then replied that the answer in every case was no. He was well aware, he said, that the plight of the farmers was intrinsically hopeless, and would probably continue so, despite doles from the treasury, for centuries to come. He had no notion that anything could be done about it by merely human means, and certainly not by political means: it would take a new Moses, and a whole series of miracles. "But you forget, Mr. Blank," he concluded sadly, "that our agreement in the premises must remain purely personal. You are not a candidate for President of the United States. *I am.*" As we left him his interlocutor, a gentleman grown gray in Washington and long ago lost to every decency, pointed the moral of the episode. "In politics," he said, "man must learn to rise above principle." Then he drove it in with another: "When the water reaches the upper deck," he said, "follow the rats."

Questions for Close Reading

1. What is the thesis of the selection? Locate the sentence(s) in which Mencken states his main idea. If he does not state the thesis explicitly, express it in your own words.
2. Mencken writes his essay as a political "insider." What are the characteristics of the politician, from this insider's perspective? What changes does a politician undergo once he or she begins campaigning?
3. Who is at fault for the deplorable political situation Mencken describes—the politicians themselves or the voters who elected them? Find evidence in the essay to support your answer.
4. Mencken is neither a politician nor a typical voter—he is a journalist. Why does Mencken say that he avoids "naming names"? How did journalists of Mencken's time view their responsibilities as reporters?
5. Refer to your dictionary as needed to define the following words used in the selection: *candid* (paragraph 1), *austere* (1), *adamantine* (2), *dipsomaniac* (2), *larval* (2), *sagacity* (4), *demagogy* (4), *succor* (5), and *interlocutor* (7).

Questions About the Writer's Craft

1. Mencken uses a variety of patterns to convince the reader to accept his definition of a politician. Identify places where exemplification, process analysis, or other patterns of development appear in the essay.

What hard evidence (facts, statistics, and so on) does Mencken use to support his ideas?

2. The humor of Mencken's essay results largely from the satiric technique known as invective, or insult. For instance, Mencken calls voters "boobs" and says they are more receptive to "hooey" than to sense. Find other examples of invective in the essay.

3. Note the things Mencken says about himself at the start of the essay and in occasional self-references. How does he create a sense of himself as a credible commentator on presidential politics? Does he consider himself to be addressing "packs of morons" or another type of audience?

4. One technique the author uses to achieve his satiric effects is to juxtapose ideas or items that are not normally related. In paragraph 2, he groups three things that make people uncomfortable: "a tight collar . . . or a speck of dust in the eye, or the thought of Hell." Find some other juxtapositions. In each case, what effect does the juxtaposition have on the point Mencken is making at the time?

Questions for Further Thought

1. This essay was written nearly fifty years ago. Is it valid now? Have our political process and our politicians changed? What similarities exist between the politicians Mencken describes and politicians today?

2. Satirists, by definition, exaggerate the vices of their targets and ignore the virtues, if any. Do you think Mencken is being unfair to those who run for office or to the American public? What good qualities of his targets is he deliberately omitting?

3. How do Americans decide whom to vote for? Do we look at the candidates' records, experience, or stands on various issues? Or are we largely swayed by physical appearance, public speaking skills, wit, and personality? How effective are advertising campaigns in determining voters' choices?

4. What constitutes the ideal training for a future politician? Mencken suggests (facetiously) "locking him up in a monastery and stuffing him with wisdom and virtue." Should a political candidate be scholarly, worldly wise, or some combination of the two?

Writing Assignments Using Definition as a Method of Development

1. Choose your favorite target: any group of people you feel is worthy of criticism. Write a satiric definition essay decrying the faults of this group. Use Mencken's techniques (insults, juxtapositions, disparag-

ing comparisons, bold slang, and a peppering of fancy words). Some possible groups to consider include the following: a teenage "type" (jock, preppie, campus queen, and so on); the boss; the doctor, lawyer, or other professional person; the teacher; the rock star or fan; the professional _____ (name a sport) player.

*2. After studying Mencken's essay and considering other examples of satire—on television, in the movies, in humor magazines and comic strips—decide how you would define satire. Before developing your definition, you might read one or more of these satirical essays: Paul Fussell's "A Well-Regulated Militia" (page 187); James Thurber's "University Days" (page 219); Stephen Leacock's "How to Live to Be 200" (page 247): Judy Syfers' "Why I Want a Wife" (page 432); Dave Barry's "In Depth, but Shallowly" (page 470); and Jonathan Swift's "A Modest Proposal" (page 579). Then write an extended definition, explaining what satire is, how it operates, and what it accomplishes. Use specific examples to support your ideas.

Writing Assignments Using Other Methods of Development

*3. Do you think that TV lessens or exacerbates the tendency of politicians to deliver "hokum"? Write an essay arguing either that television helps root out do-nothing or dishonest politicians or that it makes style the determining factor in political success. Reading what Dave Barry has to say about television ("In Depth, but Shallowly," page 470) may give you a better sense of one side of the argument.

*4. Write an essay explaining why you voted (or would have voted) for _____ in the most recent presidential election. What factors led to your choice? Be honest: were you swayed by personality, looks, the choices of friends and family, the candidate's record on public issues? How much of your choice was based on solid information? How much on image or slogans? Ann McClintock's "Propaganda Techniques in Today's Advertising" (page 502) may suggest ideas worth pursuing.

Marie Winn

Born in Czechoslovakia and brought by her family to New
York, Marie Winn was educated at Radcliffe College. The
author or editor of ten children's books, Winn developed a
special interest in the effect of television on children. She has
contributed numerous articles to such publications as *The New
York Times* and *The Village Voice*. Winn's provocative and
influential study, *The Plug-In Drug: Television, Children and
Family,* was originally published in 1977 and was revised in
1985. The selection that follows is from that book.

TV Addiction

You arrive home from work or school. Is the TV on where you
live? If not, do you automatically flick it on? You are probably
aware that television has become an overwhelming presence in
society. In the following selection, Marie Winn suggests that
television resembles such addictive substances as alcohol and
drugs. She warns us that the similarity is more than metaphori-
cal since TV addiction has real, life-damaging consequences. It
can cause people to lose jobs, families, and a normal perspective on life.

    The word "addiction" is often used loosely and wryly in   1
conversation. People will refer to themselves as "mystery book
addicts" or "cookie addicts." E. B. White writes of his annual
surge of interest in gardening: "We are hooked and are making an
attempt to kick the habit." Yet nobody really believes that reading
mysteries or ordering seeds by catalogue is serious enough to be
compared with addictions to heroin or alcohol. The word "addiction" is here used jokingly to denote a tendency to overindulge in
some pleasurable activity.

    People often refer to being "hooked on TV." Does this, too,   2
fall into the lighthearted category of cookie eating and other

pleasures that people pursue with unusual intensity, or is there a kind of television viewing that falls into the more serious category of destructive addiction?

When we think about addiction to drugs or alcohol, we 3 frequently focus on negative aspects, ignoring the pleasures that accompany drinking or drug-taking. And yet the essence of any serious addiction is a pursuit of pleasure, a search for a "high" that normal life does not supply. It is only the inability to function without the addictive substance that is dismaying, the dependence of the organism upon a certain experience and an increasing inability to function normally without it. Thus a person will take two or three drinks at the end of the day not merely for the pleasure drinking provides, but also because he "doesn't feel normal" without them.

An addict does not merely pursue a pleasurable experience 4 and need to experience it in order to function normally. He needs to *repeat* it again and again. Something about that particular experience makes life without it less than complete. Other potentially pleasurable experiences are no longer possible, for under the spell of the addictive experience, his life is peculiarly distorted. The addict craves an experience and yet he is never really satisfied. The organism may be temporarily sated, but soon it begins to crave again.

Finally a serious addiction is distinguished from a harmless 5 pursuit of pleasure by its distinctly destructive elements. A heroin addict, for instance, leads a damaged life: his increasing need for heroin in increasing doses prevents him from working, from maintaining relationships, from developing in human ways. Similarly an alcoholic's life is narrowed and dehumanized by his dependence on alcohol.

Let us consider television viewing in the light of the conditions that define serious addictions. 6

Not unlike drugs or alcohol, the television experience allows 7 the participant to blot out the real world and enter into a pleasurable and passive mental state. The worries and anxieties of reality are as effectively deferred by becoming absorbed in a television program as by going on a "trip" induced by drugs or alcohol. And just as alcoholics are only inchoately aware of their addiction, feeling that they control their drinking more than they really do ("I can cut it out any time I want — I just like to have three or four drinks before dinner"), people similarly overestimate their control over television watching. Even as they put off other activities to spend hour after hour watching television, they feel they could easily resume living in a different, less passive style. But somehow or other while the television set is present in their homes, the click doesn't sound. With television pleasures available, those other experiences seem less attractive, more difficult somehow.

A heavy viewer (a college English instructor) observes: "I 8′ find television almost irresistible. When the set is on, I cannot ignore it. I can't turn it off. I feel sapped, will-less, enervated. As I reach out to turn off the set, the strength goes out of my arms. So I sit there for hours and hours."

The self-confessed television addict often feels he "ought" to 9 do other things — but the fact that he doesn't read and doesn't plant his garden or sew or crochet or play games or have conversations means that those activities are no longer as desirable as television viewing. In a way a heavy viewer's life is as imbalanced by his television "habit" as a drug addict's or an alcoholic's. He is living in a holding pattern, as it were, passing up the activities that lead to growth or development or a sense of accomplishment. This is one reason people talk about their television viewing so ruefully, so apologetically. They are aware that it is an unproductive experience, that almost any other endeavor is more worthwhile by any human measure.

Finally it is the adverse effect of television viewing on the 10 lives of so many people that defines it as a serious addiction. The television habit distorts the sense of time. It renders other experiences vague and curiously unreal while taking on a greater reality for itself. It weakens relationships by reducing and sometimes eliminating normal opportunities for talking, for communicating.

And yet television does not satisfy, else why would the viewer 11 continue to watch hour after hour, day after day? "The measure of health," writes Lawrence Kubie, "is flexibility . . . and especially the freedom to cease when sated." But the television viewer can never be sated with his television experiences — they do not provide the true nourishment that satiation requires — and thus he finds that he cannot stop watching.

Questions for Close Reading

1. What is the thesis of the selection? Locate the sentence(s) in which Winn states her main idea. If she does not state the thesis explicitly, express it in your own words.

2. Why, according to Winn, is a gardening addiction or a mystery book addiction a humorous kind of habit? What does she call "the essence of any serious addiction"?

3. In paragraph 7, the author says that television allows the viewer "to enter into a pleasurable . . . mental state," and later that "television does not satisfy." How does Winn prepare you earlier in the essay for this seeming contradiction?

4. Since television does "not provide the true nourishment that satiation requires," what activities does Winn suggest as truly nourishing alternatives?

5. Refer to your dictionary as needed to define the following words in the selection: *wryly* (paragraph 1), *inchoately* (7), *ruefully* (9), *adverse* (10), and *satiation* (11).

Questions About the Writer's Craft

1. At the beginning of the essay, Winn uses definition by negation to clarify her interpretation of the term *television addiction*. What kinds of things does Winn say are *not* the equivalents of TV addiction? Why does she use this strategy of definition by negation?

2. How does Winn organize the two extended definitions of addiction and TV addiction? How does this organizational pattern help persuade us to accept her point that TV is addicting?

3. What does the quotation from the TV addict add to the author's argument? Why does she choose a quotation from this person?

4. Few of us would dispute Winn's discussion of serious addictions in paragraphs 3 to 5. How does this lengthy treatment of a term we already understand assist the author in convincing us that TV is addicting?

Questions for Further Thought

1. Do you agree with Winn that excess TV viewing is a problem of the same magnitude as an addiction? Or would you say instead that television viewing in excess is merely analogous to being addicted to a drug or chemical? Is using the medical idea of addiction a useful way for our society to go about understanding and solving the problem of "too much TV"?

2. Consider the characteristics of addiction as set out in paragraphs 3 to 5. Do you think all types of people are equally likely to become addicted to something? Are there any types of people who might be totally immune?

3. Do you or people you know watch too much TV? Or do you find yourself addicted to some other electronic medium — or another nondrug activity? Is your addiction humorous or serious?

4. Reformed alcoholics and drug abusers are taught to avoid places where they might feel tempted. Few families would be willing to get rid of their televisions. What methods could parents or individuals use to prevent or lessen TV addiction?

Writing Assignments Using Definition as a Method of Development

1. In her introduction, Winn describes how people often use a very serious term — *addiction* — when referring to a light or harmless experience. Think of another term that you feel is serious, but that people use lightly and apply loosely. Your choice could be *friendship, love, hate,* or another word. Begin with an example that shows how the word is misused, and then provide an extended definition clarifying the proper use of the term.

2. TV addiction is only one of the forms of addiction in our society. Many other forms exist, such as addiction to gambling, baseball games, cars, bingo, chocolate, and the latest clothing styles. Write an essay on another addiction, using one of the addictions just listed or another of your own choice.

Writing Assignments Using Other Methods of Development

*3. Many kinds of TV shows come in for criticism — "tabloid TV" talk shows, sit-coms, game shows, whatever. Pick one kind of TV show and write an essay defending the genre. Or argue that this type of show has no merit. The essay may be serious or playful. Dave Barry's satirical view of local TV news ("In Depth, but Shallowly," page 470) may spur you to imaginative thinking on your own.

4. You have probably heard from older relatives (or may yourself know) what life was like before TV. Write an essay for your future children or grandchildren describing what life was like before one or several of these new technologies: VCRs, cable TV, microwave ovens, cash cards, whatever. Persuade your descendants that life was better *or* worse before these items were invented.

Additional Writing Topics
DEFINITION

General Assignments

Use definition to develop any of the following topics. Once you fix on a limited subject, decide if the essay has an informative or persuasive purpose. The paper might begin with the etymology of the term, a stipulative definition, or a definition by negation. You may want to use a number of writing patterns—such as description, comparison, narration, process analysis—to develop the definition. Remember, too, that the paper does not have to be scholarly and serious. There is no reason it can't be a lighthearted discussion of the meaning of a term.

1. Fads
2. A family fight
3. Helplessness
4. An epiphany
5. A workaholic
6. A Pollyanna
7. A con artist
8. A stingy person
9. A team player
10. A Yiddish term like *mensch, klutz, chutzpah,* or *dreck,* or a term from some other ethnic group
11. Idiomatic expressions
12. Fast food
13. A perfect day
14. Hypocrisy
15. Inner peace
16. Obsession
17. Generosity
18. Exploitation
19. Depression
20. A double bind

Assignments with a Specific Audience and Purpose

1. *Newsweek* magazine runs a popular column called "My Turn," consisting of readers' opinions on subjects of general interest. You decide

to send in a column on today's college students, a subject about which you are knowledgeable. Your purpose is to define the college students of today, especially in light of all the generalizations made about them by the general public: "They're apathetic"; "They're not as bright as college students used to be"; "They're spoiled rich kids"; "They're interested only in making money."

2. You are an attorney arguing a case of sexual harassment—a charge your client has leveled against her boss, a business executive. If you are to win the case, you must present to the jury a clear definition of exactly what sexual harassment is and isn't. Write your definition for your opening remarks in court.

3. You have been asked to write a pamphlet to be distributed to students by the college health services clinic. In the pamphlet, you will warn students about a certain condition/ailment and detail the symptoms. Choose any of the following as your subject: depression; stress; burnout; anxiety (test or general); addiction (to alcohol, drugs, or TV); workaholic syndrome; excessive competitiveness.

4. A new position has opened in your company. You have been asked to write a job description that will then be sent to employment agencies who will do the actual screening of candidates. Select any occupational category or designation and write a job description that does the following: defines the job's purpose, states the duties or responsibilities the job entails, and outlines the position's essential qualifications.

5. Part of your job as a marriage counselor is helping troubled couples communicate better. For example, you have recently realized that when couples discuss what is missing from their marriage, each person often has a different concept of what _____ means. Choose your own term or one of these: respect; maturity; sharing; equality; fidelity; support. You decide to write a definition of this term for your clients, based on your years of counseling experience. Part of your definition employs definition by negation; you tell them what this quality is *not*.

6. You have worked for several summers at a hotel in a popular resort area. You have been so good at your job that the hotel manager has asked you to give a talk to this year's incoming summer employees. The manager wants you to define *courtesy* for the new workers. This is the factor that has made you so popular with guests, and the manager believes it is the one quality that will make or break the hotel's business. Write your speech for the new workers, using specific examples to define this term.

DIVISION–CLASSIFICATION

WHAT IS
DIVISION–CLASSIFICATION?

Try to imagine what life would be like if this is how an average day unfolded:

> You have to stop at the supermarket for only five items. But your marketing takes over an hour because all the items in the store are jumbled together. Clerks put new shipments anywhere they please; the milk might be with the vegetables on Monday but with laundry detergent on Thursday. Next, you go to the drug store to pick up some photos you left to be developed. You don't have time, though, to wait while the cashier roots through the large carton into which all the pickup envelopes have been thrown. You return to your car and decide to stop at the town hall to pay a parking ticket. But the town hall baffles you. The offices are unmarked,

451

and there's not even a directory to tell you on what floor the Violations Bureau can be found. Annoyed, you get back into your car and, minutes later, end up colliding with another car. When you wake up in the hospital, you find there are three other patients in your room: a man with a heart problem, a young boy ready to have his tonsils removed, and a woman about to go into labor.

Such a muddled world, lacking the most basic forms of organization, would make daily life chaotic. All of us instinctively look for ways to order our environment. Without systems, categories, or sorting mechanisms, we would be overwhelmed by life's complexity. An organization like a college or university, for example, is made more manageable by being divided into various schools (Liberal Arts, Performing Arts, Engineering, and so on). The schools are then separated into departments (English, History, Political Science), and each department's offerings are grouped into distinct categories — English, for instance, into Literature and Composition — before being further divided into specific courses.

Let's illustrate further this basic need to organize experience. Consider how overwhelmed people often feel when buying expensive items like stereos and cars. The multitude of choices and considerations can be perplexing. One way to plow through the tangle of possibilities is to buy a magazine like *Consumer Reports* and examine the "Best Buy," "Recommended," and "Not Recommended" categories, thereby eliminating many items from consideration.

The kind of ordering system we have been discussing is called *division – classification,* a logical method of thinking that allows us to make sense of the world. Division and classification, though separate processes, are often used together as complementary techniques. *Division* involves taking a single unit or concept, breaking the unit down into its parts, and then analyzing the connection among the parts and between the parts and the whole. For instance, if we wanted to organize the chaotic hospital described at the start of the chapter, we might think about how the single concept "a hospital" could be broken down into its components. We might come up with the following kind of breakdown for a given hospital: pediatric wing, cardiac wing, maternity wing, and so on.

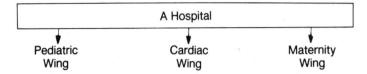

What we have just done involves division: we have taken a single entity (a hospital) and divided it into some of its component parts or wings, each with its own facilities and patients.

Classification, on the other hand, brings two or more related items together and categorizes them according to type or kind. If the disorganized supermarket described earlier were to be restructured, the clerks would have to classify the separate items arriving at the loading dock. Cartons of lettuce, tomatoes, cucumbers, butter, yogurt, milk, shampoo, conditioner, and setting lotion would be assigned to the appropriate categories:

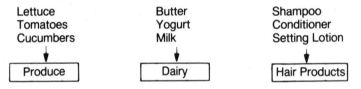

WHEN TO USE
DIVISION – CLASSIFICATION

The reorganized hospital and supermarket show concretely the way division and classification work in everyday life. But division and classification also come into play during the writing process. Because division involves breaking a subject into parts, it can be a helpful strategy when analyzing broad, complex subjects: the organization of the restaurant or store where you work; the structure of a film; the motivation of a character in a novel; the problem your community has with vandalism; the issue of school prayer; the controversy surrounding the homeless. An editorial examining a recent hostage crisis, for example, might divide the crisis into three areas: how the hostages were treated by their captors, by the governments negotiating their release, and by the media. The purpose of the editorial might be to show that the governments' treatment of the hostages was particularly exexploitative.

On the other hand, classification is useful when you want to understand how the subjects you are writing about — all of which share some common characteristics — are alike or different. Classification would, then, be a helpful strategy when you are analyzing topics like the following: techniques for impressing teachers; comic styles of talk-show hosts; views on abortion; reasons for the current rise in volunteerism. You might, for instance, use classification in a paper showing that Americans are undermining their health through their obsessive pursuit of various diets. You begin by brainstorming all the diets that have gained popularity in recent years (the Scarsdale Diet, the Rotation Diet, the Fit for Life Diet, whatever). Then you categorize the diets according to type: high fiber, low protein, high carbohydrate, and so on. Once the diets are grouped, you can discuss the problems within each category, demonstrating that none of the diets is safe or effective.

By now you may realize that division – classification can be a helpful approach to use when responding to college assignments. Consider the following:

Analyze the components that go into being an effective parent. Indicate which components you feel are most critical for raising confident, well-adjusted children.

Based on your observations, what kinds of appeals do television advertisers use when selling automobiles? In your view, do any of these appeals pose moral questions?

Describe the hierarchy of the typical high school clique, identifying the various parts of the hierarchy. Use your analysis to support or refute the view that adolescents have a strong need to conform.

Many social commentators have observed that rudeness and discourtesy are on the rise in America. Indicate whether you think this is a valid observation by characterizing the types of everyday encounters you have with people.

These assignments suggest division – classification through the use of such words as *components, kinds, parts, types.* But you generally will not receive such clear signals to write an essay using division – classification. Instead, the broad purpose of the essay —and the point you want to make—will lead you to the analytical thinking characteristic of division – classification. You will develop the essay, or part of the essay, using division – classification because the pattern allows you to meet your goal in writing.

Sometimes division – classification will be the dominant technique for structuring an essay; other times it will be used as a supplemental pattern in an essay organized mostly around another pattern of development. Here, for example, is how division – classification could be used in a number of essays. You may want to write a paper *explaining a process* (surviving adolescence; creating a hit record; shepherding a bill through Congress; using the Heimlich maneuver on people who are choking). In such a case, you would *divide* the process into parts or stages, showing, let's say, that the Heimlich maneuver is an easily mastered technique that should be taught in all public schools. Or *classification* could be used in a light essay analyzing the *effect* that increased awareness of sexually stereotyped behavior has had on the way students socialize. Perhaps you want to show that shifting gender roles make young men and women absurdly self-conscious around each other. To make your point, you might categorize the places where students scout out each other: in class, at the library, at parties, or in dorms. Then you could show how students approach each other with comic tentativeness in these four environments.

Now imagine that you are writing an *argumentation – persuasion* essay advocating that the federal government prohibit the feeding of antibiotics to livestock to stimulate their growth. The paper could begin by *dividing* the antibiotics cycle into stages: the effects of antibiotics on animals; the short-term effects on humans who consume the livestock; the possible long-term effects of consuming such meat over a period of years. To strengthen your argument, you also decide to discuss the antibiotics controversy in terms of an even larger issue: the various ways our food is treated before consumption. In this case, you would consider the different procedures (use of additives, preservatives, artificial colors, and so on), *classifying* these treatments into several types—from least harmful (some additives or artificial colors, perhaps) to most harmful (you might decide to slot the antibiotics here). Such an essay would be developed using division *and* classification: first, the division of the antibiotics cycle and then the classification of the various food treatments. Frequently, this interdependence will be reversed, and classification will precede rather than follow division.

SUGGESTIONS FOR USING DIVISION – CLASSIFICATION IN AN ESSAY

The following suggestions will be helpful whether you use division – classification as a dominant or supportive pattern of development.

1. Select a principle of division – classification consistent with your purpose. If your general purpose indicates the logic of using division – classification, you need to identify the principle of division – classification that will guide the paper. It's important to keep in mind that most subjects can be divided or classified any number of ways. An essay discussing the student senate on campus could be organized according to a number of different principles of division: the role of each senate officer; the growing dissatisfaction with students involved in campus government; the function of each senate committee; a plan for getting more students involved in the senate. The principle of division selected would depend on your purpose for writing the essay. Similarly, a paper on contemporary music groups could be classified according to various principles: the different ages that the groups appeal to (preteens, adolescents, people in their twenties); the various kinds of music played by the groups (hard rock, mainstream rock, jazz); the kinds of influence earlier musicians had on the contemporary groups. Again, your purpose for writing would determine which principle of classification you choose.

Essays may use more than one principle of division as they unfold. Consider the essay on student government. If you wanted to write a paper about the senate's lack of credibility, you might start by discussing pervasive dissatisfaction with many of the students involved in the senate (one principle of division). This point could be developed by focusing on disappointment with the following: students' meager qualifications for office; students' dubious campaign tactics; students' questionable actions once elected to the senate. Near the end, the paper might move to a second principle of division as it outlined a plan to get more students involved in campus government: editorials in the campus newspaper; announcements on the college radio station; articles in the college opinion magazine.

When writing an essay that uses classification as its primary method of development, you generally need to be careful about changing the principle of classification that focuses the paper. Imagine that you decided to write an essay showing that the success of contemporary music groups has less to do with musical talent than with the groups' ability to market themselves to a distinct segment of the listening audience. To develop your point, you might categorize several groups according to the age group they appeal to most and then analyze the marketing strategies the groups use to gain the support of their fans. The logic of the essay would be undermined if you switched to another principle of classification — let's say, the influence of earlier groups on today's music scene. In other words, most papers developed through classification generally revolve around a single principle.

The principle of division – classification you select should meet one stringent requirement: it must reinforce your essay's central point. Sometimes, a principle of division – classification seems so attractive that you latch onto it without examining whether it helps achieve your purpose. Suppose you want to write a paper asserting that several episodes of a new TV comedy are destined to become classics. Here's how you might go wrong.

You begin by doing some brainstorming about the episodes. Then, as you start to organize the prewriting material, you hit upon a possible principle of classification: grouping the characters in the show according to the frequency with which they appear: main characters (appearing in every show), supporting characters (appearing in most shows), and guest characters (appearing once or twice). You name the characters and explain which characters fit where. But is this principle of classification significant? Has it anything to do with why the shows will become classics? No, it hasn't. Such an essay would be little more than a meaningless exercise in classifying things just to classify them.

By way of contrast, a significant principle of classification might involve categorizing a number of shows according to the easily recognized human types portrayed: the Pompous Know-It-All, the Boss Who's Out of Control, the Lovable Grouch, the Surprisingly Savvy Innocent. Perhaps you illustrate the way certain episodes offer delightful twists on these stock figures, making such shows classics of comic plotting and humor.

2. Apply the principle of division – classification logically. In an essay using division-classification, you need to demonstrate to your readers that your analysis is the result of careful thought. This means, first of all, that your division – classification should be as *complete* as possible. Your analysis should include — within reason — all the parts into which you can divide your subject or all the types into which you categorize your subjects. Let's say you are writing an essay showing that where college students live is an important factor in determining how satisfied they are with college life. Keeping your purpose in mind, you classify students according to where they live: with parents, in dorms, in fraternity and sorority houses. But what about all the students who live in rented apartments, houses, or rooms off campus? If these places of residence are ignored, your classification will not be complete; you will lose credibility with your readers because they will probably realize that you have overlooked several important considerations.

Your division – classification should also be *consistent,* meaning that the parts into which you break your subject or the groups into which you place your subjects should be as mutually exclusive as possible; the parts or categories should not be mixed, nor should they overlap. Assume you are writing an essay describing the animals at the zoo in a nearby city. You decide to describe the zoo's mammals, reptiles, birds, and endangered species. But such a classification is inconsistent. You began by categorizing the animals according to scientific class (mammals, birds, reptiles), then switched to another principle when you classified some animals according to whether they are endangered. Because you drifted over to a different principle of classification, your categories are no longer mutually exclusive: endangered species could overlap with any of the other categories. In which section of the paper, for instance, would you describe an exotic parrot that is obviously a bird but is also nearly extinct? And how would you categorize the zoo's rare mountain gorilla? This impressive creature is a mammal, but it is also an endangered species. Such overlapping categories undercut the logic that gives an essay its integrity.

A helpful tip: a solid outline is invaluable when you use division – classification. The outline encourages you to do the rigorous thinking needed to arrive at divisions and classifications that are logical, complete, and consistent.

3. Prepare an effective thesis. If your essay uses division – classification as its dominant method of development, it might be helpful to prepare a thesis that does more than signal the subject of the paper and suggest your attitude toward that general subject. You also may want the thesis to state the principle of division – classification at the heart of the essay; furthermore, you may want the thesis to express your view about the part or category you regard as most important. Consider the two thesis statements below:

As the observant beachcomber moves from the tidal area to the upper beach to the sandy dunes, rich variations in marine life become apparent.

Although most people focus on the dangers associated with the disposal of toxic waste in the land and ocean, the incineration of toxic matter may pose an even more serious threat to human life.

The first thesis statement makes clear that the writer will organize the paper by classifying the varieties of marine life according to the principle of location. The shore life being described could have been classified according to another principle —seasonal differences in the marine life found at the beach, for example. But the thesis indicates that location will be the focus of the paper. Since the purpose of the essay is to inform as objectively as possible, the thesis does not suggest the writer's opinion about which category is most significant.

The second thesis signals that the essay will evolve by dividing the issue of toxic waste according to the method of disposal. Another principle of division *could* have been used to focus the subject of toxic waste — for instance, local, state, and federal legislation needed to protect workers involved in the disposal of toxins. But the thesis indicates that the organizing principle of this essay will be the method of disposal. Moreover, because the paper takes an unusual stance on an already controversial subject, the thesis is worded in such a way that it reveals the writer's view about which aspect of the topic is most important. Such a clear statement of the writer's position is an effective strategy in an essay of this kind.

You may have noted that both thesis statements above also signal each paper's organizational plan. The first essay, for example, would use specific facts, examples, and details to describe the kinds of marine life found in the tidal area, the upper beach, and the dunes, in that order. But thesis statements in papers developed primarily through division – classification do not have to be so structured. If a paper is well written, your principle of division – classification, your opinion about which part or category is most important, and the essay's plan of development will become apparent as the essay unfolds.

4. Organize the paper logically. Whether your paper has a structured thesis or is developed wholly or in part by division – classification, the essay should always have a logical structure. Within reason, you should try to discuss comparable points in each subsection of the paper. For example, in the essay on seashore life, you might describe life in the tidal area by discussing the mollusks, crustaceans, birds, and amphibians that live or feed there. You would then follow through, as much as possible, with this arrangement in the other sections of the paper (upper beach and dune). Forgetting to describe the birdlife thriving in the dunes, especially when you had discussed birdlife in the tidal and upper-beach areas, would compromise the structure of the paper. Of course, perfect parallelism is not always possible — there are no mollusks in the dunes, for instance. But striving for this sort of consistency gives the essay a solid integrity. Connecting signals should also link the various parts of the paper, making it come together as an integrated whole ("Another characteristic of marine life battered by the tides . . ."; "A final important trait of both tidal and upper-beach crustaceans is . . ."; "Unlike the creatures of the tidal area and the upper beach, the dune animals are . . ."). Such cues make clear the connections among the ideas in the essay.

5. State any conclusions or recommendations in the final section of the paper. The analytic thinking that occurs during division – classification often leads to interesting conclusions or recommendations. A paper might categorize different kinds of coaches, from unforgettably inspiring to incredibly incompetent, making the point that athletes learn a great deal about human relations simply by having to get along with their coaches — regardless of the coaches' skills. Such a paper might conclude that participating in a team sport teaches more about human nature than several courses in psychology. Or the essay might end with a proposal: rookies and seasoned team members should be paired so that novice players can get advice on dealing with coaching eccentricities. In either case, the final section of the paper is the logical spot for such conclusions or recommendations.

As products of Western culture, we consider order and exactness virtues, finding satisfaction in the process of dividing and classifying. Does our urge to divide and classify make us intolerant of that which cannot be pigeonholed? Do we lose sight of the whole by focusing on types and parts? Some cultures and philosophers believe we do and criticize our mania for dissecting and segregating. Yet dividing and classifying can be a way to understand the whole. Our achievements in science and technology are based on such analytic thinking. We use division – classification to understand everything from plants to animals, from the geologic history of earth to the mysteries of human evolution. Division – classification can, in short, be a powerful strategy for making sense of the complexities around us.

STUDENT ESSAY AND COMMENTARY

The following student essay was written by Gail Oremland in response to this assignment:

> In "Making Medical Mistakes," David Hilfiker discusses the kinds of errors made by a professional — in this case, a family physician. Choose another profession or dis-

tinct group of people and discuss the types of mistakes
that can occur. Your analysis, which may be serious or
humorous, should imply your attitude toward the people making the errors.

While reading the paper, try to determine how effectively it
applies the principles concerning the use of division –
classification. The commentary following the paper will help you
look at Gail's essay more closely.

The Truth About College Teachers

A recent TV news story told about a group of college professors   1
from a nearby university who were hired by a local school system to
help upgrade the teaching in the community's public schools. The
professors were to visit classrooms, analyze teachers' skills, and
then conduct workshops to help the teachers become more effective
at their jobs. But after the first round of workshops, the superintend-
ent of schools decided to cancel the whole project. He fired the
learned professors and sent them packing back to their ivory tower.
Why did the project fall apart? There was a simple reason. The
college professors, who were supposedly going to show the public
school teachers how to be more effective, were themselves poor
teachers. Many college students could have predicted such a disastrous outcome. They know, firsthand, that college teachers are
strange. They know that professors often exhibit bizarre behaviors,
relating to students in ways that make it difficult for students to stay
awake, or--if awake--to learn.

One type of professor assumes, legitimately enough, that her   2
function is to pass on to students the vast store of knowledge she
has acquired. But because the "Knowledgeable One" regards herself as an expert and her students as the ignorant masses, she
adopts an elitist approach that sabotages learning. The Knowledgeable One enters a lecture hall with a self-important air, walks to the
podium, places her yellowed-with-age notes on the stand, and
begins her lecture at the exact second the class is officially scheduled to begin. There can be a blizzard or hurricane raging outside
the lecture hall; students can be running through freezing sleet and
howling winds to get to class on time. Will the Knowledgeable One
wait for them to arrive before beginning her lecture? Probably not.
The Knowledgeable One's time is precious. She's there, set to begin,
and that's what matters.

Once the monologue begins, the Knowledgeable One drones on   3
and on. The Knowledgeable One is a fact person. She may be the
history prof who knows the death toll of every Civil War battle, the
biology prof who can diagram all the common biological molecules,
the accounting prof who enumerates every clause of the federal tax
form. Oblivious to students' glazed eyes and stifled yawns, the
Knowledgeable One delivers her monologue, dispensing one dry
fact after another. The only advantage to being on the receiving end
of this boring monologue is that students do not have to worry about
being called on to question a point or provide an opinion; the Knowledgeable One is not willing to relinquish one minute of her time by
giving students a voice. Assume for one improbable moment that a
student actually manages to stay awake during the monologue and
is brave enough to ask a question. In such a case, the Knowledgeable One will address the questioning student as "Mr." or "Miss."
This formality does not, as some students mistakenly suppose, indicate respect for the student as a fledgling member of the academic
community. Not at all. This impersonality represents the Knowledgeable One's desire to keep as wide a distance as possible between her and her students.

The Knowledgeable One's monologue always comes to a close   4
at the precise second the class is scheduled to end. No sooner has
she delivered her last forgettable word than the Knowledgeable One
packs up her notes and shoots out the door, heading back to the
privacy of her office where she can pursue her specialized academic
interests--free of any possible interruption from students. The
Knowledgeable One's hasty departure from the lecture hall makes it
clear she has no desire to talk with students. In her eyes, she has
met her obligations; she has taken time away from her research to
transmit to students what she knows. Any closer contact might
mean she would risk contagion from students, that great unwashed
mass. Such a danger is to be avoided at all costs.

Unlike the Knowledgeable One, the "Leader of Intellectual Dis-   5
cussion" seems to respect students. Emphasizing class discussion,
the Leader encourages students to confront ideas ("What is Twain's
view of morality?" "Was our intervention in Vietnam justified?"
"Should big business be given tax breaks?") and discover their own
truths. Then about three weeks into the semester, it becomes clear
that the Leader wants students to discover <u>his</u> version of the truth.
Behind the Leader's democratic guise lurks a dictator. When a student voices an opinion which the Leader accepts, the student is
rewarded by hearty nods of approval and "Good point, good point."
But if a student is rash enough to advance a conflicting viewpoint,
the Leader responds with killing politeness: "Well, yes, that's an

interesting perspective. But don't you think that . . . ?" Grade-conscious students soon learn not to chime in with their viewpoint. They know that when the Leader, with seeming honesty, says, "I'd be interested in hearing what you think. Let's open this up for discussion," they had better figure out what the Leader wants to hear before advancing their own theories. "Me-tooism" rather than independent thinking, they discover, guarantees good grades in the Leader's class.

Then there is the professor who comes across as the students' "Buddy." This kind of professor does not see himself as an imparter of knowledge or a leader of discussion but as a pal, just one in a community of equals. The Buddy may start his course this way: "All of us know that this college stuff--grades, degrees, exams, required reading--is a game. So let's not play it, OK?" Dressed in jeans, sweatshirt, and scuffed sneakers, the Buddy projects a relaxed, casual attitude. He arranges the class seats in a circle (he would never take a position in front of the room) and insists that students call him by his first name. He uses no syllabus and gives few tests, believing that such constraints keep students from directing their own learning. A free spirit, the Buddy often teaches courses like "The Psychology of Interpersonal Relations" or "The Social Dynamics of the Family." If students choose to use class time to discuss the course material, that's fine. If they want to discuss something else, that's fine, too. It's the self-expression, the honest dialogue, that counts. In fact, the Buddy seems especially fond of digressions from academic subjects. By talking about his political views, his marital problems, his tendency to drink one too many beers, the Buddy lets students see that he is a regular guy--just like them. At first, students look forward to classes with the Buddy. They enjoy the informality, the chitchat, the lack of pressure. But after a while, they wonder why they are paying for a course where they learn nothing. They might as well stay home and watch the soaps.

Obviously, some college professors are excellent. They are learned, hardworking, and imaginative; they enjoy their work and like being with students. On the whole, though, college professors are a strange lot. Despite their advanced degrees and their own exposure to many different kinds of teachers, they do not seem to understand how to relate to students. Rather than being hired as consultants to help others upgrade their teaching skills, college professors should themselves hire consultants to tell them what they are doing wrong and how they can improve. Who should these consultants be? That's easy: the people who know them best--their students.

After years of being graded by teachers, Gail took special pleasure in writing an essay that gave her a chance to evaluate her teachers — in this case, her college professors. Even her title, "The Truth About College Professors," implies that Gail is going to have fun knocking profs down from their ivory towers. To introduce her subject, she uses a timely news story. This brief anecdote leads directly to the essay's *thesis:* ". . . professors often exhibit bizarre behaviors, relating to students in ways that make it difficult for students to stay awake, or — if awake — to learn." You will note that Gail's thesis is not highly structured; it does not, for example, name the specific categories to be discussed. Still, the thesis suggests that the essay is going to *categorize* a range of teaching behaviors, using as a *principle of classification* the strange ways that college profs relate to students.

As with all papers developed through division – classification, Gail's essay does not use classification as an end in itself. Gail uses classification because it helps her achieve a broader *purpose.* She wants to *convince* readers — without moralizing or abandoning her humorous tone — that such teaching styles inhibit learning. In other words, there's a serious underside to her essay. This additional layer of meaning is characteristic of satiric writing.

The body of the essay, consisting of five paragraphs, presents the three categories that make up Gail's analysis. In Gail's view, college teachers can be categorized as the Knowledgeable One (paragraphs 2, 3, 4), the Leader of Intellectual Discussion (5), or the Buddy (6). Obviously, there are other ways teaching styles might be classified, but given Gail's purpose, audience, and lightly satiric tone, her categories are appropriate; they are reasonably *complete, consistent,* and *mutually exclusive.*

To make it easy for the reader to follow the progression of her analysis, Gail uses *topic sentences* to introduce the three kinds of professors: "But because the 'Knowledgeable One' regards herself as an expert and her students as the ignorant masses, she adopts an elitist approach that sabotages learning" (2); "Unlike the Knowledgeable One, the 'Leader of Intellectual Discussion' seems to respect students" (5); and "Then there is the professor who comes across as the students' 'Buddy.' This kind of professor does not see himself as an imparter of knowledge or a leader of discussion but as a pal . . ." (6).

When reading the essay, you probably were aware that Gail is able to shift smoothly and easily from one category to the next. How does she achieve such a graceful transition? Take a moment to reread the topic sentences that introduce her second and third categories. Look at the way the beginning of each sentence (in italics) links back to the preceding category or categories: *"Unlike the Knowledgeable One,* the 'Leader of Intellectual Discussion' seems to respect students" and the Buddy *"does not see himself as an imparter of knowledge or a leader of discussion* but as a pal. . . ."

Gail is equally careful about providing clear *organizational cues* within each section. For instance, she uses a chronological sequence to organize her three-paragraph discussion of the Knowledgeable One. The first paragraph deals with the beginning of the Knowledgeable One's lecture; the second paragraph, with the lecture itself; the third paragraph, with the end of the lecture. In turn, topic sentences ("Once the monologue begins, the Knowledgeable One drones on and on" and "The Knowledgeable One's monologue always comes to a close at the precise second the class is scheduled to end") signal this passage of time. Similarly, *transitions* are used in the paragraphs on the Leader of Intellectual Discussion and the Buddy to ensure a logical progression of points: *"Then* about three weeks into the semester, it becomes clear that the Leader wants students to discover *his* version of the truth" (5) and *"At first* students look forward to classes with the Buddy. . . . But *after a while,* they wonder why they are paying for a course where they learn nothing" (6).

In addition to such organizational strategies, the essay's unity can also be traced to Gail's skill in sustaining the satiric mood of the piece. Throughout the essay, Gail selects details that fit her gently mocking attitude. She depicts the Knowledgeable One lecturing from "yellowed-with-age notes . . . , oblivious to students' glazed eyes and stifled yawns," unwilling to wait for students who "run . . . through freezing sleet and howling winds to get to class on time." Then she presents another tongue-in-cheek description, this one focusing on the way the Leader of Intellectual Discussion conducts class: "Good point, good point. . . . Well, yes, that's an interesting perspective. But don't you think that . . . ?" Finally, Gail portrays with similar killing accuracy the Buddy, all decked out in "jeans, sweatshirt and scuffed sneakers." It is interesting to note that Gail's satiric depiction of her three professional types depends on many of the techniques associated with *narrative* and *descriptive writing:* she uses vigorous images, highly connotative language, and dialogue.

Although Gail's essay is unified and organized, you may have felt that the first category is out of proportion to the other two. There is, of course, no need to balance the length of the categories exactly. But Gail's extended treatment of the first category sets up an expectation that the others will be treated as fully. One way to remedy this problem is to delete some material from the discussion of the Knowledgeable One. Gail might, for instance, omit the first five sentences in the third paragraph (about the professor who addresses students as Mr. or Miss). Such a change could be made without taking the bite out of her portrayal. Even better, Gail could simply switch the order of her paragraphs, putting the portrait of the Knowledgeable One at the end of the essay. If this section were placed at the end, the extended discussion would not seem out of proportion. Rather, it would look as though Gail has used *emphatic order* to sequence her categories, saving for last the category she had most to say about.

It's apparent than an essay as engaging as Gail's must have undergone a good deal of revising. That was in fact the case. Gail made many changes in the body of the essay, but it is particularly interesting to review what happened to the introduction as she revised the paper. Reprinted below is the original introduction Gail prepared.

First Draft Version

Despite their high IQs, advanced degrees, and published papers, some college professors just don't know how to teach. Found in almost any department, in tenured and untenured positions, they prompt student apathy. They fail to convey ideas effectively and to challenge or inspire students. Students thus finish their courses having learned very little. Contrary to popular opinion, these professors' ineptitude is not simply a matter of delivering boring lectures or not caring about students. Many of them care a great deal. Their failure actually stems from their unrealistic perceptions of what a teacher should be. Specifically, they adopt teaching styles or roles that alienate students and undermine learning. Three of the most common ones are "The Knowledgeable One," "The Leader of Intellectual Discussion," and "The Buddy."

When Gail showed the first draft of the essay to her composition instructor, he laughed — and occasionally squirmed — when reading what she had prepared. On the whole, he was enthusiastic about the paper but felt that there was a problem with the tone of the introductory paragraph. It was too serious when compared to the playful, lightly satiric mood in the rest of the essay. When Gail reread the paragraph, she agreed with her instructor but was uncertain about the best way to remedy the problem. After making some changes in other parts of the essay, she decided to let the paper sit for a while before going back to rewrite the introduction.

In the meantime, Gail wanted some time to relax, so she switched on the TV. The timing couldn't have been better; she had tuned into a news story about several supposedly learned professors who had been fired from a consulting job because they turned out to know so little about teaching. This was exactly the kind of item Gail needed to start her essay. Now she was able to prepare a completely new introduction, making it consistent in spirit with the rest of the paper.

Once the essay's opening had been reworked, Gail realized she should revise her conclusion so that it would reflect the changes made in the introduction. Keeping the new introduction in mind, she decided to use the conclusion to recall the story about the fired consultants. By echoing the opening anecdote in her conclusion, Gail was able to end the paper with another poke at professors. The conclusion also gave her a chance to hint at a longed-for role reversal between students and teachers, with students — finally — having the upper hand. This was a perfect way for Gail to close her clever and insightful essay.

The selections in this chapter show how division and classification can be used to explore a variety of subjects. Dave Barry's "In Depth, but Shallowly" analyzes the components of a local news program — from smiling anchorperson to ghastly accident footage. William Zinsser describes the sorts of "College Pressures" that students typically encounter, while David Hilfiker, in "Making Medical Mistakes," confesses to the types of errors he has committed as a doctor. Classifying "Propaganda Techniques in Today's Advertising" is the method Ann McClintock uses to demonstrate how pervasive and effective such techniques can be. Finally, in "The Quick Fix Society," Janet Mendell Goldstein examines three different kinds of instant gratification and shows us the harm each causes.

Dave Barry

A Pulitzer prize–winning journalist, Dave Barry writes a syndicated humor column for the *Miami Herald*. His droll observations about the absurdities of everyday life appear in many newspapers across the country. Barry's books of collected essays and satires include *Babies and Other Hazards of Sex, The Taming of the Screw, Stay Fit and Healthy Until You're Dead,* and *Homes and Other Black Holes*. The following piece is from his 1985 book, *Bad Habits*.

In Depth, but Shallowly

Local news once imitated the national networks: sober accounts of important events read by a distinguished male with a sonorous voice—local versions of Walter Cronkite or Eric Sevareid. Then, sometime in the mid-seventies, happy-talk news took over the local stations. Friendly, attractive newscasters traded wisecracks and reported photographable disasters and fluffy human-interest stories. In the following selection, Dave Barry skewers happy-talk news with needle-sharp wit. Beneath the humor lie some unpleasant messages about the numbing effects of televised news.

If you want to take your mind off the troubles of the real 1
world, you should watch local TV news shows. I know of no better way to escape reality, except perhaps heavy drinking.

Local TV news programs have given a whole new definition 2
to the word *news*. To most people, *news* means *information about events that affect a lot of people*. On local TV news shows, *news* means *anything that you can take a picture of, especially if a local TV News Personality can stand in front of it*. This is why they are so fond of car accidents, burning buildings, and crowds: these are good for standing in front of. On the other hand, local TV news shows tend to avoid stories about things that local TV News Personalities cannot stand in front of, such as budgets and taxes

470

and the economy. If you want to get a local TV news show to do a story on the budget, your best bet is to involve it in a car crash.

I travel around the country a lot, and as far as I can tell,   3 virtually all local TV news shows follow the same format. First you hear some exciting music, the kind you hear in space movies, while the screen shows local TV News Personalities standing in front of various News Events. Then you hear the announcer:

Announcer: From the On-the-Spot Action Eyewitness News Stu-   4
            dios, this is the On-the-Spot Action Eyewitness
            News, featuring Anchorman Wilson Westbrook,
            Co-Anchorperson Stella Snape, Minority-Group
            Member James Edwards, Genial Sports Personality
            Jim Johnson, Humorous Weatherperson Dr. Reed
            Stevens, and Norm Perkins on drums. And now,
            here's Wilson Westbrook.

Westbrook: Good evening. Tonight from the On-the-Spot Ac-   5
            tion Eyewitness News Studios we have actual color
            film of a burning building, actual color film of two
            cars after they ran into each other, actual color film
            of the front of a building in which one person shot
            another person, actual color film of another burn-
            ing building, and special reports on roller-skating
            and child abuse. But for the big story tonight, we go
            to City Hall, where On-the-Spot reporter Reese Ker-
            nel is standing live.

Kernel: I am standing here live in front of City Hall being   6
            televised by the On-the-Spot Action Eyewitness
            News minicam with Mayor Bryce Hallbread.

Mayor: That's "Hallwood."   7

Kernel: What?   8

Mayor: My name is "Hallwood." You said "Hallbread."   9

Kernel: Look, Hallbread, do you want to be on the news or   10
            don't you?

Mayor: Yes, of course, it's just that my name is—   11

Kernel::   Listen, this is the top-rated news show in the three-   12
            county area, and if you think I have time to memo-
            rize every stupid detail, you'd better think again.

Mayor: I'm sorry. "Hallbread" is fine, really.   13

Kernel: Thank you, Mayor Hallbread. And now back to   14

Wilson Westbrook in the On-the-Spot Action Eye-witness News Studios.

Westbrook: Thank you, Reese; keep us posted if anything fur- 15 ther develops on that important story. And now, as I promised earlier, we have actual color film of var- ious objects that either burned or crashed, which we will project on the screen behind me while I talk about them. Here is a building on fire. Here is another building on fire. Here is a car crash. This film was shot years ago, but you can safely assume that objects just like these crashed or burned in the three-county area today. And now we go to my Co-Anchorperson, Stella Snape, for a Special Report on her exhaustive three-week investigation into the problem of child abuse in the three-county area. Well, Stella, what did you find?

Snape: Wilson, I found that child abuse is very sad. What 16 happens is that people abuse children. It's just awful. Here you see some actual color film of me standing in front of a house. Most of your child abuse occurs in houses. Note that I am wearing subdued colors.

Westbrook (reading from a script): Are any efforts under way 17 here in the three-county area to combat child abuse?

Snape: Yes. 18

Westbrook: Thank you, Stella, for that informative report. On 19 the lighter side, On-the-Spot Action Eyewitness Re- porter Terri Tompkins has prepared a three-part series on roller-skating in the three-county area.

Tompkins: Roller-skating has become a major craze in Califor- 20 nia and the three-county area, as you can see by this actual color film of me on roller skates outside the On-the-Spot Action Eyewitness News Studio. This certainly is a fun craze. Tomorrow, in Part Two of this series, we'll see actual color film of me falling down. On Wednesday we'll see me getting up.

Westbrook: We'll look forward to those reports. Our next story 21 is from Minority-Group Reporter James Edwards, who, as he has for the last 324 consecutive broadcasts, spent the day in the minority-group sector of the three-county area finding out what minorities think.

Edwards: Wilson, I'm standing in front of a crowd of minor- 22 ity-group members, and as you can see, their mood is troubled. (*The crowd smiles and waves at the camera.*)

Westbrook: Good report, James. Well, we certainly had a sunny 23 day here in the three-county area, didn't we, Humorous Weatherperson Dr. Reed Stevens?

Stevens: Ha ha. We sure did, though I'm certainly troubled 24 by that very troubling report Stella did on child abuse. But we should see continued warm weather through Wednesday. Here are a bunch of charts showing the relative humidity and stuff like that. Ha ha.

Westbrook: Ha ha. Well, things weren't nearly as bright on the 25 sports scene, were they, Genial Sports Personality Jim Johnson?

Johnson: No, Wilson, they certainly weren't. The Three- 26 County Community College Cutlasses lost their fourth consecutive game today. Here you see actual color footage of me watching the game from the sidelines. The disgust is evident on my face. I intended to have actual color film of me interviewing the coach after the game, but the team bus crashed and everyone was killed.

Westbrook: Thank you, Jim. And now, here is Basil Holp, the 27 General Manager of KUSP – TV, to present an Editorial Viewpoint:

Holp: The management of KUSP – TV firmly believes 28 that something ought to be done about earthquakes. From time to time we read in the papers that an earthquake has hit some wretched little country and knocked houses down and killed people. This should not be allowed to continue. Maybe we should have a tax or something. What the heck, we can afford it. The management of KUSP – TV is rolling in money.

Announcer: The preceding was the opinion of the management   29
of KUSP–TV. People with opposing points of
view are probably in the vast majority.

Westbrook: Well, that wraps up tonight's version of the On-   30
the-Spot Action Eyewitness News. Tune in tomor-
row to see essentially the same stories.

Questions for Close Reading

1. What is the thesis of the selection? Locate the sentence(s) in which Barry states his main idea. If he does not state the thesis explicitly, express it in your own words.
2. According to Barry, what are the typical "news personality" types on a local TV news show? Why does Barry include the drummer in his list?
3. What kinds of news items are most likely to receive coverage on local news shows? What news items don't fit in well with the formats of local news?
4. What are the subjects of the two special reports on the news show Barry describes? What information is provided in these segments?

Questions About the Writer's Craft

1. In this satiric piece, Barry uses division to identify the typical elements making up the format of a local TV news program. How does Barry's presentation of a scene from each division help him achieve his purpose? What needed changes are implied by this spoof?
2. Most of this essay is an imaginary local news show. How does this fictional show script help Barry make his point? Is the script more effective than an analytic critique of a news show?
3. Barry suggests that watching the local news is as good a way to escape reality as heavy drinking. What is the effect of putting this comparison at the start of the essay? How does it affect your expectations of what is to follow?
4. Why does Barry have the news staff repeat phrases like "actual color film"? What do you think he means to say about local news by using these repetitions? Find other examples of repeated phrases.

Questions for Further Thought

1. The title of Barry's essay, "In Depth, but Shallowly," is a paradox, that is, a statement that seems to contradict itself. How can local

news be both "in depth" and "shallow"? Why do you think Barry chose this title?

2. Besides making us laugh, Barry's essay identifies several flaws he finds in most local newscasts. What other things do you find wrong with local news shows?

3. "Happy talk" local news shows are often the highest-rated newscasts in their marketing area. Do you think the public really wants chatty, fun news shows? Why do people watch such shows?

4. Do you think the national news shows are more serious and thought-provoking than local news shows, or are they just as "shallowly in depth" in their own way? If so, how can we become better informed about the world we live in?

Writing Assignments Using Division–Classification as a Method of Development

*1. Analyze a top TV show to reveal what makes it popular. Focus on the elements that make the show so appealing: audience identification, interesting themes, escapist entertainment, and so on. Use division–classification to develop your analysis of the show's popularity. Marie Winn's "TV Addiction" (page 444) may give you some insight into people's attachment to television.

2. Select a type of TV show, other than local news, and give it "the Barry treatment." That is, write an essay using division–classification to analyze the types of people usually found in this kind of show. Develop the analysis by creating a humorous script for these stereotypical characters. You might choose daytime or night-time soaps, doctor shows, magazine shows, or whatever type seems to you most worthy of such satire.

Writing Assignments Using Other Methods of Development

3. Argue against Barry's essay, using the thesis that local news does an effective job providing the public with what it wants. You might consider the point that people do not turn to local news for insight-ful coverage of national and international stories. Instead, they look to local news for updates on what is happening in their immediate community. Provide a series of strong examples to support your argument. The essay should make clear how you feel about the expectations people have for local television.

4. Watch one TV news program, preferably local, and jot down all the

stories covered. Then compare this list with the local newspaper. Write an essay comparing and contrasting the two media in terms of stories covered, importance given to stories, depth of coverage, and so on. Use the analysis to make a judgment about the way news is treated by the two media.

William Zinsser

William Zinsser has written news journalism, drama criticism, magazine columns, and several books on American culture. Born in 1922 in New York, Zinsser attended Princeton University and worked for the *New York Herald Tribune, Life,* and *Look.* In 1970, Zinsser designed a course in nonfiction writing for Yale University; from his teaching experience at Yale came his popular guide, *On Writing Well* (1976). His other books include *The City Dwellers* (1962), *Pop Goes America* (1966), *The Lunacy Boom* (1970), and *Writing with a Word Processor* (1982). The following essay first appeared in the magazine *Country Journal* in 1979.

College Pressures

Campuses today are flooded with business majors and budding computer scientists. Many students' primary goal is to go where the money is — to transform themselves into marketable commodities who will, by the age of thirty, have luxurious homes, expensive cars, and profitable investment portfolios. William Zinsser sympathizes with the pressures that cause students' obsession with material success, yet he doubts that such a single-minded concern with a lucrative career is the surest route to happiness.

Dear Carlos: I desperately need a dean's excuse for my chem midterm which will begin in about 1 hour. All I can say is that I totally blew it this week. I've fallen incredibly, inconceivably behind.

Carlos: Help! I'm anxious to hear from you. I'll be in my room and won't leave it until I hear from you. Tomorrow is the last day for . . .

Carlos: I left town because I started bugging out again. I

477

stayed up all night to finish a take-home make-up exam
& am typing it to hand in on the 10th. It was due on the
5th. P.S. I'm going to the dentist. Pain is pretty bad.

Carlos: Probably by Friday I'll be able to get back to my
studies. Right now I'm going to take a long walk. This
whole thing has taken a lot out of me.

Carlos: I'm really up the proverbial creek. The problem
is I really *bombed* the history final. Since I need that
course for my major I . . .

Carlos: Here follows a tale of woe. I went home this
weekend, had to help my Mom, & caught a fever so
didn't have much time to study. My professor . . .

Carlos: Aargh! Trouble. Nothing original but everything's piling up at once. To be brief, my job
interview . . .

Hey Carlos, good news! I've got mononucleosis.

Who are these wretched supplicants, scribbling notes so   1
laden with anxiety, seeking such miracles of postponement and
balm? They are men and women who belong to Branford College, one of the twelve residential colleges at Yale University, and
the messages are just a few of the hundreds that they left for their
dean, Carlos Hortas — often slipped under his door at 4 A.M. —
last year.

But students like the ones who wrote those notes can also be   2
found on campuses from coast to coast — especially in New England and at many other private colleges across the country that
have high academic standards and highly motivated students.
Nobody could doubt that the notes are real. In their urgency and
their gallows humor they are authentic voices of a generation that
is panicky to succeed.

My own connection with the message writers is that I am   3
master of Branford College. I live in its Gothic quadrangle and
know the students well. (We have 485 of them.) I am privy
to their hopes and fears — and also to their stereo music and

their piercing cries in the dead of the night ("Does anybody *ca-a-are?*"). If they went to Carlos to ask how to get through tomorrow, they come to me to ask how to get through the rest of their lives.

Mainly I try to remind them that the road ahead is a long one and that it will have more unexpected turns than they think. There will be plenty of time to change jobs, change careers, change whole attitudes and approaches. They don't want to hear such liberating news. They want a map — right now — that they can follow unswervingly to career security, financial security, Social Security and, presumably, a prepaid grave. 4

What I wish for all students is some release from the clammy grip of the future. I wish them a chance to savor each segment of their education as an experience in itself and not as a grim preparation for the next step. I wish them the right to experiment, to trip and fall, to learn that defeat is as instructive as victory and is not the end of the world. 5

My wish, of course, is naïve. One of the few rights that America does not proclaim is the right to fail. Achievement is the national god, venerated in our media — the million-dollar athlete, the wealthy executive — and glorified in our praise of possessions. In the presence of such a potent state religion, the young are growing up old. 6

I see four kinds of pressure working on college students today: economic pressure, parental pressure, peer pressure, and self-induced pressure. It is easy to look around for villains — to blame the colleges for charging too much money, the professors for assigning too much work, the parents for pushing their children too far, the students for driving themselves too hard. But there are no villains; only victims. 7

"In the late 1960s," one dean told me, "the typical question that I got from students was 'Why is there so much suffering in the world?' or 'How can I make a contribution?' Today it's 'Do you think it would look better for getting into law school if I did a double major in history and political science, or just majored in one of them?'" Many other deans confirmed this pattern. One said: "They're trying to find an edge — the intangible something that will look better on paper if two students are about equal." 8

Note the emphasis on *looking* better. The transcript has 9

become a sacred document, the passport to security. How one appears on paper is more important than how one appears in person. *A* is for Admirable and *B* is for Borderline, even though, in Yale's official system of grading, *A* means "excellent" and *B* means "very good." Today, looking very good is no longer good enough, especially for students who hope to go on to law school or medical school. They know that entrance into the better schools will be an entrance into the better law firms and better medical practices where they will make a lot of money. They also know that the odds are harsh. Yale Law School, for instance, matriculates 170 students from an applicant pool of 3,700; Harvard enrolls 550 from a pool of 7,000.

It's all very well for those of us who write letters of recommendation for our students to stress the qualities of humanity that will make them good lawyers or doctors. And it's nice to think that admission officers are really reading our letters and looking for the extra dimension of commitment or concern. Still, it would be hard for a student not to visualize these officers shuffling so many transcripts studded with *A*s that they regard a *B* as positively shameful.   10

The pressure is almost as heavy on students who just want to graduate and get a job. Long gone are the days of the "gentleman's *C*," when students journeyed through college with a certain relaxation, sampling a wide variety of courses — music, art, philosophy, classics, anthropology, poetry, religion — that would send them out as liberally educated men and women. If I were an employer I would rather employ graduates who have this range and curiosity than those who narrowly pursued safe subjects and high grades. I know countless students whose inquiring minds exhilarate me. I like to hear the play of their ideas. I don't know if they are getting *A*s or *C*s, and I don't care. I also like them as people. The country needs them, and they will find satisfying jobs. I tell them to relax. They can't.   11

Nor can I blame them. They live in a brutal economy. Tuition, room, and board at most private colleges now comes to at least $7,000, not counting books and fees. This might seem to suggest that the colleges are getting rich. But they are equally battered by inflation. Tuition covers only 60 percent of what it costs to educate a student, and ordinarily the remainder comes from what colleges receive in endowments, grants, and gifts.   12

Now the remainder keeps being swallowed by the cruel costs—higher every year—of just opening the doors. Heating oil is up. Insurance is up. Postage is up. Health-premium costs are up. Everything is up. Deficits are up. We are witnessing in America the creation of a brotherhood of paupers—colleges, parents, and students, joined by the common bond of debt.

Today it is not unusual for a student, even if he works part $\quad$ 13 time at college and full time during the summer, to accrue $5,000 in loans after four years—loans that he must start to repay within one year after graduation. Exhorted at commencement to go forth into the world, he is already behind as he goes forth. How could he not feel under pressure throughout college to prepare for this day of reckoning? I have used "he," incidentally, only for brevity. Women at Yale are under no less pressure to justify their expensive education to themselves, their parents, and society. In fact, they are probably under more pressure. For although they leave college superbly equipped to bring fresh leadership to traditionally male jobs, society hasn't yet caught up with this fact.

Along with economic pressure goes parental pressure. Inevi- $\quad$ 14 tably, the two are deeply intertwined.

I see many students taking pre-medical courses with joyless $\quad$ 15 tenacity. They go off to their labs as if they were going to the dentist. It saddens me because I know them in other corners of their life as cheerful people.

"Do you want to go to medical school?" I ask them. $\quad$ 16

"I guess so," they say, without conviction, or "Not really." $\quad$ 17

"Then why are you going?" $\quad$ 18

"Well, my parents want me to be a doctor. They're paying all $\quad$ 19 this money and . . ."

Poor students, poor parents. They are caught in one of the $\quad$ 20 oldest webs of love and duty and guilt. The parents mean well; they are trying to steer their sons and daughters toward a secure future. But the sons and daughters want to major in history or classics or philosophy—subjects with no "practical" value. Where's the payoff on the humanities? It's not easy to persuade such loving parents that the humanities do indeed pay off. The intellectual faculties developed by studying subjects like history and classics—an ability to synthesize and relate, to weigh cause and effect, to see events in perspective — are just the faculties that make creative leaders in business or almost any general field. Still, many fathers would rather put their money on courses that point toward a specific profession — courses that are pre-law, pre-medical, pre-business, or, as I sometimes heard it put, "pre-rich."

But the pressure on students is severe. They are truly torn. 21 One part of them feels obligated to fulfill their parents' expectations; after all, their parents are older and presumably wiser. Another part tells them that the expectations that are right for their parents are not right for them.

I know a student who wants to be an artist. She is very 22 obviously an artist and will be a good one — she has already had several modest local exhibits. Meanwhile she is growing as a well-rounded person and taking humanistic subjects that will enrich the inner resources out of which her art will grow. But her father is strongly opposed. He thinks that an artist is a "dumb" thing to be. The student vacillates and tries to please everybody. She keeps up with her art somewhat furtively and takes some of the "dumb" courses her father wants her to take — at least they are dumb courses for her. She is a free spirit on a campus of tense students — no small achievement in itself — and she deserves to follow her muse.

Peer pressure and self-induced pressure are also intertwined, 23 and they begin almost at the beginning of freshman year.

"I had a freshman student I'll call Linda," one dean told me, 24 "who came in and said she was under terrible pressure because her roommate, Barbara, was much brighter and studied all the time. I couldn't tell her that Barbara had come in two hours earlier to say the same thing about Linda."

The story is almost funny — except that it's not. It's sympto- 25 matic of all the pressures put together. When every student thinks every other student is working harder and doing better, the only solution is to study harder still. I see students going off to the library every night after dinner and coming back when it closes at midnight. I wish they would sometimes forget about their peers and go to a movie. I hear the clacking of typewriters in the hours before dawn. I see the tension in their eyes when exams are approaching and papers are due: *"Will I get everything done?"*

Probably they won't. They will get sick. They will get 26 "blocked." They will sleep. They will oversleep. They will bug out. *Hey, Carlos, help!*

Part of the problem is that they do more than they are 27
expected to do. A professor will assign five-page papers. Several
students will start writing ten-page papers to impress him. Then
more students will write ten-page papers, and a few will raise the
ante to fifteen. Pity the poor student who is still just doing the
assignment.

"Once you have twenty or thirty percent of the student 28
population deliberately overexerting," one dean points out, "it's
bad for everybody. When a teacher gets more and more effort
from his class, the student who is doing normal work can be
perceived as not doing well. The tactic works, psychologically."

Why can't the professor just cut back and not accept longer 29
papers? He can, and he probably will. But by then the term will be
half over and the damage done. Grade fever is highly contagious
and not easily reversed. Besides, the professor's main concern is
with his course. He knows his students only in relation to the
course and doesn't know that they are also overexerting in their
other courses. Nor is it really his business. He didn't sign up for
dealing with the student as a whole person and with all the
emotional baggage the student brought along from home. That's
what deans, masters, chaplains, and psychiatrists are for.

To some extent this is nothing new: a certain number of 30
professors have always been self-contained islands of scholarship
and shyness, more comfortable with books than with people. But
the new pauperism has widened the gap still further, for professors who actually like to spend time with students don't have as
much time to spend. They are also overexerting. If they are
young, they are busy trying to publish in order not to perish,
hanging by their finger nails onto a shrinking profession. If they
are old and tenured, they are buried under the duties of administering departments—as departmental chairmen or members of
committees—that have been thinned out by the budgetary axe.

Ultimately it will be the students' own business to break the 31
circles in which they are trapped. They are too young to be
prisoners of their parents' dreams and their classmates' fears.
They must be jolted into believing in themselves as unique men
and women who have the power to shape their own future.

"Violence is being done to the undergraduate experience," 32
says Carlos Hortas. "College should be open-ended: at the end it
should open many, many roads. Instead, students are choosing
their goal in advance, and their choices narrow as they go along.

It's almost as if they think that the country has been codified in the type of jobs that exist — that they've got to fit into certain slots. Therefore, fit into the best-paying slot.

"They ought to take chances. Not taking chances will lead to 33 a life of colorless mediocrity. They'll be comfortable. But something in the spirit will be missing."

I have painted too drab a portrait of today's students, making 34 them seem a solemn lot. That is only half of their story; if they were so dreary I wouldn't so thoroughly enjoy their company. The other half is that they are easy to like. They are quick to laugh and to offer friendship. They are not introverts. They are unusually kind and are more considerate of one another than any student generation I have known.

Nor are they so obsessed with their studies that they avoid 35 sports and extracurricular activities. On the contrary, they juggle their crowded hours to play on a variety of teams, perform with musical and dramatic groups, and write for campus publications. But this in turn is one more cause of anxiety. There are too many choices. Academically, they have 1,300 courses to select from; outside class they have to decide how much spare time they can spare and how to spend it.

This means that they engage in fewer extracurricular pursuits 36 than their predecessors did. If they want to row on the crew and play in the symphony they will eliminate one; in the '60s they would have done both. They also tend to choose activities that are self-limiting. Drama, for instance, is flourishing in all twelve of Yale's residential colleges as it never has before. Students hurl themselves into these productions — as actors, directors, carpenters, and technicians — with a dedication to create the best possible play, knowing that the day will come when the run will end and they can get back to their studies.

They also can't afford to be the willing slave of organizations 37 like the *Yale Daily News*. Last spring at the one-hundredth anniversary banquet of that paper — whose past chairmen include such once and future kings as Potter Stewart, Kingman Brewster, and William F. Buckley, Jr. — much was made of the fact that the editorial staff used to be small and totally committed and that "newsies" routinely worked fifty hours a week. In effect they belonged to a club; Newsies is how they defined themselves at Yale. Today's student will write one or two articles a week, when he can, and he defines himself as a student. I've never heard the word Newsie except at the banquet.

If I have described the modern undergraduate primarily as a driven creature who is largely ignoring the blithe spirit inside who keeps trying to come out and play, it's because that's where the crunch is, not only at Yale but throughout American education. It's why I think we should all be worried about the values that are nurturing a generation so fearful of risk and so goal-obsessed at such an early age. **38**

I tell students that there is no one "right" way to·get ahead —that each of them is a different person, starting from a different point and bound for a different destination. I tell them that change is a tonic and that all the slots are not codified nor the frontiers closed. One of my ways of telling them is to invite men and women who have achieved success outside the academic world to come and talk informally with my students during the year. They are heads of companies or ad agencies, editors of magazines, politicians, public officials, television magnates, labor leaders, business executives, Broadway producers, artists, writers, economists, photographers, scientists, historians—a mixed bag of achievers. **39**

I ask them to say a few words about how they got started. The students assume that they started in their present profession and knew all along that it was what they wanted to do. Luckily for me, most of them got into their field by a circuitous route, to their surprise, after many detours. The students are startled. They can hardly conceive of a career that was not pre-planned. They can hardly imagine allowing the hand of God or chance to nudge them down some unforeseen trail. **40**

Questions for Close Reading

1. What is the thesis of the selection? Locate the sentence(s) in which Zinsser states his main idea. If he does not state the thesis explicitly, express it in your own words.
2. According to Zinsser, why are the pressures on college students today so harmful?
3. Zinsser says that some of the pressures are "intertwined." What does he mean? Give examples from the essay.

4. What actions or attitudes on the part of students can help free them from these pressures?
5. Refer to your dictionary as needed to define the following words used in the selection: *privy* (paragraph 3), *venerated* (6), *exhorted* (13), *tenacity* (15), *vacillates* (22), *furtively* (22), and *circuitous* (40).

Questions About the Writer's Craft

1. When analyzing a subject, writers usually try to identify divisions and classifications that are — within reason — mutually exclusive. But Zinsser acknowledges that the four pressures he discusses can be seen as two distinct pairs, with each pair consisting of two "deeply intertwined" pressures. How does this overlapping of categories help Zinsser make his point?
2. In addition to using classification in this essay, what other mode of development does Zinsser use?
3. Why did the author use the notes to Carlos as his introduction? What profile of college students do you get from these notes?
4. In paragraph 4, the author writes that students want a map "they can follow unswervingly to career security, financial security, Social Security and, presumably, a prepaid grave." What tone is Zinsser using here? Where else does he use this tone?

Questions for Further Thought

1. Zinsser is a college professor at Yale. Do you think he is well qualified to advise students about career choices? Do you think he knows enough about the real world to advise students to "relax" and take a wide range of courses, instead of focusing on a practical "pre-rich" major?
2. Is it possible to both major in something "safe" and practical, and take electives to become liberally educated? Is it desirable?
3. Zinsser states that today's students "engage in fewer extracurricular pursuits than their predecessors." Do you agree that students are focusing more on their majors? Are extracurricular activities at your college suffering low membership and lack of interest?
4. What does the author mean by saying that "One of the few rights that America does not proclaim is the right to fail"? Do you agree that students should take more risks? If so, what kinds of risks should they take?

Writing Assignments Using Division – Classification as a Method of Development

1. Zinsser writes as if all students are the same — panicky, overwrought, and materialistic. Take a position counter to his and write an essay explaining that campuses contain many students different from those Zinsser writes about. To support your point, categorize students into types, giving examples of what each type is like. Be sure that the categories you identify refute Zinsser's analysis of the typical student. The tone of your essay may be serious or playful.

2. Is economic security the only kind of satisfaction that students should pursue? Write an essay classifying the various kinds of satisfactions that students could aim for. At the end of the paper, include brief recommendations about ways students could best spend their time preparing for these different kinds of satisfactions.

Writing Assignments Using Other Methods of Development

3. Using Zinsser's analysis of the pressures on college students, write an essay explaining how these pressures can be reduced or eliminated. Give practical suggestions as to how students can avoid or get around the pressures. Also, indicate what society, parents, and college staff can do to help ease the situation.

4. Zinsser's essay indicates that today's students are "slotting" themselves into preordained careers and not leaving themselves open to later opportunities that may present themselves. Write an essay arguing that this inclination to specialize is either beneficial or disastrous for students. Consider such issues as individual freedom, career confusion, changing job markets, changes in society, and the like.

David Hilfiker

Dr. David Hilfiker (1945–) spent his childhood years in Buffalo, New York, graduated from Yale University, then earned his medical degree from the University of Minnesota Medical School. He now works in two Washington, D.C., clinics caring for disadvantaged patients. In *Healing Wounds: A Physician Looks at His Work* (1985), Hilfiker reveals the pressures, doubts, and anxieties endured by the ordinary family doctor. The following excerpt is taken from this book.

Making Medical Mistakes

We want our doctors to be human: sympathetic and generous-spirited. We also want them to be godlike: all-knowing and infallible. But physicians do make mistakes, no matter how much we — and they — don't like to recognize this fact. In this selection, Hilfiker confesses that he has made several errors in medical judgment. By breaking the usual code of silence, Hilfiker explores what society can do to ease the burden of perfection imposed on doctors.

A warm July morning. I finish my rounds at our small coun- 1
try hospital around nine o'clock and walk across the parking lot to the clinic. I am a primary-care practitioner, a family doctor; my partners and I work together in a small office building. After greeting the receptionist, I look through the list of my day's appointments and notice that Barb Daily will be in for her first prenatal examination. "Wonderful," I think, recalling the joy of helping her deliver her first child two years ago. Barb and her husband, Russ, had been friends of mine before Heather was born, but we grew much closer with the shared experience of her birth. In a rural family practice such as mine, much of every workday is taken up with disease; I look forward to the prenatal visit with Barb, to the continuing relationship with her over the next months, to the prospect of birth.

At her appointment that afternoon, Barb seems to be in good 2 health, with all the signs and symptoms of pregnancy: slight nausea, some soreness in her breasts, a little weight gain. But when the nurse tests Barb's urine to determine if she is pregnant, the result is negative. The test measures the level of a hormone that is produced by a woman and shows up in her urine when she is pregnant. But occasionally it fails to detect the low levels of the hormone during early pregnancy. I reassure Barb that she is fine and schedule another test for the following week.

Barb leaves a urine sample at the clinic a week later, but the 3 test is negative again. I am troubled. Perhaps she isn't pregnant. Her missed menstrual period and her other symptoms could be a result of a minor hormonal imbalance. Maybe the embryo has died within the uterus and a miscarriage is soon to take place. I could find out by ordering an ultrasound examination. This procedure would give me a "picture" of the uterus and of the embryo. But Barb would have to go to Duluth, 110 miles from our village in northern Minnesota, for the examination. The procedure is also expensive. I know the Dailys well enough to know they have a modest income. Besides, by waiting a few weeks, I should be able to find out for sure without the ultrasound: Either the urine test will be positive or Barb will have a miscarriage. I call her and tell her about the negative test result, about the possibility of a miscarriage, and about the necessity of seeing me again if she misses her next menstrual period.

I work in a summer resort area, and it is, as usual, a hectic 4 summer; I think no more about Barb's troubling state until a month later, when she returns to my office. Nothing has changed: still no menstrual period, still no miscarriage. She is confused and upset. "I feel so pregnant," she tells me. I am bothered, too. Her uterus, upon examination, is slightly enlarged, as it was on the previous visit. But it hasn't grown any larger. Her urine test remains negative. I can think of several possible explanations for her condition, including a hormonal imbalance or even a tumor. But the most likely explanation is that she is carrying a dead embryo. I decide it is time to break the bad news to her.

"I think you have what doctors call a 'missed abortion,'" I 5 tell her. "You were probably pregnant, but the baby appears to have died some weeks ago, before your first examination. Unfortunately, you didn't have a miscarriage to get rid of the dead tissue from the baby and the placenta. If a miscarriage doesn't occur within a few weeks, I'd recommend a re-examination, another pregnancy test, and, if nothing shows up, a dilation and curettage procedure to clean out the uterus."

Barb is disappointed; there are tears. She is college educated, and she understands the scientific and technical aspects of her situation; but that doesn't alleviate the sorrow. We talk at some length and make an appointment for two weeks later.   6

When Barb returns, Russ is with her. Still no menstrual period; still no miscarriage; still another negative pregnancy test, the fourth. I explain to them what has happened. The dead embryo must be removed or there could be serious complications. Barb could become sterile. The conversation is emotionally difficult for all three of us. We schedule the dilation and curettage for later in the week.   7

Friday morning, Barb is wheeled into the operating room of the sixteen-bed county hospital. Barb, the nurses, and I all know one another—small-town life. The atmosphere is warm and relaxed; we chat before the operation. After Barb is anesthetized, I examine her pelvis again. Her muscles are now completely relaxed, and it is possible to perform a more reliable examination. Her uterus feels bigger than it did two days previously; it is perhaps the size of a small grapefruit. But since all the pregnancy tests were negative and I'm so sure of the diagnosis, I ignore the information from my fingertips and begin the operation.   8

Dilation and curettage, or D & C, is a relatively simple surgical procedure performed thousands of times each day in this country. First, the cervix is stretched by pushing smooth metal rods of increasing diameter in and out of it. After about five minutes of this, the cervix has expanded enough so that a curette can be inserted through it into the uterus. The curette is another metal rod, at the end of which is an oval ring about an inch at its widest diameter. It is used to scrape the walls of the uterus. The operation is done completely by feel after the cervix has been stretched, since it is still too narrow to see through.   9

Things do not go easily this morning. There is considerably more blood than usual, and it is only with great difficulty that I am able to extract anything. What should take ten or fifteen minutes stretches out into a half-hour. The body parts I remove are much larger than I expected, considering when the embryo   10 died. They are not bits of decomposing tissue. These are parts of a body that was recently alive!

I do my best to suppress my rising panic and try to complete the procedure. Working blindly, I am unable to evacuate the uterus completely; I can feel more parts inside but cannot remove them. Finally I stop, telling myself that the uterus will expel the rest within a few days.   11

Russ is waiting outside the operating room. I tell him that Barb is fine but that there were some problems with the operation. Since I don't completely understand what happened, I can't be very helpful in answering his questions. I promise to return to the hospital later in the day after Barb has awakened from the anesthesia.   12

In between seeing other patients that morning I place several almost frantic phone calls, trying to piece together what happened. Despite reassurances from a pathologist that it is "impossible" for a pregnant woman to have four consecutive negative pregnancy tests, the realization is growing that I have aborted Barb's living child. I won't know for sure until the pathologist has examined the fetal parts and determined the baby's age and the cause of death. In a daze, I walk over to the hospital and tell Russ and Barb as much as I know for sure without letting them know all I suspect. I tell them that more tissue may be expelled. I can't face my own suspicions.   13

Two days later, on Sunday morning, I receive a tearful call from Barb. She has just passed some recognizable body parts; what is she to do? She tells me that the bleeding has stopped and that she now feels better. The abortion I began on Friday is apparently over. I set up an appointment to meet with her and Russ to review the entire situation.   14

The pathologist's report confirms my worst fears: I aborted a living fetus. It was about eleven weeks old. I can find no one who can explain why Barb had four negative pregnancy tests. My meeting with Barb and Russ later in the week is one of the hardest things I have ever been through. I describe in some detail what I did and what my rationale had been. Nothing can obscure the hard reality: I killed their baby.   15

Politely, almost meekly, Russ asks whether the ultrasound examination would have shown that Barb was carrying a live baby. It almost seems that he is trying to protect my feelings, trying to absolve me of some of the responsibility. "Yes," I   16 answer, "if I had ordered the ultrasound, we would have known the baby was alive." I cannot explain why I didn't recommend it.

Mistakes are an inevitable part of everyone's life. They happen; they hurt — ourselves and others. They demonstrate our fallibility. Shown our mistakes and forgiven them, we can grow, perhaps in some small way become better people. Mistakes, understood this way, are a process, a way we connect with one another and with our deepest selves.   17

But mistakes seem different for doctors. This has to do with the very nature of our work. A mistake in the intensive care unit, in the emergency room, in the surgery suite, or at the sickbed is different from a mistake on the dock or at the typewriter. A doctor's miscalculation or oversight can prolong an illness, or cause a permanent disability, or kill a patient. Few other mistakes are more costly.   18

Developments in modern medicine have provided doctors with more knowledge of the human body, more accurate methods of diagnosis, more sophisticated technology to help in examining and monitoring the sick. All of that means more power to intervene in the disease process. But modern medicine — with its invasive tests and potentially lethal drugs — has also given doctors the power to do more harm.   19

Yet precisely because of its technological wonders and near-miraculous drugs, modern medicine has created for the physician an expectation of perfection. The technology seems so exact that error becomes almost unthinkable. We are not prepared for our mistakes and we don't know how to cope with them when they occur.   20

Doctors are not alone in harboring expectations of perfection. Patients expect doctors to be perfect, too. Perhaps patients have to consider their doctors less prone to error than other people: How else can a sick or injured person, already afraid, come to trust the doctor? Further, modern medicine has taken much of the treatment of illness out of the realm of common sense; a patient must trust a physician to make decisions that he, the patient, only vaguely understands. But the degree of perfection expected by patients is no doubt also a result of what we doctors have come to believe about ourselves, or, better, have tried to convince ourselves about ourselves.   21

This perfection is a grand illusion, of course, a game of   22 mirrors that everyone plays. Doctors hide their mistakes from patients, from other doctors, even from themselves. Open discussion of mistakes is banished from the consultation room, from the operating room, from physicians' meetings. Mistakes become gossip, and are spoken of openly only in court.

Unable to admit our mistakes, we physicians are cut off from healing. We cannot ask for forgiveness, and we get none. We are thwarted, stunted; we do not grow.   23

During the days, and weeks, and months after I aborted Barb's baby, my guilt and anger grew. I did discuss what had happened with my partners, with the pathologist, with obstetric specialists. Some of my mistakes were obvious: I had relied too heavily on one test; I had not been skillful in determining the size of the uterus by pelvic examination; I should have ordered the ultrasound before proceeding to the D & C. There was no way I could justify what I had done. To make matters worse, there were complications following the D & C, and Barb was unable to become pregnant again for two years.   24

Although I was as honest with the Dailys as I could be, and although I told them everything they wanted to know, I never shared with them my own agony. I felt they had enough sorrow without having to bear my burden as well. I decided it was my responsibility to deal with my guilt alone. I never asked for their forgiveness.   25

When I began at the age of thirty to practice medicine, I was certainly not prepared for the reality of my mistakes or my emotional responses to them. Like many other physicians, I had entered medical school out of a deep desire to serve people and to relieve suffering. I chose to practice in a remote rural area because it desperately needed physicians, because it seemed to offer the opportunity to establish a practice with the kind of personal care I wanted to provide, and because it seemed to be a good place for me and my family to live.   26

Along with three other doctors also committed to personal medical care, I practiced for seven years in that small Minnesota town. Marja and I raised our family, entered into the life of our community, and tried to live out our dreams. Finally, however, I could no longer tolerate the stresses, and I chose to leave. Dealing with my mistakes was among the stresses.   27

Doctors' mistakes come in a variety of packages and stem   28 from a variety of causes. For primary-care practitioners, who see every kind of problem, from cold sores to cancer, the mistakes are often simply a result of not knowing enough. One evening during my years in Minnesota a local boy was brought into the emergency room after a drunken driver had knocked him off his bicycle. I examined him right away. Aside from swelling and bruising of the left leg and foot, he seemed fine. An X-ray showed what appeared to be a dislocation of the foot from the ankle. I consulted by telephone with an orthopedic specialist in Duluth, and we decided that I could operate on the boy. As was my usual practice, I offered the patient and his mother a choice: I could do the operation or they could travel to Duluth to see the specialist. My pride was hurt when she decided to take her son to Duluth.

My feelings changed considerably when the specialist called 29 the next morning to thank me for the referral. He reported that the boy had actually suffered an unusual muscle injury, a posterior compartment syndrome, which had twisted his foot and caused it to appear to be dislocated. I had never even heard of such a syndrome, much less seen or treated it. The boy had required immediate surgery to save the muscles of his lower leg. Had his mother not decided to take him to Duluth, he would have been permanently disabled.

Sometimes a lack of technical skill leads to a mistake. After I 30 had been in town a few years, the doctor who had done most of the surgery at the clinic left to teach at a medical school. Since the clinic was more than a hundred miles from the nearest surgical center, my partners and I decided that I should get some additional training in order to be able to perform emergency surgery. One of my first cases was a young man with appendicitis. The surgery proceeded smoothly enough, but the patient did not recover as quickly as he should have, and his hemoglobin level (a measure of the amount of blood in the system) dropped slowly. I referred him to a surgeon in Duluth, who, during a second operation, found a significant amount of old blood in his abdomen. Apparently I had left a small blood vessel leaking into the abdominal cavity. Perhaps I hadn't noticed the oozing blood during surgery; perhaps it had begun to leak only after I had finished. Although the young man was never in serious danger, although the blood vessel would probably have sealed itself without the second surgery, my mistake had caused considerable discomfort and added expense.

Often, I am sure, mistakes are a result of simple carelessness.   31
There was the young girl I treated for what I thought was a minor
ankle injury. After looking at her X-rays, I sent her home with
what I diagnosed as a sprain. A radiologist did a routine follow-
up review of the X-rays and sent me a report. I failed to read it
carefully and did not notice that her ankle had been broken. I
learned about my mistake five years later when I was summoned
to a court hearing. The fracture I had missed had not healed
properly, and the patient had required extensive treatment and
difficult surgery. By that time I couldn't even remember her
original visit and had to piece together what had happened from
my records.

Some mistakes are purely technical; most involve a failure of   32
judgment. Perhaps the worst kind involve what another physician
has described to me as a "failure of will." She was referring to
those situations in which a doctor knows the right thing to do but
doesn't do it because he is distracted, or pressured, or exhausted.

Several years ago I was rushing down the hall of the hospital   33
to the delivery room. A young woman stopped me. Her mother
had been having chest pains all night. Should she be brought to
the emergency room? I knew the mother well, had examined her
the previous week, and knew of her recurring bouts of chest pains.
She suffered from angina; I presumed she was having another
attack.

Some part of me knew that anyone with all-night chest pains   34
should be seen right away. But I was under pressure. The delivery
would make me an hour late to the office, and I was frayed from a
weekend on call, spent mostly in the emergency room. This new
demand would mean additional pressure. "No," I said, "take her
over to the office, and I'll see her as soon as I'm done here."
About twenty minutes later, as I was finishing the delivery, the
clinic nurse rushed into the room. Her face was pale. "Come
quick!" she told me. "Mrs. Helgeson just collapsed." I sprinted
the hundred yards to the office, where I found Mrs. Helgeson in
cardiac arrest. Like many doctors' offices at the time, ours did not
have the advanced life-support equipment that helps keep patients alive long enough to get them to a hospital. Despite everything we did, Mrs. Helgeson died.

Would she have survived if I had agreed to see her in the   35
emergency room, where the requisite staff and equipment were
available? No one will ever know for sure. But I have to live with

the possibility that she might not have died if I had not had a "failure of will." There was no way to rationalize: I had been irresponsible, and a patient had died.

Many situations do not lend themselves to a simple determi-   36
nation of whether a mistake has been made. Seriously ill, hospital-ized patients, for instance, require of doctors almost continuous decision-making. Although in most cases no single mistake is obvious, there always seem to be things that could have been done differently or better: administering more of this medication, starting that treatment a little sooner . . . The fact is that when a patient dies, the physician is left wondering whether the care he provided was adequate. There is no way to be certain, for it is impossible to determine what would have happened if things had been done differently. In the end, the physician has to suppress the guilt and move on to the next patient.

Maiya Martinen first came to see me halfway through her   37
pregnancy. I did not know her or her husband well, but I knew that they were solid, hard-working people. This was to be their first child. When I examined Maiya, it seemed to me that the fetus was unusually small, and I was uncertain about her due date. I sent her to Duluth for an ultrasound examination and an evalua-tion by an obstetrician. The obstetrician thought the baby would be small, but he thought it could be safely delivered in the local hospital.

Maiya's labor was quite uneventful, except it took her longer   38
than usual to push the baby through to delivery. Her baby boy was born blue and floppy, but he responded well to routine newborn resuscitation measures. Fifteen minutes after birth, how-ever, he had a short seizure. We checked his blood-sugar level and found it to be low, a common cause of seizures in small babies who take longer than usual to emerge from the birth canal. We immediately administered intravenous glucose, and baby Marko seemed to improve. He and his mother were discharged from the hospital several days later.

It was about two months later, a few days after I had given   39
him his first set of immunizations, that Marko began having short spells. Not long after that he started to have full-blown seizures. Once again the Martinens made the trip to Duluth, and Marko was hospitalized for three days of tests. No cause for the seizures was found, and he was placed on medication. Marko continued

to have seizures, however. When he returned for his second set of immunizations, it was clear to me that he was not doing well.

The remainder of Marko's short life was a tribute to the faith and courage of his parents. He was severely retarded, and the seizures became harder and harder to control. Maiya eventually went east for a few months so Marko could be treated at the National Institutes of Health. But nothing seemed to help, and Maiya and her baby returned home. Marko had to be admitted frequently to the local hospital in order to control his seizures. At two o'clock one morning I was called to the hospital; the baby had had a respiratory arrest. Despite our efforts, Marko died, ending a year and a half struggle with life.

No cause for Marko's condition was ever determined. Did something happen during the birth that briefly cut off oxygen to his brain? Should Maiya have delivered at the high-risk obstetric center in Duluth, where sophisticated fetal monitoring is available? Should I have sent Marko to the neonatal intensive care unit in Duluth immediately after his first seizure in the delivery room? I subsequently learned that children who have seizures should not routinely be immunized. Would it have made any difference if I had never given Marko the shots? There were many such questions in my mind and, I am sure, in the minds of the Martinens. There was no way to know the answers, no way for me to handle the guilt I experienced, perhaps irrationally, whenever I saw Maiya.

The emotional consequences of mistakes are difficult enough to handle. But soon after I started practicing I realized I had to face another anxiety as well: It is not only in the emergency room, the operating room, the intensive care unit, or the delivery room that I can blunder into tragedy. Medicine is not an exact science; errors are always possible, even in the midst of the humdrum routine of daily care. Was that baby I just sent home with a diagnosis of mild viral fever actually in the early stage of serious meningitis? Will that nine-year-old with stomach cramps whose mother I just lectured about psychosomatic illness end up in the hospital tomorrow with a ruptured appendix? Did that Vietnamese refugee have a problem I didn't understand because of the language barrier? A doctor has to confront the possibility of a mistake with every patient visit.

My initial response to the mistakes I did make was to ques- 43
tion my competence. Perhaps I just didn't have the necessary
intelligence, judgment, and discipline to be a physician. But was I
really incompetent? My University of Minnesota Medical School
class had voted me one of the two "best clinicians." My diploma
from the National Board of Medical Examiners showed scores
well above average. I knew that the townspeople considered me a
good physician; I knew that my partners, with whom I worked
daily, and the consultants to whom I referred patients considered
me a good physician, too. When I looked at it objectively, my
competence was not the issue. I would have to learn to live with
my mistakes.

A physician is even less prepared to deal with his mistakes 44
than is the average person. Nothing in our training prepares us to
respond appropriately to the mistakes we will inevitably make.
Medical school is a competitive place, discouraging any sharing
of feelings. And resident doctors are typically so overburdened
with work that there is literally no time to reflect. An atmosphere
of precision pervades the teaching hospital; there is little opportunity to confront the emotional consequences of making mistakes.

Physicians in private practice are no more likely to find errors 45
openly acknowledged or discussed, even though they occur regularly. My own mistakes represent only some of those of which I
am aware. I know of one physician who administered a potent
drug in a dose ten times that recommended; his patient almost
died. Another doctor examined a child in an emergency room late
one night and told the parents the problem was only a mild viral
infection. Only because the parents did not believe the doctor,
only because they consulted another doctor the following morning, did the child survive a life-threatening infection. Still another
physician killed a patient while administering a routine test: a
needle slipped and lacerated a vital artery. Whether the physician
is a rural general practitioner with years of experience but only
basic training or a recently graduated, highly trained neurosurgeon working in a sophisticated technological environment, the
basic problem is the same.

Because doctors do not discuss their mistakes, I do not know 46
how other physicians come to terms with theirs. But I suspect
that many cannot bear to face their mistakes directly. We either
deny the misfortune altogether or blame the patient, the nurse,

the laboratory, other physicians, the System, Fate — anything to avoid our own guilt.

The medical profession seems to have no place for its mistakes. Indeed, one would almost think that mistakes were sins. If the medical profession has no room for doctors' mistakes, neither does society. The number of malpractice suits filed each year is symptomatic of this. In what other profession are practitioners regularly sued for hundreds of thousands of dollars because of misjudgments? I am sure the Dailys could have successfully sued me for a large amount of money had they chosen to do so.   47

The drastic consequences of our mistakes, the repeated opportunities to make them, the uncertainty about our culpability, and the professional denial that mistakes happen all work together to create an intolerable dilemma for the physician. We see the horror of our mistakes, yet we cannot deal with their enormous emotional impact.   48

Perhaps the only way to face our guilt is through confession, restitution, and absolution. Yet within the structure of modern medicine there is no place for such spiritual healing. Although the emotionally mature physician may be able to give the patient or family a full description of what happened, the technical details are often so difficult for the layperson to understand that the nature of the mistake is hidden. If an error is clearly described, it is frequently presented as "natural," "understandable," or "unavoidable" (which, indeed, it often is). But there is seldom a real confession: "This is the mistake I made; I'm sorry." How can one say that to a grieving parent? to a woman who has lost her mother?   49

If confession is difficult, what are we to say about restitution? The very nature of a physician's work means that there are things that cannot be restored in any meaningful way.   50

What can I do to make good the Dailys' loss? . . .   51

Questions for Close Reading

1. What is the thesis of the selection? Locate the sentence(s) in which Hilfiker states his main idea. If he does not state the thesis explicitly, express it in your own words.

2. What led Hilfiker to believe that Mrs. Daily was no longer pregnant? Why didn't he order an ultrasound test?
3. What does the author mean by a mistake caused by a "failure of will"? Why is this the worst kind of mistake?
4. What was Hilfiker's reaction to his own medical errors? How does the medical profession in general deal with the issue of diagnostic and treatment mistakes?
5. Refer to your dictionary as needed to define the following words in the selection: *alleviate* (paragraph 6), *rationale* (15), *thwarted* (23), *angina* (33), *rationalize* (35), *culpability* (48), and *absolution* (49).

Questions About the Writer's Craft

1. How does the author classify the typical mistakes of doctors? What is the principle of classification that he uses to establish these categories?
2. Why does Hilfiker begin with a narrative? What tone does it set for the rest of the essay? What image of the author does it create in your mind?
3. In addition to division and classification, what other modes of development does the author use?
4. Locate places where Hilfiker uses questions. What is the effect of these questions? Are they merely rhetorical, or are they questions with answers?

Questions for Further Thought

1. If you had been Mr. or Mrs. Daily, would you have sued Dr. Hilfiker for his mistake? Why or why not? Is legal action a solution to errors in medicine?
2. The author writes, ". . . mistakes seem different for doctors." Is this true? How should doctors deal with their mistakes?
3. Why does Hilfiker reveal so many of his own mistakes—and such serious ones? Might this essay serve a personal purpose for him, as well as act as a place for him to communicate his message about how all doctors make mistakes?
4. "Mistakes . . . are a process, a way we connect with one another and with our deepest selves." What do you think Hilfiker means by this statement? How do we in our everyday lives come to terms with mistakes we make?

Writing Assignments Using Division – Classification as a Method of Development

1. Hilfiker writes, "Mistakes are an inevitable part of everyone's life." Using Hilfiker's statement as your point of departure, write a paper that classifies three or four typical kinds of mistakes all of us tend to make. So that you prepare an essay unified by a common theme, make sure your categories are based on the same principle of classification. You might, for instance, use as a principle of classification the kinds of errors you think many parents make relating to their teenage children: they are overly critical; they are suspicious; they are insensitive. Your essay may be serious or light. In either case, the paper should indicate clearly your attitude toward the mistakes described.

2. Classify the types of stress experienced by people in a particular occupation. This occupation may be one you know about through friends, relatives, your reading, or your own experience. For example, an essay on waiting on tables might discuss the stresses of close supervision, physical exertion, and customers' demands. Develop your essay by providing examples of the kinds of incidents that cause these stresses. End the essay with some recommendations about ways to ease the stresses you have identified.

Writing Assignments Using Other Methods of Development

3. Physicians are high-status professionals in this country. In other countries, such as Russia, this is not so — there, physicians are more like technicians and are not highly paid. Write an essay arguing that the high status and pay of physicians in the United States is or is not a good thing for American health care.

4. Through interviews and/or library research, find out what kind of training medical students receive in this country. Then write an essay explaining the process involved in becoming a doctor. The concluding section of your paper should evaluate this process and explain why it is or is not adequate for producing competent, ethical, and responsible physicians.

Ann McClintock

Ann McClintock (1946–   ) was educated at Temple University in Philadelphia and later earned an advanced degree from the University of Pennsylvania. Currently Director of Occupational Therapy at Ancora State Hospital in New Jersey, she has also worked as a freelance editor and writer. A frequent speaker before community groups, McClintock is especially interested in the effects of advertising on American life. This essay is part of a work in progress on the way propaganda techniques are used to sell products and political candidates.

Propaganda Techniques in Today's Advertising

Propaganda is not just the tool of totalitarian governments and dictators. Rather, propaganda is all around us—in the form of commercials and advertisements. The author of this selection shows how Madison Avenue uses many of the techniques typical of political propaganda to convince us that we need certain products and services. After reading the essay, you may regard in a different light the jingles, endorsements, and slogans characteristic of today's commercials.

Americans, adults and children alike, are being seduced. 1
They are being brainwashed. And no one protests. Why? Because the seducers and the brainwashers are the advertisers we willingly invite into our homes. We are victims, content—even eager—to be victimized. We read advertisers' propaganda messages in newspapers and magazines; we watch their alluring images for hours at a time on television. We absorb their messages and images into our subconscious. We all do it—even those who claim to see through advertisers' tricks and therefore feel immune to advertising's charm. Advertisers lean heavily on propaganda to sell their products, whether the "products" are a brand of toothpaste, a candidate for office, or a particular political viewpoint.

502

Propaganda is a systematic effort to influence people's opin-   2
ions, to win them over to a certain view or side. Propaganda is
not necessarily concerned with what is true or false, good or bad.
Propagandists simply want people to believe the messages being
sent. Often, propagandists will use outright lies or more subtle
techniques to sway people's opinions. In a propaganda war, any
tactic is considered fair.

When we hear the word "propaganda," we usually think of it   3
as some kind of foreign menace: anti-American radio programs
broadcast by the Soviets or brainwashing tactics practiced on
helpless G. I. prisoners-of-war. But the vast majority of us are,
right this minute, targets in the advertisers' propaganda war.
Every day, we are bombarded with slogans, print ads, commercials, packaging claims, billboards, trademarks, logos, and designer brands — all forms of propaganda. One study claims that
each of us, during an average day, is exposed to over *five hundred*
advertising claims of various types. This intensive saturation may
even increase in the future, for current trends include showing
ads on movie screens, shopping carts, pay-cable TV services, even
public television.

What kind of propaganda techniques do advertisers use?   4
There are seven basic types:

1. *Name Calling*   Name calling is a propaganda tactic in   5
which negatively-charged names are hurled against the opposing
side or competitor. By using such names, propagandists try to
arouse feelings of hate, fear, and mistrust in their audiences. For
example, political advertisements may label opposing candidates
as "losers," "fence-sitters," and "back-room politicians"; or ads
may state that rival candidates are "inconsistent," "dishonest,"
"radical," or "warmongers." Depending on the advertiser's target market, labels such as "big government," "big business," or
"the old politics" can be the epithets that damage an opponent.
Ads for products may also use name calling. An American manufacturer may refer, for instance, to a "foreign car" in its
commercial — not an "imported" one. The label of foreignness
clearly has unpleasant connotations in many people's minds.
Unlike the childhood rhyme which states that "names can never
hurt me," name calling is an effective way to damage the opposi-

tion, whether it is another car maker or a Congressional candidate.

2. *Glittering Generalities*   Using glittering generalities is the 6 opposite of name calling; in this case, advertisers surround their products with attractive — and slippery — words and phrases. They use vague terms that are difficult to define and that may have different meanings to different people: "freedom," "democratic," "all-American," "progressive," "Christian," and "justice." As you can see, many of these words also have patriotic echoes. This kind of language stirs positive feelings in people, feelings that may spill over to the product or idea being pitched. As with name calling, the emotional response may overwhelm logic. Target audiences accept the product without thinking very much about what the glittering generalities mean — or whether they even apply to that product. After all, how can anyone oppose "truth, justice, and the American way"?

The ads for politicians and political issues often use glitter- 7 ing generalities because such "buzz words" can influence votes. For example, election slogans include high-sounding but basically empty phrases like the following:

> "He cares about people." (That's nice, but is he a better candidate than his opponent?)
> "Vote for progress." (What kind of progress? And is progress automatically good?)
> "Vote for the future." (What kind of future?)
> "If you love America, vote for Phyllis Smith." (If I don't vote for Smith, does that mean I don't love America?)
> "He'll make this country great again." (What does "great" mean? Does "great" mean the same thing to others as it does to me?)

Ads for consumer goods are also sprinkled with glittering 8 generalities. Product names, for instance, are supposed to evoke good feelings: Luvs diapers, New Freedom feminine hygiene products, Joy, Futura, Home Pride, Loving Care, Almost Home, Yankee Doodles. Product slogans lean heavily on vague but comforting phrases: Kinney is "The Great American Shoe Store," General Electric "brings good things to light," and for years, Westinghouse claimed that "progress" was their most important product. Old Grand-Dad bourbon portrays pastoral scenes labeled "The Spirit of America," and Chrysler calls the Dodge 600 "The American Dream: Built by Americans for Americans." Chevrolet used a jingle about "baseball, hot dogs, apple pie, and Chevrolet," probably the most obvious string of glittering generalities ever assembled to support a product. And it worked.

3. *Transfer* In transfer, advertisers try to improve the 9 image of a product by associating it with a symbol many people respect or admire, such as the cross, the American flag or Uncle Sam. In this way, the advertisers hope to carry over the same feelings of respect and prestige to the product. Many companies use transfer devices to identify their products: Lincoln Insurance shows a profile of the President; Continental Insurance portrays a Revolutionary War minuteman; Amtrak's logo is red, white, and blue; Liberty Mutual's corporate symbol is the Statue of Liberty; Allstate's name is cradled by a pair of protective, fatherly hands; IBM creates a friendly image by featuring a Charlie Chaplin double in its ads.

Corporations also use the transfer technique when they 10 sponsor prestigious shows on radio and television; these shows function as symbols of dignity and class. Kraft Corporation, for instance, sponsored a "Leonard Bernstein Conducts Beethoven" concert, while Gulf Oil is the sponsor of *National Geographic* specials and Mobil supports public television's *Masterpiece Theater.* In this way, corporations can reach an educated, influential audience and, perhaps, improve their public image by associating themselves with quality programming.

Political ads, of course, practically wrap themselves in the 11 flag. Ads for a political candidate often show either the Washington Monument, a Fourth of July parade, the Stars and Stripes, a bald eagle soaring over the mountains, or a little white-steepled church on the village green. The National Anthem or "America the Beautiful" may play softly on the soundtrack. Such appeals to Americans' patriotism and love of country can surround the candidate with an aura of respectability and integrity.

4. *Testimonial* The testimonial is one of the advertisers' 12 most-loved and most-used propaganda techniques. Similar to the transfer device, the testimonial uses the admiration people have

for a celebrity to make the product shine more brightly — even though the celebrity is not an expert on the product being sold.

Print and television ads offer a nonstop parade of testimonials: here's Cher for Holiday Spas; then Bruce Jenner touts orange juice; Cliff Robertson, Joan Rivers, and Burt Lancaster appear for various telephone services; Michael Jackson sings about Pepsi; American Express features a slew of well-known people with lesser-known faces who ask "Do you know me?" and then assure us that they never go anywhere without their American Express card. Testimonials can sell movies — read the movie reviewers' comments in the newspaper ads. They can sell books — see the blurbs by celebrities and critics on the backs of paperbacks. 13

Political candidates — as well as their ad agencies — know the value of testimonials. Carroll O'Connor endorses Senator Ted Kennedy, and Robert Redford lends his star appeal to Gary Hart's campaign. Even controversial social issues are debated by celebrities. The nuclear freeze, for instance, stars Paul Newman for the pro side and Charlton Heston for the con. 14

As illogical as testimonials sometimes are (Michael Jackson, for instance, is a Jehovah's Witness who does not drink Pepsi), they are effective propaganda. We like the *person* so much that we like the *product* too. 15

5. *Plain Folks*   The plain folks approach says, in effect, "Buy me or vote for me. I'm just like you." Regular folks will surely like Bob Evans' Down on the Farm Country Sausage or good old-fashioned Countrytime Lemonade. Some ads emphasize the idea that "we're all in this boat together." We see people making long-distance calls for just the reasons we do — to put the baby on the phone to Grandma or to tell Mom we love her. And how do these folksy, warmhearted (usually saccharine) scenes affect us? They're supposed to make us feel that A T & T — the multinational corporate giant — has the same values we do. Similarly, we are introduced to the little people at Ford, the ordinary folks who work on the assembly line, not to the bigwigs in their exclusive offices. What's the purpose of such an approach? That's easy. It's to encourage us to buy a car built by these honest, hardworking "everyday Joes" who care about quality as much as we do. 16

Political advertisements make almost as much use of the "just folks" appeal as they do of transfer devices. Candidates wear 17 hard hats, farmers' caps, jeans, lab smocks, butchers' aprons, and T-shirts; they jog around the block and carry their own luggage through the airport. The idea is to convince voters that the candidates are real people, not wealthy lawyers and executives (as they often are) who might otherwise appear too elitist or out of touch with the common man.

6. *Card Stacking* When people say that "the cards were stacked against me," they mean that they were never given a fair chance. Applied to propaganda, card stacking means that one side may suppress or distort evidence, tell half-truths, oversimplify the facts, or set up a "straw man"—a false target—to be attacked while the main issue is overlooked. Card stacking is a difficult form of propaganda both to detect and dispute. When a candidate claims that an opponent has "changed his mind five times on this important issue," we must do some research into—or already know about—the subject in order to be objective. Did the candidate, for instance, have good reasons for changing his mind? What is his side of the story? But many people do not investigate before making up their minds; instead, they are swayed by what may be one-sided or distorted evidence.   18

Advertisers often stack the cards in favor of the products they are pushing. They may, for instance, use what are called "weasel words." These are small words that usually slip right past us, but that make the difference between reality and illusion. The weasel words are underlined in the following claims: 19

> "<u>Helps</u> <u>control</u> dandruff symptoms." (The audience usually interprets this as <u>stops</u> dandruff.)
>
> "Most dentists <u>surveyed</u> recommend sugarless gum for their patients <u>who</u> <u>chew</u> <u>gum</u>." (We hear the "most dentists" and "for their patients," but we don't think about how many were surveyed or whether or not the dentists first recommended that the patients not chew gum at all.)
>
> "Sticker price $1000 lower than <u>most</u> <u>comparable</u> cars." (How many is "most"? What cars does the advertiser consider "comparable"?)

Advertisers also use a card stacking trick when they make an unfinished claim. For example, they will say that their product has "twice as much pain reliever." We are left with a favorable   20 impression; we don't usually ask, "Twice as much pain reliever as what?" Or advertisers may make extremely vague claims that sound alluring on the surface, but that have no substance: Toyota's "Oh, what a feeling!"; Vantage cigarettes' "the taste of success"; "the spirit of Marlboro"; "the real thing"; "the right stuff," for example. Another way to stack the cards in favor of a certain product is to use scientific-sounding claims that are not supported by sound research. Ford, for example, claimed that the LTD model was "400% quieter." Consumers believed that the car was quieter than all other cars but, when taken to court, Ford admitted they meant that it was 400% quieter inside the car than outside. Other scientific-sounding claims use mysterious ingredients that are never explained as selling points: "Retsyn," "special whitening ingredients," "the ingredient doctors recommend," "cleaning agents."

7. *Bandwagon*   In the bandwagon technique, advertisers urge, "Everyone's doing it. Why don't you?" This kind of propaganda often succeeds because people have a deep desire not to be different. Political ads tell us to vote for the "winning candidate"; the advertisers know we want to do what the majority is doing; we want to be on the winning team. Or ads show a series of people proclaiming, "I'm voting for the Senator. I don't know why anyone wouldn't." Again, the audience feels under pressure to conform to what everyone else is doing.   21

In the marketplace, the bandwagon approach lures buyers. Ads tell us that "nobody doesn't like Sara Lee" (the message is that you must be weird if you don't). They tell us that "most people prefer Brand X two to one over other leading brands" (to be like the majority, we should buy Brand X). If we don't drink Pepsi, we're left out of "the Pepsi generation." We are told to "join the switch to Burger King." We are even treated to a tour around the country intended to prove that most American women wear Underalls: "Come on, America! Show us your Underalls!" In other words, join the crowd and wear Underalls. Honda motorcycle ads sing to us of the virtues of being a follower and tell us to hop on the bandwagon: "Follow the leader. He's on a Honda."   22

Why do these propaganda techniques work? Why do we buy   23

the products, viewpoints, and candidates urged on us by propaganda messages? They work, first of all, because some of them appeal to prejudices and biases we already have. For example, if we are convinced that environmentalists are radicals who want to destroy America's record of growth and progress, then we will agree with the candidate who uses a name-calling approach — "treehugger" — against an opponent. The main reason propaganda techniques work, however, is that they appeal to our emotions, not to our minds. Clear thinking requires hard work: analyzing a claim, researching the facts, examining both sides of an issue, using logic to see the flaws in an argument. Many of us would rather let the propagandists do our thinking for us. We are content to sit back and let our emotions be manipulated by others.

Because propaganda is so effective, it is important to track it down and understand how it is used. We may eventually agree with what the propagandist says because all propaganda isn't necessarily bad; some advertising, for instance, urges us not to drive drunk, to have regular dental checkups, to contribute to the United Way. Even so, we must be aware that propaganda is being used. Otherwise, we will have consented to handing over our independence, our decision-making ability, and our brains.   24

Questions for Close Reading

1. What is the thesis of the selection? Locate the sentence(s) in which McClintock states her main idea. If she does not state the thesis explicitly, express it in your own words.
2. What is propaganda? What mistaken associations do people often have with this term?
3. What are "weasel words"? How do they trick listeners?
4. Why does McClintock believe we should be better informed about propaganda techniques?
5. Refer to your dictionary as needed to define the following words in the selection: *seduced* (paragraph 1), *warmongers* (5), and *elitist* (17).

Questions About the Writer's Craft

1. Before explaining the categories into which propaganda techniques can be grouped, McClintock provides a definition of propaganda. Is

the definition purely informative, or does it have a larger objective? If you think the latter, what is the definition's broader purpose?

2. In her introduction, McClintock uses loaded words like *seduced* and *brainwashed*. What effect do these words have on the reader?
3. Locate places where McClintock uses questions. Which ones are rhetorical, and which ones are real questions?
4. What kind of conclusion does McClintock provide for the essay?

Questions for Further Thought

1. Do you agree with McClintock that we are subjected to commercial propaganda every day? Is *propaganda* the right term to use for today's advertising techniques?
2. Which of these advertising techniques are easiest to identify in an ad? Which are the least obvious? Can you recall examples of ads that make use of these techniques?
3. Do you suspect that advertising really influences you? Or do you think that you are relatively immune to it? What factors influence your decision to purchase a particular brand or product?
4. Since propaganda is so effective, is it ethical for advertisers and politicians to use it? Is awareness enough to protect us from the effects of such propaganda — or do we need stronger protection? What other means could we use to protect ourselves?

Writing Assignments Using Division – Classification as a Method of Development

1. McClintock cautions us to be sensitive to propaganda in advertising, but of course young children aren't capable of this kind of awareness. Watch some commercials aimed at children, such as those for toys, cereals, and fast food. Take notes, and then analyze the use of propaganda techniques in these commercials. Using division– classification, write an essay describing the main propaganda techniques you observe. Support your analysis with examples and illustrations drawn from the commercials studied. Remember to provide a thesis that signals your opinion of the advertising techniques.
2. Develop an essay around the point that popular TV shows can be categorized into three types. Avoid the obvious system of classifying according to game shows, sitcoms, detective shows, and so on. Instead, categorize the shows according to your own original principle of classification. For example, you could classify shows according to any one of the following: how family life is depicted; the way the world of work is presented; how male and female relationships are portrayed. Refer to specific shows to support your classification

system, and be sure to make clear your attitude toward the shows being discussed.

Writing Assignments Using Other Methods of Development

*3. McClintock says that card stacking "distort[s] evidence, tell[s] half truths, oversimplif[ies] the facts." Focusing on either an editorial, a political campaign, a print ad, or a television commercial, analyze the extent to which card stacking is used as a persuasive strategy. Paul Fussell's "A Well Regulated Militia" (page 187) and H. L. Mencken's "The Politician" (page 437) may provide some insight into the way card stacking hides the truth.

4. To increase your sensitivity to the moral dimensions of propaganda, write a proposal describing an ad campaign for a real or imaginary product or politician. The introduction to your proposal should identify the product being promoted, and the thesis or plan of development should indicate the specific propaganda techniques you propose. Use the paper's supporting paragraphs to explain how these techniques will be utilized to promote your product or candidate.

Janet Mendell Goldstein

Born in Philadelphia in 1940, Janet Mendell Goldstein did her undergraduate work at Radcliffe College and earned advanced degrees at Harvard University and the University of Pennsylvania. She divides her time between teaching English at Friends Select School in Philadelphia and working as an editorial consultant, freelance writer, and textbook author. Co-author of a recently published college reading text, Goldstein is also an essayist and poet. Her work has appeared in a variety of newspapers and magazines, including the *English Journal, Faith and Inspiration,* and the *Philadelphia Inquirer.* The selection below is drawn from a series of pieces Goldstein has written about contemporary life.

The Quick Fix Society

Not so long ago, we were told that if we worked hard and never gave up, we would eventually get what we wanted. These days, however, "eventually" isn't good enough for many people. Janet Mendell Goldstein urges us to consider where we are going in such a rush. And what, she asks, are we missing along the way?

My husband and I just got back from a week's vacation in 1
West Virginia. Of course, we couldn't wait to get there, so we took the Pennsylvania Turnpike and a couple of interstates. "Look at those gorgeous farms!" my husband exclaimed as pastoral scenery slid by us at 55 mph. "Did you see those cows?" But at 55 mph, it's difficult to see anything; the gorgeous farms look like moving green checkerboards, and the herd of cows is reduced to a sprinkling of dots in the rear-view mirror. For four hours, our only real amusement consisted of counting exit signs and wondering what it would feel like to hold still again. Getting there certainly didn't seem like half the fun; in fact, getting there wasn't any fun at all.

So, when it was time to return to our home outside of 2
Philadelphia, I insisted that we take a different route. "Let's
explore that countryside," I suggested. The two days it took us to
make the return trip were studded with new experiences. We
toured a Civil War battlefield and stood on the little hill that
fifteen thousand Confederate soldiers had tried to take on another hot July afternoon, one hundred and twenty-five years ago,
not knowing that half of them would perish in the vain attempt.
We meandered through main streets of sleepy Pennsylvania
Dutch towns, slowing to twenty miles an hour so as not to crowd
the horses and buggies on their way to market. We admired toy
trains and antique cars in county museums and saved 70% in
factory outlets. We stuffed ourselves with spicy salads and homemade bread pudding in an "all-you-can-eat" farmhouse restaurant, then wandered outside to enjoy the sunshine and the herds
of cows — no little dots this time — basking in it. And we returned home refreshed, reeducated, revitalized. This time, getting
there had *been* the fun.

Why is it that the featureless turnpikes and interstates are the 3
routes of choice for so many of us? Why doesn't everybody try
slowing down and exploring the countryside? But more and
more, the fast lane seems to be the only way for us to go. In fact,
most Americans are constantly in a hurry — and not just to get
from Point A to Point B. Our country has become a nation in
search of the quick fix — in more ways than one.

Now instead of later: Once upon a time, Americans under- 4
stood the principle of deferred gratification. We put a little of
each paycheck away "for a rainy day." If we wanted a new sofa or
a week at a lakeside cabin, we saved up for it, and the banks
helped us out by providing special Christmas Club and Vacation
Club accounts. If we lived in the right part of the country, we
planted corn and beans and waited patiently for the harvest. If we
wanted to be thinner, we simply ate less of our favorite foods and
waited patiently for the scale to drop, a pound at a time. But
today we aren't so patient. We take out loans instead of making
deposits, or we use our VISA or Mastercard to get that furniture
or vacation trip — relax now, pay later. We buy our food, like our
clothing, ready-made and off the rack. And if we're in a hurry to
lose weight, we try the latest miracle diet, guaranteed to shed ten

pounds in ten days . . . unless we're rich enough to afford liposuction.

Faster instead of slower: Not only do we want it now; we don't even want to be kept waiting for it. This pervasive impatience, the "I-hate-to-wait" syndrome, has infected every level of our lives. Instead of standing in line at the bank, we withdraw twenty dollars in as many seconds from an automatic teller machine. Then we take our fast money to a fast convenience store (why wait in line at the supermarket?), where we buy a frozen dinner all wrapped up and ready to be popped into the microwave . . . unless we don't care to wait even that long and pick up some fast food instead. And if our fast meal doesn't agree with us, we hurry to the medicine cabinet for — you guessed it — some fast relief. We like fast pictures, so we buy Polaroid cameras. We like fast entertainment, so we record our favorite TV show on the VCR so we can "zap" each commercial, and stop watching if nothing exciting happens in the opening thirty seconds. We like our information fast, too: messages flashed on a computer screen, documents FAXed from your telephone to mine, current events in 90-second bursts on *Eyewitness News,* history reduced to "Bicentennial Minutes." Symbolically, the American eagle now flies for Express Mail. How dare anyone keep America waiting longer than overnight?

Superficially instead of thoroughly: What's more, we don't even want *all* of it. Once, we lingered over every word of a classic novel or the latest best-seller. Today, since faster is better, we read the condensed version or pop an audio cassette of the book into our car's tape player to listen to on the way to work. Or we buy the *Cliff's Notes,* especially if we are students, so we don't have to deal with the book at all. Once, we listened to every note of Beethoven's Fifth Symphony. Today, we don't have the time; instead, we can enjoy 26 seconds of that famous "da-da-da-DUM" theme — and 99 other musical excerpts almost as famous —on our "Greatest Moments of the Classics" record. After all, why waste 45 minutes listening to the whole thing when someone else has saved us the trouble of picking out the best parts? Our magazine articles come to us pre-digested in *Reader's Digest.* Our news briefings, thanks to *USA Today,* are more brief than ever. Even our personal relationships have become compressed. Instead of devoting large segments of our days to our loved ones —

5

.

6

after all, we *are* busy people—we substitute something called "quality time," which, more often than not, is no time at all. As we rush from book to music to news item to relationship, we do not realize that we are living our lives by the iceberg principle—paying attention only to the top and ignoring the ⅞ that lies just below the surface.

When did it all begin, this urge to do it now, to get it over 7
with, to skim the surface of life? Why are we in such a hurry to save time? And what, pray tell, are we going to do with all the time we save—besides, of course, rushing out to save some more? The sad truth is that we don't know how to use the time we save, because all we're good at is *saving* time . . . not *spending* time.

Don't get me wrong. I'm not saying we should go back to 8
growing our own vegetables or knitting our own sweaters or putting our paychecks into piggy banks. I'm not even advocating a mass movement to cut all our credit cards into little pieces. But I am saying that all of us need to think more seriously about putting the brakes on our "we-want-it-all-and-we-want-it-now" lifestyle before we speed completely out of control. Let's take the time to read every word of that story, hear every note of that music, savor every nuance of that countryside—or that other person. Let's rediscover life in the slow lane.

Questions for Close Reading

1. What is the thesis of the selection? Locate the sentence(s) in which Goldstein states her main idea. If she does not state the thesis explicitly, express it in your own words.
2. Goldstein and her husband enjoy looking at toy trains and antique cars, eating homemade pudding, and watching cows basking in sunshine. What do all of these pleasures have in common?
3. What evidence does Goldstein give to support her contention that in the past Americans were willing to defer gratification?
4. In paragraph 6, Goldstein describes "the iceberg principle." What does she mean by this term? How, in Goldstein's view, does this principle apply to the way many people live their lives?
5. Refer to your dictionary as needed to define the following words used in the selection: *pastoral* (paragraph 1), *meander* (2), *bask* (2), *revitalize* (2), *pervasive* (5), *syndrome* (5), and *nuance* (8).

Questions About the Writer's Craft

1. The body of Goldstein's selection is divided into three ways Americans seek a quick fix. Are the three subdivisions of the "quick fix" syndrome mutually exclusive?

2. In addition to division–classification, Goldstein uses comparison–contrast to develop her essay. What are some contrasting images in the first and second paragraphs? Where else in the essay do you find similar juxtapositions? What purpose do these contrasts serve?

3. Goldstein often uses *rhetorical questions* — questions she does not expect her readers to answer — as when she asks "why wait in line at the supermarket?" (paragraph 5). Where else does she use rhetorical questions? What purposes do such questions serve?

4. Goldstein uses a number of contemporary expressions, abbreviations, and quoted clichés. What is the effect, for example, of "FAXed"? Why does she put "zap" and "quality time" in quotation marks?

Questions for Further Thought

1. According to Goldstein, Americans suffer from the "I-hate-to-wait" syndrome. In which aspects of your life are you willing to defer gratification; in which do you require immediate satisfaction?

2. Goldstein repeats the word *fast* throughout paragraph 5, always with negative implications. Think, however, of some modern convenience (a microwave oven, a word processor, a vacuum cleaner) that speeds up mundane chores. Discuss ways this device has freed you to spend more time in personally meaningful ways.

3. Goldstein's outgoing trip was planned to minimize travel time. The return trip, however, seems to have been more a matter of following impulse and finding surprises. What spontaneous thing have you ever done that led to some discovery or special pleasure? When, on the other hand, have you gone on impulse and found the consequences to be disastrous?

4. Most Americans, Goldstein believes, don't know how to spend their time. If you were free of pressures and obligations, how would you spend your time? What would you do differently?

Writing Assignments Using Division–Classification as a Method of Development

*1. Goldstein urges readers to slow down and appreciate life more fully. Consider the different activities of your everyday life. Write an essay classifying the activities according to those you like to give time to and those you like to speed through. Reach some conclusions about what is and is not important to you. Anne Morrow Lindbergh's "Channelled Whelk" (page 200) will help you do some serious thinking about your priorities.

2. Goldstein laments the superficiality of many relationships. Consider those people with whom you spend time. Brainstorm and then categorize the characteristics these people do or do not have in common. Use your analysis to identify the qualities you value in others.

Writing Assignments Using Other Methods of Development

3. Goldstein seems to find the natural and rural more appealing than the technological. Taking the opposite point of view, write a descriptive piece conveying the beauty made possible by modern technology—an aerial view of a bayside city, the lit span of a suspension bridge, the graphics of your favorite computer program. Build your description around a dominant impression, selecting details that express your sense of wonder.

4. Although Goldstein writes that Americans like their clothing and food ready-made, many people take pleasure in a more leisurely approach to satisfying their basic needs. Think of something you enjoy cooking, building, or crafting. Or you might consider activities like planting a vegetable garden or going fishing. Write a how-to essay guiding the reader, step by step, in the process you select. Your essay should capture the contentment and pride you experience in the process.

Additional Writing Topics
DIVISION – CLASSIFICATION

General Assignments

Choose one of the following subjects and write an essay developed wholly or in part through division – classification. Start by determining the purpose of the essay. Do you want to inform, compare and contrast, or persuade? Apply a single, significant principle of division or classification to your subject. Do not switch the principle midway through your analysis. Also, be sure that the types or categories you create are as complete and mutually exclusive as possible.

Division

1. A shopping mall
2. A video and/or stereo system
3. A fruit such as a pineapple, an orange, or a banana
4. A tax dollar
5. A particular kind of team
6. A word-processing system
7. A human hand
8. A meal
9. A meeting
10. A favorite poem, story, or play
11. A favorite restaurant
12. A school library
13. A basement
14. A playground, gym, or other recreational area
15. A church service
16. A wedding or funeral
17. An eventful week in your life
18. A college campus
19. A TV show or movie
20. A homecoming or other special weekend

Classification

1. People in a waiting room
2. Holidays
3. Closets
4. Roommates
5. Salad bars
6. Divorces
7. Beds
8. Students in a class
9. Shoes
10. Summer movies
11. Teachers
12. Neighbors
13. College courses
14. Bosses
15. TV watchers
16. Mothers or fathers
17. Commercials
18. Vacations
19. Trash
20. Friends

Assignments with a Specific Audience and Purpose

1. You are a dorm counselor. During orientation week, you will be talking to students on your floor about "what to expect in college." As part of the talk, you plan to tell them about the different types of instructors they are likely to encounter. Write your talk, labeling each "kind" of instructor and describing the behaviors and/or attitudes of each.
2. You are a driving instructor. As part of the classroom work you do with neophyte drivers, you give a lecture on the types of drivers your students are likely to encounter on the road. Write your lecture, categorizing drivers according to a specific principle and showing the behaviors of each type.
3. You have been asked to write a booklet for "new recruits" — new workers on your job, new students in your college class, new members of the team, and so on. The title of the booklet is "How to Succeed Now That You're Here." In the booklet, identify at least three general qualities needed for success in this organization.
4. A seasoned camp counselor, you have been assigned to orient new counselors to their jobs. You prepare an informational sheet on the

kinds of emotional needs that children have. Decide exactly what those needs are and give examples of what the counselors should do to make the summer psychologically rewarding for the youngsters in their care.

5. You are the television critic for *People* magazine, reviewing the new fall shows. You are upset by the fact that the networks show little originality in the shows they televise. The problem is especially apparent in the comedies and crime-drama shows on the air. In order to show how stereotypical the programs are, you divide one of these two kinds of shows into subtypes, based on a specific principle — which could be "level of reality on the show," "appeal of the leading character(s)," or any other principle. Remember that your goal is to prove how poor *all* the current programs are.

6. You have been asked to write an editorial for the campus paper. You decide to do a semiserious piece on taking "mental health" days off from classes. Your essay is structured around three kinds of occasions when "playing hooky" is an absolute necessity for one's sanity.

ARGUMENTATION– PERSUASION

WHAT IS
ARGUMENTATION – PERSUASION?

"You can't possibly believe what you're saying."
"Look, I know what I'm talking about, and that's that."

When most of us hear the word *argument*, we think of a heated situation with one person pitted against another. We may even picture a verbal battle that deteriorates into hostile accusations or worse. All of us have been involved in arguments that were propelled more by stubbornness and irrational thinking than by reason and logic. When caught up in the heat of an argument — whether it is about which candidate to vote for or which baseball team will win the World Series — we often assume that our perspective is the only valid one. Or we may become so emotionally involved in a contest of wills that we end up forgetting the point we're trying to make and get sidetracked by unrelated and often personal issues. That's how unreasonable we can be.

Unlike person-to-person arguing, *argumentation* in writing emphasizes careful thought. Using reason and logic, the writer tries to convince readers of the soundness of a particular opinion or position on a controversial issue. If, while trying to convince, the writer uses emotional language and highly charged appeals to the readers' concerns, beliefs, and values, then the piece is called *persuasion*. In addition to encouraging the audience to accept a specific opinion, persuasion often attempts to convert agreement to action. Assume that you are writing an essay about the controversial use of animals in medical research. If your purpose is to document, coolly and objectively, the way animals are mistreated in medical experiments, you would prepare an argumentation essay. But if your purpose is to distress your instructor and the other students, perhaps even prod them to write letters to their congressional representatives urging stricter controls, you would write a persuasive essay. Similarly, your paper would have a persuasive intent if you described steps that medical facilities should take to eliminate abuses in animal laboratories.

Because people respond rationally *and* emotionally to situations, argumentation *and* persuasion are usually combined. Suppose you decide to write an article for the campus newspaper advocating a pre – Labor Day start for the school year. You know that your readers will include the college administration, students, and faculty. The article might begin by *arguing* that several schools have discovered that beginning the academic year earlier allows them to close for the month of January, thus reducing heating and other maintenance expenses. Such an argument, supported by documented facts and figures, would help convince the administration. Realizing that you also have to gain student and faculty support for your idea, you decide to add a second point: The proposed change means that students and faculty could leave for winter break with the semester behind them — papers written, exams taken, grades calculated and recorded. To make this part of your argument especially compelling, you might adopt a *persuasive* strategy, using emotional appeals and positively charged language to dramatize the pleasures gained by faculty and students under your plan: "Think how pleasant it would be to relax, visit friends, and toast the New Year — without having to worry about work awaiting you back on campus."

When argumentation and persuasion blend, as in the example above, emotion *supports* logic and sound reasoning. But sometimes writers and speakers resort to emotional appeals to the *exclusion of* rational thought. In your writing, you want to use emotion to *reinforce* rather than *replace* reason. In this chapter, the term *argumentation – persuasion* refers to writing that advances a position through a balanced appeal to reason and emotion.

WHEN TO USE ARGUMENTATION – PERSUASION

At this point, you might be thinking that much of the writing you do involves argumentation – persuasion. Indeed it does. When you prepare a *causal analysis*, *descriptive piece*, *narrative*, or *definition essay*, you advance a specific point of view: Rock videos have a negative influence on young teens' view of sex; Cape Cod in winter is imbued with a special kind of magic; a disillusioning experience can teach people much about themselves; character can be defined as the willingness to take unpopular.positions on difficult issues. In fact, an essay organized around any of the patterns described in this book may have a persuasive intent. You may, for example, encourage readers to try out for themselves a *process* you have explained, or you could urge them to see one or two movies you have *compared*.

An argumentation – persuasion essay, however, does more than present a point of view and provide supporting evidence. Unlike other forms of writing, argumentation – persuasion assumes controversy and recognizes that opposing viewpoints are a certainty. Consider the following assignments. Since all of them require the writer to take a position on a debatable issue, argumentation – persuasion would be appropriate.

> In various parts of the country, communities established for older citizens or childless couples have refused to rent to families with children. How do you feel about this situation? What do you think are the rights of the parties involved?

Citing the fact that the highest percentage of automobile accidents involve young men, insurance companies consistently charge young males their highest rates. Is this fair? Why or why not?

For years, debate raged over the registration of young men for the draft. Now there is a controversy regarding the registration of women to serve in the armed services. Should women as well as men be compelled to register for the draft?

It is impossible to predict with 100 percent certainty what will make readers accept the view you advance or take the action you propose. But the ancient Greeks, who formulated our basic concepts of logic, isolated three factors that help determine the effectiveness of argumentation – persuasion messages. The key factors they discussed were *logos*, *pathos*, and *ethos*.

Your main concern in an argumentation – persuasion essay should be with the *logos*, or the soundness, of your argument: the facts, statistics, examples, and authoritative statements you marshal to support your viewpoint. This supporting evidence must be unified, specific, sufficient, accurate, and representative. (See pages 31 – 34.) Imagine that you want to write a piece convincing people that a popular charity misappropriates the money it receives from the public. Your readers, inclined to believe in the good works of the charity, are likely to dismiss your argument unless you can substantiate your claim with valid, well-documented evidence. Later in this chapter we offer suggestions for selecting evidence and structuring an essay to enhance its logic. The important point here is that clear thinking, or *logos*, is at the heart of effective argumentation – persuasion.

Sensitivity to the *pathos*, or emotional power, of the written word is another key consideration for writers of argumentation– persuasion essays. *Pathos* appeals to readers' needs, values, and attitudes, encouraging them to commit to a viewpoint or course of action.

The *pathos* of a piece derives partly from the language the writer uses. *Connotative* language — words with strong emotional overtones — can move readers to accept a point of view and may even spur them to action. Propaganda is perhaps the most dramatic example of the way *pathos* can be used to influence and even manipulate people. And every day we see the way *pathos* is used in advertisements, another kind of persuasive writing that relies heavily on connotative language. Compare these pitches for a man's cologne and a woman's perfume; the language — and the attitudes to which the language appeals — are different in each case:

> Brawn: Experience the power. Bold. Yet subtle. Clean, masculine. The scent for the man who's in charge.

> Black Lace is for you — the woman who dresses for success but who dares to be provocative, slightly naughty. Black Lace. Perfect with pearls by day and with diamonds by night.

The appeal to men plays on the impact that words like *Brawn*, *bold*, *power*, and *in charge* have for some males. Similarly, the charged words *Black Lace*, *provocative*, *naughty*, and *diamonds* are intended to appeal to businesswomen who — in the advertiser's mind, at least — are looking for ways to reconcile sensuality and professionalism.

When writing an argumentation – persuasion essay, you must — like a copywriter — pay careful attention to the emotional content of words. Your language must reinforce your viewpoint. In a paper urging support of an expanded immigration policy, you might use charged phrases like "land of liberty," "a nation of immigrants," "America's open-door policy," and "hard-working freedom seekers." On the other hand, if you were arguing for strict immigration quotas, you might use language like "save jobs for unemployed Americans," "flood of unskilled labor," and "illegal aliens." Remember, though, such emotionally charged language should support, not supplant, clear thinking.

Finally, whenever you write an argumentation – persuasion essay, you should establish your *ethos*, that is, your credibility and reliability. If readers are going to accept and even act on your point of view, you have to convince them you know what you are talking about and that you are worth listening to. You will seem knowledgeable and trustworthy if you present a logical, reasoned argument that takes opposing views into account. You should also be careful that your appeals to emotion are not excessive. Overwrought emotionalism undercuts credibility.

It's important to keep in mind that *ethos* is not constant. Because *ethos* is closely linked with subject matter, you may have credibility on one subject but not on another. An army general might be a reliable source for information on military preparedness but not for information on federal funding of day care.

Writing an effective argumentation – persuasion essay involves an interplay among *logos*, *pathos*, and *ethos*. The exact balance between these factors is determined by your purpose — whether you want the audience simply to agree with you or whether you want them to take action — and by the way you expect the audience to react to you, your topic, and your viewpoint.

In general, readers will fall into one of three broad categories. They will be supportive, wavering, or hostile.

1. A supportive audience. You may be fortunate: Your audience may agree with your position and trust your credibility. In this situation, a highly reasoned argument dense with facts, examples, and statistics is not needed. Rather, you may rely primarily on *pathos*, on a strong emotional appeal, to reinforce readers' commitment to your common viewpoint. Assume that you belong to the National Rifle Association (NRA) and have volunteered to write an article encouraging members to support efforts to preserve hunting rights in state parks. Your essay might briefly review why hunting in state parks is beneficial: By eliminating the weakest animals, hunting actually strengthens the wildlife population. Since your audience would certainly be familiar with this concept, you would not devote much time to it. Instead, you would attempt to move them emotionally. You might evoke the camaraderie among hunters, the exhilarating confrontation between humans and wildlife, the beauty of the outdoors, and conclude, "If you wish these pleasures to continue, please make a generous contribution to our fund."

2. A wavering audience. At times readers may be interested in what you have to say but may not have committed themselves fully to your view. Or perhaps they are not as informed about the subject as they should be. In either case, because the audience needs to be encouraged to give their complete support, you should concentrate on *ethos* and *logos*, bolstering your image as a reliable source and providing the evidence needed to advance your position. If you want to convince an audience of high school seniors to take a year off to work between high school and college, you might establish your credibility by recounting the year you spent working, being sure to show the positive effects it had on your life (*ethos*). In addition, you could cite two studies showing that delayed entry into college often leads to higher grade-point averages. This is so, you would explain, because the year's savings free students to study rather than worry about their ability to pay tuition (*logos*).

3. A hostile audience. It should come as no surprise that an apathetic, skeptical, or downright hostile audience is the most difficult to convince. With such readers, you should avoid emotional appeals, which might seem irrational, sentimental, or even comical. Instead, weight the essay heavily in favor of logical reasoning and hard-to-dispute facts (*logos*). Assume your college administration is working to ban liquor from the student pub. You plan to submit to the college newspaper an open letter in support of this unpopular effort. To sway readers, many of whom are students, you cite the positive experiences of schools that have gone dry and show how your college could reap the same benefits. Many colleges, you explain, have found their tavern revenues actually increase because all students — not just those of drinking age — can now support the pub. With the greater revenues, some schools have upgraded the food served in the pubs and hired disk jockeys or musical groups to provide entertainment. You could also point out that many schools have seen a sharp reduction in alcohol-related vandalism. By arguing soundly and giving your readers a hard dose of facts, you encourage them to reconsider their position. They may not be totally convinced, but they may modify or reshape their views when brought face to faace with your logical, well-supported argument.

SUGGESTIONS FOR USING ARGUMENTATION – PERSUASION IN AN ESSAY

1. At the beginning of the paper, identify the controversy being discussed and your position. Your assessment of the audience will determine how much background to supply in the introduction. Even if only minimal background information is needed, the introduction should clarify in a general way the controversy surrounding the issue.

The thesis of an argumentation – persuasion paper is often called the *assertion* or *proposition*. Occasionally the proposition will appear at the end of the paper, but usually it is stated at the beginning. If you present the thesis right away, your audience knows where you stand and is better able to evaluate the evidence for your position.

Remember, argumentation – persuasion assumes conflicting viewpoints. Be sure your proposition focuses on a controversial issue and signals your view. Avoid a proposition that is merely factual; a fact is demonstrably true and allows little room for debate. To see the difference between a factual statement and an effective thesis, examine the two statements below:

Fact: In the past few years, the nation's small farmers have suffered financial hardships.

Thesis: Because traditional methods for operating farms are costly and inefficient, small farmers should adopt the management techniques of modern agribusiness.

The first statement is inarguably true. It would be difficult to find anyone who believed that these are easy times for the farming community. Because the statement invites little opposition, it cannot serve as the focal point of an argumentation – persuasion essay. The second statement, though, takes a controversial stance on a complex issue. Such a proposition can be a valid starting point for a paper.

In addition to being obvious and factual, the first statement is also too general. Vague and excessively broad, it would not provide the boundaries needed to write a focused essay. Remember to keep the proposition narrow and specific. Having such clarity of purpose allows you to focus your thoughts in a purposeful way. Consider the following statements:

> *Broad thesis:* The welfare system has been abused over the years.

> *Narrow thesis:* No one except the handicapped and mothers of pre-school-age children should be eligible to receive welfare payments.

If you tried to write a paper based on the first statement, you would face an unmanageable task — showing all the ways that welfare has been abused. Your readers would also be confused about what to expect in the paper. Will you discuss unscrupulous bureaucrats, fraudulent bookkeeping, dishonest recipients? By way of contrast, the revised thesis is limited and specific. It signals that the paper will propose limiting welfare payments to two groups. Such a proposal will surely have its opponents and is thus an appropriate subject for an argumentation – persuasion essay.

The thesis in an argumentation – persuasion essay can simply state your opinion about the issue in question, or it can go a step further and call for some action.

> *Opinion:* The lack of affordable day care centers discriminates against lower-income families.

> *Call for action:* The federal government should help underwrite corporations' efforts to establish on-site day care centers.

In either case, your stand on the issue being discussed must be clear to your readers.

2. Generate strong support for the thesis. Finding convincing evidence is a crucial part of writing an argumentation – persuasion essay. Much support will be accumulated during the prewriting stage. As in any effective essay, your evidence must be unified, adequate, and specific. It might consist of personal experience or observation. Or it could be gathered from outside sources — statistics, facts, examples, expert authority taken from books, articles, reports, interviews, and documentaries. A paper arguing that elderly Americans are better off than they used to be might incorporate the following kinds of evidence:

- A description of the writer's grandparents who are living comfortably on Social Security and pensions (*personal observation or experience*)
- A statement that the per capita after-tax income of older Americans is $335 greater than the national average (*statistics from a report*)
- The point that the majority of elderly Americans do not live in nursing homes or on the street; they have their own houses or apartments (*fact from a newspaper article*)
- Accounts of several elderly couples living in retirement villages in Florida (*examples from interviews*)
- A statement by Dr. Marie Sanchez, a specialist in geriatrics: "An over-65 American today is likely to be healthier, and have a longer life expectancy, than a 50-year-old living only a decade ago." (*expert authority cited in a documentary*)

Always keep in mind, of course, that the evidence you collect must also be accurate and representative; otherwise, your argument and credibility will be undermined.

When using outside sources, you should be sure to *document* or give credit to those sources. Otherwise, readers may dismiss your evidence as nothing more than your subjective opinion, or they may regard as dishonest your failure to cite your indebtedness. Your instructor can provide information about ways to document sources.

3. Organize the supporting evidence. The support for an argumentation paper can be organized in a variety of ways. Any of the patterns described in this book — description, narration, definition, causal analysis, and so on — may be used to develop the essay's proposition. Imagine you are writing a paper arguing that car racing should be banned from television. The essay might contain a *description* of a horrifying accident that was televised in graphic detail; you might devote part of the paper to a *causal analysis* showing that the broadcast of such races encourages teens to drive carelessly; you could include a *process analysis* to explain how young drivers "soup up" their own cars in a dangerous attempt to imitate the races seen on television.

When presenting evidence, arrange it so that you create a strong, convincing effect. That means you often will end with your most compelling point, leaving readers with dramatic evidence that underscores the validity of your proposition.

4. Acknowledge and perhaps refute differing viewpoints.   If your essay has a clear thesis and strong logical support, you have taken important steps toward winning readers over to your way of thinking. However, because argumentation – persuasion essays focus on controversial issues, you should also try to take opposing points of view into account. As you think and read about your subject, seek out arguments on the other side. A good argument does not ignore dissenting views; it admits that other positions exist, perhaps even acknowledges that others have ideas worthy of consideration. Mentioning dissimilar views shows you to be a reasonable person and may even disarm readers, leaving them receptive to your argument. Investigating opposing viewpoints also helps you anticipate and counter objections, alerting you to weaknesses and flaws in your own position; you learn to avoid the *either – or thinking* that so often plagues argumentation.

As you will see in the professional essays in this chapter, writers can use a number of techniques to deal with dissenting positions. Here are three particularly effective strategies.

First, you can simply *acknowledge* the competing viewpoint when you present your proposition. You begin by recognizing the opposing opinion, and then you state your own position, implying that your view stands on more solid ground. With such an approach, you may not have to discuss the opposing opinion. The thesis below illustrates this strategy (the opposing viewpoint is underlined once, and the writer's position is underlined twice):

> <u>Although</u> <u>compulsory</u> <u>drug</u> <u>testing</u> <u>is</u> <u>not</u> <u>without</u> <u>prob-lems,</u> <u>colleges</u> <u>should</u> <u>nonetheless</u> <u>mandate</u> <u>the</u> <u>testing</u> <u>of</u> <u>all</u> <u>their</u> <u>athletes.</u>

Second, you can *summarize* the competing viewpoint, admit (when appropriate) the validity of some of its points, and then go on to present evidence for your position.

Third, you can *refute* the competing position. Refutation

means pointing out problems with the dissenting view, thus highlighting the superiority of your own position. You may focus on the inadequacies or inaccuracies in the opposing side's evidence, or you may point to flaws in its logic. Pages 536 – 541 identify some common examples of illogical thinking.

Here is how the competing position could be refuted in an essay arguing in favor of sex education in public schools. You might start by acknowledging the opposing viewpoint's key argument: "Sex education should be the prerogative of parents." Then, while granting the validity of this view in an ideal world, you might continue by showing that many parents do not meet their responsibilities in this area. You could provide statistics showing the number of parents who are uncomfortable talking about sex with their children and therefore avoid doing so; you could cite studies revealing that children in single-parent homes are likely to receive even less parental guidance about sex; you could describe several young people whose parents provided sketchy, even misleading, information about sex.

There are various ways to present and develop the refutation section of your paper. The method used will depend on the length of the paper and the complexity of the issue in question. Two possible sequences are outlined below:

First Strategy	**Second Strategy**
State your proposition.	State your proposition.
Cite the opposing viewpoint and the evidence for its position.	Cite the opposing viewpoint and the evidence for its position.
Refute the opposing viewpoint by presenting counterarguments to its evidence.	Refute the opposing viewpoint by presenting counterarguments to its evidence.
	Present additional evidence for your position.

In the first strategy, your whole argument is based on a refutation of all or part of the opposing position. When using the second strategy, you present *additional* evidence that is *different from* the points made in the refutation. This additional evidence may appear at the end of the essay (as in the preceding table) or at the start (after the proposition). The additional evidence may even be split up, some presented at the beginning and some at the end. Moreover, when refuting the opposing view, you may refute its argument *in toto* or one point at a time.

5. Think logically about your argument. The chain of reasoning used to develop an argument is the surest indicator of how rigorously you have thought through your position. There are two basic ways to think about a subject: through *inductive* and *deductive* reasoning. Though the following discussion treats induction and deduction as separate processes, the two often overlap and complement one another.

Inductive reasoning examines an issue or problem by looking closely at specific cases, facts, or examples. Based on these specifics, you then draw a conclusion or make a generalization. This is the kind of thinking scientists use when they examine evidence or facts (the results of experiments, for example) and then draw a *conclusion*: Smoking causes cancer. All of us use inductive reasoning in everday life. We might think the following: "My head is aching" (evidence). "My nose is stuffy" (evidence). "I'm coming down with a cold" (conclusion). Based on the conclusion, we might go a step further and decide to take some action: "I think I'll take an aspirin."

When inductive reasoning is used, the conclusion reached serves as the proposition for an argumentation essay. (Of course, the essay will most likely include elements of persuasion since strict argumentation — with no appeal to emotions — is uncommon.) If the paper advances a course of action, the proposition often states the action proposed, thus signaling that the essay has a distinctly persuasive purpose.

Let's suppose that you are writing a paper about the current crime wave in the small town where you live. You might use inductive thinking to structure the argument for the essay:

Several people were mugged last week while shopping in the center of town. (evidence)

A number of homes and apartments were burglarized the past few weeks. (evidence)

A growing number of cars have been stolen from people's driveways. (evidence)

The police force has been negligent about protecting town residents. (conclusion or proposition for an argumentation essay with probable elements of persuasion)

The police force needs to take steps to upgrade its protection of town residents. (conclusion or proposition for an argumentation essay with a clearly persuasive intent)

This inductive sequence helps point the way to a possible structure for the essay. For example, after providing a clear statement of your proposition, you might detail recent mugging, burglary, and stolen car incidents. Then you could move to the opposing viewpoint: a description of the steps the police say they have taken to protect town members. At that point, you would refute the police's claim, citing additional evidence that shows the measures taken have not been sufficient. Finally, if you wanted your essay to have a decidedly persuasive purpose, the paper could end with specific action the police should take to improve protection of the community.

As in all essays, your evidence should be specific, unified, adequate, and representative. These last two characteristics are critical when you think inductively. You want to be certain your conclusion is based on sufficient and representative evidence, guaranteeing that the conclusion would be equally valid even if other evidence were presented. Insufficient and atypical evidence often leads to *hasty generalizations* that mar the logic of an essay. For example, you might think the following: "Some elderly people are very wealthy and do not need Social Security checks" (evidence), and "Some Social Security recipients illegally collect several checks" (evidence). On the basis of this evidence, you might conclude, "The Social Security system is a waste of the taxpayers' money." But your conclusion would be invalid and hasty because it would be based on only a few atypical examples. Millions of Social Security recipients are not wealthy and do not abuse the system. Because you failed to consider the full range of evidence, any action you propose ("The Social Security system should be disbanded") will probably be considered suspect by thoughtful readers. It is possible, of course, that Social Security should be disbanded, but the evidence leading to such an argument must be sufficient and representative. Such is not the case in this situation.

When reasoning inductively, you should also be careful that the evidence you collect is recent and accurate. No valid conclusion can result from dated or erroneous evidence. To ensure that your evidence is sound, you need to evaluate the reliability of your sources. Gossip, hearsay, and biased opinions are not authoritative sources. When a person who is legally drunk claims to have seen a flying saucer, the evidence is shaky, to say the least. But if two respected scientists, both with 20-20 vision, saw the saucer, their evidence is worth considering.

Finally, it is important to realize that there is always an element of uncertainty in inductive reasoning. The conclusion can never be more than an *inference*, involving what logicians call an *inductive leap*. There could be other explanations for the evidence cited and thus other positions to take and actions to urge. For example, based on the evidence concerning a crime wave in a small town, you might conclude not that the police force has been remiss, but that people in the town are careless about protecting themselves and their property. In turn, you might call for a different kind of action: the police force should conduct workshops for the public in self-defense and home security. In an inductive argument, your task is to weigh the evidence, consider alternative explanations, and then choose the conclusion and course of action that seem most valid.

With inductive reasoning, you start with specific cases and move toward a generalization or conclusion. But in *deduction*, you begin with a generalization, then apply that generalization to a specific case so a conclusion can be drawn. This movement from general to specific involves a three-step form of reasoning called a *syllogism*. The first part of a syllogism is called the *major premise*, a general statement about a large group. The second part of a syllogism is a *minor premise*, a statement about an individual within that group. The syllogism ends with a *conclusion* about that individual.

Just as we use inductive thinking in everyday life, so we use deductive thinking — often without being aware of it — to sort out our experiences. When trying to decide which car to buy, you might think as follows:

Major premise:	In an accident, large cars are safer than small cars.
Minor premise:	The Chevy Cruiser is a large car.
Conclusion:	In an accident, the Chevy Cruiser will be safer than a small car.

Based on your conclusion, you might decide to take a specific action, buying the Cruiser rather than the smaller car you had first considered.

In order to create a valid syllogism and thus a sound conclusion, you should be aware of two major pitfalls when reasoning deductively. First, you want to be sure not to start with a *sweeping* or *hasty generalization* as your *major premise*. Second, you need to be careful about accepting as truth a *faulty minor premise* or *conclusion*. Let's look at each of these problems in turn.

Perhaps you are concerned about a trash-to-steam incinerator scheduled to open near your home. Although you are not fully conscious of your reasoning, your thinking about the situation might follow along these lines:

Major premise:	Trash-to-steam incinerators have had serious problems and pose significant threats to the well-being of people living near the plants.
Minor premise:	The proposed incinerator in my neighborhood will be a trash-to-steam plant.
Conclusion:	The proposed trash-to-steam incinerator in my neighborhood will have serious problems and pose significant threats to the well-being of people living near the plant.

Having arrived at this conclusion, you might decide to join organized protests against the opening of the incinerator. But your thinking is somewhat illogical. Your *major premise* is a *sweeping* one that indiscriminately groups all trash-to-steam plants into a single category. It is unlikely that you are familiar with the operations of all the trash-to-steam incinerators in this country and abroad. Moreover, it is probably not true that all plants have had serious difficulties that endangered the public safety. For your argument to reach a valid conclusion, the major premise must be based on repeated observations or verifiable fact. You would have a better argument, and thus reach a more valid conclusion, if the major premise were restricted or qualified — if it were applied to some, not all, of the group. The qualified syllogism would more likely be valid.

Major premise:	A number of trash-to-steam incinerators have had serious problems and posed significant threats to the well-being of people living near the plants.
Minor premise:	The proposed incinerator in my neighborhood will be a trash-to-steam plant.
Conclusion:	It is possible that the proposed trash-to-steam incinerator in my neighborhood will run into serious problems and pose significant threats to the well-being of people living near the plant.

This new conclusion, the result of more careful reasoning, would probably encourage you to learn more about trash-to-steam incinerators in general and about the proposed plant in particular. If further research still left you feeling uncomfortable about the plant, you would probably decide to join the protest. On the other hand, your research might convince you that the plant has incorporated into its design a number of safeguards that have been used with great success at other plants. This added information could reassure you that your original fears were unfounded. In either case, the revised deductive process would lead to a more informed conclusion and course of action.

Your syllogism will also be invalid if your *minor premise or conclusion reverses the if . . . then relationship implied in the major premise*. Assume you are writing a letter to the college newspaper urging the resignation of the student government president. Perhaps you pursue a line of reasoning that goes like this:

Major premise:	Students who plagiarize term papers must appear before the Faculty Committee on Academic Policies and Procedures.
Minor premise:	Yesterday, Jennifer Kramer, president of the student government, appeared before the Faculty Committee on Academic Policies and Procedures.
Conclusion:	Jennifer must have plagiarized her term paper.
Action:	Jennifer should resign her position as president of the student government.

Such a chain of reasoning is illogical and unfair. Here's why. *If* students plagiarize their term papers, *then* they must appear before the committee. However, the converse isn't necessarily true — that *if* they appear before the committee, *then* they must have plagiarized. Jennifer could have been speaking on behalf of another student; she could have been protesting some action that the committee took; she could have been seeking the committee's help on an article she plans to write about academic honesty. The minor premise and conclusion fail to take into account these other possible explanations.

Now that you have a clear sense of the problems that can occur when thinking deductively, let's look more closely at the way syllogistic reasoning might be used to structure an argumentation – persuasion essay. Suppose you decide to write a paper advocating support for a projected space mission. You are aware that controversy surrounds the space program, especially since seven astronauts died in a 1986 launch. Confident that the tragedy has led to more rigorous controls, you want to urge support of an upcoming mission, arguing that the mission's benefits outweigh its risks. An essentially deductive pattern could be used to develop your argument. In fact, outlining your thinking as a syllogism might help you formulate a proposition, organize your evidence, deal with the opposing viewpoint, and — if appropriate — propose a course of action.

Major premise:	Space programs in the past have led to important developments in technology, especially in medical science.
Minor premise:	The Cosmos Mission is the newest space program.
Proposition (essay might be persuasive):	The Cosmos Mission is likely to lead to important developments in technology, especially in medical science.
Proposition (essay clearly persuasive):	Congress should continue its funding of the Cosmos Mission.

Having outlined the deductive pattern of your thinking, you might begin by stating your proposition and then discuss some new procedures developed to protect the astronauts and the structural integrity of the rocket system. With that background established, you could detail the opposing claim that little of value has been produced by space programs of the past. You could then move to your refutation, citing the significant medical advances emerging from former space missions. Finally, the paper might conclude on a persuasive note, with a plea to Congress to continue funding of the latest space mission.

6. Recognize logical fallacies in your own and other people's thinking. When writing an argumentation – persuasion essay, you want to avoid *logical fallacies*, gaps in logic that reveal serious flaws in the thinking process. Logicians have identified many logical fallacies — including *sweeping* or *hasty generalizations* (pages 534–537), *faulty minor premises* or *conclusions* (pages 537–538), and *either–or thinking* (page 531). But there are other fallacies for you to be wary of. The ability to detect these fallacies enables you to identify weaknesses in the opposition's view, providing a solid basis for the refutation portion of your essay.

Post hoc thinking (short for a Latin phrase meaning "After this, therefore because of this") occurs when you conclude that a cause – effect relationship necessarily exists simply because one event preceded another. For example, it would be illogical to argue in an essay that recently arrived immigrants are the sole cause of the economic slump in a nearby city. To support your argument, perhaps you cite two pieces of evidence: the growing number of immigrants who have settled in the city and the city's fiscal decline. Such a chain of thinking is faulty because it assumes a cause – effect relationship based purely on the coincidence of time. Perhaps the immigrants' arrival was a factor, but there could also be other reasons for the situation: the lack of financial incentives to attract business to the city, restrictions on the size of the manufacturing facilities built in the city, citywide labor disputes that make companies leery of settling in the area. Your argument should also consider these possibilities.

An even more blatant muddying of cause – effect relationships occurs in *non sequitur thinking* (Latin for "it does not follow"), when a conclusion is drawn that has no logical connection to the evidence cited: "Millions of Americans own cars, so there is no need to fund public transportation." Not only does the faulty conclusion disregard the millions of Americans who don't own cars, but it also ignores pollution and road congestion — both of which could be reduced if people had access to safe, reliable public transportation.

Ad hominem argument (from the Latin meaning "to the man") occurs when you attack a person rather than an issue. Suppose you want to write a letter to the school newspaper, arguing against the college's plan to sponsor a symposium on the abortion controversy. The symposium would be attended by physicians on both sides of this complex issue. The letter starts with your reasons for protesting the proposed symposium. But soon you get sidetracked and take swipes at the doctors who support the right to abortion. You mention that one physician has serious marital difficulties and has just filed for divorce; you indicate that the other doctor is alleged to have a drinking problem. By hurling personal invective, you avoid discussing possible loopholes in their position and the merits of your stance. Mudslinging is a poor substitute for reasoned argument.

Sometimes, rather than discrediting others, writers may try to bolster their arguments by appealing to *authority* that may, in reality, be *questionable* or downright *faulty*. Most of us have developed a healthy suspicion of phrases like "sources close to," "an unidentified spokesperson states," "experts claim," and "studies show." If these people and these reports are so reliable, why aren't they acknowledged more specifically? (For more on logical fallacies, see "Propaganda Techniques in Today's Advertising," page 502.)

Begging the question involves reasoning that never establishes proof for a debatable point. Instead, the writer starts with an arguable premise and expects readers to accept as given a premise that is actually controversial. You would have trouble convincing readers that prayer in public schools should be banned if you based your argument on the premise that school prayer violates the Constitution. Perhaps the Constitution does, either explicitly or implicitly, prohibit the use of prayer in public education. But your essay must demonstrate that fact. You cannot build a sound argument if you pretend there is no controversy surrounding your premise.

Few of today's critical problems — arms control, terrorism, care for the homeless — lend themselves to quick solutions. Overwhelmed by endless facts and speculations, many of us look to experts to help us arrive at meaningful positions on these complex issues. We may read one article and conclude, "Yes, this position makes sense," only to read another article that advances an opposing but equally compelling viewpoint. Perhaps the key to finding answers is to rely on ourselves — not on the experts — to sort out information and ideas. Writing an argumentation – persuasion essay is the perfect vehicle for such an investigation. The very act of writing helps us discover how we feel and what we think. Weighing fact against fact, stipulation against stipulation, we use reason to draw conclusions that make sense. Argumentation – persuasion also gives us a chance to share that point of view with others, perhaps even convincing readers of the soundness of our view. Indeed, as average people with limited political clout or recognized expertise, we may find that argumentation – persuasion provides us with one of our strongest sources of personal power.

STUDENT ESSAY AND COMMENTARY

The following student essay was written by Mark Simons in response to this assignment:

> In "My Pistol-Packing Kids," Jean Marzollo refutes the popular notion that parents should prohibit their children's aggressive games and use of warlike toys. Select a controversial issue you feel strongly about and, using logic and solid evidence, convince your readers of the validity of your viewpoint.

While reading Mark's paper, try to determine how effectively it applies the principles concerning the use of argumentation – persuasion. The commentary following the paper will help you look at Mark's essay more closely.

Compulsory National Service

Our high school history class spent several weeks studying the events of the 1960s. The most intriguing thing about that decade was the spirit of service and social commitment in young people. In the Sixties, young people thought about issues beyond themselves; they joined the Peace Corps and participated in freedom marches against segregation. They accepted President Kennedy's urging to "Ask not what your country can do for you; ask what you can do for your country." Most young people today, despite their obvious concern with careers and getting ahead, would also like an opportunity to make a worthwhile contribution to society. By instituting a program of compulsory national service, our country could tap this desire in young people. Such a system would yield significant benefits.   1

Compulsory national service means that everyone between the ages of 17 and 25 would serve their country for two years. Young people could choose between two major options: military service or a public-service corps. They could serve their time at any point within the eight-year span. The unemployed or the uncertain could join   2 immediately after high school; college-bound students could complete their education before joining the national service.

The idea of compulsory national service has been discussed for   3
many years, and some nations such as Israel have embraced it wholeheartedly. The idea could also be workable in this country. Unfortunately, detractors have prevented the idea from taking hold. Opponents contend, first of all, that the program would cost too much; they argue that a great deal of money would have to be spent administering the program. In addition, young people would have to receive at least a minimum wage for their work, and some of them would need housing--both costly items. Another argument against compulsory national service is that it would demoralize young people; the plan would prevent the young from getting on with their careers and would make them feel as though they were engaged in work that had no personal reward. A final argument is that compulsory service would lay the groundwork for a military state. The picture is painted of an army of young robots totally at the mercy of the government, like the Hitler Youth of the Second World War.

Despite opponents' claims that compulsory national service   4
would involve exorbitant costs, the program would not have to be that expensive to run. The program might use as a model the Peace Corps, which has achieved great benefits even while being administered on a fairly modest budget. Also, the sums required for wages and housing could be reduced considerably through payments made by the towns, cities, and states using the corps' services. And the economic benefits of the program could be significant. The public-service corps could repair deteriorating bridges, highways, public buildings, and inner-city neighborhoods. The corps could organize recycling projects; it could staff public health clinics, day care centers, legal aid centers, and homes for the handicapped. The corps could also monitor pollution, clean up litter, and help care for the country's growing elderly population. All of these projects would help solve many of the problems that plague our nation, and they would probably cost much less than if they were handled by traditional government bureaucracies or the private sector.

Also, rather than undermining the spirit of young people, as   5
opponents contend, the program would be likely to boost their morale. Many young people feel enormous pressure and uncertainty. They are not sure what they want to do, or they have trouble finding a way to begin their careers. Compulsory national service could give young people a much-needed breathing space and could even equip them with the skills needed to start a career. Moreover, participating in compulsory national service could provide an emotional boost

for the young; all of them would experience the pride that comes from working hard, reaching goals, acquiring skills, and handling responsibilities. A positive mind-set would also result from the sense of community that would be created by serving in the national service. All young people--rich or poor, educated or not, regardless of sex or social class--would come together during this time. Young people would grow to understand one another and learn that every person has an ability to aid the welfare of the whole group. Each young person would have the satisfaction of knowing that he or she has made a real contribution to the nation.

Finally, contrary to what opponents claim, compulsory national   6 service would not signal the start of a dictatorship. Although the service would be required, young people could have complete freedom to choose any two years between the ages of 17 and 25. They would also have complete freedom to choose the branch of the military or public-service corps which suits them best. Nor would there be any need to outfit the public-service corps in military uniforms or to keep the corps confined to barrack-like camps. The corps could be set up like a regular job, with young people living at home as much as possible, following a nine-to-five schedule, enjoying all the personal freedoms that would ordinarily be theirs. Also, a dictatorship would no more likely emerge from a program of compulsory national service than it has from our present military system. We would still have a series of checks and balances to prohibit the taking of power by one group or individual. We should also keep in mind that our system is different from that of fascist regimes; our long tradition of personal liberty makes improbable the seizing of absolute power by one person or faction. A related but even more important point to remember is that freedom does not mean people are guaranteed the right to pursue only their individual needs. That is mistaking selfishness for freedom. And, as everyone knows, selfishness leads only to misery. It cannot lead to a happy life. The national service would not take away freedom. On the contrary, it would help young people grasp this larger concept of freedom, a concept that is badly needed to counteract the deadly "look out for number one" attitude that is spreading like a poison across the nation.

Perhaps there will never be a time like the 1960s when so many   7 young people were concerned with remaking the world. Still, a good many of today's young people want meaningful work. They want to feel that what they do makes a difference. A program of compulsory national service would tap this willingness in young people, helping them realize the best in themselves. Such a program would also allow us as a nation to make substantial headway against the social problems that haunt the country. It is apparent that compulsory national service is an idea whose time has come.

In his *argumentation – persuasion* essay, Mark tackles — as the assignment required — a complex and controversial issue. He takes the position that compulsory national service would benefit both the country and its young people. Mark's essay is a good example of the way argumentation and persuasion often mix; although the paper presents Mark's position in a focused, thoughtful manner, it also appeals to readers' personal value systems and suggests a course of action to be taken.

When planning the essay, Mark realized that most of his audience — his composition class — would consist of two kinds of readers. Some people, not sure of their views, would be inclined to agree with him if he presented his case well. Others would probably be reluctant to accept his view. Because of this mixed audience, Mark knew he could not depend on *pathos* (an appeal to emotion) to convince his readers of the soundness of his position. Rather, his argument had to be based mainly on *logos* (reason) and *ethos* (his own credibility). So, after thinking through the pros and cons of the issue, Mark decided to organize his essay around a series of logical arguments. He also decided to evoke his own authority, drawing on his "inside" knowledge of young people as well as his knowledge of history.

Mark introduces his subject by discussing an earlier decade when large numbers of young people worked for societal change. Mark's references to the Peace Corps, freedom marches, and President Kennedy reinforce his image as a knowledgeable source and establish a context for the position he will take. These historical references also provide a smooth lead-in to the two-sentence thesis at the end of the introduction: "By instituting a system of compulsory national service, our country could tap this desire in young people to serve. Such a system would yield significant benefits."

The next paragraph is developed around a *definition* that clarifies what is meant by compulsory national service. The definition guarantees that Mark and his readers have a common understanding. Without this paragraph, readers might be unprepared to grasp the concept at the heart of the essay.

Mark is now in a good position to launch his argument. Like

most argumentation – persuasion essays, the paper addresses a controversial issue, and, as we have seen, Mark wisely recognizes that some people will not agree with him. Rather than ignoring the opposing point of view, he acknowledges its existence in the *topic sentence* of the essay's third paragraph: "Unfortunately, detractors have prevented the idea from taking hold in America." He then summarizes the main points the dissenting opinion might advance: compulsory national service would be expensive, demoralizing to young people, and dangerously authoritarian. Mark uses the rest of the essay to argue against these three criticisms.

You probably realized that Mark did not conduct any library research on the opposing point of view. Since the assignment did not require outside sources, Mark brainstormed with friends to discover some of the reservations people might have about compulsory national service. If he had been writing a longer paper, or if the assignment had required library research, Mark would have been obligated to read what critics of compulsory national service say about such a program. Indeed, such research would have strengthened Mark's argument. By investigating the dissenting position, he would have become more aware of possible weaknesses in his own position. Moreover, research would have enabled him to quote advocates of the opposing viewpoint, thus appearing even more authoritative to his audience. But in an essay of this kind, it is acceptable not to conduct such outside research.

The next three paragraphs *refute* the opposing stance and represent Mark's evidence for his position. Mark structures the essay so that readers can follow his *counterargument* with ease. Each paragraph argues against one opposing point and begins with a *topic sentence* that serves as Mark's response to his opponents. In fact, note the way the italicized portion of each topic sentence recalls a dissenting point cited earlier: "Despite opponents' claims that *compulsory national service would involve exorbitant costs*, the program would not have to be that expensive to run" (paragraph 4); "Also, rather than *undermining the spirit of young people*, as opponents contend, the program would be likely to boost their morale" (5); "Finally, contrary to what opponents claim, *compulsory national service would* not *signal the start of a dictatorship*" (6). Mark also guides the reader through the various points in the refutation by using *transitions* within paragraphs:

"*And* the economic benefits . . . could be significant" (4); "*Moreover*, participating in compulsory national service would provide an emotional boost . . ." (5); "*Also*, a dictatorship would no more likely emerge . . ." (6).

As we have seen, Mark's essay is not based on researched facts, statistics, or other hard evidence. Just as he used brainstorming to generate material on the opposing view, Mark brainstormed his counterarguments, arriving at his position *inductively* — through an *inference* or *inductive leap*. Starting with a number of specific observations, Mark moved to a general *conclusion* that compulsory national service would be both workable and beneficial. In other words, Mark's support, as thoughtful and convincing as it may be, takes the form of reasonable speculation. The evidence for his argument constitutes a kind of *causal analysis* that assumes that certain things will happen if compulsory national service is implemented. Of course, Mark cannot be sure that the consequences he envisions will actually occur, but he has worked hard to show the logic behind his thinking. Moreover, since Mark's projected consequences cannot be proven, he seeks to reinforce his position by infusing the essay with several *persuasive* or emotional appeals. For example, he points to consequences that most people would endorse with enthusiasm: If the program were in operation, pollution would be reduced, the nation's elderly would be cared for, deteriorating highways would be repaired. Such attractive prospects make Mark's argument all the more compelling.

When reading the essay, you may have felt that Mark loses some control over his argument in the last part of the sixth paragraph. Beginning with "And as everyone knows . . . ," Mark falls into the *logical fallacy* called *begging the question*. He also indulges in charged emotionalism. For one thing, he shouldn't assume that everyone agrees that a selfish life inevitably brings misery. Also, when he refers — somewhat melodramatically — to the "deadly 'look out for number one' attitude that is spreading like a poison across the nation," he assumes that readers agree with his assessment; he presents his view as truth when actually it needs to be proven. These presumptions, especially when combined with the overwrought language, somewhat undercut Mark's credibility and the effectiveness of his argument.

Despite this problem, Mark recovers and comes up with a

solid concluding paragraph. This final section echoes the point Mark made in the introduction about the Sixties and also restates his thesis. The essay then ends with a crisp assertion that suggests a course of action to be taken.

Given the complex nature of his argument, Mark found that he had to revise his essay several times. One way to illustrate some of the changes he made is to compare his final introduction with the original draft reprinted here:

First Draft Version

"There's no free lunch." "You can't get something for nothing." "You have to earn your way." In America, these sayings are not really true. In America, we gladly take but give back little. In America, we receive economic opportunity, legal protection, the right to vote, and, most of all, a personal freedom unequaled throughout the world. How do we repay our country for such gifts? In most cases, we don't. This unfair relationship must be changed. The best way to make a start is to institute a system of national compulsory service for young people. This system would be of real benefit to the country and its citizens.

When Mark met with a classmate for a feedback session, he found that his partner had a number of helpful suggestions for revising various sections of the essay. But Mark's partner focused most of her comments on the essay's introduction because she felt it needed special attention. Mark read the paragraph aloud and agreed that the opening was weak. For one thing, it was choppy and awkward. More important, though, Mark's partner helped him see that the introduction did not provide an effective lead-in to the essay's thesis. The original introduction referred in a general way to the one-sided relationship between America and Americans. The paragraph did not help readers see that Mark was concerned specifically with young people. Mark reconsidered his opening paragraph and decided to focus it exclusively on American youth. When revising the paragraph, he also decided to mention the social commitment characteristic of young people in the Sixties. This reference to an earlier period provided the discussion with an important historical perspective and lent a note of authority to Mark's argument.

These are just a few of the many changes Mark made while reworking his essay. Because he budgeted his time carefully, he was able to do a thorough job of revising. Thus, with the exception of the problem mentioned in the sixth paragraph, Mark was able to prepare a well-reasoned, convincing essay.

The selections ahead demonstrate that argumentation – persuasion can stimulate thinking on numerous issues. In "My Pistol-Packing Kids," Jean Marzollo contends that the violence in children's play does not lead to aggressive lives. Adamantly opposed to censorship, Loudon Wainwright argues that a "A Little Banning Is a Dangerous Thing." Mark Twain ("The Damned Human Race") and Frank Trippett ("A Red Light for Scofflaws") makes some compelling points about flaws in human nature. With scathing irony, Jonathon Swift advocates in "A Modest Proposal" a solution to the agony of Ireland's poor. Finally, while Ed Koch and David Bruck take opposing stands on capital punishment, Louis Nizer and Beth Johnson Ruth tackle different sides of the controversy surrounding the legalization of drugs.

Jean Marzollo

A Connecticut native, Jean Marzollo received her B.A. in English from the University of Connecticut and her M.A. from Harvard University. Before becoming a freelance writer, Marzollo taught high school and directed educational programs for disadvantaged children. Her articles have appeared in many popular magazines, including *Redbook, Parents, Mademoiselle,* and *Working Mother*. The author of several books for children and teenagers, she has recently started an adult novel. The following selection was first published in *Parents* magazine.

My Pistol-Packing Kids

Marbles, hopscotch, and hide-and-seek are all old, familiar childhood games. But the most favorite of all may be "Bang, bang, you're dead." All children seem to enjoy games of make-believe violence, played with sticks, pointed fingers, or toy weapons that shoot plastic darts, "laser" beams, or rubber projectiles. Parents debate whether such games are healthy or damaging to young minds. Jean Marzollo maintains that such shoot-'em-up games have hidden dimensions that parents may not at first appreciate.

One day as I was loading the dishwasher, I glanced over at 1 my two boys, Danny and David, ages seven and five, respectively, and thought how sweet and quiet they are. I wonder what they are drawing so intently; I think I'll go see. I went over to the kitchen table and found, rather to my dismay, two lurid pictures of outer space battles. Blood and destruction was everywhere.

These frail little babes I held in my arms, what made them 2 grow up and want to create things like this? Repeatedly? Given clay, they make monsters and destroy them limb by limb with home-made clay bombs. Given yarn, they devise tarantula traps behind the couch. Given board and blocks they rig ramps to crash their cars into each other at high speed.

550

Outdoors, straight sticks are knives and bent ones are guns. 3
Danny and David stick them into their belts and swagger around
on the grass like John Wayne and Burt Reynolds.

Oh, sure, they also like to roll out cookie dough, play the 4
piano, build sand castles, and pet cats, but nothing, I have noticed, quite catches their fancy as does violence.

With their friends they are superheroes or spacemen, and, as 5
I watch them run around shooting each other, I sometimes feel
guilty that it was I who took them to (and enjoyed) the movies
Superman, *Star Wars*, and *The Empire Strikes Back*. Adding to this
guilt is the fact that my husband and I let them watch Saturday
morning cartoons so we can sleep late.

On a slow, regular basis their innocent little minds have been 6
contaminated with kiddie media culture. It's excessively violent,
which is why Danny and David, at the ripe old ages of five and
seven, like it so much. They are at the ages when they know what
they see on television is not real. Instead of worrying about reality
as they did when they were three or four, they now spend their
energy memorizing the exact order in which their favorite cartoons appear.

What About the Kids of Parents Who Say "No"?

Good and stalwart friends of ours, wishing to protect their 7
children's minds from nefarious influences, do not buy TVs, do
not permit guns, and do not take their children to ungentle
movies. But when their children come to visit, they dive into the
box in the entryway that contains two squirt guns, a plastic laser
gun, an orange pistol that shoots rubber darts (all of which have
been lost), and a homemade wooden machine gun. Although
these kids have never watched morning TV, they know exactly
how to play with toy weapons, and they do so with the passion of
converts.

Secretly, wickedly, I feel better. Why? Because I'm haunted 8
by the idea that our actions, or the lack of them, may be bringing
out in our children a natural tendency toward aggressive violence
that should be suppressed. In a time of assassinations, political
terrorism, nuclear buildup, and much publicized violence in people's daily lives, we desire more consciously than ever peace and

safety in the world. It is out of this concern that we worry about the place and legitimacy of toy guns in the lives of our children.

What if, we wonder, all parents kept all children from toy   9
weapons and the media that glorifies them; wouldn't the world be better off? We could take the TV and the laser guns to the dump. But what about the sticks, yarns, and crayons? Should we take them, too?

We could also lay down the law: no more torpedoes in the   10
bathtub. Play only with rubber ducks. No more bows and arrows may be made out of construction toys. Make houses instead. No more clay bombs. Make bowls. Our laws would require rigid surveillance and strict discipline, but the means (our dictatorship) would be justified by the end (their innocence). Childhood, after all, should be a time of kittens, mittens, gingerbread, and yo-yo's.

Think positive. Be happy. Play nice, our laws would say.   11

But our children don't want to play nice. They want to have   12
fun. And they have so much fun *pretending* to wipe each other out.

Kids Want Both Sides

It seems kids want to learn about *both* sides of childhood, not   13
just the mittens and kittens side, full of discovery and nurturing, but also the ghosts and ghouls side, full of dread and helplessness. Watching our children and their friends at play, it is clear to me that the mock violence in their play has a great deal to do with their need to *do* something about the underside of their lives. In order to fight back the witches, giants, and werewolves that menace them in the night, they run around in the daytime with toy pistols, toy knives, and toy swords. When I stop to think about their play in these terms, I find I can accept it.

I'm not talking about condoning real violence, nor am I   14
suggesting we avoid the responsibilities to teach morals and ethics to our children. As a matter of course, we teach them that no matter how mad they are at someone else, they must not hit, bite, pull hair, and pinch. We teach them to protest verbally, to negotiate a deal if they can, or simply to say, "I'm not going to play with you anymore if you do that." We teach them basically not to hurt others to get their own way. And just as we teach our children safety precautions about cars, roads, matches, broken

glass, and electrical outlets, we caution them about real knives and guns. We tell them how very dangerous these things are, how they must be used correctly, and that the use of guns is prohibited for young children.

"Your Thing, Not Mine"

Guns are a particularly sensitive topic for parents, and many 15 of us feel uncomfortable when our children lust for plastic ones. Although I do not prohibit my children from playing with them, I try to make it clear that such activity is their thing, not mine. I say, "Don't point that rifle at me because it reminds me of a real gun and I don't like real guns." I also insist that gunplay take place outside.

Some friends of mine won't buy toy guns but permit their 16 children to do so with their own money. Others will not allow any toy guns in their homes but do not interfere if their children play guns with sticks or their fingers. Still other parents own real guns, go hunting, and bring home carcasses on the top of the car. Their children, we hope, learn the ethic of the hunter: one must be a good shot, one must kill only for food.

But the use of real guns is not really the point here. Danny 17 and David do not use real guns nor would they want to. *They are using toys and they are only pretending.* While I admit that it can be unsettling to see how truly inspired they can be at their games, I am impressed by their powers of invention and the fact that what they are doing is not only fun, but refined, effective, and safe.

It is refined in the sense that the children organize them- 18 selves to take the different parts involved. They also know how to act out all the parts and how to cooperate with each other to enhance the overall drama. They have a remarkable ability to improvise scenes and an almost professional attitude about giving and taking directions. Listening to them play with their little men dolls, it is almost as if I were listening to puppeteers or movie directors.

"All right," says Danny. "You land our guy behind the 19 mountain, and I'll find him and blast him out of the water."

"Okay, here goes." (Realistic landing sounds.) "Let's set up 20 camp here. Oh no! They found us. Watch out!" (Explosion sounds. Swimming sounds.) "Look, here's an underwater cave!

Let's go in!" (Aside) "Let's pretend the cave is really a giant shark."

"Yeah, and I'll kill it and save you."   21

"Okay. Oh no! It's a giant shark! Look at those teeth!"   22

Their Own Play Therapy

It seems to me that fantasy play is effective in the sense that it   23
allows children to blow off a lot of steam. Let's face it, on some
level every child lives with tyrants (us) on whom he or she is
absolutely dependent. We may be benevolent tyrants, but we are
tyrants nonetheless, and the whole thrust of our children's growing up is to liberate themselves from us.

By playing out fantasies, children release frustrations and   24
experience illusory control over things, such as big people's
power and the threat of death, over which, in fact, they have no
control at all. Day after day, they take turns acting out scene after
scene in which they as good guys heroically defend themselves
against horrible bad guys. Every child I have watched can play
both roles.

In a way children are their own play therapists, helping each   25
other cope with pent-up rage. They seem to know how long each
session should last. The game is over when the kids are bored, or
tired, or someone thinks of something else to do and everyone
agrees; in short, when enough steam has been blown off.

As far as I can see, violent fantasies are safe precisely because   26
they are not real. They are thrilling for the same reason. Children
don't want to get hurt. From my observation, the kids who enjoy
playing with toy guns in the yard are those who have already
learned to be cautious around cars, ovens, and climbing equipment. *They don't want to get hurt and they know how not to.* Just
because they crash toy cars now does not mean they will drive real
ones over cliffs when they are twenty. And just because they love
to shoot each other with imaginary guns now does not mean they
will abuse guns when they grow up.

It takes more than toy guns to make a killer. Conversely,   27
many peace-loving grown-ups I know tell me they played war
with a vengeance when they were little.

No Winners, No Losers?

Another important point: Have you ever noticed that in 28
mock violent play no one ever wins or loses? You get shot, you
fall down, you get up, you shoot someone else. A five-year-old
can play as skillfully as an eight-year-old. The weakest child is on a
par with the strongest. The game is safe emotionally as well as
physically.

Paradoxically, games that involve less violent imagination 29
but more real jeopardy are harder for children to play, and one
has to be mature enough to handle them. To play baseball, for
example, you have to be able to strike out without bursting into
tears. In Monopoly you have to be able to land on Park Place
when someone else owns it and lose all your money. In a class
play you have to be able to keep going even though some kid in
the back row whistles.

I don't want to see my kids strike out or forget their lines, 30
but I know they may, that they have to, and that they will put up
with such discomfort in order to participate in the next stage of
life. On their own, I suspect, they will realize eventually that
fantasy violence is for little kids. What's for big kids? Real violence? No, at least not for kids who have learned about love and
respect for others.

Graduating into Life

For older kids there is a stage of activity that moves closer to 31
real life. Sports, science projects, model making, music lessons, dancing, arts and crafts — all these activities help children
sharpen their skills, develop their imagination, and explore their
interests. The toy guns, toy dolls, and toy cars will be given away
or collect dust on a shelf in the basement. Real tools and real
equipment will have replaced them.

Eventually, Danny and David will move on to real life with 32
its possibilities for real jeopardy, real success, real independence,
and satisfaction. By then I hope they will have gained whatever
skills and strength of character they need to play this last, and
hardest, and most rewarding game of all. I trust that part of their
maturity will be based upon the ability they gained at an early age
to distinguish between fantasy and reality.

Questions for Close Reading

1. What is the thesis of the selection? Locate the sentence(s) in which Marzollo states her main idea. If she does not state the thesis explicitly, express it in your own words.
2. Why, according to the author, do kids want to play at violence?
3. Marzollo suggests children progress through different stages of maturity. What are these? In which stages do children focus on reality and in which on fantasy?
4. What does Marzollo mean by saying that play with toy guns is "refined"? How is it "effective" and safe?
5. Refer to your dictionary as needed to define the following words used in the selection: *stalwart* (paragraph 7), *legitimacy* (8), *condoning* (14), *improvise* (18), and *vengeance* (27).

Questions About the Writer's Craft

1. Why do you think the author chooses the first person point of view to develop her argument? How does the first person affect the persuasiveness of the essay?
2. What contrast makes the introduction dramatic? How does this contrast underlie the theme of the essay?
3. Examine the places where Marzollo uses direct quotations as opposed to reporting conversation indirectly. What is gained by using exact words at these points?
4. Marzollo asks rhetorical questions at several points in the essay. How do these questions help focus her argument? How do these questions function as transitional devices?

Questions for Further Thought

1. What kinds of games involving pretended violence, destruction, and death did you play as a child? What was your parents' reaction? Were you aware of playing with something adults considered very serious?
2. From your experience, do you think all children (both male and female, from all ethnic groups and backgrounds) play games of pretended violence? Would you say such play is normal?
3. It has been said that play is "the child's work," in that through play children try on new behaviors and skills and test their abilities. Would Marzollo agree? What things specifically can children learn through play?
4. What might be some of the reasons for the popularity with adults of violent action movies (such as the Rambo and Dirty Harry series)? Do you see any connection between child's fantasy play and the popular-

ity of these films? Are these films beneficial, harmless, or dangerous for people to view?

Writing Assignments Using Argumentation – Persuasion as a Method of Development

1. In paragraphs 15 and 16, Marzollo mentions four different parental attitudes toward guns. Write an essay that makes a case for parents' adopting one of these attitudes. After citing possible counterarguments, support your proposition with reason and emotional appeals. Draw, as Marzollo does, on your own experience as a child, babysitter, neighbor, parent, and so on.

2. One of Marzollo's points is that physical play and fantasy have important, healing roles in the lives of children. Write an essay defending the role of physical activity and/or fantasy in adults' lives as ways to release pent-up rage about things adults cannot control. Make your proposition as specific as possible, supporting it with examples from your own life and with references to films, TV, and books. At some point in the essay, you should acknowledge briefly the opposing view that escaping from reality can have negative repercussions.

Writing Assignments Using Other Methods of Development

3. Write an essay about the games (physical, fantasy, or other) that helped you grow up. These may have been games that taught you about yourself, others, feelings, or life in general. Describe the games that absorbed you and explain their benefits.

4. Marzollo contends that childhood play with weapons is not a cause of violence among adults. What, then, are the causes of the violence in our world? Write an essay explaining the causes of a particular kind of violence in your town or city, the United States, or the world. Be specific. Focus on only one type of violence and account for its existence.

Loudon Wainwright

A native New Yorker, Loudon Wainwright graduated from the
University of North Carolina. After leaving the Marine Corps
in 1945, Wainwright began his career at *Life* magazine, where
he worked as a writer, assistant picture editor, articles editor,
and assistant managing editor. Now retired, he nonetheless
continues to write "A View from Here," *Life*'s first and longest-running column. Focusing on a wide range of personal and
social issues, Wainwright has written essays dealing with such
subjects as the parent–child relationship, drug abuse, and — as
in the selection reprinted here — censorship.

A Little Banning Is a
Dangerous Thing

Which books should children in school be allowed to read?
Should a book with a character called "Nigger Jim" be banned
because it appears racist? Should a book about a woman who
bears an illegitimate child be prohibited because it deals with a
touchy subject? But what if the books in question are two
masterpieces of American writing, *Huckleberry Finn* and *The
Scarlet Letter*? In the following selection, Loudon Wainwright
argues that book banners understand neither the material they
want to censor nor the needs and good sense of children.

My own introduction to sex in reading took place about   1
1935, I think, just when the fertile soil of my young mind was
ripe for planting. The exact place it happened (so I've discovered
from checking the source in my local library) was the middle of
page 249, in a chapter titled "Apples and Ashes," soon after the
beginning of Book III of a mildly picaresque novel called *Anthony
Adverse*. The boy Anthony, 16, and a well-constructed character
named Faith Paleologus ("Her shoulders if one looked carefully
were too wide. But so superb was the bosom that rose up to

support them. . . .") made it right there in her apartment where he'd gone to take a quick bath, thinking (ho-ho) that she was out.

Faith was Anthony's sitter, sort of, and if author Hervey   2
Allen was just a touch obscure about the details of their moon-drenched meeting, I filled in the gaps. "He was just in time," Allen wrote, "to see the folds of her dress rustle down from her knees into coils at her feet. . . . He stood still, rooted. The faint aroma of her body floated to him. A sudden tide of passion dragged at his legs. . . . He was half blind, and speechless now. All his senses had merged into one feeling. . . . To be supported and yet possessed by an ocean of unknown blue depths below you and to cease to think! Yes, it was something like swimming on a transcendent summer night."

Wow! Praying that my parents wouldn't come home and   3
catch me reading this terrific stuff, I splashed ahead, line after vaguely lubricious line, exhilarated out of my mind at Anthony's good fortune. "After a while he was just drifting in a continuous current of ecstasy that penetrated him as if he were part of the current in which he lay." I still don't understand *that* line, but I sure feel the old surge of depravity. And reading it again, I thank God there was no righteous book banner around at the time to snatch it from me. *Anthony Adverse* doesn't rank as literature, or even required reading, but I'm convinced it served a useful, even educational, purpose for me at the time.

Alert vigilantes of the printed word worked hard to suppress   4
the novel then. The wretched little war to keep the mind of children clean is always going on. In fact, it has heated up considerably since President Reagan came to power, with libraries around the country reporting a threefold increase in demands that various volumes even less ruinous than *Anthony Adverse* be withdrawn. School boards, too, are feeling the cleansing fire of assorted crusaders against dirty words and irreverent expressions of one sort or another. Protesters range from outraged individual parents to teachers to local ministers to such well-organized watchdog outfits as the Gabler family of Texas, Washington's Heritage Foundation and, of course, the Moral Majority.

The victims are fighting back. Writers are leading public   5
"read-ins" of their banned works. One school board case, which actually dates to 1976, has gone all the way to the U.S. Supreme Court. Before the end of the current term, the court is expected to

rule on whether or not the First Amendment rights (to free expression) of five students in Island Trees, N.Y., were denied when the board took nine books out of circulation. A far more personal thrust against censorship was made recently by author Studs Terkel. At the news that his book *Working* was in danger of being banned in Girard, Pa., Terkel went there and standing before the whole school in assembly made his own eloquent case for the book, for the so-called bad language in it and for reading in general. Six weeks later the school board voted unanimously to keep *Working* in the reading program where it had initially been challenged. Presumably they were persuaded, in part at least, that Terkel was *not*, as Kurt Vonnegut wrote in a furious and funny defense of his own *Slaughterhouse-Five*, one of those "sort of ratlike people who enjoy making money from poisoning the minds of young people."

What gets me is the weird presumption that the book ban- 6 ners actually know something about the minds of young people. Vonnegut, among others, suspects that a lot of censors never even get around to reading the books they suppress. And just the briefest scanning of the list of titles currently banned or under threat in various communities calls the banners' credentials to rude question. *The Scarlet Letter, The Great Gatsby, A Farewell to Arms, Huckleberry Finn, The Grapes of Wrath* are a few of the variously seminal works challenged as somehow being dangerous to the stability of impressionable young minds. *Mary Poppins* and *The American Heritage Dictionary* have been under attack, too, the former after protests that its black characters were stereotypes, the latter presumably as a storehouse of words that shouldn't be viewed by innocent eyes, much less defined.

More critically, the censors forget, if they ever knew, many of 7 the needs of childhood. One, obviously, is the need for privacy, for a place to get away from the real world, a place where one is safe from — among other things — difficult or boring adult demands. The world that a reader makes is a perfect secret world. But if its topography is shaped by adults pushing their own hardened views of life, the secret world is spoiled.

Yet the world of the young human mind is by no means a 8 comfy habitat, as much as a lot of interfering adults would like to shape it that way. In *The Uses of Enchantment*, Bruno Bettelheim's book about the great importance of folk and fairy tales to child development, the author writes: "There is a widespread refusal to let children know that the source of much that goes wrong in life is due to our very own natures — the propensity of all men for acting aggressively, asocially, selfishly, out of anger and anxiety. Instead, we want our children to believe that, inherently, all men are good. But children know that *they* are not always good; and often, even when they are, they would prefer not to be." In the fantasies commonly churned out in the mind of a normal child, whatever that is, bloody acts of revenge and conquest, daredevil assaults and outlandish wooings are common currency. To achieve the bleak, cramped, sanitized, fear-ridden state of many adults takes years of pruning and repression.

Books, as everyone but the censors knows, stimulate growth   9
better than anything — better than sit-coms, better than *Raiders of the Lost Ark*, better than video games. Many books, to be sure, are dreadful heaps of trash. But most of these die quickly in the marketplace or become best-sellers incapable of harming the adults who buy them.

It's often the best books that draw the beadiest attention of   10
the censors. These are the books that really have the most to offer, the news that life is rich and complicated and difficult. Where else, for example, could a young male reader see the isolation of his painful adolescence reflected the way it is in *The Catcher in the Rye*, one of the *most* banned books in American letters. In the guise of fiction, books offer opportunities, choices and plausible models. They light up the whole range of human character and emotion. Each, in its own way, tells the truth and prepares its eager readers for the unknown and unpredictable events of their own lives.

Anthony Adverse, my first banned book, was just a huge   11
potboiler of the period. Still, it tickled my fantasy. And it sharpened my appetite for better stuff, like *Lady Chatterley's Lover*. Actually I didn't read that tender and wonderful book until I was almost 50. I wish I'd read it much sooner while we were both still hot.

Questions for Close Reading

1. What is the thesis of the selection? Locate the sentence(s) in which Wainwright states his main idea. If he does not state the thesis explicitly, express it in your own words.

2. What was Wainwright's initial reaction to *Anthony Adverse*? Why does he say it served a "useful, even educational" purpose in his childhood?

3. Who are the book banners, according to the author? What kind of people are they—and what motivates them?

4. According to Wainwright, what benefits do children get from reading books, even ones with "bannable" characteristics? Are these the same benefits of reading that educators stress?

5. Refer to your dictionary as needed to define the following words in the selection: *lubricious* (paragraph 3), *ecstasy* (3), *depravity* (3), *vigilantes* (4), and *potboiler* (11).

Questions About the Writer's Craft

1. In describing those who would ban books, Wainwright uses negatively charged words. For example, he calls them "vigilantes" in paragraph 4. Find other examples of vivid words and phrases that contain negative connotations. What effect do these loaded words have on the argument against banning?

2. You probably have heard the expression, "A little learning is a dangerous thing." Why does Wainwright use a variant of this saying as his title? How is a little banning "dangerous"?

3. Why does the author use the agricultural metaphor "the fertile soil of my young mind was ripe for planting" in the first sentence? What does this farming image have to do with reading a sexy passage in a book?

4. What is Wainwright's tone in the final paragraph? Why do you think he chose to conclude with this reference to a renowned banned book rather than present a conventional summary or concluding argument?

Questions for Further Thought

1. Should any books be banned? If so, which ones, and why? Should the reading of children and young people be closely monitored?

2. Does it really matter what children read, see, listen to, in books and the media? Is their moral development determined by their home life and upbringing, their community environment, their formal education, or by such cultural experiences as books and TV?

3. The quotation from psychologist Bruno Bettelheim suggests that children are aware they are capable of wrong, yet adults often try to shelter them from life's realities. Should children be kept innocent, or should they be taught about all aspects of life?

4. Are books the best way of educating children, or are TV, films and

video better for stimulating children intellectually? Is Wainwright old-fashioned in his preference for books?

Writing Assignments Using Argumentation–Persuasion as a Method of Development

1. Wainwright is concerned about attempts to ban literary works and middle-brow books, those that make the bestseller list. But what about books and magazines that cater to the basest parts of human nature — for example, publications that feature sadism, child pornography, and racism? Should society censor these publications? Or should we have total freedom of the press? Write an essay arguing for or against control of such material.

2. As a Moral Majority member, you have read Wainwright's essay and have decided to respond. Write an essay rebutting three of Wainwright's statements. Or base the essay on three reasons why the reading of young people should be controlled by responsible adults. In either case, your argument should take the opposing view into account.

Writing Assignments Using Other Methods of Development

3. Choose three books and/or magazines you read as a child that would have upset your parents (or grandparents) if they had known. Write an essay showing that the materials you read are precisely the kinds of publications that children should be allowed *or* forbidden to read. Support your point of view with convincing examples.

4. Discuss the amount of explicit sexual content in one of the following:

Movies	Popular song lyrics	TV miniseries
Soap operas	Magazine ads	Billboards

Your working thesis might be that there is *or* there is not too much explicit sexual content in today's ———————————.

Mark Twain

Mark Twain is a central figure in American literature. *The Adventures of Huckleberry Finn*, his finest work, is the story of a journey down the Mississippi by two memorable figures, a white boy and a black slave. Twain was born Samuel Langhorne Clemens in 1835 and was raised in Hannibal, Missouri. During his early years, he worked as a riverboat pilot, newspaper reporter, printer, and gold prospector. Although his popular image is as the author of such comic works as *The Adventures of Tom Sawyer, Life on the Mississippi,* and *The Prince and the Pauper,* Twain had a darker side that may have resulted from the bitter experiences of his life: financial failure and the deaths of his wife and daughter. His last writings are savage, satiric, and pessimistic. The following selection is taken from *Letters from the Earth,* one of his later works.

The Damned Human Race

Did today's newspaper contain a headline about people—Irish, Lebanese, Chilean—fighting somewhere in the world? Most likely, it did. In the following selection, Mark Twain concludes that the combative and cruel nature of human beings makes them the lowest of creatures, not the highest. With scathing irony, he supplies a startling reason for humans' warlike nature.

I have been studying the traits and dispositions of the "lower animals" (so-called), and contrasting them with the traits and dispositions of man. I find the result humiliating to me. For it obliges me to renounce my allegiance to the Darwinian theory of the Ascent of Man from the Lower Animals; since it now seems plain to me that the theory ought to be vacated in favor of a new and truer one, this new and truer one to be named the *Descent* of Man from the Higher Animals.

In proceeding toward this unpleasant conclusion I have not

1

2

guessed or speculated or conjectured, but have used what is commonly called the scientific method. That is to say, I have subjected every postulate that presented itself to the crucial test of actual experiment, and have adopted it or rejected it according to the result. Thus I verified and established each step of my course in its turn before advancing to the next. These experiments were made in the London Zoological Gardens, and covered many months of painstaking and fatiguing work.

Before particularizing any of the experiments, I wish to state   3
one or two things which seem to more properly belong in this place than further along. This in the interest of clearness. The massed experiments established to my satisfaction certain generalizations, to wit:

1. That the human race is of one distinct species. It exhibits slight variations — in color, stature, mental caliber, and so on — due to climate, environment, and so forth; but it is a species by itself, and not to be confounded with any other.
2. That the quadrupeds are a distinct family, also. This family exhibits variations — in color, size, food preferences and so on; but it is a family by itself.
3. That the other families — the birds, the fishes, the insects, the reptiles, etc. — are more or less distinct, also. They are in the procession. They are links in the chain which stretches down from the higher animals to man at the bottom.

Some of my experiments were quite curious. In the course of   4
my reading I had come across a case where, many years ago, some hunters on our Great Plains organized a buffalo hunt for the entertainment of an English earl — that, and to provide some fresh meat for his larder. They had charming sport. They killed seventy-two of those great animals; and ate part of one of them and left the seventy-one to rot. In order to determine the difference between an anaconda and an earl — if any — I caused seven young calves to be turned into the anaconda's cage. The grateful reptile immediately crushed one of them and swallowed it, then lay back satisfied. It showed no further interest in the calves, and no disposition to harm them. I tried this experiment with other

anacondas; always with the same result. The fact stood proven that the difference between an earl and an anaconda is that the earl is cruel and the anaconda isn't; and that the earl wantonly destroys what he has no use for, but the anaconda doesn't. This seemed to suggest that the anaconda was not descended from the earl. It also seemed to suggest that the earl was descended from the anaconda, and had lost a good deal in the transition.

I was aware that many men who have accumulated more millions of money than they can ever use have shown a rabid hunger for more, and have not scrupled to cheat the ignorant and the helpless out of their poor servings in order to partially appease that appetite. I furnished a hundred different kinds of wild and tame animals the opportunity to accumulate vast stores of food, but none of them would do it. The squirrels and bees and certain birds made accumulations, but stopped when they had gathered a winter's supply, and could not be persuaded to add to it either honestly or by chicane. In order to bolster up a tottering reputation the ant pretended to store up supplies, but I was not deceived. I know the ant. These experiments convinced me that there is this difference between man and the higher animals: he is avaricious and miserly, they are not.

In the course of my experiments I convinced myself that among the animals man is the only one that harbors insults and injuries, broods over them, waits till a chance offers, then takes revenge. The passion of revenge is unknown to the higher animals.

Roosters keep harems, but it is by consent of their concubines; therefore no wrong is done. Men keep harems, but it is by brute force, privileged by atrocious laws which the other sex were allowed no hand in making. In this matter man occupies a far lower place than the rooster.

Cats are loose in their morals, but not consciously so. Man, in his descent from the cat, has brought the cat's looseness with him but has left the unconsciousness behind—the saving grace which excuses the cat. The cat is innocent, man is not.

Indecency, vulgarity, obscenity—these are strictly confined to man; he invented them. Among the higher animals there is no trace of them. They hide nothing; they are not ashamed. Man, with his soiled mind, covers himself. He will not even enter a drawing room with his breast and back naked, so alive are he and his mates to indecent suggestion. Man is "The Animal that Laughs." But so does the monkey, as Mr. Darwin pointed out; and so does the Australian bird that is called the laughing jackass. No — Man is the Animal that Blushes. He is the only one that does it — or has occasion to.

At the head of this article we see how "three monks were burnt to death" a few days ago, and a prior "put to death with atrocious cruelty." Do we inquire into the details? No; or we should find out that the prior was subjected to unprintable mutilations. Man — when he is a North American Indian — gouges out his prisoner's eyes; when he is King John, with a nephew to render untroublesome, he uses a red-hot iron; when he is a religious zealot dealing with heretics in the Middle Ages, he skins his captive alive and scatters salt on his back; in the first Richard's time he shuts up a multitude of Jew families in a tower and sets fire to it; in Columbus's time he captures a family of Spanish Jews and — but *that* is not printable; in our day in England a man is fined ten shillings for beating his mother nearly to death with a chair, and another man is fined forty shillings for having four pheasant eggs in his possession without being able to satisfactorily explain how he got them. Of all the animals, man is the only one that is cruel. He is the only one that inflicts pain for the pleasure of doing it. It is a trait that is not known to the higher animals. The cat plays with the frightened mouse; but she has this excuse, that she does not know that the mouse is suffering. The cat is moderate — unhumanly moderate: she only scares the mouse, she does not hurt it; she doesn't dig out its eyes, or tear off its skin, or drive splinters under its nails — man-fashion; when she is done playing with it she makes a sudden meal of it and puts it out of its trouble. Man is the Cruel Animal. He is alone in that distinction.

The higher animals engage in individual fights, but never in organized masses. Man is the only animal that deals in that atrocity of atrocities, War. He is the only one that gathers his brethren about him and goes forth in cold blood and with calm pulse to exterminate his kind. He is the only animal that for sordid wages will march out, as the Hessians did in our Revolution, and as the boyish Prince Napoleon did in the Zulu war, and help to slaughter strangers of his own species who have done him no harm and with whom he has no quarrel.

Man is the only animal that robs his helpless fellow of his 12
country—takes possession of it and drives him out of it or
destroys him. Man has done this in all the ages. There is not an
acre of ground on the globe that is in possession of its rightful
owner, or that has not been taken away from owner after owner,
cycle after cycle, by force and bloodshed.

Man is the only Slave. And he is the only animal who en- 13
slaves. He has always been a slave in one form or another, and has
always held other slaves in bondage under him in one way or
another. In our day he is always some man's slave for wages, and
does that man's work; and this slave has other slaves under him
for minor wages, and they do *his* work. The higher animals are the
only ones who exclusively do their own work and provide their
own living.

Man is the only Patriot. He sets himself apart in his own 14
country, under his own flag, and sneers at the other nations, and
keeps multitudinous uniformed assassins on hand at heavy expense to grab slices of other people's countries, and keep *them*
from grabbing slices of *his*. And in the intervals between campaigns he washes the blood off his hands and works for "the
universal brotherhood of man"—with his mouth.

Man is the Religious Animal. He is the only Religious Ani- 15
mal. He is the only animal that has the True Religion—several of
them. He is the only animal that loves his neighbor as himself,
and cuts his throat if his theology isn't straight. He has made a
graveyard of the globe in trying his honest best to smooth his
brother's path to happiness and heaven. He was at it in the time
of the Caesars, he was at it in Mahomet's time, he was at it in the
time of the Inquisition, he was at it in France a couple of centuries, he was at it in England in Mary's day, he has been at it ever
since he first saw the light, he is at it today in Crete—as per the
telegrams quoted above—he will be at it somewhere else tomorrow. The higher animals have no religion. And we are told that
they are going to be left out, in the Hereafter. I wonder why? It
seems questionable taste.

Man is the Reasoning Animal. Such is the claim. I think it is 16
open to dispute. Indeed, my experiments have proven to me that
he is the Unreasoning Animal. Note his history, as sketched
above. It seems plain to me that whatever he is he is *not* a
reasoning animal. His record is the fantastic record of a maniac. I

consider that the strongest count against his intelligence is the fact that with that record back of him he blandly sets himself up as the head animal of the lot: whereas by his own standards he is the bottom one.

In truth, man is incurably foolish. Simple things which the other animals easily learn, he is incapable of learning. Among my experiments was this. In an hour I taught a cat and a dog to be friends. I put them in a cage. In another hour I taught them to be friends with a rabbit. In the course of two days I was able to add a fox, a goose, a squirrel and some doves. Finally a monkey. They lived together in peace; even affectionately.   17

Next, in another cage I confined an Irish Catholic from Tipperary, and as soon as he seemed tame I added a Scotch Presbyterian from Aberdeen. Next a Turk from Constantinople; a Greek Christian from Crete; an Armenian; a Methodist from the wilds of Arkansas; a Buddhist from China; a Brahman from Benares. Finally, a Salvation Army Colonel from Wapping. Then I stayed away two whole days. When I came back to note results, the cage of Higher Animals was all right, but in the other there was but a chaos of gory odds and ends of turbans and fezzes and plaids and bones and flesh—not a specimen left alive. These Reasoning Animals had disagreed on a theological detail and carried the matter to a Higher Court.   18

One is obliged to concede that in true loftiness of character, Man cannot claim to approach even the meanest of the Higher Animals. It is plain that he is constitutionally incapable of approaching that altitude; that he is constitutionally afflicted with a Defect which must make such approach forever impossible, for it is manifest that this defect is permanent in him, indestructible, ineradicable.   19

I find this Defect to be *the Moral Sense*. He is the only animal that has it. It is the secret of his degradation. It is the quality *which enables him to do wrong*. It has no other office. It is incapable of performing any other function. It could never have been intended to perform any other. Without it, man could do no wrong. He would rise at once to the level of the Higher Animals.   20

Since the Moral Sense has but the one office, the one capacity—to enable man to do wrong—it is plainly without value to him. It is as valueless to him as is disease. In fact, it manifestly *is* a disease. *Rabies* is bad, but it is not so bad as this   21 disease. Rabies enables a man to do a thing which he could not do when in a healthy state: kill his neighbor with a poisonous bite. No one is the better man for having rabies: The Moral Sense enables a man to do wrong. It enables him to do wrong in a thousand ways. Rabies is an innocent disease, compared to the Moral Sense. No one, then, can be the better man for having the Moral Sense. What, now, do we find the Primal Curse to have been? Plainly what it was in the beginning: the infliction upon man of the Moral Sense; the ability to distinguish good from evil; and with it, necessarily, the ability to *do* evil; for there can be no evil act without the presence of consciousness of it in the doer of it.

And so I find that we have descended and degenerated, from some far ancestor — some microscopic atom wandering at its pleasure between the mighty horizons of a drop of water perchance — insect by insect, animal by animal, reptile by reptile, down the long highway of smirchless innocence, till we have reached the bottom stage of development — namable as the Human Being. Below us — nothing.   22

Questions for Close Reading

1. What is the thesis of the selection? Locate the sentence(s) in which Twain states his main idea. If he does not state the thesis explicitly, express it in your own words.
2. Humans are usually called the highest animal, on the basis of intelligence. What are the specific traits that make humans the lowest animal for Twain?
3. How does the story of the earl who hunted down seventy-two buffalo prove that an anaconda is superior to an earl?
4. What does Twain mean when he points out that humankind is the only animal that "has occasion to" blush? What are some of the occasions for blushing he highlights in the essay?
5. Refer to your dictionary as needed to define the following words used in the selection: *confounded* (paragraph 3), *anaconda* (4), *wantonly* (4), *chicane* (5), *heretics* (10), *constitutionally* (19), *ineradicable* (19), and *smirchless* (22).

Questions About the Writer's Craft

1. Most writers do not tell the reader outright the reasoning process they used to arrive at their essay's proposition. But Twain, with

scathing irony, states that he reached his conclusion about human beings inductively—through the use of the "scientific method." Why does Twain make this claim?

2. Where in the essay does Twain try to shock the audience? What might be his purpose in using this technique?

3. In some paragraphs Twain piles on the examples of political and religious atrocities. Wouldn't one or two examples be enough? Why does he supply so many?

4. Black humor is defined as "the use of the morbid and the absurd for comic purposes." What elements of the morbid and the absurd do you find in Twain's essay? Would you say "The Damned Human Race" is an example of black humor?

Questions for Further Thought

1. Twain wrote this essay in the early 1900s. Is what he says about humans true today? Have people improved in a century's time? If Twain were writing today, what events and situations would he include in this essay as proof of humanity's lowness?

2. After reading this satire, are you incensed at humanity's failures—or at Mark Twain for taking this approach to exposing them? Has Twain gone overboard here? Or do we humans deserve this attack?

3. If a person behaved like the cat with a mouse that Twain describes in paragraph 10, would that person be evil, or innocent like the cat? Is it really behavior that is the problem for Twain? Or something else?

4. Twain's essay hinges on an idea most of us take for granted—that the human species tops a hierarchy of creatures. We are, we assume, the ultimate creature, the end result of nature's evolutionary process. What would happen if we became aware that we were not the cleverest, most powerful creature in the universe? What beliefs, habits, actions of ours might change?

Writing Assignments Using Argumentation– Persuasion as a Method of Development

1. Twain focuses on the atrocities committed by human beings in order to show that we are desperately flawed. Write an essay arguing it is our everyday meannesses, unkindnesses, and cruelties that make us the "lowest animal." Use real incidents as your examples, and include whatever description and dialogue you wish. Some situations you might choose include:

Violence or abuse toward children
Neglectful or abusive behavior toward animals

Insults or prejudice of a racial, sexist, or religious nature
Indifference to homeless or injured people
Sarcasm and jesting that humiliates people, friends, family

Use the introduction or conclusion of the essay to acknowledge briefly the opposing viewpoint.

*2. In an essay, argue that human beings are worthy of being considered the "highest animal." The paper should acknowledge and then refute Twain's charges that people are miserly, vengeful, foolish, and so on. To support your proposition, use specific examples of how human beings can be kind, caring, generous, and peace-loving. You might find it helpful to read Bob Greene's "Handled with Care" (page 142), an essay focusing on the more positive aspects of human nature.

Writing Assignments Using Other Methods of Development

*3. What failings of human decency do you see around you every day in your town, on your campus, or at your job? Write an essay showing that inhumanity resides not just in atrocities but also in ordinary life. Before planning the paper, you might want to see what William McKibben ("Ugly," page 427) has to say about people's often uncaring attitude toward the homeless. In your essay, you may use Twain's kind of bitter sarcasm. Or you may adopt a more objective, less vitriolic tone.

4. How could humans become less cruel? Write an essay outlining a new process for raising children or "recivilizing" adults — processes, which if instituted, would improve the morality of humanity. You may wish to approach the essay seriously, or you may take a humorous tone.

Frank Trippett

Now senior editor of *Time* magazine, Frank Trippett (1926–) has had a lifelong career in journalism. He has served as a writer and editor at such national publications as *Look* and *Newsweek* and is the author of three books: *The States: United They Fall* (1967), *The First Horseman* (1974), and *Child Ellen* (1975). The following essay first appeared in *Time*.

A Red Light for Scofflaws

You drive 60 in a 55 mph zone. You fib a bit on your income tax return and your job application. You hide beer in your jacket and bring it into the stadium, although alcohol is prohibited. Are you a criminal? Of course not, you say; everybody does these little things and no one gets hurt. In "A Red Light for Scofflaws," Frank Trippett takes a wider view of what happens when individuals bend small laws for their own convenience.

Law-and-order is the longest-running and probably the best-loved political issue in U.S. history. Yet it is painfully apparent that millions of Americans who would never think of themselves as lawbreakers, let alone criminals, are taking increasing liberties with the legal codes that are designed to protect and nourish their society. Indeed, there are moments today—amid outlaw litter, tax cheating, illicit noise and motorized anarchy—when it seems as though the scofflaw represents the wave of the future. Harvard Sociologist David Riesman suspects that a majority of Americans have blithely taken to committing supposedly minor derelictions as a matter of course. Already, Riesman says, the ethic of U.S. society is in danger of becoming this: "You're a fool if you obey the rules." 1

Nothing could be more obvious than the evidence supporting Riesman. Scofflaws abound in amazing variety. The graffiti-prone turn public surfaces into visual rubbish. Bicyclists often 2 ride as though two-wheeled vehicles are exempt from all traffic laws. Litterbugs convert their communities into trash dumps. Widespread flurries of ordinances have failed to clear public places of high-decibel portable radios, just as earlier laws failed to wipe out the beer-soaked hooliganism that plagues many parks. Tobacco addicts remain hopelessly blind to signs that say NO SMOKING. Respectably dressed pot smokers no longer bother to duck out of public sight to pass around a joint. The flagrant use of cocaine is a festering scandal in middle- and upper-class life. And then there are (hello, Everybody!) the jaywalkers.

The dangers of scofflawry vary widely. The person who illegally spits on the sidewalk remains disgusting, but clearly poses less risk to others than the company that illegally buries hazardous chemical waste in an unauthorized location. The fare-beater on the subway presents less threat to life than the landlord who ignores fire safety statutes. The most immediately and measurably dangerous scofflawry, however, also happens to be the most visible. The culprit is the American driver, whose lawless activities today add up to a colossal public nuisance. The hazards range from routine double parking that jams city streets to the drunk driving that kills some 25,000 people and injures at least 650,000 others yearly. Illegal speeding on open highways? New surveys show that on some interstate highways 83% of all drivers are currently ignoring the federal 55 m.p.h. speed limit. 3

The most flagrant scofflaw of them all is the red-light runner. The flouting of stop signals has got so bad in Boston that residents tell an anecdote about a cabby who insists that red lights are "just for decoration." The power of the stoplight to control traffic seems to be waning everywhere. In Los Angeles, red-light running has become perhaps the city's most common traffic violation. In New York City, going through an intersection is like Russian roulette. Admits Police Commissioner Robert J. McGuire: "Today it's a 50 – 50 toss-up as to whether people will stop for a red light." Meanwhile, his own police largely ignore the lawbreaking. 4

Red-light running has always ranked as a minor wrong, and so it may be in individual instances. When the violation becomes habitual, widespread and incessant, however, a great deal more than a traffic management problem is involved. The flouting of basic rules of the road leaves deep dents in the social mood. 5

Innocent drivers and pedestrians pay a repetitious price in frustration, inconvenience and outrage, not to mention a justified sense of mortal peril. The significance of red-light running is magnified by its high visibility. If hypocrisy is the tribute that vice pays to virtue, then furtiveness is the true outlaw's salute to the force of law-and-order. The red-light runner, however, shows no respect whatever for the social rules, and society cannot help being harmed by any repetitious and brazen display of contempt for the fundamentals of order.

The scofflaw spirit is pervasive. It is not really surprising   6
when schools find, as some do, that children frequently enter not knowing some of the basic rules of living together. For all their differences, today's scofflaws are of a piece as a symptom of elementary social demoralization — the loss by individuals of the capacity to govern their own behavior in the interest of others.

The prospect of the collapse of public manners is not merely   7
a matter of etiquette. Society's first concern will remain major crime, but a foretaste of the seriousness of incivility is suggested by what has been happening in Houston. Drivers on Houston freeways have been showing an increasing tendency to replace the rules of the road with violent outbreaks. Items from the Houston police department's new statistical category — freeway traffic violence: (1) Driver flashes high-beam lights at car that cut in front of him, whose occupants then hurl a beer can at his windshield, kick out his tail lights, slug him eight stitches' worth. (2) Dump-truck driver annoyed by delay batters trunk of stalled car ahead and its driver with steel bolt. (3) Hurrying driver of 18-wheel truck deliberately rear-ends car whose driver was trying to stay within 55 m.p.h. limit. The Houston Freeway Syndrome has fortunately not spread everywhere. But the question is: Will it?

Americans are used to thinking that law-and-order is threat-   8
ened mainly by stereotypical violent crime. When the foundations of U.S. law have actually been shaken, however, it has always been because ordinary law-abiding citizens took to skirting the law. Major instance: Prohibition. Recalls Donald Barr Chidsey in *On and Off the Wagon:* "Lawbreaking proved to be not painful, not even uncomfortable, but, in a mild and perfectly safe way, exhilarating." People wiped out Prohibition at last not only because of the alcohol issue but because scofflawry was seriously undermining the authority and legitimacy of government. Ironi-

cally, today's scofflaw spirit, whatever its undetermined origins, is being encouraged unwittingly by government at many levels. The failure of police to enforce certain laws is only the surface of the problem: they take their mandate from the officials and constituents they serve. Worse, most state legislatures have helped subvert popular compliance with the federal 55 m.p.h. law, some of them by enacting puny fines that trivialize transgressions. On a higher level, the Administration in Washington has dramatized its wish to nullify civil rights laws simply by opposing instead of supporting certain court-ordered desegregation rulings. With considerable justification, environmental groups, in the words of *Wilderness* magazine, accuse the Administration of "destroying environmental laws by failing to enforce them, or by enforcing them in ways that deliberately encourage noncompliance." Translation: scofflawry at the top.

The most disquieting thing about the scofflaw spirit is its   9 extreme infectiousness. Only a terminally foolish society would sit still and allow it to spread indefinitely.

Questions for Close Reading

1. What is the thesis of the selection? Locate the sentence(s) in which Trippett states his main idea. If he does not state the thesis explicitly, express it in your own words.
2. According to Trippett, what is the most dangerous and common kind of "scofflawry" today? Why is it so dangerous?
3. What does the author mean by "hypocrisy is the tribute vice pays to virtue"?
4. What more serious problem underlies the looseness with which Americans adhere to traffic rules? Why is this skirting of the law more than just "poor etiquette"?
5. Refer to your dictionary as needed to define the following words in the selection: *illicit* (paragraph 1), *blithely* (1), *derelictions* (1), *flouting* (5), *brazen* (5), *incivility* (7), and *nullify* (8).

Questions About the Writer's Craft

1. At what point in this essay did you realize that Trippett was concerned with more than just traffic violators? Do you feel Trippett proves that scofflawry will spread "indefinitely"? Or is his argument founded on a fallacy?

2. Where does Trippett support his argument with statistics? Are these statistics convincing? Where else might he have used facts and figures effectively?
3. Why does Trippett add "(hello, Everybody!)" in the middle of a sentence in paragraph 2? Who is his intended audience?
4. Examine Trippett's conclusion. Why is it so short? What effect does this conclusion have on you? What conclusion strategy is he using?

Questions for Further Thought

1. Is scofflawry the major danger to law-and-order in this country? What other kinds of antisocial behavior might be just as or even more dangerous?
2. Do you agree with the sayings, "You're a fool if you obey the rules" and "Rules are made to be broken"? What sound arguments are there against these maxims?
3. Should police do more to curb minor infractions on the road, on subways, on streets? How could we help bring this about?
4. One kind of lawbreaking is the deliberate organized resistance to unjust laws known as civil disobedience. It has been practiced in India to win independence and in the American South to overturn segregation, to name just two instances. Is this kind of lawbreaking justifiable? Does widespread scofflawry undermine the effectiveness of civil disobedience?

Writing Assignments Using Argumentation– Persuasion as a Method of Development

1. Write an essay from the point of view of a scofflaw arguing that some laws are worthless and should be ignored. Support your argument by providing reasons why the laws are of no value and thus should be ignored. Part of the essay should cite and, if possible, rebut the opposing view.
2. Trippett contends that driving violations are the worst form of scofflawry. Think of another form you feel is just as destructive — for example, drug abuse, environmental damage, noise pollution, cheating, or some other type of lawbreaking. Argue that if this type of behavior continues, society will be in great danger.

Writing Assignments Using Other Methods of Development

3. Identify some law or restriction that people tend to ignore. You might focus on dorm regulations, library rules, speeding restrictions

on our highways, and so on. In an essay, illustrate the consequences of ignoring these regulations and then describe the advantages that would result if the regulations were honored.

*4. Research the term *civil disobedience* by looking it up in an encyclopedia and the *Readers' Guide to Periodical Literature*. You might also want to read Martin Luther King, Jr.'s "Three Kinds of Resistance to Oppression" (page 629). Then write an essay that defines civil disobedience, using for support the material you researched. Show how civil disobedience could be an effective force for change in a current situation that needs remedying. The situation could be on campus, in your hometown, or on the national or international scene.

Jonathan Swift

The foremost satirist in the English language, Jonathan Swift (1667–1745) is most famous as the author of *Gulliver's Travels* (1726), an often scorching indictment of human conduct. Born in Ireland, Swift moved to London at a young age and in 1694 was ordained an Anglican priest. In 1714 he was appointed the Dean of St. Patrick's Cathedral in Dublin, a minor post the ambitious Swift accepted with reluctance. For most of his life, Swift was an outspoken public figure, writing satiric poems, plays, and essays aimed at political and religious targets. His major works include *A Tale of a Tub* (1704) and *The Battle of the Books* (1704). Later, outraged by the British government's treatment of the Irish people, Swift wrote "A Modest Proposal," the classic essay reprinted here.

A Modest Proposal

In 1729, Ireland was in tragic condition. Poverty was widespread, a devastating famine was in its third year, and people were starving. Moreover, the British government, which ruled Ireland, imposed high taxes on the already impoverished populace. Angered by these injustices, Swift wrote a powerful satire attacking the English and wealthy Irish who ignored the existence of the suffering masses. Speaking not as himself but in the guise of a disinterested observer, Swift suggested an outrageous solution to Ireland's problems, a solution in keeping with the inhumanity he saw rampant in Ireland.

It is a melancholy object to those who walk through this great town[1] or travel in the country, when they see the streets, the roads, and cabin doors, crowded with beggars of the female sex, followed by three, four, or six children, all in rags and importuning every passenger for an alms. These mothers, instead of being

[1] Dublin.

579

able to work for their honest livelihood, are forced to employ all their time in strolling to beg sustenance for their helpless infants, who, as they grow up, either turn thieves for want of work, or leave their dear native country to fight for the Pretender in Spain, or sell themselves to the Barbadoes.[2]

I think it is agreed by all parties that this prodigious number   2
of children in the arms, or on the backs, or at the heels of their mothers, and frequently of their fathers, is in the present deplorable state of the kingdom a very great additional grievance; and therefore whoever could find out a fair, cheap,and easy method of making these children sound, useful members of the commonwealth would deserve so well of the public as to have his statue set up for a preserver of the nation.

But my intention is very far from being confined to provide   3
only for the children of professed beggars; it is of a much greater extent, and shall take in the whole number of infants at a certain age who are born of parents in effect as little able to support them as those who demand our charity in the streets.

As to my own part, having turned my thoughts for many   4
years upon this important subject, and maturely weighed the several schemes of other projectors, I have always found them grossly mistaken in their computation. It is true, a child just dropped from its dam may be supported by her milk for a solar year, with little other nourishment; at most not above the value of two shillings, which the mother may certainly get, or the value in scraps, by her lawful occupation of begging; and it is exactly at one year old that I propose to provide for them in such a manner as instead of being a charge upon their parents or the parish, or wanting food and raiment for the rest of their lives, they shall on the contrary contribute to the feeding, and partly to the clothing, of many thousands.

There is likewise another great advantage in my scheme, that   5
it will prevent those involuntary abortions, and that horrid practice of women murdering their bastard children, alas, too frequent among us, sacrificing the poor innocent babes, I doubt, more to avoid the expense than the shame, which would move tears and pity in the most savage and inhuman breast.

The number of souls in this kingdom being usually reckoned   6

---

[2]Many poor Irish were leaving the country to try to find a living elsewhere.

one million and a half, of these I calculate there may be about two hundred thousand couples whose wives are breeders, from which number I subtract thirty thousand couples who are able to maintain their own children, although I apprehend there cannot be so many under the present distress of the kingdom; but this being granted, there will remain an hundred and seventy thousand breeders. I again subtract fifty thousand for those women who miscarry, or whose children die by accident or disease within the year. There only remain an hundred and twenty thousand children of poor parents annually born. The question therefore is, how this number shall be reared and provided for, which, as I have already said, under the present situation of affairs, is utterly impossible by all the methods hitherto proposed. For we can neither employ them in handicraft nor agriculture; we neither build houses (I mean in the country) nor cultivate land. They can very seldom pick up livelihood by stealing till they arrive at six years old, except where they are of towardly parts;[3] although I confess they learn the rudiments much earlier, during which time they can however be looked upon only as probationers, as I have been informed by a principal gentleman in the county of Cavan, who protested to me that he never knew above one or two instances under the age of six, even in a part of the kingdom so renowned for the quickest proficiency in that art.

I am assured by our merchants that a boy or a girl before 7 twelve years old is no salable commodity; and even when they come to this age, they will not yield above three pounds, or three pounds and half a crown at most on the Exchange; which cannot turn to account either to the parents or the kingdom, the charge of nutriment and rags having been at least four times that value.

I shall now therefore humbly propose my own thoughts, 8 which I hope will not be liable to the least objection.

I have been assured by a very knowing American of my 9 acquaintance in London, that a young healthy child well nursed is at a year old a most delicious, nourishing, and wholesome food, whether stewed, roasted, baked, or boiled; and I make no doubt that it will equally serve in fricassee or a ragout.

I do therefore humbly offer it to public consideration that of 10 the hundred and twenty thousand children, already computed, twenty thousand may be reserved for breed, whereof only one

[3]Prematurely developed.

fourth part to be males, which is more than we allow to sheep, black cattle, or swine; and my reason is that these children are seldom the fruits of marriage, a circumstance not much regarded by our savages, therefore one male will be sufficient to serve four females. That the remaining hundred thousand may at a year old be offered in sale to the persons of quality and fortune through the kingdom, always advising the mother to let them suck plentifully in the last month, so as to render them plump and fat for a good table. A child will make two dishes at an entertainment for friends; and when the family dines alone, the fore or hind quarter will make a reasonable dish, and seasoned with a little pepper or salt will be very good boiled on the fourth day, especially in winter.

11   I have reckoned upon a medium that a child just born will weigh twelve pounds, and in a solar year if tolerably nursed increaseth to twenty-eight pounds.

12   I grant this food will be somewhat dear, and therefore very proper for landlords, who, as they have already devoured most of the parents, seem to have the best title to the children.

13   Infant's flesh will be in season throughout the year, but more plentiful in March, and a little before and after. For we are told by a grave author, an eminent French physician,[4] that fish being a prolific diet, there are more children born in Roman Catholic countries about nine months after Lent, than at any other season; therefore, reckoning a year after Lent, the markets will be more glutted than usual, because the number of popish infants is at least three to one in this kingdom; and therefore it will have one other collateral advantage, by lessening the number of Papists among us.

14   I have already computed the charge of nursing a beggar's child (in which list I reckon all cottagers, laborers, and four fifths of the farmers) to be about two shillings per annum, rags included; and I believe no gentleman would repine to give ten shillings for the carcass of a good fat child, which, as I have said, will make four dishes of excellent nutritive meat, when he hath only some particular friend or his own family to dine with him. Thus the squire will learn to be a good landlord, and grow

[4] François Rabelais, a sixteenth-century comic writer.

popular among the tenants; the mother will have eight shillings net profit, and be fit for work till she produces another child.

Those who are more thrifty (as I must confess the times 15 require) may flay the carcass; the skin of which artifically[5] dressed will make admirable gloves for ladies, and summer boots for fine gentlemen.

As to our city of Dublin, shambles[6] may be appointed for this 16 purpose in the most convenient parts of it, and butchers we may be assured will not be wanting; although I rather recommend buying the children alive, and dressing them hot from the knife as we do roasting pigs.

A very worthy person, a true lover of his country, and whose 17 virtues I highly esteem, was lately pleased in discoursing on this matter to offer a refinement upon my scheme. He said that many gentlemen of his kingdom, having of late destroyed their deer, he conceived that the want of venison might be well supplied by the bodies of young lads and maidens, not exceeding fourteen years of age nor under twelve, so great a number of both sexes in every county being now ready to starve for want of work and service; and these to be disposed of by their parents, if alive, or otherwise by their nearest relations. But with due deference to so excellent a friend and so deserving a patriot, I cannot be altogether in his sentiments; for as to the males, my American acquaintance assured me from frequent experience that their flesh was generally tough and lean, like that of our schoolboys, by continual exercise, and their taste disagreeable; and to fatten them would not answer the charge. Then as to the females, it would, I think with humble submission, be a loss to the public, because they soon would become breeders themselves; and besides, it is not improbable that some scrupulous people might be apt to censure such a practice (although indeed very unjustly) as a little bordering upon cruelty; which, I confess, hath always been with me the strongest objection against any project, how well soever intended.

But in order to justify my friend, he confessed that this 18 expedient was put into his head by the famous Psalmanazar,[7] a

---

[5]Skillfully.

[6]Slaughterhouses.

[7]A Frenchman, Georges Psalmanazar, who fooled London society into thinking he was from the exotic land of Formosa.

native of the island Formosa, who came from thence to London above twenty years ago, and in conversation told my friend that in his country when any young person happened to be put to death, the executioner sold the carcass to the persons of quality as a prime dainty; and that in his time the body of a plump girl of fifteen, who was crucified for an attempt to poison the emperor, was sold to his Imperial Majesty's prime minister of state, and other great mandarins of the court, in joints from the gibbet, at four hundred crowns. Neither indeed can I deny that if the same use were made of several plump young girls in this town, who without one single groat to their fortunes cannot stir abroad without a chair,[8] and appear at the playhouse and assemblies in foreign fineries which they never will pay for, the kingdom would not be the worse.

Some persons of a desponding spirit are in great concern about that vast number of poor people who are aged, diseased, or maimed, and I have been desired to employ my thoughts what course may be taken to ease the nation of so grievous an encumbrance. But I am not in the least pain upon that matter, because it is very well known that they are every day dying and rotting by cold and famine, and filth and vermin, as fast as can be reasonably expected. And as to the younger laborers, they are now in almost as hopeful a condition. They cannot get work, and consequently pine away for want of nourishment to a degree that if any time they are accidentally hired to common labor, they have not strength to perform it; and thus the country and themselves are happily delivered from the evils to come. — 19

I have too long digressed, and therefore shall return to my subject. I think the advantages by the proposal which I have made are obvious and many, as well as of the highest importance. — 20

For first, as I have already observed, it would greatly lessen the number of Papists, with whom we are yearly overrun, being the principal breeders of the nation as well as our most dangerous enemies; and who stay at home on purpose to deliver the kingdom to the Pretender, hoping to take their advantage by the absence of so many good Protestants, who have chosen rather — 21

---

[8]A groat was a coin worth several pennies; a chair was a sedan chair in which a person was carried by servants.

to leave their country than to stay at home and pay tithes against their conscience to an Episcopal curate.

Secondly, the poorer tenants will have something valuable of their own, which by law may be made liable to distress,[9] and help to pay their landlord's rent, their corn and cattle being already seized and money a thing unknown.   22

Thirdly, whereas the maintenance of an hundred thousand children, from two years old and upwards, cannot be computed at less than ten shillings a piece per annum, the nation's stock will be thereby increased fifty thousand pounds per annum, besides the profit of a new dish introduced to the tables of all gentlemen of fortune in the kingdom who have any refinement in taste. And the money will circulate among ourselves, the goods being entirely of our own growth and manufacture.   23

Fourthly, the constant breeders, besides the gain of eight shillings sterling per annum by the sale of their children, will be rid of the charge for maintaining them after the first year.   24

Fifthly, this food would likewise bring great custom to taverns, where the vintners will certainly be so prudent as to procure the best receipts for dressing it to perfection, and consequently have their houses frequented by all the fine gentlemen, who justly value themselves upon their knowledge in good eating; and a skillful cook, who understands how to oblige his guests, will contrive to make it as expensive as they please.   25

Sixthly, this would be a great inducement to marriage, which all wise nations have either encouraged by rewards or enforced by laws and penalties. It would increase the care and tenderness of mothers toward their children, when they were sure of a settlement for life to the poor babes, provided in some sort by the public, to their annual profit instead of expense. We should see an honest emulation among the married women, which of them could bring the fattest child to the market. Men would become as fond of their wives during the time of pregnancy as they are now of their mares in foal, their cows in calf, or sows when they are ready to farrow; nor offer to beat or kick them (as is too frequent a practice) for fear of a miscarriage.   26

Many other advantages might be enumerated. For instance,   27

[9]Seizure for the payment of debts.

the addition of some thousand carcasses in our exportation of barreled beef, the propagation of swine's flesh, and improvements in the art of making good bacon, so much wanted among us by the great destruction of pigs, too frequent at our tables, which are no way comparable in taste or magnificence to a well-grown, fat, yearling child, which roasted whole will make a considerable figure at a lord mayor's feast or any other public entertainment. But this and many others I omit, being studious of brevity.

Supposing that one thousand families in this city would be constant customers for infants' flesh, besides others who might have it at merry meetings, particularly weddings and christenings, I compute that Dublin would take off annually about twenty thousand carcasses, and the rest of the kingdom (where probably they will be sold somewhat cheaper) the remaining eighty thousand.   28

I can think of no one objection that will possibly be raised against this proposal, unless it should be urged that the number of people will be thereby much lessened in the kingdom. This I freely own, and it was indeed one principal design in offering it to the world. I desire the reader will observe; that I calculate my remedy for this one individual kingdom of Ireland and for no other that ever was, is, or I think ever can be upon earth. Therefore, let no man talk to me of other expedients: of taxing our absentees at five shillings a pound: of using neither clothes nor household furniture except what is of our own growth and manufacture: of utterly rejecting the materials and instruments that promote foreign luxury: of curing the expensiveness of pride, vanity, idleness, and gaming in our women: of introducing a vein of parsimony, prudence, and temperance: of learning to love our country, in the want of which we differ even from Laplanders and the inhabitants of Topinamboo[10]: of quitting our animosities and factions, nor acting any longer like the Jews,[11] who were murdering one another at the very moment their city was taken: of being a little cautious not to sell our country and conscience for nothing: of teaching landlords to have at least one degree of mercy toward their tenants: lastly, of putting a spirit of honesty, in-   29

[10]A place in the Brazilian jungle.
[11]Rival factions were at war within Jerusalem when the city was seized by the Romans in 70 A.D.

dustry, and skill into our shopkeepers; who, if a resolution could now be taken to buy only our native goods, would immediately unite to cheat and exact upon us in the price, the measure, and the goodness, nor could ever yet be brought to make one fair proposal of just dealing, though often and earnestly invited to it.

Therefore, I repeat, let no man talk to me of these and the like expedients, till he hath at least some glimpse of hope that there will ever be some hearty and sincere attempt to put them in practice. 30

But as to myself, having been wearied out for many years with offering vain, idle, visionary thoughts, and at length utterly despairing of success, I fortunately fell upon this proposal, which, as it is wholly new, so it hath something solid and real, of no expense and little trouble, full in our own power, and whereby we can incur no danger in disobliging England. For this kind of commodity will not bear exportation, the flesh being of too tender a consistence to admit a long continuance in salt, although perhaps I could name a country which would be glad to eat up our whole nation without it. 31

After all, I am not so violently bent upon my own opinion as to reject any offer proposed by wise men, which shall be found equally innocent, cheap, easy, and effectual. But before something of that kind shall be advanced in contradiction to my scheme, and offering a better, I desire the author or authors will be pleased maturely to consider two points. First, as things now stand, how they will be able to find food and raiment for an hundred thousand useless mouths and backs. And secondly, there being a round million of creatures in human figure throughout this kingdom, whose sole subsistence put into a common stock would leave them in debt two millions of pounds sterling, adding those who are beggars by profession to the bulk of farmers, cottagers, and laborers, with their wives and children who are beggars in effect; I desire those politicians who dislike my overture, and may perhaps be so bold to attempt an answer, that they will first ask the parents of these mortals whether they would not at this day think it a great happiness to have been sold for food at a year old in this manner I prescribe, and thereby have avoided such a perpetual scene of misfortunes as they have since gone through by the oppression of landlords, the impossibility of paying rent without money or trade, the want of common suste- 32 nance, with neither house nor clothes to cover them from the inclemencies of the weather, and the most inevitable prospect of entailing the like or greater miseries upon their breed forever.

I profess, in the sincerity of my heart, that I have not the least 33 personal interest in endeavoring to promote this necessary work, having no other motive than the public good of my country, by advancing our trade, providing for infants, relieving the poor, and giving some pleasure to the rich. I have no children by which I can propose to get a single penny; the youngest being nine years old, and my wife past childbearing.

Questions for Close Reading

1. What is the thesis of the selection? Locate the sentence(s) in which Swift states his main idea. If he does not state the thesis explicitly, express it in your own words.
2. The author mentions several economic, social, and political realities in Ireland that prompted him to write this essay. Identify a few of them.
3. What twisted reasoning does the speaker use to argue that his proposal will improve relationships between husbands and wives and between parents and children?
4. What problems does the speaker contend the British government will solve if it permits the butchering and sale of infants from impoverished families?
5. Refer to your dictionary as needed to define the following words in the selection: *importuning* (paragraph 1), *alms* (1), *prodigious* (2), *raiment* (4), *prolific* (13), *repine* (14), *discoursing* (17), *encumbrance* (19), and *vintners* (25).

Questions About the Writer's Craft

1. *Satire* uses humor to criticize a situation and create awareness of the need for change; *irony*, often used in satire, involves writing or saying one thing but meaning the opposite. How do satire and irony help Swift accomplish what a more conventional approach to persuasion would not?
2. Swift uses language laden with emotion to convey a sarcastic, downright bitter tone. Locate several examples of emotionally charged language. How does this language support Swift's real purpose for writing "A Modest Proposal"?

3. In paragraph 20, the speaker apologizes for having "digressed" in the last few paragraphs. Do paragraphs 17, 18, and 19 really represent a digression, or are they germane to the issue? Explain.
4. Writers of argumentation–persuasion essays often anticipate and then refute opposing opinions. In what paragraph does the speaker in "A Modest Proposal" refute the dissenting viewpoint? What is the real purpose of this refutation?

Questions for Further Thought

1. Are the causes of the poverty Swift saw in eighteenth-century Ireland similar to some of the economic problems we experience in this country? Explain.
2. In paragraph 29, the speaker rejects several proposals that Swift actually believes would help alleviate poverty in Ireland. Which of these proposals might be used to address the problem of poverty in our nation?
3. Do the well-off, even the merely comfortable, have a responsibility to the poor? If so, what is the nature and extent of this responsibility?
4. Swift's epitaph reads, "He has gone where savage indignation can no longer lacerate his heart." About what do you feel "savage indignation"? What can you do about the situations that distress you?

Writing Assignments Using Argumentation– Persuasion as a Method of Development

1. Choose an issue about which you feel strongly: the shortage of student parking spaces at your college, the poor sex education curriculum in local high schools, the inefficient trash-recycling program in your town, whatever. Then, like Swift, use an ironic approach to convince readers of your position. In other words, argue for one point of view while pretending to advance the opposite. For example, if you are opposed to permitting people to smoke in public places, write an essay arguing the "advantages" of breathing in second-hand smoke and defend the "rights" of smokers to pollute the air.
*2. Read what William McKibben has to say in "Ugly" (page 427) about one segment of this country's poor—the homeless. Then write an essay advocating the steps ordinary citizens can take to help alleviate the problem. As you draft your proposal, keep in mind what McKibben says about people's insensitivity and apathy. What persuasive strategies will you adopt to puncture this callous disregard?

Writing Assignments Using Other Methods of Development

3. At the start of "A Modest Proposal," Swift describes briefly the poverty he witnessed in his native land. How would *you* describe the face of poverty? Write an essay describing an impoverished, blighted area. What are its streets, houses, stores, and people like? Organizing the essay around a dominant impression, depict what you see, smell, hear, and feel.

4. Seeking to improve the Irish economy, Swift advocates boycotting foreign-made products. Do you believe the United States should impose restrictive tariffs and import limits on goods manufactured abroad? Write a paper in which you identify the positive and negative consequences of such protective measures. Gather information by brainstorming with others and, if necessary, go to the library to locate several articles on this issue.

Edward I. Koch

Edward I. Koch, mayor of New York City since 1978, calls himself "the sort of person who might give other people ulcers." Controversial and outspoken, Koch was elected mayor after campaigning on an anti-crime and anti-spending platform. Active in New York City politics throughout the 1960s, Koch also served in the U.S. House of Representatives from 1966 until the time he became mayor. Koch, trained as an attorney, has written two autobiographical books: *Mayor* (1984) and *Politics* (1985). The following essay, "Death and Justice," was published in *The New Republic* in 1985.

Death and Justice

Critics of capital punishment call the death penalty state-sanctioned murder. On the contrary, says New York City Mayor Ed Koch, the death penalty "affirms the value of human life." To develop his position, Koch examines his opponents' arguments point by point, concluding that execution is the only adequate punishment for cold-blooded killings.

Last December a man named Robert Lee Willie, who had 1 been convicted of raping and murdering an 18-year-old woman, was executed in the Louisiana state prison. In a statement issued several minutes before his death, Mr. Willie said: "Killing people is wrong. . . . It makes no difference whether it's citizens, countries, or governments. Killing is wrong." Two weeks later in South Carolina, an admitted killer named Joseph Carl Shaw was put to death for murdering two teenagers. In an appeal to the governor for clemency, Mr. Shaw wrote: "Killing is wrong when I did it. Killing is wrong when you do it. I hope you have the courage and moral strength to stop the killing."

It is a curiosity of modern life that we find ourselves being 2 lectured on morality by cold-blooded killers. Mr. Willie previously had been convicted of aggravated rape, aggravated kidnapping, and the murders of a Louisiana deputy and a man from Missouri. Mr. Shaw committed another murder a week before the two for which he was executed, and admitted mutilating the body of the 14-year-old girl he killed. I can't help wondering what prompted these murderers to speak out against killing as they entered the death-house door. Did their newfound reverence for life stem from the realization that they were about to lose their own?

Life is indeed precious, and I believe the death penalty helps   3
to affirm this fact. Had the death penalty been a real possibility in the minds of these murderers, they might well have stayed their hand. They might have shown moral awareness before their victims died, and not after. Consider the tragic death of Rosa Velez, who happened to be home when a man named Luis Vera burglarized her apartment in Brooklyn. "Yeah, I shot her," Vera admitted. "She knew me, and I knew I wouldn't go to the chair."

During my 22 years in public service, I have heard the pros   4
and cons of capital punishment expressed with special intensity. As a district leader, councilman, congressman, and mayor, I have represented constituencies generally thought of as liberal. Because I support the death penalty for heinous crimes of murder, I have sometimes been the subject of emotional and outraged attacks by voters who find my position reprehensible or worse. I have listened to their ideas. I have weighed their objections carefully. I still support the death penalty. The reasons I maintained my position can be best understood by examining the arguments most frequently heard in opposition.

1. The death penalty is "barbaric." Sometimes opponents of   5
capital punishment horrify with tales of lingering death on the gallows, of faulty electric chairs, or of agony in the gas chamber. Partly in response to such protests, several states such as North Carolina and Texas switched to execution by lethal injection. The condemned person is put to death painlessly, without ropes, voltage, bullets, or gas. Did this answer the objections of death penalty opponents? Of course not. On June 22, 1984, *The New York Times* published an editorial that sarcastically attacked the new "hygienic" method of death by injection, and stated that "execution can never be made humane through science." So it's not the method that really troubles opponents. It's the death itself they consider barbaric.

Admittedly, capital punishment is not a pleasant topic. How- 6
ever, one does not have to like the death penalty in order to
support it any more than one must like radical surgery, radiation,
or chemotherapy in order to find necessary these attempts at
curing cancer. Ultimately we may learn how to cure cancer with a
simple pill. Unfortunately, that day has not yet arrived. Today we
are faced with the choice of letting the cancer spread or trying to
cure it with the methods available, methods that one day will
almost certainly be considered barbaric. But to give up and do
nothing would be far more barbaric and would certainly delay the
discovery of an eventual cure. The analogy between cancer and
murder is imperfect, because murder is not the "disease" we are
trying to cure. The disease is injustice. We may not like the death
penalty, but it must be available to punish crimes of cold-blooded
murder, cases in which any other form of punishment would be
inadequate and, therefore, unjust. If we create a society in which
injustice is not tolerated, incidents of murder — the most flagrant
form of justice — will diminish.

2. *No other major democracy uses the death penalty.* No other 7
major democracy — in fact, few other countries of any
description — are plagued by a murder rate such as that in the
United States. Fewer and fewer Americans can remember the days
when unlocked doors were the norm and murder was a rare and
terrible offense. In America the murder rate climbed 122 percent
between 1963 and 1980. During that same period, the murder
rate in New York City increased by almost 400 percent, and the
statistics are even worse in many other cities. A study at M.I.T.
showed that based on 1970 homicide rates a person who lived in
a large American city ran a greater risk of being murdered than an
American soldier in World War II ran of being killed in combat.
It is not surprising that the laws of each country differ according
to differing conditions and traditions. If other countries had our
murder problem, the cry for capital punishment would be just as
loud as it is here. And I daresay that any other major democracy
where 75 percent of the people supported the death penalty
would soon enact it into law.

3. *An innocent person might be executed by mistake.* Consider 8
the work of Adam Bedau, one of the most implacable foes of
capital punishment in this country. According to Mr. Bedau, it is
"false sentimentality to argue that the death penalty should be

abolished because of the abstract possibility that an innocent person might be executed." He cites a study of the 7,000 executions in this country from 1893 to 1971, and concludes that the record fails to show that such cases occur. The main point, however, is this. If government functioned only when the possibility of error didn't exist, government wouldn't function at all. Human life deserves special protection, and one of the best ways to guarantee that protection is to assure that convicted murderers do not kill again. Only the death penalty can accomplish this end. In a recent case in New Jersey, a man named Richard Biegenwald was freed from prison after serving 18 years for murder; since his release he has been convicted of committing four murders. A prisoner named Lemuel Smith, while serving four life sentences for murder (plus two life sentences for kidnapping and robbery) in New York's Green Haven Prison, lured a woman corrections officer into the chaplain's office and strangled her. He then mutilated and dismembered her body. An additional life sentence for Smith is meaningless. Because New York has no death penalty statute, Smith has effectively been given a license to kill.

But the problem of multiple murder is not confined to the nation's penitentiaries. In 1981, 91 police officers were killed in the line of duty in this country. Seven percent of those arrested in the cases that have been solved had a previous arrest for murder. In New York City in 1976 and 1977, 85 persons arrested for homicide had a previous arrest for murder. Six of these individuals had two previous arrests for murder, and one had four previous murder arrests. During those two years the New York police were arresting for murder persons with a previous arrest for murder on the average of one every 8.5 days. This is not surprising when we learn that in 1975, for example, the median time served in Massachusetts for homicide was less than two and a half years. In 1976 a study sponsored by the Twentieth Century Fund found that the average time served in the United States for first-degree murder is ten years. The median time served may be considerably lower.

4. *Capital punishment cheapens the value of human life.* On the contrary, it can be easily demonstrated that the death penalty strengthens the value of human life. If the penalty for rape were lowered, clearly it would signal a lessened regard for the victims'

suffering, humiliation, and personal integrity. It would cheapen their horrible experience, and expose them to an increased danger of recurrence. When we lower the penalty for murder, it signals a lessened regard for the value of the victim's life. Some critics of capital punishment, such as columnist Jimmy Breslin, have suggested that a life sentence is actually a harsher penalty for murder than death. This is sophistic nonsense. A few killers may decide not to appeal a death sentence, but the overwhelming majority make every effort to stay alive. It is by exacting the highest penalty for the taking of human life that we affirm the highest value of human life.

5. *The death penalty is applied in a discriminatory manner.* This   11
factor no longer seems to be the problem it once was. The appeals process for a condemned prisoner is lengthy and painstaking. Every effort is made to see that the verdict and sentence were fairly arrived at. However, assertions of discrimination are not an argument for ending the death penalty but for extending it. It is not justice to exclude everyone from the penalty of the law if a few are found to be so favored. Justice requires that the law be applied equally to all.

6. *Thou shalt not kill.* The Bible is our greatest source of moral   12
inspiration. Opponents of the death penalty frequently cite the sixth of the Ten Commandments in an attempt to prove that capital punishment is divinely proscribed. In the original Hebrew, however, the Sixth Commandment reads, "Thou Shalt Not Commit Murder," and the Torah specifies capital punishment for a variety of offenses. The biblical viewpoint has been upheld by philosophers throughout history. The greatest thinkers of the 19th century — Kant, Locke, Hobbes, Rousseau, Montesquieu, and Mill — agreed that natural law properly authorizes the sovereign to take life in order to vindicate justice. Only Jeremy Bentham was ambivalent. Washington, Jefferson, and Franklin endorsed it. Abraham Lincoln authorized executions for deserters in wartime. Alexis de Tocqueville, who expressed profound respect for American institutions, believed that the death penalty was indispensable to the support of social order. The United States Constitution, widely admired as one of the seminal achievements in the history of humanity, condemns cruel and inhuman punishment, but does not condemn capital punishment.

7. The death penalty is state-sanctioned murder. This is the   13
defense with which Messrs. Willie and Shaw hoped to soften the
resolve of those who sentenced them to death. By saying in effect,
"You're no better than I am," the murderer seeks to bring his
accusers down to his own level. It is also a popular argument
among opponents of capital punishment, but a transparently
false one. Simply put, the state has rights that the private individual does not. In a democracy, those rights are given to the state by
the electorate. The execution of a lawfully condemned killer is no
more an act of murder than is legal imprisonment an act of
kidnapping. If an individual forces a neighbor to pay him money
under threat of punishment, it's called extortion. If the state does
it, it's called taxation. Rights and responsibilities surrendered by
the individual are what give the state its power to govern. This
contract is the foundation of civilization itself.

Everyone wants his or her rights, and will defend them jeal-   14
ously. Not everyone, however, wants responsibilities, especially
the painful responsibilities that come with law enforcement.
Twenty-one years ago a woman named Kitty Genovese was as-
saulted and murdered on a street in New York. Dozens of neighbors heard her cries for help but did nothing to assist her. They
didn't even call the police. In such a climate the criminal understandably grows bolder. In the presence of moral cowardice, he
lectures us on our supposed failings and tries to equate his crimes
with our quest for justice.

The death of anyone — even a convicted killer — diminishes   15
us all. But we are diminished even more by a justice system that
fails to function. It is an illusion to let ourselves believe that
doing away with capital punishment removes the murderer's deed
from our conscience. The rights of society are paramount. When
we protect guilty lives, we give up innocent lives in exchange.
When opponents of capital punishment say to the state: "I will
not let you kill in my name," they are also saying to murderers:
"You can kill in your *own* name as long as I have an excuse for not
getting involved."

It is hard to imagine anything worse than being murdered   16
while neighbors do nothing. But something worse exists. When
those same neighbors shrink back from justly punishing the murderer, the victim dies twice.

Questions for Close Reading

1. What is the thesis of the selection? Locate the sentence(s) in which Koch states his main idea. If he does not state the thesis explicitly, express it in your own words.
2. According to Koch, what is it about the death penalty that its opponents find objectionable? Are such objections, in Koch's opinion, justified? Why or why not?
3. What arguments does Koch use to try to convince readers that the death penalty does not run counter to traditional religious and philosophical thought?
4. In Koch's view, how does the death penalty affirm the fact that "life is . . . precious"? Why would punishing murderers with anything less than the death penalty be unjust?
5. Refer to your dictionary as needed to define the following words in the selection: *reverence* (paragraph 2), *constituencies* (4), *heinous* (4), *reprehensible* (4), *lethal* (5), *implacable* (8), and *sophistic* (10).

Questions About the Writer's Craft

1. Where does Koch try to establish his *ethos*? What does this attempt to establish his credibility say about Koch's perception of his audience's point of view?
2. Where does Koch draw on hard evidence to develop his argument? What is the effect of this evidence?
3. What instances do you find in Koch's essay of emotional appeals and connotative language? How do you think Koch intends readers to react to such appeals and emotionally charged language?
4. Why might Koch have decided to conclude his essay with the Kitty Genovese anecdote? How does this anecdote contribute to his arguments in support of capital punishment.

Questions for Further Thought

1. If you were opposed to capital punishment before reading "Death and Justice," in what way, if any, has Koch's essay prompted you to re-examine your views? Which of Koch's arguments do you find most convincing? Which are least convincing? Why?
2. According to Koch, "had the death penalty been a real possibility," the three convicted murderers he quotes early in the essay "might well

have stayed their hand." Do you agree? Can you think of situations in which fear of the death penalty might *not* deter a potential killer?

3. Consider the religious and philosophical principles Koch uses to defend capital punishment (paragraph 12). In what ways are or aren't those principles in keeping with your own?

4. Koch calls the failure of Kitty Genovese's neighbors to help a case of moral cowardice. Do you agree this is an age of moral cowardice, or can you dispute such a negative assessment by citing examples of significant moral courage? Explain.

Writing Assignments Using Argumentation – Persuasion as a Method of Development

*1. Koch bases his refutation of the standard arguments against capital punishment on a number of principles to which he is strongly committed. Some of these are stated clearly in the text:

If we create a society in which injustice is not tolerated, incidents of murder — the most flagrant form of injustice — will diminish. (paragraph 6)

. . . it is "false sentimentality to argue that the death penalty should be abolished because of the abstract possibility that an innocent person might be executed." (8)

. . . the death penalty strengthens the value of human life. (10)

Using what you have read in "Death and Justice" and what you know about the issue of capital punishment, write an essay which supports or refutes one of these principles or any other that Koch makes in his essay. Part of your paper should acknowledge and, if possible, refute the opposing viewpoint. To become more familiar with that viewpoint, you might want to read David Bruck's "The Death Penalty" (page 600).

2. Using the same organizational strategy as Koch, write an argumentation – persuasion essay that argues for or against a particular stand on a controversial issue. Begin by stating and defending your position. Then, identify and refute several of the standard opposing arguments. Possible topics include the banning of college fraternities and sororities, allowing prayer in public schools, and implementing new graduation requirements at a college.

Writing Assignments Using Other Methods
of Development

*3. Read David Bruck's "The Death Penalty" (page 600), written in
response to Koch. Then write a strictly informative essay comparing
and contrasting Koch and Bruck's view. Don't ally yourself with
either side, but do focus on those points you consider most important to an objective discussion of the capital punishment issue.

4. Have you or anyone you know well ever witnessed or been a victim
of violence? If so, write a narrative about the incident. Use taut
sentences, descriptive detail, and climactic time order to convey the
fear, helplessness, anger you or the person you are writing about felt.
End with a statement about the impact of the event on your or the
other person's life.

David Bruck

In 1980, attorney David Bruck left his job as a public defender so that he could specialize in the defense of death-row inmates. He has since represented numerous death-row clients in South Carolina and Florida. A frequent lecturer and consultant on the death penalty, Bruck has had his analyses of legal issues published in the *Washington Post* and *The New York Times*. He has also discussed capital punishment on a variety of television programs, including the *MacNeil/Lehrer Newshour* and *Nightline*. The following article, written in response to New York Mayor Ed Koch's argument in favor of the death penalty, first appeared in *The New Republic* in May 1985.

The Death Penalty

Few topics evoke such heated emotional response as capital punishment. Advocates call the death penalty the only fitting punishment for murderers; opponents consider the execution of a killer as immoral as the original crime. Opposed to capital punishment, David Bruck believes that the lust for vengeance blinds supporters of the death penalty to many injustices.

Mayor Ed Koch contends that the death penalty "affirms 1 life." By failing to execute murderers, he says, we "signal a lessened regard for the value of the victim's life." Koch suggests that people who oppose the death penalty are like Kitty Genovese's neighbors, who heard her cries for help but did nothing while an attacker stabbed her to death.

This is the standard "moral" defense of death as punish- 2 ment: even if executions don't deter violent crime any more effectively than imprisonment, they are still required as the only means we have of doing justice in response to the worst of crimes.

Until recently, this "moral" argument had to be considered 3 in the abstract, since no one was being executed in the United

States. But the death penalty is back now, at least in the southern states, where every one of the more than 30 executions carried out over the last two years has taken place. Those of us who live in those states are getting to see the difference between the death penalty in theory, and what happens when you actually try to use it.

South Carolina resumed executing prisoners in January with   4 the electrocution of Joseph Carl Shaw. Shaw was condemned to death for helping to murder two teenagers while he was serving as a military policeman at Fort Jackson, South Carolina. His crime, propelled by mental illness and PCP, was one of terrible brutality. It is Shaw's last words ("Killing was wrong when I did it. It is wrong when you do it. . . .") that so outraged Mayor Koch: he finds it "a curiosity of modern life that we are being lectured on morality by cold-blooded killers." And so it is.

But it was not "modern life" that brought this curiosity into   5 being. It was capital punishment. The electric chair was J. C. Shaw's platform. (The mayor mistakenly writes that Shaw's statement came in the form of a plea to the governor for clemency: actually Shaw made it only seconds before his death, as he waited, shaved and strapped into the chair, for the switch to be thrown.) It was the chair that provided Shaw with celebrity and an opportunity to lecture us on right and wrong. What made this weird moral reversal even worse is that J. C. Shaw faced his own death with undeniable dignity and courage. And while Shaw died, the TV crews recorded another "curiosity" of the death penalty— the crowd gathered outside the death-house to cheer on the executioner. Whoops of elation greeted the announcement of Shaw's death. Waiting at the penitentiary gates for the appearance of the hearse bearing Shaw's remains, one demonstrator started yelling, "Where's the beef?"

For those who had to see the execution of J. C. Shaw, it   6 wasn't easy to keep in mind that the purpose of the whole spectacle was to affirm life. It will be harder still when Florida executes a cop-killer named Alvin Ford. Ford has lost his mind during his years of death-row confinement, and now spends his days trembling, rocking back and forth, and muttering unintelligible prayers. This has led to litigation over whether Ford meets a centuries-old legal standard for mental competency. Since the Middle Ages, the Anglo-American legal system has generally pro-

hibited the execution of anyone who is too mentally ill to understand what is about to be done to him and why. If Florida wins its
case, it will have earned the right to electrocute Ford in his
present condition. If it loses, he will not be executed until the
state has first nursed him back to some semblance of mental
health.[1]

We can at least be thankful that this demoralizing spectacle   7
involves a prisoner who is actually guilty of murder. But this may
not always be so. The ordeal of Lenell Jeter — the young black
engineer who recently served more than a year of a life sentence
for a Texas armed robbery that he didn't commit — should remind us that the system is quite capable of making the very worst
sort of mistake. That Jeter was eventually cleared is a fluke. If the
robbery had occurred at 7 P.M. rather than 3 P.M., he'd have had
no alibi, and would still be in prison today. And if someone had
been killed in that robbery, Jeter probably would have been sentenced to death. We'd have seen the usual execution-day interviews with state officials and the victim's relatives, all complain-
ing that Jeter's appeals took too long. And Jeter's last words from
the gurney would have taken their place among the growing
literature of death-house oration that so irritates the mayor.

Koch quotes Hugo Adam Bedau, a prominent abolitionist,   8
to the effect that the record fails to establish that innocent de-
fendants have been executed in the past. But this doesn't mean, as
Koch implies, that it hasn't happened. All Bedau was saying was
that doubts concerning executed prisoners' guilt are almost never
resolved. Bedau is at work now on an effort to determine how
many wrongful death sentences may have been imposed: his list
of murder convictions since 1900 in which the state eventually
admitted error is some 400 cases long. Of course, very few of
these cases involved actual executions: the mistakes that Bedau
documented were uncovered precisely because the prisoner was
alive and able to fight for his vindication. The cases where someone is executed are the very cases in which we're least likely to
learn that we got the wrong man.

I don't claim that executions of entirely innocent people will   9

---

[1]On June 26, 1986, the Supreme Court prohibited the execution of convicted murderers who are so insane they do not understand they will be executed.
However, if Ford regains his sanity, Florida may execute him.

occur very often. But they will occur. And other sorts of mistakes already have. Roosevelt Green was executed in Georgia two days before J. C. Shaw. Green and an accomplice kidnapped a young woman. Green swore that his companion shot her to death after Green had left, and that he knew nothing about the murder. Green's claim was supported by a statement that his accomplice made to a witness after the crime. The jury never resolved whether Green was telling the truth, and when he tried to take a polygraph examination a few days before his scheduled execution, the state of Georgia refused to allow the examiner into the prison. As the pressure for symbolic retribution mounts, the courts, like the public, are losing patience with such details. Green was electrocuted on January 9, while members of the Ku Klux Klan rallied outside the prison.

Then there is another sort of arbitrariness that happens all 10
the time. Last October, Louisiana executed a man named Ernest Knighton. Knighton had killed a gas station owner during a robbery. Like any murder, this was a terrible crime. But it was not premeditated, and is the sort of crime that very rarely results in a death sentence. Why was Knighton electrocuted when almost everyone else who committed the same offense was not? Was it because he was black? Was it because his victim and all 12 members of the jury that sentenced him were white? Was it because Knighton's court-appointed lawyer presented no evidence on his behalf at his sentencing hearing? Or maybe there's no reason except bad luck. One thing is clear: Ernest Knighton was picked out to die the way a fisherman takes a cricket out of a bait jar. No one cares which cricket gets impaled on the hook.

Not every prisoner executed recently was chosen that ran- 11
domly. But many were. And having selected these men so casually, so blindly, the death penalty system asks us to accept that the purpose of killing each of them is to affirm the sanctity of human life.

The death penalty states are also learning that the death 12
penalty is easier to advocate than it is to administer. In Florida, where executions have become almost routine, the governor reports that nearly a third of his time is spent reviewing the clemency requests of condemned prisoners. The Florida Supreme Court is hopelessly backlogged with death cases. Some have taken five years to decide, and the rest of the Court's work waits in line

behind the death appeals. Florida's death row currently holds more than 230 prisoners. State officials are reportedly considering building a special "death prison" devoted entirely to the isolation and electrocution of the condemned. The state is also considering the creation of a special public defender unit that will do nothing else but handle death penalty appeals. The death penalty, in short, is spawning death agencies.

And what is Florida getting for all of this? The state went through almost all of 1983 without executing anyone: its rate of intentional homicide declined by 17 percent. Last year Florida executed eight people — the most of any state, and the sixth highest total for any year since Florida started electrocuting people back in 1924. Elsewhere in the U.S. last year, the homicide rate continued to decline. But in Florida, it actually rose by 5.1 percent. 13

But these are just the tiresome facts. The electric chair has been a centerpiece of each of Koch's recent political campaigns, and he knows better than anyone how little the facts have to do with the public's support for capital punishment. What really fuels the death penalty is the justifiable frustration and rage of people who see that the government is not coping with violent crime. So what if the death penalty doesn't work? At least it gives us the satisfaction of knowing that we got one or two of the sons of bitches. 14

Perhaps we want retribution on the flesh and bone of a handful of convicted murderers so badly that we're willing to close our eyes to all of the demoralization and danger that come with it. A lot of politicians think so, and they may be right. But if they are, then let's at least look honestly at what we're doing. This lottery of death both comes from and encourages an attitude toward human life that is not reverent, but reckless. 15

And that is why the mayor is dead wrong when he confuses such fury with justice. He suggests that we trivialize murder unless we kill murderers. By that logic, we also trivialize rape unless we sodomize rapists. The sin of Kitty Genovese's neighbors wasn't that they failed to stab her attacker to death. Justice does demand that murderers be punished. And common sense demands that society be protected from them. But neither justice nor self-preservation demands that we kill men whom we have already imprisoned. 16

The electric chair in which J. C. Shaw died earlier this year   17
was built in 1912 at the suggestion of South Carolina's governor
at the time, Cole Blease. Governor Blease's other criminal justice
initiative was an impassioned crusade in favor of lynch law. Any
lesser response, the governor insisted, trivialized the loathsome
crimes of interracial rape and murder. In 1912 a lot of people
agreed with Governor Blease that a proper regard for justice required both lynching and the electric chair. Eventually we are
going to learn that justice requires neither.

Questions for Close Reading

1. What is the thesis of the selection? Locate the sentence(s) in which
   Bruck states his main idea. If he does not state the thesis explicitly,
   express it in your own words.
2. Bruck refers to Mayor Koch's belief that being lectured on morality
   by convicted killers is a "curiosity of modern life." Bruck then goes
   on to mention things he finds even more curious about the death
   penalty. What are they?
3. What does Bruck's essay reveal about the J. C. Shaw case that Koch's
   essay does not? How do these new facts support Bruck's thesis?
4. In paragraph 12, Bruck writes that states now executing prisoners are
   "learning that the death penalty is easier to advocate than . . . to
   administer." What does he mean? What evidence does he give to
   support this point?
5. Refer to your dictionary as needed to define the following words in
   the selection: *semblance* (paragraph 6), *retribution* (9), *impaled* (10),
   clemency (12), *spawning* (12), *tiresome* (14), and *trivialize* (16).

Questions About the Writer's Craft

1. Where does Bruck use appeals to reason to support his argument?
   Where does he use appeals to emotion? Which does he emphasize?
   What does this emphasis say about the way Bruck perceives his
   readers?
2. Like many writers of argumentation–persuasion essays, Bruck spends
   time refuting opposing opinions, in this case those of New York City
   Mayor Ed Koch. Which points raised by Koch provide the organizational framework for Bruck's argument? Why might Bruck have selected these points and not others?
3. In paragraph 10, Bruck uses a series of *rhetorical questions* — questions

he does not expect his readers to answer. What is the effect of these questions?

4. In the essay's conclusion, Bruck explains that the electric chair in which J. C. Shaw died had been built at the suggestion of Governor Cole Blease, a man who also fervently supported lynch law. Why does Bruck introduce this new fact at the very end of the essay? What purpose does it serve?

Questions for Further Thought

1. If you were in favor of the death penalty before reading this essay, in what way have your views been altered? Which of Bruck's arguments do you find most convincing?

2. Bruck reports the crowd's blood-thirsty reaction at J. C. Shaw's execution. What other examples can you think of to illustrate this human tendency to gawk at the plight of others? Why do humans react this way?

3. Bruck implies that, because J. C. Shaw's crime was "propelled by mental illness and PCP," he should not have been put to death. Do you believe that we should stay the executioner's hand in special cases? Explain.

4. According to Bruck, the claim that "we trivialize murder unless we kill murderers" is as wrong-headed as the idea that "we trivialize rape unless we sodomize rapists." Do you agree, or do you feel that in some instances the penalty for a crime should be as severe as the crime itself? Explain.

Writing Assignments Using Argumentation – Persuasion as a Method of Development

*1. Bruck bases his argument against the death penalty on several important key points, the following among them:

The death penalty negates the sanctity of human life.
The death penalty offers no more practical deterrent to violent crime than imprisonment.
The death penalty is pronounced disproportionately against minorities.
The death penalty may result in the execution of innocent people.

Write an essay either defending or challenging *one* of these points. No matter which position you take, one section of your paper should recognize and, if possible, rebut the opposing viewpoint. Ed

Koch's "Death and Justice" (page 591) will familiarize you with a viewpoint in sharp contrast to Bruck's.

2. Develop an argument in which you try to persuade your readers that life imprisonment is a just way of punishing convicted murderers and that there is no need to impose the death penalty. Try to anticipate and refute objections others might have to your position.

Writing Assignments Using Other Methods of Development

3. Bruck believes that many people support the death penalty out of frustration with the criminal justice system rather than out of commitment to a particular ideology. Write an essay analyzing the consequences of this disillusionment with the criminal justice system. What other effects does it have on our beliefs and on the way we lead our lives?

4. Think of a law, regulation, procedure, or policy that has, like the death penalty, run into difficulty being implemented. Possible subjects include banning alcohol from campus parties, legalizing gambling, and building low-income housing in middle-income neighborhoods. Write an essay explaining the steps that should be taken to make things run more smoothly. Before presenting your step-by-step discussion, describe problems with the current law or policy.

Louis Nizer

One of this country's best-known attorneys, Louis Nizer (1902–   ) has shared his legal expertise and courtroom experiences in such bestsellers as *My Life in Court, The Jury Returns,* and *Reflections Without Mirrors.* Portions of his books have been adapted for the theater, cinema, and television. Respected for his lucid prose style, Nizer has written for such diverse publications as *The New York Times, Reader's Digest, McCall's,* and scholarly legal journals. Nizer seems able to express himself in almost any medium; in addition to being a skilled attorney, author, and lecturer, he is an accomplished painter and composer.

Low-Cost Drugs for Addicts?

Drug addiction and drug-related crimes cost the nation millions of dollars and thousands of lives each year. Louis Nizer argues that many of the ills associated with drug use exist only because narcotics are illegal. Legalizing drugs, he contends, would sharply reduce what many believe is the number one problem facing our nation today.

We are losing the war against drug addiction. Our strategy is   1
wrong. I propose a different approach.

The Government should create clinics, manned by psychia-   2
trists, that would provide drugs for nominal charges or even free
to addicts under controlled regulations. It would cost the Government only 20 cents for a heroin shot, for which the addicts
must now pay the mob more than $100, and there are similar
price discrepancies in cocaine, crack and other such substances.

Such a service, which would also include the staff support of   3
psychiatrists and doctors, would cost a fraction of what the nation now spends to maintain the land, sea and air apparatus

necessary to interdict illegal imports of drugs. There would also be a savings of hundreds of millions of dollars from the elimination of the prosecutorial procedures that stifle our courts and overcrowd our prisons.

We see in our newspapers the triumphant announcements by Government agents that they have intercepted huge caches of cocaine, the street prices of which are in the tens of millions of dollars. Should we be gratified? Will this achievement reduce the number of addicts by one? All it will do is increase the cost to the addict of his illegal supply. 4

Many addicts who are caught committing a crime admit that they have mugged or stolen as many as six or seven times a day to accumulate the $100 needed for a fix. Since many of them need two or three fixes a day, particularly for crack, one can understand the terror in our streets and homes. It is estimated that there are in New York City alone 200,000 addicts, and this is typical of cities across the nation. Even if we were to assume that only a modest percentage of a city's addicts engage in criminal conduct to obtain the money for the habit, requiring multiple muggings and thefts each day, we could nevertheless account for many of the tens of thousands of crimes each day in New York City alone. 5

Not long ago, a Justice Department division issued a report stating that more than half the perpetrators of murder and other serious crimes were under the influence of drugs. This symbolizes the new domestic terror in our nation. This is why our citizens are unsafe in broad daylight on the most traveled thoroughfares. This is why typewriters and television sets are stolen from offices and homes and sold for a pittance. This is why parks are closed to the public and why murders are committed. This is why homes need multiple locks, and burglary systems, and why store windows, even in the most fashionable areas, require iron gates. 6

The benefits of the new strategy to control this terrorism would be immediate and profound. 7

Fist, the mob would lose the main source of its income. It could not compete against a free supply for which previously it exacted tribute estimated to be hundreds of millions of dollars, perhaps billions, from hopeless victims. 8

Second, pushers would be put out of business. There would be no purpose in creating addicts who would be driven by desperate compulsion to steal and kill for the money necessary to main- 9

tain their habit. Children would not be enticed. The mob's macabre public-relations program is to tempt children with free drugs
in order to create customers for the future. The wave of street
crimes in broad daylight would diminish to a trickle. Homes and
stores would not have to be fortresses. Our recreational areas
could again be used. Neighborhoods would not be scandalized by
sordid street centers where addicts gather to obtain their supply
from slimy merchants.

Third, police and other law-enforcement authorities, domes- 10
tic or foreign, would be freed to deal with traditional nondrug
crimes.

There are several objections that might be raised against such 11
a salutary solution.

First, it could be argued that by providing free drugs to the 12
addict we would consign him to permanent addiction. The answer is that medical and psychiatric help at the source would be
more effective in controlling the addict's descent than the extremely limited remedies available to the victim today. I am not
arguing that the new strategy will cure everything. But I do not
see many addicts being freed from their bonds under the present
system.

In addition, as between the addict's predicament and the 13
safety of our innocent citizens, which deserves our primary concern? Drug-induced crime has become so common that almost
every citizen knows someone in his immediate family or among
his friends who has been mugged. It is these citizens who should
be our chief concern.

Another possible objection is that addicts will cheat the sys- 14
tem by obtaining more than the allowable free shot. Without
discounting the resourcefulness of the bedeviled addict, it should
be possible to have Government cards issued that would be
punched so as to limit the free supply in accord with medical
authorization.

Yet all objections become trivial when matched against the 15
crisis itself. What we are witnessing is the demoralization of a
great society: the ruination of its school children, athletes and
executives, the corrosion of the workforce in general.

Many thoughtful sociologists consider the rapidly spreading 16
drug use the greatest problem that our nation faces — greater and
more real and urgent than nuclear bombs or economic reversal.

In China, a similar crisis drove the authorities to apply capital punishment to those who trafficked in opium — an extreme solution that arose from the deepest reaches of frustration.

Free drugs will win the war against the domestic terrorism 17 caused by illicit drugs. As a strategy, it is at once resourceful, sensible and simple. We are getting nowhere in our efforts to hold back the ocean of supply. The answer is to dry up demand.

Questions for Close Reading

1. What is the thesis of the selection? Locate the sentence(s) in which Nizer states his main idea. If he does not state the thesis explicitly, express it in your own words.
2. Nizer believes his plan would yield numerous benefits. What are they?
3. Nizer acknowledges some possible objections to his plan. What are they? How does he refute these arguments?
4. How much concern does Nizer have for those addicted to drugs? How do you know?
5. Refer to your dictionary as needed to define the following words used in the selection: *nominal* (paragraph 2), *interdict* (3), *cache* (4), *macabre* (9), *salutary* (11), *consign* (12), and *illicit* (17).

Questions About the Writer's Craft

1. Page 532 presents two possible strategies for organizing argumentation–persuasion essays. Which strategy does Nizer use?
2. Nizer's essay starts with a brief introductory paragraph consisting of three crisp, almost clipped sentences. What is the effect of this unusually brief introduction?
3. What words with militaristic connotations does Nizer use in his essay? What might have been Nizer's reason for using such language?
4. To what audience does Nizer seem to be addressing his proposal? How do you know?

Questions for Further Thought

1. Besides those Nizer mentions, what additional objections might people have to legalizing drugs? How valid are these objections?
2. Nizer holds drug users accountable for their acts. Do you think that courts should take into account the environmental and psychological factors that may have precipitated a crime? Explain.

3. Can any of Nizer's ideas be used to argue that other "vices" should be legalized? Consider, for example, gambling or prostitution.
4. Nizer suggests that organized crime is mostly responsible for this country's drug problem. Can you identify other players in this tragedy?

Writing Assignments Using Argumentation – Persuasion as a Method of Development

*1. Nizer argues that legalizing drugs would not necessarily increase the number of addicts and that it would definitely strike a blow at crime. Write an essay supporting or challenging *one* of these conclusions. No matter which side you take, assume that some readers are opposed to your point of view. Acknowledge and try to dismantle as many of their objections as you can. Beth Johnson Ruth's "Our Drug Problem (on page 613) will familiarize you with some counterarguments to Nizer's position.

2. If you do not believe that legalizing narcotics would help solve the problem, offer your own proposal. Focus on what *one* of the following should do to eliminate drug trafficking and to educate people about the disastrous effects of drug addiction: public schools; federal, state, or local governments; colleges or universities; parent groups. Put your proposal in the form of a letter to the appropriate person (a high school principal, president of a college, and so on). Try to anticipate and rebut possible objections to your proposal.

Writing Assignments Using Other Methods of Development

3. Psychologists point out that some individuals have an "addictive personality." How would you define this term? Do you know people who are addicted to alcohol, tobacco, danger, love, junk food? Illustrate your definition through reference to people you know well, showing what characteristics these outwardly quite different people share.
4. Assume that the Dean of Students has asked you to write an open letter to be published in next year's freshmen orientation brochure. Your assignment is to warn incoming students about the long-term effects of drug abuse, too much partying, or excessive procrastination — anything that might affect their well-being and success in college. Develop your letter by drawing on your own and other people's experience. You might even cite relevant facts, statistics, and expert testimony, using the *Readers' Guide to Periodical Literature* to track down helpful articles.

Beth Johnson Ruth

A journalist and freelance writer, Beth Johnson Ruth received an advanced degree in literacy education from Syracuse University. Ruth's crisp, no-nonsense prose style has served her well in the public relations writing she has done for a college news bureau and a community mental health center. Formerly on the faculties of Goshen College and New England College, Ruth has also written for a number of publications, among them *The Starke County Ledger* and *The New Hampshire Business Review*. The selection reprinted below is taken from a collection of Ruth's essays dealing with the impact of drugs on society.

Our Drug Problem

Nearly everyone agrees that drug abuse is an overwhelming national problem. But a solution to that problem finds far less consensus. Some advocate such drastic measures as the automatic execution of drug dealers. Others favor the legalization of narcotics, believing that the illicit nature of the drug trade is largely responsible for our predicament. In the author's view, the removal of legal restraints would be the beginning of a drug-induced nightmare from which America might never awaken.

Imagine, if you will, the final reel of a trashy "B" movie 1
based on the Biblical story of Sodom and Gomorrah. You remember the tale of two cities so given over to evil practices, immortality, and mindless self-indulgence that God finally destroyed them by raining down fire and brimstone.

What sort of activity do you suppose a filmmaker would 2
choose in order to portray, in an updated fashion, the wickedness of Sodom and Gomorrah? The perfect catch-all choice, in my mind, would be unrestricted drug use. Think of the potential for related decadent behavior. There would be plenty of room for self-annihilation through drug overdose; sexual excesses with no

613

concern for the consequences; any number of reckless acts leading to crippling or fatal accidents; obsession with narcotics to the
point of ignoring the needs of one's family . . . the possibilities
go on and on. Unlimited access to drugs would provide the
perfect metaphor for the legendary evil that was Sodom and
Gomorrah.

Incredibly, voices are being heard in America today — voices   3
belonging to supposedly responsible and intelligent persons in
positions of some authority — that are recommending the legalization of narcotics. The war on drugs has been lost, they say; it's
time to stop wasting the enormous resources that American society has been pouring into a futile battle and start addressing the
issue of drug abuse as a massive public health problem, not a legal
one.

Has a more ludicrous proposal ever been seriously intro-   4
duced for public discussion? Are we honestly being asked to
consider raising our children in a society that says, "Yes, we know
that these substances will very likely ruin your and your family's
lives and will probably kill you sooner or later, and we'd really
rather you didn't use them, but it's just too inconvenient to try to
enforce the law"?

Apparently we are. Conservative columnist William F. Buck-   5
ley, Jr., Nobel Prize–winning economist Milton Friedman,
Mayor Kurt Schmoke of Baltimore, and U.S. Reps. Fortney
Stark of California and Steny Hoyer of Maryland have been
among the respected — and presumably not drug-addled — folks
who have suggested that legalization of drugs is an idea whose
time may have come.

Let's look at their arguments one by one. But be forewarned;   6
dismantling them will not take too much time or effort.

"Legalizing drugs would mean the end of drug-related   7
crime." Presumably it's true that if all forms of narcotics were
given blanket legalization, the role of druglords, corrupt government officials, pushers and drug gangs would be phased out of
existence. It does not follow that addicted persons would be any
less driven to desperate measures to obtain their needed fix, legal
or otherwise. Killings, robberies, muggings and prostitution for
cash to be spent on narcotics would not cease. With the enormous growth in the number of addicts each year, the opposite
would very likely be true.

"The government could tax drug sales and regulate the pu-   8 rity of narcotics if they were sold legally." The advocates of legalization point out that two other addictive substances — alcohol and tobacco — are legal and subject to government regulation. True enough. But what's the point? Alcohol and tobacco combined are responsible for about 400,000 deaths each year. In 1985, the death toll from all illegal drugs was only 3,562. Would we consider it progress to have more people dying from injecting, inhaling and consuming purer forms of poison?

"The war on drugs is simply too expensive and too ineffec-   9 tive. The country can't afford to continue spending money at this rate." No doubt about it, the price tag attached to fighting drug abuse is phenomenal. It's estimated that federal, state and local governments are spending about $8 billion a year on direct drug-enforcement activities. Add to that the uncounted billions spent on feeding and housing those imprisoned for drug-related crimes (more than a third of all federal prisoners fall in this category) and you end up with some breathtaking sums.

And true, the war on drugs is not being won. The courts are   10 overflowing with cases waiting to be tried; huge seizures of narcotics stop only a tiny fraction of the drugs coming into the country; countless arrests — usually of the small-time pusher, not the big wheel in a drug organization — don't make a dent in the enormous population of the drug underworld. Clearly, as being waged now, the national fight against drug abuse is a futile one.

The only thing more expensive than continuing the current   11 war on drugs would be the legalization of narcotics. To send that double-sided message to our already confused society — that drug abuse is such an enormous problem that we're going to give it the official stamp of approval — would create a nightmare from which America might never awaken.

The economic and spiritual toll of legalizing narcotics is one   12 that can barely be guessed at. Addiction would claim innumerable citizens. "People say only 10 percent of those who drink are problem drinkers, so they assume that only 10 percent of the people who take drugs will become addicts," said Mitchell Rosenthal, president of Phoenix House, a New York City–based drug rehabilitation program. "But there is no reason to believe that if we made crack available in little crack shops that only 10 percent would be addicted; the number would probably be more like 75 percent."

Currently, drug abuse costs American industry something   13 over $70 billion per year through lost productivity. Imagine how that figure would soar if the restraints were off currently law-abiding citizens. If we didn't have to drive into a seedy neighborhood . . . if we didn't risk arrest and disgrace . . . if we could justify our actions as legal . . . how many of us could resist trying some seductive-sounding drug "just once"? And how many addicts started out by experimenting with drugs "just once"? Every one of them, that's how many. And just what would be the fate of addicts if narcotics were available legally? In the words of one Los Angeles musician, addicted to cocaine for three years, "I'd be dead . . . I'd just sit down with a big pile of the stuff and snort it until I dropped. Only a real cocaine connoisseur can appreciate what I mean."

One more number to consider: Today, the health costs of   14
treating drug abuse are estimated at $60 billion per year. Care to guess what that figure might become if drugs were made legal?

As if the above facts weren't enough to dissuade anyone from   15
the belief that legalizing narcotics has anything to recommend it, let's examine what's lurking just below the surface of the supposedly reasonable arguments cited above. And that is a sickening current of immorality, racism and elitism that says, in essence: "These people are going to kill themselves anyway; I'm not going to have my tax dollars used to try to save them." Isn't that what it boils down to? Isn't there a still small voice whispering through middle-class America: "What does it matter if drugs wipe out a generation — as long as it's a generation of poor black and Hispanic kids who will just drain our society of welfare dollars throughout their lives?"

Isn't it true? If not, where is the compassion for "these people" and their agonizing problems? Where is the public outcry over our country's gutting of education and job-training programs — the only kinds of "drug prevention" that address the real cause of most drug abuse: poverty and despair? When the minimum wage has fallen to its lowest level in terms of buying power since 1955, is it so amazing that poor teenagers choose the lucrative jobs offered them by druglords over flipping hamburgers? Where is the public protest when federal aid to college students dropped 16 percent between 1980 and 1987, while the cost of college nearly doubled? When the number of families living beneath the poverty level increased six-fold between 1979 and 1987, did more fortunate Americans rise up to offer a hand? Why in God's name do people think the underprivileged turn to drugs in such massive numbers? The reason is tragically obvious: because drugs offer the only available escape from their wretched existence.

The devastating drug problem in America today is an illus-   17
tration of our country's reaping what it has sowed: a harvest of broken lives, violence and despair grown from the roots of poverty and neglect. That the problem has grown to this extent is immoral in itself; to encourage it further through the legalization of narcotics would not only be impractical but also unethical to an incredible degree. Unless this once-great country acts quickly to address the drug problem in the only way that can work—through providing real education and employment opportunities for its people—it will truly deserve comparison with cities that suffered the fate of fire and brimstone.

Questions for Close Reading

1. What is the thesis of the selection? Locate the sentence(s) in which Ruth states her main idea. If she does not state the thesis explicitly, express it in your own words.
2. Why, according to Ruth, would "supposedly responsible and intelligent persons in positions of some authority" want to advocate the legalization of narcotics?
3. How does the number of deaths each year from illegal drug abuse compare with the number of deaths caused by the abuse of alcohol and tobacco?
4. Ruth admits that, as it is currently being fought, the war against drugs is ineffectual and costly. Why, then, is she against legalizing narcotics? What does she advocate instead?
5. Refer to your dictionary as needed to define the following words in the selection: *decadent* (paragraph 2), *ludicrous* (4), *addled* (5), *forewarned* (6), *dismantling* (6), *dissuade* (15), and *elitism* (15).

Questions About the Writer's Craft

1. Ruth often employs provocative, even inflammatory language, as when she refers to the idea of legalizing narcotics as "ludicrous" (paragraph 3). Find additional examples of such language. What

assumptions about her audience might have motivated Ruth to adopt this style?

2. Ruth also draws on facts, statistics, illustrations, and expert testimony to support her argument. Identify examples in the essay of each kind of evidence. What is the effect of this evidence?

3. Ruth creates an interesting *metaphor* when she compares the consequences of legalizing narcotics to the fate of Sodom and Gomorrah. What purpose does this metaphor serve? Where else does the author use metaphors? What is their function?

4. Ruth works to refute the arguments of her opponents. But she also concedes points to the opposing view, as in paragraph 9 when she admits, "No doubt about it, the price tag attached to fighting drug abuse is phenomenal." Why does she make such concessions?

Questions for Further Thought

1. In paragraph 13, Ruth argues that narcotics abuse would soar if there were no risk attached to buying drugs. Is this a fair conclusion? Do you know people who would begin using or would increase their consumption of drugs if legal restraints were removed?

2. The author claims that the real causes of most drug abuse are poverty and despair. What, then, accounts for the abuse of illegal substances like cocaine and marijuana among the middle class and the rich?

3. Some people believe that drug addicts are criminals and should, if convicted, suffer stiff prison sentences. Others consider drug abuse a disease that can be corrected only through careful, compassionate medical attention. What's your opinion? Why?

4. For Ruth, "real education and employment opportunities" are the only genuine solutions for the drug problem. What specific measures do you think should be taken to help stem the tide of drug abuse in this country?

Writing Assignments Using Argumentation – Persuasion as a Method of Development

*1. Ruth contends that a "sickening current of . . . racism and elitism" is behind the proposal to legalize drugs. Do you agree? Remembering to mention and, when possible, refute opposing arguments, write an essay in which you defend or challenge Ruth's charge. Louis Nizer's "Low-Cost Drugs for Addicts?" (page 608) will give you insight into a viewpoint sharply different from Ruth's.

2. Assume that your college's Office of Student Life has just hired you as a peer counselor whose job it is to reach out to students in

distress. Your first task is to write a letter to students with drug and/or alcohol problems, persuading them to seek out the college's professional and peer counseling services. The letter will be posted on campus bulletin boards and will appear in the student newspaper. As you write the letter, keep in mind that people in difficulty often resist offers of help. What persuasive strategies will you use to overcome this resistance?

Writing Assignments Using Other Methods of Development

3. What are the effects of discovering that star athletes have been found using steroids or other drugs? Write an essay discussing the effects of athletes' illegal drug use on one or two of the following: participants, fans, youngsters for whom these athletes are role models, the sporting events themselves. End with a brief proposal about what should be done. What penalties should be imposed and who should be penalized?

4. Assume that you are a student member of your college's Disciplinary Action Committee. On this week's agenda is the case of a student who has been found selling drugs on campus. Write a position paper detailing the step-by-step procedure you think the college administration should follow when dealing with this (and similar) case(s).

Additional Writing Topics
ARGUMENTATION – PERSUASION

General Assignments

Using argumentation – persuasion, develop any of the following topics. After choosing a topic, think about your purpose and audience. Remember that the paper's thesis should state the issue under discussion as well as your position on the issue. As you work on developing evidence, you might want to do some outside research. Keep in mind that effective argumentation – persuasion usually means that some time should be spent acknowledging and refuting opposing points of view. Be careful not to sabotage your argument by basing your case on a logical fallacy.

1. Mercy killing
2. Hiring quotas
3. Giving birth control devices to teenagers
4. Prayer in the schools
5. Living off campus
6. The drinking age
7. Spouses sharing housework equally
8. Smoking in public places
9. Big-time sports in college
10. Music videos
11. Mothers of young children going out to work
12. Acid rain
13. Drugs on campus
14. Political campaigns
15. Making personal computers mandatory for all college students
16. 55-mile-per-hour speed limit
17. Putting elderly parents in nursing homes
18. An optional pass/fail system for courses
19. The homeless
20. Nonconformity in a neighborhood: allowing a lawn to go wild, keeping many pets, painting house an odd color, or some other atypical behavior.

Assignments with a Specific Audience and Purpose

1. Your supervising editor at *Time* magazine has given you an important assignment: choosing the "Man or Woman of the Year" to be featured on the cover of the December 31 issue. Make your decision and write a report to your boss arguing in favor of this choice.

2. Your eighteen-year-old son or daughter sent off a college application but was rejected because of low SAT scores. Write to the college admissions director, arguing that an injustice has been done. Give reasons why the SAT scores are not a fair indicator of your child's abilities and potential.

3. You and your parents don't agree on some aspect of your romantic relationship (you want to live with your boyfriend/girlfriend and they don't approve; you want to get married and they want you to wait; they simply don't like your partner; or any other conflict). Write your parents a letter explaining why your preference is reasonable. Try hard to win them over to your side.

4. As a member of a high school faculty, you support the adoption of a controversial behavior code for students. Write an article for the school newspaper, justifying this new rule to the student body. The rule might be "no radios in school," "no T-shirts," "no food in class," "no smoking on school grounds," or any other rule you think appropriate.

5. Your parents are convinced that the music you listen to is nothing more than deafening noise. Write an essay proving to your parents that your music has value. Use specific examples of lyrics, groups, or musical styles to support your points.

6. You are part of a minority group (racial, ethnic, female teenagers, college students, the elderly, or any other group). On a recent television show or in a TV advertisement, you saw something that depicts your group in an offensive way. Write a letter (to the network or the advertiser) expressing your feelings and explaining why you feel the material should be taken off the air.

FOR
FURTHER
READING

Martin Luther King, Jr.

Nearly a quarter of a century after his assassination, Martin Luther King, Jr. (1929–1968), is still recognized as the towering figure in the struggle for civil rights in America. Born in Atlanta, Georgia, King earned doctorates from Boston University and Chicago Theological Seminary and served as pastor of a Baptist congregation in Montgomery, Alabama. Advocating a philosophy of nonviolent resistance to racial injustice, he led bus boycotts, marches, and sit-ins that brought about passage of the 1964 Civil Rights Act and the Voting Rights Act of 1965. Dr. King was awarded the Nobel Peace Prize in 1964. The first of the following selections is taken from *Where Do We Go From Here: Community or Chaos?* (1967). The second comes from *Strive Toward Freedom* (1958).

Where Do We Go From Here: Community or Chaos?

Political leaders present convincing arguments for military aggression. They advocate supplying weapons to countries that are fighting communist insurgents; they urge the stockpiling of deadly warheads as a defense strategy; they argue for the funding of nuclear missiles euphemistically called "peace-keepers." But to Dr. King the belief that war can lead to peace is absurd. In this essay, he maintains that only nonviolent methods can bring stability and peace to a troubled world.

A final problem that mankind must solve in order to survive 1
in the world house that we have inherited is finding an alternative to war and human destruction. Recent events have vividly reminded us that nations are not reducing but rather increasing their arsenals of weapons of mass destruction. The best brains in the highly developed nations of the world are devoted to military technology. The proliferation of nuclear weapons has not been halted, in spite of the limited-test-ban treaty.

In this day of man's highest technical achievement, in this day of dazzling discovery, of novel opportunities, loftier dignities and fuller freedoms for all, there is no excuse for the kind of blind craving for power and resources that provoked the wars of previous generations. There is no need to fight for food and land. Science has provided us with adequate means of survival and transportation, which make it possible to enjoy the fullness of this great earth. The question now is, do we have the morality and courage required to live together as brothers and not be afraid?

One of the most persistent ambiguities we face is that everybody talks about peace as a goal, but among the wielders of power peace is practically nobody's business. Many men cry "Peace! Peace!" but they refuse to do the things that make for peace.

The large power blocs talk passionately of pursuing peace while expanding defense budgets that already bulge, enlarging already awesome armies and devising ever more devastating weapons. Call the roll of those who sing the glad tidings of peace and one's ears will be surprised by the responding sounds. The heads of all the nations issue clarion calls for peace, yet they come to the peace table accompanied by bands of brigands each bearing unsheathed swords.

The stages of history are replete with the chants and choruses of the conquerors of old who came killing in pursuit of peace. Alexander, Genghis Khan, Julius Caesar, Charlemagne and Napoleon were akin in seeking a peaceful world order, a world fashioned after their selfish conceptions of an ideal existence. Each sought a world at peace which would personify his egotistic dreams. Even within the life span of most of us, another megalomaniac strode across the world stage. He sent his blitzkrieg-bent legions blazing across Europe, bringing havoc and holocaust in his wake. There is grave irony in the fact that Hitler could come forth, following nakedly aggressive expansionist theories, and do it all in the name of peace.

So when in this day I see the leaders of nations again talking peace while preparing for war, I take fearful pause. When I see our country today intervening in what is basically a civil war, mutilating hundreds of thousands of Vietnamese children with napalm, burning villages and rice fields at random, painting the valleys of that small Asian country red with human blood, leaving broken bodies in countless ditches and sending home half-men, mutilated mentally and physically; when I see the unwillingness of our government to create the atmosphere for a negotiated settlement of this awful conflict by halting bombings in the North and agreeing unequivocally to talk with the Vietcong—and all this in the name of pursuing the goal of peace—I tremble for our world.[1] I do so not only from dire recall of the nightmares wreaked in the wars of yesterday, but also from dreadful realization of today's possible nuclear destructiveness and tomorrow's even more calamitous prospects.

Before it is too late, we must narrow the gaping chasm   7
between our proclamations of peace and our lowly deeds which precipitate and perpetuate war. We are called upon to look up from the quagmire of military programs and defense commitments and read the warnings on history's signposts.

One day we must come to see that peace is not merely a   8
distant goal that we seek but a means by which we arrive at that goal. We must pursue peaceful ends through peaceful means. How much longer must we play at deadly war games before we heed the plaintive pleas of the unnumbered dead and maimed of past wars?

President John F. Kennedy said on one occasion, "Mankind   9
must put an end to war or war will put an end to mankind." Wisdom born of experience should tell us that war is obsolete. There may have been a time when war served as a negative good by preventing the spread and growth of an evil force, but the destructive power of modern weapons eliminates even the possibility that war may serve any good at all. If we assume that life is worth living and that man has a right to survive, then we must find an alternative to war. In a day when vehicles hurtle through outer space and guided ballistic missiles carve highways of death through the stratosphere, no nation can claim victory in war. A so-called limited war will leave little more than a calamitous legacy of human suffering, political turmoil and spiritual disillusionment. A world war will leave only smoldering ashes as mute testimony of a human race whose folly led inexorably to ultimate

---

[1]Only after more than 58,000 Americans had been killed did the United States withdraw from Vietnam. The civil war then continued until the North Vietnamese, aided by the Vietcong, took over all of Vietnam.

death. If modern man continues to flirt unhesitatingly with war, he will transform his earthly habitat into an inferno such as even the mind of Dante could not imagine.

Therefore I suggest that the philosophy and strategy of nonviolence become immediately a subject for study and for serious experimentation in every field of human conflict, by no means excluding the relations between nations. It is, after all, nation-states which make war, which have produced the weapons that threaten the survival of mankind and which are both genocidal and suicidal in character.   10

We have ancient habits to deal with, vast structures of power, indescribably complicated problems to solve. But unless we abdicate our humanity altogether and succumb to fear and impotence in the presence of the weapons we have ourselves created, it is as possible and as urgent to put an end to war and violence between nations as it is to put an end to poverty and racial injustice.   11

The United Nations is a gesture in the direction of nonviolence on a world scale. There, at least, states that oppose one another have sought to do so with words instead of with weapons. But true nonviolence is more than the absence of violence. It is the persistent and determined application of peaceable power to offenses against the community—in this case the world community. As the United Nations moves ahead with the giant tasks confronting it, I would hope that it would earnestly examine the uses of nonviolent direct action.   12

I do not minimize the complexity of the problems that need to be faced in achieving disarmament and peace. But I am convinced that we shall not have the will, the courage and the insight to deal with such matters unless in this field we are prepared to undergo a mental and spiritual re-evaluation, a change of focus which will enable us to see that the things that seem most real and powerful are indeed now unreal and have come under sentence of death. We need to make a supreme effort to generate the readiness, indeed the eagerness, to enter into the new world which is now possible, "the city which hath foundation, whose Building and Maker is God."   13

It is not enough to say, "We must not wage war." It is necessary to love peace and sacrifice for it. We must concentrate not merely on the eradication of war but on the affirmation of peace. A fascinating story about Ulysses and the Sirens is pre-   14 served for us in Greek literature. The Sirens had the ability to sing so sweetly that sailors could not resist steering toward their island. Many ships were lured upon the rocks, and men forgot home, duty and honor as they flung themselves into the sea to be embraced by arms that drew them down to death. Ulysses, determined not to succumb to the Sirens, first decided to tie himself tightly to the mast of his boat and his crew stuffed their ears with wax. But finally he and his crew learned a better way to save themselves: They took on board the beautiful singer Orpheus, whose melodies were sweeter than the music of the Sirens. When Orpheus sang, who would bother to listen to the Sirens?

So we must see that peace represents a sweeter music, a   15
cosmic melody that is far superior to the discords of war. Somehow we must transform the dynamics of the world power struggle from the nuclear arms race, which no one can win, to a creative contest to harness man's genius for the purpose of making peace and prosperity a reality for all the nations of the world. In short, we must shift the arms race into a "peace race." If we have the will and determination to mount such a peace offensive, we will unlock hitherto tightly sealed doors of hope and bring new light into the dark chambers of pessimism.

Martin Luther King, Jr.

Three Kinds of Resistance to Oppression

The architect of the modern American civil rights movement analyzes two common reactions to the experience of being oppressed. He then offers a third response, explaining that it provides the only path to a lasting and honorable freedom.

Oppressed people deal with their oppression in three charac- 1
teristic ways. One way is acquiescence: the oppressed resign themselves to their doom. They tacitly adjust themselves to oppression, and thereby become conditioned to it. In every movement toward freedom some of the oppressed prefer to remain oppressed. Almost 2800 years ago Moses set out to lead the children of Israel from the slavery of Egypt to the freedom of the promised land. He soon discovered that slaves do not always welcome their deliverers. They become accustomed to being slaves. They would rather bear those ills they have, as Shakespeare pointed out, than flee to others that they know not of. They prefer the "fleshpots of Egypt" to the ordeals of emancipation.

There is such a thing as the freedom of exhaustion. Some 2
people are so worn down by the yoke of oppression that they give up. A few years ago in the slum areas of Atlanta, a Negro guitarist used to sing almost daily: "Been down so long that down don't bother me." This is the type of negative freedom and resignation that often engulfs the life of the oppressed.

But this is not the way out. To accept passively an unjust 3
system is to cooperate with that system; thereby the oppressed become as evil as the oppressor. Noncooperation with evil is as much a moral obligation as is cooperation with good. The oppressed must never allow the conscience of the oppressor to slumber. Religion reminds every man that he is his brother's keeper. To accept injustice or segregation passively is to say to the

629

oppressor that his actions are morally right. It is a way of allowing his conscience to fall asleep. At this moment the oppressed fails to be his brother's keeper. So acquiescence—while often the easier way—is not the moral way. It is the way of the coward. The Negro cannot win the respect of his oppressor by acquiescing; he merely increases the oppressor's arrogance and contempt. Acquiescence is interpreted as proof of the Negro's inferiority. The Negro cannot win the respect of the white people of the South or the peoples of the world if he is willing to sell the future of his children for his personal and immediate comfort and safety.

A second way that oppressed people sometimes deal with oppression is to resort to physical violence and corroding hatred. Violence often brings about momentary results. Nations have frequently won their independence in battle. But in spite of temporary victories, violence never brings permanent peace. It solves no social problem; it merely creates new and more complicated ones.   4

Violence as a way of achieving racial justice is both impractical and immoral. It is impractical because it is a descending spiral ending in destruction for all. The old law of an eye for an eye leaves everybody blind. It is immoral because it seeks to humiliate the opponent rather than win his understanding; it seeks to annihilate rather than to convert. Violence is immoral because it thrives on hatred rather than love. It destroys community and makes brotherhood impossible. It leaves society in monologue rather than dialogue. Violence ends by defeating itself. It creates bitterness in the survivors and brutality in the destroyers. A voice echoes through time saying to every potential Peter, "Put up your sword." History is cluttered with the wreckage of nations that failed to follow this command.   5

If the American Negro and other victims of oppression succumb to the temptation of using violence in the struggle for freedom, future generations will be the recipients of a desolate night of bitterness, and our chief legacy to them will be an endless reign of meaningless chaos. Violence is not the way.   6

The third way open to oppressed people in their quest for freedom is the way of nonviolent resistance. Like the synthesis in Hegelian philosophy, the principle of nonviolent resistance seeks to reconcile the truths of two opposites—acquiescence and violence—while avoiding the extremes and immoralities of both.   7

The nonviolent resister agrees with the person who acquiesces that one should not be physically aggressive toward his opponent; but he balances the equation by agreeing with the person of violence that evil must be resisted. He avoids the nonresistance of the former and the violent resistance of the latter. With nonviolent resistance, no individual or group need submit to any wrong, nor need anyone resort to violence in order to right a wrong.

It seems to me that this is the method that must guide the actions of the Negro in the present crisis in race relations. Through nonviolent resistance the Negro will be able to rise to the noble height of opposing the unjust system while loving the perpetrators of the system. The Negro must work passionately and unrelentingly for full stature as a citizen, but he must not use inferior methods to gain it. He must never come to terms with falsehood, malice, hate, or destruction.   8

Nonviolent resistance makes it possible for the Negro to remain in the South and struggle for his rights. The Negro's problem will not be solved by running away. He cannot listen to the glib suggestion of those who would urge him to migrate en masse to other sections of the country. By grasping his great opportunity in the South he can make a lasting contribution to the moral strength of the nation and set a sublime example of courage for generations yet unborn.   9

By nonviolent resistance, the Negro can also enlist all men of good will in his struggle for equality. The problem is not a purely racial one, with Negroes set against whites. In the end, it is not a struggle between people at all, but a tension between justice and injustice. Nonviolent resistance is not aimed against oppressors but against oppression. Under its banner, consciences, not racial groups, are enlisted.   10

Joan Didion

Known for her taut prose style and sharp social commentary, Joan Didion (1934–) graduated from the University of California at Berkeley. Her essays have appeared in *The Saturday Evening Post*, *The American Scholar*, and *The National Review*, as well as in two collections: *Slouching Towards Bethlehem* (1969) and *The White Album* (1979). *Salvador* (1983) is a book-length essay about a 1982 visit to Central America. She has also written several novels, including *River Run* (1963), *Play It As It Lays* (1971), *A Book of Common Prayer* (1977), and *Democracy* (1984). The first essay below is taken from *The White Album;* the second from *Slouching Towards Bethlehem*.

In Bed

Perhaps you are skeptical of people who take to bed with a bad headache, or maybe you use the term "migraine" to describe your own occasional discomfort. If so, reading this essay will put you in your place. A chronic migraine sufferer since childhood, Joan Didion frequently falls victim to bouts of debilitating pain. Brace yourself for some excruciating details; you'll never use the term "migraine" loosely again.

Three, four, sometimes five times a month, I spend the day 1
in bed with a migraine headache, insensible to the world around me. Almost every day of every month, between these attacks, I feel the sudden irrational irritation and flush of blood into the cerebral arteries which tell me that migraine is on its way, and I take certain drugs to avert its arrival. If I did not take the drugs, I would be able to function perhaps one day in four. The physiological error called migraine is, in brief, central to the given of my life. When I was fifteen, sixteen, even twenty-five, I used to think that I could rid myself of this error by simply denying it, character over chemistry. "Do you have headaches *sometimes? frequently?*

never?" the application forms would demand. "Check one." Wary of the trap, wanting whatever it was that the successful circumnavigation of that particular form could bring (a job, a scholarship, the respect of mankind and the grace of God), I would check one. *"Sometimes,"* I would lie. That in fact I spent one or two days a week almost unconscious with pain seemed a shameful secret, evidence not merely of some chemical inferiority but of all my bad attitudes, unpleasant tempers, wrongthink.

For I had no brain tumor, no eyestrain, no high blood pressure, nothing wrong with me at all: I simply had migraine headaches, and migraine headaches were, as everyone who did not have them knew, imaginary. I fought migraine then, ignored the warnings it sent, went to school and later to work in spite of it, sat through lectures in Middle English and presentations to advertisers with involuntary tears running down the right side of my face, threw up in washrooms, stumbled home by instinct, emptied ice trays onto my bed and tried to freeze the pain in my right temple, wished only for a neurosurgeon who would do a lobotomy on house call, and cursed my imagination.

It was a long time before I began thinking mechanistically enough to accept migraine for what it was: something with which I would be living, the way some people live with diabetes. Migraine is something more than the fancy of a neurotic imagination. It is an essentially hereditary complex of symptoms, the most frequently noted but by no means the most unpleasant of which is a vascular headache of blinding severity, suffered by a surprising number of women, a fair number of men (Thomas Jefferson had migraine, and so did Ulysses S. Grant, the day he accepted Lee's surrender), and by some unfortunate children as young as two years old. (I had my first when I was eight. It came on during a fire drill at the Columbia School in Colorado Springs, Colorado. I was taken first home and then to the infirmary at Peterson Field, where my father was stationed. The Air Corps doctor prescribed an enema.) Almost anything can trigger a specific attack of migraine: stress, allergy, fatigue, an abrupt change in barometric pressure, a contretemps over a parking ticket. A flashing light. A fire drill. One inherits, of course, only the predisposition. In other words I spent yesterday in bed with a headache not merely because of my bad attitudes, unpleasant tempers, and wrongthink, but because both my grandmothers had migraine, my father has migraine, and my mother has migraine.

No one knows precisely what it is that is inherited. The chemistry of migraine, however, seems to have some connection with the nerve hormone named serotonin, which is naturally present in the brain. The amount of serotonin in the blood falls sharply at the onset of migraine, and one migraine drug, methysergide, or Sansert, seems to have some effect on serotonin. Methysergide is a derivative of lysergic acid (in fact Sandoz Pharmaceuticals first synthesized LSD-25 while looking for a migraine cure), and its use is hemmed about with so many contraindications and side effects that most doctors prescribe it only in the most incapacitating cases. Methysergide, when it is prescribed, is taken daily, as a preventive; another preventive which works for some people is old-fashioned ergotamine tartrate, which helps to constrict the swelling blood vessels during the "aura," the period which in most cases precedes the actual headache.

Once an attack is under way, however, no drug touches it. Migraine gives some people mild hallucinations, temporarily blinds others, shows up not only as a headache but as a gastrointestinal disturbance, a painful sensitivity to all sensory stimuli, an abrupt overpowering fatigue, a strokelike aphasia, and a crippling inability to make even the most routine connections. When I am in a migraine aura (for some people the aura lasts fifteen minutes, for others several hours), I will drive through red lights, lose the house keys, spill whatever I am holding, lose the ability to focus my eyes or frame coherent sentences, and generally give the appearance of being on drugs, or drunk. The actual headache, when it comes, brings with it chills, sweating, nausea, a debility that seems to stretch the very limits of endurance. That no one dies of migraine seems, to someone deep into an attack, an ambiguous blessing.

My husband also has migraine, which is unfortunate for him but fortunate for me: perhaps nothing so tends to prolong an attack as the accusing eye of someone who has never had a headache. "Why not take a couple of aspirin," the unafflicted will say from the doorway, or "I'd have a headache, too, spending a beautiful day like this inside with all the shades drawn." All of us who have migraine suffer not only from the attacks themselves but from this common conviction that we are perversely refusing to cure ourselves by taking a couple of aspirin, that we are making ourselves sick, that we "bring it on ourselves." And in the most immediate sense, the sense of why we have a headache this Tuesday and not last Thursday, of course we often do. There certainly is what doctors call a "migraine personality," and that personality tends to be ambitious, inward, intolerant of error, rather rigidly organized, perfectionist. "You don't look like a migraine personality," a doctor once said to me. "Your hair's messy. But I suppose you're a compulsive housekeeper." Actually my house is kept even more negligently than my hair, but the doctor was right nonetheless: perfectionism can also take the form of spending most of a week writing and rewriting and not writing a single paragraph.

But not all perfectionists have migraine, and not all migrainous people have migraine personalities. We do not escape heredity. I have tried in most of the available ways to escape my own migrainous heredity (at one point I learned to give myself two daily injections of histamine with a hypodermic needle, even though the needle so frightened me that I had to close my eyes when I did it), but I still have migraine. And I have learned now to live with it, learned when to expect it, how to outwit it, even how to regard it, when it does come, as more friend than lodger. We have reached a certain understanding, my migraine and I. It never comes when I am in real trouble. Tell me that my house is burned down, my husband has left me, that there is gunfighting in the streets and panic in the banks, and I will not respond by getting a headache. It comes instead when I am fighting not an open but a guerrilla war with my own life, during weeks of small household confusions, lost laundry, unhappy help, canceled appointments, on days when the telephone rings too much and I get no work done and the wind is coming up. On days like that my friend comes uninvited. 7

And once it comes, now that I am wise in its ways, I no longer fight it. I lie down and let it happen. At first every small apprehension is magnified, every anxiety a pounding terror. Then the pain comes, and I concentrate only on that. Right there is the usefulness of migraine, there in that imposed yoga, the concen- 8 tration on the pain. For when the pain recedes, ten or twelve hours later, everything goes with it, all the hidden resentments, all the vain anxieties. The migraine has acted as a circuit breaker, and the fuses have emerged intact. There is a pleasant convalescent euphoria. I open the windows and feel the air, eat gratefully, sleep well. I notice the particular nature of a flower in a glass on the stair landing. I count my blessings.

Joan Didion

The Santa Ana

A wind blows through Southern California — not a wind to cool the air and refresh the spirit, but one that oppresses, agitates, and destroys. Filled with eerie foreboding, Didion's description is every bit as unsettling as the Santa Ana. How much control, Didion makes us wonder, do we puny humans have when confronted by such impersonal natural forces?

There is something uneasy in the Los Angeles air this afternoon, some unnatural stillness, some tension. What it means is that tonight a Santa Ana will begin to blow, a hot wind from the northeast whining down through the Cajon and San Gorgonio Passes, blowing up sandstorms out along Route 66, drying the hills and the nerves to the flash point. For a few days now we will see smoke back in the canyons, and hear sirens in the night. I have neither heard nor read that a Santa Ana is due, but I know it, and almost everyone I have seen today knows it too. We know it because we feel it. The baby frets. The maid sulks. I rekindle a waning argument with the telephone company, then cut my losses and lie down, given over to whatever it is in the air. To live with the Santa Ana is to accept, consciously or unconsciously, a deeply mechanistic view of human behavior. 1

I recall being told, when I first moved to Los Angeles and was living on an isolated beach, that the Indians would throw themselves into the sea when the bad wind blew. I could see why. The Pacific turned ominously glossy during a Santa Ana period, and one woke in the night troubled not only by the peacocks screaming in the olive trees but by the eerie absence of surf. The heat was surreal. The sky had a yellow cast, the kind of light sometimes called "earthquake weather." My only neighbor would not come out of her house for days, and there were no lights at night, and her husband roamed the place with a machete. 2

One day he would tell me that he had heard a trespasser, the next a rattlesnake.

"On nights like that," Raymond Chandler once wrote about the Santa Ana, "every booze party ends in a fight. Meek little wives feel the edge of the carving knife and study their husbands' necks. Anything can happen." That was the kind of wind it was. I did not know then that there was any basis for the effect it had on all of us, but it turns out to be another of those cases in which science bears out folk wisdom. The Santa Ana, which is named for one of the canyons it rushes through, is a *foehn* wind, like the *foehn* of Austria and Switzerland and the *hamsin* of Israel. There are a number of persistent malevolent winds, perhaps the best known of which are the mistral of France and the Mediterranean sirocco, but a *foehn* wind has distinct characteristics: it occurs on the leeward slope of a mountain range, and although the air begins as a cold mass, it is warmed as it comes down the mountain and appears finally as a hot dry wind. Whenever and wherever a *foehn* blows, doctors hear about headaches and nausea and allergies, about "nervousness," about "depression." In Los Angeles some teachers do not attempt to conduct formal classes during a Santa Ana, because the children become unmanageable. In Switzerland the suicide rate goes up during the *foehn,* and in the courts of some Swiss cantons the wind is considered a mitigating circumstance for crime. Surgeons are said to watch the wind, because blood does not clot normally during a *foehn*. A few years ago an Israeli physicist discovered that not only during such winds, but for the ten or twelve hours which precede them, the air carries an unusually high ratio of positive to negative ions. No one seems to know exactly why that should be; some talk about friction and others suggest solar disturbances. In any case the positive ions are there, and what an excess of positive ions does, in the simplest terms, is make people unhappy. One cannot get much more mechanistic than that.

Easterners commonly complain that there is no "weather" at all in Southern California, that the days and the seasons slip by relentlessly, numbingly bland. That is quite misleading. In fact the climate is characterized by infrequent but violent extremes: two periods of torrential subtropical rains which continue for weeks and wash out the hills and send subdivisions sliding toward the sea; about twenty scattered days a year of the Santa Ana, which, with its incendiary dryness, invariably means fire. At the first prediction of a Santa Ana, the Forest Service flies men and equipment from northern California into the southern forests, and the Los Angeles Fire Department cancels its ordinary nonfirefighting routines. The Santa Ana caused Malibu to burn the way it did in 1956, and Bel Air in 1961, and Santa Barbara in 1964. In the winter of 1966–67 eleven men were killed fighting a Santa Ana fire that spread through the San Gabriel Mountains.

Just to watch the front-page news out of Los Angeles during 5 a Santa Ana is to get very close to what it is about the place. The longest single Santa Ana period in recent years was in 1957, and it lasted not the usual three or four days but fourteen days, from November 21 until December 4. On the first day 25,000 acres of the San Gabriel Mountains were burning, with gusts reaching 100 miles an hour. In town, the wind reached Force 12, or hurricane force, on the Beaufort Scale; oil derricks were toppled and people ordered off the downtown streets to avoid injury from flying objects. On November 22 the fire in the San Gabriels was out of control. On November 24 six people were killed in automobile accidents, and by the end of the week the Los Angeles *Times* was keeping a box score of traffic deaths. On November 26 a prominent Pasadena attorney, depressed about money, shot and killed his wife, their two sons, and himself. On November 27 a South Gate divorcee, twenty-two, was murdered and thrown from a moving car. On November 30 the San Gabriel fire was still out of control, and the wind in town was blowing eighty miles an hour. On the first day of December four people died violently, and on the third the wind began to break.

It is hard for people who have not lived in Los Angeles to 6 realize how radically the Santa Ana figures in the local imagination. The city burning is Los Angeles's deepest image of itself: Nathanael West perceived that, in *The Day of the Locust;* and at the time of the 1965 Watts riots what struck the imagination most indelibly were the fires. For days one could drive the Harbor Freeway and see the city on fire, just as we had always known it would be in the end. Los Angeles weather is the weather of catastrophe, of apocalypse, and, just as the reliably long and bitter winters of New England determine the way life is lived there, so the violence and the unpredictability of the Santa Ana affect the entire quality of life in Los Angeles, accentuate its impermanence, its unreliability. The wind shows us how close to the edge we are.

GLOSSARY

Abstract and Concrete Language refers to two different qualities of
words. Abstract words and phrases convey concepts, qualities, emotions, and ideas that we can think and talk about but not actually see
or experience directly. Examples of abstract words are *conservatism,
courage, avarice, joy,* and *hatred.* Words or phrases whose meanings
are directly seen or experienced by the senses are concrete terms.
Examples of phrases using concrete words are *split-level house, wad-
dling penguin,* and *short pink waitress uniform.*

Adequate — see *Evidence.*

Ad Hominem Argument — see *Logical Fallacies.*

Analogy refers to an imaginative comparison between two subjects that
seem to have little in common. Often a complex idea or topic can be
made understandable by comparing it to a more familiar subject,
and such an analogy can be developed over several paragraphs or
even an entire essay. For example, to explain how the economic
difficulties of farmers weaken an entire nation, a writer might create
an analogy between failing farms and a cancer that slowly destroys a
person's life.

Argumentation – Persuasion tries to encourage readers to accept a writer's point of view on some controversial or significant issue. In *argumentation,* a writer uses objective reasoning, facts, and hard evidence to demonstrate the soundness of a position. In *persuasion,* the writer uses appeals to the readers' emotions and value systems, often in the hope of encouraging them to take a specific action. Argumentation and persuasion are frequently used together in an essay. For example, a writer might argue for the construction of a highway through town by pointing out that the road would bring new business, create new jobs, and lighten traffic. The writer also might try to persuade readers to vote for a highway appropriations bill by appealing to their emotions, claiming that the highway would allow people to get home faster, thus giving them more time for family life and leisure activities. A whole essay can be organized around argumentation–persuasion, or an essay developed chiefly through another mode may contain elements of argumentation–persuasion.

Assertion refers to the *thesis* of an *argumentation–persuasion* essay. The assertion, or *proposition,* is a point of view or opinion on a controversial issue or topic. The assertion cannot be merely a statement of a fact. Such statements as "Women still experience discrimination in the job market," "General Rabb would make an ideal mayor for our town," and "This university should devote more funds to raising the quality of the food services" are examples of assertions that could serve as theses for argumentation–persuasion essays.

Audience refers to the writer's intended readers. In planning the content and tone of an essay, you should identify your audience and consider its needs. How similar are the members of your audience to you in knowledge and point of view? What will they need to know for you to achieve your *purpose?* What *tone* will make them open to receiving your message? For example, if you were to write a description of a trip to Disney World, you would have to explain a lot more to an eighty-year-old grandmother who had never seen a theme park than to a young parent who had probably visited one. If you wrote about the high cost of clothing for an economics professor, you would choose a serious, analytic tone and supply statistical evidence for your points. If you write about the same topic for the college newspaper, you might use a tone tinged with humor and provide helpful hints on finding bargain clothing.

Begging the Question — see *Logical Fallacies.*

Brainstorming is a technique used in the *prewriting* stage. It helps you discover the limited subject you can successfully write about and also generates raw material — ideas and details — to develop that subject. In brainstorming, you allow your mind to play freely with the subject. You try to capture fleeting thoughts about it, no matter how random, minor, or tangential, and jot them down rapidly before they disappear from your mind.

Causal Analysis—see *Cause–Effect.*

Causal Chain refers to a series of causes and effects, in which the result or effect of a cause becomes itself the cause of a further effect, and so on. For example, a person's alarm clock failing to buzz might begin a causal chain by causing the person to oversleep. Oversleeping then causes the person to miss the bus, and missing the bus causes the person to arrive late to work. Arriving late causes the person to miss an important phone call, which causes the person to lose a chance at a lucrative contract.

Cause–Effect, sometimes called *causal analysis,* involves analyzing the reasons for or results of an event, action, decision, or phenomenon. Writers develop an essay through an analysis of causes whenever they attempt to answer such questions as "Why has this happened?" or "Why does this exist?" When writers explore such questions as "What happens or would happen if a certain change occurs?" or "What will happen if a condition continues?" their essays involve a discussion of effects. Some cause–effect essays concentrate on the causes of a situation, some focus on the effects, and others present both causes and effects. Causal analysis can be an essay's central pattern, or it can be used to help support a point in an essay developed primarily through another mode.

Characteristics—see *Formal Definition.*

Chronological Sequence—see *Narrative Sequence* and *Organization.*

Circularity is an error in *formal definition* resulting from using variations of the to-be-defined word in the definition. For example, "A scientific hypothesis is a hypothesis made by a scientist about the results of an experiment," is circular because the unknown term is used to explain itself.

Class—see *Formal Definition.*

Comparison–Contrast means explaining the similarities and/or differences between events, objects, people, ideas, and so on. The comparison–contrast format can be used to meet a purely factual purpose ("This is how *A* and *B* are alike or different"). But usually writers use comparison–contrast to make a judgment about the relative merits of the subjects under discussion. Sometimes a writer will concentrate solely on similarities *or* differences. For instance, when writing about married versus single life, you would probably devote most of your time to discussing the difference between these lifestyles. Other times, comparison and contrast are found together. In an essay analyzing two approaches to U.S. foreign policy, you would probably discuss the similarities *and* the differences in the goals and methods characteristic of each approach. Comparison–

contrast can be the dominant mode of development in an essay, or it can be used as a supplemental pattern in an essay developed chiefly through another mode.

Conclusion   refers to the one or more paragraphs that bring an essay to an end. Effective conclusions give the reader a sense of completeness and finality. Writers often use the conclusion as a place to reaffirm the *thesis* and to express a final thought about the subject. Methods of conclusion include summarizing main points, using a quotation, predicting an outcome, or recommending an action.

Conflict   creates tension in the readers of a *narration*. It is produced by the opposition of characters or other forces in a story. Conflict can occur between individuals, between a person and society or nature, or within a person. Readers wonder how a conflict will be resolved and read on to find out.

Connecting Devices   signal the relationships among ideas in an essay. They help the reader follow the train of thought from sentence to sentence and from paragraph to paragraph. There are three types of connectives. *Transitions* are words that briefly indicate the coming flow of meaning. They can signal an additional or contrasting point, an enumeration of ideas, the use of an example, or other movement of ideas. For a list of transitional devices, see page 45. *Linking sentences* summarize a point just made and then introduce a follow-up point. *Repeated words, synonyms,* and *pronouns* create a sense of flow by keeping important concepts in the mind of the reader.

Connotative and Denotative Language   describe the ability of language to emphasize one or another aspect of a word's range of meaning. *Denotative language* stresses the dictionary meaning of words. *Connotative language* emphasizes the echoes of feeling that cluster around some words. For example, the terms *weep, bawl, break down,* and *sob* all denote the same thing: to cry. But they have different associations and call up different images. A writer employing the connotative resources of language would choose the term among these that suggested the appropriate image.

Controlling Idea — see *Thesis*.

Deductive Reasoning   is a form of logical thinking in which general statements believed to be true are applied to specific situations or cases. The result of deduction is a conclusion or prediction about the specific situation. Deduction is often expressed in a three-step pattern called a *syllogism*. The first part of the syllogism is a general statement about a large class of items or situations, the *major premise*. The second part is the *minor premise,* a more limited statement about a specific item or case. The third part is the *conclusion*, drawn from the major premise, about that specific case or item. Deductive reasoning is very common in everyday thinking. For example, you might use deduction when car shopping:

In an accident, large cars are safer than small cars.
(Major premise)

The Chevy Cruiser is a large car.
(Minor premise)

In an accident, the Chevy Cruiser will be safer than a small car.
(Conclusion)

Definition explains the meaning of a word or concept. The brief formal definitions found in the dictionary can be useful if you need to clarify or restrict the meaning of a term used in an essay. In such cases, the definition is short and to the point. But you may also use an *extended definition* in an essay taking several paragraphs, even the entire piece, to develop the meaning of a term. You may use extended definition to convey a personal slant on a well-known term, to refute a commonly held interpretation of a word, or to dissect a complex or controversial issue. Definition can be the chief method of development in an essay, or it can be used as a supplemental mode in an essay organized around another pattern.

Definition by Negation is a method of defining a term by first explaining what it is not, and then going on to explain what it is. For example, you might begin a critical essay about television with a definition by negation: "Television, far from being a magical medium of light entertainment and immediate information, actually disseminates a distorted view of how Americans live and what they want from life, their government, and society." *Definition by negation* can provide a stimulating introduction to an essay.

Description involves the use of vivid word pictures to express what the five senses have experienced. The subject of a descriptive essay can be a person, place, object, or event. Description can be the dominant pattern in an essay, or it can be used as a supplemental method in an essay developed chiefly through another pattern.

There are two main types of description. In an *objective description,* a writer provides details about a subject without conveying the emotions the subject arouses. For example, if you were involved in a traffic accident, your insurance agent might ask you to write an objective description of the events leading up to and during the crash. But in a *subjective description,* the writer's goal is to evoke in the reader the emotions felt during the experience. For example, in a cautionary letter to a friend who has a habit of driving dangerously, you might write a subjective description of your horrifying close call with death during a car accident.

Development—see *Evidence.*

Dialogue is the writer's way of directly presenting the exact words spoken by characters in a *narration.* By using dialogue, writers can convey people's individuality and also add drama and immediacy to an essay.

Directional Process Analysis—see *Process Analysis.*

Division–Classification refers to a logical method for analyzing a single subject or several related subjects. Though often used together in an essay, division and classification are separate processes. *Division* involves breaking a subject or idea into its component parts. For instance, the concept "an ideal vacation" could be divided according to its destination, accommodations, or cost. *Classification* involves organizing a number of related items into categories. For example, in an essay about the overwhelming flow of paper in our everyday lives, you might classify the typical kinds of mail most people receive: personal mail (letters, birthday cards, party invitations), business mail (bills, bank statements, charge card receipts), and junk mail (flyers about bargain sales, solicitations to donate, contest announcements). Division–classification can be the dominant pattern in a paper, or it may be used to support a point in an essay organized chiefly around another pattern of development.

Dominant Impression refers to the purpose of a descriptive essay. While some descriptive essays have a thesis, some do not; instead, they convey a dominant impression or main point. For example, one person writing a descriptive essay about New York City might use its architectural diversity as a focal point. Another person writing a description of Manhattan might concentrate on the overpowering sense of hustle and speed about everyone and everything in the city. Both writers would select only those details that supported their dominant impressions.

Dramatic License refers to the writer's privilege, when writing a narrative, to alter facts or details to strengthen the support of the *thesis* or *narrative point.* For example, a writer is free to flesh out the description of an event whose specific details may be partially forgotten or to modify or omit details of a narrative that do not contribute to the meaning the writer wishes to convey.

Emphatic Sequence—see *Organization.*

Ethos refers to the necessity for a writer to establish an image of reliability or credibility in the readers of an *argumentation–persuasion* essay or piece. This is done by using reason and logic to argue points, by being moderate in any appeals to the emotions, and by demonstrating overall knowledgeability of the subject. Effective argumentation – persuasion should possess *ethos, logos,* and *pathos.*

Etymology refers to the history of a word or term. All English words have their origins in other, usually ancient, languages. Giving a brief etymology of a word can help a writer establish the context for developing an *extended definition* of the word. For example, the word *criminal* is derived from a Latin word meaning "accusation/accused." Today, our word *criminal* goes beyond the concept of "accused" to mean "guilty."

Evidence lends substance to your main idea and so assists the reader to accept your viewpoint. Evidence should meet three criteria. First of all, it should be *unified,* in the sense that all supporting ideas and details should relate directly to the point you are making. Second, the evidence should be *adequate;* there should be enough evidence to convince the reader to agree with your thesis. Third, evidence should be *specific,* that is, vivid and detailed, rather than vague and general. The bulk of an essay is devoted to supplying evidence. Supporting the thesis with solid evidence is the third stage of a writing process.

Exemplification, at the heart of all effective writing, involves using concrete specifics to support generalizations. In exemplification, writers provide examples or instances that support or clarify broader statements. You might support the thesis statement, "I have a close-knit family," by using such examples as the following: "We have a regular Sunday dinner at my grandmother's house with at least ten family members present"; "My sisters and brothers visit my parents every week"; "I spend so much time on the phone talking with my sisters that sometimes I have trouble finding time for my new college friends." Exemplification may be an essay's central pattern, or it may supplement an essay developed mainly around another pattern.

Extended Definition — see *Definition.*

Fallacies — see *Logical Fallacies.*

Figures of Speech are imaginative comparisons between two things usually thought of as dissimilar. Some major figures of speech are *simile, metaphor,* and *personification. Similes* are comparisons that use the signal words *like* or *as:* "Superman was as powerful as a locomotive." *Metaphors,* which do not use signal words, directly equate unlike things: "The boss is a tiger when it comes to landing a contract." "The high-powered pistons of the boxer's arms pummeled his opponent." *Personification* attributes human characteristics to inanimate things or nonhuman beings: "The angry clouds unleashed their fury on the town"; "The wind caressed the trees"; "The turtle shyly poked his head out of his shell."

First Draft refers to the writer's first try at producing a basic, unpolished version of the whole essay. It is often referred to as the "rough" draft, and nothing about it is final or unchangeable. The process of writing the first draft often brings up new ideas or details. Writers sometimes break off writing the draft to *brainstorm* or *freewrite* as new ideas occur to them and then return to the draft with new inspiration. You shouldn't worry about spelling, grammar, or style in the first-draft stage; instead, you should keep focused on casting your ideas into sentence and paragraph form. Writing the first draft is the fifth stage in the writing process.

Flashback — see *Narrative Sequence.*

Flashforward — see *Narrative Sequence.*

Formal Definition involves stating a definition in a three-part pattern of about one sentence in length. In presenting a formal definition a writer puts the *term* in a *class* and then lists the *characteristics* that separate the term from other members of its class. For example, a formal definition of a word processor might be, "A word processor (term) is an electronic machine (class) that is used to write, edit, store, and produce typewritten documents (characteristics)." Writers often use a formal definition to prepare a reader for an extended definition that follows.

Freewriting can help a writer during the *prewriting* stage in coming up with ideas for developing the limited topic. To use this method, write nonstop for five or ten minutes about everything your topic brings to mind. Disregard grammar, spelling, and organization as you keep your pen and mind moving. Freewriting is similar to *brainstorming,* except that the result is a rambling, detail-filled paragraph rather than a list.

Hasty Generalization — see *Logical Fallacies.*

Inductive Reasoning is a form of logical thinking in which specific cases and facts are examined in order to draw a wider-ranging conclusion. The result of inductive reasoning is a generalization that is held to apply to situations or cases similar to the ones examined. Induction is typical of scientific investigation and of everyday thinking. For example, on the basis of specific experiences, you may have concluded that when you feel chilly in a room where everyone else is comfortable, you are likely to develop a cold and fever in the next day or two. In an *argumentation–persuasion* essay, the conclusion reached by induction would be your *assertion* or *thesis.*

Inference is the term for a conclusion based on *inductive reasoning.* Because the reasoning behind specific cases may not be simple, there is usually an element of uncertainty in an inductive conclusion. Choosing the correct explanation for specific cases is a matter of carefully weighing and selecting alternative conclusions.

Informational Process Analysis — see *Process Analysis.*

Introduction refers to the first paragraph or several paragraphs of an essay. The introduction serves three purposes. It informs readers of the general subject of the essay, it catches their attention, and it presents the controlling idea or thesis. The methods of introducing an essay include the use of an anecdote, a quotation or surprising statistic or fact, or questions. Or you may narrow your discussion down from a broad subject to a more limited one.

Irony occurs when writers or speakers say the opposite of what they actually mean. The listener or reader is able to comprehend the true meaning because of the style, the tone, or context of the ironic statement. Author Betty Rollin describes a simple example of verbal irony (also known as *sarcasm*) in "Allene Talmey" (page 194). When her boss at *Vogue* asked her, "What are you trying to say, dear?" Rollin understood that her boss really meant "moron," not "dear."

Journal Writing can be seen as a form of prewriting, with many writers making daily entries in a private journal, much as they would in a diary. Whether they focus on one topic or wander freely, journal writers jot down striking incidents, images, and ideas encountered in the course of a day. Such journal material can lead to themes for more formal essays.

Logical Fallacies are easily committed mistakes in reasoning that writers must be on guard against, especially when writing *argumentation-persuasion* essays. There are many kinds of logical fallacies. Here are six:

Ad hominem argument occurs when you attack a person's point of view by criticizing the person, not the issue. Often called "mud-slinging," ad hominem arguments try to invalidate a person's ideas by revealing unrelated, past or present, personal or ethical flaws. For example, to claim a person cannot govern the country well because it can be proven he has had an extramarital affair is to use an ad hominem argument.

Begging the question is a fallacy in which the writer assumes something that should be proven and directs the reader's attention to an opinion that is usually easier to prove. To argue that "A law should be passed to require that dangerous pets like German shepherds and Doberman pinschers be restrained by fences, leashes, and muzzles at all times" would be to beg the question of whether such dogs are always dangerous.

Hasty generalizations are unsound *inductive inferences* based on too few instances of a behavior, situation, or process. For example, it would be a hasty generalization to conclude that you are allergic to a food such as curry because you once ate it and became ill. There are several other possible explanations for your illness, and only repetitions of this experience or a lab test could prove conclusively that you are allergic to this spice.

Non sequiturs are faulty conclusions about cause and effect. Here's an example: "Throughout this country's history, most physicians have been male. Women apparently have little interest in becoming doctors." The faulty conclusion accords one factor — the possible vocational preferences of women — the status of sole cause. The conclusion fails to consider pressures on women to devote themselves to husband and home and to avoid an occupation sexually stereotyped as "masculine."

Post hoc thinking results when you presume that one event caused another just because it occurred first. For instance, if your car broke down the day after you lent it to your brother, you would be committing the post hoc fallacy to blame him, unless you knew he did something to your car's engine.

Questionable authority, revealed by such phrases as "studies show" and "experts claim," undercuts a writer's credibility. Readers become suspicious of such vague and unsubstantial appeals to authority. Writers should demonstrate the reliability of their sources by citing them specifically.

Logos is a major factor in creating an effective argument. It refers to the soundness of *argumentation,* as created by the use of facts, statistics, information, and commentary by authoritative sources. The most effective arguments involve an interplay between *logos, pathos,* and *ethos.*

Major Premise — see *Deductive Reasoning.*

Minor Premise — see *Deductive Reasoning.*

Narration means recounting an event or a series of related events to make a point. Narration can be an essay's principal mode of development, or it can be used to supplement a paper organized primarily around another pattern. For instance, to persuade readers to avoid drug use, a writer might use the narrative mode by recounting the story of an abuser's addiction and recovery.

Narrative Point refers to the meaning the writer intends to convey to a reader by telling a certain story. This narrative point might be a specific message or lesson, or it might be a feeling about the situation, people, or place of the story. This underlying meaning is achieved by presenting details that support it and editing out any that are nonessential. For example, in an essay about friendship, a writer's point might be that friendships change when one of the friends acquires a significant partner of the opposite sex. The writer would focus on the details of how her close female friend had less time for her, changed their habitual times of getting together, and confided in her less. The writer would omit judgments of the friend's choice of boyfriend and her declining grades because these details, while real for the writer, would distract the reader from the main narrative point.

Narrative Sequence refers to the order in which a writer recounts events. When you follow the order of the events as they happened, you are using *chronological sequence*. This sequence, in which you begin at the beginning and end with the last event, is the most basic and commonly used narrative sequence. If you interrupt this flow to present an event that happened before the beginning of the narrative sequence, you are employing a *flashback*. If you skip ahead to an event later than the one that comes next in your narrative, you are using the *flashforward* technique.

Non Sequiturs—see *Logical Fallacies*.

Objective Description—see *Description*.

One-Side-at-a-Time Method refers to one of the two techniques for organizing a *comparison–contrast* essay. In using this method, a writer discusses all the points about one of the compared and contrasted subjects before going on to the other. For example, in an essay titled "Single or Married?" a writer might first discuss single life in terms of amount of independence, freedom of career choice, and companionship. Then the writer would discuss married life in terms of these same three subtopics. The issues the writer discusses in each half of the essay would be identical and presented in the same order. See also *Point-by-Point Method*.

Organization refers to the process of arranging your evidence to support your thesis in the most effective way. In organizing, you decide what ideas come first, next, and last. In *chronological* sequence, you arrange details according to occurrence in time. In *spatial* sequence, details appear in the order in which they occur in space. In *emphatic* sequence, ideas are sequenced according to importance, with the most significant, outstanding, or convincing evidence being reserved for last. Organizing is the fourth stage of the writing process.

Outlining is making a formal plan before writing a *first draft*. Writing an outline helps you determine whether your supporting evidence is logical and adequate. As you write, you can use the outline to keep yourself on track. Many writers use the indentation system of Roman numerals, letters, and Arabic numbers to outline; sometimes writers use a less formal indented list.

Paradox refers to a statement that seems impossible, contrary to common sense, or self-contradictory, yet that can be seen after consideration to be plausible or true. For example, Oscar Wilde produced a paradox when he wrote that "When the gods wish to punish us, they answer our prayers." The statement does not contradict itself because often, Wilde believes, that which we wish for turns out to be the very thing that will bring us the most pain.

Pathos refers to the emotional power of an *argumentation–persuasion* essay. By appealing to the needs, values, and attitudes of readers and by using highly *connotative language,* writers can increase the chances that readers will come to agree with the ideas in an essay. Writing very strong in *pathos* is usually persuasive in *purpose,* but all effective argumentation–persuasion essays are built upon three factors, *pathos, logos,* and *ethos.*

Plan of Development refers to a useful but not essential means of supplying the reader with a brief map of the main points to be covered. If used, the plan of development occurs as part of the *thesis* or in a sentence following the thesis. In it, the main ideas are mentioned in the order they will appear in the supporting paragraphs. Longer essays and term papers usually need a plan of development to maintain unity, but shorter papers may do without.

Point-by-Point Method refers to one of the two techniques for organizing a *comparison–contrast* essay. A writer using this method covers each point of comparison or contrast in relation to each subject of the comparison before going on to the next point. For example, in an essay titled "Single or Married?" a writer might first discuss the amount of independence a person has when single and when married. Then, the writer might go on to discuss how the single or married state affects career choice. Finally, the writer might discuss the amount of companionship available in each of the two lifestyles. See also *One-Side-at-a-Time Method.*

Point of View refers to the perspective a writer chooses when writing about a subject. In *narration,* the point of view should be consistent throughout. If you narrate events as you experienced them, you are using the first-person point of view. You might say, for example, "I noticed jam on the child's collar and holes in her shirt." If you relate the events from a distance, as if you know about them but did not experience them, you are using the third-person point of view. For example, "Jam splotched the child's collar, and her shirt had several holes in it."

Post Hoc Thinking—see *Logical Fallacies.*

Prewriting is the first stage of the writing process. During prewriting, you jot down rough ideas about your subject without yet moving to writing a draft of your essay. Your goals at this stage are to (1) understand the boundaries of the assignment, (2) discover the limited subject you could write well about, (3) generate raw material about the limited subject, and (4) organize the raw material into a very rough *scratch outline.* If you keep in mind that prewriting is "unofficial," it can be a low-pressure, even enjoyable activity.

Process Analysis refers to writing that explains the steps involved in doing something or the sequence of stages in a recurring event or behavior. There are two types of process analysis. In *directional process analysis,* readers are shown how to do something step by step. Cookbook recipes, tax form instructions, and how-to books are some typical uses of directional process analysis. In *informational process analysis,* the writer explains how something is done or occurs, without expecting the reader to attempt the process. "A Senator's Road to Political Power," "How a Bee Makes Honey," and "How a Convict Gets Paroled" would be titles of essays developed through informational process analysis. Process analysis can be the dominant mode in an essay, as in these examples, or it may be used in an essay of another mode to support a point. For example, in a cause–effect essay that explores the impact of the two-career family, process analysis might be used to explain how parents arrange for day care.

Proofreading involves rereading a final draft carefully to catch any errors in spelling, grammar, punctuation, or typing that have slipped by to this stage. While such errors are minor, a significant number of them can seriously weaken the effectiveness of an essay. Proofreading is the last stage in the writing process.

Proposition—see *Assertion.*

Purpose is the reason you have in mind for writing a particular essay. Usually, writers frame their purposes in terms of the effect they wish to have on their *audience.* They may wish to express themselves, explore a subject or experience, explain an idea or process, provide information, influence opinion, or entertain. Many essays have more than one purpose. As a writer, you will find you will be most effective if you establish one primary purpose for your essay and plan it accordingly.

Refutation is an important strategy in *argumentation–persuasion.* In refutation, writers acknowledge that there are opposing views on the subject under discussion, and go on to do one of two things. They may admit the opposing views are somewhat valid, but assert that their own position has more merit and devote their essay to demonstrating that merit. For example, a writer might assert, "While many business majors graduate to find interesting and lucrative jobs, liberal arts graduates have many more advantages in the job market in the long run, because they think better, learn faster, and communicate more successfully." This writer would concentrate on proving the advantages liberal arts graduates have. On the other hand, writers may choose to argue actively against others' views before going on to support their own thesis. Such refutation of opposing views can strengthen the writer's own arguments.

Repeated Words, Synonyms, and Pronouns—see *Connecting Devices.*

Revision means, literally, "reseeing" your *first draft* with a fresh eye, as if you were a new reader. In revising, you make whatever changes are necessary to increase the essay's effectiveness. You might eliminate weak phrasing or examples, change the organization, add transitions, or rework whole paragraphs. Such changes often make the difference between mediocre and superior writing. Revision is the last stage of the writing process.

Satire is a humorous form of social criticism usually aimed at society's institutions or human behavior. Often irreverent as well as witty, satire is serious in purpose: to point out evil, injustice, and absurdity and bring about change through an increase in awareness. Satire ranges widely in tone: it may be gentle or biting; it may sarcastically describe a real situation or use fictional characters and events to spoof reality. Satire often makes use of *irony*. Examples of satire in this book include "In Depth, but Shallowly," "How to Live to Be 200," and "A Modest Proposal."

Scratch Outline refers to your first informal plan for an essay, devised at the end of the *prewriting* stage. In making a scratch outline, you select ideas and details from your raw material for inclusion in your essay and discard the rest. You also arrange these ideas into an order that makes sense and that will help you achieve your *purpose*. A scratch outline is tentative and flexible, and can be reshaped as needed.

Sensory Description vividly evokes the sights, smells, taste, sounds, and physical feelings of a scene or event. It allows the reader to feel imaginatively present. For example, if a writer carefully chooses words and images, readers can see the vibrant reds and oranges of falling leaves, taste the sourness of an underripe grapefruit, hear the growling of motorcycles as a gang sweeps through a town, smell the spicy aroma of a grandmother's homemade tomato soup, and feel the pulsing pain of a jaw after Novocaine wears off. Sensory description is particularly important in writing *description* or *narration*.

Sentence Variety adds interest to the style of an essay or paragraph. In creating sentence variety, writers mix different kinds of sentences and sentence patterns. For example, you might make sure some of your sentences are short and some long, some simple, some complex, and some compound-complex, and that your sentences use a number of different transitional and opening phrases. Repetitive sentence patterns tend to make readers pay less attention.

Spatial Sequence — see *Organization*.

Specific — see *Evidence*.

Stipulative Definition is a way of restricting a term for the purposes of discussion. Many words have multiple meanings that can get in the way of clarity when a writer is creating an extended definition. For example, you might stipulate the following definition of *foreign car:* "While many familiar American cars these days use parts or even whole engines made in foreign countries by foreign car manufacturers, for the purposes of discussion, 'foreign car' refers only to those automobiles wholly designed and manufactured by a company based in another country. By this definition, a Volkswagen made in Pennsylvania is a foreign car."

Subjective Description — see *Description.*

Support — see *Evidence.*

Syllogism — see *Deductive Reasoning.*

Term — see *Formal Definition.*

Thesis is the central idea in any essay, usually expressed in a one- or two-sentence thesis statement. Writers accomplish two things by providing a *thesis* statement in an essay; they indicate the essay's limited subject and express an attitude about that subject. Also called the *controlling idea,* the *thesis statement* consists of a particular slant, angle, or point of view about the limited subject. Stating the thesis is the second stage of the writing process.

Tone conveys your attitude toward yourself, your purpose, your topic, and your readers. As in speaking, tone in writing may be serious, playful, sarcastic, and so on. Generally, readers detect tone more by how you say something rather than by what you say.

Topic Sentence is the term for the sentence or two conveying the main idea of a paragraph. Such sentences are often, but not always, found at the start of a paragraph. They provide a statement of the subject to be discussed and an indication of your attitude toward that subject. Writers concern themselves with topic sentences during the writing of the first draft, the fifth stage of the writing process.

Transitions — see *Connecting Devices.*

Unified — see *Evidence.*

Acknowledgments

"The Santa Ana." From "Los Angeles Notebook" in *Slouching Towards Bethlehem,* by Joan Didion. Copyright © 1967, 1968 by Joan Didion. Reprinted by permission of Farrar, Straus and Giroux, Inc.

"Sexism and Language," from "Sexism as Shown Through the English Vocabulary." Alleen Pace Nilsen, from *Sexism and Language,* by Alleen Pace Nilsen, Haig Bosmajian, H. Lee Gershany, and Julia P. Stanley (1977). Copyright © 1977 by the National Council of Teachers of English. All rights reserved.

"Shooting an Elephant" from *Shooting an Elephant and Other Essays* by George Orwell, copyright 1950 by Sonia Brownell Orwell and renewed 1978 by Sonia Pitt-Rivers, reprinted by permission of Harcourt Brace Jovanovich, Inc.

"Shopping with Children." From *Night Lights,* by Phyllis Theroux. Copyright © 1987 by Phyllis Theroux. All rights reserved. Reprinted by permission of Viking Penguin Inc.

"That Lean and Hungry Look." Suzanne Britt, from a "My Turn" column in *Newsweek.* Reprinted by permission of Suzanne Britt.

Excerpt of "Three Types of Resistance to Oppression" from *Stride Toward Freedom* by Martin Luther King, Jr. Copyright © 1958 by Martin Luther King, Jr. Reprinted by permission of Harper and Row, Publishers, Inc.

"TV Addiction." From *The Plug-InDrug* by Marie Winn. Copyright © 1977, by Marie Winn. Reprinted by permission of Viking Penguin, a division of Penguin Books USA, Inc.

"Ugly" by William McKibben. From "Notes and Comments" in the June 11, 1984 issue of *The New Yorker.* Reprinted by permission of *The New Yorker.*

"University Days." James Thurber. Copyright © 1933, 1961 by James Thurber. From *My Life and Hard Times,* published by Harper & Row, Publishers, Inc.

"Wanting an Orange." Larry Woiwode, from *The Paris Review,* Winter 1984. Copyright © 1984 by Larry Woiwode. Reprinted by permission of Candida Donadio & Associates.

"A Well-Regulated Militia." Paul Fussell, from *Thank God for the Atom Bomb.* Copyright © 1988 by Paul Fussell. Reprinted by permission of Summit Books, a division of Simon & Schuster, Inc.

INDEX

661

(*Continued*)

To the Student from the Authors

By now, you realize that almost all writing goes through a series of revisions. The same was true for this book. *The Macmillan Reader, Second Edition* has been reworked a number of times, with each revision taking into account student and instructor reaction to drafts of material.

Before we prepare the next edition of *The Macmillan Reader*, we'd like to know how you, the student, feel about the book. We hope you'll spend a few minutes completing this brief questionnaire. You can be sure that your responses will help shape subsequent editions. Please send your completed survey to the College English Editor, Macmillan Publishing Company, 866 Third Avenue, New York, New York 10022.

Thanks for your time.

College _____ City and state _____

Course title _____ Instructor _____

DESCRIPTION	I really liked.	It was okay.	I didn't like.	I didn't read.
Woiwode, *Wanting an Orange*	___	___	___	___
Baker, *In My Day*	___	___	___	___
Dillard, *In the Jungle*	___	___	___	___
White, *Once More to the Lake*	___	___	___	___
Anderson, *Children's Hospital*	___	___	___	___

NARRATION

	I really liked.	It was okay.	I didn't like.	I didn't read.
Orwell, *Shooting an Elephant*	___	___	___	___
Greene, *Handled with Care*	___	___	___	___
Watkins, *Little Deaths*	___	___	___	___
Hughes, *Salvation*	___	___	___	___
Keillor, *Eloise*	___	___	___	___

EXEMPLIFICATION

Fussell, *A Well-Regulated Militia*	___	___	___	___
Rollin, *Allene Talmey*	___	___	___	___
Lindbergh, *Channelled Whelk*	___	___	___	___
Nilsen, *Sexism and Language*	___	___	___	___
Thurber, *University Days*	___	___	___	___

PROCESS ANALYSIS

Leacock, *How to Live to Be 200*	___	___	___	___
Hubbell, *The Beekeeper*	___	___	___	___
Mitford, *The American Way of Death*	___	___	___	___
Roberts, *How to Say Nothing in 500 Words*	___	___	___	___
Theroux, *Shopping with Children*	___	___	___	___

COMPARISON–CONTRAST

Britt, *That Lean and Hungry Look*	___	___	___	___
Carson, *A Fable for Tomorrow*	___	___	___	___
Spikol, *High Noon*	___	___	___	___
Thoreau, *The Village*	___	___	___	___
Rodriguez, *Workers*	___	___	___	___

	I really liked.	It was okay.	I didn't like.	I didn't read.

CAUSE – EFFECT

	I really liked.	It was okay.	I didn't like.	I didn't read.
Gallup, *The Faltering Family*	___	___	___	___
Farb, *In Other Words*	___	___	___	___
Wolfe, *O Rotten Gotham — Sliding Down into the Behavioral Sink*	___	___	___	___
Walker, *Beauty: When the Other Dancer Is the Self*	___	___	___	___
Thomas, *The Lie Detector*	___	___	___	___

DEFINITION

Cole, *Entropy*	___	___	___	___
McKibben, *Ugly*	___	___	___	___
Syfers, *Why I Want a Wife*	___	___	___	___
Mencken, *The Politician*	___	___	___	___
Winn, *TV Addiction*	___	___	___	___

DIVISION – CLASSIFICATION

Barry, *In Depth, but Shallowly*	___	___	___	___
Zinsser, *College Pressures*	___	___	___	___
Hilfiker, *Making Medical Mistakes*	___	___	___	___
McClintock, *Propaganda Techniques in Today's Advertising*	___	___	___	___
Goldstein, *The Quick Fix Society*	___	___	___	___

ARGUMENTATION – PERSUASION

Marzollo, *My Pistol-Packing Kids*	___	___	___	___
Wainwright, *A Little Banning Is a Dangerous Thing*	___	___	___	___
Twain, *The Damned Human Race*	___	___	___	___

	I really liked.	It was okay.	I didn't like.	I didn't read.
Trippett, *A Red Light for Scofflaws*	___	___	___	___
Swift, *A Modest Proposal*	___	___	___	___
Koch, *Death and Justice*	___	___	___	___
Bruck, *The Death Penalty*	___	___	___	___
Nizer, *Low-Cost Drugs for Addicts?*	___	___	___	___
Ruth, *Our Drug Problem*	___	___	___	___

FOR FURTHER READING

King, *Where Do We Go From Here: Community or Chaos?*	___	___	___	___
King, *Three Kinds of Resistance to Oppression*	___	___	___	___
Didion, *In Bed*	___	___	___	___
Didion, *The Santa Ana*	___	___	___	___

Any general comments or suggestions?

Name ——————————— Date ———————————

Address ———————————————————————

THANKS AGAIN!